The Royal Manor of Penkhull

and the surrounding areas of Stoke and Newcastle

Richard Talbot, M.Phil

The Talbot Press
2010

Published by

The Talbot Press

88 Newcastle Lane, Penkhull,

Stoke-on-Trent. ST4 5DR

ISBN 978-0-9566866-0-2

9 780956 686602 >

Printed in the UK by

Creative Copy-n-Colour

Eccleshall, Staffordshire

Dedicated to the memory of

Sir Oliver Lodge

a son of Penkhull
1851 - 1940

Chapters

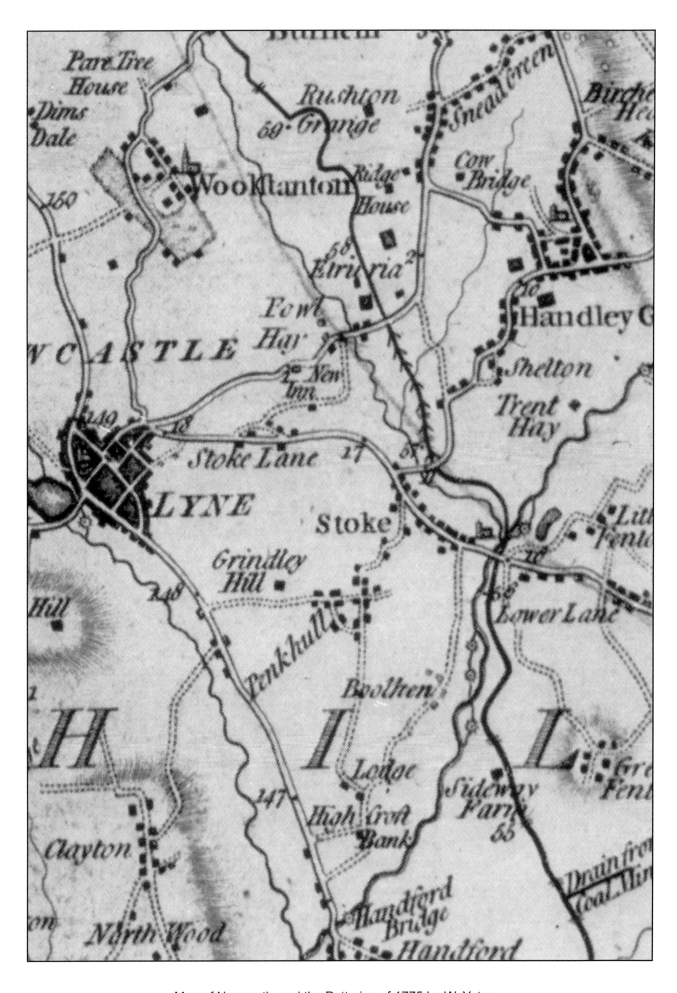

Map of Newcastle and the Potteries of 1775 by W. Yates

Foreword

The recent discovery of the Staffordshire Hoard – that treasure-chest of Anglo-Saxon riches scattered in the soil surrounding Lichfield – alerted us once more to the ancient history embedded in north Staffordshire. For too long the enormity of the Industrial Revolution and the transformation of the Six Towns' townscape into a brutal maelstrom of pot banks, pit shafts and steel works hid the old past from our view. Yet from the 13th century ruins of the Cistercian Abbey of St. Mary at Hulton to the ancient landmarks of Stoke, the city of Stoke-on-Trent has a pre-history stretching back long before the advent of steam.

So it is with great pleasure that one of our leading urban scholars, Richard Talbot, has brought out this new book charting the history of one of the oldest communities in North Staffordshire, the Royal Manor of Penkhull together with the surrounding areas of Stoke and Newcastle. Today, we can still see hints of this history in the form of The Greyhound Inn or the artefacts unearthed by the construction of the garden village in 1911 and later at the new University Hospital of North Staffordshire. But it is Mr Talbot's achievement to provide a narrative thread tracing this history from Bronze Age settlements up to 'The Kingdom of Spode' and mass urbanisation. In the process, we are offered a series of compelling insights into the everyday life of medieval Penkhull; the social history of its people from hospitals to pubs; the advent of industry as well as the sad history of enforced migration and the treatment of the poor.

What this work also touches on is the terrible destruction of old Penkhull in the 1960s. Blindly, the old was knocked down for the new with little feeling for the concerns of residents or the long-term interests of the city. That has been the case too often in Stoke on Trent, as some of our great landmarks and civic icons have fallen victim to the wrecker's ball. Explaining the remarkable history of Stoke-on-Trent is part of the process of valuing the past and protecting its legacy today.

Richard Talbot's book is an important and fascinating contribution to that process.

Tristram Hunt., PhD, FRHistS

Penkhull 1880s
Taken from 'The Romance of Staffordshire'
by William Wedgwood

Introduction

It is more than forty years since I was introduced to the subject of local history. I had been loaned a copy of a small pamphlet-type book written to commemorate the centenary of Penkhull Church by the Rev. V.G. Aston in 1942. Although small, certainly limited in its research and simply written, it conveyed the art of communicating history to ordinary folk of the things that mattered in their communities. It was not the stereotypical historical account of a series of dates and events and how they changed the world that one would experience in school but that of local people and how they lived, worked and how national events can affect simple village life.

I would acknowledge above all else this single contribution which has stimulated my interest and enthusiasm during four decades to produce a book which has ended up being the largest local history book ever published in North Staffordshire. The last book of any significance was Ernest Warrillow's Sociological History of Stoke-on-Trent in 1960. Nearly all books since that date have been of pictures or old postcards with captions. This book is a book to be read as well as a place of reference. The facts and results of research are presented in a way to be read like a story, bringing to life the very soul of the past in an illuminating and interesting way. I believe that much of the contents will be used for sociological study by students for generations to come.

This is my sixth book and certainly the most informative and academic work produced so far. Within the twenty-three chapters, just about every topic of a community or district has been meticulously researched. Much of the material is from the manorial court rolls of Newcastle-under-Lyme of which the Queen remains as Duchy of Lancaster. These parchment records date from 1350 and have never previously used before to support a history of this kind and my archives contain the largest transcribed database of court records for the manor in the world. Therefore the contents of this book are backed up by original research, which, in many cases re-write previously assumed historical information.

I have over the last number of years produced three local films on different aspects of the history of Penkhull. A further film was already scripted on the subject of the workhouse and Penkhull Cottage Homes but unfortunately the experiences of breach of my copyright through illegal copying turned my thoughts to a new publication. The end result has surpassed the original expectation of size and content.

In the early years, when the first shoots of interest were beginning to show, I was supported by two wonderful friends both now no longer with us, Ken Nutt and Ronald Foster. In addition a former evening class tutor of forty years ago, George Baugh encouraged me into the field of research. It is to these that a huge debt is owed. I was further encouraged to undertake a degree as a mature student at the University of Keele, gaining a Masters of Philosophy degree. This experience has enabled me to move forward in undertaking the huge task of compiling this book.

To my knowledge there is only one other person Mr Peter Roden who has extensively used the manor court rolls from 1700-1832 in his study of early potworks within the manor *(Copyhold Potworks and Housing in the Staffordshire Potteries).* For referencing and availability of these records and untold advise my gratitude to Peter.

Finally, I acknowledge the kind support of so many local residents, many no longer with us who have over the years allowed me free access to their property deeds, together with the availability of many old photographs.

And lastly to Dr. Valery McKay for helping with the proof reading and advice.

Richard Talbot, M.Phil. (Keele)
November 2010

Acknowledgements

The author acknowledges the kind assistance given to him by the following.

Stoke-on-Trent Archives and Museum

National Archives, Kew

County Archives, Stafford

County Archives, Shropshire

The National Archives of Wales, Aberystwyth University

University of Keele Special Collection Library

The William Salt Library, Stafford

Church Commissioners, London

Diocesan Record Office, Lichfield

The National Society, London

Stoke-on-Trent City Council Legal Dept.

Spode Limited

Peter Roden

Dr. David Barker

Chris Emms

Jackie Gregory

The Evening Sentinel for extensive use of material

BBC Radio Stoke

Dr. Valery McKay

Gary Richardson and Steven Crossley, for the reproduction of maps and plans

Those former children and staff of Penkhull Cottage Homes

The support of my family over many years

And those numerous kind residents of Penkhull who have allowed me access to the deeds to their properties and to probably hundreds of people, past and present who have communicated their knowledge of the history of Penkhull over the last four decades.

Chapter 1
Penkhull – In the Beginning.

Penkhull, in all but name, formed a part of the middle lands left dormant after the ravages of subsequent ice ages where little but thick mists oozed from the mass of fermenting earth swamps, where from thousands of years of new life and then decay covered all. Forests formed and were impenetrable except where the River Trent ran unhindered, a mile wide, bringing witness to a life yet to come. Here, shelter provided home to the wild ox, the elk, the bear, red deer, wolf and beaver, all food for those who would come to hunt and build a village at the end of the wood, Penkhull.

It is an area where the uplands of the Pennine hills meet the rolling midland countryside overlooking the southern lower reaches of the River Trent. The chief topographical feature of the district is its elevated position. The physical relief of Celtic Penkhull is an important factor when considering the origins of our village. The ridge upon which Penkhull sits dominating the forested valleys of the Trent, Lyme and Fowley the waters of which would be clear and well-stocked, stands at the entrance of the North Staffordshire Potteries conurbation and juts out between two valleys. It rises sharply from the junction of the Trent and Lyme at Hanford, to an altitude of five hundred and fifty feet above sea level. From this point, it commands extensive views over the surrounding North Staffordshire landscape and, more importantly, the Trent Valley, which invaders, if any, would follow.

To understand the history of the area known as the Potteries, we first have to understand the underground riches it inherited from the Carboniferous period. The Penkhull area was part of a vast tropical coastal swamp stretching from Birmingham to Edinburgh. It is from the natural processes of life and death of plants, and the successive rise and fall of the landscape, that alternate layers of coal and sandstone were laid. This combination of raw materials would lead to the formation of the pottery industry within the wider area of North Staffordshire.

After that, during the Triassic period two hundred million years ago, desert conditions prevailed. Gravels and red sandstones were deposited by flash floods and large rivers, forming the rocks beneath Trentham, Sideway and Parkhall. Much wearing away of the top surface took place before the sands and gravels of the Triassic formation were laid down on the old coal measure rocks. At Penkhull, the whole of the gravels have been washed off the high ground into the rivers below, leaving the Keele group of sandstone exposed at the summit.

Much of Penkhull's landscape is the product of the last two and a half million years, during which time developments included the advance of ice sheets across the region. This is the background of pre-historic Penkhull, where man had not yet trod the soils that would later sustain some of the first settlers to North Staffordshire.

Thousands of years before man trod the soils there roamed the Bos Primigenius. Evidence of this, the skull and horns were discovered whilst excavating for a diversion of the Fowley Brook in 1877.

Bos Primigenius

The River Trent lies along the eastern side of the Penkhull ridge and its valley shows features, which indicate that the river could well have been a mile wide at this time stretching from almost the bottom of Penkhull New Road to half way up City Road, Fenton. At Sideway, half a mile to the south east, there is significant glacial displacement, suggesting a history of land disturbance in the area as the Great Ice Age came to its close. Further evidence was found in 1892 whilst excavating Hanley Park lake when a huge boulder, originating from the north, which had been carried with the melting ice to settle, was uncovered. This was for many years displayed as a feature outside the entrance to the old Stoke swimming baths adjacent to the public library in London Road. What happened to this I wonder?

Penkhull lies neatly between two main geological features, notably the Etruria marls and the Newcastle and Keele group of sandstones. The district formed part of a large basin during the final phase of the Carboniferous sedimentation. The Etruria marl group, consisting of red marl and green grit, extends along the Trent valley from Hanford. At Mayne Street, and Trentham Road there has been extensively excavations of the red marls from quarries for use in the manufacture of bricks and tiles during the nineteenth and early twentieth centuries. These red marls were the result of grinding down the Newcastle and earlier sandstones, particularly by the glaciers. It was used in medieval times mixed with limestone to make mortar, but later became the basis of the earthenware production.

Marl Hole at Trent Vale

11

North of Hanford, at the junction of Rookery Lane, Trent Vale, stood a further marl hole, at the side of which was excavated a Roman kiln in the 1950s. We shall discuss the significance of this later. Half a mile to the north, in the direction of Newcastle stood Wheatley Tileries, now demolished and replaced by Springfields Retail Park. I recall that it took many years to fill in this huge hole, which stretched from the rear of the properties in Springfield Road almost to the A34.

Passing to the east of Trent Vale, a geological fault throws down the marls to form the lower slopes of Penkhull on the easterly side between Boothen and Stoke. On the north side of Penkhull New Road, near to where Ashfields Cottage once stood, the natural junction of the Newcastle group of sandstone and red marls becomes visible in the remaining open excavation to a depth of twenty feet. Thomas Doody, who was producing coarse brown pottery in Penkhull in the mid-seventeenth century, could well have obtained his raw material here. On the lower slopes of Penkhull hill, facing north at Hartshill and Etruria, the Etruria marls were again quarried on a commercial basis.

During the Middle Ages, quarries were dug in the centre of the village and presumably formed part of the economy of Penkhull. The one in the middle of the village although filled with water forming a pond existed until the 1840s. It was a place where young lads were immersed in some form of medieval rite upon reaching puberty to become either a Penkhullite or Penkhull Pile. Other quarries were located along the length of Newcastle Lane and the area of Whalley Avenue. Local stone was used to build the parish church at Hartshill. In recent times, work to lay new power cables to the hospital complex exposed just a few inches from the surface the red sandstone whilst marl was the product to be negotiated from Hunters Way down the hill to the north.

It was not until ten thousand years ago, when the landscape was not unlike that of Iceland today, that humans are known to have ventured into the region. Evidence of this in the form of tiny flint tools and butchered reindeer bones have been found in limestone caves of the Peak district some twenty miles away but not in Penkhull. Lack of agricultural expertise, however, resulted in the early settlers of North Staffordshire being unable to make little use of the productive soil of the area. They probably operated as hunters in the great forests that formed a large part of the landscape and grazed cattle in the lower fields and pastures available to them.

Some two thousand years B.C., farmers of the Neolithic period entered North Staffordshire from the south via the only access, the river valley. Invading Britain from Europe via the Humber Estuary they would follow the River Trent

to the point known as Hanford. It is from here that the land rises up sharply almost in a triangular shape to provide a natural defensive location. Penkhull, with its extensive views surrounded by dense forests would provide ideal hunting grounds for food while grassland on its western slopes was a perfect location for the early tribes to settle.

Penkhull was probably the first inhabited settlement within the city and three prehistoric finds in the area confirm its early occupation. The first is an early Bronze Age cup dating c2000-1500 B.C. found by Mr R. Scrivener, a local architect, during the excavations for Penkhull Garden Village in 1911. This type of cup is known as a Pygmy Cup. The discovery of this cup strongly suggests a burial mound as other pygmy cups found in the county were all discovered in burial mounds, but extensive developments of the surrounding area over the following fifty years have probably destroyed all other physical evidence.

The significance of this important find should not be under estimated. From around 2,500 BC, we see a new type of monument on the landscape. This is an individual burial under a round barrow and it signals a departure from the common older Neolithic custom of deposing the remains of the ancestors in repositories like earthen and megalithic barrows. A round barrow is essentially a single grave albeit a rather grand one that could only have been afforded by the better-off. This fact can either suggest that wealth was being accumulated in individual hands, or even more likely in the case for Penkhull, that it was built for the use of a local chieftain.

Pygmy Cup

The cup is handmade from clay, pinched and decorated with regular impressions, probably done by a stick end. The top rim decorated with a criss-cross pattern has a similarity to other pygmy cups found elsewhere in the country. Around the rim of the base there is a thin line around the circumference probably made by the pressure of a thread of hemp being pressed into the clay. The cup measures 32mm high, 75mm in diameter at its rim 59mm and 59mm at its base. There are no signs inside of any heated material which rules out the burning of incense. Nor could it have been made to contain any liquid because there are two small neat holes found half way down the vessel on one side. Although the exact purpose of these holes has not been confirmed, they could suggest that they were placed in that position to enable the vessel to be hung in some way on an upright support and not hung from a roof support otherwise the holes would have been spaced out equally for balance.

The cup was presented by the son of Mr Scrivener to Hanley Museum in 1931. Based upon the evidence available, archaeologist Dr. Barker suggests that it may have been used to contain something such as pot-pours, giving off a sweet scented smell within the burial mound.

Technically, this cannot be called a 'cup' since two deliberate holes in the body would have precluded its holding liquid; holes are common, but by no means universal in these vessels. The term 'incense cup' has been used in the past, assuming that such vessels were used to burn incense, or to hold pot-pours. No explanation is really satisfactory. Whether this vessel found at Penkhull was primarily domestic, adopted for a funerary use, or primarily funerary, is not known, but certainly their presence in graves is well-known and frequently they accompany cinerary urns. The discovery of this cup at Penkhull strongly suggests that an Early Bronze Age burial was disturbed during the ground works for the Garden Village.

It should be remembered that a British Barrow was found in 1858 at Northwood, Trentham in which were found male and female human remains, probably those of a chieftain. Here would be placed alive his wife and his dog to provide for the chief's future life.

The second pre-historic find is a fine flintleaf-shaped arrow head of Neolithic period 2000-2500 B.C. This fine example of workmanship was found in the garden of a house in Chamberlain Avenue near to its junction with Hunters Way.

Its length measures 30mm and its width 25mm. Although now over 4,000 years old the workmanship is still clearly visible. It was chipped into its leaf shape, the point of which remains sharp

Arrow head found off Hunters Way

enough to penetrate if used as a head to an arrow. Also associated with the same period, is a stone axe head, fashioned from a basic ingenious rock. Although found in Penkhull, probably by a pupil of Penkhull Senior School, but no exact location is recorded.

Hammer head found in Penkhull

The first settlement of Penkhull would be a little further to the north than the present churchyard. It would be a simple clearing around the junction area of St. Thomas Place bounded by Honeywall and Doncaster Lane. In this clearing there would be a few huts erected close together for mutual protection from wild beasts, invading tribes and to give social and economic support. It would also have a wooden fence around its perimeter to add further security at night. In the centre there would be a hut, probably whitewashed, placed apart for the chieftain. This clearing in the centre of a huge forest would be where the day to day work of coming and going took place, women talking and children playing, the never ending need to cook. cut wood and the like. It would be into this clearing, or a further clearing in the forest, perhaps where the present church stands, that early pagan worshippers brought oak branches from the forests at Oakhill and mistletoe for their rites. It is here that in all probability, thousands of years ago, human sacrifices were made. Evidence of such a ritual was discovered in 1984 in a peat bog in Cheshire. The victim, known as the *Lindow Man* had been struck on the head, strangled and had his throat cut, perhaps to drain the body of blood. He was young, fit and well-groomed, suggesting high social status. There were traces of mistletoe, suggesting a definite druidical connection. It is not beyond possibility that this form of sacrifice was executed here in Penkhull.

Any animals such as goats would be bought into huts at night for safety and warmth during the winter months. Later, as knowledge grew of how to smelt metal and forge tools, as the Bronze Age gathered momentum a smithy would follow. So too a pinfold to keep live-stock safe. No doubt hunters would travel within a few miles radius of the village to obtain their daily kill. and there would be the happy homecoming into the village clearing at dusk, with animals from the forests or fish from the rivers to the excitement of adults and children alike.

We still retain the names that relate to this time in Hunters and Brisley, an area which was until the mid 18th century known as Bearshill. Proof of hunting slightly away from the village was found when a further arrow head was discovered some years ago in Leawood Road, Trent Vale possibly left behind by a hunter after missing its target.

Iron Age Fort

The Iron Age in Britain covers the period from about 700 BC to 43 AD, following the Bronze Age and before the Roman period, when the working and use of iron gradually spread throughout the region. Of course, the introduction of iron-making did not happen overnight; nor did it take place everywhere at the same time.

Early studies of the British Iron Age tended to emphasise the importance of continental influence, with foreign invasions being responsible for the big changes that took place during the period. It is also thought to have been behind the emergence of large, fortified hill forts during the fifth and sixth centuries BC.

Although no direct evidence has yet been uncovered, the physical appearance of the hill of Penkhull in the area of Hunters Way with almost sheer drops to the valley below, strongly suggests a Celtic Iron Age Fort. Such a fort, dating c400 B.C. in that locality would have had extensive views over the Trent Valley, thereby being in a position to protect itself against any invading tribe coming from the direction of the south via the Trent. There is much evidence of such hill forts locally, Bury Bank at Darlaston, at the Wrekin and others. Any evidence of such a fort at Penkhull has been worn away with the passing of time as the geology of Penkhull was in the main sandstone. Primrose Hill, on the other side of the Trent Valley, overlooking the ford at Hanford bears similar features, and like the hill at Penkhull

could well have been a perfect location, the two guarding the entrance to North Staffordshire.

Old Owestry Hill Fort

The Hill Fort at Penkhull may have looked like this.

Evidence of early settlements is found in the use of place names towards the end of the first millennium B.C. Both the names of Penkhull and Honeywall are Celtic in origin and therefore pointers to the pattern of settlement in pre-Roman times. These two names of such importance will be discussed in full detail.

With the Roman Conquest, beginning with the invasion by Emperor Claudius 1 in AD43, a Roman garrison had been established at Trent Vale within seven years, guarding the approaches to the ford. A network of roads was established, including that across north Staffordshire linking Derby to Chesterton.

During excavation of the hill adjoining the southern end of Campbell Road, Stoke in 1971, for factory development, the ramparts of a Roman Fort were exposed indicating a

settlement in the locality. The University of Manchester investigated, stating that the results were better than expected, there being two clear V-shaped ditches indicating a Roman military site, the rampart of which had been destroyed probably by the second century A.D. The question must be asked whether this fort was so placed as to dominate any last remains of an Iron Age population situated just higher up the hill and to control, as slaves, the inhabitants of the largest settlement in the area, Penkhull.

In the late 1920s and early 30s there were numerous Roman finds in the area, mostly documented by the late Thomas Pape of Newcastle. It was a further twenty years later in July 1955, when a group of volunteers excavated a series of trial holes in the same area in which Pape had worked.

Two excavations were made, the first of which showed the first signs of occupation as a post hole was discovered. Adjacent to this lay a charcoal deposit, intermixed with pottery sherds and on the floor lay pottery consisting of lamp-holders, cooking pot lids, platters, flagons and an incense burner. A crude hearth was found together with an iron poker. The pots were fashioned from local clay but at this point no kiln was unearthed. At the end of the first session it was possible to deduce that the post holes supported a wattle and daub structure and with the profusion of potsherds, indicated a potter's workshop. The building it would seem had been burnt to the ground.

In March the following year, an up-draught kiln was found and can be classed as a typical first century up-draught type. Certain factors make it an important discovery. No other Roman kiln of this type has previously been located in this area of the north midlands and as such became the earliest known example. Exhibits from the kiln are on display at the City Museum in Hanley.

The second ditch was found to contain a dark powder silt, in which were found several coarse potsherds, fragments of amphora and two pieces of Samian pottery dating from the middle of the first century were found. The two locations are situated on the slopes of the hill overlooking the Trent valley. The evidence at this site, together with the ramparts found much later near to Campbell Road goes along way to providing early evidence of a Roman occupation in that part of Penkhull Township at Trent Vale. From this it must be recognized that it was an important site in first-century Roman occupation. In all probability, there would have been a hurried withdrawal from the site, perhaps the rebellion of Boudicca (A.D.61) demanding the return of all Roman outposts.

It is generally understood, in keeping with established facts, that where a fort is located there would be an adjacent civil camp where there would be found camp followers, taverns, shops, and probably Turkish baths. The site of St Joseph's College, the other side of Rookery Lane, is considered a most likely area for those purposes.

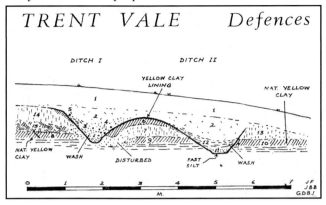

Picture of the site, off Campbell Road

It is interesting that the field on the other side of the River Trent which forms a triangular field where the Lyme Brooke joins the Trent was called Mythorne Meadow in old documents. It has been suggested that this name could have been derived from Mythrus, a God favoured by Roman soldiers and the nearness of the field to the fort could indicate the site of an early temple. However, as always all may not be as it seems as the old English word mythe simply means the confluence of two rivers which can be found in many others places, Mytholmroyd in Yorkshire and Mythathome in Staffordshire. The name continued to be listed in the manor court rolls until the 19th century as belonging to the Doody family.

At Campbell Place, Stoke, excavations undertaken by Mr Charles Lynam in 1903 exposed at a depth of just under ten feet a cobbled pavement covered with one foot five inches of silt, black and ashy, apparently washed and deposited by water suggesting a lengthy period of flooding. This was followed by a layer of potters refuse amounting to thirteen inches and topped by a previous road. A procedure continued once more to provide a total of three road surfaces before the present road

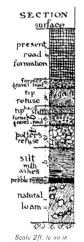

level was reached. The question remains of how this discovery can be interpreted? A further excavation in 1910 outside the White Lion Inn in Honeywall uncovered a boulder channel to carry water. At the time of excavation both were suggested to be of Roman origin. No written evidence of the latter has been discovered except the markings on an old O.S. map indicating the excavation. I last saw this map in what used to be the City Surveyor's Office sometime in the late 1960s.

With regards to the excavations in Campbell Place, Charles Lynam compiled a report published in the Transactions of the North Staffordshire Field Club. On the basis of these facts, even though they are limited, it may be assumed that the early settlers of Penkhull would have an almost daily contact with their Roman masters via a network of minor roads whilst being based at the fort at Trent Vale. Without further conclusive evidence on the subject any further assumption would be unfounded, but clearly with the evidence of Stoke churchyard, Campbell Place and Penkhull, points to a much earlier settlement for the Celts.

Evidence is sparse and our understanding of the early Saxon settlers limited, but it is with the Saxons the first proper settlement in Penkhull may be associated. In the 5th and 6th centuries AD these Germanic peoples migrated to Britain from the North Sea coast lands between the Netherlands and Norway. The progress of their settlements, and the tribal nature of their societies characterised by personal loyalty to a chief, was reflected in the place names. When Penkhull became occupied by the Saxons, they found that the hill was called Pencet or Penno.

Not understanding the word, they tacked onto it our word for hill, which in the West Midlands dialect was called hull, whereas it took the form of Hyll elsewhere. 'Cet' meant 'wood'. The modern Welsh is 'coed'. Penn is a little more difficult, literally meaning *head* but its meaning in place-names is more uncertain and varied. It sometimes meant *headland* or *promontory*, a description fitting the hill of Penkhull as seen from the south. It could simply mean 'hill' but recent interpretations would suggest 'end' to be a better description.

Thus it seems clear that Penkhull is the Anglo-Saxon name for an 'end of wood hill' which the British population had called Pencet. The Anglo-Saxons were settlers from the German regions of Angeln and Saxony who made their way over to Britain after the fall of the Roman Empire. They were masters in a new land and they did little to keep the legacy of the Romans alive replacing any Roman stone buildings with their own wooden ones, and spoke their own language, which gives rise to the English spoken today.

The Domesday entry of 1086 records a wood one mile long, and therefore the interpretation of the end of the wood seems appropriate. Although other local names have survived from this period, it must not be assumed however that each has a similar or identical meaning to Penkhull.

Different spellings of Penkhull and the dates they occur:

Pinchetel	- Domesday Book 1086
Pencil	- Inquisition 1249
Penciled	- Pleas 1262
Penket	- Inquisition 1298
Penkhill	- Final Concords 1272-1372
Penkhul	- Subsidy Roll 1327
Pencle	- Muster Roll 1563-1576-1640
Penckull	- Copyhold Court 1558-1689
Penghall	- Subsidy Roll 1331-3
Penckylle	- De-Banco 1444
Penchehull	- De-Banco 1444
Penkyll	- Ecclesiastical Survey 1535
Penkcull	- Muster Roll 1539
Penckull	- Duchy of Lancaster Map 1777
Penkhull	- Copyhold Court 1798

With the Anglo Saxons came field systems, new rural settlements, and better cultivation and draining of the soil. There are many other local settlements of the same period which can date their origin to the Anglo Saxon occupation such as Wolstanton, Knutton, Clayton, Butterton, Chesterton, Blurton, and Brampton, all of which were sited on the upper coal measures of the Keele and Newcastle beds. It may be deduced, therefore, that the location of an Anglo Saxon homestead village indicated a preference, firstly for high and dry sites, and secondly for where the upper coal measures outcropped.

Saxon Cross

Further evidence of Saxon occupation comes with the origins of Stoke Church. Here stands the Saxon cross, a listed ancient monument, which is dated c750-780. It was discovered buried in the churchyard in 1876 and at one time was used as a door lintel for the 10th century Saxon church. This stone church, the remains of which form two arches in Stoke Churchyard, replaced the first 8th century timber Saxon church. The significance of this is important

Reconstructed arches of Stoke old church

as it indicates a substantial occupation by the Anglo-Saxons in the area. The village would be situated in Penkhull, but the site of the church in Stoke would be chosen for two reasons; it was situated by the 'ford' over the River Trent on a highway to encourage travelers to worship and secondly to replace any remains of pagan worship which had previously occupied the site.

The battle which secured the Saxon Staffordshire Hoard took place near to Lichfield dates from the same period as the Saxon cross in Stoke. As warriors for any battle would come from far and wide it may rightly be assumed that the men of Penkhull would have been involved in that battle.

Recent studies suggest that Roman-British countryside could well have been settled with scattered farmsteads, hamlets and field systems. Nevertheless, the Early Saxon period had at times far reaching disruptions. Life was already localised and violent compared with what had gone before and what was to follow. There was a substantial fall in population and by the end of the sixth century the invaders were in permanent control of half of Britain.

The villagers who settled on this hill of Penkhull, shut in by the vast woodlands, had lived very easily in Saxon times, with respect to forest laws. But after the Conquest things changed, and Saxon laws were put away to make room for stringent Norman Laws. The husbandman may have hunted under his old rulers, and regaled himself with animals that the forest produced, the flesh of which was the Saxon's greatest luxury.

All this ended with the advent of the Normans, as every piece of forest land had its forest officers, whose tyranny knew no bounds. The people were not allowed to venture near these grounds without risk of pain and penalties. Under the Norman conquerors, if a person was determined to hunt without permission, (and permission was seldom granted) it depended upon the status of that person as to the punishment they would receive.

For Penkhull, all were serfs, under the feudal system of Lordship. Therefore, punishment would be at its most painful and a much more cruel method pursued. In some cases their property would be confiscated, but depended upon the possessions of the offender. Killing any beast of the forest would render the offender liable to abacination, which is a red hot iron to be held before the delinquent's eyes until he became blind. Enclosing, ploughing or putting any beast to pasture on part of the King's forests was punished with the forfeiture of the offender's property. Other punishments included having an ear cut off or a hand amputated at the wrist.

In the seventh century, a pattern of kingdoms emerged, Penkhull being a part of the Kingdom of Mercia. It was a time of assessments, based upon a measurement called 'hide'; an area necessary to support a free man. During the Saxon period, Christianity reached Staffordshire and the remains of a preaching cross from this period still stands witness in Stoke churchyard.

Chapter 2
Domesday Penkhull
and the origins of Newcastle-under-Lyme.

William the Conqueror landed unopposed at Pevensey Bay on the 28th September 1066 A.D. and later won the Battle of Hastings against King Harold at nearby Senlacc (later renamed Battle) on the 14th October 1066. William the Conqueror was crowned King of England in Westminster Abbey on Christmas Day 1066 a date that is embedded in the mind of almost every British citizen.

England in 1066 was probably the wealthiest and most well governed kingdom in Western Europe. On inheriting the kingdom, William confiscated most of the land from the Saxon nobility and divided it up between his Norman barons and the church. At Christmas 1085, intent on knowing more about the land he had reigned over for nearly twenty years and stamping his authority over it, William commissioned the survey that became known as the Domesday Book. The survey was much more than a means to satisfy William's fascination with his new kingdom. It recorded the value of land he held personally and that held by his barons and the church. Where there were disputes over land it helped settle disagreements.

William's reasons for compiling the Domesday Book will never be known for certain. However, Domesday was probably the result of a geld (land tax) inquest to raise funds for the realm's defence. In 1085, William's kingdom had come under threat from King Canute of Denmark and King Olaf of Norway. Additionally, unrest in France, Normandy and Scotland contributed to an uneasy winter. Geld was collected in the year of Domesday

Others authorities suggest William wanted an account of the lands held by his tenants-in-chief (land holders) so that he could exercise his rights as feudal overlord. There is also the school of thought that William wanted to assess the burden of mercenaries upon his vassals and redistribute the burden fairly. A new theory is that several years lapsed between the inquest and the making of Domesday and it was written after the death of William and was commissioned by his son, William II, as a result of a revolt in 1088. Some have also put forward the theory that William simply wished to learn more about the country he had conquered 20 years earlier and to bring order from the chaos of the Norman Conquest. *'To bring the conquered people under the rule of written law'* wrote one chronicler.

Some indication of the extent of clearance, occupation and relative prosperity established in the first phase of settlements can be gleaned from the Domesday survey. There is no mention of Stoke as such but the valuation of the church is recorded under the entry for Caverswall, as the Lord of Caverswall held half of the advowson of Stoke Church.

Many manors were recorded as 'waste', and for those listed locally it is unlikely that the description presented an accurate picture or physically equated with reality. In all probability it could have simply meant uninhabited or uncultivated or just lying in common.

Even if there had been extensive destruction in 1066, it would be expected that by 1086 that all the damage caused over twenty years earlier would have been made good. The word 'waste' is more likely to be interpreted as meaning that the taxable value was not worthy of either assessment or collection. Of those manors confirmed as agricultural units, Penkhull stands alongside Wolstanton as of the highest value, with Trentham a close third. All three have at their disposal the fertile loams of the Keele and Newcastle beds. Penkhull was valued at £6 0 0d as was Wolstanton; Trentham's valuation was at £5 15 0d, three times as valuable as the next richest manor of the area, and over twelve times higher than the majority of the North Staffordshire manors. In comparison, Madeley, the richest of the drift manors, possessing only four plough lands and three ploughs was valued at thirty shillings. Other drift manors were valued at ten shillings or less, but in contrast many had large areas of appurtenant woodland, suggesting that land clearance, except that of Madeley, had not progressed very far towards a more general agricultural landscape.

Domesday details life in eleventh century England. The wealth of information that Domesday provides helps create a snap shot of the rich landscape that William inherited. The survey reveals what areas of the countryside were worked as plough land, pasture, meadow or woodland, and suggests regional variations. It tells us something about the people who held or worked the land and the social relationships between them. As an Anglo-Saxon chronicler wrote, *not one ox nor one cow nor one pig which was there left out and not put down in his record.* In spanning twenty years, Domesday also tells of how the landscape changed as a result of activities aimed at protecting Norman England.

The Domesday entry for Penkhull reads:
The King holds Pinchetel, which was aforetime held by Earl Alfgar. There are two hides of land and their appurtenances. The arable land consists of eleven carucates, two ploughs are in the demesne and seventeen villeins and six bordars have eight ploughs. There are two acres of meadow, also a wood one mile long and two furlongs broad, the value of the whole being six pounds.

The first impression is of Penkhull as an extensive farming community embracing arable, meadow and woodland well supplied with farm machinery. The implications of the organised presentation of the entry, suggests a community, which had been established for some time. At its highest point, Penkhull village, no farming was possible because of the visible outcrop of red sandstone. It is this area that would have been chosen for early huts and a community settlement. The western and northern slopes provided ample opportunity for good farming. These later became the principal sites of the mediaeval 'open field' farming community.

The exact measurement of a 'hide' (the basis upon which tax assessments were made) varied depending on the state of cultivation. It was the amount of land that could be ploughed in a day using one plough with an eight oxen team. The measurement differed from around sixty acres to around one hundred and eighty acres according to the degree in which the terrain restricted farming techniques. An average of one hundred and twenty acres is generally accepted as an approximate measurement equal to one hide.

Where the Danes settled in England, the word 'carucate' replaced that of 'hide'. Domesday records for Penkhull eleven carucates indicating a manor of approximately one thousand three hundred acres; in addition there are a further two acres of meadow. Thus from a simple calculation, the size of Penkhull in 1086 may be assumed to reach far beyond the boundaries of the village of today.

The number of ploughs employed in the Demesne was two. This was the land set aside for the Lord of the Manor (absentee) who, with the assistance of compulsory labour from his villeins and bordars had the benefit of its crop or at least the value of it. A further eight ploughs; the villagers used each consisting of a team of eight oxen. This amounted to a total of eighty oxen employed within Penkhull. The six bordars each had a cottage, with a small plot of land attached for their own domestic needs. They would work in the Lord's demesne, farming a number of strips of land in the open fields in lieu of rent, and probably hired themselves out to other farmers with large holdings of land during harvest time.

From the Domesday Book entry a picture can be gleaned of what Penkhull was like in 1086. First of all to place Penkhull in the context of its importance and value, a comparison should be made with other villages of the area. Yates' Domesday settlements and relief map shows those in North Staffordshire and the immediate locality of Penkhull. It is significant that nearly all are four to six hundred feet above sea level.

List of Domesday Manors in North Staffordshire and value:

Penkhull	£6 0 0d
Wolstanton	£6 0 0d
Trentham*	£5 15 0d
Bucknall	waste
Norton	£2 0 0d
Madeley	£1 10 0d
Burslem	10 0d
Clayton	£1 0 0d
Fenton	waste
Hanford	2 0d

Trentham may well have included the immediate area of the castle site at Newcastle-under-Lyme.

This list clearly emphasizes the value of the Royal Manor of Penkhull at the time of Domesday, but it also lists two manors, Fenton and Bucknall as waste. Why this is so remains a question not easily answered and in the end any conclusion can only be subjective. First, it is known that after 1066, the army of William continued their conquest to the west, the midlands and to the north. The term *waste* or *wasted* appears several times; most often describing settlements the army had passed through, bringing death and destruction.

It could mean, however, that because parts of the district of Fenton and Bucknall are high and the soil thin they would be considered as moorland areas and as such the word 'waste' would describe them.

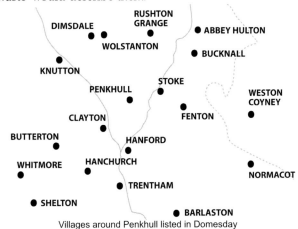
Villages around Penkhull listed in Domesday

The seventeen bordars of Penkhull's Domesday and their appurtenances appear to have continued their status as later they would become known as yeoman farmers of the mediaeval period. The manorial records for the manor of Newcastle contain numerous references to 'ancient messuages', numbering seventeen in Penkhull until the early part of the nineteenth century.

So where did these original homesteads lie? The majority of the manorial records for Newcastle-under-Lyme have survived in the National Archives. With research it has been possible with the use of these records combined with others, to accurately identify the exact spot of the homestead for nearly all of the seventeen villains.

With the use of these court records, together with Reeve Books almost an intimate knowledge of the area can be gathered for centuries. The Reeve (the person responsible to the Steward of the Manor for the administration and duties of its officers) for the Manor of Newcastle-under-Lyme was elected by his fellow tenants on an annual basis. Because of this he was quite often their spokesman in negotiations with the Deputy Steward of the manor appointed by the Lord of the manor. He was in charge of the agricultural policy and the livestock and was there to ensure the smooth running of the courts.

This Reeve Book of 1796 makes possible a connection with an earlier listing of 1714 of all the 'ancient holdings' and linking this to an earlier Reeve book which dates from 1579 and then to at least 1815. Through the use of over six hundred years of manorial records. The record of 1796 lists all the seventeen ancient messuages and the years that the tenant of that messuage performed on a rota basis the duty of manorial Reeve. The description of the property recorded in 1796 can easily be identified. The year 1415 is some time after 1086, but in reality it is most unlikely that there would have been any change of location for an 'ancient messuage' as it was a period of little or no change. Communities remained static except for the labouring classes, who, during periods of failing harvests, often moved to find work elsewhere. It may therefore be taken as certain that the 'ancient messuages' listed throughout the Reeve Books up to the early 20th century, are the same smallholdings but not the same buildings as were listed in Domesday. The significance of being able to identify the holdings of the early settlers should not be under estimated.

The wood listed in the Domesday entry would be the Kings and, as such no hunting or public access would be allowed. The way from the town of Stoke to Newcastle would be via Honeywall to Penkhull and then down what is now called Doncaster Lane. It is here at this junction that the early village of Penkhull would be identified with the majority of homesteads dotted around the clearing in the forest. The following map has been drawn up to identify those early homesteads.

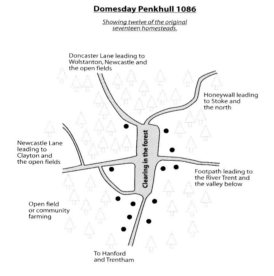

Domesday Penkhull 1086

Showing twelve of the original seventeen homesteads.

Doncaster Lane leading to Wolstanton, Newcastle and the open fields

Honeywall leading to Stoke and the north

Newcastle Lane leading to Clayton and the open fields

Clearing in the forest

Footpath leading to the River Trent and the valley below

Open field or community farming

To Hanford and Trentham

To summarise, Penkhull had a total of around thirteen hundred acres of arable and meadow, and a section of woodland, a much greater area than its occupation today. The Lord of the Manor held land sufficient for the work of two ploughs and the local population was obliged to tend his land as well as to cultivate their own. There was a minimum of twenty-three dwellings and eighty oxen. Using a formula for population trends it may be estimated that approximately one hundred and twenty-seven people lived in the Royal Manor of Penkhull at the time of Domesday.

Most villages at the time of Domesday were comparatively simple. Many were little more than scattered hamlets, not yet settled into the nucleated pattern of the medieval village. However, some settlements like Penkhull were well established with their open fields and even a church,

although this was situated down the hill in the town of Stoke (Stoches) and listed in Domesday as part of the estate belonging to Robert de Stafford as part of his fee of Caveswall.

Life for the Domesday peasant was harsh. Peasant houses were made of wood, wattle and mud, which needed frequent maintenance after harsh winters. Families shared a single large room with their animals for warmth in winter, and cooking was over an open fire. Clothes made of wool, flax and skins were rarely changed. Only the elite, the lord, the priest and the reeve, the lord's steward and perhaps some of the wealthier inhabitants would enjoy better housing, clothing and have sufficient to eat throughout the year.

Village life revolved around the agricultural calendar. In spring animals grazed in the pasture, and seed was sown. Summer was the busiest period; particularly when the harvests of wheat, barley, rye, hay, vegetables and fruit were being gathered. In autumn, animals grazed on the remains of the crops and manure provided for fields, which were then ploughed. Winter was the time when family and those animals not killed for meat stayed indoors.

In an attempt to identify the area covered by the Domesday record of Penkhull, an assessment of the surrounding area together with available documentary evidence has to be viewed and evaluated. The high estimated acreage of agricultural land recorded in the Domesday entry for Penkhull has led to the belief that its boundaries included parts of what is now known as Newcastle, stretching up to Parliament Row at Hanley to the north and to Hanford in the south.

Newcastle-under-Lyme

There is no mention of Newcastle-under-Lyme in the Domesday Book, which raises many questions. Was Newcastle as we know it part of the Royal Manor of Penkhull? Did the new castle at Newcastle replace an older one perhaps at Chesterton, Trentham or even Penkhull?

William Camden, the earliest writer to present a theory on the origins of Newcastle suggested in his 'Britannia' of 1586 that the castle replaced a previous castle three miles to the north at Chesterton. This assertion by Camden remained unchallenged for over two hundred and fifty years. Few historians, however, have attempted to solve the question of its origin. William Pitt in the early nineteenth century argued that the perpetuation of the error by which Newcastle succeeded Chesterton as the urban centre of North Staffordshire was due to a misreading of Camden's 'Britannia'. Other historians, notably Mr S A H Bourne, successfully argued in 1912 against Camden's observations, presenting an alternative argument that the *old* castle, was in fact located at nearby Trentham, two miles to the south of Newcastle. On the other hand, Thomas Pape, writing in the 1920s, supported the view taken by Camden stating *there seems no good reason for departing from the view that Newcastle was so called to distinguish it from the old castle at Chesterton.*

In 1973, Professor David Palliser writing in a *History of Newcastle*, which celebrated the octocentenary of the town, did not argue the case of Bourne, but, like Pape, presented no alternative argument. He maintained without any supportive evidence Camden's 'Britannia' theory of a new castle to replace the old one at Chesterton and commented *the site of the future town was simply an area between the villages of Trentham, Penkhull and Wolstanton where two main roads forked.*

Dr. Robin Studd of the University of Keele presents an authoritative argument to substantiate his theory that a settlement, later known by the name of Newcastle was in existence at the time of Domesday, hidden within the entry for the Royal Manor of Trentham. Studd qualifies his hypothesis successfully arguing the errors of the Domesday commissioners, along with a considered assessment of the entry for the Manor of Trentham.

> There is land for 3 ploughs. In demesne is
> 1 plough: 5 villeins, 1 bordar and a reeve have 3½
> Ploughs: The priest and a free man have 2 ploughs,
> 3 villeins and 6 bordars 1 plough.
> The woodland is 1 league long and ½ wide.

Studd points out that the first part of the entry conforms to standard commissioner's dialogue. Immediately after being informed of the priest and the freeman and their plough-teams, the entry continues with an additional three villein tenants and six small-holders with only a single plough between the three of them in the manor. It is from this additional *tagged-on* entry that Studd develops the subject and points to a detached part of the manor of Trentham, situated where the castle stood at Newcastle. Similarities are to be found elsewhere including Stoke, which held Tittensor as part of its ancient parish even though it was four miles to the south. Studd concludes: *If this view is correct, then a number of consequences follow. First, if this is Domesday Newcastle, then we can be sure that a settlement whatever it was called - Market Trentham perhaps - and that Newcastle existed before the Norman Conquest, for at least local trading as a place of "voluntary association for the purposes of trade".*

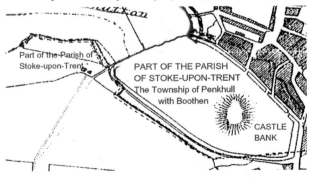

Plan showing the area of the former area of the castle belonging to the parish of Stoke-upon-Trent until 1875

To substantiate his argument, Studd then follows with an accumulation of related documents examining all the available evidence, which are published in 'Staffordshire Studies' Vol.III 1990. These conclusively point to the existence of the castle called Newcastle and its situation

within a detached section of the manor of Trentham and correspond to the second part of the Domesday entry for Trentham.

The question of the size of this additional part of Trentham Manor, now known as Newcastle and its boundaries has never been addressed. The Domesday entry lists enough land for a team of oxen sufficient to cultivate the area in one year. It was calculated that one team of oxen could work an area between sixty and one hundred and eighty acres, depending on soil quality and the lie of the land. The figure used to analysis the approximate size of Penkhull is one hundred acres per team of oxen. If the formula is applied to the castle pool area at Newcastle, forty acres are accounted for.

This figure suggests that *the appurtenances* referred to in the grant of 1140/46 amounted to at least a further sixty acres of land refering to the adjacent early settlement of traders in the immediate vicinity of the castle site. Further calculations of the surrounding area indicate that an area approximately one and a half times the size of Pool Dam would be a reasonable assessment of the detached part of the manor of Trentham as pointed out by Studd. If this were the case, what would be the boundaries of such a section of Trentham manor? So often boundaries of a manor or parish are distinguished by natural features, such as a river, brook or main highway.

Both Studd and Pape point to an early settlement, providing for and exploiting any commercial opportunity in the vicinity of the castle itself. This is an established pattern used from the Roman occupation of Britain.

A Royal Charter of 1162 further suggests that a detached part of the Manor of Trentham was situated two miles away at what is now called Newcastle: *whereby John, the prior of the church of the Blessed Virgin Mary and All Saints confirmed the priory endowments among which was 'a certain small township of Newcastle which is the territory of the parish of Trentham.* This statement at such an early period of Newcastle's history ought to be sufficient to resolve the issue.

Early town maps of Newcastle show that a market existed in the Upper Green area that may have formed the boundary to the west along with what is now known as Bridge Street and High Street with the Manor of Penkhull. The Lyme Brook formed the eastern boundary. If this was the case, the area to the east of High Street would be under the jurisdiction of Stoke, presenting for the first time the case that most of the area known as Newcastle Borough today would at the time of Domesday be included in the entry for Penkhull.

Calculating the area of the former site of the castle and its surrounding pool and drawing a comparison with current maps, almost mirror each other, add further support for the theory of Dr. Studd.

Chapter 3
The Royal Manor of Penkhull
and Newcastle-under-Lyme.

If the Domesday Book had not been compiled a detailed insight into many hamlets, villages and towns would be denied to us. Domesday records the first documented evidence we have for Penkhull and its importance with regard to its higher recorded monetary value than that of many other villages in North Staffordshire during that period. Penkhull, as we know it today, is a small rural suburb overlooking the town of Stoke, whereas for hundreds of years Penkhull comprised a huge slice of Stoke-on-Trent stretching from parliament Row, Hanley to Hanford, and incorporated around half of what is today considered the Borough of Newcastle-under-Lyme.

We have already discussed and explored the significance of Domesday when Penkhull was recorded as a Royal Manor but to further the task of exploring its significance within the context of North Staffordshire it is necessary to view other records that can identify Penkhull as a place of importance and integrity.

The Royal Manor of Penkhull retained its own title and independence for some time after 1086, indicating its value to the crown. The Pipe Rolls of 1168/9 inform us that Penkhull men pay seven marcs as 'aid', amounting to £4 13s 4d on the marriage of Princess Matilda to the Duke of Saxony. To place this sum into context, the men of Newcastle paid slightly less at £4 6s 8d and by further comparison, the men of Wolverhampton paid £2 13s 4d. The tax paid by Penkhull during the same year to the crown amounted to £1 4s 8d. Various amounts of tax were paid by the villagers of Penkhull: 1185 – 24s 6d, 1195 – 20s, 1198 four marks, 1205 - £9 9s 4d and in 1206 - £7 0s 0d. These sums reflect the agricultural wealth of an area and show that Penkhull's monetary worth was substantial compared with most areas, which today greatly exceed the size of Penkhull.

The Pipe Roll of II Richard I and 1 John is dated Michaelmas, 1195. (King John's Coronation took place on Ascension Day May 27th 1199. (Therefore the Pipe Roll is entitled 'first of John') This document lists the Royal estates of Penkhull, Wolstanton, Meertown, Tettenhall, and Alrewas which had all been supplied with fresh stock at the expense of the crown. From the fact that Penkhull is included in this pipe roll it is clear that Penkhull and other manors remained in the Sheriff's care and were of ancient escheat (land reverted back to the Lord or Crown when a tenant died without heirs, or where the heir had not reached his majority, or else where the tenant had committed an offence which involved the forfeiture of his estate)

It is not known why the king decided to re-stock the manor of Penkhull, in 1198/9. It might have been because it contributed such high taxes that it was considered necessary to invest in its wealth to produce even more tax: *at the King's expense with sixteen oxen the sheriff charges 48s for two cart horses; 6s, for twenty-five cows; 75s one bull; 3s for fifteen sows and 1 boar 16s.*

It was in 1212 that the first list appears recording that military service was part of the duty of the men of Newcastle manor. In the great inquest of service included in this register entitled 'Testa de Neville', there is no specific entry for Penkhull of military service to the castle at Newcastle, even though King John had requested all such service to be accounted for. Nor in this document is Penkhull listed as paying rent to the King, even though the surrounding districts did under the title of 'ancient right'. Those that did pay are estates belonging to the castle at Newcastle; which include Knutton; Dimsdale; Hanchurch; Clayton; Hanford; Whitmore; Longton; Hanley; Fenton; Chatterley; Normacot; Tunstall; Bradwell and Thursfield. It may be assumed therefore, that Penkhull at this point in history could still be regarded as a Royal Manor in its own right and not a part of the larger community incorporated in the Manor of Newcastle-under-Lyme. The Plea Rolls of 1227/8 confirm that Penkhull retained its independent title as a manor: *The Manor of Penkhull appeared by twelve jurors at the assizes at Lichfield.*

An inquisition into the lands held, introduced by Henry III in 1249, recorded the following: *also, they say that the Lord the King has in the demesne of the vill of Penchul, one carucate of land with appurtenances, which the men of the same vill render 15 shillings. In addition the men of the same vill hold 8½ virgates of land and render yearly 34 shillings. Also, the men of Penchul hold eight bovates of bondmen land (a man bound to service without wages) for 20s 8d. Also William Muriel holds the vill of Penchul the fields of Caldhock in the King's demesne and renders by the year 11s and 4s.* (Murial was also keeper of the King's Park at Cliffe Vale and his name recurs in Merrial Street, Newcastle).

In 1251 a further record confirms the independent status of Penkhull: *The Abbot of Hulton has entered into the Manor of Bradenop and of Mixen, which was a Royal domain of the King, through Henry de Audley, after the time of the death of Earl Ranulf* (1232). Item: *the service of Bradenop and Mixen which was of the Royal domain of the King is subtracted, that is to say 5s 2d and four loads of hay, which used to be rendered yearly to the Royal Manor of Penkhull.*

What was actually involved in this transaction is accounted for 24 years later. The Staffordshire Hundred Rolls of 1275 records: the Abbot of Hulton who held Mixen, which used

21

to be held of the king in fee farm by the service of five shillings and a cartload of hay and an iron fork paid to the Royal Manor of Penkhull.

A further inquisition held during the 25th year of King Edward 1st, 1296 records: *The land in the demesne there are eight bovates (a variable measure related to the soil quality of the amount of land an ox could plough in a year, usually one-eighth of a Hide) which the customary tenants of Penchul hold, each bovate renders 5s. Total 40s. There are also 34 bovates of land, which eighteen sokemen hold and each bovate renders 12d at four times a year and for certain works which they are accustomed to do for the said bovates 7s 6d at two terms a year. Total 41s 6d.* The document continues to list other lands, amounting a total of nearly two hundred acres to the value of £8 3s 2d.

Until this time there is little evidence to suggest otherwise than that Penkhull still remained a Royal Manor despite the fact that a castle had been established at Newcastle and a Manor had been created to provide an income for its maintenance. The following document is the last confirmation of Penkhull's status as a Royal Manor. It is an Assize Roll taken at Stafford on the Friday following the feast of the Exaltation of the Holy Cross, 2nd year of the reign of Edward II, (19th September 1308) *The steward of Thomas Earl of Lancaster names the Earl's Manor of Penkhull as of ancient demesne of the Crown and where no writ would run but the writ of right.* A modern interpretation would be that only the rule of law would exist in the Royal Manor of Penkhull.

In 1327, a subsidy was granted by the first Parliament of King Edward III to meet the expenses of the Scottish War. The statute has been lost, but the King's Commission, dated 23rd November, in the 1st year of Edward III, recites that the Earls, Barons, Knights, Citizens and Burgesses of the Kingdom, had granted to him a twentieth part of all moveable goods for the defence of the kingdom against the Scots. Each vill, were to elect four, or six, as assessors to make inquiry into the goods possessed by every man of the vill on Michaelmas Day, 1 Edward III, in the house or out of the house, and to tax the same according to their true value. A number of items were exempt from the tax such as armour, jewels and robes of knights and the goods of those whose moveable property did not reach the amount of 10s. The commission made no distinction between freemen and others, and it is probable therefore that the villein tenants such as those in Penkhull would be taxed.

	s.	d.
De Johne de Tytnesovere		xij.
Willmo de Boys	ij.	vj.
Willmo de Tytnesovere		xv.
Rogero del Boys	x	viij.
Willmo filio Willelmi	x	ij.
Johne Speremon	xiiij.	ob.
Thoma filio Willelmi	xiiij.	ob.qu.
Willmo Attende		xij.
Willmo filio Henrici		xv.
Johne Atte lake	ij.	o
Willmo le Faunt	ij.	o
Ricardo de Fulford	ij.	ob. qu.
Roberto de Fulford	ij.	iij.
Willmo de Suede	iij.	o
Stephano Dyke	ij.	ij.
Willmo le Faunt	ij.	o
Johne del Hu	ij.	ob.qu.
Margareta Croket		xviij.
Adam Molendinario		xv.
Thoma le Taylor		xvj.
Ricardo de Ays		xij.
Willmo Amys		xv.
Willmo filio Willelmi le Hayward		xij.
Ricardo fratre ejus		xj.
Willmo Broun	ij.	o
Roberto de Wythemor	ij.	j.ob.
Symone Schakespere		xij.ob.
Willmo de Scheperigge		xviij.
Nicholao filio Ade		xij.
John Symond		xiiij.
Willmo Attetouneshende		xij.
Willmo in le Wro	ij.	o
Ricardo le Smethessone		xvj.
Johne Lovot	ij.	o
Summa	lij.s.x.d.	ob.qu. p'b'.

Many of these names continually appear in the manor court rolls for the next 400 years. The list comes under the heading of Penkhull and not a part of Newcastle, which is listed separately. There were twelve people paying over 2s. twenty paying over 1s to 1s 11d and only one paying under 1s. There were a total of 34 paying the Subside Tax. A total of eleven were exempt from paying the tax. If the multiple of five is used for the average family size, it could be reasoned that the population for Penkhull amounted to 225. The total value collected amounted to £2 12s 10d.

In comparison there were only twelve who paid between the sum of 2s and 3s listed in the Subsidy Tax of 1332/3.

From 1335, there is no clear date from which the Royal Manor of Penkhull ceased to exist and become part of the manor of Newcastle. Like other parts of the Newcastle manor, Penkhull contained land which was farmed by serfs as part of their rental and also performed duties as castle guard for a set number of days per year as part of their obligation to the Lord in exchange for service.

It seems that by gradual process the manor of Penkhull became an appendage of Newcastle at some date after 1308, (that being the last reference of the manor of Penkhull) and 1335 when it was included in the Manor Court Rolls of Newcastle.

To emphasize the importance of the district of Penkhull following its attachment to the manor of Newcastle the Poll Tax of 1337 points to a Penkhull retaining its agricultural wealth, only second to Newcastle, Stone and Eccleshall.

Newcastle	£9 13 4d
Eccleshall	£8 10 4d
Stone	£3 19 0d
Penkhull	£3 16 4d
Biddulph	£3 5 0d
Tunstall	£2 11 0d
Fenton	£1 15 0d
Trentham	£1 8 8d
Ashley	£1 3 0d
Hanchurch	£0 15 4d

During John of Gaunt's overlordship of Newcastle, there is a very long list of revenues raised for the Duchy of Lancaster from his manor of Newcastle, one of which was collected in the 10th year of the reign of Richard II (1386). The provost of Newcastle, William Bateson, prepared the account and shows Penkhull retaining its position as a wealthy farming community.

Penkhull	£15 10 9d
Clayton and Seabridge	£13 19 3d
Wolstanton	£10 4 7d
Shelton and Hanley	£7 1 1d
Knutton	£4 11 6d

When the Borough of Newcastle applied for the renewal of its charter in 1344, Alice - widow of Thomas, Earl of Lancaster, executed for treason - received for life by royal grant many of his estates including the manor of Newcastle-under-Lyme. She died without issue in 1348 and her nephew Henry became the lord of the manor. He was the son of Henry, third earl of Lancaster, and brother of Thomas, the second earl.

Other aspects of the history of Penkhull can be gleaned from the Plea Rolls of the Crown. The following dated 1364/5 lists a murder: The jury of Pyrhull presented that Hugh de Stredeley, the brother of John de Stredeley, living at Penkhull, had feloniously killed Simon le Meleward at Penkhull on the Thursday the feast of St. James. A further entry for the 14th century is dated Easter, 4, Richard II (1380); John, King of Castile and Leon; and Duke of Lancaster, sued Thomas de Podmore, Ralph de Podmore, and James de Podmore, for breaking, vier armis, together with John de Podmore and Ralph Stynges into his free warren at Penkhull with that of Wolstanton, Clayton and Shepbrugge and taking hares and rabbits, pheasants and partridges. None of the defendants appeared and the sheriff returned they could not be found. The sheriff ordered their arrest and to produce them at the Quindene of Holy Trinity. (Free Warren is an area within the manor that is for the private hunting of the crown or those obtaining this approval. Any person found poaching without approval, were classed as common criminals).

The 12th century was a period of draconian legislation. Penkhull, like much of the country lay under the iron grip of the Royal Forest laws, with all hunting reserved to the King. The penalty for poaching was severe. For killing a deer on the King's land for example, the punishment would be the amputation of a hand or an ear. An eye could be gouged out as a further form of punishment, or even a death penalty imposed. The King's foresters, notorious for their greed and corruption, rigorously upheld these harsh laws. The laws became increasingly unpopular during the 12th century, and the Magna Carta 1215 mitigated some of the grievances. Vivian de Stoke, the first recorded Parson of the parish church of St. Peter ad Vincula in 1154 was much favoured by John, who besides appointing him to Stoke gave also the vicarage of Wolstanton. Vivian was known for his prowess in the hunting field. He was once fined the sum of one mark for the ravages committed by his dogs in the King's forest, which was called Hay of Clive, an area now covered by the districts of Cliffe Vale and Hartshill. Vivian seemed reluctant to pay, for it was returned by the sheriff as being in arrears. Vivian was again fined four pence on numerous occasions for not attending the manorial courts at Newcastle.

A charter attributed to 1173 to create the Borough of Newcastle was granted to the people to liberate them from feudalism which involved restrictions - social, economical and political - that were associated with the manorial status of neighbouring lands. The borough was to all intents and purposes carved out and separated from the manorial system. This is what is meant by a 'free borough', freedom from payment of traditional manorial dues, but Newcastle was still subjected to an annual cash payment to the crown. This charter however, relates only to the town of Newcastle and did not include the castle or the Pool Dam area, which by 1215 formed the focal point of the Manor of Newcastle-under-Lyme situated then, not in the parish of Trentham, but in the ancient parish of Stoke-upon-Trent.

Before 1175, Trentham priory had owned the chapels of Newcastle and Whitmore, but gave them to Robert de Constentin. Robert later shared his interest in Newcastle with Vivian, Rector of Stoke, (1154-1189). By an agreement, Robert and Vivian surrendered their interest to the priory and Vivian received in exchange a life holding in Whitmore chapel. Thomas Pape (1928) records further complicated disputes over the ownership of the advowsons together with that of Wolstanton, but concludes by asking the question when was Newcastle chapel attached to Stoke as the mother church suggesting either 1215 when the manor was granted to Ranulf de Blundeville, earl of Chester, or when the King caused the prior of Trentham to surrender its claim to Whitmore chapel between 1250 and 1257. It is from this period that the whole of Newcastle remained within the parish of Stoke-upon-Trent until the Rectory Act of Stoke-upon-Trent, dated 1807.

In effect, this Act of 1807 separated the town from the ancient parish of Stoke, creating a new independent parish of Newcastle. The site of the castle and pool dam were not included in the transfer thereby leaving this detached wedge-shaped section of Stoke parish to be governed by the Select Vestry of Stoke, who were superseded in 1839 by Stoke Improvement Commissioners and Overseers.

The castle may have contained some ancient chantry so would have been the beneficiary of land and financial benefit for the daily rendering of prayers for the faithful departed until its decay. The site of the castle, once decayed remained a poorly drained area, marshy and of little use commercially and as such was unsuitable for any commercial development or residential purposes. It is quite remarkable however, that mid-nineteenth century maps still marked the Pool Dam area as a detached part of the parish of Stoke-upon-Trent and within the township of Penkhull with Boothen.

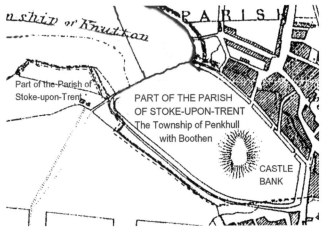

Pool Dam area, once the site of the castle moat

This area of Pool Dam remained the property of the Duchy of Lancaster and thereby of copyhold tenure until it was sold in 1829. At the time of its sale, the area extending some forty acres but remained within the parish of Stoke and consequently under its community provision. To continue to designate the area as part of Stoke-upon-Trent was both impractical and expensive to service for sanitation, policing, refuse, health and education. There was also a further provision under the obligation of Stoke, that of maintenance of the poor.

That part of Newcastle including Lower Street, housed some of the most under-privileged people in the Borough, and formed a burden to Stoke. It was therefore decided to apply to parliament under the Local Poor Law Amendment Act, 1867, for this detached part of Stoke to be transferred from the parish and administration of Stoke-upon-Trent to that of Newcastle in 1875 for all purposes connected with the relief of the poor, the repair of the highways, the making and collection of all rates and lists of voters etc. (Local Govt. Board poor 28 & 29 Victoria 1875 p.8-10).

Penkhull for centuries was dependent entirely upon the market town of Newcastle-under-Lyme just over a mile away for trade and commerce. It was here that produce of its land was sold, cattle auctioned and household items and husbandry purchased. It was also by way of Newcastle that the stagecoach linked Penkhull to other parts of the country. Even during the 19th century, properties in Penkhull were advertised not as near to the town of Stoke with its industries polluting the atmosphere, poor housing and little sanitation, but to the prosperous market town of Newcastle.

It is not surprising; therefore, that in April 1831 a special meeting of the townsfolk of Stoke was called in the upper room of Stoke Town Hall, in what is now Hill Street. Initially it was to discuss the forthcoming Reform Bill then before Parliament, which was being put forward by Lord John Russell. Under the chairmanship of Herbert Minton, the first item on the agenda was a proposal to apply for permission from parliament to transfer the township of Penkhull and Boothen to the Borough of Newcastle. This would then be included in the Reform Bill. Thomas Minton, spoke at the meeting to support the motion. Minton was convinced the scheme would be advantageous to all parties. It would benefit his property and that of his neighbours by giving them an efficient police force. However, Mr John Boyle spoke against the plan. He felt that the idea was nothing less than an attempt to separate the interests of Stoke from that of the rest of the Potteries. At this, there was a huge sound of cheers from the meeting. The minutes of the meeting make interesting reading with claims, counterclaims, fists raised, people evicted, and accusation that Mr Boyle had brought in a rabble to oppose the proposition. In the end, the proposal was defeated and the township of Penkhull with Boothen remained within the Borough of Stoke-upon-Trent.

A view from the south of the former Royal Manor of Penkhull

Chapter 4
Medieval Hospital of St Loye.

Just before the lower reaches of Penkhull as the land slopes down to the valley of the Lyme Brook, on a site now occupied by the University Hospital teaching buildings for student doctors, once stood a hospital dating from around the middle of the 13th century.

The University Hospital of North Staffordshire

The site of the Hospital of St. Loye

Hargreaves Map 1832

Documentary evidence of this Hospital of St Loye has been known for many years, but the exact location remained a mystery until 1985, when excavations to the west of the new hospital wards was being carried out.

Then, two skeletons and some stone foundations were uncovered together with a few sherds of medieval pottery. No serious archaeological work was carried out and the site was covered over to enable a car park to be established. From this time, whatever secrets these 'finds' held were to remain hidden for a further sixteen years.

Before 1985, there had been discussions to the origins of this hospital. It was first thought that it could have been attached to the parish church of St Peter in Stoke even a perhaps a leper hospital. There is little substance in this argument. It is more likely that a hospital evolved naturally in the vicinity of the Royal castle at Newcastle and with its adjacent trading community.

The location, described above (within the present hospital grounds) is on one of the earliest roads through North Staffordshire, from London to Carlisle. However, it is of sufficient distance from the towns of Newcastle and the village of Penkhull to be set in isolation and to offer to both communities a refuge when ill, as well as being available to travellers.

Documentation for the Hospital of St Loye.

There has been much confusion over the hospital's dedication. By 1266, there was a hospital 'without' Newcastle dedicated to St. John the Baptist when in that year the master and the Crown granted brethren protection for three

years. In 1437, it was reported that it was dedicated to St Louis and St John followed by St Louis, were given as alternative dedications in 1454, 1459 and 1460 although St Eloy was given as the sole dedication in 1485 and 1546. In 1485, 1516 and 1551 it was referred to as St Leo.

In 1546, the Chantry Commissioners reported that the rent of certain lands amounting to £2 13s 4d a year was paid to a priest called the Master of the Hospital of St. Loye. The incumbent did not know the name of the founder or the purpose of its foundation. This suggests that it had been founded for several hundred years.

So who was St Loye? All authorities agree that Loy, Loi, or Loye are English corruption of the French Eloy or Eloi a form of Latin Eligius.

St Loye lived in the 7th century and was of obscure origin but he rose to become a famous worker in metals. Having excelled at his craft he went to Paris where, through the good offices of the King's Treasurer, he was given an important commission by Clotaire II. He was placed in a high position of trust that of making a throne out of an allotted amount of gold and jewels. He succeeded in making two thrones.

Under Clotaire's successor Dagobert, Eloy was promoted Master of the royal mint during which time he studied much and practiced a life of great piety. So much so that after the death of Dogobert in 645 A.D., Eloy, having taken Holy Orders was consecrated Bishop of Noyon at the King's behest. St Loye was known for his work with the poor and crippled where it is stated that he performed many miracles. He died at the age of seventy.

It would appear likely, from the fact that the hospital, in the patronage of the Duchy of Lancaster was given to retired royal servants, who were probably not in Holy Orders. At some date before the first facts of its history are known it had ceased to serve any charitable purpose

The patron may have contemplated an attempt at reform when it was granted to Thomas Chamberlayn in 1408, during his pleasure only apparently on condition that he observed all the charitable obligations 'according to the first foundation'. In fact it is unlikely that any permanent reform was made for Chamberlayn's successors were all granted the hospital for life and they probably enjoyed the whole of its endowment and the benefit of its land.

There are no references to the hospital recorded in thy Duchy copyhold records confirming that the land was given by direct grant of the crown.

In 1437, Henry VII gave the hospital to John Ryder. The citation reads: *To all greetings. Know that of our especial grace and in consideration of the good service which John Ryder has performed both for our most dear lord and father, the late King and for us in our wars with France, and because he was maimed in our wars and has become so feeble that he cannot support*

Excavations taking place 2001

Burial excavations

Remains of structure

Master John Carpenter appointed 1459.

Nicholas Morely, appointed 1460, occurs also in 1464

Thomas Goship, died 1479

John Badeley, was appointed 1485, son of Henry in consideration of his father's good and faithful service.

John Badeley, the younger, appointed 1516.

Richard Smith, Edward VI grant of 1551 to hold for life.

The hospital was not suppressed under the Act of 1547 but evidently had been suppressed by the end of the century, for in 1590 the hospital formed a part of a large grant of former ecclesiastical property to William Tipper and Robert Dawe.

Archaeology of the site

As part of the new development at the University Hospital it was decided that a full archaeological investigation should proceed on the site previously uncovered in 1985 before extensive building took place. It was undertaken between June and December 2001 by Birmingham University Archaeology Department. The writer acknowledges their report on the excavations published in 2009 in compiling much of the following.

The excavation revealed a series of boundary ditches partly enclosing a small burial ground comprising of 22 burials and the partial remains of a rectangular, stone-built structure. Sadly, the human remains were so badly decomposed that little information could be learned from them.

The remains of the stone structure show that it was a rectangular building measuring 11m-east west by c.6.5m north south. In places only a foundation trench survived, but the foundations of the north and west wall were reasonably well preserved. They were c. 1m wide and survived to a depth of 0.4m. On the basis of these measurements, it would appear that this was a fairly substantial building whose walls could have stood to a height of 5m or more. Two separate builds were identified for the north wall, while buttresses were added against the corners of the southern wall, possibly to remedy the effects of land-movement over the centuries.

himself or help himself, we have granted the said John the keepership of the hospital of St. Louis near our castle under Lyme, vacant, so it is said, by the death of a certain Thomas Chamberlain, and our gift. To hold it with all its rights and appurtenances. In witness whereof etc, on the 12th October in the 16th year. By signet letter.

Other Masters

Thomas Chamberlayn, appointed 1409, died 1437

John Ryder, appointed 1437

John Crecy, appointed 1454, resigned 1459

Of the 22 burials identified within the ditched enclosure, only two pre-dated the remains of the building discovered on the site. One contained a skeleton, laid on an extended supine position with the arms crossed over the chest, possibly an adult. The back-fill of this grave produced a single sherd of 13th to 14th century pottery. Other burials are later in date, but for the vast majority the skeletal remains were poorly preserved.

Skeleton discovered

have just been discarded by travellers or even by Roman soldiers, as it has been established that a 1st century Roman fort with an adjacent settlement existed at Trent Vale one mile to the south. Roman finds are not unusual in this part of North Staffordshire, and clearly there was a settlement of some sort in the area for much of the period the 1st to late 4th centuries.

15th century hospital

A few sherds of post-medieval pottery were also found, but again these were in poor condition. One vessel was a possible stoneware waster in the form of a rim-neck sherd, similar in form to 17th century Rhenish Bartmann type jug. It is unclear whether these few sherds represent any significant post-medieval activity on the site.

The function of the stone building is unknown and no evidence was found for accommodation or domestic arrangements. (These may well have been situated in a different area of the site that was subsequently used for road widening or the building of the original 19th century workhouse) The suggestion that this was a chapel associated with the medieval hospital can neither be proved nor disproved on the evidence recovered. No finds that might be of an ecclesiastical nature, such as tiles, glass, or dressed

Some burials were worthy of note. One of the graves appeared to contain the remains of multiple individuals, including three distinct skulls. Unfortunately, the remains were so fragmented as to obscure the relationship between the bodies, but it is possible that this represents a charnel pit. A further burial produced evidence for a large pillow stone being placed to support the head. The use of pillow stones was current during the 11th and 12th centuries, but its significance remains unclear and it is believed to have developed from an earlier Christian tradition. Unfortunately the poor preservation of the body here precluded any judgement on the custom, but as it post-dates the known period for pillow burials, it seems to represent a late survival of the practice.

The excavations yielded 26 sherds of medieval pottery, many of which were small and badly abraded. All were of the 13th to 14th century date and were of types found previously in the area. Iron-rich sandy wares included sherds of cooking pots, while whitewares included two bottles of roughly cylindrical form and an unusual small pedestal base. The pottery provides no clear dating evidence for activity on the site, and it is only possible to suggest an early 13th century foundation.

Pre-medieval activity in the area was indicated by a single piece of Roman pottery, a jar rim tempered with Malvernian rock. How this arrived at this spot is unknown. It may simply

15th century blood-letting

stone were found and a direct relationship between the burial ground and the structure could not be proved. This leaves open the possibility that the structure was built after the suppression of the hospital in 1547 and the disuse of the burial ground.

Other parts of the excavations

It is known that the main road, London Road, was re-aligned early in the 19th century, possibly because of the building of the Newcastle canal. Its original line was much further towards the Lyme Brook. Therefore the intervening land between the excavated site and the old line of the road would have been quite extensive and may well have supported the living accommodation and domestic arrangements, with the chapel and burial ground being situated further up on higher ground.

Whatever else may have existed on the site would now either lie beneath the present dual-carriageway or even beneath the new hospital buildings. It is certain that there would have been far more burials considering the length of the period of its existence. No doubt some remains may have been removed as development commenced in that area early in the late 18th and early 19th centuries.

The exact reason for the hospital's situation, set apart from the castle and town of Newcastle, can only be speculated upon. Maybe its location near to the important road from London, or, more likely because of the abundant supply of fresh water needed for a hospital running down from the hill of Penkhull to find its way into the Lyme Brook. During this period hospitals were more spiritual than medical, and what medical care there was, was fairly rudimentary. Their main function fell into four categories: housing the poor, caring for the sick, secluding lepers, and providing accommodation for travellers. Anyone or all of these reasons could apply to this hospital.

Exactly what part this hospital played in the daily life of the villagers of Penkhull can only be speculated upon, but it is probable that local people would have been employed in some way or another in the cultivation of the lands attached, or in daily domestic duties as found in so many religious houses at this period.

Chapter 5
The Manor Courts of Newcastle-under-Lyme.

The workings of the Manor Courts

The Manor records for Newcastle under Lyme provide an almost complete record of events, transactions, valuations and surveys for a period extending over five-hundred years. The study of these records stored in the National Archives, has, until recently been limited to a few isolated quotations found within the Historical Collections of Staffordshire, Thomas Pape's history of Medieval Newcastle-under-Lyme (1928) and John Ward's history of Stoke-on-Trent (1843).

It is important from the outset for those readers, who are not familiar with the term *Manor Court*, or its functions and responsibilities to first explain all that a manor court is not the same as a Crown or Magistrates court, an assumption that some local amateur historians have made in recent years.

The manor court was the lowest court of law in England, and is the direct result of feudalism, a structure of social organisation which developed from the 11th century based on dependent land holding in return for services rendered. It was know as Court Baron. Its governance was applied only to those who resided in or held lands within the manor. The Manor of Newcastle-under-Lyme was such. The court met every three weeks throughout the year, although meetings could be more irregular than this. This Court Baron or manorial court, was where all copy holders within their terms of tenure were obliged to attend. Firstly, the term copyhold is important.

Today we have freehold and leasehold tenure. Those living within the manorial system held land by permission from the Lord of the manor. The transactions covering the exchange of property or land consisted of a system of surrender and admittance carried out at a manor court. The current tenant of land, property, smallholding or farm would come to the court and surrender to the lord via the deputy steward his property or land. The person who was to become the new tenant of a property or land, (*a messuage, tenements and appurtenance*) would then pray to the deputy steward to be admitted. Hence the word admittance.

The transaction was recorded upon the court roll for the manor. Afterwards a copy of the entry of the court roll was given to the new tenant giving authority to occupy what was agreed in court. Upon receipt of the copy of the court roll, the tenant was then called a 'copyholder'. Copyhold tenure ceased in 1922 by Act of Parliament and was changed to freehold tenure by the payment of a small charge known as a Compensation Agreement.

Within Penkhull, there were seventeen ancient messuages at least from the time of Domesday. As time moved forward, original plots of land were divided and copyhold tenants multiplied as a result. However, those who occupied the original seventeen ancient messuages would form the

Homage or jury at the court. The court records always commence with the Homage. The Homage acknowledgement, which continued until 1922 was a hangover from the feudal period. The significance of the Homage varied from manor to manor, but it was common for many decisions of the court to be taken by the homage, i.e. by the tenants collectively sitting as the jury sometimes twelve, sometimes far fewer, sometimes more. Court rolls for the Manor of Newcastle-under-Lyme always included in the opening statement a list of the homagers who were present.

In addition to copyhold land transfers, the court also managed the open fields, settled disputes between individuals and manorial offences. There was, in addition to the Court Baron, a court known as Court Leet held twice a year usually after Michaelmas and after Easter, which all residents of the manor were obliged to attend. Business included a 'View of Frankpledge', at which all men over the age of twelve were bound to appear and make their *pledge* to keep the king's peace. The Court Leet, sometimes known as the Great Court dealt with petty offences from common affray, the breaking of the assize of bread and ale to the maintenance of highways and ditches. At court the cases were presented by a method known as View of Frankpledge. This was a system of policing and law enforcement found within the manorial feudal system dating back to Anglo-Saxon times. The word frank pledge (Lat. Francium plegium) simply means *free and upon oath*. This relied upon the knowledge of the accused neighbours to vouch for guilt or innocence. This involved what was known as the 'hue and cry' which was the process by which villagers were summoned to both assist in the apprehension of a villain and also to bear witness to the crime.

Courts described as Court Leet continue to appear well into the 19th century, but soon after the middle of the 18th century, their business, as recorded in the minutes, seems no different from the Court Baron, and there are many minutes starting with a joint heading for both courts, for example, 'The Court Leet and Court Baron for the said Manor held at Penkhull', etc.

Penkhull, covering a large area at the time, would be divided into tithings whereby ten or twelve adult males would group to form a tithing. Henry Ist ordered that every person of substance over twelve years of age be enrolled in a frank-pledge. The group (tithing) would have a mutual responsibility for ensuring that if any of its members accused of a crime would appear at the Court Leet to answer before the six monthly visit of the Sheriff. At a later date the Frankpledge became known as the Headborough.

In addition, the Court Leet dealt with the election and swearing of the jury, election of constables and the presentment of offences, including those relating to matters of Crown jurisdiction franchised to the manorial lord (*e.g., brewing and baking for sale*). There was often an overlap, however, in the type of business conducted in the Court Baron and Court Leet. In a large manor, the steward would summon the court by instructing its officers to fix a notice to the church door or have it read out in church. While in theory all men over twelve attended each court, it is likely that in practical terms only the manorial officers, offenders, jurymen, witnesses, litigants and pledges and those involved in land transfers came to the court.

Although a married woman had no legal existence of her own from her husband until the early twentieth century, the customs of the Manor did recognize that she had some rights if she had owned land before her marriage. Women could and did become customary tenants if they had inherited land either as a spinster or widow. If they married, their property became the husband's property, but the court did not allow a man to deal with the wife's land without her agreement. When her land was surrendered at a manor court, it was surrendered jointly by husband and wife, with a special note in the court proceedings. This referred to the fact in the opening sentence of the court record that the steward had secretly or separately examined the wife to confirm that she makes the surrender of her own free will without any compulsion by her husband.

However elementary the organization, or however complex, within the manorial system the one official, the Reeve, played a central part whereas in some manors the authority lay with Bailiff. This person would know every field and every person who lived within the township. The Reeve was chosen once a year, generally at Michaelmas on an established rota basis between those seventeen copyholders of the original ancient messuages.

Strictly speaking, the Reeve would deal with the daily business of the manor such as the enforcement of the agricultural policy, as well as the livestock held in the village pinfold. He would also be the spokesperson for the villagers in matters relating to the running of the manor and for this he would receive some financial benefit.

For the Township of Penkhull with Boothen two Reeve Books have survived the first dates from 1579 the second from c1754. The Manor of Newcastle was divided into three defined areas, Penkhull and Boothen; Shelton and Hanley; Clayton; Seabridge and Wolstanton. The books list the names of those who undertook the office of Reeve from the year 1579 to 1835 and in what year and from which township the obligation was undertaken. Towards the end of the period the Reeve Book records a number of those under obligation to serve the office that willingly paid others to undertake the responsibilities of office on their behalf.

The system of succession to copyhold land was, in simple terms, as follows: Upon a copyholder's death, his estate owed a heriot *(a manorial tax payable to the Lord on the death of a tenant, something like today's death duty)* to the lord of the manor, usually a best beast or a fixed sum of money instead. At the next court after the death, the homage would present *(i.e. report)* the death of a tenant and make a proclamation for the heir, defined by local custom, to come forward and be 'admitted' to the land upon payment of the heriot and an

entry *fine (an 'arbitrary' but 'reasonable' sum fixed by custom)*. The heir would be admitted by the rod *(a billet of wood or other ceremonial object placed in his hands, usually by the steward. This ceremony was not unlike the use of a judge's hammer the striking of which confirmed the action)*. By this ritual the heir would, take seisin *(possession)* from the land. After doing fealty *(making oath of fidelity and allegiance to the Lord of the Manor)* and promising to pay the accustomed annual rent usually a small fixed sum, and perform services *(usually insignificant after the 16th century)*, the succession was complete and the heir became the copyholder.

By the sixteenth century, the status of villeins had changed dramatically as a result of social and economic developments. The intervention of the courts to protect villein tenants and the growing acknowledgement of custom appeared to create a secure place in law for protecting the rights of villein tenants. Tenure in villeinage had become a newly recognised secure form of tenure by copy of court roll *'at the will of the lord according to the custom of the manor'*. This created tenure independent of the will of the lord in everything but name. Copy holders, as they became known, were as well protected as freeholders.

After reform in 1660 only one freehold or *'free'* tenure survived. Copyhold or customary tenure, with its peculiar and varied administrative procedures or customs *(general and particular)* and 'incidents' *(liabilities and obligations of tenure)*, was retained as the only other recognised tenure. Still administered by the Manor Court Baron and dependent on local custom it was, however, the subject of a growing body of case law and legal definition and, despite its often idiosyncratic nature, could be freely bought and sold, mortgaged, settled, sub-let, and otherwise conveyed. By the late 18th century copyhold tenure was the main business of the manor court and seen as ripe for reform and much copyhold land had already been assimilated to freeholds. A series of Copyhold Acts in the 1840s encouraged voluntary enfranchisement (turning copyhold into freehold) and further 19th century Acts enabled compulsory enfranchisement. By this time a great deal of court business was transacted privately in the offices of solicitor-stewards, manor courts meeting infrequently if at all. By the Law of Property Act 1922 all copyhold land was converted into land of freehold tenure.

Other business of the court, while producing useful profits for the lord, could also have benefits for the community of the manor. The enforcement of village or manor bylaws and regulations through the presentment and amercing of offenders enabled the open-field system to operate effectively and discouraged breaches of the peace. The court also offered arbitration in disputes between individuals *(debt, trespass, detention or breach of agreement)*. Each case was brought by a plaintiff, and both the plaintiff and defendant would often produce named pledges, especially in the medieval period, to stand surety. Most defendants were allowed three summonses, three distraints *(for failing to appear)* and three essoins *(excused absences)* before being required to defend the case, so that cases could be pending for months. The jury would finally decide the outcome, but many times the case was agreed out of court before the final stage was reached; if so, there was still a fee to be paid for licence to agree.

Quite by chance a number of years ago, I came across a significant document drawn up by Mr Thomas Fenton, the Deputy Steward of the Manor of Newcastle c1730. This document is an account of the exact wording used at the time in a manor court and the oaths made by manor officials. It was probably written to ensure that future court officials, especially the town crier, maintained the established pattern of legal wording.

> *Court called from outside the court building by the crier.* "O yes, O yes, O yes, all manner of persons that owe suit and service to this Court Leet and View of Frankpledge of our Sovereign Lord the King, held of the Manor of Newcastle-under-Lyme come in and show your suit and service upon pain and peril that may fall thereon".
> *Call over the suitors and march them into the court room. Crier to make and proclaim the law.* "If any man will be essoined *(excused for non-attendance) or enters any plaints, let him come in and there shall be heard, and all such as were essoined at the last court are now to come in and with their assigns, or also they will be amerced* (fined in a manor court) *both for this, and the last court".*
> *If the jury of the last court has to me given to this court to bring into their protestation, then call them over and if they all appear, say:* "Gentlemen, you all agreed to these your protestation and you allow the same to be drawn up and altered in forms but not in substance". *Then swear as follows:* "You, and each of you do swear that you will truly and indifferently tax, assess all such amercement *(fine in a manor court) as are now delivered in by the jury. And that you will swear no man for love, favour or affection, but shall tax access according to the quality of the offence or faults committed to the best of your knowledge. So help you God".*

The document continues with the swearing in of court officials, the Headboroughs, the Aleconers, Constables etc. The Headboroughs Oath: *You swear that you will well and truly serve our Sovereign Lord the King and the Lord of this Leet as the Headborough until another shall be chosen in your room* (place). *In the constables presence you shall be aiding and assisting to him and in his absence shall supply his place. And in everything well and sufficiently execute the office of the Headborough to the best of your judgement, so help you God.*

The Newcastle-under-Lyme Court Rolls.

The early manorial records of Newcastle-under-Lyme were written on parchment rolls in Latin. These rolls were superseded at the end of the sixteenth century by hardback books. It was not until 1733 that the language changed from Latin to English. Information gleaned from these records provides an insight into the daily events of the community

and enables land transactions to be plotted over centuries showing family growth and land ownership for nearly six hundred years.

The National Archive at Kew holds a large series of Court Rolls for the Manor of Newcastle-under-Lyme. The first court roll is dated 24th January in the ninth year of Edward III (from 23rd January 1335 – 24th January 1336). The next roll is dated 1348 and thereafter the rolls are almost continuous from the time of Henry II down to modern times. The courts met every three weeks, on a Saturday at the castle until the reign of Henry VII. All tenants of the manor were obliged to attend.

Suitors came from the various districts within the manor as well as those from Penkhull, thereby confirming the appendage of Penkhull to the Manor of Newcastle by that date. The first court rolls commences:

John de Knynardsley recently parson of the Church in Stoke is mentioned and John of Stoke, Clerk is complainant against Thomas Shakspeare in a plea of debt.

The second rolls consist of six decayed membranes of the 22nd year of Edward III (25th January, 1348 – 24th January, 1349). All court rolls commence by first informing the reader of the date and where the courts were held, in this case they were held at Newcastle. The business consisted in the main of that of debt and transfers of land, the first being in the district of Wolstanton. In 1368, the frank pledges of Penkhull presented the death of the parson of Stoke who held of the Lord his church. A heriot *(a tax upon a person's wealth)* of one bull valued at 8 shillings was due to the Lord.

The court rolls of 1379 are much better preserved. *The Frankpledge present that John Symenson, miller owes suite and has not come, fined 2d, and that Henry Atte Boothes assaulted Thomas Tyttensor, fined 3d, and the same Thomas Tyttensor assaulted Alan Bateson, fined 4d, and that Marjorie the wife of Thomas Tyttensor justly raised the hue after Alan Bateson, fined 4d, and the son of Thomas Tyttensor assaulted Alan, fined 2d, and that Roger le Peyntor, fined 2d, and that Roger le Reyntor assaulted Thomas Tyttensor, fined 2d.*

A further entry of the same date lists that John the son of Thomas Mason assaulted William Atte Boothes and overpowered him and drew blood from which he was fined a total of 2 shillings and 6 pence.

In the first year of Henry V, at a court held at Newcastle on Saturday 30th September 1413, *the Frankpledge presents Henry de Lyme brewed once against the assize (6d) and that Thomas Jackson did the same (6d) and that Thomas Harryson and John Passall did the same and that William le Paynton attacked the wife of William le Smyth (4d) and that the said wife justly raised the hue on the said William (4d) and that the wife of the said William Smythe attacked the son of William Paynton (4d) and that the same justly raised the hue on him (4d).*

In the same roll a further court dated 22nd April 1414 presented that *William of Stoke, John Tok, John Paynton, John Huchon, Roger Gent all brewed once and broke the assize and each was fined 6d and that Thomas de Mulneton ought to appear and has not come therefore he is in mercy (6d) and that a ditch has been blocked up by the said Thomas Mulneton (4d) and that John Tomkynson of Hanley did the same in 'le marclych' (4d) and that John Bateson blocked up a road to the prejudice of the inhabitants of Penkhull.*

A court held on Saturday 19th October (5th Henry V) 1418 *For Penkhull and Boothen John of Boothen the elder, William Persall and William Lake, frankpledges there present that Thomas de Greve ought to appear and has not come; and that William de Wroo, who held certain lands and tenements in the said manor (died) and there is due to the Lord, 2s, called 'farefee', and the land remains...* (this is the amount due to the Lord when someone surrendered all his copyhold property and thus ceased to be a copyhold tenant) *And that Richard Symson attacked Richard the son of John Payntor with his fists and beat him (6d); and that Agnes Smythe justly raised the hue on Thomas Dawson (4d); and that Thomas Huchon attacked Richard the son of John of Boothen with a (?) (6d); and that Thomas Huchon holds a parcel of land in 'le Placehough' separately – where by rights it ought to be held in common to the prejudice of the inhabitants dwelling there (4d) Total fines 4 shillings.*

The next presentation on the same roll was held on 26th April 1419, when frankpledges John Huchon, William Smythe and Thomas Harryson (of Boothen) presented *that John of Boothen concealed the attack made on John Kydde with a staff by John the son of Thomas of Boothen (3d) and that Thomas Harryson and his son John, overburdened the common with their cattle more than they ought (4d) and that William Passall and his son John did the same thing (4d) and that Thomas Huchon attacked Agnes, wife of William Smythe with a staff and shook her by the shoulders (2d) and that Agnes is a common ale wife (4d) and that Richard Broad, John Harryson and William Smythe had all withdrawn their labour from the mill to the prejudice of the Lord, fined 2d each and that a bargain had been made between William Smyth and Agnes his wife on the one side and William, the son of William T..., of Chesterton, on the other side concerning 2½ messages with the lands adjoining to them in Penkhull.*

The good name of Penkhull seems to have been further darkened by the ill treatment of servants as the assize roll of 1444 states that: *Thomas Bokenall sued William Pesale of Penkhull, yeoman and two others for beating wounding and ill treating his men servants. The defence did not appear and the Sheriff was ordered to arrest and produce them on the festival of St. Hilary.*

From at least 1335 to c1500 the castle, at Newcastle-under-Lyme was the meeting place for the manor courts. John Leyland a 16th century traveller and writer wrote in 1541: *All the castle is down, save one great tower.* Although it is not known what condition the tower was in, or if inhabitable it gives a possible starting point to the location of the courts as historians have considered by this time the castle would be derelict. If then by 1541 the castle was in ruin, the courts must have vacated the castle much earlier. They could not be held in the town of Newcastle as first thought, because at an earlier date attributed to 1173, the townsfolk of Newcastle had petitioned the King to become separated from the old feudal system of authority to become an independent Borough, a democracy, and with the authority to set its own taxes and have a different legal system. The courts for the manor, based upon the feudal system therefore had to be held somewhere within the manor but no information to their location exists. It may have been Penkhull, it may have been elsewhere.

From about 1530 until 1829 the manor courts for most of the time were held at Penkhull in what is now known as The Greyhound Inn. But why at Penkhull? Because it was in the centre of the farming community and the main function of the court was its association with land occupation under the copyhold system.

The court minute books show from time to time that other private residences were used. On the 18th Jan 1742/3 they were held at the home of Thomas Dytchfield, on the 24th May 1754 at the home of John Terrick where 'The Views' now stand. On the 17th September 1806 at the home of Samuel Doncaster and on the 10th December 1807 at 'The Mount', the home of Josiah Spode. In Whites Trade Directory dated 1834 reference is made to the fact that all the courts were then being held in the 'Wheatsheaf Inn' at Stoke.

Peter Roden covers this issue in his book *Copyhold Potworks and Housing,* and writes that from *October 1738 to April 1739 the courts were held at the home of Sam. Jenny in Penkhull.* Other places included the 'Wheatsheaf Inn' at Stoke, 'The Swann Inn', in Hanley and at various times at the home the Deputy Steward, Thomas Fenton of 'Stoke Lodge', which was situated at the bottom of Trent Valley Road near to where 'New Lodge' now stands.

The court records show that at Penkhull the courts were held every three weeks in an old farmhouse. In 1536 this was described as being *recently built.* Unfortunately the word *recently* cannot be relied upon to mean what it says, nor can the limited description of the property be accurately aligned to that of what is now the 'Greyhound'. In many cases a description such as *'recently built'* can be carried forward from one entry within court documents to the next for many years, as on each occasion the previous wording being copied without change. One thing is for certain, the old farmhouse was standing in 1536 but it could date from a much earlier period and even have been the location for the courts after the necessity arose to vacate the castle, probably in the late 14th century or even earlier.

Chapter 6
Courts throughout Regnal Years.

The study of the court records for the Manor of Newcastle-under-Lyme over the past two decades is the largest ever undertaken. The subject has already been introduced under the heading of Manor Court. This chapter includes subjects so wide ranging that to present it in any logical format would be difficult. The subjects chosen not only deal with the transfer of copyhold estates from one person to another which was the main function of the manor court, the court Baron held ever three weeks but also those transactions of the court Leet, held every six months which deals with the view of frankpledge.

Until around the mid 18th century to identify a messuage or land in respect of its location recorded at the court Baron is difficult and for most impossible. These court transactions fail to give locations or descriptions of the properties until the early 19th century. They form the overwhelming business of the court. Subsequently only a few examples have been included as most are repetitive in format and content.

In addition to the court Baron, the other court, that of Court Leet dates from the early Middle Ages and exercised powers of jurisdiction over petty offences and civil affairs. The court met twice a year, and were overseen in Penkhull by the steward of the manor or his deputy. They were known by the name of View of Frankpledge. The presentations by the View of Frankpledge dealt with differing incidents one following on from the other. Examples of these are given in the following entries. The figure in brackets, following a name, relates to the amount of fine imposed by the court.

To enable the reader to gain an insight into the way of life and its social workings and implications the examples are extensive in their variety. They record many of the social and economic issues found within the system of manorial governance.

Whilst the archive is huge and comprehensive, the purpose in this chapter is to list entries that may be of interest to readers. For example, in the mid 17th century, when the pottery industry was in its infancy, records enable a better understanding of how the mining and ceramic industry first evolved. They could be used to re-write the history of North Staffordshire.

Other records relating to the Commonwealth period extend further the knowledge of this period locally. There are also records that cover the appointment of clergy to the Rectory of Stoke, proving that there is nothing new with regards to corruption in appointments. Every effort is made to place entries into context but this may not always be possible. The only work previously published on the subject of manor courts, and then limited in its content to just a few was by Thomas Pape. *Medieval Newcastle-under-Lyme.* (1928)

Many of the early court records relate to those people who have brewed ale or baked bread against the assize. This was based upon the Assize of Bread and Ale Act. c1266, which set standards of quality, measurement, and pricing for bakers and brewers. At a local level, this resulted in regulatory licensing systems with arbitrary recurring fees, fines and punishments for lawbreakers whereby in each locality the price of bread and ale was laid down based upon the prevailing prices of corn or malt.

22nd April 1414
The Frankpledge present that William of Stoke brewed once and broke the assize therefore he is in mercy (6d) and that John Tok did the same (6d) and that John Paynter did the same (6d) and that John Huchon did the same (6d) and that Roger Gent did the same (6d), and that Thomas de Mulueton ought to appear and has not come therefore he is in mercy (6d), and that a ditch has been blocked up by the said Thomas Mulueton (4d) and that John Tumkynson of Hanley did take the same and that John Bateson blocked up a road to the prejudice of the inhabitants of Penkhull (4d) - Total fined 4s 2d.

The trail of murder or of a serious offence, the manor court was not used. Such offences were held at Stafford but a manor court was used however for minor offences or assaults in addition to transactions of land transfer.

Saturday 24th April 1417
Township of Penkhull and Boothen. The frankpledge there present that John Colclough junior (2d) Thomas Wyg (2d), Henry Tupp (4d), Adam Dutton (2d), John Swanyld (2d), the wife of Thomas Bren who owe do not come and are in mercy. And that Henry de Mer (4d) assaulted William son of John Tetonsor with a drawn knife. And that John Toke (6d) brewed against the assize. And that John Payntour (2d) and Benedict Machon (2d) owe appearance and do not come. And that John Andrewe (6d) broke into the enclosure of animals that were impounded by order of the lord king.
(Note here also the reference to a Pinfold at such an early date.)

Saturday 26th June 1417
Richard Penkhull and John Sadeler, the lessees, complain of William Rughleg (2d) in a plea of trespass; William did not attend, therefore an order to distrain so that he attends the next court.

The said Richard and John, lessees, complain of John (2d) son of Henry de Bech in a plea of trespass in that he failed to grind his corn at the mill to the loss of 6s 8d; who came and acknowledged the trespass in part and sought an assessment, therefore through his acknowledgement, is in mercy.

The following case refer to assaults and the damage caused to the village enclosure.

Richard Pekforde (2d) defendant in an action, which he had previously contested for trespass brought by Richard and John as above, therefore in mercy. Let it be executed.

John Colclogh the elder complains of William Leke (2d) and his servant in a plea of trespass for entering the wood of the said John against his wishes to the damage of 6s 8d; who did not come, therefore to be distrained to attend the next court. The mill referred to was a water mill situated on the River Trent at Stoke, probably belonging to the Rector as part of his Glebe.

Saturday 5th June 1417
Small court of the above manor held there. Edmund Orpe (2d) is not present in a plea of debt against John Symson, therefore in mercy - the other is acquitted.

John Godeyere (2d) came into court and acknowledged the debt of 6d for rent on his account, therefore through his acknowledgement is in mercy.

John de Bothus complains of John Smyth (2d) of Shelton in a plea of trespass in that the defendant trespassed with cattle through his growing rye to the damage of one quarter of rye; who came and acknowledged the trespass in part and submitted himself to an assessment, therefore through his acknowledgement is in mercy.

John Godeyere complains of Tibet Shakesper (2d) in a plea of trespass in that the defendant's wife damaged his oats in his barn and the said barn to the damage of half a quarter of oats together with two cows; who came and acknowledged the trespass in part and submitted to an assessment.

Henry VI. (Note here various reports to the use of the common fields and the first indication of enclosures.)

Friday 3rd October 1427
Great court held at Newcastle Penchull and Bothus. Thomas Huchon, Thomas Haryson of Bothus and William Smyth, thirdboroughs, present that William Chaumber (4d) owes suit of court and has not come and that John Toke (2d) because he was poor brewed once and broke the assize of ale with one pot of ale.

And that a parcel of land and meadow called Ackeforde within the township of Penchull is a close which ought to be by right in common in the open season after corn and hay are carried away, through the fault of Thomas Huchon to the prejudice of the neighbours. And that a parcel of land and meadow called Platehalgh within the township of Penchull is enclosed which by right ought to be in common in the open season after corn and hay are carried away, through the fault of Thomas Huchon, to the prejudice of the neighbouring occupiers. And that John Huchon and Thomas Huchon (2d) have been challenging to William Smyth and Agnes Smyth his wife in that they accused the aforesaid William and Agnes of stealing various property from

various people to the grave shame of their names. And that Thomas Huchon (3d) assaulted and hit Thomas son of Richard Bonde with a staff in the township of Penchull. And that Joan de Colclough did not clean her ditch out around Stevunparroke to the prejudice of the neighbours. And that William Tetonsore (2d) challenged John Bothus the elder on the way from Seabridge. Wm. Tetonsore (2d) fact rebell John Bothus senior via de leynyng in Seabridge. And that John de Bothus (4d) made affray on William Tetonsore in the church of Stoke and touched his dagger with malice.

The above mentions the possible use of a dagger whilst the following refers to the drawing of blood.

10th October 1422
The heirs of Richard de Colclough who owe suit and do not come. And that Roger de Hanley (2d) assaulted William Tetonsore with a stick, and struck him and drew blood (6d). And that the same William Tetonsore assaulted (2d) the said Roger with a stick, and struck him and drew blood (6d) And that Thomas de Bothus (2) and his son stopped up the watercourse within Onywallonesyche in Penchulle, to the injury of the neighbours there. And that John Bothus (2d) the elder broke the pinfold, taking a horse that Henry Mere impounded.

Edward IV
Great Court held at Newcastle on 19th October 1476
John Fenton. Roger Symson and Thomas Nicson, thirdboroughs, (another word for Frankpledge) present that Roger Machon (4d) overcharged the pasture(s) with beasts.

26th April 1477
Roger Machon, John Fenton and John Boothen, thirdboroughs, present that John Polson (2d) made affray on John Machon of Botteslowe and struck him with a staff. And that William Mer (2d) made affray on Thomas Hudson the younger and intended to strike him with a staff. And that the same Thomas (2d) did the same. And that Stephen Houdson (2d) made affray on William Mere and intended to strike him with a staff.

3rd October 1478
Thomas Bradley, John Kent and John Boothen, thirdboroughs, present that Roger Vernon (14d) made affray on Oliver Grendon and tried to strike him with a staff and drew blood from him. And that Thomas Huchon (12d) the elder and his household made a pound-breach and took beasts, which had been impounded, in the common fold. And that the servants of Thomas Tettonshor made a pound-breach and took beasts of the household of Thomas Huchon. And that Nicholas (1d), servant of Elen Whyt, made affray on Henry Nykson and intended to strike him with a staff. And Henry did the same. And that the servants of Thomas Tettonshor (8d) made a forestall and took animals from the servants of Thomas Huchon. And Thomas Vernon dug and made a trap within the lord's pool, which is a great harm. And that William Clayton (14d), chaplain, made affray on Stephen

Botorton the younger and struck him and drew blood from him. And that Stephen (2d - later altered to 4d) did the same and intended to strike him with a staff. And that John Haywood, arrested by a constable and thirdborough because of a lawsuit on behalf of the lord the King, broke arrest. And he made affray on John Kent, the thirdborough there, and struck him with a bill and drew blood from him. And the said John Haywood (3s 4d) broke a fetter and fetters and broke arrest.

Henry VII

Great Court held at the manor of Newcastle-under-Lyme on Thursday 15 March 1509

Thomas Tyttensor, John Dale and Roger Fenton of the frankpledge present that Henry Symson was a tenant of the lord who died since the last great court, after whose death 2s are due to the lord in the name of 'farfee'. And that Richard Huchyn (2d) assaulted Richard Browde and Richard Browde (2d) assaulted Richard Huchyn. And they present Margaret wife of John Patson (3s 4d) who was rebellious of words with malice and rebuke at an inquiry of the lord king.

They present that John Patson (8d) and his wife and servant took a sheaf of wheat from John Huchyn steward at Penkyll against the law.

Today this would be a charge of 'contempt of court'.

One of the functions of the court was to receive notifications of any death of a copyholder and deal with the surrender and admittance. In addition wills were presented to assess the value of a heriot. A heriot could be best described as an Anglo Saxon inheritance tax assessed upon the value of an estate at the time of death. The obligation applied to both freemen and villeins but later tended to be associated only with copyhold tenants. A heriot was originally in the form of the best beast of the deceased paid by the heir but this form of payment was later superseded to a monetary payment.

Henry VIII 1509

Thomas Eldurshawe, Thomas Dale and William Symson, freeholders there present that Thomas Peysall, who was a tenant of the lord, died since the last court after whose death there fell to the lord an ox of black colour price 10 shillings. Also they present that Thomas Machyn, jun. overcharged the common with cattle, beasts and sheep 4 shillings.

The small court of the manor held on Saturday next after the feast of St. Chad, Bishop, 1509.

John Tetynsore complains against Hugh Wodcoke 2d on a plea of debt of 13d. The defendant seeks licence to agree. Mercy 2d. The same John Tetynsore complains against Thomas Eldurshawe on a plea of trespass because he destroyed oats at his house and barley at Herdall Heyth to a loss of two shillings. The attorney comes on behalf of the complainant and seeks payment. Mercy 2d.

Margaret Symson 2d complains against John Dale on a plea of debt of 18d on one side and 20d on the other side, which she does not pursue.

John Tetynsor complains against John Leghton 2d on a plea of trespass, because he destroyed four strips of plough land of oats at Hartushyll to a loss of 6s 8d. The attorney comes and on behalf of the complainant and seeks payment. Mercy 2d.

The same John complains against the same John 2d on a plea of trespass, because he destroyed his meadow called Rudmede and his barley with his horses in Penkyllfyld to a loss of 3s 4d. The attorney comes and on behalf of the complainant and seeks payment.

Philip and Mary

Note: the second entry under Philip and Mary refers to the first time to the name of Penkhull being given as the location for the courts.

1st October 1557

View of Frankpledge with court of the lord King and lady Queen held at Newcastle-under-Lyme on Bartholomew Bowyer, Roger Dale and John Amos, frankpledges there, being sworn, present that Thomas Belton (2d); and Roger Fenton (2d) made an affray on each other. Therefore they are separately in mercy etc. And that John Bagnall (2d), Richard Wynkull (2d), Hugh Adderley (2d), and John Hansley (2d) brewed in common and sold their beer contrary to the assize. Therefore they are separately in mercy etc. And that Thomas Machyn, John Huchyn and Roger Fenton shall be frankpledges there the year following.

30th September 1558

Held at Penkhull. View of Frankpledge John Hachyn, Thomas Machyn and John Fenton, frankpledges present there, being sworn present that Stephen Huchyn (4d) made an assault on John Hachyn contrary to the peace, therefore he is in the Lord's mercy etc.

Also they present John Turner (12d) because he broke into the park of the lord King and lady Queen etc.

This would be the Royal Park, which covered much of what are now covered by the districts of Hartshill and Basford.

1st October 1558 Penkhull - John Huchyn, Thomas Machyn and John Fenton present that Stephen Huchyn (4d) made an assault on John Huchyn against the peace, therefore in mercy. And also that John Huchyn (4d) made an assault on Stephen against the peace, therefore he is in mercy. *They present John Turner (12d) for breaking the pound of the lord the King and the lady the Queen and taking out a horse impounded there or tied up, therefore he is in mercy. And furthermore they present that Thomas Wood, Roger Huchyn and Margaret Machyn, widow, will be thirdboroughs for the following year.*

Elizabeth 1st

16th June 1559

Thomas Lovatt died since the last court seized of one cottage and certain lands adjoining thereto, and one pasture in Clayton. By his death there happens to the Queen, one ox of twenty shillings price for a heriot. John Lovatt is his son and next heir and of the age of 17 years.

John Lovatt died since the last court seized of one messuage and certain lands, meadows and pastures in Clayton and Seybryge and of one pasture in Penkhill. By his death there happens to the Queen for a heriot one ox of 20ˢ price. John Lovatt is his nephew and next heir and 18 years of age.

2nd Sept 1559

Randall Bothes in mercy of the lady the Queen being present in court refused to answer two pleas of Bartholomew Bower according to the customs of the manor but preferred evil and contumacious words to the disturbance of the court and refused to obey the order of the court on the premises to the bad example of other tenants, in contempt of the court and against the Queen's peace.

4th October 1560

Penkhull - John Hanley, George Fenton and John Huchyn, thirdboroughs, on their oath present:
That John Copnall (4ᵈ) clerk (meaning under Holy Orders, probably from the church in Stoke) owes appearance at this court and is in default, therefore he is in mercy.

They also present that John Hunt died since the last court seised of one meadow called Flaxbutts in Penkhull and that Robert Hunt is his son and of full age. They also present that Hugh Adderley (2d), John Bagnold (2d) and Richard Wyncle (2d) commonly sold ale and broke the assize. Thus they are in mercy.

And, they present that Anne Huchen, the daughter of Roger Huchen of Penkhull aforesaid who died during the last year, as appears more clearly in the court roll of the preceding year, is the heir of the aforesaid Roger, and she is aged one year etc.

25th January 1561

James Hudson by the assent, consent and licence of all the tenants there takes seisin of waste land (3 perches in length and 2 perches in breadth) in a lane called Meyre lane leading from Stoke to Newcastle, near his dwelling house, to build a barn in, and to make a certain enclosure there. He pays to the Queen in new rent [amount not quoted].

6th July 1566 This is an interesting record for it is known that the current Franklin Road was previously called Outlane.
In answer to a number of questions from Randall Bouthes. The jurors present that the way for all necessary goings and returnings from the township of Penkhull as far as the pasture called the

Polehaugh is by a lane called the Outlane and so descending by a hedge into a close called Cramferlonges as far as an olive tree in the said close and then across the butts to the corner of the Polehaugh and into Polehaugh.
The way for all necessary goings and returnings from the township of Penkhull as far as the pasture called Harrysfieldes is to the Polehaugh, and then onto a head butt into the lower end of Cromferlonges as far as the close called Bowstyche and so across the ends of the butts as far as Wadgearlanes end and by Wadgear lane and into a close called Whatley going up by Charles hay hedge as far as the middle hade and so to Harrisfieldes. The way from Penkhull to Hongryhill is across the middle of the hade on fulla hill, and upon the shorter side, as these jurors have allotted.

Could Hungryhill an early name for Hartshill? Polehough later became known as Poolhough which was situated in an area of the botton of what is now Franklin Road.

17th December 1559

This entry lists a mill in Shelton.
Nicholas Barrett surrenders the fourth part of Shelton Mylne with all lands, waters, gutters, rivers, pools and easements belonging to it. To Richard Tunstall and his assigns for 40 years, paying yearly to the Queen, her heirs and successors 3ˢ 4ᵈ, and keeping not only the said fourth part but the whole mylne in repair all the term and so yielding it up at the end of it; and well and effectively grinding the corn of Nicholas and his assigns when he can without lawful let, taking the twentieth part of the grain for toll. Richard Tunstall admitted. Fine 2ˢ.

Note: Barrett was at this time owner of the Ridghouse in Shelton and paid a fourth part of all services belonging to the town and received a fourth part of the mylne profits as here appears, which mylne at this time belonged to the tenants of Shelton, and for it they paid yearly 13s 4d to the Queen.

3rd October 1589 *View of frankpledge.*

The lower section of what is now Honeywall once went under the name of Castle Cliff. There is no evidence however to suggest there was a castle in the vicinity despite this name.

Verdict of customary jury.
They confirm the thirdboroughs' presentments.
And further they present, by the acknowledgement of Ralph Greene gentleman and on the oaths of the jurors that six trees have been cut down in Castyll Clyffe, of which five and part of a sixth have been converted into gates, posts and other necessary things on this side of Castyll Clyff, and the rest of the sixth tree has been used around Stoke mill belonging to the Rector of Stoke to the value of 16ᵈ. And the stones, which were carried from the Castyll, we present as the aforesaid jurors have presented before this, and the afferers of the court have assessed the fine for it at this court and others held before.

This is an interesting entry in as much that the lower reaches of Honeywall were once called Castle Cliff. The area would have been well stocked with timber, but the reference to stones being carried from the castle is not easily explained. Could this be the remains of a pervious Iron Age fort that once occupied the hill of Penkhull?

2nd December 1589 before Wm. Bishop of Coventry. A case of attempted murder.

Thomas Lovatt of Cleyton, yeoman, John Clayton of the same, yeoman, Francis Whythurst, late of the same, weaver, Thomas Fenton, late of Fenton, yeoman, Thomas Fenton, late of Boothen, husbandman and Richard Lovatt, late of Penkhull, yeoman (with other male persons to the number of eight) for assembly at Stone in the highway on the 11th December 1580 and for assault and battery against Edward Palyn there continued Thomas Lovatt of Cleyton etc. with intent to murder William Palyn and for assault upon him. Thomas Lovatt and Thomas Fenton of Boothen struck William on the head with two staves value 6d, giving him two wounds two inches wide and three inches long so that he was ill from 11th December - 10th January following. Reported 13th January, 32nd year of Elizabeth 1st that they did not appear in court.

2nd April 1596

Thomas Hichen surrenders 1¼ day's math of meadowing in great Ackford in Penkhull or Clayton in mortgage for three lives. To Francis Lysatt for the payment of £6 13s 4d on 25th March 1599 at Lysatt's house in Penkhull. Lysatt admitted; fine 12d. Thomas Browne surrenders a close called Whatfurlong alias Grinley field and another close called the Haugh in Penkhull. To Jone Machen, wife of Joan Machen, her heirs and assigns forever. Jone Machen admitted; fine 2s 6d.

18th November 1598

Jone Ames surrenders a messuage or tenement in Hanley and all buildings, gardens and orchards belonging to it, and a pasture called Ten Acres as it is now divided to Thomas Wood and Jane Wood his wife for 5 years to commence on the next Lady Day or Michaelmas day following the death of Elianor Bourne, wife of Jone Bourne of Chesterton, at the yearly rent of 10s. Fine 8d.

Thomas Lovatt, son of Richard Lovatt of Great Cleyton deceased, through Thomas Browne and William Turner his attorneys, by virtue of a letter dated 30th October 1599, surrenders half of a meadow with the appurtenances called little Ackeford now in the holding of Nicholas Lovatt or his assigns, half of a pasture called Plathaugh hey with the appurtenances now in the holding of Francis Lysatt or his assigns, one and a half days maths in a certain meadow called great Ackford now in the holding of Roger Dale or his assigns in Penkhull, half of a close or pasture called the Paddocke alias Heald in Cleyton and Seabridge, half of a meadow called Ackford in Cleyton & Seabridge now in the holding of Thomas Lovatt and Nicholas Lovatt or their assigns and half of a meadow called Plathaugh meadow in Penkhull now in the occupation of Francis Lysatt or his assigns. To Nicholas Lovatt, his heirs and assigns forever. Admitted; fine 2s.

Jone Huchen releases and quitclaims to Nicholas Lovatt all his claim in the little Ackford meadow, in one and a half day maths of meadowing in great Ackford meadow in Roger Dale's holding, in a meadow called Plathaugh meadow, in a close or pasture called Plathaugh hey, in half of a close called the Cliff, in half of a cottage and a croft called the further croft alias furcroft, and half of the pits, in which cottage Jone Machen now lives, in Penkhull and Cleyton.

James 1st

3rd March 1604. Roger Dale questions the authority of the copyhold court to have the exclusive right to grant sezin of a property or can this be done elsewhere on condition that that there were two customary tenants to witness the transaction.

Roger Dale in his own person seeks 12 lawful men who are customary tenants of the manor for 12d to be sworn, according to the custom of the manor, to enquire into the following:

1. Whether any person or persons being lawfully possessed of, or having an interest in, any customary or copyhold lands that are part of the manor for a term of years by surrender in the manor court and according to the custom of the manor, may lawfully assign them for the said term to any person or persons out of the manor court in the presence of two customary tenants of the manor or more; and whether such an assignment is good and lawful according to the custom of the manor or not.

2. And whether Richard Dodye being possessed or interested according to the custom of the manor by copy of court roll bearing the date 5th October 1588 of and in one pasture or close called New Leasowe alias Crabtree flat in Penkhull for the term of 80 years from Michaelmas last past before the date of the said copy did lawfully assign the same copy and his term therein specified to Roger Dale and his assigns in presence of customary tenants of the said manor according to the custom of the manor or not.

Verdict

1. They present that a customary tenant by the custom of this manor may lawfully assign a copy for term of years for his term to any person or persons out of the court in the presence of two customary tenants of the said manor or more, and that such assignment is good and lawful by the custom of the manor.

2. They present that by the oaths of Thomas Bagnall senior, Thomas Barrett and Nicholas Barrett, Richard Dodye did assign over to Roger Dale and his assigns one copy of court roll of the manor bearing date 5th October 1588 of and in one pasture called New Leasowe alias Crabtree flat in Penkhull for the term of 80 years from Michaelmas last past before the date of the said copy, for all the term contained in the copy.

1st October 1607 View of Frankpledge held at Stoke.
Note the early reference to coal mines in Hanley and Shelton and filling in the same once exhausted.
Thirdboroughs of Cleyton & Seabridge - John Malpas, Nicholas Lovatt and Thomas Lovatt.
And that John Austen (12d) and John Gryffen (12d) overcharged the lord's common, and that Thomas Warrelowe and Henry Meyre senior have incurred a fine of 10s for not filling in the coal mines in Shelton & Hanley.

31st March 1608
The Freehold jury confirm the thirdboroughs' presentments and present that all is well.
A fine of £3 6s 8d will be imposed on Anne Hunt, widow if she does not fill all her coal and stone pits on Meir Heath within the manor before 29th September next.

19th May 1608
A fine of £5 is to be imposed on Anne Hunt, widow, unless she fills up all the pits of coal and stone on the Meir heath within the manor before 25th March next year.

4th October 1611
Thomas Bagnold senior and Thomas Bagnold junior in person surrender a messuage, an orchard, a garden, a barn and the rest of the buildings belonging to it, a croft called Kylne croft, a croft called Barne croft, two parcels of land called Longcroft and Longcroft meadow, a parcel of land called Longoe, formerly the land of John Bradshawe deceased, a cottage, a garden and a yard adjoining it, situated in Penkhull, and three pastures or closes called the Astewoodes, as they are now divided, lying in Hanley, now occupied by Thomas Bagnold senior and Thomas Bagnold junior or their assigns. To Joan Hexam, widow, and assigns for her life.

7th April 1618
Thomas Lovatt surrenders two parcels of land called the Hales fields, a parcel of meadow-ground called Stonewall meadow, and another parcel of land called Moswall leasowe in Cleyton. To Richard Lovatt, Nicholas Lovatt and William Machin for 21 years at 12d yearly rent. Admitted. fine 2s 6d.

Tyttensor down in the town of Penkhull admitted. Thomas Tyttensor junior is admitted to a messuage and all the lands of which Robert Tyttensor his father died seized in Penkhull, Bothon and Cleyton; fine 12s.

Thomas Tyttensor junior, Elizabeth Tyttensor his wife and Margarett Tyttensor widow surrender a parcel called the Heigh wall furlong, abutting on the Clough, and another pasture called the Haugh and another pasture called the Cliff, and all his land in Bearswall Waste in Penkhull in the holding of John Machen and Jone Baddeley. To John Machen, his heirs and assigns forever. Admitted. Fine 2s 6d.

30th May 1620
Jone Bagnall widow desires according to the custom of the manor to have twelve men to enquire and find a way from Hanley Green to those lands called Astwoods now in the occupation of the said Jone Bagnall or her assigns, and to set forth the same by means and bonds.

In margin: Verdict for a way to Machin's Astwoods. *The jury present that, on the evidence given to them, the way from Hanley Green to the lands called Astwoods for all necessary uses, is first into a parcel of ground called Shorthays at a gate at the upper end of the same, and so along after the hedge at the west side of Shorthays till it come almost to the lower end of it, leaving the old pits on the east side, and so into a piece of ground called the Delphgutter field, and so down the same directly to two trees standing on the east side of the footway there in the Astwoods hedge, and so between the two trees into the Astwoods.*

19th March 1622
The copyhold jury present that Hugh Doody died since the last court, seized of a messuage and certain lands &c belonging to it in Penkhull and Clayton. A heriot is due. John Doody is his son and next heir and about 15 years old.

5th May 1625
View of frankpledge with court baron held at Stoke
The Freehold jurors present that Thomas Clarke (40s) infringed the liberty of this manor by arresting Richard Thorley with a warrant beyond the writ of the lord the King.
The Copyhold Jurors present again the death of Elizabeth Bagnall, one of the daughters and heirs of Thomas Bagnall of the Spout House in Penkhull, and now find that she died seized of the fourth part of a messuage and the fourth part of two cottages and various lands and hereditaments in Penkhull, and of the fourth part of various lands in Shelton & Hanley (which was omitted before). And that Jane Bagnall, Ann Bagnall and Catharine Bagnall are her sisters and nearest heirs.

Charles I
21st June 1625
Roger Dale senior, surrenders a cottage or tenement in which he now lives with all buildings belonging to it, a garden a croft called the backside, two parcels of land lying together called the Cliffs, the Stonewall croft meadow, one butt of land in Collins moore, three butts of land in the Highcroft head, two pieces of land called New Peace & Further Flatt, a parcel of meadowing called Acford meadow, two parcels of land called Highomes, and one parcel of land called Plat hill in Penkhull.

To his son Roger Dale and Margery Dale, his son's wife, for their lives, with remainder to the heirs begotten between them, with remainder to the heirs to be begotten by Roger the son, with remainder to Margaret daughter of Roger the father and the heirs of her body to be begotten, with remainder to the right heirs of

Roger the son for ever.
Roger Dale and his wife Margery Dale admitted. Fine 5ˢ 7ᵈ.

6th October 1625

This entry records that a property previously stood on the site of the old Penkhull Square in Trent Valley Road before a further property was built which went by the name of Turner or Ingrams. The old property referred to must have dated from at least the 13/14th century.

View of frankpledge.
The Copyhold Jurors present that Agnes Turner (40ˢ), widow, copyholder for the term of her life of a certain messuage and land, the inheritance of William Turner, caused certain old timber and stones, which had been used as a foundation for a previous old part of the premises, to be set at another copyhold messuage in Penkhull. And that Agnes Turner had had certain oak and ash plants and trees cut down on the aforesaid premises. And that Margaret Turner, Agnes' daughter, now wife of William Hunt sold twenty-four rods commonly called a Trined of spokes from the aforesaid plants and trees to a certain John Machen. And that the aforesaid William Hunt cut down (fined 20ˢ) various large trifolia and two crab-apple trees on the premises.

16th Jauary 1626

Rowland Cotton, knight, William Bowyer, knight, and William Cotton, gentleman, by attorney surrender the messuage or tenement where John Terrick junior lately dwelt, (area now occupied by The Views in Penkhull New Road) *and all lands, tenements, meadows, feedings, pastures and hereditaments belonging to it, late the inheritance of Walter Baddiley, gentleman. And also the half messuage, a house called the New House, a barn with a fold and backside belonging to the half messuage, a yard called Bradshawes yard,* (this confirms the entry dated the 6th October 1625 of a new house being erected to replace a previous one) *another yard called the little yard, a croft called Green croft,* (where Henry Ward Place now lies) *a meadow called Hodgmeadow, a pasture called New Leasowe, a pasture called Townsend,* (the section of land between Queens Road and Franklin Road) *a pasture called Further flatt, a pasture called Poole haugh, a parcel of land called Poolwalsitch, 8 butts and a headland in Woodfield, with their appurtenances in Penkhull, Cleyton & Bowden, late the inheritance of Randle Boothes, deceased. To John Terrick the elder, gentleman, his heirs and assigns forever.*
Admitted; fine 23ˢ 2ᵈ.

Village Stocks

A Statute of 1405 ordered that every manor should also provide stocks. There were many crimes that could be covered by the punishment. A statute dated to the 27th year of the reign of Henry VIII for example, made it law for children from 5-14 to be put to husbandry (farm work) and those who refused to work could be whipped. Anyone refusing to implement the punishment was to be set in the stocks for two days and fed only on bread and water.

Rogues and vagabonds were also stocked. One statute of 1495 required that vagabonds were set in the stocks for three days on bread and water and then sent away. If they returned then it was to be another six days in the stocks. These punishments were however seen as excessively harsh and the periods soon reduced to one and three days respectively.

Drunkards were another group for whom the stocks were a common punishment. Another statute of 1605 required that anyone convicted of drunkenness would have six hours in the stocks and those convicted of being a drunkard (as opposed to be caught drunken) should suffer 4 hours in the stocks or a three shilling and four pence fine. A slightly later statute made it legal to set those caught swearing in the stocks for one hours, if they could not pay a twelve pence fine. In actual fact the authorities preferred the offenders to pay fines as the monies were used to fund poor relief.

Although there are no records available to suggest punishment was administered from the manor courts in Penkhull, there a number of references which reflect upon the subject of punishment. Stocks are recorded as early as May 1628 as the method of punishment for petty crimes: *and that Penkhull's stocks are not in good repair.* In all probability as they were reported *as not in good repair,* it may be assumed that they had been in use for many years previous.

Even though the report was bought to the court in May, nothing was done. In July the matter was once more reported to the courts, but this time the inhabitants of Penkhull were fined five shillings. The stocks were listed again the following October as still un-repaired and a further fine of five shillings was imposed upon the villagers.

Maj. Gen. Thomas Harrison

The following note makes interesting reading as it refers to Maj. Gen. Thomas Harrison who was the son of a Newcastle butcher and became second in command after Oliver Cromwell. Following the restitution, Harrison was hung, drawn and quartered for treason.

On the wall outside of the HSBC Bank in High Street, there is a bronze plaque with the appropriate wording recording the birth of Thomas Harrison in Newcastle. Either the Deputy Steward or the clerk to the court wrote the following after the restitution. Although it is not dated the contents point to a date after 1660.
View of frankpledge
William Bolton and John Asbury are thirdboroughs' for Shelton. Both the Freehold and Copyhold Jury confirm the thirdboroughs' presentments.

Plaque recording the birth of Thomas Harrison

Humphrey Steventon & Elizabeth Steventon his wife surrender a meadow called Danniells alias Fowley meadow in Penkhull to Richard Harrison, his heirs and assigns for ever.

The said Richard Harrison was a butcher in Newcastle and had two sons viz Thomas and Richard. Thomas engaged himself in the English civil wars against King Charles Ist and became so great a man as to be made Major General of the rebels' army, and after the death of King Charles the first, and the exile of King Charles the second, became possessed of some part of the Crown rights and particularly to be the lord de facto of this manor. Richard the father died in the lifetime of his sons Thomas & Richard junior.

Upon the restoration of King Charles II to his rightful throne Thomas was charged with high treason, condemned and executed, and all his estate (whereof this Daniells alias Fowley was a part) was forfeited to the king and by him given to his brother James Duke of York and by him granted to other person, and by him or them sold to Randle Lovatt by whose son and heir this said meadow was sold to a gentleman in London, who hath again sold it to Thomas Baddely of Newcastle under Lyme, carrier, who now enjoys it. It is now by these grants made of it from the Crown, become freehold land but pays the xii^d yearly rent, with the copyhold rent.

Mrs Cooke of Newcastle, widow, purchased the most of the aforesaid forfeited lands about Newcastle. And William Boughey purchased the house and buildings in Newcastle, but hath since taken down most of the old house and built a new brick house over against the cross where the old house stood was called Lovatt's of the cross.
Mr Hatrill hath since bought the Cross Heaths from Mrs Cooke, which was part of Harrison's land.

5th October 1631 View of frankpledge
The copyhold jury presents that Tittensor down in the town of Penkhull his death and heir presented.
Thomas Tittensor has died since the last court seized of a messuage or tenement and diverse lands belonging to it in Penkhull. A heriot of 17^s is due [implying a customary acreage of 17 acres]. And that Roger Tittensor is his son and next heir and of full age.

And that Richard Bolton, William Hunt, Jone Machen and Roger Dale have incurred the fine of 30^s for failing to pay for the office of reeve.

26 April 1633
Be it remembered that Nicholas Lovatt the elder, paid Richard Broad of Fenton Vivian, Staffs, yeoman, the sum of £10 in the south porch of the parish church of Stoke upon Trent for Thomas Lovatt, his heirs and assigns for and in consideration of an abortive surrender of a meadow called Broadmeadow and of land known as Plathaugh meadow with the appurtenances made at a court of this manor 28th February 1632, so that this surrender now is of no effect. Witnesses of the payment who have sworn to this effect in open court: Thomas Fenton and John Machen junior.

21 April 1636
Admittance of John Mainwaring as Rector of Stoke. Two very interesting entries regarding the Rector of Stoke Dr Mainwaring.
The copyhold jurors say and present on their oath that the reeve or bailiff of the manor ought to be served for the following year by Raphe Keeling, gentleman, and by the rest of the occupiers of the lands that were formerly Nickson's in Penkhull. And further, that John Weston, doctor of civil law, rector of the parsonage or rectory of Stoke upon Trent in right of his rectory paid 2^s 6^d to the lord the King for certain parcels of meadow containing 5½ acres of meadow in Penkhull and Shelton, and owes suit of court and other services for the meadow to the lord the King just as the other tenants of the manor do for similar lands. And that William Prymrose, formerly Rector of the parsonage of Stoke, has died, seized of it, and a heriot is due. And that John Mainwaring, clerk, now rector of the parsonage of Stoke, holds the meadow and renders the services.
John Mainwaring, clerk, admitted; [fine 2^s 11^d]

Note by John Fenton c.1688 Mr Prymrose immediately before mentioned who was Rector of the Church of Stoke-upon-Trent was buried the 24th day of 1631. And the reason why Mr Mainwaring was not presented by the homage as his successor until the 21st day of April 1636 was because after he had by ways and means obtained the presentation from Roger Brereton of Newcastle-under-Lyme Esq. who was at that time patron, and his institution and induction; he was presented by Sir William Bowyer of Knypersley for simony, *(the selling and selling of ecclesiastical privileges such as a benefice of the size and wealth of Stoke)* which cost him a long and tedious law suit, but at last with much hardship he prevailed against Sir William and held the parsonage, yet (I doubt) I suspect guilty enough of the crime whereof he was charged.

The Commonwealth Period.
13th April 1637
After the execution of King Charles 1st on 30th January 1649, the kingship was abolished and a government by Council of State was set up on the 14th February 1649. This Council of State was dissolved on the 20th April 1653 and replaced by another Council of State on the 29th April 1653. Oliver

40

Cromwell took the office of Lord Protector on the 16th December 1653 and held it until his death on 3rd September 1658. His son Richard Cromwell succeeded to the same office on the day of his father's death and abdicated on 24th May 1659. After a year of parliamentary government Charles II was proclaimed king on 5th May 1660 and arrived in London on 29th May 1660.

It is interesting to note that in the first year of the Commonwealth period, no one is named as having the Lordship of the Manor. It was a Royal manor and the executed King had been the Lord of the Manor, by right. In the early years of the Commonwealth, period there was uncertainty regarding who was going to replace the King as Lord of the Manor. This is indicated by the adjustment to the wording of the usual surrender phrase *into the hands of the Lord of the said Manor*, which was changed to *into the hands of the Custodians of the liberty of England by act of Parliament*. There are also a number of references in the opening sentence of 'to the court of Major General Thomas Harrison'.

On a number of occasions, Major General Harrison sat as head of the court. In the Great Court of October 1649, those making presentations are described in Latin as the Franc pledge. This has been translated as Frankpledgers, though in other translations the term 'Thirdboroughs' has been used. The term Headboroughs was used post 1733, but not the term Thirdboroughs.

The first court held following the execution of Charles 1st was held on the 7th October 1649. The contents of the entry suggest that the courts continued to deal with the manorial business as previously even though there had been a lapse of over ten months.

7th October 1649
This court entry once more refers to the village pinfold being out of repair.
Penkhull & Bothon. John Terrick, Nicholas Woodcock and Robert Shelley, thirdboroughs, present that Henry Stevenson (2d), William Walter (2d), Ellice Griffith (2d), Randle Brownsword (2d), Elizabeth Till, widow (2d), Edward Poulson (2d), Roger Whittlelars (2d), Randle Brett (2d), Joan Ingram, widow (2d), Ellice Bagnall (2d), Randle Shawe (2d) and Edward Poulson (2d) have broken the assize. They present that the pinfold of Penkhull (18d) is not in good repair. And they present Roger Machen senior and William Meare and Nicholas Barrett as thirdboroughs for the following year.
Henry Stevenson was sworn in as constable for this year.

1st day of November 1649
Small Court of the said Manor held at Penckhull
To this Court came German Tittensor, in his proper person, and surrendered into the hands of the Custodians of the liberty of England by act of parliament.

One meadow called Ridd Meadow, with the appurtenances in the occupation of Nicholas Woodcock, lying in Penckhull aforesaid. To the use and behoof of Richard Cooke, his heirs and assign forever, under the conditions following. However, if the said German, his heirs executors or administrators, pay or cause to be paid to the said Richard Cooke, his executors or administrators, the sum of £30 of legal money of England, on the 2nd day of February which will be in the year of our Lord 1658, at or within the mansion house of Henry Stevenson in Penckhull, or within the space of 10 days next after the said 2nd day of February 1658, that then and henceforth this present surrender shall be void and of no value.

4th October 1650
View of frankpledge with court baron of the keepers of the liberty of England by authority of Parliament held at Penckhull before the steward John Byrche, gentleman.

Essoins: Thomas Hill and Thomas Machen have failed to attend as appears in the court roll over their names therefore in mercy.

Knutton - John Beech constable is sworn in and John Low in place of William Gibson, headborough, presents that all is well. And that John Low has been chosen as constable for the following year and John Badley as headborough for the following year.

Whitmore - Edward Asbury, headborough, presents that John Cotton (3s 4d) headborough failed to present, therefore in mercy. And that Isaac Low (2d) is a brewer of ale. And presents Thomas Brough and Thomas Sanders as headboroughs for the year following, and Edward Asbury as constable for the year following, and all is well.

Longton and Mere Lane end - Edward Alcock and George Townsend, headboroughs, present Edward Brindley (2d) John Bullock (2d) and Walter Hamersley because they have been brewers of ale &c. And all is well. And that Richard Mynors and Richard Fallows are the headboroughs.

Hanchurch - Thomas Collyer and Richard Foxe, headboroughs, says all is well. And present John Doody (3s 4d) and Richard Goodwin as headboroughs for the following year.

Hanford - John Whitehurst, headborough, presents Thomas Brerehurst, gentleman, as headborough for the following year, and all is well.

Included in the following entry are references to the erection of 'cottages contrary to the statue'. In modern terms that they were built without permission of the steward of the manor whereby the property was encroached onto the manorial land.

It would be a term used direct from the *1589 Act against erecting or maintaining cottages, the statute of 31.Eliz.,cap.7.,* which requires that 'no man may at this day build such a cottage for habitation, unless he lay into it foure acres of freehold land, except in market-towns, or cities, or within a mile of the sea, or for habitation of labourers in mines, saylors, foresters, sheepeheards etc.

The idea was that cottagers who did not have four acres of land were more likely to become a burden on the poor law rates. By c1670 most presentments had ceased. The Act was repealed by 15 Geo 111, c 32.

However from this date, 1650, it would seem that they were tolerated because it created additional rent to the lord of the manor. In reality these cottages were situated on the uncultivated waste patches of land found on the side of the roads.

Botoslow and Fenton Vivian - Richard Broade and William Badley, headboroughs, present William Poulson (2d) and William Barker (2d) are brewers of ale and that John Serjant and Edward Cock are the headboroughs for next year and that Thomas Mihoard (3s 4d) erected a cottage contrary to the statute, therefore he is in mercy.
Hanley - William Stevenson in place of Robert Asten, headborough, presents William Meare (2d), Sara Sherratt, Katherin Keeling (2d) and William Daton (2d) because they are brewers &c. And that Raphe Simpson (3s 4d), Anthonie Keeling (3s 4d), John Ellis (3s 4d), William Daton (3s 4d) and Thomas Waldron (3s 4d) have erected cottages contrary to the statute, therefore &c. And further he presents William Meare for headborough for the following year.

Wolstanton - William Harrison, headborough, presents William Burslem (2d), John Eaton (2d), Elizabeth Tunstall, widow (2d) and Robert Hancock (2d) are brewers of ale and broke the assize, therefore &c. And presents that Richard Fatherson (2s) Thomas Woolfe (2s) and Francis Johnson (2s) have erected cottages contrary to the statute, therefore and that Richard Badley and Richard Cartwright and John Williams are headboroughs for the following year.

Penckhull and Bothon - Roger Machen the elder and Nicholas Barrett, headboroughs, present that Roger Whittekurs (4d), Ellen Shawe (2d) Randall Brett (2d) William Johnson (2d) Edward Polson (2d) Elizabeth Till, widow (2d), Raphe Brownsword (2d) Henry Stevenson (2d) William Walter (2d) Ellic Griffith (2d) and Joan Ingram, widow (2d) are brewers of ale and have broken the assize. And present Roger Machen and John Terrick, gentleman, constables and Thomas Tittensor and Roger Machen as headboroughs for Penckhull and John Seabridge for Bothon for the year following.

Shelton - Robert Sympson and John Cartwright, headboroughs, present William Barlow (2d), George Banckes (2d), Thomas Bloore (2d), Robert Fendall (2d) and William Sympson (2d) because they are brewers and broke the assize, therefore &c. And that the pound there has not been repaired. And further they present John Middleton and John Cartwright headboroughs for the following year. Robert Simpson sworn in place of John Middleton.

Cleyton and Seabrige - Henry Shaw and Robert Byddulph and Nicholas Lovatt, headboroughs, present that Robert Carter (6d) erected a cottage contrary to the statute. And that William Anyan encroached on the common of Cleyton. And that William Anyan, thrower, (2d) and William Anyan, Robert Walker and Elizabeth Dawson are brewers of ale and broke the assize. And present Thomas Lovatt, Thomas Fenton and Richard Lovatt for headboroughs for the year following.

A further reference also reflects the period with regards to claims on the poor law. *That John Tyler lives with several inmates'.* In all probability this came about because of the fear that overcrowding of cottages would mean that many would not be able to find work. As a result of this they would become a burden on the Poor Law rate payers or that to encourage a long period of stay would affect the 'law of settlement' and therefore not encouraged or allowed.

4th October 1650
Verdict of the small inquest
They confirm the headboroughs' presentments. Further, they present that George Hales (12d) and Robert Hales erected a cottage contrary to the statute in which John Tyler lives and several inmates. And present that Thomas Stanley (12d) erected a cottage contrary to the statute and made an incroachment. They present Richard Stanley (12d) for a similar offence. And present Robert Cotgreave (12d) because he made an incroachment. And present William Sympson (12d) because he erected a cottage contrary to the statute and made an incroachment. And present Elizabeth Lovatt (12d) similarly for a cottage contrary to the statute, therefore &c. They present [word missing] Hancock (12d) because he/she made an incroachment. They present separately the ponds of Cleyton (12d) and Shelton (12d) because they are not well repaired, but are now in repair. They present Robert Butterton (10s) who lives outside the manor has burdened the inhabitants of Seabridge in the fields there with his beasts.

14th October 1653
View of frankpledge with court baron held at Penckhull for the keepers of the liberty of England by authority of Parliament before William Hill, deputy steward.
We present Thomas Stevenson to be constable of Penckhull. And all those persons that hold any part of the land for which he is to serve to contribute to him for his service at the amount of £3 10s. We find John Machen son and heir of Thomas Machen his

late father who died seized of 8 acres of copyhold land who died and a heriot of 8s is due. And he is of full age.
We fyne the sum of 30s forfeited by those who ought to make the Spittle yate. (gate) And we lay a fyne of 30s on those persons that ought to make the gate, so that it is effectively made and set up before 25th March next. We confirm the presentments of the headbarrows (except the part of the pinfold in Shelton that belongs to Richard Cartwright and John Cartwright).

It is impossible to say what was the importance of Spittle Gate. Perhaps it was an early form of Toll Gate or one of the main gates into one of the former open fields?

29th September 1653 Small court held at Penckhull
John Terrick, gentleman, through Roger Machen his attorney by virtue of a letter of attorney made to him and Nicholas Woodcock dated 29th April last, surrenders a close called Townsend, a pasture or close of land called Poole haugh, a parcel of land called Further flatt, part of a pasture of land called Wood field, one parcel of land called Greene Croft and one little nook of land previously Nicholas Woodcock's with the appurtenances now or recently in John's holding or that of his assignes in Penckhull. To Jane Terrick, widow, and Richard Badley for two years from March 25th last, the rent of 6d to be paid to John and his heirs. Admitted. Fine 12d.

26th January 1654
At the Small Court of Thomas Harrison of his manor of Newcastle-under-Lyme holden at Penkhull within the said manor the sixth and twentieth daie of January in the year of our Lord God one thousand, six hundred and fifty and four before Thomas Bagnall, gent steward there.

To this court comes Randall Brownsword and Roger Machen in their own persons and surrender into the hands of the said lord of the manor one messuage in Penkhull also one garden, one croft called Honniewell Croft to the said Messuage belonging now in the occupation of William Meare to the use and behoof of the said William Meare. And there upon in the same court cometh the said William Meare in his own person and desireth seizin of the premises To whom the lord by his said steward granteth seizin of by the rod to have and to hould the premises unto the said William Meare according to the custome of the said manor by rents and services thereof due and of right accustomed And give to the lord for his fine six pence and is admitted tenant.

5th October 1654
Penckhull & Bothon - John Bowyer, Roger Machen and Robert Shelley, headbarrows, present Randle Brett (2d), Ellis Griffis (2d), Joane Ingrum, widow (2d), William Hodgskyns (2d), Thomas Munford (2d), Anne Stevenson, widow (2d), Randle Brownsword (2d), Marie Walker, widow (2d), Roger Whittekurs (2d) and Edward Poulson (2d) for breaker[s] of the assize of ale. And present Dorothie Machen, widow, John Lovatt of Shelton

and Alice Boulton, widow for new headbarrows. And Roger Dale to be constable. And that Sara Poulson (4d), wife of Edward Poulson, struck Thomas Stevenson on the face with her hands and made him bleed. And that Nicholas Barrett (12d) and Thomas Butterton (12d) lay dunghills in the street in Boden and annoy their neighbours with them. And present that Alice Boulton, widow, keeps two gates out of repair into the Rie Feild in Bothon.

Most have heard of the saying 'upon payne of death' meaning that if a certain order was not carried out, the person would be executed. The same principle in the following entries applies except that if certain work is not carried out under the instructions of the court, the person involved would be fined the sum stated along side their name.

We lay a payne of 20ˢ upon John Lee that he repairs a messuage in Penkhull in John Lovatt's holding before 25ᵗʰ March next. We present Sara Terrick (10ˢ) for making a pound-breach.
We lay a payne of 39ˢ on those persons that ought to make the Spittle gate in Penkhull, that they or some of them make an effective gate and hang it up in the usual place in the highroad near the Spittle ground, and to make the fence at both ends of it at or before 2ⁿᵈ February next.

The following entry gives an unusual reference to The Cromwellian conquest of Ireland (1649-53) whereby Jerman Tittensor of Penkhull enlisted in the army of Cromwell. According to the court minute it was at Clonmel. The Siege of Clonmel took place in April - May 1650 during the Cromwellian conquest of Ireland when the town of Clonmel in County Tipperary, Ireland was besieged by Oliver Cromwell's New Model Army. Cromwell's 8000 men eventually took the town from its 1000 Irish defenders, but not before they suffered heavy losses, between 2000-2500 army soldiers being killed after being caught in a trap by Hugh Dubh ("Black Hugh") O'Neill. Cromwell suffered the biggest defeat of his military career at Clonmel.

The family of Tittensor was well established in Penkhull and held considerable land. This reference is one of the very few that give an indication of which side the folk of Penkhull took during the Commonwealth period and as such is an important contribution to our history.

2nd November 1654 Small court held at Penckhull before William Hill, deputy steward.
Thomas Yardley an enlisted soldier under Major Jones, governor of Dublin castle, upon his corporal oath affirms that he received from the hands of William Shacoe, captain, the certificate produced and shown to the court, which attests the death of Jerman Tittensor:

I do hereby certify all whom it may concern that Jerman Tittensor late of Penckhull-cum-membris in the parish of Stoake within the county of Stafford enlisted as a soldier under my command in May 1650 for the service of Ireland, whither with myself he transported himself, where he was mustered in my foot company in the regiment of the late Lord Deputy Ireton till December following the said year 1650, in which month the said Jerman died in Clonmell in the county of Tipperarie in Ireland. In witness whereof I have hereunto put my hand and seal this 27th May 1653.

Major Michael Jones was chosen by the parliamentary army as governor of Dublin.

The following entry points to considerable mining of coal taking place towards the end of the Commonwealth period.

27th April 1655

We present that Mary Crockett, the wife of John Crockett (20ˢ 20ᵈ) who is a copyholder of this manor, on 14th June 1654 stopped William Anyon and others who came in the right of the lord of the manor to sink pits and to get coal.

13th September 1655

Small court of Thomas Harrison Esq. held at Penkhull before William Hill deputy steward. We lay a payne of 10s against Elizabeth Baylie that she forms the watercourse through the Hall Meadow betwixt [omission] and the first day of April next. We lay a payne of 10s against Thomas Ward that he scours his ditch betwixt Patsons high greaves and the Milne home. We lay a payne of 10s against the occupiers of the lower croft meadow and Whitfeilde Meadow that they form the brooke down to the Whitfeild yate (gate) before the first day of April next.

The following entry gives an insight to the old parish church of Stoke, which was surrounded by a moat for protection in its early years or to allow the water from the River Trent to flow through to the water mill channels which was situated around where the old Victoria Football Ground once stood to return into the river at a lower point.

We lay a payne of 10s against John Mainwaring doctor of divinitie (The Rector of Stoke church) that he either remove his flood gates to the Ancient place, or keep his water going to the Mill out of the foot way leading betwixt Stoake and Bowden before the 10th of November next. We lay a payne of 10ˢ against the occupiers of lands on both sides the Waste land that they scour their ditches there before the 20ᵗʰ March next upon every mans default to forfeit 10ˢ. We present Richard Bowker and Jane Beech that they have not made their fences in Eglow field according to a former payne of 10ˢ, which was laid against them. We continue a payne against all the occupiers of the fences betwixt Holditch mill Brooke and Margarett Beeches Meadow

That they and every one of them make the fences there sufficient before 20th March next. We lay a payne upon Mr Thomas Smith that he scours the head of Marian Tayliers Banck in the ancient place leading betwixt Bucknall and Newcastle before the 20th November next. We continue the payne of 20ˢ against those that dig pits to get Clay in the Lanes of Shelton and Hanley. We continue a payne upon the inhabitants of Penkhull to lay a Bridge at Spittle Brook We lay a payne upon Mr Thomas Burslem of 10ˢ to shift his stile in Bosleys meadow to the lower ends thereof against the Castle Cliffe before the first day of January next.

16th April 1657

Handley: A payne laid upon Thomas Smyth of ten shillings to be forfeited by him if he cause not two pits at Hanley green to be filled up before the four and twentieth day of June next.

16th April 1657

By the time of this court entry there appear to be wide-ranging social issues that are addressed by the Manor Court.

First they present Raphe Biddulph for making an affray and bloodwipe on Thomas Lovatt of Clayton. Also they present Thomas Lovatt of Clayton for making an affray and bloodshed upon Raphe Biddulph. Also they present Walter Collyer and John Corkersole have broken a payne of thirty shillings layd upon them at the last court that they not make sufficient gate at the Lower End of Clayton Leas Leasow. Also they present that Thomas Blarkwall hath broken a payne of ten shillings as layd at the last court in that he hath not get up sufficient styles and opened the way in his backsides to Ederley. Also they present Robert Creswall xxxixs xid for serving ale and issuing forth of Darlaston Court upon the goods of Thomas Harding within liberty of the Duchy to the breath if the liberty. Also they present John Rowson (fined iijd) for carrying gravel into the watercourse near Shelton Mill whereby the water is turned upon the land of John Cartwright and they present Andrew Deane (fined iiid) for the like Also they present Thomas Moyles the younger, (fined iis iijd). Nicholas his brother (fined iis iiid) Samuel Simpson (fined iis iijd) for getting of clay in Shelton Lane contrary to aforementioned payne that since the last court next. Also they present John Cartwright of Shelton who has erected a new hand mill at Shelton whereby he hath sworn the suit and malt grist of the Lords tenants from the mill, anciently the lord's mill in Shelton contrary to the custom there used. A payne laid upon Nicholas Lovatt of Clayton that he put up a sufficient gate at a place called the Blessa Pitt and make up the four at either end before the 24ᵗʰ day of July next or else forfeit five shillings. Also they continue a payne of ten shillings upon Richard Heath and Thomas Shawe that they scower their ditches between diglakes and dungsmore meadow at or before the first day of May next.

44

Also, they continue a payne of twenty shillings upon every person that doth dig pits or get clay within the lands belonging to the township of Shelton and Hanley.

A payne laid of thirty-nine shillings eleven pence half penny upon any one that doth bring in any stranger or foreigner within this manor that is like to be chargeable to the same.

Also they present Thomas Tittensor of Penkhull to serve the office of Reeve for the year to come and that contribution shall be made to him from those that hold land chargeable to the service according to the custom. And afterwards Thomas Machin upon the request of the said Thomas Tittensor was admitted to serve the office of Reeve for him.

12th October 1659 The following entries relate to a number of coal and brass mines being sunk-

Also they find and present that the respective of the lords manor of Newcastle under Lyme aforesaid have where the time whereof the memory of man is not to the contrary by their farmers under tenants against servants or workmen entered into or upon any copyhold or customary lands within the said manor where any coal myne or mynes below the ground and have therein at their wills and pleasure sunk pit or pits for the getting of coal and have taken, carried away, sold and converted to their own use the said coals there in so begotten as of right they then did and still may do.

And they find and present that Balthazer Bell, gent, Robert Pope and other farmers or tenants to the lord of the manor of several coal mynes within the same did on or about the month of October in the year of our lord God, one thousand, six hundred and fifty and four set out or employ John Wright, John Griffin ground colliers to make a pit in the copyhold land of Thomas Smyth of Handley, gent lying on the southwest side of the Woodhouses within the said manor then and now in the occupation of one Christopher Chatterley for the perfecting bettering and recovering of one coal myne lying there which by lease hold from the lord of the said manor called the Bassemyne. And that the said Thomas Smyth on or about the time of the aforesaid did molest, interrupt and hinder the said John Wright and John Griffin from going on in their said work by giving them various threatening speeches and pulling one of them by the hair of the head thereby did cause him to desist work.

And they find and present that the said Balthazer Bell, Robert Pope and other farmers or tenement to the Lord of the said manor of the coal mynes aforesaid did on or about the month of August in the year of our Lord God 1656 in the copyhold land of the said Thomas Smyth within the manor likewise in the holding or occupation of the said Christopher Chatterley, employ workmen to get Bassetone or boylom (iron ore) as of right the same might do to have five employed for the use of some of the said coal mynes and gutter, to which said workmen then got there so much Bassetone, boyloam as cost the said farmers or tenants of the said coal mynes forty shillings of there about for the getting thereof

which Bassetone or boylom the said Thomas Smyth or caused to be carried away and converted the same to his own use.

Also they find and present that John Crockett the younger son of John Crockett of Shelton within the manor did in or upon the eighth day of this instant molest, stop and hinder the servants or workmen of the said farmers or tenants or coal mynes from amending the way in a gate within the copyhold land of the said John Crockett his father leading the usual and most convenient way from the lane to the said coal mynes and gave out various threatening speeches against the said workmen or any others that should offer to amend the same. All, which the said John Crockett the younger then said, and he did by the command of the said John Corbett the father.

And they lay a payne of xxx shillings upon all those persons that have or hold any land or meadow within the said manor of Newcastle-under-Lyme adjoining the brook or river called Fowley or long bridge water that they and everie of them do and shell well and sufficiently farm and clean the bottom of the said brook or water course so far as their respective lands or meadows do or shall adjoin that water in the said brook may have free passage away and also all by brooks from and between the meadow called Wood Meadow now in the occupation of one William Clowse and the bridge called the Fowlea Bridge at or before the 20th May next coming.

23rd April 1660

A payne layd of Thomas Smyth, gent, Robert Keelinge and Anthony Keelinge that they fill or arranged to be filled in two coal pits that they have made and left open at or before the tenth day of May next.

Paynes layd of Edward Foster that he sufficiently scour his ditch at the open end of pavement Leasow at or before the tenth day of May next or to forfeit ten shillings.

The following is a copy of a Warrant under the sign manual of King Charles 2nd, authorising Sir John Bowyer to work the King's mines north of the Trent.

The following was written after the restitution referring to the discovery of coal, ironstone and limestone by the former head of the manor, Maj. Gen. Thomas Harrison.

Charles R.

Whereas we are informed that a number of our Lands and Manors on the North side of the River Trent have in them several mines of coal, ironstone and limestone, and that some part thereof hath been discovered by Thomas Harrison and more might be found out to the benefit of us and our subjects if diligent search were made. Our will and pleasure is that our trusty and well beloved Sir John Bowyer Knt. do prosecute and he is authorised to prosecute such works as are already begun for that purpose by the said Thomas Harrison and also to search for more of the *foresaid mines giving us an account from time to time of his proceedings. And for so doing this shall be his Warrant. Given in the Court of Whitehall the 26th day of June 1660 in the twelfth year of our Reigne.*

By his Maties command William Morice.

The following entry is interesting as it refers to a park and the park gates. What or where this is would be only speculation. However, the fields flowing from the lower section of Honeywall down to what is now London Road were known as Park fields. Spark Street covers this area.

4th May 1682

They present John Dale of Penkhull for forestalling the way in the park betwixt the park gate and several pieces of ground called the wastes in Penkhull.

It was also an offence not to maintain hedges and to clean out ditches and not to obstruct the flow of water.

A fine of 20s on John Terrick and Andrew Corbett to sufficiently lop and crop their hedges and scour their ditches in their closes called Knowles Meadow in Penkhull and the Dig Lakes betwixt by the 15th May next.

Thomas Dale, John Tittensor, Robert Machin and John Fenton obstruct the course of the ancient watercourse, the stonewall wellspring, they being some of the occupiers on either side of the said spring.

James II

22nd December 1685 This refers to property where The Views, off Penkhull New Road now stands.

To this court comes John Terrick, son and heir of John Terrick deceased in his own person and seeks to be admitted tenant of one messuage or tenement and all lands in Penkhull of which John Terrick, senior lately died seized except all lands and tenements before this surrender to the use of John Terrick, junior to which John the son was admitted before this admittance. To whom the said lady granted seizin thereof by the rents and services and he gives to the lady for a fine of 9s 3d and is admitted tenant thereof.

7th April 1686

View of Frankpledge with Court Leet and Court Baron held at Penkhull the jury of customary tenants present that Bird, widow (2d) John Ward (2d) William Webb (2d) Peter Gilworth (2d) Robert Cooper (2d) Thomas Edge (2d) [blank] Massey, widow (2d) and Mark Scarrat (2d) inhabit cottages and made encroachments on the waste give of fines as is shown above their heads.

William and Mary

4th June 1690

John and Elizabeth Tittensore's rendering of seizin. The Court Baron of Catherine, the present Dowger Queen of England etc. held at Penkhull within the aforesaid manor on the 4th day of

June in the second year of the reign of William and Mary, King and Queen of England before William Wright, gent, deputy for the right honourable Robert Lord Ferrers, Baron de Chartley, and the High Steward there.

William III

31st January 1699/0

(Would this be the origins of Twyfords factory in Shelton?)

Richard Bagnall of Highgate, Middlesex, Esq., for a lease of 21 years from 25th March next at £26 p.a., to Joshua Twyford all that messuage or tenement in Shelton in which Richard Coten now lives, and all barns edifices stables and gardens to the same belonging, and all those pieces or parcels of land meadow or pasture to the same messuage belonging etc., called by the various names of the two Croshawes, the Arbor Field, the Wheat Croft, the Gorsty Field, the Great Crowshaw Meadow, the Little Meadow at Fowlea Bridge, the Brindley Bank and the Bank House Croft, all which premises are in Shelton; fine 1s 2d.

31st Jan 1699/0

John Fenton Gent, for a 6 year lease commencing 25th March 1701 at £80 p.a., to John all that capital messuage or tenement in Shelton in which John Marsh now lives, and all barns edifices stables and malt kilns, cowsheds structures orchards gardens and folds to the same belonging etc., and all those closes and parcels of land meadow and pasture called the Greensitch Croft, the Lower Croft, the Turmishaw Meadow, all those three closes called Ends, the Horsford Meadow, the Cocksitch, the Steels Meadow, the Little Coton, the Household Flatt, the Brown Hill, the Farther Cotons Hey, the Nearer Cotons Hey, the Heath Meadow, the further Horsford with the Pingle adjoining the same, the Nearer Horsfords and all his part or portion of and in a certain close in Shelton called the Great Coton, and all ways waters etc., all which premises are in Shelton; fine 6s 9¾d.

16th October 1700

Comes to this court John Adams and surrenders two closes called le two crane furlongs in Penkhull in the occupation of John Bowyer to the use of Thomas Doody.

Thomas Doody surrenders messuage situated and standing in Penkhull, within the said manor in which Thomas Tittensor now lives . . . . . and all those closes, enclosures, pieces or parcels of land lying in Penkhull commonly called or known as le Pease field or Over field, le Lower field, le Lambfitch, le Townsend in the several tenures of the said Thomas Doody and Thomas Tittensor to the use of Esther Stockton, spinster for 1,000 years paying annually a pepper corn rent on the first day of May provided that the said Thomas Doody pay the said Esther two hundred and fifty pounds with interest at 5% p.a. on the 29th March next or this surrender will be void. Esther Stockton asks for admission and pays one shilling and is admitted.

5th June 1700

John Woodcock to John Bowyer Sen[r]

re. a messuage or tenement in Penckhull with all buildings barns stables cowsheds gardens orchards and flax butts to the same messuage belonging and all those closes inclosures or parcels of land called by the various names of the Green Croft, one other piece called the Townsend and one other piece of land called the Little Townsend, with all ways waters etc., all which premises are in Penckhull and are now in the holding or occupation of John Philips or his assigns, and all other customary tenements of the same John Woodcock within the Manor; fine 10[d]; fair fee 2s.

Queen Anne

9th February 1703/4

Thomas Tittensor, for a mortgage of £115, to William Low.
One close pasture or parcel of land called the Townsend, one other close pasture or parcel of land called the Ridding, one meadow called Green Meadow Moore, one parcel of land called Honywall Dole, and one close or pasture called the Pitt Croft, with all ways etc., in Penckhull; fine 6[d]½.

7th January 1707/8

Richard Colley and Margery his wife to Richard and Mary Harrison for life, then their children but of none, back to Richard Colley – four days math of arable land, more or less in a certain common field called the Stubbs in Penkhull, now in the holding of Richard Harrison adjoining a certain place walled the Whorston; fine 1d.

14th August 1708

John Bowyer and Margaret Bowyer, widow, his mother, surrenders a messuage or tenement with the appurtenances in Penckhull now in the tenure of Thomas Blakeman and the messuage or tenement with the appurtenances called Woodcocks house in Penckhull in the tenure of John Philips, and a close, piece or parcel of land of meadow and pasture called the meadow below the house and Duncall Lee, the Hoo waste, the Hancocks meadowe, the Honeywall dole, the Hoo Cranefurlong, the little Hough, the Boothen heath, the Heathhouse in separate parts divided, the new piece, the greencroft, the little Townsend with all houses, barns, stables, gardens, orchards, ways, waters and hereditaments belonging to the messuage or property, all of which are in Penkhull & Boothen and now in the tenure or occupation of John Bowyer. To Margaret Bowyer for life, unless John Bowyer pays her £30 a year on 25th December and 24th June, the first payment being 25th December next during her life; in which case John Bowyer and his heirs can have and enjoy all the property and the rents from it, notwithstanding anything in this surrender to the contrary. Margaret Bowyer admitted: fine 5s 7¼d.

Indenture made 28th April 1714

The following is a marriage settlement.

Between Roger Townsend of Penkhull Yeoman of the first part and Katherine Smith of Penkhull Spinster on the second part and Robert Smith of Penkhull yeoman and Richard Smith of Penkhull on the 3rd part.

Whereas Katherine Smith is now possessed of a personal estate in money of sixty pounds and whereas Roger Townsend is now in possession of a copyhold estate of a messuage which he now inhabits in Penkhull together with a croft and garden lying on the Backfield of the messuage with the out buildings belonging which he possesses and called by the name of Spittle and whereas Roger Townsend likewise is entitled to another copyhold messuage with land belonging in Penkhull as the inheritance of Thomas William D.... and now in the inheritance of John Knight of Whitmore, gent by virtue of a mortgage made by surrender dated the 17th July 1690 subject to redemption of payment of £50 and interest for the same.

And where a marriage is intended firstly to be held and solemnised between Roger Townsend and Katherine Smith. Now this Indenture witnessed that in consideration of a marriage for the setting of property, possession of maintenance upon the said Katherine and her issue in life marriage shall effect it is agreed between all parties to this document Roger Townsend for himself and his heirs etc. doth covenant and promise and grant to with Robert Smith and Richard Smith that he the said Roger Townsend shall at the next Court Baron or some other following court to be held within the Manor of Newcastle within the space of two months after the marriage shall surrender to the Lord of the said manor according to the customs all and singular that copyhold messuage lands called by the name Spittals Houses with those crofts into the hands of Robert Smith and Richard Smith, nevertheless for the Roger Townsend for and during the term of his natural life without impeachment of or for any matter and from and after his wife to the life and behoof of Katherine Smith for and during the term of her natural life and after the marriage to Katherine Smith which shall first happen to the use of the said Roger Townsend upon the body Katherine Smith lawful to begotten and of default of such issue to the use of Roger Townsend.

After his death shall yearly pay the interest to the use and behoof of Katherine Smith.

On or after her death or marriage, which shall first happen that, they shall be to Roger Townsend.

They were married on the 3rd May 1714 at Newcastle, Roger, Townsend and Katherine Smith, both of Stoke.

George I

27th April 1715

Formal presentment of the death and will of John Bourne of Newcastle, Inn holder. John Bourne died since the last View of Frankpledge seized of 8½ acres of customary land within the Manor, by his death there happened to the Lord for a heriot 8s 6d; John Bourne, gent. is his son and heir and of full age; the Jury then presented his last will and testament.

27th April 1715

Formal admittance of John Bourne, the son of John Bourne dec'd. All and singular the customary land of which the said John Bourne died seized; fine 8s 9d; heriot 8s 6d.

25th January 1715/6

John Bourne, to Ralph Beech, all those pieces or parcels of land meadow or pasture in Penkhull now in the holding of Ralph Beech or his assigns called the Nearer Mill Field, adjoining a certain common field called the Stubbs, with all ways etc; fine 1s.

30th December 1720

And as concerning all that messuage or tenement in Penkhull called the Greenhead House in which Joseph Lovatt now lives and all malt houses barns stables outhouses gardens orchards fold curtelages and easements to the same belonging, and all that close or parcel of land meadow and pasture in Penkhull called the Stonycroft, the two Stonycroft meadows, the two Stepping Stone meadows, the four Cliffs, the Slade, and the Little Heighwall adjoining the land of Richard Hewit and a lane. To the use and behoof of the said Mary Lovatt, her heirs and assigns forever, for her share of the land of the said Thomas Dale; fine 4s ¾d.

And as concerning all that messuage or tenement, in Penkhull called Tittensor's House now in the holding of Robert Tittensor, with all barns stables outhouses gardens and orchards to the same belonging, and all those closes or parcels of land meadow and pasture in Penkhull and Clayton called the two Long Fields, the Hassell Croft, with the barns to the same belonging, the two Townsends, the Woodfield, the New Leasowe, the Minorsley and Boothen Heath, with their appurt's, To the use and behoof of the said Margery Bourne, her heirs and assigns for ever, for her share of the land of the said Thomas Dale; fine 4s ¾d.

30th December 1720

John Bourne and wife Margery, to themselves and their surviving heirs and assigns re: all that messuage or tenement, in Penkhull called Tittensor's House and now in the holding of Robert Tittensor, with all barns stables outhouses gardens orchards folds curtelages and easements to the same belonging, and all those closes or parcels of land meadow and pasture in Penkhull and Clayton called the two Long Fields, Hassell's Croft, with the barns to the same belonging, the two Townsends, the Woodfield, the New Leasowe, the Minorsley and the Boothen Heath, with their appurt's; fine 4s 0d.

11th May 1726

Anne and Jemima Barratt, both spinsters and daughters of Elizabeth Barratt, widow, to Thomas Buxton. All that parcel of land on which an ancient barn once stood, containing by estimation 12yds in length and 6yds in breadth, adjoining to the house of Thomas Bloor and the garden of Richard Buxton, with the Maerecino lying on the same, which premises are in Boothen; fine 1d.

George II

26th March 1729 This court record refers to what is now The Greyhound Inn.

Joseph Lovat and Mary, for a mortgage of £209, to Martha Minors Sen', widow, and Martha Minors Jun', Spinster re: all that messuage called Greenhead House in which the said Joseph now lives, and all malthouses, barns stables outhouses gardens orchards folds, curtelages to the same belonging, and all those closes pieces or parcels of land meadow and pasture called the Big Cliff, the Gorsty Cliffe, the two Stepping Stone Meadows, the Slade, the Little Heighwall adjoining to land of Richard Hewit and the lane to the same belonging, and all ways etc., all which premises are in Penckhull and in the possession of the said Joseph; [fine 1s 4¼d; adm. on 9 July.

12th May 1736

James Taylor surrenders that entire messuage in Penkhull in the occupation of John Dutton containing stables, gardens, orchards, meadows belonging, closes and inclosures. Spittle meadow, Spittle croft and also five days work of arable land lying in Penkhull in a common field called Stubbs and also other day's work of arable in the Stubbs. That James Taylor shall pay unto Ralph Taylor his heirs the sum of £500 at the rate of £4. 10s p.a. interest. Ralph Taylor admitted; find 2d.
Signed James Taylor.

28th March 1738

Comes Francis Taylor Gent, John Terrick gent and Ralph Taylor in their proper persons and surrenders that property now in the possession of John Dutton and other tenants − all those houses, outbuilding, barns, stables, gardens, orchards called Little Piece, Grindley Hill, Grindley Field adjoining land of John Taylor formerly John Bolton also great Stubbs and little Stubbs, gardens, crofts, all to Thomas Fenton.

6th April 1743

Joseph Lovatt the younger surrendered all the property surrendered to him on 12th January last by his father, and all other customary land within the manor except a meadow lying on Newcastle Brook called Brewthen Lake (7 days math) and 2 little meadows called Stepping Stones meadow (½ days math) lying opposite each other and adjoining the high road from Newcastle to Trentham, to the use of himself for life, after the use of Dale Lovatt and Thomas Baddeley gentleman during Lovatt's life to preserve contingent remainders, after to secure a rent charge of £50 to Anne Sherman his intended wife and after her death to raise £500 for younger children of the marriage. After to the first son and sons in succession and issue, for want of issue, to daughters. Joseph Lovatt the younger admitted.

24th May 1754

For whatever reason the following court was held at the home of John Terrick which once occupied the site of The Views. It refers to the old workhouse stood at the top of what is now Garden Street and overlooked the parish church.

Held at Penckhull by adjournment at the house of John Terrick, on the twenty fourth day of May in the year of our Lord one thousand seven hundred and fifty four.

To this Court came John Terrick the elder, and surrendered All that cottage or tenement, with its appurtenances, standing in Penckhull aforesaid, with the outbuildings gardens orchards to the same belonging, now used for a workhouse, and formerly purchased from the exec'rs of Richard Godwyn deceased.

To the use & behoof of John Fenton Esq, Thomas Broad Esq, Jeremiah Smith Gent. and John Terrick the younger, in trust to be employed for a workhouse for the poor of the parish of Stoake upon Trent.

October 1758

This refers to the previous site of Spode Works in the town of Stoke, but Stoke at this time was within the Township of Penkull.

To this court comes William Clarke of Caverswall in this county of Stafford in his own person and surrender unto the Lord of the manor all that newly erected messuage in Penkhull of the said William Clarke now in the possession of Joseph Brindley and all waterways etc, those newly erected workhouses, pot-ovens and warehouses formerly a barn standing to the west of Madeley Meadow, thirteen yards northwards in breadth and always etc. to the use of William Banks and John Turner; fine 2d.

23rd May 1759

To this court comes William Harrison in his proper person and surrenders all that cottage with appurtenances situated in Penkhull in which Josiah Spode lately occupied and which John Wilkinson now doth inhabit to the use of John Slaney for the sum of £20 to be paid on the 13th day of June.

John Slaney is admitted tenant; fine ½d.

7th November 1759

Comes Benjamin Lewis and surrenders to the court all that tenement leading from the highway from Newcastle to Uttoxeter through a certain piece of land where Banks and Turner had lately erected a new building. Banks and Turner admitted.

In the following entry Banks and Turner surrender to the Lord another piece of land to Benjamin Lewis.

7th November 1759

Comes William Clarke of Caverswall, gent and surrenders all that now erected messuage tenement in Penkhull of the said William Clarke now in the possession of Joseph Brindley and all gardens, ways etc. to the same belonging. And all the now erected work houses, pot ovens, warehouses being formerly a barn standing in Penkhull now rented out from the rest of Madeley Meadow thirteen yards northwards in breadth and all ways etc. to the same belonging, except a house reserved unto Benjamin Lewis, the two roads into and from the said meadow out of a high [?] To the use of William Banks, John Turner there belonging as tenants in common; fine 2d.

George III
28th May 1764.

This entry refers to the site of the current Victoria House in St.Thomas Place.

Comes Joseph Bourne in his own proper person and surrenders to the court all that messuage standing in Penkhull now in the holding of Sampson Bagnall and in which the said Joseph Bourne now inhabits and all houses, outhouses yards and Hempbutts belonging and those pieces of land, meadow or pasture lying in Penkhull and Boothen known by the names of Barnfield or Bankside/Backside? Formerly called The Meadow and all other closes or parcels of land in Penkhull called the Two Townsends and the Two Longfields, the Hassell's Croft with the barn standing by the same Woodfield. The New Leasow, the Boothen, to the use of John Mare provided always that he firstly pays into the hands of John Mare the full and just sum of £1,600 of lawful English money at the rate of £2 5s per year for £100 to be completed from the 5th day of April. J. Mare is admitted; fine of 4s 1½ d.

29th February 1776

Again referring to the works later to be owned by Josiah Spode.

Comes Jeremiah Smith of Great Horton in Stafford and surrenders all that pothouses, works, warehouses, barns, stables, cow house back yards marl banks belonging situate in Penkhull late in the holding of Wm. Banks and by the said Wm. Banks surrendered into the hands of Jeremiah Smith at a court held on the 29th July 1764 whom the deputy stewards granted seizin to have and to hold and Jeremiah Smith is admitted.

To this court comes Jeremiah Smith and surrenders all that meadow lying in Penkhull called Madeley Meadow and all those pot ovens, hot houses, workhouses, ware houses, comprising stables, cow houses marl bank. To the use and behoof of Josiah Spode.

To this court comes Josiah Spode of Penkhull, potter one of the copyholders of the manor and surrenders into the hands of the lord all that meadow with appurtenances called Madeley Meadow. Also all those potworks, pot ovens, pot houses, workhouses etc now late in the holding of William Banks, potter to the use of Jeremiah Smith of provided that the said Josiah Spode to Jeremiah Smith the sum of £1,000 from the 25th day of March and the 29th September. Jeremiah Smith admitted.

26th October 1768

This entry refers to the first parish workhouse situated in Garden Street Penkhull, later demolished and replaced by a new one known by the name Victoria Buildings.

To this court comes Eliza Alsager, Sarah Alsager, Mary Alsager, Margery Alsager and Judith Alsager by Joseph Jackson and George Bell their attorney and surrendered into the hands of the Lord All that copyhold pair of buildings forming two copyhold cottages now converted into a workhouse for the use of the parish of Stoke-upon-Trent situate at Penkhull with all ways, etc. To the use and behoof of Jeremiah Smith of Great Horton Esq., his heirs assigns etc.

4th March 1778

Comes Thomas Smith of Penkhull and Margaret his wife late Margaret Pickin being previously examined, surrenders into the hands of the Lord, all that messuage situated in Penkhull now in the possession of Thomas Smith, late of Margery Pickin, with barnes, stables, gardens etc. now belonging together with the small croft lying on the back of the house. Also those 2 crofts lying in Penkhull called Smithfields in the holding of J. Smith and all that meadow called Honeywall.

30th August 1800

This refers to the street known by the name Eardley Street.

Comes John Eardley of Penkhull, potter and surrenders all that piece of land marked and staked out and from a piece of land called Bowyers Meadow containing 23 yards in width and 8 yards for the new intended street upon which a dwelling house has been erected to the use of David Bostock of Stoke and John Hatton of Newcastle for the sum of £60.

29th July 1801

Refers to the estate which was to become the site for the new Parish Workhouse, the Spittals, later the City General Hospital.

Comes Josiah Wedgwood, late of Etruria, now of Gunville near Blandford in Dorset by John Rudyard, his attorney and surrenders all that Farm and Tenement with stables, buildings, grounds belonging to him known by the name of Spittle's Farm and also Stoke Lane Farm now in the use and occupation of Messrs Walker and Co. and also all other erections upon the said Spittle's Farm now converted by the said Messrs Walker and Co. as a white lead manufactory.

2nd April 1803

Entry refers to the site and property now known as The Views.

To this court comes Mary Terrick and Elizabeth Terrick both of Newcastle-under-Lyme, spinsters and surrender All that plot of land part of a certain close of Mary and Elizabeth Terrick called Boyers Meadow containing 376 square yards and a half land by the same more or less and adjoining to a plot of land part of the said Bowyers meadow lately sold and surrendered by Mary and Elizabeth Terrick to William Hulse. Together with full liberty for Daniel Greatbatch, the purchaser of the said plot of land to whom the same is herein after surrendered and his heirs to use and occupy the road or public street already made or intended to be made adjoining the said plot of land the said Daniel Greatbatch. To the use and behoof of the said Daniel Greatbatch of Penkhull Engrave; fine 4d.

12th September 1803

This property, Tittensors House, was to be demolished and replaced by the mansion known by the name The Mount by Josiah Spode.

Comes John Baddeley, Miles Mason and William Booth assignees of the estate and effects of John Harrison, duly appointed by virtue of a commission of bankrupt.

Surrenders - all that messuage or farmhouse, called Tittensor's House, near Penkhull Green with barns, stables and other outbuildings, gardens, orchards. And also two crofts or parcels of land called Barn Croft and also that large close called Brickkiln Field etc. Surrendered to John Harrison by William Ward with other land at a court held on 1st May 1789. Josiah Spode admitted tenant.

25th Apr 1806

Record refers to the Malt House to the rear of what is now The Greyhound Inn.

Robert Smith of Penkhull Lane, gent. and John Townsend of Penkhull, assigning the security for Townsend's mortgage of £350 to William Adams of Cobridge in the parish of Burslem, Manufacturer of Earthen Ware.

All that copyhold or customary messuage or dwelling house with the malt kiln buildings garden and orchard thereunto belonging, in Penkhull, containing by measurement 1^a 1^r 9^p or thereabouts, now and for several years past in the holding of the said John Townsend, and also the seats or pews and sitting places in the parish church of Stoke upon Trent appurtenant or belonging to the aforesaid messuage or dwelling house and every other messuage or dwelling house, late the estate of Thomas Lovatt, late of Chirk in the County of Denbigh dec'd, together with all rights etc., which said premises were late the estate of Thomas Lovatt dec'd, previous of William Lovatt dec'd, and formerly of Joseph Lovatt the younger; fine 1d.

View of Penkhull from Sideway

Chapter 7
Early Road Network.

Until the first quarter of the 20th century, Penkhull remained almost untouched from mediaeval times, except for limited housing development by a mixture of gentry and the working classes. The industrial revolution from the 17th century onwards was attracted to areas more easily accessed than the steep hill of Penkhull. As a result Penkhull remained little more than a farming community with its produce going to the nearby market town of Newcastle.

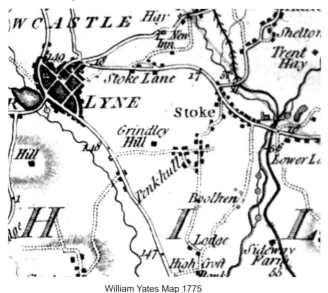

William Yates Map 1775

Penkhull had experienced little change for probably a thousand years. The centre of the village, now focused around the church with its graveyard is almost a modern addition in comparison with the time-line of change. From time immemorial the village centre was waste, common land, and a place for community use, for early religious festivals, even possibly human sacrifice. It could have been the place where the chieftain occupied his white hut and where village animals would be kept at night in the pinfold for safety, or where the village smithy smelted early bronze followed by iron during the time when Penkhull was a hill fort.

The area from the centre of the village extended northwards, wide and unhindered until it reached where the present Penkhull Service Station stands and the road junctions of Honeywall and Doncaster Lane become one. Few maps exist that help in the identification of an early roads until 1775 when William Yates produced his map of Staffordshire.

Early invaders from the continent doubtless followed the line of the river from the Humber Estuary into the River Ouse then into the Trent continuing to North Staffordshire long before roads were laid, as we know them today. The first 'ways' often sought the higher ground, away from marshes, the frequent flooding of rivers and dense undergrowth. The 'way' from the south, long before the Romans laid their roads came via Barlaston Old Road, New Inn Lane through to Hanford before the Trentham, estate was created. At a later

date a new section would have been laid, missing out Barlaston and leading onto Trentham - the line of which followed that of the present A34 to about where Bankhouse Road forks off to the right. This road then led onto the Domesday settlement village of Hanford overlooking the ford below over the Trent.

Standing at the top of Mayne Street, and imagining just fields and forests, the view of the ancient road to what is now Stoke-on-Trent is still visible amongst the 19th and 20th century developments.

Looking towards Penkhull, where the church tower rises to identify that once stronghold of the Celts, the road from Hanford crosses the River Trent

View from the top of Mayne Street, Hanford looking towards to hill of Penkhull with its church steeple in the far distance.

and continues towards the town of Newcastle-under-Lyme. This was the major road linking London to Carlisle and is listed on the oldest surviving map of Britain, the Gough Map c1360.

From this major road, Rookery Lane forks off to the right only a few hundred yards after crossing the River Trent. This narrow twisting lane, an ancient highway continued for a distance then on the same line as the present London Road until it forks to the left into what is now Trent Valley Road. In a map dated 1777 this lane was referred to as *Crabtree Lane*. London Road was a Turnpike Road stretching from the Black Lion to the centre of Stoke and was so built as to avoid the steep hill into Penkhull and then down again to Stoke via Honeywall.

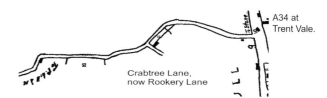

This new road was built in 1791/92 under an Act of 1791 below the steep hill of Penkhull to join with the road from Derby to Newcastle at what is now Campbell Place; continuing on the other side of this main road by the construction of Liverpool Road (the new road to Shelton) to join Shelton Old Road near to the canal.

At the junction of Trent Valley Road stood a tollgate, built in 1792. It went by the names of either The Gate House or Lodge Gate, because of its nearness of Stoke Lodge, a large house which stood a little further up Trent Valley Road near to the current mansion, New Lodge. The tollgate existed until at least 1878. In 1861, William Kimber, aged 61, was the toll collector. He came from Middlesex and had an additional occupation as a tailor. He lived with his wife Lucy, age 60, together with two teenage daughters and a granddaughter aged 8.

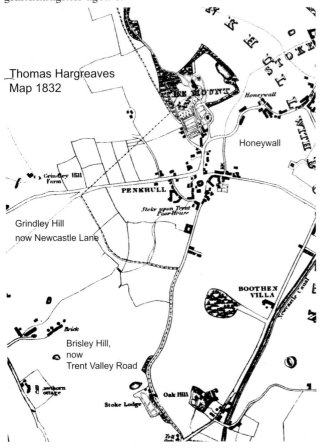

Thomas Hargreaves Map 1832

The name by which the road was known had the general name of the hill, Brisley Hill, a name that is retained in a small road off Trent Valley Road near to the centre of the village. Unfortunately early forms of the name have not survived. In Norfolk there is a village called Brisley which probably means Gadfly-ley, and that may possibly be an explanation. There are other possibilities however including something as mundane as ownership by a person or family called Brisley. It is interesting that the nearby fields are called Bearshill and the two names are just close enough to make you wonder whether one could be a corruption of the other, but dissimilar enough to cast doubt on a connection.

The only record of the name Brisley found in the manor court records is dated 1830. Not very significant! What is significant is that Trent Valley Road went by the name of The Lane. The first reference to this occurs in the 16th century. From modern times it was known as Trentham Road, changing its name in the 1950s to that of Trent Valley Road.

Entering the centre of the village, Garden Street, to the left was formerly appropriately named Farm Lane, and before this it went by its original name, Tyttensor's Lane, because the Tyttensor family lived in what is now Elm Tree House, which since medieval times went by the name Tyttensor's

Messuage. To distinguish Penkhull Village from the rest of the township of Penkhull with Boothen, it was often referred to as 'Penkhull up in the town', a title which has caused confusion in the past.

The next road to be identified is Newcastle Lane linking Penkhull to the main artery road to Newcastle from Trentham. The lower section still retains an atmosphere of times past, narrow, twisting with high banks on either side. It was not until the 1930s and 40s as a result of housing development that the character of the upper section of the lane changed. It is this ancient road that would be used by early settlers and peddlers as they travelled from one village to the next, which would have been Clayton. The hill leading from this important road to Penkhull went by the general name of Grindley Hill from at least the early 16th century. Early spellings of this word are not easy to find but in 1572 it went by the name Grindle; in 1586, Gryndley Hill and in 1596, Grinley. It could well mean 'green' from the word 'grind', for if the area is compared with the other side of the hill overlooking the town of Stoke, the word 'grind' would be an appropriate description. It was here, at Grindley Hill that two of the village's 'open fields' operated from early medieval times.

By 1841 its name was Castle Street then Newcastle Street and finally in 1950 it became Newcastle Lane. In a record of 1752 London Road. The bottom of Newcastle Lane, went by the name of Gt. London Road but 19th century census records name the section at the bottom of the lane as Turnpike Road, Trent Vale.

At the bottom of Newcastle Lane, to the right before its junction with the main turnpike road, stood a further 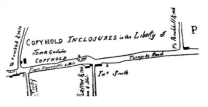 tollgate. From the fact that it was known as Knapper's Gate it was always assumed that the tollgate keeper went by the name Knapper. And indeed in the 1777 survey, the first name listed as occupiers in the schedule attached to the map was Richard Knapper. However, the manor court records point to an earlier date of 1752 when James Taylor surrendered to Richard Knapper: *All that small part of a certain meadow called the Spittals meadow, lying near the Great London Road on which part there is built or made a cellar and part of a parlour, now in the possession of Richard Knapper.*

This is an interesting entry as the wording includes a *cellar* and *part of a parlour* a description not often used. It could mean that the property was only partly built. A further court entry when Knapper sold the property to Job Hulse in 1757 contained the same words. In a much later court entry dated

1783 there is a further reference, which may help to clear the issue of *the cellar and the part of a parlour*. It refers to James Godwyn, a butcher from Newcastle who obtained a mortgage from John Garratt. Reference is made to a *small house and garden and a close of land in two parts divided on the back thereof*. Perhaps, therefore, the description of part parlour reflects that one half could have been built on a piece of land, which was in the hands of someone else? The same entry and a further entry of the following year, both refer to the toll gate house and also *a meadow lying opposite thereto on the back of Richard Knapper's house which premises are now in the holding of James Godwyn*. Perhaps this means that the tollhouse was attached to Knapper's house?

As said it has always been wrongly assumed that Knapper was the tollgate keeper because of the use of his surname. The family name of Knapper was found in the parish registers of Stoke from the mid 1600s. Probably since the establishment of an inn run by Richard Knapper the area became known and recorded as 'Knapper's', with no association whatsoever in the first instance with the word 'gate'.

When this main highway to Newcastle was turnpiked initially in 1714, a tollgate was established at Hanford Bridge. In June 1775, the trustees of the Tittensor Turnpike Trust decided to close this toll gate and build a new one nearer to the town of Newcastle *at a place known by the name Knapper's*. This was to enable a toll charge to be collected from people and traffic entering the road from the villages of Penkhull and Clayton. Later the same month the trustees met to approve plans for the toll house prepared by Mr Thomas Bloor and gave the contract to Thomas Brook *being paid the sum of £50 for building if the same be executed to the satisfaction of the Trustees.*

In September 1782 the toll gate, situated at the bottom of Newcastle Lane, (before its junction with the turnpike road) was rented out to Samuel Hulse for the sum of £430p.a but when this lease finished the trustees had difficulty in letting out the toll gate and therefore installed as toll collector Mr Richard Tomkinson who received a weekly wage of 8s. from the 11th December 1783.

The following year, following an advertisement for the letting of the toll house, it was leased out to Edward Brad for the sum of £520 p.a. but reduced to £400 in August 1786, probably because the fees collected did not justify the lease price. Again in 1790, a lessee could not be found, so as previous a weekly wage of 8s was offered to William Broomfield who took the position of toll collector.

For the villages of Hanchurch, Clayton and Penkhull concessions were made with regard to the toll fees. They were reduced by half except for the passage of coal, bricks or tiles carried by either horse or carriage.

In 1830, an advertisement appeared in the press for the letting of a number of tollgates. Among them were Knapper's gate and Lodge gate at Oakhill. After expenses the sum of £1,200 was the profit produced for the two gates. The advertisement continued: *Whoever happens to be the best bidder, they must immediately, after the letting pay one month in advance of the year's rental and give security with sufficient sums to the satisfaction of the trustees for payment of the remaining.*

In 1851 George Roberts and his family occupied the tollhouse.

Newcastle Lane 1910

If we retrace our steps up Newcastle Lane, the first side path off the lane would be on the right, just about where the present Harpfield Road commences. This path dropped down to the turnpike road already discussed where it entered opposite to what is now The Orange Tree, formerly The Springfields Hotel. From almost the same point on Newcastle Lane, a path also ran to the left dropping through the fields now occupied by the hospital complex to join the main highway approximately where the new University of Keele teaching unit stands.

A little higher up Newcastle Lane, where it joins Thistley Hough, a path turned to the right and followed the current line of Thistley Hough until its junction with Trent Valley Road. A little higher up Newcastle Lane, to the left, is Franklin Road. From the middle of the 17th century this road went by the name of Out Lane. Why 'Out Lane' is difficult to explain. Perhaps the name of 'Out Lane' could have been the road out of the Iron Fort leading the ancient village of Wolstanton.

Later the name became Franklins Lane taking its name from the field name of Frankland at the bottom of the narrow cart road. Frankland means *freehold land* but there is no evidence to suggest that it was other than copyhold land. The road now goes under the name of Franklin Road.

Returning to the centre of Penkhull village and turning left, Doncaster Lane comes into view. This previously went by the name of Swynnerton's Lane because Swynnerton Works, a small engraving business of copper printing plates for the pottery industry was situated on the corner. For many years Henry Doncaster owned it, hence the name Doncaster Lane. The lane originally was much narrower than today and continued considerably beyond the present 'dead end' following the line of boundary wall of the Mount. This wall still remains behind the properties in Queens Road and slowly curved to the current line of Queens Road.

The old way continued behind the 1930's properties to the left of Queens Road and came out almost opposite the entrance to Hartshill parish church joining the old way which continued from the bottom of what is now Franklin Road. From this point at Hartshill the path continued to Wolstanton, also a one time Domesday settlement.

Honeywall: Castle Cliff

Retracing our steps to the top of Doncaster Lane, the road bears to the left and continues to Honeywall, a name steeped in history and of ancient origin. The name is now associated with the whole length of the road but this was not always the case. In fact, the name Honeywall did not start from the bottom as it does today. That area was originally called Castle Cliff then the name changed to Cliff Bank. The section higher was called Upper Cliff Bank followed by Princess Street before it all changed to one name, Honeywall. The name of Castle Cliff is interesting as to its origins and yet there is no evidence to support this name in the form of castle remains. The area known as Honeywall commences from just about where The Beehive now stands to its junction with Penkhull Terrace and refers to the Hamlet of Honeywall, which was a separate identity from Penkhull and not the road name.

To gain an insight to the meaning of any name, early records and spellings are important. The earliest reference to Honeywall is in October 1566 when Thomas Tittensor leased fields called Honeywall to Richard Pateson for a period of eight years. In May 1606 the area was referred to as Honnie Meadow, but by 1627, it was called Honeywall. Robert Nicholls, in his short history of 1929 assumes that Honeywall comes from the early English 'onnig' - a hill fortress. Piecing together facts this could be correct, for Penkhull is now thought to have supported an Iron Age fort. Perhaps this explains why parts of what is now Honeywall went by the name of Castle Cliff. Food for thought! Then to add further to the mystery, in 1870, whilst digging near to The White Lion Inn an ancient boulder pathway was found. Could this have any connection with some form of early settlement?

Aston, in his little book of 1942 suggests that the name could mean *Hole in the Wall*, pointing to a possible wall around the ancient royal forest where a hole in the wall was used for game hunters! However, this suggestion should not be taken seriously in this context but could possibly relate to some former iron age fort the entrance of which was in this locality. In saying this there could be an argument presented for that part of Honeywall being the boundary of the once Iron Age fort that capped the hill of Penkhull. Why? We have

the name of Castle Cliff and we have the evidence of a boulder pathway being uncovered outside The White Lion. Also the name of Honeywall could derive from the old English – 'hill fortress' and lastly the name given to a small hamlet not a road. People would be known by the place where they lived (not a street name, but a district) and the name Hole in the Wall, the entrance point of the hill fort, could be just that place where a group of traders gathered to do business. Near to Grantham in Lincolnshire there is a known Iron Age fort by the name of Honington Camp. Does the similarity of Honington and this section of Honeywall support the assumption given here?

The final suggestion is that Honeywall is connected with the keeping of bee hives on the slopes of the hill as honey was the only sweetening agent available until quite modern times.

So where does this hamlet of Honeywall lie, in Stoke or Penkhull? From the earliest map of the area it is clearly separated from the town of Stoke by fields. The give-away probably lies with the origins of The White Lion public house, the second known longest established inn in Penkhull. From what records are available, from the early part of the 18th century it has always been referred to as being in Penkhull.

At the bottom end of Honeywall, at Cliff Bank, there once stood a tollgate where it joined the new turnpike road from Derby to Newcastle now called Hartshill Road.

Yates map of 1775 shows a road from the centre of Penkhull village leading down to what is now known as West Bank, that small terrace of Georgian properties overlooking the valley of the Trent. Originally, the narrow carriageway would have supported access to the fields for both agricultural equipment and farm animals for grazing. Once London Road, Stoke was laid in 1791/2 a footpath would have appeared across this stretch of land as a shortcut to the town of Stoke and places of work. Josiah Spode laid the lower section of Penkhull New Road from West Bank into London Road in around 1812. In reality, Spode had advertised two small fields for sale along a section of London Road, the turnpike road in July 1809. It was the area, which is now occupied by Commercial Buildings and the Commercial Inn. The advertisement recorded the intention of Spode to lay a new street: *a spacious street is proposed to be opened from the front of it (meaning London Road), leading to the well known rural village of Penkhull, where purchasers may be accommodated with land for the erection of many houses.* The land referred to here is Penkhull New Road itself and its adjacent streets reaching to the area of West Bank.

Chapter 8
The Changing Nature of
Population and Trade.

There is a real difficulty in establishing early population trends for the area of Penkhull and the immediate surrounding district as it forms just a section of a the vast ancient parish of Stoke which included nearly all the pottery towns, in addition to Newcastle, Seabridge, Clayton and Whitmore. The parish was divided into numerous townships, and the village of Penkhull formed only a section within the township of Penkhull with Boothen, the title of the area given for administration purposes before the town of Stoke-upon-Trent was recognised as the head following its new status of Borough in 1876.

For early periods occupations are difficult to quantify as the copyhold courts make little reference to these. There would be for example in most communities of the size of Penkhull, corn dealers, wheelwrights, blacksmiths, butchers, farmers, victuallers and small manufacturing trades all existing side-by-side to provide services to the community but we have only fragmentary documentation for them.

A survey of the manor dated 1416 lists Nicholas, potter of Penkhull paying 23 pence in rental for his land. A discovery just a few years ago was made at the bottom of a garden at the top of Trent Valley Road over looking the town of Stoke with a significant drop. It would appear that this was a waste dump for pottery sherds. A part of discovery was a section of a rim from a dish or cooking pot dating from the 13th or 14th century approximately two feet in diameter. It is also known that the site of the present Victoria House in St Thomas Place was once the site of a mid 17th century manufactory, producing curse brown pottery under the name of Thomas Doody. This was one of three recorded as being in Penkhull in 1600. A small part of this sandstone building still remains today converted into an office and store. In Manchester museum there is an 18th century 12" plate manufactured by Thomas Bird of Penkhull.

The following year, 1417, Richard Lagow, butcher of Penkhull is recorded in the court rolls in a plea of debt to the value of 20d. The first listing of a victualler was recorded in May 1587 when Thomas Bagnold appeared at the Quarter Sessions. No doubt there would have been victuallers dating back to the time of Penkhull's first occupation. In the 18th century, blacksmiths and wheelwrights were listed for the first time, both trades being held by Michael Henny.

Muster roll 1539

The Muster Roll for Penkhull of 1539 lists *those able men with bowes and have hornes and artillarie as foloith their names. Thomas Boothes, William Hitchyn, John Hitchyn, Hugh Audley, John Strynger, Thomas Hairchcock, Robert Pye, Roger Wood, Thomas Foxe, Thomas Telricke*. The Rolls then continues to lists those persons *of able men with billes and have hernes and artillarie as follows their name. Laurence Hordern, Thomas Hitchyn, Bartholomew Wagg, Nicholas Turner, Thomas Barrett, Ralph Bradshawe, John Turner.* It is an interesting fact that just over 500 years since the Domesday entry that the combined totals add up to seventeen, the same number of ancient messuages listed in 1086.

Church Lunes

The next reliable source available is the churchwardens' accounts for Stoke-upon-Trent of 1595, which list those heads of families in Penkhull that were paying church lunes. Church Lunes (as in lunar) was the charge made on each property to support the parish poor and also known as the Poor Rate.

From the nineteen names listed, in 1595, fifteen can be identified as residents of Penkhull with the remaining four residents of the hamlet of Boothen. Using the multiplier of 4.4 as suggested by Gregory King of Lichfield, the 17th century first great economic government statistician, a population of around eighty persons seems possible but in practice a further 15% should to be added for marginal error to account for those poor who were exempt from the payment of church lunes. It may therefore be reasonable to conclude that the total population of Penkhull in 1595 would be approximately seventy-six.

The detail in the churchwardens' accounts allows us to believe that there had been little demographic change in Penkhull from the time of Domesday, which listed an identical figure of seventeen families, and which multiplied by an average family size of 4.4 would again produce a figure of approximately seventy-five.

When we come to the mid 17th century, the Hearth Tax affords a further method of calculation. This tax was introduced in England and Wales in 1662 to provide a regular source of income for the newly restored monarch, King Charles II. Parliament had accepted in 1662 that the King required an annual income of £1.2 million to run the country, much of which came from customs and excise. The previous year, 1661 the amount collected was short by £300,000, a figure that the hearth tax was projected to yield but a sum which proved to be a hopeless over estimate.

Sometimes the tax was referred to as chimney money but was essentially a property tax on dwellings graded according to the number of their fireplaces. The 1662 Act stated that *every dwelling and other house and edifice should be chargeable for every fire hearth and stove by the sum of two shillings by the yeare.* The money was to be paid in two equal instalments at Michaelmas, 29th September and Lady Day, 25th March by the occupier or, if the house was empty, by the owner.

Thus it may be hoped that the Staffordshire Hearth Tax, some two generations after 1595 will provide our next snapshot of population trends in Penkhull. Even on the assumption that hearth-tax estimates are accurate, the problem of converting the number of households into a head-count of population remains. Gregory King set out to estimate the average number of people in a household. The number of households recorded in the Hearth Tax return could then be multiplied by the average to arrive at a population count. As a result of his researches, King projected the following multipliers: Towns 4.40, Villages 4.00 persons per household.

The Hearth Tax Records the lists for 1662, 1666 and 1671 are complete. A list of exemptions exists but unfortunately there is no breakdown of numbers into districts only a collective list for all the districts except for the year 1666. The list of people with exemptions for 1672 amount to around 190. In addition the 1672 list for Stoke and Penkhull does not include Boothen as this is shown separately listing six, which, when making comparisons this number should be deducted from the number of properties listed in 1666. In 1662, there were 22 houses paying tax, in 1666, 43 in addition to 18 certified as none chargeable and in 1672, only 33 but the same year there were 190 exemptions, a figure for the whole parish from which those for the district of Penkhull cannot be separated. It is clear that because of insufficient local information to make any accurate estimate of population numbers is almost impossible.

In an attempt to move the debate further a general view of the parish creates an image in the third quarter of the 17th century as a district subject to the demographic changes of people hoping to gain employment in the expanding pottery industry. Shelton in particular was a district of high occupancy as well as the town of Stoke. Boothen and Penkhull still remained as rural farming communities. Yates' map of 1775 and Hargreaves of 1832 confirm that even after a significant period since the introduction of the Hearth Tax, there were few properties in either district whilst the town of Stoke, Shelton and Hanley had expanded beyond all recognition. The copyhold records of land transactions clearly point to buildings, industrialisation and increase of land transfers from the end of the Commonwealth period.

To place Penkhull into context with its neighbouring villages the following chart indicates Penkhull as a leading district for population in 1662.

Number in household of Hearths.	Penkhull	Clayton	Wolstanton	Shelton	Seabridge
13	1				
8			1		
7	1				
5	1	2		4	2
4	1				
3	3	1	1	2	
2	6	5	6	5	4
1	30	9	12	25	9

Total number of hearths chargeable	131	57.7%
Hearths not chargeable	96	42.3%
Total Hearths	227	

From these figures, Penkhull stands alone both for the highest number of properties with one hearth at 30 to which can be added on average a further 16 properties (indicating those exempt from the tax) (42.3%) bringing a total of 46 and a population of just over two hundred. The figures also point to the fact that Penkhull contains a higher proportion of the larger properties above one hearth as well as the highest number of one to three hearths that seem to indicate not only social status but also a mixed economy.

To give a contrast to the population figure for Penkhull, comparisons of population are listed for the 1666 entry taking into account the number of approximate exempt households.

Population count based on the Hearth Tax 1666, for Penkhull and the surrounding areas in North Staffordshire

Penkhull	200	Newcastle	255-394
Bagnall	121-135	Norton	454-505
Bucknall	283-315	Whitmore	135-150
Burslem	391-435		

The figures for Penkhull reflect little increase in population numbers while, in reality, over the intervening years there were a number of additional cottages erected upon the Lord's waste. Despite the fact that the intervening years were *good and abundant,* historians agree that they were also years with an excess of burials over conceptions due to epidemic disease. The parish records for Stoke confirm that from 1669-1672, the average number of deaths increased by 51%. A further reason for a reduction of one-hearth cottagers is that there was an increase in larger copyhold tenancies, the smaller being pushed out in the process. Evidence points to larger houses of four hearths upwards being recorded by the growth from one in 1666 to six in 1672.

Out of a total of six properties listed with four hearths, only three, those belonging to James Newton, Robert Newton and James Bowyer, were listed in both assessments: John Terrick, William Kendle and Thomas Dale all had acquired their property since the first assessment. In 1666 Thomas Dale was resident with his father, Roger, who declared five hearths. Six years later, there was no mention of Roger, only Thomas, who may well have inherited his father's house and blocked up one hearth to reduce the burden of taxation, a common practice as only five hearths are recorded against his name.

Hearth Tax figures and the years in which each name appears

Name	1662	1666	1672
Adamson William			1
Ash John			1
Basford Robert			1

Bedson John (or Betson)	1	1	1
Beech Andrew		2	
Boulton Richard			1
Brownser Randulph			
Bowyer John	3	3	4
Brayfort Randle		1	
Brerehurst Randle		3	
Brett Nicholas (Senior)		1	
Brett Randle		1	
Brownsword William	1		
Burd William	1	1	
Burn John			1
Butterton Nathaniell		1	1
Clay Philip	1	1	
Cleveley Philip			1
Colclough John	7	7	
Corbett William			1
Dale Roger		5	
Dale Thomas			4
Dale			2
Daniell John		1	
Doody (Mr)			3
Fenton John		1	2
Fenton William	1		1
Fenton (widow) & Bourne		2	
Gennings			2
Griffiths Eliz		1	2
Heath Robert			1
Hewett Richard		1	1
Hewett Henry		1	
Kendal William			4
Lycett Francis		1	
Machin John	1	1	
Machin Robert		1	
Machin Robert		3	4
Machin Roger (Junior)	1	1	1
Machin Roger (Senior)	3	1	
Mainwaring Dr (Rector)	13	13	13
Marshall (widow)			1
Massey Ralph		1	
Meare William	2	1	1
Mountford Henry		4	
Muchell Thomas		1	
Newton Thomas	2	1	1
Omimford Henry	5		
Philips John			1
Podmore William			2
Pouston Edward	1	1	
Seabridge John		1	
Shawe (Widow)		1	
Stevenson Thomas		2	
Terrick John			4
Tittensor John		1	1
Tittensor Roger		1	1
Tittensor Thomas	1	1	
Tittensor Williamm	2	2	
Tittensor William		1	
Tittensor (Widow)			2
Townsend Roger	2	2	
Vinsor William		1	
Winson William	1		
Whittaker Roger	1		
Wilson Nicholas	1		
Woodcock Nicholas (descendants)	1	1	
Woodcock (widow)			1
Yawood John	1		
Yong John		1	

In an area such as Penkhull, a low or even negligible mobility of population would be expected. In farming communities before the onslaught of industrialisation, young people left home to become domestic farm servants or to be apprenticed to a craft or profession. Once a single member of a family moved to another district, other member displacements followed. In some villages as many as five out of one hundred and fifty families moved out each year, meaning that the entire population changed over a thirty-year period. Of those who reached the age of fifteen, 64% of the boys and 57% of the girls probably moved on to find work in larger towns either in service or in various trades. Families were not limited to the bounds of their home, but operated in a rather wider area.

Pre-industrial villagers were conversant with neighbouring villages as intimately as they knew their own. When a cottage became vacant, someone from the next village snapped it up immediately. Besides this, high mortality coupled with a low expectation of life encouraged movement for men who grasped at the smallest opportunity of self-advancement. Those who moved into Penkhull came seeking employment. The nearness of the expanding pottery towns and an opportunity to find employment was sufficient incentive to move to a community that was growing and ideally situated. The lack of copyhold land transfers during this period indicates that few came seeking land, although the manorial waste was made full use of by squatters. The fact that Penkhull contained no freehold land, reduced any interest in its acquisition.

Harvest failures in Penkhull could mean little or no work for several months of the year, producing in its wake potential hunger for families during the unproductive seasons of the year. Such a threat of starvation made mobility inevitable, fuelled by the need to maintain even the poorest of living conditions.

Inadequate clean water supplies, non-existent sanitation and the lack of warmth in the winter months took their toll thereby influencing the hearth tax figures for 1672. The coming of the bubonic plague in 1665/66 dramatically interrupted the demographical progress of Penkhull. It began in London in the poor, overcrowded parish of St. Giles-in-the-Fields. It started slowly at first but by May of 1665, 43 had died. In June 6,137 people died, in July 17,036 and at its peak in August, 31,159 people died. In all 15% of the population perished during that terrible summer which resulted in more than 70,000 deaths nationally.

By 1669, smallpox, cholera and measles had become the main causes of epidemic mortalities. This helps to explain the difference between the hearth-tax assessments of 1666 and of 1672.

Gregory King, prepared figures in 1679/80 on the projected population of England. In his notebook for that date he recorded that there were 40-50 houses in Penkhull Township, which would produce a population size of between 176 and 220 in 1679. These figures almost mirror the conclusions drawn from Hearth Tax records.

Early parish records for Stoke do not give separate figures for the area of Penkhull; they include the whole of the ancient parish. Even so, indications of the effects of the plague and other epidemics on the area as a whole, including Penkhull may be determined.

Burial records in the Stoke Registers 1662-1684

1662 – 19	1671 – 29	1681 – 56
1663 – 22	1672 – 47	1682 – 55
1666 – 23	1678 – 51	1683 – 51
1669 – 53	1679 – 49	1684 – 58
1670 – 52	1680 – 42	

From the figures above, we see that the number of deaths more than doubled from nineteen in 1662, to fifty three in 1669 and remained nearly constant thereafter at an average figure of forty-nine.

Many births would not be recorded for reasons of poverty, absentee incumbents, parish clerks who were not diligent in their duties, infants buried alongside adults, private burials and baptisms, all of which raise questions as to the reliability of such figures from church registers. To allow for these factors a 10% to 15% increase to these figures is necessary. As numbers suffering from poverty in the areas should not be under estimated, and therefore, the tendency to include one burial with that of another, the higher percentage of fifteen has been chosen.

Average Births/Burials over a 5-year period for the parish of Stoke.

Years	Births	Years	Burials
1662-1667	43	1662-1667	32
1676-1700	95	1676-1700	71

Early records to evaluate death through plagues and various epidemics are difficult to come by. The only source for accurate information is from parish records for burials. For Stoke, they do not commence until 1630, for Newcastle they commence in 1563. Newcastle, like Stoke and Penkhull would have been visited by plague and pestilence many times. The plague was so severe in 1593 that it was recorded in the parish records of Newcastle that a *great plague raged*. The number of burials in the churchyard reflects this at 57. In the following year their number had fallen to only 10.

In 1647 the Bubonic plague struck again with devastating consequences. In Stafford it was recorded as *catastrophic and the mortality arising ravaged the town*. It the pottery towns of North Staffordshire it was also recorded as severe. In Burslem it was particularly severe, so much so that the

Justices of the Peace levied a rate on the neighbouring towns to support the people of Burslem. The records from Stoke and Newcastle show that the plague reached Penkhull in 1651 as both parishes recorded significant increases in burials that year, Stoke from 22 in 1650 to 50 in 1651 and Newcastle from 39 in 1650 to 56 in 1651.

The two main causes of high mortality in the seventeenth century were disease and dearth, often associated together making the situation even more devastating. Living conditions for an increasing number of pottery workers in the town of Stoke and agricultural labourers in Penkhull was dismal; inadequate ventilation; extensive over-crowding; communal privies; lack of a clean water supply and low wages, all contributing to the natural causes of death.

A run of bad harvests was caused by inclement weather. At the same time the associated cold and damp in the accommodation of the poorer classes lowered resistance to disease. Not only disease, but also the general weather pattern could inflict a higher death rate among the young and the old. The crisis years for Penkhull in this decade were 1684 and 1685, when the average annual death rate increased from 59.3 to 84.5 but exactly what caused this upturn is not known. In the southeast of England the following year 'Spotted Fever' raged, which gave all the symptoms of meningococcal infection, proving fatal in over 50% of cases. In 1684 evidence exists that the 'King's Evil' visited the Potteries, scrofula, a form of tuberculosis. Two certificates were issued to sufferers from this disease in the hope of a healing from the King by his touch. *That the Minister and Churchwardens of Stoke, give unto Cather Ffluit, ye daughter of Arthur Ffluit and Mary his wife, upon the 3rd day of May 1684 a certificate under their hands and seal in order to her obtaining of His Majesties sacred touch for the healing of the disease called Kings Evil.* The king's touch did not heal Cather, the young girl from Fenton. For after the arduous journey to London in the hope of a cure from the king's touch, she was buried in Stoke churchyard on the 3rd March 1685 The second certificate relates to a child from Cobridge, three miles north of Stoke.

Parish Registers

As parish registers are used for local population studies attention is usually concentrated upon annual totals of baptisms, marriages and burials and on the resulting statistics. It is not, however, always realised that there is a great deal to be learned from a study of seasonality. That is, the fluctuations from month to month within a specific year. Questions may be asked, for example as to how the monthly distribution of marriages was affected by the seasonal nature of employment, such as farming in Penkhull.

Conclusions drawn from these statistics indicate that the months of April and August were the highest months for conception in the village. April would be accounted for by Easter, a time to celebrate after a period of abstinence of sexual intercourse during Lent in keeping with old Canon Law. It may too be a time for a few days off from work, coupled with the feel of spring in the air after the long dreary months of winter. August was also a time of holiday from work. The parish church in Stoke celebrated its patronal festival during the first week of August using the opportunity to promote *church ales*, brewed in a Penkhull malt house. On this occasion the inhabitants of Penkhull rallied around the church carrying out minor repairs, painting and cleaning, while the church provided the necessary ale to encourage parishioners. These *church ales* were considered, not so much as a chore as of a working celebration for the whole family.

Illegitimacy in Penkhull recorded from the mid-17th to mid-18th century was practically negligible with only three cases recorded, one in 1702 and two in 1704, representing .036 per annum whereas national figures based on the registers of twenty-five rural villages over a period of forty years, 1660 to 1700 amount to 3.25 per annum. Other comparisons with both Newcastle and Stoke parishes for 1701-05 are significant as Penkhull with the smaller community is represented by the highest percentage of illegitimacy.

	Newcastle	Stoke	Penkhull
Baptised	549	542	103
Illegitimate	7	5	3
Percentage	1.27%	0.92%	2.91%

Although there is little evidence of illegitimacy for the years 1701 to 1740, a number of marriages were followed by baptisms within nine months of marriage. Out of seven marriages between 1703/4 three of the brides were pregnant at the time of marriage.

The baptismal figures for 1746/50 suggest a younger population for the town of Stoke, whereas the falling numbers for Penkhull confirm an ageing population as this brings in itself a decrease in the number of childbearing couples, although emigration could have out weighed immigration as an important factor, something that may have contributed to the figures for Penkhull.

The Marriage Duty Act.
Secular records, by contrast with the historical recording of data in church records, are more episodic, commemorating such fiscal measures as the Hearth Tax, Poll Taxes, Land Tax, and Window Tax and so on. Although they may be of use in providing estimates of population, they have so far yielded no listings that could be properly termed as censuses. One such fiscal measure, however, which goes a long way towards providing census-like accuracy, was enacted in 1694.

In the midst of William III's struggle with Louis XIV, an Act was passed, *(possibly under the influence of Gregory King, a notable statistician from Lichfield)* to raise money for carrying on the war with France. It imposed duties on births, marriages and deaths, which is why it is usually called *The Marriage Duty Act.* These duties, graduated according to status and to property, were to be in force for five years commencing 1st May 1695, but remained on the statute books for eleven years.

For demographers, this list is invaluable. Unfortunately there is no trace of the vast majority of these returns in the National Archives. The only ones which remain being for London, its suburbs, parts of Kent, and a few other townships including Lichfield (1695) and a part of the ancient parish of Stoke-upon-Trent (1701).

The listing was prepared by or under the instructions of Thomas Allen, Rector of Stoke from 1697-1732. It is dated 2nd June 1701. Although Allen was probably the person who organised the taking of this list, the writing up was evidently left to his curate, John Ward, and the parish clerk, John Poulson. The heading reads *A collection of the names of every particular and individual person in the parish of Stoke-upon-Trent as they are now residing within their respective liberties (townships) and families, together with the age of every such person, as near as can conveniently be known, as also the number of families and souls qualified (as their ages) for communicating, in each family.*

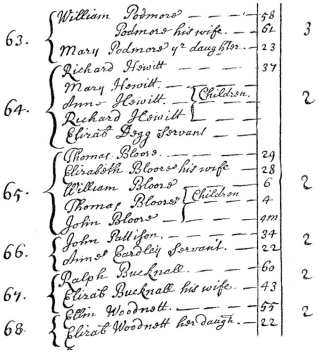

Sample page of the 1701 Parish Listing

Regrettably, the record for the townships within the substantial parish of Stoke is not complete. This was not the fault of the curate, but much more probably that of the transcribers, who made the only surviving copy in 1705 and failed to finish their task. Significant comparisons however, can be made using the townships that remain: Shelton, Hanley, Fenton Culvert, Seabridge, Clayton and Penkhull.

Population of Penkhull and districts adjacent 1701

Townships	No. of Houses	Female	Male	Missing	Total	Av.Family.
Penkhull	95	230	189	1	419	4.4
Clayton	26	53	52	0	105	4.0
Seabridge	19	38	38	1	77	4.1
Fenton Culvert	51	102	95	3	200	3.9
Shelton	108	257	243	0	500	4.6
Hanley	74	168	153	6	327	4.4

The sex of eleven individuals is unknown because their first names did not appear in the listing. The smallest liberties, Clayton and Seabridge, had roughly equal numbers of males and females. The other four liberties had more females than males.

It should be remembered that the males could well have relocated to other parts of the city or further a field to find work and therefore no firm conclusions should be drawn from these results, as Penkhull was mostly agricultural. Even so, the mean family size for the whole, of 4.4 people per family, is very similar to the figures of 4.3 people per household calculated for England for the period of 1662-1712.

It is noticeable that Shelton shows the largest number as Shelton was the most populous area, although not the largest of the districts covered in the listing. The high density of housing and house occupation of 4.5 persons arose from the expanding pottery industry in that area. Penkhull, though rural came second with 419 residents at a house occupation of 4.4.persons. Even though the town of Stoke had hardly developed by 1701, Penkhull still remained the main area for population.

It should also be noted that in Penkhull there were some of the largest families. A further dimension to investigate is that in Penkhull a higher proportion of couples were found with a significant difference in age.

When making attempts to evaluate the status or wealth of an area there is the need to evaluate the number of properties that employ servants, a common indication of status. In the listing there are a total of ninety-seven households, sixteen of which employ either one or two servants numbering thirty-two in total representing 16.4% of the population. A rural area such as Penkhull with a total of six yeomen recorded all but one yeoman employed servants. The Rector of Stoke, his widowed mother and the curate also employed servants, leaving seven other properties employing servants.

The population of Staffordshire and indeed of the whole of England (except London) grew only slowly during the seventeenth and early eighteenth century, the average increase over each decade being 0.33%. In a number of regions the influence of plagues and of a succession of poor harvests even led to decline. From 1651-1661 a decrease of 0.11% is recorded nationally. To assess such findings the statistics for Penkhull are aggregated and then compared with the aggregates of other local areas so that the results for Penkhull can be evaluated in relation to those of other rural farming communities.

A full list of names for the 1701 Parish Listing is reproduced in Appendix vii

The main source of demographic research for seventeenth century Penkhull, can be obtained from: Parish Registers and Ecclesiastical returns for the ancient parish of Stoke-upon-Trent; the Hearth Tax returns for 1662, 1666 and 1672; the parish listings of inhabitants dated 1701 and Church Lune books, Tithe schedules, Land Tax returns and other documents. For the period of the 19th century we have the census returns to work upon.

Many academics produce statistical pyramids that point to many facts, especially when looking at the numbers of either gender within each age range. Only a few can conclude why more are in some age range than others looking at external reasoning such as the plague, disease, harvests, famine and wars just to mention a few.

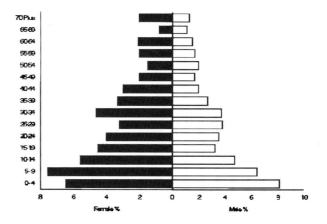

Age/Sex Pyramid
Stoke-upon-Trent 1701

The demand for food and dairy produce followed the population growth of the district. Farmers from Penkhull supplied the Pottery towns more cheaply than producers from other areas because of low transport costs. Moreover their produce could be fresher. This factor protected Penkhull from early urban growth.

There has survived a list of those landowners in the Township of Penkhull, who in 1740 paid the annual rent to the Duchy of Lancaster during the reign of George II. These rentals vary considerably reflecting the range in size and value of estates, some of which held just a small messuage and some to a much larger home with considerable land attached. The main land occupiers are John Amory paying £3 15s 9d, Thomas Moss £2 15s 0d and William Terrick at £2 3s 2d. The list gives no further details apart from the rental due. However, the court records for the period do give some information. John Amory owned land in what was called Bearscroft, the area of Brisley Hill and Hunters Way. He also owned land at the top of Newcastle Lane, an area called Townsend. It would appear that Thomas Moss was the tenant of both a large house and two small cottages in Penkhull while William Terrick owned a large property which once stood where the current house, The Views now stand.

The list continues: Thomas Bill £1 6s 0d, William Myatt £2 1s 6d, Richard Hewitt 12s 8d, Robert Smith 17s 8d, Thomas Whittaker 4s 0d, Stephen Amason 8s 0d, William Terrick £2 3s 2d, William Lovatt £1 4s 0d, William Pickin £4 15s 0d, John Slany 14s 0d, Oliver Astbury 14s 0d, Miss Jenkins 16s 6d, Thomas Moss £2 15s 0d, William Bagnall 6s 8d, Thomas Fenton 3s 9d, George Buxton 6s 8d, John Amory £3 15s 9d, John Ridgway 15s 9d Thomas Edwards 18s 0d, Thomas Taylor 1s 8d, John Baxter 8s 3d, William Bailey 18s 0d, Solar Broomer 5s 3d, John Cartwright 4s 6d, Ralph Bagnall 14s 8d. The total rentals amounted to £27 10s 5d.

Censuses

The 1841 census is rather different from the later enumerations since it was involved only a simple household schedule including name, age, (rounded down to the nearest term of five if over fourteen), sex, profession, trade, and employment, or if of independent means, whether born in the same county (yes or no) or whether born in Scotland or foreign parts. The 1851 and further successive censuses asked for the same details, but new precision was called for in the recording of place of birth and ages that were no longer, as with over fifteens in 1841, to be given to the lowest term of five. Two additional requirements listed the relationship of each individual to the household head and their marital status.

The changes of male age-groups over the period 1701-1881

AGE	1701	1841	1851	1861	1881
85-89	0	0	3		2
80-84	3	3	2	4	2
75-79	3	2	3	2	5
70-74	3	7	5	5	5
65-69	1	5	6	18	7
60-64	15	8	14	16	14
65-59	9	8	14	16	17
50-54	9	12	12	25	15
45-49	4	16	24	24	34
40-44	11	15	31	31	30
35-39	12	28	36	37	35
30-34	24	30	33	54	35
25-29	17	40	50	67	51
20-24	18	39	55	59	62
15-19	22	39	60	77	71
10-14	30	43	57	71	62
05-09	30	73	67	93	66
00-04	25	73	77	109	82

The changes of female age-groups over the period 1701-1881

AGE	1701	1841	1851	1861	1881
85-89	1	1	0	0	0
80-84	3	2	3	0	0
75-79	0	2	3	1	2
70-74	6	8	8	5	3
65-69	5	5	7	6	5
60-64	3	5	7	12	16
55-59	5	4	16	15	14
50-54	5	8	16	21	22
45-49	6	14	19	23	29
40-44	7	23	31	31	22
35-39	11	25	20	45	24
30-34	18	38	40	51	39
25-29	16	38	41	60	30
20-24	10	35	57	59	51
15-19	12	49	53	70	61
10-14	16	45	75	63	58
05-09	22	60	54	84	67
00-04	42	83	78	111	85

Where census returns for large towns are concerned, sampling is the accepted practice for analysing numbers. If high numbers are involved, a 10% or 20% sampling can produce figures sufficient to enable meaningful conclusions.

In Penkhull the numbers are relatively small, amounting to 886 in 1841 and 1,110 in the 1851 census, which included twenty-nine pupils residing at The Mount Residential School for Girls. These residential scholars and four people listed as visitors in the census return have been deducted from the total, leaving 1,077 people residing. It is this total that is the basis for analysis that enables a more progressive picture of early Victorian Penkhull to be formed and its transition from its agrarian background to a residential suburb. For this purpose the districts of Burslem, Hanley and Longton are evaluated alongside that of Penkhull. To enable comparisons the following contrasting studies have been used: Burslem (Stuart 1971); Penkhull (Pattinson 1972); Longton (Breeze 1976) and Hanley (Gatley 1991).

Burslem, described as the mother-town of the Potteries, is situated five miles north of Penkhull. Similarly, Hanley, two miles to the north, and Longton, three miles to the east were all growing manufacturing pottery towns with concentrated terraced dwellings mingled with the early pottery works and bottle ovens.

The difficulty immediately confronts us, is that the label of 'Penkhull' has been applied to an area of variable extent having no factual boundary. The descriptive area of earlier records for Penkhull was much wider than the village associated with the twentieth-century. Pattinson was aware of this dilemma and eliminated the sub-districts of Cliff Bank and Honeywall. These contained scattered groups of houses and densely-congested dwellings mostly built for pottery workers at various times in the form of squares with communal privies.

However advantageous Pattinson thought if the 1851 census was compared with that of 1841, the fundamental problem of identification remained. The 1841 census has often been over-looked by historians because of the lack of birthplace, exact age of adults over the age of fourteen and the relationship to the head of the family. Regardless of these omissions, this document can yield valuable information if used in conjunction with the 1851 listings. Pattinson describes his methodology: *Our difficulty in selecting the area to be studied came from the lack of a detailed map of the area in, or around 1851 and from the frustrating absence of street or house numbers on the Enumerators returns. It was decided that the subject of our analysis should be those households whose 'address' column had been marked 'Penkhull' i.e. we eliminated the households marked Honeywall and Trent Vale which respectively preceded and succeeded the Penkhull households.*

The description on the 1851 census return for the district covered continues: *All that part of the township of Penkhull that comprises the ecclesiastical district of Penkhull (including Honeywall, Village of Penkhull, Harden Cottage Knapper's Gate, Grindley Farm, Stubbs Cottage and Little Mount).* The 1841 census, however, was divided into two divisions and gave a greater indication as to the path the enumerator travelled in compiling his return along with basic addresses against the names: *All that part of the township of Penkhull lying west of Hill Street, comprising, Farmyard, The Mount, Doncaster Lane and that part of Penkhull commencing at Robert Archers, taking the houses on the left as far as the Marquis of Granby from there keeping to the left down to the farm occupied by Wm Hemmings including Seven Row and Ten Row.* The second division continues: *Comprising the houses opposite Ten Row and the houses on the East and West of the Marl Pit including Brisley Hill, Penkhull Square, Taylor's Buildings, the Old Workhouse, Farm Lane, Penkhull Lane taking in Bostock's Cottage and Grindley Hill House.*

From this 1841 introduction, a fair and reasonable adjustment could have increased the value of Pattinson's study. His concern, however, was to place Penkhull into context with an earlier study of Burslem of the same date.

1851 Main Findings of Local Census Studies

	Burslem	Penkhull	Longton	Hanley
Population Totals	1,886	1,077	1,555	3,327
% Male	52.3	49.0	50.4	50.5
% Female	47.7	51.0	49.6	49.5
Aged 0-14	34.3	37.9	34.5	37.5
% Aged 15-49	54.2	51.1	58.0	52.6
% Aged 50 +	14.5	11.0	7.5	9.7

Marital Status (aged 16 and over)				
% Unmarried	37.5	34.2	39.1	34.0
% Married	50.0	58.4	51.0	57.9
% Widowed	12.5	7.4	9.9	8.2
Place of Birth				
% The Town	48.5	55.4	48.0	53.5
% Within five miles	13.6	18.6+	11.8	24.3
% Ireland	8.2	1.1	13.4	1.5

+ Born in other Pottery towns and Newcastle

The first set of figures indicates that Penkhull was slightly weighted in favour of female against of male as compared with the other three districts. Penkhull, a long-established village, probably retained stability, even in an unstable era. Neither Breeze nor Gatley give an explanation for this difference in gender, except that Breeze suggests that perhaps the more rural setting influenced the findings.

When the figures are looked at as a whole, Penkhull records the highest ratio of married people at 58.4%, reflecting, as expected, the highest number of females recorded compared with the other three surveys. Besides this, the solution may also be gleaned from the fact that Penkhull shows the lowest number of widows of the four districts. Explanations are not easy, but the rural environs, coupled with the more settled life pattern of Penkhull compared with those of the manufacturing towns with their higher immigration, could provide the answer.

Further pointers to this conclusion are supported by the statistics showing Penkhull as having the lowest percentage of population in the middle-age group, 15-49 years at 51.1%. These figures therefore suggest that the majority of the population in Penkhull was native compared with those of Burslem, Hanley and Longton, where the population suddenly grew to numbers greatly in excess of Penkhull. The hypothesis is supported by the fact that 55.4% of the population of Penkhull was born locally, while those of Burslem (48.0%) and Longton (48.5%) shows immigration into the industrial towns influences the calculations.

One noticeable feature from the population statistics of 1851 is the youthfulness of the population in all the districts of study. Whilst Penkhull recorded the highest number of persons between the ages of 0-14 years at 37.9%, Hanley just fell short at 37.5% while both Longton and Burslem produce similar figures at 34.4% and 34.5%.

Ages in Penkhull for Census returns of 1851 - 1861 - 1881

AGE	1851	1861	1881
0 - 14	37.9%	39.2%	39.8%
15 - 49	51.1%	50.1%	48.8%
50 plus	11.0%	10.7%	11.4%

Trends in occupation in Penkhull indicate both the status and wealth of a village. For example we mentioned earlier in this chapter that the number of servants employed in 1701 gives an indication of the wealth and standing of a number of householders at that time.

During the 19th century, Britain became the world's first industrial society. It also became the first urban society for by 1851 more than half the population lived in towns. The population of Britain boomed during the century. In 1801 it was about 9 million but had increased to about 41 million by 1901.

Nineteenth century Britain was an oligarchy. Only a small minority of men (and no women) was allowed to vote. In order to be considered middle class you had to have at least one servant. Most servants were female. (Male servants were much more expensive because men were paid much higher wages). Throughout the century being *in service* was a major employer of women.

It is suggested that Penkhull, because of its annexation to the town of Stoke and as a consequence through the development of pottery industry its rural background of agrarian traditions changed to accommodate an influx of working class people from the town of Stoke. The following is extracted from the census returns of 1851, 1861 and 1901 and represent a reasonable balance with fifty years between the first and later figures, which should identify any major changes in occupational trends. The area used for this analysis is quite small but includes the centre of Penkhull. The area commences from the top of Honeywall to the other side of the village to Brisley Hill and from West Bank to what is now Hilton Road, (half way down Newcastle Lane).

Census details for 1851, 1861, and 1901

The following lists in details the main occupations that may be found in census returns of 1851, 1861 and 1901. To add a further dimension, the places of birth and age have also been listed to indicate the extent of places of birth for those deciding to settle in Penkhull and find work in the locality.

Occupations over a period of 50 years

Occupation	1851	1861	1901
Adultress	1		
Agricultural Labourer	9	3	1
Beer Seller	1	1	1
Blacksmith		1	1
Boatman	1		
Butcher	1	1	1
Charwoman	1		3
Coal Merchant		1	
Draper	1		
Dress Maker	5	3	0
Errand Boy	3	1	1
Engraver	1		
Farmer	7	2	4
Grocer	2	4	3
Maltster	1	0	0
Milk seller	1		
Miller of flour			1
Nursery maid	1		
Nurseryman	4	2	0
Policemen	1	1	1
Prostitute	1		
Publican	3	3	4
School master	1	1	1
School Mistress	1	1	1
Scullery Girl	1		
Servant	29	41	26
Shoemaker	3		
Shop Keeper			2
Timber merchant	1	3	
Veterinary surgeon	1		
Vicar	1	1	1
Wheelwright	1	1	

Looking first at the figures for those employed in domestic service there were 32 in 1851. From those only 11 came from either Penkhull or the town of Stoke. Two came from Ireland, one from North Wales. Other places of origin included Worcester, Lancashire, Derby, Tipton as well as the villages and towns of North Staffordshire. It was not unusual for girls as young as thirteen to leave their home to find employment. The 1851 census unfortunately does not give the address of residents, only those being identified as being employed at Beech Grove, The Mount, The Views and Grindley House.

By 1861, the number of servants being employed in the area had increased to 41, reflecting the social standing and wealth of a number of residents who had moved into new properties during the intervening ten years. Once more the places of birth reflected a wide area, Ireland, Shropshire, Cheshire, Yorkshire, as well as the local towns and villages of North Staffordshire. Sixteen were recorded as being born either in Stoke or Penkhull, a very similar portion as the 1851 census.

But what type of properties in Penkhull employed a servant it may be asked? As well as the large houses listed in the 1851 summary, the more genteel properties were those in West Bank where four households employed servants. The same numbers were also resident in properties in Penkhull Terrace. Others included Victoria Place, Trentham Road, the Vicarage, Newcastle Street and local farms.

The 1901 census reveals a different Penkhull forty years later. The number of local servants had fallen to only 5 out a total of 26. Whereas the large properties such as The Mount, The Views and Beech Grove remained substantial employers. Other areas such as West Bank showed a reduction of 50%.

The local pubs still retained live-in staff, the Marquis 1:

Greyhound 1: Terrace 2 and the White Lion 2. The vicarage now employed two servants, Sarah Bennion, aged 23, from Tittensor and Jane Brammer, aged 22, from Bucknall.

In 1851 there were 10 self employed farmers or seeds men and 28 agricultural labourers. By 1901 there were only 5 self employed farmers and 1 agricultural labourer. This is possibly accounted for by the fact that they no longer lived on the farms but outside the area, which would mean they are not shown on the Penkhull census.

Other occupations are listed such as errand boys, one as young as 11, and in 1901, three charwomen are working in the area. In 1851 there were 5 dressmakers, by 1901 there was only 1 remaining. The village policeman occupied a house in East Street, known locally as 'Bobbies Row' in all three-census returns. Tax collectors, railway clerks, wheelwrights, blacksmiths and trades people all had a part to play in village life throughout the fifty years of comparison. In the earlier census returns, two entries are quite surprising. The first comes from Penkhull Square where a young lady describes herself as a prostitute and the second is living with a local farmer who classes herself as an adulteress.

Placing Penkhull further under the microscope for 1901 the vast majority worked in the pottery industry or tile manufacture at Wheatley Tileries at Springfield's. Considering next the occupations found in the new housing developments such as in Queens Road and Princes Road, the statistics would reflect a different picture as the larger better class properties attracted pottery manufactures, managers, artists and professional people.

Local Newspapers

The last remaining documents that are used to indicate the occupations in the area are reproduced from directories compiled by The Sentinel newspaper. At the turn of the century many local newspapers compiled directories listing each address and the head and occupation of the family in each street. Those, which cover Penkhull, are dated 1907 and 1912.

Church Street, now Manor Court Street

	1907		1912	
1.	Turnock, Jas.	Stonemason	Challinor. J.	Poultry dealer
2.	Mayor, Edgar	Potters printer	Mayer, Edgar	Potter
3.	Bradbury, Henry		Hemmings, John	Labourer
4.	Smith, Wm	Boot & shoemaker	Smith, Wm	Boot & shoemaker
6.	Simcock, Alfred	Greyhound	Henley, George	Greyhound
7.	Powner, Leonard	Labourer	Powner, Leonard	Labourer
8.	Bradbury, Lewis	Potters Placer	Bradbury, Lewis	Potters Placer
9	Mansfield, Wm.	Potter		
10.	Hissey, Arthur		Rushton, Tom's	Butcher
11.	Turnock, John	Labourer	Turnock, John	Labourer
12.	McLean, Harry	Grocer	Clarke, Wm	Grocer
13.	Berrisford, James	Butcher	Berrisford, James	Butcher
14.	Bradbury, Richard	Sub-Postmaster	Bradbury, Richard	Sub-postmaster/confectioner
15.	Roberts, Walt.	Goods porter	Roberts, Walt.	Goods porter

Eardley Street

2.	Johnson, Wm	Potter	Johnson, Wm	Potter
3.	Deakin, Mary Mrs		Deakin, Mary Mrs	
4.	Bennett, Josiah	Boiler Maker	Bennett, Josiah	Boiler Maker
5.	Smith, Herbert	Potter	Smith, Herbert	Potter
6.	Lawton, Wm	Potter	Lawton, Wm.	Potter
7.	Smith, Henry	Potter	Smith, Henry	Potter

East Street, now Rothwell Street

1.	Underwood, John	Quarry worker	Smith, Henry	House Painter
2.	Allen, Edwin,	Brass Miller	Poulton, Geo	Hairdresser
3.	Harrison, Frances		Salt, Frederick	Potter
4.	Clowes, Henry	Labourer	Whitmore, Josiah	Potter
5.	Hill, Arthur, House	Painter	Hawkins, Henry	Fireman
6.	Maddock, Wm	Collier	Bailey, J	Estate Agent
8.	Wilshaw Mrs		Barker, Mrs	
9.	Shenton, Oscar	Butcher	Shenton, Oscar	
10.	Lake, Mrs Sarar		Poole, Leonard	Labourer
11.	Bardell, Moses	Grocer	Bardell, Moses	Grocer
12.	Bennett, Mrs Eliza		Bennett, Mrs Eliza	
13.	Thursfield, Wm	House Painter	Thursfield, Wm	House painter
14.	Alcock, John,	Police constable	Hopkins, Geo	Signalman
15.	Simpson, Edward	Labourer	Simpson, Ed.	Labourer
16.	Ford, Wm	Potter	Ford, Wm	Potter
18.	Colclough, Miss Ada		Deakin, Wm	Potter
19.	Colclough, Wm		Colclough, Wm	
20.	Clowes, Sam	Labourer	Bradbury, Wm	Potter
21.	Bloor, Joseph	Potter	Bloor, Joseph	Potter
22.	Harvey, Elijah		Harvey, Elijah	
23.	Clowes, Robert	Potter	Clowes, Robert	Potter
24.	Hall, Robert	Grocer/beer	Stone, Harry	
25.	Ford, Mrs Lily		Poole, Mrs	
26.	Richardson, Henry		Richardson, Henry	
27.	Richardson, Henry	Beer retailer	Richardson, Hy	Beer retailer
28.	Sanders, Stephen	Grocer	Sanders, Step'en	Grocer
29.	Turner, Alfred	Plumber	Turner, Alfred	Plumber
30.	Stone. Thomas	Potter	Stone, Thomas	Potter
31	Haddrell, Chas	Labourer	Underwood, Jn	Brick maker
32.	Cliff, Joseph	Labourer	Cliff, Joseph	Labourer
33.	Baggley, Bert	Greengrocer	Redman, Fred	Fried fish dealer

Garden Street, Victoria Buildings

1.	Gotham,Thomas		Furber, John	Potter
2.	Bradley, Thomas	Potter	Bradley, Thomas	Potter
3.	Parkes, Herbert	Grocer	Parkes, E	Grocer
4.	Webster, Sarah		Gibson, John	Collier
5.	Stewart, John	Potter	Banks, Alfred	Electrician
6.	Comley, Alfred	Greengrocer	Henley, Wm	
7.	Banks, Alfred		Stanley, Sydney	Painter
8.	Rushton, Thomas	Potter	Bishop, Wm	House painter
9.	Plants, Thomas	Labourer	Plant, Thomas	Labourer
10.	Broomfield, Harry	Labourer	Broomfield, H.	Labourer
11.	Roberts, Martha		Roberts, Thomas	Potter
12.	McPherson, Eliz	Grocer/b'r retailer	McPherson, Eliz	Grocer/beer retailer

Farm Lane

	Jervis, Arthur	Farmer	Jervis, Arthur	Farmer
16	Wilkinson, Eliza	Elm Tree Hs	Blois, Bazin	Land Agent
	Shenton, A.	Timekeeper		

Newcastle Lane

1.	Clay, Alfred	House Painter	Woolley, Wm	Potter
1a	Lockley, John	Stoker		
3.	Rowley, Thomas	House Painter	Rowley, Thomas	House Painter

5.	Simpson, Emma	Grocer	Simpson, Emma	Grocer
9.	Simpson, James	Labourer	Plant, Thomas	House Painter
11.	Odell, Frederick	Engraver		
13.	Tedstone, Chas	Postman	Tedstone, Chas	Postman
15.	Gittins, Alf	Engine Driver	Gittins, Alf	Engine Driver
17.	Bosley, Thomas	Labourer		
19.	Hand, Wm	Confectioner	Roberts, Wm	Labourer
21.	Rushton, Walter	Plumber	Rushton, Thomas	Watchman
23.	Williams, Charles		Handley, Wm.	Potter
25.	Woolley, Mrs Jane		Sutton, Frederick	Labourer
27.	Woolley, Wm	Potter	Ashcroft, Mrs	
29.	Sandham, James		Sandham, James	Wood Machinist
31.	Ford, Joseph	Potter	Till, Herbert	Baker

Penkhull New Road commencing from 'The Views'

1.	Gamon, H.	Solicitor	Gamon, H.	Solicitor
2.	Whittaker, Wm	Bank Clerk	Whittaker, Wm	Bank Clerk
3.	Minton, S.	Manufacturer	Swettenham, Miss	
94.	Downes, L	Boiler Tenter		
96.	Cliff, Earnest	Fishmonger	Ryder, Richard	Potter
100.	Radford, Frank.	Terrace Inn	Radford, Frank	Terrace Inn
104.	Dooley, James	Labourer	Parkes, Samuel	Potter
106.	Swetnam, M.A.	Newsagent	Swetnam, M.A.	Newsagent
108.	Cope, J.T.	Potter	Cope, J.T.	Potter
110.	Colley, Sam	Potter	Simpson, Colin	Railwayman
112.	Parkes, Sam	Potter	Wheeler,	

This list may be used as a study into occupations of those residing in the centre of Penkhull. It indicates two important factors. Firstly there are only four occupations that could be deemed as 'professional', two were residents of The Views, one an estate agent living in East Street and the last a land agent, living at Elm Tree House in Garden Street. All the other occupations recorded apart from traders and shopkeepers that amounted to fourteen were classified as at the lower end of the social scale.

Secondly viewing the variation of residential names within various streets the number of properties where residents changed between these dates is significant. Two streets, Garden Street that included Victoria buildings and East Street show a 50% change of residents, whereas Penkhull New Road shows a 45% turnover and slightly less in Newcastle Lane at 36% but in Eardley Street, containing only seven dwellings the turnover is recorded as nil. A quite different picture is found for Penkhull Terrace, located just on the periphery of the centre of the village. In 1907 there were nine professional residents recorded but in 1912 the number had increased to 10. This is because the properties in Penkhull Terrace were larger and considered more genteel than those situated around the church. The turnover for that Penkhull Terrace between the two dates was 31%.

During this period the overwhelming majority of houses were rented with absentee landlords. Employment was so precarious and as such weekly incomes were not dependable which unfortunately resulted in a high proportion of families doing a *moonlight flit* to avoid bad debts and being made homeless.

Rate Books

Further information regarding ownership and value of properties can be obtained from the Rate Books. The valuation return lists occupier, owner, rentable and rateable value with a short description of the property, i.e. house and garden, house and yard, shop etc. They are a source little used by historians but their value to students of economic social change is fundamental.

To continue from the previous two listings the general valuation of Stoke for rates in 1914 is used as it is the nearest to the Sentinel listing of 1912. The findings will substantiate the issue of tenanted properties.

This information has been arranged into context with the previous streets shown in the study to enable comparisons. Eardley Street continues to maintain 100% retention of tenants from 1907. There was only one owner for the whole street, Mr J.G. Whalley. The gross rental for each property was listed at £6 13 0d p.a. Just around the corner in East Street, the situation is quite different with 50% of the properties changing hands. The houses in this street were built at different periods and in different styles and sizes, which reflect a difference in rental values from £6 13 0d to £8 2s 0d. Shops are listed at No's 11, 24, 26, 28, and 32. These varied in rentals from £9 7s 0d to a maximum of £22 10 0d for No. 22 East Street. None of these properties was owner occupied. Mr Whalley owned eleven houses and others were divided between Angelina Reeves with four and James Morris with three. The remainder of the houses were owned by just two other people.

In Church Street, now known as Manor Court Street, a 50% turn around of tenants was noted. None was owner occupied. The central block of terraced properties were owned by Sarah Bagnall, a family member of the original builder. Mr Beresford's butcher's shop and the following two shops were owned by Julia Lowe and remained in the same family until they became subject to compulsory purchase by the city council in the mid 1960s. Mr Edwin Foreshaw owned the Greyhound, and Elizabeth McPherson owned the property next door and the three cottages adjacent just before the entrance into Garden Street. She also owned the majority of the cottages in Garden Street including the outdoor beer house.

The Bagnall Row of cottages in Church Street were superior to the old cottages in East Street the rentable value being £8 0s 0d while the old cottages in East Street were listed at £6 13 0d. 'The Greyhound Inn' was valued at £40 0s 0d. The shops belonging to Julia Lowe were valued at between £9 0s 0d and £12 10s 0d depending upon size.

These properties in East Street were occupied by the lower end of the working classes as compared with other properties in the village. For example, in Penkhull Terrace rentable annual values varied considerably and reflected the status of those living there. The highest rent paid was at No. 19 at

£24 12s. Most were around the £17 to £18 figure and the two lowest were the very old 18th century cottages situated almost at the junction of Penkhull Terrace with Penkhull New Road at £8 each. For the first time we come across owner-occupiers, nine being listed. The only large owner of multiple properties was John Brunt, who owned four and lived at No.3 the rent being valued for house, stabling and yard at £16 15s.

The last group of properties, which reflect the importance of Penkhull as a residential area for the professional elite, is Queens Road. In 1914 most of the properties were relatively new but later developed over the years to what it is today. John Charlesworth, the father of the late Miss Charlesworth *(who used to own the little sweet shop at the corner of Princes Road and Honeywall)* owned eight. The short terraced row on the right and two following pairs varied in rentable values from £19 4s to £40 4s a huge difference from those of Eardley Street. There was one property in the occupation of Harold Robinson, described as 'house and grounds', which was assessed at £72. The old parsonage fronting Queens Road was assessed at the sum of £54.

These figures point to a wide-ranging mixture of professional, manual workers, trades people, managers and manufacturers living at Penkhull.

Trade Directories

Nineteenth-century trade directories are of major importance to the historian when establishing the period and extent of growth in an area. The first publication of Trade Directories commenced in the late 1700s, mainly on a national scale.

The town of Stoke from an early date would have been supplied with a wide range of shops to cater for most of the daily needs. As Stoke was an industrial town, and the majority of its workers being employed in the pottery industry, there would have been a shortage of quality shops, especially for ladies. There would certainly be no stores for agricultural supplies or equipment so these items would have been purchased from the nearby market town of Newcastle.

Penkhull traders listed in 1800

Michael Baxter	Huckster
John Burgess	Gardener
Mary Broad	Huckster
John Chapman	Miller
Cotton Mrs.	Crate Maker
Richard Cyples	Tailor
Thomas Egirton	Victualler
William Hill	Huckster
William Kettle	Victualler
John Merry	Blacksmith
William Simcock	Tailor

No doubt building upon the success of the first directory and its value to the community, at least to those who could read and write, Thomas Allbut set about in 1802 compiling his next. It should be remembered that in 1800 the vast majority of the working classes would be illiterate. But it was with the well-to-do people and other traders that Allbut's work found favour. It would be seen almost as something of a status symbol to have your name in print and therefore encourage others to contribute to the publication. It is therefore not surprising that this later directory produced by Thomas Allbut would contain additional names.

Penkhull traders 1802

Michael Baxter	Huckster (peddler) Penkhull
John Burgess	Gardener, Penkhull
John Chapman	Miller, Penkhull
Mrs Cotton	Crate Maker, Penkhull
Richard Cyples	Tailor, Penkhull
Thomas Eggerton	Victualler, Penkhull
William Hill	Huckster, Penkhull
William Hulse	Nailer, Penkhull
Hulse Miss	Milliner, Penkhull mantua maker *(a woman's loose gown)*
William Kettle	Victualler, Penkhull
John Merry	Blacksmith, Penkhull
John Young	Dealer in earthenware, Penkhull

The next directory is dated 1818 and published by Parsons and Bradshaw, and due to the commercial success of this trade directory as it was the first locally to list individuals in alphabetical order as well as by trades. For the first time a directory contained the names of working class people many of whom are listed as potters especially those living at Honeywall. The section for Stoke Town commences with a brief description of the collection times for mail. South mail arrives at forty-five minutes past eight in the morning, and departs at half past one after noon. North mail arrives at half past seven in the evening and departs at half past ten at night. The postmaster was Mr James Hazlehurst.

There were three stage coaches in 1818, which stopped at The Wheatsheaf Inn, Stoke. *The Light Post* to London, through Burton every day at four o'clock. To Liverpool, every morning at nine o'clock. *The Prince Cobourg* to London, through Lichfield and Coventry every evening at six o'clock. To Liverpool every day at twelve o'clock. *The Regulator* to Liverpool and Birmingham, every Sunday, Tuesday and Thursday at one o'clock at noon.

List of names that appear in the Parsons and Bradshaw Directory for Penkhull in 1818

James Atkins	Victualler	White Lion
Michael Baxter	Grocer, flour dealer	Penkhull
Elizabeth Benner	Dress maker	Honeywall
Joseph Brandreth	Farmer	Honeywall
Mary Broad	Grocer, flour dealer	Honeywall
John Burgess	Gardener, seeds man	Penkhull
Edward Candland	Marquis of Granby	Penkhull
John Kirkham	Timber merchant	Penkhull (House)

William Mills	Grocer, flour dealer	Penkhull
Edward Salt	Shop Keeper	Honeywall
Thomas Sutton	Farmer	Penkhull
Mary Tilstone	Gentlewoman	The Grove, Penkhull
Joseph Tilstone	Gentleman	The Grove, Penkhull
William Warrilow	Maltster	Penkhull
William Hill	Baker, flour	Penkhull
William Mills	Baker, flour	Penkhull
Simeon Thorley	Baker, flour	Penkhull

The list still included only two Inns, but six names are shown for the supply of grocery and provisions indicating an expanding community.

Trade Directories appear to have been worthwhile for local traders, as Thomas Allbut published a further directory in 1822. From this date new directories appeared at regular intervals increasing in size with each edition. Unfortunately, many did not go to the trouble to update previous details and as such errors could be carried forward. There is no doubt that with the growth of the village came an increasing number of listed traders although this could have been down to the popularity of directories and well as an increase of population and demand.

Trade Directory dated 1822.

Robert Archer,	Gentleman	The Grove, Penkhull
Michael Baxter	Maltster, miller	Penkhull
William Bird	Victualler	White Lion
Thomas Brammer	Boot/ shoe maker	Penkhull
Charles Brindley	Boot/ shoe maker	Penkhull
John Burgess	Gardener/seeds man	Penkhull
John Burgess Jun.	Gardener/seeds man	Penkhull
Edward Candland	Victualler	Marquis of Granby
John Edge	Draper	Penkhull
Daniel Greatbatch	Engraver	Penkhull
William Henshall	Farmer	Penkhull
William Hill	Grocer/Baker	Penkhull
William Mills	Grocer	Penkhull
Thomas Moore	Farmer	Penkhull
Thomas Palmer	Traveller	Penkhull Cottage
Samuel Philips	Baker	Penkhull
Christopher Preston	Guardian of the Poor	Honeywall
Joseph Reeves	Farmer	Penkhull
John Shufflebotham	Gov'r/ Poor House	Penkhull
Robert Simcock	Tailor	Penkhull
Josiah Spode	Manufacturer	The Mount
John Sutton	Farmer	Penkhull
Samuel Warrilow	Maltster	Penkhull

This directory lists for the first time four farms, two maltsters, two boot and shoemakers and Daniel Greatbatch, a self-employed engraver whose home was situated in what is known as 'The Views' off Penkhull New Road. Greatbatch Avenue is named after him. Once more only two Inns are listed the White Lion and the Marquis of Granby.

The gentry for the first time were listed, no doubt for their patronage. As in many directories of the time the real issues of health, housing, sanitation and working conditions in the towns are glossed over. We read only of the manufacturers

being philanthropic to the workers and their dependants. The real picture of living and working conditions are hard to ascertain for the period except through government reports. Even these can be misleading as employees being interviewed rarely spoke the truth for fear of losing their jobs. By 1861 street names started to appear in the town of Stoke for the first time. Unfortunately it remained many more years, before streets and lanes in the village of Penkhull were identified by name.

The entry for Stoke-upon-Trent identifies those people of traders in the village who considered themselves to be of importance: David Anderson, gent; Robert Archer, gent; John and William Burgess, nursery and seeds men; John Eardley; Daniel Greatbatch, engraver; George Hemmings, farmer; Miss Cathleen Williamson; Walter Willett; John Fenton, attorney, Stoke Lodge.

Trade Directory 1861

John Heath	Boot and shoe maker	Penkhull
John Evans and Son	Builders	Penkhull
Thomas Tatton	Butcher	Penkhull
Daniel Steele	Crate Maker	Penkhull
Marquis of Granby Inn		Penkhull
The White Lion Inn		Penkhull
James Grocott	Beer house keeper	Penkhull
John Sanders	Beer house keeper	Penkhull
Thomas Tatton	Beer house keeper	Penkhull
Thomas Trickett	Beer house Keeper	Knapper's Gate
Michael Baxter	Maltster	Penkhull
Henry Hill	Maltster	Penkhull
Thomas Lowndes	Shop keeper	Penkhull
Joseph Mountford	Shop keeper	Penkhull
Thomas Lysett	Shop keeper	Honeywall
Elizabeth Martin	Shop keeper	Penkhull
Nicholas Richards	Shop keeper	Penkhull
Hugh Pickering	Shop keeper	Penkhull
James Taylor	Shop keeper	Penkhull

The significance in this directory is the introduction of beer house keepers. This was not an outdoor retail outlet for beer, but in the majority of cases a converted front parlour, for under the Beer House Act it was permissible to sell beer or ale from such premises but no spirits. This Act was to provide an alternative to an Inn, where spirits could be purchased, and to encourage social intercourse between the working classes. The large number of shop keepers listed reflected the increasing demand by an expanding population.

Trade Directories from 1802-1887 together with the numbers of occupations

Occupations	1802	1818	1822	1834	1851	1864	1869	1887
Academies				1	2	2	2	1
Agent	1							
Artists						1	1	1
Baker			1					
Beer House				4	1	2	6	2
Blacksmith	1							
Boot and Show Repairs			1	1	2	2		
Butchers				1	1	1	2	1

	1	2	3	4	5	6	7	8
Chemists						1		
Colour Manufacturers								1
Coal Dealer						2	1	1
Cordwinder		2						
Crate Maker	1	1	1	1				
Farmer		1	4	4	4			
Inns	2		2	2	2	2	2	3
Gardener/Seeds man	1	1	1	1	1	1	1	1
Maltster		1	2	2	2			
Millener/Dressmaker	1					3	2	
Miller	1							
Nailor	1		1					
Shop keepers	2	3	1	7	4	6	6	7
Bonet Makers						1		
Tailor	2			1	2	1	2	
Victualler	2	2	2	2	2	2	2	2

The White Lion Inn started as an old established Coaching Inn as it was situated on a steep hill from the town of Stoke-upon-Trent.

Indeed this road probably dates from prehistoric times. The White Lion is shown on a 1777 Duchy of Lancaster Map as in the occupation of Mr Thomas Appleton. The county records for the Justices of the Peace record the issue of a licence from the mid 18th century. In 1823 the property became part of the estate of Josiah Spode II. It stood at the corner of the Old Coach Road, which ran as a private road between the Mount, and Honeywall.

In 1861, The White Lion was owned by Richard Stone who sold the plot of land at the rear of the Inn to Frederick Bishop to enable a new road to be built from Honeywall to Princes Road thereby opening up the area for building development from 1865. Note the name Stone Street.

It is likely that the White Lion was extended in around 1900 to accommodate the increased demand from the nearby housing development called The Allotments.

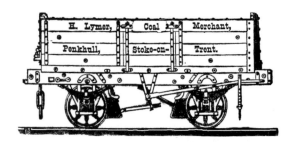

H. LYMER,
Family Grocer, Provision Dealer
AND
COAL MERCHANT,
PENKHULL, STOKE-ON-TRENT.

Chapter 9
Land - Occupation and Agriculture.

In the last hundred years there has been speculation by historians as to the historical importance of Penkhull. There were stories of early castles, preceding that of Newcastle on the basis that 'new' implied there was an 'old' castle, and suggested a Manor House with resident Lord. I recall the late Deaconess Smee making the serious suggestions that a 'Hall' was previously on the site of her home, The Views, on the evidence that the land upon which the house was built was at one time called Halls Meadow. Unfortunately this almost reckless assumption appeared in the local press and so now appears in a local history publication almost as fact.

Penkhull as in the past remains under two different layers of authority, civic and manorial. Before 1818 it was based upon ecclesiastical and manorial authorities. For the purposes of correlation, manorial records for the manor of Newcastle-under-Lyme have been used to illustrate the growing agricultural and domestic scene. Ecclesiastical records are used to provide an insight into property, wealth, social conditions and genealogy.

Manorial Surveys 1414 and onwards

The early layout of Penkhull has previously been discussed at the time of Domesday and so we follow on from this time using various documents. The first is a manorial survey taken on the 4th February in the second year of the reign of Henry 5th 1414/15. The document is found in the National Archives (Ref: DL 42/4 folios 168-174) but why was this survey complied at this time? The answer is that during the years 1411/12 most of Europe was engulfed in an epidemic of the Black Death, which was one of the most deadly pandemics in human history. It is said to have killed one third of the population of Europe.

Following this period of national demographic and population changes followed by a short period of stability it would have become necessary to re-asses and update records of the tenants, their land occupation and rentals. This conclusion is arrived at by the contents of the survey, listing not only the current tenant of the land, but also the previous tenant. No doubt there may have been a previous survey of the manor prior to 1414/15 but if there if is it has not survived.

The following is only a guide to this extensive document, which covers the whole of the manor which included Penkhull and Boothen, Clayton and Seabridge with Wolstanton and Shelton with Hanley. It lists the rentals charged for land, a description of the tenure of the land and its measurement.

(Further entries can be found in Appendix ii).

Survey of the Manor of Newcastle - 1414 (Penkhull)

John Tyttensor holds half a messuage 20 lands of socage [22d] two acres [2s] and 1 part of an acre of land of demesne [2d] formerly held by William Tyttensor & pays per annum at the terms of Saint Andrew the Apostle, the Annunciation of the Blessed Mary and the Nativity of Saint John the Baptist and St Michael equally: 4s 4½d.

William Tyttensor holds half a messuage 8 lands of socage [53/4d] 3 lands of demesne [6d] & the third part of an acre called Holeplane [9d] 4½ acres and one rood of land of waste [2s 3½d] formerly held by the aforesaid William & pays per annum at the same terms: 4s 3¾d.

Henry de Lyme holds one cottage, three and a half lands of socage formerly held by the aforesaid William pays per annum at the same terms 4½d.

The Procurator of the Blessed Mary holds one half-land of socage formerly held by the aforesaid William pays per annum at the same terms ½d.

Roger Fenton chaplain holds half an acre of land of waste formerly held by the same William pays per annum at the same terms 3d.

The aforesaid Procurator holds half an acre of land of waste formerly held by the same William pays per annum at the same terms: 3d.

John Toke holds one messuage 4 lands of socage land at a halfpenny, 12 lands of socage land at 1d; 5 lands of demesne formerly held by John Atteke pays per annum at the same terms 2s 8d.

Roger Fenton chaplain holds half an acre of land of waste formerly held by the said John pays per annum at the same terms: 3d.

Although this above is only a small section of the survey it paints a vivid picture of life in the early 15th century. First, it should be remembered that even though the date of this record is over three hundred years after the time of Domesday, in reality there would have been little change.

Penkhull at this time was still an open field village with perhaps more than three open fields divided into strips or lands, as they would be called. They went by the name Akford, Stubbs field (a field shared with the town of Newcastle), Wood field and possibly Whatley. The other townships within the manor also had a number of open fields. There is no evidence to suggest that the present names of Barnfield and Springfields have any roots in history to substantiate them as names of previous 'open fields'.

It is interesting to note that even at this early date, there is mention of Nicolas, potter of Penkhull who paid 23d in rent. We can also note that Roger Fenton was the chaplain at Stoke Church. No doubt the Rector, Richard of Monmouth would be an absentee cleric like so many during this period living off the income from tithes and land. A number of 'lands' were held in socage; others in the demesne meaning that copyholders labour was used in cultivating lands as a 'service to the lord', a form of rental.

It is possible to calculate individual properties, land holdings, how much waste, the total of land cultivated for the lord of the manor and rentals paid. There were 85 acres of waste, 368 acres of land cultivated in socage, and over 100 acres farmed in the demesne, totalling 553 acres. Calculations can also be made of the number of cottages. They number just 17, the exact number of farmers listed in 1086 which upholds the premise that little woodland would have been put under the plough throughout the intervening three hundred years and the farming community remained almost static. Names that appear at this date, Tyttensor, Fenton, Bothes, Bateson, Pesedale, Machin, Nikson, and Peyntor are among those that we shall come across in the study of Penkhull over the following four hundred years.

In an attempt to present a clearer picture of the events for the period, let us look at just a few of the court records during the reign of Henry V. The courts at this time would still be held within the castle at Newcastle.

We read in the year 1414 that *Richard and John, lessees, complain of John son of Henry de Bech in a plea of trespass in that he failed to grind his corn at the mill to the loss of 6s 8d; John was fined 2d. John Colclogh the elder complains of William Leke and his servant in a plea of trespass for entering the wood of John against his wishes to the damage of 6s 8d; William did not attend court and was therefore ordered to be detained to attend the next court. Fined 2d. William Fossebroke complains of William Glover in a plea of debt of 16½d; who did not come, therefore detain [him] to attend the next court. Fined 2d.*

The next entry deals with the conveyance of property from Richard Lovot who surrendered a quarter of a cottage of a socage tenure in great Clayton. *To John Lovot, the son of Richard Lovot. Admitted. Fine 2d.*

Saturday 7th August 1417 *John Colclogh the younger surrenders 8 acres of land of waste on the Stubbs in the tenure of Thomas de Godemere and 6 acres of land of waste on the Stubbs formerly belonging to Thomas Podmore to John Colclogh and Agnes his wife and their legally born heirs, to hold for the whole of her life so long as she stays un-married, and after Agnes death parcels of the lands should stand as a newly added parcel with other lands which have been granted. Fine 2s.*

Thomas Astley, son of John Astley, binds himself, his heirs and executors to Agnes Rughley, wife of Roger Rughley, in the sum of 20s that if he deprives Agnes of her possession of a cottage.

Saturday 18th September 1417 *small court of the above manor held there. Adam Colclogh complains of John Housbond in a plea of trespass in that he took a hundred of wooden shingles and he transported them downhill against Adams wishes to the damage of 10s who came and contested it and had it heard at this court.*

Saturday 26th April 5 Henry V (1418) Penkhull and Boothen. (The amount in brackets following their names is the fine charged) *John Huchon, William Smyth and Thomas Haryson of Boothen, frankpledges there present that William Chaumber fined (4d), Roger de Hanley (4d) and the heir of Richard de Colclogh ought to appear and have not come and that John of Boothen, the frankpledge, concealed that attack made on John Kydde with a staff by John, the son of Thomas of Boothen, the frankpledge concealed in the same way (3d); and that Thomas Harryson of Boothen and his son John over burdened the common with their cattle more than they ought to do (4d) and that William Pessall and John his son did the same there in the same way (4d) and that Thomas Huchon attacked Agnes the wife of William Smyth with a staff and 'shook' her by the shoulders (2d) and that John Brode, the servant of John Huchon attacked William Smyth with a staff (2d) and that the said John Brode attacked the said William in his house with the said staff (4d) and that the said Agnes, wife of the said William is a common ale wife (4d) and that Richard Bond (2d), John Harryson (2d) of Boothen and William Smyth have withdrawn their writ of the mill to the prejudice of the lord (2d); and that a bargain has been made between William Smyth and Agnes his wife on the one side and William, the son of William T . . . of Chesterton, on the other side concerning 2 and half messuages with the lands adjoining to them in Penkhull, and the lands remain.*

The next survey, dated 1516 in the 8th year of Henry VIII was taken by Richard Lovatt, a surname that is continually found in Penkhull until the 19th century. The document is stored in the British Library under the title of Harley Roll K.9.

Rental of the Manor of Newcastle-under-Lyme made by Richard Lovatt in the year 8 Henry VIII
William Synson holds and the rent p.a. 14s 2d Richard Barrett 4s 6d, Richard Woodcock 4s 6d, Ranulph Machyn 21s 11d Ranulph Machyn (the same) holds in Clayton & Shepbridge 6s 11d, Thomas Bothus 18s 6d, Procurator of St. Mary of Stoke 4s ½d, Procurator of St. Mary in Chelton 11½d, Procurator of St. Mary in Chelton & Shepbridge 8½d, Roger Turner 10s 10d, Richard Amys 10s 8d, Ralph Pare 9d, John Huchyns 13s 3d, John Huchyns 12s 4d, Roger Handley 7s 8d, John Dale 7s 10d, William Tyttensor 12s 4d, David Hudson 8d Thomas Peysall 5s 11d, Thomas Elkyn 2s 1d, Roger Fenton 2s 6d for a pasture called Neyderley 4d, Mychaell Wulfley 1s 5d, Ranulph Bagnold

3s 4d, The same Ranulph for land in Wolstanton ½d, William Vernam 10d, Agnes Orpe 3d, Ralph Bagnold 6d, John Leghton 2s 11d.

By the time this survey was carried out in 1516 the open fields had partly become enclosed except for that of Stubbs, which was shared with the town of Newcastle. We read the addition of new family names such as Bagnold and Dale, which we shall come across many times in future court records.

The largest landowners are the procurator of St. Mary (the Catholic Church) with lands valued at 35s 8d. followed by Machyn at 28s 10d and Huchyn at 25s 7d.

As we move to take a glimpse of events during the years of Henry VIII, we come across a new title, that of Reeve. The Reeve was the person who was elected each year by the tenants of the 'seventeen ancient messuages' and responsible for the running of the manorial court on behalf of the steward or his deputy.

At a small court of the manor on Saturday next before the feast of the Lord's Ascension, 1st year of the reign of King Henry VIII, 1509.

Saturday, 11th January 1509
Thomas Tyttensor, John Dale and Roger Fenton, freeholders there present Henry Symson who was a tenant of the lord died since the last great court, after whose death there fell to the lord 2 shillings in the name of farfee. And that Richard 2d Huchyn made an assault on Richard Browde, and Richard 2d Browde made an assault on Richard Huchyn. Also they present Margaret 3s 4d wife of John Patson, who was a rebel (spoke) in words of malice and rebutting the lord king's inquisition. They also present John Patson 8d and his wife and servants took sheaves of wheat from John Huchyn, senior at Penkyll, contrary to the law.

It is ordered by the steward that no man make affray, battery or evil warfare while the court is sitting, under penalty of 6s 8d.

John Tyttensor complains against John Huchyn, junior on a plea of debt of four shillings. The defendant complains fined 17d.

Thomas Amys, Thomas Rowley, Thomas Burne, Stephen Hyll, Thomas Hyll, John Heth, Robert Sponer and Richard Amiss elect John Turner to the office of Reeve for this year.

Thomas Eldurshawe complains against Thomas Johnson 2d on a plea of trespass because he detained one sythe for three days to a loss to the complainant of 16d. The attorney comes and seeks payment.

The same John Tyttensor complains against Thomas Eldurshawe on a plea of trespass because he destroyed oats at his house and

barley at Herdall Heyth to a loss of two shillings. The attorney comes on behalf of the complainant and seeks payment. Mercy 2d.

Margaret Symson 2d complains against John Dale on a plea of debt of 18d on one side and 20d on the other side, which she does not pursue.

The following entry points to the fact that the open field system of farming was still operating in certain areas of Penkhull at this time as 'strips of plough land' are being referred to. *John Tyttensor complains against John Leighton 2d on a plea of trespass, because he destroyed four strips of plough land of oats at Hartshyll to a loss of 6s 8d. The attorney comes and on behalf of the complainant and seeks payment. Mercy 2d.*

The same John complains against the same John 2d on a plea of trespass, because he destroyed his meadow called Rudmede and his barley with his horses in Penkyll fyld to a loss of 3s 4d. The attorney comes and on behalf of the complainant and seeks payment.

Thomas Jonson complains against Thomas Eldurshawe 2d on a plea of debt for half a day's mowing. The defendant comes and complains of the account.

A court held at Newcastle view of frankpledge on 24th November 32nd year of Henry VIII (1542)
Penkhull – Thomas Bothes, Thomas Tyttensor of the frankpledge there present that Hugh Awerley (2d) Henry Bradshawe (2d) John Bagnold (2d) and Richard Wyncull (2d) are common brewers against the assize (of ale).

If we moved on to the time of Edward VI once more the names of Tyttenshore, Huchyn, Fenton and Dale reoccur time and again. The first entry refers to the death of Thomas Huchyn and as a result an ox to the value of 20s was due to the lord as a heriot, which was a form of inheritance tax.

14th April 1553 7th year of Edward VI, Thomas Tyttensor, senior, Bartholomew Bowyer and Roger Fenton frankpledges were sworn present: *Thomas Huchyn who holds one messuage half an acre of certain lands, tenement, meadow, feedings and pasture in Penkhull and Clayton died since the last court seized thereof, after which death there falls to the lord a heriot one ox price 20s. And that John Huchyn is his son and next heir and aged 17 years. And they say that Roger Dale who held of the lord, one messuage and certain lands and tenements, meadows and feedings or pasture in Penkhull by copy of the court roll according to the custom of the manor died seized thereof, after whose death there falls to the lord a heriot one cow price ten shillings. And that John Dale is his son and next heir and of full age.*

The next entry appears in the time of Philip and Mary and records that the courts were by this time being held at Penkhull.

Small court held at Penkhull 1st October 5 & 6 Philip and Mary 22nd October 1558.
To this court comes Stephen Hyll in his own proper person and surrendered all his messuages, cottages, lands, tenements, meadows, feedings and pastures whatsoever with all and singular their appurtenances lying in Penkhull and Shelton to the use and behoof of Robert Hyll, and his heir apparent of Stephen, his heirs and assigns for ever. And at this same court came Robert Hyll in his own proper person and took from the lord King and lady Queen all the messuages, cottages, lands, tenements and rest of the premises to have and hold to Robert, his heirs and assigns for ever by the rent and services therefore due and of right accustomed. And he gives to the lord King and lady Queen a fine at entry of 5 shillings and is admitted tenant thereof. This fine of five shillings would be the court charges due to the crown and value of such was based upon the value of the estate.

The next period we come to is that of the reign of Elizabeth 1st who remained on the throne for forty-five years from 1558-1602.

At a small court held at Penkhull on 14th day in the third year of the reign of the lady Queen Elizabeth June 1561 *To the court comes John Huchen in his own proper person and he renders seizin into the hands of the lady Queen of two closes or pastures of land, namely one called the Long Cliff and another called the Hawghtes with appurtenances, lying within the township of Penkhull, now in the tenure of the aforesaid John Huchen to the use and behoof of John Fenton and his assigns.*

Having and holding the aforesaid to the aforesaid John Fenton and his assigns from the feast of St. Michael the Archangel (29th September) which shall be in the year of our Lord 1562 until the end of the term of 30 years from the next following and to be fully completed.

The View of frankpledge dated 3rd October 1567 refers to lands seized by the Court Reeve for non-payment of rent due to the Lord.
Richard Tunstall, collector of rents for the Queen, lord of the manor, says that on 30th September 1567 one messuage with all lands, tenements, meadows, feedings and pastures belonging to the said messuage in Penkhull in the possession or occupation of Thomas Tyttensor, son of John Tyttensor deceased, (which Thomas formerly had upon a surrender by Ralph Bagnall, knight, in this court) was seized and taken into the hands of the lady the Queen, in the presence of John Ames, Thomas Dawson, Ranulph Boothes and Richard Meare, customary tenants of the manor.

In the next entry we read of land passing into the hands of the Dale family.

28th May 1580 *Randle Booths surrenders a messuage, a hemp yard, a pasture called Trenthay, 6 butts of land in Bearswall waste and a half day math of meadow near a wood called Castyll cliff in Penkhull or Bothen.*
To Roger Dale and Emma Dale his wife for their lives, at the yearly rent of one red rose for the first eight years of the term, and afterwards 12s a year and two capons at Christmas, and a heriot at the decease of each of them if Emma outlives her husband, and they are to pay and do all services and duties, and keep the property in effective repair, and do not waste (cause destruction), nor assign any part without consent. Roger and Emma admitted. Fine 12d.

The next entry is one of many which refer to land in Penkhull, which was being transferred to the Dale family.
11th December 1598 *Robert Wood surrenders a close or pasture called New leasow and one close or pasture called Townsend in Penkhull in the holding of Robert or his assigns.*

To John Dale and his assigns for the lives of Elizabeth Baddeley, Jane Baddeley and John Baddeley children of John Baddeley of Knutton deceased and whoever of them lives the longer, paying yearly to Randle Bothes and his heirs 2s during the term, provided that if Randle pays £60 to Robert Wood on any Michaelmas day during the term at Robert Wood's dwelling-house in Knutton, then this surrender is to be void. Dale admitted. Fine 3s 4d.

From Elizabeth we now move to that of James 1st.
11 Feb 1607/8   Settlement by Randall Woodcocke to his wife Ann for her life *a tenement or cottage and all his lands in Penkhull and Bothen in the holding of Lawrence Willat, and half of a messuage and half of all lands in Penkhull and Bothen in the holding of himself, Margaret Tittensor, widow, Roger Dale, John Machin, Nicholas Barrett and Joan Baddeley, widow; fine 3s*

I wish there was more time to investigate the following entry in detail as it refers to Turner's being of ancient date. Turner's stood on the current site of Jeremy Close, where previously stood Penkhull Square. There are records of the early 19th century to indicate that an ancient messuage owned by Turner was demolished to make way for Penkhull Square, the foundations for which were discovered during the excavation of the site for Jeremy Close. I recall they were hurriedly covered over so not to delay building work. But first let us look at the entry and then come back afterwards with more points.
13th March 1606 *William Turner senior and Agnes Turner his wife surrender a messuage and all lands, tenements, meadows, feedings and pastures in Penkhull, Bothen and Clayton, now in the holding of Thomas Turner, his father; and two cottages with all the lands belonging to them in Penkhull in the holding of Thomas Fenton alias Chismaye and Bartholomew Hewitt; and*

a messuage and all lands, tenements, meadows, feedings and pastures in Penkhull and Bothen, now in the holding of William or one of his assigns; and a cottage and adjoining yard in Penkhull in the holding of William Harding to William Turner, son and heir apparent of William, his heirs and assigns for ever. Admitted. Fine 19s.

Note. Turner had anciently one messuage and lands of his own inheritance in Penkhull which stood northward over against John Bowyers house which is now taken down and removed away by Dale, but a barn yet stands there; It is said that very anciently John Hassalls house which stands upon a part of that land was the chief meese place, but I conceive at the time of the present surrender, it was reckoned as a cottage and that Thomas Fenton alias Chismaye did dwell there, and that Bartholomew Huett did then and long after dwell in the other cottage at Penkhull bank, which is now the inheritance of Richard Fenton.

A note written in the margin of this document reads: 24th April 1579 Also the aforesaid William Turner senior by marrying Agnes the daughter and heir of Roger Huchen had another messuage and lands in Penkhull, which was Hutchens' in the Lane, and also with some of the lands thereto belonging now is the inheritance of Thomas Dale of the Greenhead.

Where Harding's cottage was at the time is not clear. The meaning of 'chief meese place' refers to land intended to be occupied, or actually occupied, as a site for a dwelling house. In modern legal language, a dwelling house with its outbuildings and adjacent land assigned to its use. So, the interpretation is that John Hassell's messuage was built on part of the land that was intended and set apart for that purpose. Bowyer's meadow was the land on the left at the top of Penkhull New Road where some thirty years ago Deaconess Smee discovered some old cut sandstone blocks in her garden, The Views. One reference is certain 'Green Head' that refers to the large farmhouse situated at the head of the village green, (Head of Green) this now forms the basis of the current Greyhound Inn. It is known that the family of Dale lived there for over a century but I will return to this when the history of that place is discussed.

The last entry for the time of James 1st refers to land at Hunters Croft and the area known as Bearshill, which is the area at the end of Hunters Way and covers the current road of Brisley Hill. The land known as Townsend until the 19th century is on the north side of Newcastle Lane where the newsagent is situated. Note that the names of Turner and Dale appear once more in an entry: 15th May 1621. William Turner and Agnes Turner his wife surrender a close called Smeyfield in Penkhull containing by estimation 1½ acres. To Hugh Benson and Alice Benson his wife. Admitted. Fine 6d.

We return to the Court Roll of 1606. William Turner and Agnes Turner his wife surrender two closes called the Bruthens and the Bruthens lakes meadow containing by estimation 4½ acres in Penkhull to Roger Dale junior, son of Roger Dale, his heirs and assigns for ever. Roger Dale junior admitted. Fine 2s.

William Turner and Agnes Turner his wife surrender a close called New Leasowe, one close called the Townsend and another close called the Hunters croft in Penkhull to themselves for their respective lives, with remainder to their son Thomas Turner, his heirs and assigns for ever. William, Agnes and Thomas admitted. Fine 5s 6d.

The same William Turner surrenders one messuage with all the lands belonging called backsides, and one close called Bearshill, two parcels of land called the waste as they now lie, and one parcel of land called the Bothen heath in Penkhull, in the holding of Agnes Turner his mother. To Agnes Turner his wife for her life. Fine 18d.

The next survey dated 31st October 1615 is found in John Ward's history of Stoke-on-Trent 1843. (Appendix xxii). The survey is a huge piece of work listing every plot of land together with its tenants. It is twenty-eight pages long but Ward only summarises the totals. However, to enable the reader to have a glimpse of the survey I list below the entry for the largest landowner in Penkhull at that time, Roger Machin.

The opening comments are interesting. We present and say that we have called before us the copyholders of this manor, and do find there several copyhold lands to be anciently held and enjoyed by copy of the court roll to them and their heirs. And that every year once the steward of the manor court has sworn four freehold and copyhold tenants to assess and write down such fines as have been due to the King.

Roger Machin son of Roger to him and his heirs by Copy of Court Roll and pays 35s 7¼d One messuage and a half messuage with appurtenances six closes called the new fields containing in arable and pasture 15 acres two Crofts called the Over and Lower crofts containing arable and pasture 2 acres. Two closes called the Acres. 2 acres and one called the Plat Hill Acre, containing arable 1 acre and in the other 3 acres. One close called Spittle Croft containing in arable and pasture 3 acres. One meadow called Steales meadow containing 2 acres, six closes called Knoolles containing in arable and pasture 11 acres. One meadow called Rid meadow containing in meadow 1 acre. Two parts of one Messuage called Bates House, a Hemp Butt. A croft of arable containing 1 acre and one close called Townsend, arable and pasture 2 acres. Certain land on a close called Hough Acres, and one close called Eight Acres Meadow. Trent leasow and one called the Homme, containing arable and pasture 4 acres and 52 acres of arable and pasture. Two parts of one close called the *common peace, one butt in Collinsmore flat, and two butts in Trent leasow containing in arable containing ½ acre. One Croft called the Waste containing in arable and pasture 1 acre. One meadow called the Lowke meadow, a parcel of one meadow called Stanwall and one meadow, the waste meadow adjoining to Fowley in meadow. 2 acres. One half messuage and lands thereto adjoining containing in arable and pasture 2½ acres. Certain Land in Collinsmore and Collinsmore flatt containing arable and pasture 4 acres. One croft called little Hordow containing arable ½ an acre and 1 rode. One dole, in doles meadow containing 1 rode. Two Closes, called Swarstons Hayes or Harriesfield containing in arable and past 5 acres. The value in rent amounted to £1 15s 7¼d.*

John Terrick, a name previously mentioned is the next largest land owner with 38 acres, paying an annual rental of £1 3s 4d, followed by that of Roger and John Dale at 25 acres and having an annual value of 14s 8d.

There are over forty-two names listed in the survey but as the whole document includes the districts of Stoke, Hartshill and Boothen it is difficult in some cases to distinguish which plots actually belong to the village of Penkhull. One needs to remember at the time of this survey all this area would be called Penkhull.

The next surveys of 1618 follow on quickly and is dated the following year, 1619. It is found in the County Record Office dated the 16th year in the reign of James 1st.

List of rental for the Manor of Newcastle-under-Lyme for the 16th year of James 1st (1618) - Penkhull
Ralph Keeling - late Agnes his wife 1 acre; Stephen Hales 5 acres; Thomas Bagnold late of Randall Leigh's 5 acres; Thomas Jennings for ¼ and ⅛ acre; Robert Rodes ⅛ acre; Thomas Brome 9½ acres; John Terrick (Gent) 36½ acres; Richard Bagnold 3 acres; Ralph Caldwall late John Caterall 8 acres; William Hume 8 acres; William Boulton 8 acres; John Machin 2 acres; William Hall 4 acres; Thomas Tittensor the younger 17 acres; Thomas Fenton 16 acres; Ralph Keeling 1 acre; John Brownsword a tenement late of William Knight Ann, Elizabeth, Jane, Katherine, the daughters to Thomas Bagnall late of Thomas 8 acres; John Boothes ½ acre; Thomas Barrett 18 acres; Nicholas Barrett 3 acres; John Barrett 1 acre; John Riggs 1½ acres; Thomas Rawlins in Penkhull and Shelton 17 acres; Randall Bagnall of Cheadle 2 acres; Roger Dale 23½ acres; Thomas Crompton Esq. 22 acres; Roger Machin - son of Roger Machin 60 acres; Francis Lisatt - son of Thomas and the said Thomas 10 acres; William Turner, John Dale and Thomas Barnett 39 acres; Randall Woodcock 15 acres; Roger Machin - son of John Machin 30 acres; Joan Machin – widow 4 acres; James Hudson 1 acre; Roger Dale - late of Thomas Hutchin ¼ acre; Edward Master (Gent) and Kathleen his wife 1 acre and Thomas Hunt 1½ acres.

From this survey a clear picture created is who were the main land occupiers of that time.

Roger Machin remains the largest landowner with 60 acres followed by John Terrick with 36½ acres and Roger Dale who was tenant of 24 acres. His brother John shared land amounting to 39 acres with William Turner and Thomas Barnett, all are names that we frequently come across in court transactions.

Following the execution of Charles 1st on the 30th January 1649 all former crown lands, estate and possessions were to be disposed of by an Act of Parliament dated 16th July 1649 which was one of the first fruits of the Cromwellian army's political mastery of England and represented the first effective measures to eliminate military pay arrears. A quarter of former crown lands were sold to civilians, while the other three-quarters remained in military hands, namely the officer class. Sir Richard Leveson was the steward of the Manor of Newcastle during the time of Charles 1st but following the execution of Charles the manor was handed over by Cromwell to his second in command Major General Thomas Harrison a native of Newcastle.

After the restitution Harrison was executed as a Regicide. All the former lands belonging to the crown were valued prior to the sale or transfer. In June 1650 the manor of Newcastle was valued. The original valuation is located in the National Archives. (E317/Staffs 38) In 1654 Thomas Bagnall, the Town Clerk of Newcastle was appointed by Harrison to the office of Steward of the former royal manor. As a result the benefits and income of the manor were handed over to Major General Thomas Harrison. *(A later chapter on manorial courts will highlight the attendance at such courts of Major General Thomas Harrison.)*

It was during the Commonwealth period that a further survey was carried out to the extent and value of the former Royal Manor. It was done under an Act of Parliament dated June 1650: *A Survey of the Manor of Newcastle under Lyme being in the County of Stafford late parcel of the possessions of Charles Stewart late king of England in Right of the Dutchie of Lancaster made and taken by us whose names are hereunto subscribed in the month of June one thousand six hundred and fifty by virtue of a Commission granted upon an Act of the Commons assembled in Parliament for sale of the Honours Manors and Lands heretofore belonging to the late King Queen and Prince under the hands and seals of five or more of the Trustees in the said Act named and appointed.*

Ralph Keeling late James Till and Agnes his wife for one acre; Stephen Hales for five acres; Thomas Bagnall for five acres; Thomas Jennings for the fourth and eight part of an acre; Robert Rodes for the eight part of an acre; Thomas Browne for nine acre and a half; Ralph Caldwall for eight acre late John Caldwalls, William Hume for eight acres; William Bolton for three acres; John Machin for two acres and a half; John Terrick gent for thirty six acres and a half; Richard Bagnall for three acres; William Hall for two acres; Thomas Tittensor jun. for seventeen acres; Thomas Fenton for sixteen acres; Ralph Keeling for one acre; John Brownsword for a tenement late William Knight; John Rigg for one acre and a half; Ann, Elizabeth, Jane and Katherine Daughters and Coheirs of Thomas Bagnall for eight acres; late the said Thomas John Boothes for half an acre; Thomas Rawlins for seventeen acres in Shelton and Penkhull; Thomas Barrett for eighteen acres; Nicholas Barrett for three acres; John Barrett for one acre; Randall Bagnall of Cheadle for two acres; Thomas Crompton Esq. for twenty acres; Roger Dale for twenty three and a half acres; Roger Machin, son of Roger Machin for thirty six acres; Francis Lysat son of Thomas Lysat for fourteen acres; William Turner, John Dale and Thomas Barrett for forty nine acres; Randall Woodcock for fifteen acres; Roger Machin son of John Machin for thirty acres; Joan Machin widow for four acres; James Hudson for one acre; Thomas Hunt for one acre and a half; Roger Dale for a quarter of an acre; Edward Muster (or Master) gent and Katherine his wife one acre.

The two lists that of 1618 and 1650, despite there being thirty-two years between them, are almost identical. The only significant land change is associated with Frances Lisatt or Lysat where a difference of four acres is recorded. Even so during the intervening years there is a significant number of copyhold transactions listed in the court rolls. Perhaps, therefore it may be assumed that the new list was almost copied from that of 1618, the appraisers not being content with the new Parliamentarian authority over the former royal manor. The following are just a few entries extracted from the court rolls as a taster from the time of Charles 1st, and during the Commonwealth period.

21st June 1625 *Roger Dale senior surrenders a cottage or tenement in which he now lives with all buildings belonging to it, a garden a croft called the backside, two parcels of land lying together called the Cliffs, the Stonewall croft meadow, one butt of land in Collinsmore, three butts of land in the Highcroft head, two pieces of land called New Peace & Further Flatt, a parcel of meadowing called Akford meadow, two parcels of land called Highomes, and one parcel of land called Plat hill in Penkhull. To his son Roger Dale and Margery Dale, his son's wife, for their lives, with remainder to the heirs begotten between them, with remainder to the heirs to be begotten by Roger the son, with remainder to Margaret daughter of Roger the father and the heirs of her body to be begotten, with remainder to the right heirs of Roger the son for ever. Roger Dale and his wife Margery Dale admitted. Fine 5ˢ 7ᵈ.*

6th February 1626 John Terrick senior and Elizabeth Terrick surrender 5 butts and 2 pykes of arable land in Tunstall field on High croft bank containing by estimation half an acre of land in Penkhul to John Doody, his heirs and assigns for ever. Fine 1ᵈ.

John Terrick senior and Elizabeth Terrick surrender a croft called Smeafield croft between Roger Machin's Stonewall meadow and the highway and one butt of arable land with part of two balks adjoining in Plat hill on the north side in Penkhull. To William Hunt, his heirs and assigns forever. Fine 3ᵈ.

We now move on to a further snapshot, this time to the Commonwealth period. First of all the traditional introductions to the court records have changed by act of parliament from the 'Lord of the Manor' to that of the 'Custodians of the Liberty of England'.

1st day of November 1649 (DL30/240/1) Small Court of the said Manor held at Penckhull. To this Court comes German Tittensor, and surrendered into the hands of the Custodians of the liberty of England by act of parliament. One meadow called Ridd Meadow, with the appurtenances in the occupation of Nicholas Woodcock, lying in Penckhull aforesaid, to the use and behoof of Richard Cooke.

However, if the said German, his heirs executors or administrators, pay or cause to be paid to the said Richard Cooke, his executors or administrators, the sum of £30 of legal money of England, on the 2nd day of February which will be in the year of our Lord 1658, at or within the mansion house of Henry Stevenson in Penckhull, or within the space of ten days next after the said 2nd day of February 1658, then and henceforth this present surrender shall be void and of no value, this present surrender not withstanding.

It is interesting to read that there was a Mansion House in Penkhull belonging to Henry Stevenson but unfortunately despite their being a number of references to this, its location cannot be identified.

The next three entries are dated 1656. By now it was the court of Thomas Harrison Esq., held of his manor. He was also referred to as the Lord of the Manor. Thomas Bagnall from Newcastle was the Steward.

A Small Court of Thomas Harrison Esq., held of his manor of Newcastle-under-Lyme at Penkhull within the said manor the 15th day of October in the year of our lord, one thousand, six hundred, fifty and six before Thomas Bagnall, gent, steward there.

To this court comes Jane Terrick, widow by Richard Bradshaw her attorney by virtue of a letter of attorney to him and to Richard Boulton being the date bearing the date the first day of October and now showed in Court and surrender into the hands of the Lord of the manor, one close called Green Croft, one other close called the Little Croft lying at the bottom of Out lane situated in Penkhull within the said manor and now in the occupation of the said Jane to the use and behoof of Walter Bagnall from the first day of October last for and during the said term of forty years if Elizabeth Brereton, wife of William Brereton of Swynnerton, gent so long shall live by the rents and services therefore due. And at the same court comes Walter Bagnall and taketh possession thereof by the rod to have and to hold etc. for the term of the said forty years and giveth to the lord for his fine two pence and is admitted tenant. (Green Croft is situated where Beech Grove stands and Outlane was the old name given for Franklin Road).

To this court cometh Roger Machin in his own person and surrenders into the hands of the lord one parcel of land called Bearswall croft situated in Penkhull now in the occupation of Roger Machin to the use and behoof of Thomas Ruffell his heirs and assigns etc. provided always that of the said Roger Machin or his assigns etc. or anyone of them do or shall well and truly pay unto the said Thomas Ruffell the sum of twenty one pounds and four shillings of lawful English money at or upon the sixteenth day of October which shall be in the year of the Lord God, one thousand six hundred and fifty and seven at or in the church porch of Stoke-upon-Trent then this surrender be voyd and there upon at the same court comes Thomas Ruffell and desireth seizin of the said premises to whom the Lord granteth seizin by the rod and pays his fine of eight pence and is admitted. (Bearswall Croft covers the area now known as Brisley Hill and Hunters Way. For where the money was to be paid, in the porch of Stoke Parish Church this would be chosen as a public place, on public view for confirmation of payment).

Between the years 1520 and 1700, the population of England rose from between two and a half to five million. This is viewed by many academics as phenomenal, the product of better economic conditions leading to younger marriages, and thereby a higher marital fertility, coupled with a drop in mortality rates.

Penkhull, seen as wedged between the expanding market town of Newcastle to the west and a string of pottery producing hamlets to the north and east was an ideal location for surplus population that could not easily be absorbed into the humble industrial conurbations. The six towns of the Potteries gradually became incapable of accommodating the increasing demand of migrants from the countryside for work. The number of congested towns of the Potteries consisted in the vast majority of squares or hovels, back to back adjacent to the bottle ovens. Their daily dose of thick black smoke from the ovens polluted all within five hundred yards. There were cesspits brimming over, no running water, and the stench of filth and disease covering many areas. As in the rest of Europe, the plague was an affliction every few years. In 1647, there was a visitation of the plague to the Potteries and Newcastle bringing suffering so great that the County Justices levied a rate on all the neighbouring towns for the relief of the afflicted. There is no evidence found in Stoke church records of any significant increase in the death rate but just four years later in 1651, the return of the plague to Stoke saw a 30% increase of deaths in Penkhull alone.

As the thriving town of Newcastle and the pottery hamlets grew, the demand for foodstuffs increased. The farmers of Penkhull situated on the periphery of the towns, were ideally situated to supply the increasing needs. Seeking a chance of employment in the district was an increasing flow of newcomers claiming the right to use the manorial waste, those small pieces of land on the side of the road not already in copyhold tenure, where it was not possible to cultivate because of thistle, un-even ground or rocks.

The issue found throughout the manor was but a reflection of a great national problem. In 1589 the Cottages Act was implemented to deal with the very problem found in almost every area, and the burden it presented to small rural communities such as Penkhull. The main provision of the Act was that no cottage was to be erected or a conversion made unless the person assigns and adds to the cottage four acres of ground which was to be continually occupied and manured so long as the same cottage was to be inhabited, or a fine of 10s made for every offence. The large amount of land required was to ensure that any resident would not become a burden upon the poor rate.

The declared purpose of the statue was to halt the number of cottages being erected but it was considered that the real intention was to refuse accommodation to undesirables. The manor of Newcastle is one of the few manors that implemented this Act to any degree. The first record for Penkhull dated 27th May 1611 when the court agreed *to lay a paine upon all the copyhold tenants within the manor that they shall take noe strangers into their houses except they have been three yeares resident within the said manor, or else they shall put in sufficient sureties to discharge the parish of them upon paine of any one offending to forfeit xxxixs xid. And likewise lay a paine upon all the copyhold tenants that they shall avoyd all such tenants as they have lately received betwixt this and the feast of St. John next under the paine of any one that offendeth to forefite xxxxixs xid likewise.*

The second entry is dated the 28th April 1612 appears harsh. The frankpledges present *that Isabel Bourne, widow lately received John Woodward into her house as a wanderer despite a paine of 39s 11d.* At the same court present *that John Gilbert; senior received into a cottage Thomas Bayly and George Trotte as inmates, contrary to the statue. Fined 10d.* 9th October 1638 *The frankpledges present that John Benson erected a cottage contrary to the form in which Margaret Harding, widow now lives, and therefore she is in mercy.*

By the following entry it would appear that the problem for the manor was increasing. 4th October 1650 *Presented that George Hales and Robert Hales erected a cottage contrary to the statute in which John Tyler lives and several inmates. Fined 12d each and that that Thomas Stanley and Richard Stanley both erected a cottage. Fined 12d each. And that Robert Cotgreave find 12d because he made an incroachment and that William Sympson find 12d because he erected a cottage.* There are many other presentations for this period but the next entry shows that others outside the manor of Newcastle were often in conflict. *They present Robert Butterton who lives outside the manor has burdened the inhabitants of Seabridge in the fields with his beasts, find 12d.*

It appears that any new cottages should have been erected to standards approved by the steward of the manor, for at a court held at Penkhull also in April 1616: *Roger Machin and Joan Machin erected a cottage contrary to the statue in which Richard Taylor now lives.* Again, in October 1638 *came John Bedson and Henry Stevenson who had erected a cottage contrary to the form of the statute.* In some communities it was often the case that if a poor man could build himself a cottage on the waste of a manor overnight, he could occupy it un-disturbed. There are also other entries that give a day-to-day account of life such as the following entry which also gives one of the first entries that present the case for early industrialisation of the area: *At the same court the following entry they present that Thomas Tyttensor and Thomas Turner dug a marl pit on the King's highway in Penkhull to the great hurt and danger of the villagers.*

As an absentee landlord, the Duchy of Lancaster owned the Manor of Newcastle squatters took advantage even though a steward was appointed to oversee land administration. Evidence of the extent of this can ascertained from court records of fines being charges on those exploiting the situation. In 1671 the steward presented twelve squatters to the court who had encroached onto the Lord's waste and erected cottages.
Name, amount and fine. *William Barlow 0s 6d; Thomas Byrd 2s 0d; Henry Cooper 1s 0d; Thomas Ward 4d; John Weston 8d; John Hewitt 10d; John Machin 1s 0d; John Webber 1s 0d; William Webb 1s 0d; Peter Gillworth 1s 0d; Thomas Edge 4d and Ralph Cooper 4d.*

No indication is given as to how the fines were calculated but the list divides neatly into three distinctive categories. Thomas Byrd who was fined two shillings and six pence, five squatters were fined one shilling, and six who were fined only a few pence. Fines that were charged in other districts show similar grouping and values. Unfortunately the manorial copyhold records do not list any of the names

recorded as being fined after 1671. It would therefore appear that those listed would have been sub-tenants and not the copyhold tenants.

The baptism records for Stoke Parish Church show that Messrs Byrd, Cooper, Machin and Webber were all recorded as being born locally and by 1671 had attained the ages between sixteen and thirty-five. The fine of two shillings and six pence upon Thomas Byrd stands out as substantial by comparison. He was the son of William and Eliza Byrd and baptised in 1636. The Byrd family of Penkhull were early potters of the district.

For the district of Shelton there were forty three encroachments and for Seabridge three but others were recorded as fined for *keeping swine un-ringed and un-yoked, for not cleaning out ditches and causing a nuisance on the path to the church.* There were also eight fined 4d each for breaking the assize of ale.

It was not only squatters that claimed manorial waste. The following entry shows that existing copyhold tenants extended their boundaries without permission.
At a court held on 14th April, Charles II 33 (1682) the frankpledges Thomas Tyttensor; Thomas Blakeman; John Fenton; Tithingmen, present that Richard Massey; Henry Cooper senior; Ann Byrd, widow; Jane Barlow, widow; John Walton; John Machin; Thomas Ward; William Webb and Peter Gilworth as copyhold tenants were fined for encroaching on the Lord's waste land.

Others were also presented to the same court for erecting property on the Lord's waste. *They were separately held in mercy for as much as appears over their heads.* These are words used in court records which means that the amount fined written above their name on the court roll. By 1686, further cases appeared at a Court Leet held in Penkhull: 2 James 11 (1686) The tithing men present *(fourteen names given)* who enclosed part of the Lord's waste, a fine of two pence to be charged as above their heads. Domestic disagreements between copyhold tenants of the manor were also heard at a Court Leet held at Penkhull. The subjects of such courts are clearly identified: 4th May Charles II 23 (1682) *They present that John Dale of Penkhull for forestalling the way in the park between the park gate and several places of waste in Penkhull. A fine of twenty shillings on John Terrick and Andrew Corbett for failing to lop and crop hedges and scour their ditches in Penkhull.* This is an interesting entry confirming that a royal park from mediaeval times was still being upheld.

The last document we look at under this category is a map entitled 'A Plan of Cottages and Encroachments in the Liberty of Penkhull belonging to the Duchy of Lancaster in the County of Stafford 1777'.

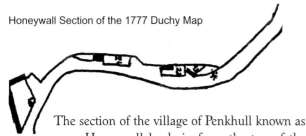

Honeywall Section of the 1777 Duchy Map

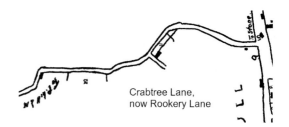

Crabtree Lane, now Rookery Lane

The section of the village of Penkhull known as Honeywall leads in from the top of the map from Stoke to Penkhull Green, following down what is now Newcastle Lane to the A34. A small number of cottages, which have encroached upon the Lord's waste, are identified by a reference number, which corresponds with a list of names. It was drawn up in preparation for the renewal of the Lease of the manor to from the Duchy of Lancaster to the Rt. Hon. Granville Leveson Earl Gower of Trentham in 1781.

However, by the third quarter of the eighteenth century considerable growth of the pottery industry was attracting migrant workers both from the land and from other industrial towns. There became an urgent need for housing to accommodate the ever-increasing numbers and not to house them was considered a threat to the growth of the pottery industry.

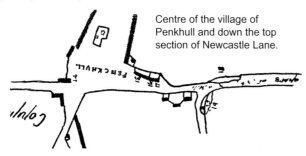

Centre of the village of Penkhull and down the top section of Newcastle Lane.

The existing expansion onto the waste of the manorial land in the districts of Penkhull and Shelton increased the annual rentals. A memorandum dated the 2nd day of March 1781 attached to the Duchy plans dated 1777 states that the rent would be set at a tenth part of the annual value of properties elsewhere.

The reason for this reduction was that the buildings had been erected on the waste by and at the expense of the reputed owners thereof with permission of the Duchy of Lancaster. Furthermore, the document refers to the fact that the local inhabitants would not have suffered the waste being used for building if the benefit had been for the Crown, but as it benefited the increase of trade and commerce it was agreed to.

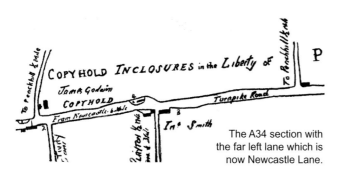

The A34 section with the far left lane which is now Newcastle Lane.

Those properties shown as thick lines are existing cottages and barns belonging to copyholders and paying rental to the Duchy:

1. Richard Knapper, a house and garden, 2. James Godwin, house and encroachments, 3. James Godwin, an encroachment; 4. Richard Marlow, house and garden; 5. John Smith; 6. Sam. Glover a garden; 7. John Tomlinson, house and garden; 8. John Shaw, house and garden; 9. John Shaw, an encroachment; 10. Robert Bill, a cow house, 11. Widow Hulse, a garden; 12. In. Emery, an encroachment; 13. Josh. Botham, a house and garden, 14. John Slaney, Smiths shop; 15. James Burne, three houses and a garden; 16. William Fox, one house and a garden; 17. John Hancock, a house and a garden; 18. Geo Cowper, garden; 19. Margaret Cowper, house and a garden; 20. Waley an encroachment and 21. Thomas Appleton, house and garden.

On the original document, found written next to occupier of the property is the name of the road where the names appear No's 1-19 are on the side of the great Turnpike Road leading from London to Liverpool. However at the side of No's 10-12 it reads – *These are in Crabtree Lane leading from Penkhull to the above turnpike road.* Crabtree Lane commences with what is Rookery Lane leading into Trent Valley Road. The list above also points to the fact that there were a total of six encroachments upon the lord's land. Copyhold tenants for the Manor of Newcastle-under-Lyme did not hold the same rights and privileges of land tenure as freehold farmers elsewhere. The situation became so strained that the fullest declaration of the customary rights of the manorial copyholders was decided at a Copyhold Court Baron, held at Penkhull in 1714.The following copyholders sit as the jury.

Samuel Machin, Gent,	Thomas Machin
Joshua Twyford	Thomas Doody, Gent,
John Moreton,	David Edwards,
Thomas Lea Gent,	Ralph Moreton,
Thomas Keeling,	Thomas Lovatt,
Richard Fenton,	Joshua Stevenson,
Thomas Machin,	John Adams,
Thomas Stevens.	

To this court comes John Fenton, John Terrick and Richard Beech being copyholders, or customary tenants, of the Manor and with several other copyholders or customary tenants of the said Manor, who desired that a special jury enquired into several customs of the Manor. This was granted as follows:

1. Power to make wills without surrender of land to the Lord of the Manor. 2. Wife, one third unless surrender during

lifetime of copyholder, or wife has dower. 3. Entail. *(This means that the property could only be passed to direct descendants, often only the male.)* 4. Copyhold lands may be let for three years without surrender. 5. Transfers. 6. Power of Attorney. 7. Absence from Court. 8. Costs. 9. To the ninth article the jurors upon their oaths present and say that anciently and from the time whereof the memory of man is not to the contrary, the following course and method has been kept and observed with respect to the service of the office of Reeve within the manor. They say with regard to the service of the office the manor is divided into three parts whereof Penkhull and Boothen make one, Shelton and Hanley make another, Clayton and Seabridge and Wolstanton make a third, and that the office of Reeve goes its round making a perpetual circle through the three parts of the manor successively. They further say and present upon oath that according to the evidence now produced to them there are in parts of the manor consisting firstly of Penkhull with Boothen seventeen ancient messuages or places to which the office of Reeve is and time out of mind has been incident so named in order. According to their antiquity in point of service beginning with that which served the longest time since and is to serve again the next time, the office of Reeve falls into that part of the manor.

In the above a number of words have been changed to bring the language up to date. The most important fact is that the information is based clearly upon what had always been *'from a time that was so long ago it had been forgotten'.* This was probably referring from at least the time of Domesday or even earlier when only seventeen tenants were recorded. By 1714, there were far more than seventeen tenants in the area of Penkhull and Boothen as the court records bear witness, but it was only those seventeen of ancient tenure who held the right to become an official of the court.

The record continued to lists each messuage, with a brief description; the name of the owner and in some instances the previous copyhold tenant. In isolation, this list may be considered to be of little value for researchers but if it is used as a link from what facts we have, it then enables information from previous documents to be identified. One such document is the Reeve Book.

Until recently it was thought that the only Reeve Book which has survived was located in the National Archives and records those who served the office of Reeve from as early as 1657 until 1836. However, quite by chance an earlier book came to light at the County Records Office at Stafford hidden away under the title of 'Fenton's Law Book'. This discovery contains an earlier list of those holding the office of Reeve, the first dating from 1572. However the format is very different from the later Reeve book in as much that it would appear that the Reeve would serve the whole of the

manor and not just the township of Penkhull with Boothen. The later book was distinguished by each township being identified separately and the person serving the office for which year. This discovery enables the assessment to go back further to the third quarter of the 16th century with regards to who occupied each of the seventeen ancient messuages.

The Reeve Book provides a brief description of each ancient messuage (seventeen), its current copyhold tenant and if sub-let, the occupier. The two Reeve books together with the 1714 listing enables a comparison to be made of land, estate, occupancy and value. As a result a fairly accurate picture of the layout of the village can be ascertained, both in 1714 back to the 16th century and up to the early 19th century. It provides a snapshot of Penkhull until the office of Reeve ceased in 1835. The locality of these messuages recorded in all three documents has probably remained static for several centuries, possibly from the time of Domesday as seventeen farmers and homesteads were listed from this date. The following identifies the messuages by number, followed by the appropriate Reeve Book entry, with a final comment as to where this property would lie today.

1st 1714 - First a place called the Bear yard, adjoining to William Machin's over-croft.
Fenton's Book - 1663 Robert Machin for his messuage which formerly was his grandfather's which is now pulled down, heretofore called Little Beare Yard. 1716 Mr Thomas Machin for Beare Yard, served by George Machin his father, and served for before 1663.
Reeve Book - *An ancient messuage called Beare Yard of late Mr Machin's now Mr Whaley's. This messuage is now down, the site is now a hollow place at the top of Hunters Croft and opposite Mr Spode's square erected upon Turner's messuage.* (On land opposite Jeremy Close*).

2nd 1714 - A toft or meese place, where a messuage, formerly called Turner's and Ingram's stood, now in the holding of Thomas Dale and adjoining to Nelson's yard.
Fenton's Book - 1666 Thomas Dale for old Turner's alias Ingram's house in Penkhull being one of his three services in Penkhull. 1719 Thomas Dale for one of his services, viz an house formerly Ingram's, and served for before viz.1666.
Reeve Book - *An ancient messuage formerly Turner and Ingram's now Mr Joseph Bourne's. This stands adjoining the poor house belongs to John Chapman sold by him to Spode. This is now pulled down and land sold by Spode to the poor house.* (Site of the current Donald Bates House, off Garden Street).

3rd 1714 - A place called the Hunters croft-head, now belonging to Roger Machin, father of the said Thomas.
Fenton's Book - 1669 Thomas Dale for an ancient messuage standing heretofore in Hunters Croft being his third service. This is now sold to Roger Machin. 1772 Rebecca Machin,

widow of Roger Machin, for the Hunters Croft Head in Penckhull, formerly served for 1669; executed by Cleaton Lea.

Reeve Book - *An ancient messuage called Hunters Croft Head formerly Machin's now Mr Whaley's. This is near the poor house in the crofts of this name and now held by Mr Thomas Wolfe.* (Probably the site of the old school, now Penkhull Church Hall).

4th 1714 - A toft whereon a messuage lately stood, lately belonging to John Bowyer and now belonging to John Terrick and now a part of Orchid Meadow.

Fenton's Book – 1672 John Bowyer Junr. For his father's house. 1725 John Terrick for the messuage in Penkhull lately by him purchased of John Bowyer, served for before 1672.

Reeve Book - *An ancient messuage formerly Bowyer's now Mr Terrick's. This is taken down it was in the meadow where Michael Henney's house stands. Several houses on the meadow. Daniel Greatbatch's house stands on the site of the old messuage.* (This is the site of The Views, just off Penkhull New Road).

5th 1714 - A messuage, formerly Fenton's and now belonging to Thomas Doody.

Fenton's Book - Thomas Doody junr. For his own house in Penkhull. 1728 John Doody for his messuage in Penkhull, served for before 1675; served now by Mr Jenkinson.

Reeve Book - *An ancient messuage formerly Thomas Doody now Mr Joseph Bourne. This house is where John Chapman lives now purchased by Mr Spode.* (This is the site current Victoria House in St. Thomas Place).

6th 1714 - A messuage formerly Baddeley's and now belonging to and inhabited by the said John Terrick.

Fenton's Book - 1624 Mr Jon Terrick for Badeley's messuage in Penckhull served by Cranage Wilcockson. 1678 John Terrick of Penckhull for his messuage anciently one Badeley's served by Richard Cartwright of Fowlea at the wages of £2 15s.

Reeve Book - *An ancient messuage formerly Baddeley now Mr Terrick's. This is near to Mr Joseph Booth's house late in the holding of Thomas Swinnerton but now of Machin.* (This is an area situated at the top of Doncaster Lane)

7th 1714 - A messuage formerly belonging to John Dale and now belonging to Joseph Bourne.

Fenton's Book - 1627 Roger Dale for John Dale's messuage in Penckhull. 1681 John Dale for Draw Well House served by Richard Cartwright of Flowlea at the wages of £3 beside the aforesaid 24s. 1734 Mr Wm Bourne of Chess for the Draw Well House, served by Thomas Marsh before 1681.

Reeve Book - *An ancient messuage called Drawwell formerly Dales now Mr Alsager's. This was Harvey Boulton's now held by Mr Spode.* (This Alsager's now. Penkhull Farm, Harvey Boulton was a tenant farmer)

8th 1714 - A messuage formerly belonging to Roger and John Tittensor now belonging to Daniel Edwards.

Fenton's Book - 1630 William Hill for Thomas Tittensor's messuage down in the Towne. 1684 Roger and John Tittensor his sonne for their messuage in Penckhull served by Richard Cartwright at the wages last aforesaid; this was the Tittensor downe in the towne of Penckhull. 1737 Mr Pickin for his house in Penkhull, serv'd for 1684.

Reeve Book - *An ancient messuage formerly Roger Tittensor's now Mr Joseph Bourne's belonging to Chapman. This is in the possession of Gardener Burgess.* (Elm Tree House in Garden Street).

9th 1714 - Place called Bradshaw's Yard, adjoining to Penkhull Town Street.

Fenton's Book - 1633 Henry Shawe hired for Henry Stevenson to serve for Bradshawe's House and land in Penckhull. 1687 Robert Machin for Bradshaw's messuage, the messuage house long since stood in Robert Machin's yard but not within the memorie of man. Thomas Stevenson usually serveth or hireth the offices served for the said messuage because he hath most of the lands now known as being to the said messuage and he hired Thomas Dale to serve the Reeve's office for the said messuage and lands this present year, at the wages of three pounds beside 24s allowed from the Kings Auditt.

Reeve Book - *An ancient messuage called Bradshaw's Yard formerly Machin's now to be served by Mr Benjamin Lewis. Mr Spode, Bostock, Greaves and Turner. Attached note: Reeve's office for the year 1792. It comes to the turn of a messuage in Penkhull called Bradshaww's Yard formerly Machin's, afterwards of Mr Benjamin Lewis's (deleted: 'now I believe Mr Ephram was Hugh Booth's and called the Honeywall'), afterwards trustees of Taylor Lewis's, sold of to Mr Malkin and sold to Bostock, Greaves, Spode Turner.* (This additional information confirms that Bradshaw's Yard was situated at the bottom of Honeywall, formerly known by the name of Penkhull Town Street).

10th 1714 - A toft and meese place, formerly Woodcock's, now a barn belonging to the said Thomas Doody and Thomas Blakeman and for which Thomas Doody and Thomas Blakeman serve alternately.

Fenton's Book - 1636 Nicholas Woodcocke for Nickson's House and land in Penkhull. 1691 Woodcock's messuage in Penkhull, serv'd by George Hanson for the wages of three pounds six shillings and eight pence, besides the 24s due from Auditt. 1743 Mr Tho. Lovatt for a messuage in Penkhull formerly Woodcock's served before 1692 and now executed by Mr Tho Pickin. Tho. Blakeman for a message in Penkhull now belonging to Mr Lovatt of Fulford and Jon Terrick, and served by them alternately; it was formerly Halton's Nicson's and Woodcock's.

Reeve Book - *An ancient messuage formerly Woodcocks and Blakeman's Mr Joseph Booth's house stands where this messuage was.*

11th 1714 - A place called Booths', adjoining to or being part of the fold up in the town and now belonging to the said Thomas Machin.

Fenton's Book - 1639 William Hill hired Mr Jon. Terrick, Roger Machin of Bate Lake and others to serve for one of the houses and lands called Boothe's land in Penkhull. 1694 Mrs Elizabeth Machin for a messuage in Penckhull formerly Boothe's and served for before 1839. Now executed by George Hanson. 1746 *(no name quoted)* for a messuage in Penkhull now or lately Machin's and formerly Boothe's, served for before 1694 and executed now by Robert Machin for Boothe's messuage in Penkhull now Whalley's. 1799 Daniel Whalley's

Reeve Book - *An ancient messuage formerly Roger Machin's called Booths now Mr Whaley's. This is where Masgreave did live when he rented the farm, lies near Mr Spode's new stable.* (Spode's new stables that once stood at the south end of Greatbatch Avenue and the corner of Tilson Avenue).

12th 1714 - A toft called Dunross Lee, adjoining to Penkhull Town Street and the yard wherein the said demolished messuage lately Bowyers stood. This is now also belonging to the said John Terrick and is part of the orchid meadow.

Fenton's Book - 1642 Roger Machin of the Greenhead for one of Boothe's his service in Penkhull; viz for an ancient meese place called Duncott Leigh. This now belongs to Mr John Fenton of Shelton. 1698 John Bowyer for the place in Penkhull where the messuage called Duncott Leigh formerly stood; served for before Ano. 1642. 1749 Mr Terrick for Duncott Lee.

Duncott Lea, formerly Bowyers, and now Mr Terrick's. (In the area of The Views or the top of Penkhull New Road or just off Rothwell Street).

13th 1714 - A messuage formerly called Hutchins's in the town, now belonging to Samuel Astbury.

Fenton's Book - 1648 John Simkin for one of the Hutchins's of the Green his land in Penckhull now Richard Huett's House, now sold to Thomas Astbury. 1701 Thomas Astbury for ye house on ye green in Penkhull; formerly Hutchins' and serv'd for before 1648; now executed by Thomas Astbury assistente Tho. Doody, Senr. 1752 Thomas Astbury for a messuage in Penkhull, late Hitchin's, and serv'd by Henry Mountford. Thomas Astbury for a messuage in Penckhull, served by Henry Mountford; it was late Hutchin's in the town.

Reeve Book - *An ancient messuage called Hutchin's in the town, now near Catherine Asbury's, now Daniel Cotton's and in his own possession. (An area situated around the junction of Eardley and Rothwell Street.)*

14th 1714 - A messuage formerly called Turners in the lane, now belonging to the said Thomas Dale.

Fenton's Book - 1651 Roger Dale for the other Hitchin's land in Penckhull viz. Hichwen's in the land since Turner's in the lane and now Thomas Dale's. 1704 Thomas Dale for his house in Penkhull, once Hitchen's in the lane then Turner's and serv'd for before 1651.

Reeve Book - *An ancient messuage called Turners now in Mr Joseph Lovatt's. Mr Spode has purchased and pulled down this house and built 20 houses upon the site.* (This is the site of the former Penkhull Square, the current site of Jeremy Close).

15th 1714 - A toft whereon a messuage formerly stood called Hutchin's in the lane, lying over against the last mentioned messuage and now belonging to the said Roger Machin.

Fenton's Book - 1654 Robert Machins for Wood's House in Penckhull (alias Machin in the lane) served by Thomas Doody being one of his four services in Penkhull. 1707 Mr Roger Machin for a house now demolished (formerly inhabited by one Thornton), lately standing in Penckhull and serv'd for before Ano. 1654; now serv'd by John Terrick.

Reeve Book - *An ancient messuage called Hutchin's in the lane now Mr Whaley's. A barn is standing and several small houses are erected upon the back of the old messuage.* (Somewhere in Trent Valley Road, perhaps where Brisley Hill now stands).

16th 1714 - A messuage formerly Thomas Tittensor's, now belonging to the said Thomas Doody.

Fenton's Book - 1657 Thomas Tittensor for his messuage in Penckhull up in the Town, serv'd by Thomas Machin of Botteslow. 1710 Mr Thomas Doody for the house in Penkhull lately purchased by him of Thomas Tittensor and serv'd formerly Ano.1657; the office of Reeve now executed by Richard Fenton.

Reeve Book - *An ancient messuage formerly Thomas Tittensor's, now belonging to Mr Lovatt of Fulford afterwards Peggy Ward. Purchased by Mr Spode from Harrison and pulled part down and new stables erected on site. Mr Spode's own stables.* (These were the old stables at the end of Greatbatch Avenue, demolished in the 1960s).

17th 1714 - A messuage called the Batch Lake, now belonging to the said Roger Machin.

Fenton's Book - 1660 Robert Machin for Bate Lake House belonging one of his four services, served by Thomas Doody. 1713 Mr Roger Machin for the Bate Lake House in Penckhull; serve for before 1660; executed by himself.

Reeve Book - *An ancient messuage called Bate Lake anciently Roger Machin's now Mr Whalley's divided into four dwellings. Stands opposite the old pit in Penkhull near an old barn.* (This would be in what is now Rothwell Street or where Eardley Street stands.

(The full list is found under Appendix viii)

What are seen here in this list of ancient messuages are properties, which had stood for probably in excess of three or four hundred years. Some were demolished by the mid 18th century, others remained until Josiah Spode acquired land and property then demolished them. They may have been built of stone from the local quarries or half stone and timber or all timber.

The agrarian land in Penkhull from this period remained almost untouched in a time warp for five hundred years until the period between the two great wars.

It must be at least nearly forty years ago that whilst visiting the William Salt Library in Stafford I was introduced to the late S A H Burne who was probably the most important historian for Staffordshire during the last century. He was in his 80s and had been publishing his researches from the early part of the 20th century. Mr Burne married a Miss Ashwell who used to live at Beech Grove, so he knew Penkhull well.

As a young, rather naive historian reading much of the debate over the origins of Penkhull I wrongly drew the conclusion that Penkhull may have been the site for an old castle, a forerunner to that of Newcastle. Mr Bourne stating that Penkhull's history lay only in its agrarian past, with no resident lord, manor house or castle, quickly put me on the right track.

The basis upon which early farming was carried out, that of community farming has already been discussed. Penkhull, unlike most other manors, changed from openfield to enclosures, with the exception of part of Stubbs field at sometime during the late 15th or early 16th century. A working example of this method of farming is still retained in places like Laxton in Nottinghamshire.

Enclosure here meant consolidation of all the scattered strips of land belonging to a given villager in the large open fields, to be re-allocated into just one section then enclosed by fences, hedges or ditches. For most other towns and villages, this feature did not come about until the early 19th century. Many people benefited from this practice, as farming in this way would be far more economical; encourage better use of machinery and make the land more productive and therefore profitable. In some areas, the anti-enclosure movement organised riots; breaking down fences, burning barns and violently disrupted communities.

Within the court rolls, there is just an occasional reference regarding conflict between the copyholders of Penkhull. We go to the time of Henry VI for the first entry. DL 3O/232/5

Saturday 19th October 1426 (5 Henry VI) Great court held at Newcastle for Penkhull & Bothus: *John de Bothus the elder, William Persall and William Lake, thirdboroughs, present that Thomas de Green owes appearance at court and has not come. And that William de Wroo who held from the lord certain demesne land and tenements has died and a farefee of 2s is due to the lord and the land remains. And that Richard Symson (fined 6d) assaulted Richard son of John Payntor by punching him and that Agnes Smyth (fined 4d) without right raised the hue on Thomas Dawson. And Thomas Huchon (fined 6d) assaulted Richard son of John de Bothus with his heel extended. And that Thomas Huchon (fined 4d) holds a parcel of land in the Placehalgh in severalty (separateness) when by right it should be in common, to the prejudice of neighbouring occupiers of land.*

The second entry comes the following year describes Agnes Smith quarrelling again but with another neighbour. DL 30/232/6

Friday 3rd October 1427 Great court held at Newcastle for Penkhull and Bothus
And that Joan and the heirs of Richard Colclogh deceased, who held of the lord certain lands and tenements within the manor has died, and 2s is due to the lord as a fare fee, and that a parcel of land and meadow called Ackeford within the township of Penchull is a close which ought to be by right in common in the open season after corn and hay are carried away, through the fault of Thomas Huchon to the prejudice of the neighbours and Thomas Huchon (fined 2d) have been challenging to William Smyth and Agnes Smyth his wife in that they accused the aforesaid William and Agnes of stealing various property from various people to the grave shame of their names. And that Thomas Huchon assaulted (fined 3d) and stopped (fined 3d) Thomas son of Richard Bonde with a staff in the township of Penchull. And that Joan de Colclogh did not clean her ditch out around to the prejudice of the neighbours.

The Pinfold

In most ancient rural communities there was always a pinfold *(a place for the holding of cattle or sheep etc.)* The earliest for Penkhull

What Penkhull Pinfold may have looked like.

is found in 1417 when *John Andrew broke into the enclosure for animals, fined 6d.* Again in 1422 *And that John the elder broke the pinfold, taking a horse which Henry Mere impounded. Fined 2d.* Again in 1478 when Thomas Huchon the elder and his servants *took beasts, which had been impounded, in the common fold.* It is clear from the court records that a pinfold in Penkhull continued for many years as on the 1st October

1558, John Turner was fined 12d *for breaking the pound of the lord king and taking out a horse impounded there.* All fines would go the Steward of the Manor.

Again, some years later in 1632 Thomas Smyth is fined 30s as a penalty for not repairing the pinfold. The pinfold remained a part of village life at least until the middle of the 17th century as the court held on the 7th October 1649 the frankpledges *reported that the pinfold of Penkhull is not in good repair.*

Penkhull, unlike many other manors commenced the process of enclosure some time during the third quarter of the 15th century, whereas others only commenced several hundreds of years later. It is difficult to give a precise reasoning for this but it must be remembered that many of the 'strips' were in the demesne, being farmed on behalf of the lord, as a form of rental even though the lord of the manor was an absentee. The castle at Newcastle had fallen into ruin by the late 15th century, so there would be no garrison. It would be reasonable, therefore, to suggest that the produce or the rents of the lord's demesne could well have been used in the maintenance at the castle and its staff before its demise. So by the late 15th century with no castle to support and no local authority to enforce the cultivation of the lord's demesne it possibly fell into disuse. As a direct result the lord or his steward of the manor may have encouraged, or even stipulated a re-alignment of the land as a process of increasing the rent values to the crown. However, the position is not clear, as odd references occur in the court rolls which show that at least one of the great open fields remained, even if only in part, until the 17th century whilst Stubbs field, shared with the borough of Newcastle, remained much longer into the mid 19th century.

Ackford Field

30th October 1599 *Thomas Lovatt surrenders half a meadow with the appurtenances called little Ackford now in the holding of Nicholas Lovatt and one half and a half days work in a certain field called great Ackford in the holding of Roger Dale. Nicholas Lovatt admitted. Fine 2d.*

We can still read of this open field until the mid 17th century: *6th November 1633, Memorandum that whereas Roger Tittensor son and heir of Thomas Tittensor of Penkhull deceased. Item for a parcel of meadowing in Great Ackford bought of John Machin 3d.* By the early 18th century Ackford field must have been reduced from its original size as it was referred to as Little Old Ackford: *3rd April 1700, Ralph Lander of Hardwick, gent (releasing mortgage security) to Samuel Smith, gent. A pasture or parcel of land lately in the possession of Joseph Glass, and a close pasture or parcel of land called the Little Old Ackford now in the holding or occupation of William Poole. Fine 6d*

One field name, which has survived from this period, is that of Stubbs. This was a huge open field stretching from roughly the lower section of Newcastle Lane, to the current Stubbs Walk in Newcastle. The first record of the name is found in an Inquisition dated 1296, when the field was recorded as containing 38½ acres.

The next time the name appears in the court rolls for the manor is dated the 22nd Sept 1564: *that Randle Brett past died seized of 6 acres of socage land in Penkhull fields and 6 acres of land in the Stubbs and 3 acres of waste there and 16 acres of new assart in Castell Clyff by charter, and 3 acres of land of waste below Kingesfield in Penkhull and one meadow called the Whoreston meadow in Wolstanton. And that Edward Brett gentleman is his son and next heir and of full age.*

The following entry, however, presents a different picture, that of a growing community. It would appear that there were two Stubbs, a great and a little, with a lane between the two. One of them is recorded as being enclosed. There is also mention of a property being erected, barns, water mill and land provided for the mill, along with a mill dam. It concluded that an adjacent pasture was overgrown as it was to be cleared.

9th April 1580 Randle Booths *surrenders the great Stubbs in Penkhull and the little Stubbs, and the lane between them as it is now enclosed to Richard Collyer and his assigns for 21 years at the yearly rent of 6d to Booths and his heirs. Provided that Randle Booths, his heirs or assigns is allowed sufficient space in the pasture called the great Stubbs in the lower part next to the hollow there for constructing a house of two bays for the mill to be set up there, and sufficient space for making the waste water course belonging to the mill, and for making a mill dam, without any enclosure by gates or hedges to be made and they give and yield up to Randle and his heirs during the term as much of the adjoining pasture as will be cut off and cleared in the aforesaid beating down of the undergrowth. Provided also that Richard, his executors and assigns are not allowed to plough and sow any seed in the aforesaid pasture nor in any part of it during the term of the lease. Admitted. Fine 2s.*
Twenty years later however we can read that the Stubbs open field remained in use.

5th April 1605 *Stephen Hales and Alice his wife surrender 3 days work of arable land abutting on the Hightree, in a certain common field called the Stubbs in Penkhull. To Richard Harrison for 12 years at the yearly rent of 1d. Admitted. Fine 3d.*

12th April 1616 *Randall Lee, son and heir of Randall Lee deceased, is admitted to three closes called Charles hay and to 6 days work of arable land in a common field called Stubbs. Fine 3s 9d.*

25th April 1633 *Benson and his wife surrender a close called the great Stubbs and another parcel of land called the Greaves, as now divided and 11 butts of land which are three days work of plough land in a common field belonging to the borough of Newcastle under Lyme called the Stubbs lying in Penkhull. To Thomas Boulton, his heirs and assigns forever. Boulton admitted. Fine 5d.*

28th October 1657 *To this court comes Thomas Boulton the younger in his own person and surrenders into the hands of the Lord, one croft or parcel of land called Little Stubbs and one days work of arable land lying in one Townfield called Stubbs situate in Penkhull being the nearer day worked to Newcastle under Lyme and now in the possession of the said Thomas Boulton the elder. To the use and behoof of Thomas Boulton the elder father of the said Thomas for and during the term of his natural life.*

14th April 1710 *together with three acres or days works of arable land, lying and being in certain common field called The Stubbs in the respective tenures of Thomas Lovatt and Thomas Machin adjoining to the land of Thomas Stonier on the one side and the upper side thereof to a certain close called Harry field lying and being in Penckhul to the use of John Fenton his heirs and assigns etc. Fine 5d.*

12th August 1802. In the Will of Richard Lovatt, deceased presented to the court dated 12th August 1802 refers to his holding two days work of copyhold land in a common field called Stubbs.

There is little evidence available to suggest the exact date when the farms recorded in the early 19th century were established. Penkhull Farm, Mount Farm, Grindley Farm, Franklins Farm, and Terrace Farm all existed within living memory and all except Penkhull Farm, now neglected, have completely disappeared. There are available, however, various references in court records and other documents from which reckoning can be made of dates or acreage of these farms.

Grindley Hill Farm

Grindley Hill Farm was situated on the southern western slopes of Penkhull, (the site of the present pensioners' bungalows set back from Hilton Road). The problem in tracing the history of this farm is that the name of Grindley Hill has been associated with that area from at least 1572 when the manor court rolls record that John Huchyn surrendered a pasture in that area called Grindle field to Thomas Badeley for a term of twenty one years. Land at Grindley Hill was recorded in the 1615 survey of the manor in the ownership the John Dale, a prominent local farmer. Dale surrenders this land consisting of five butts *(a piece of land in an open arable field which, because of the irregular shape*

of the field, was shorter than the normal strip) at a copyhold court held on 1st May 1617 to Thomas Barrett.

The next relevant entry is dated 27th July 1624 when Grindley Hill was the subject of a legal dispute between John Riggs on the grounds that there is no right of way between the house of John Terrick, gentleman *(formerly the house of Randle Booths senior deceased)* to certain parcels of land called the great Stubbs and various other plots formerly the lands belonging to Randle Booths.

Verdict of the jurors: who say (with only Thomas Tittensor disagreeing with the rest of the jurors) *on their oath that the way for John Riggs for all necessities from the house to the close or pasture called the great Stubbs is from the house down a certain lane called the Greenway lane, then into a gate called Grindley hill gate, and so down the Grindley hill field by a hedge from the east part near the middle of the said Grindley hill field, and so down the end of the aforesaid close by a certain place called 'the gapp', and so into and through the close called the Greaves in the holding of John Barrett, and so into the great Stubbs.*

In 1656, during the commonwealth period we read of one Ralph Keeling, gent, surrendering many plots of land both in Penkhull and in Clayton. The court roll is dated 1st February 1656 when Keeling surrendered Grindley Hill to Roger Tittensor who was also recorded as the occupier. In September the following year the lands were returned to Ralph Keeling.

During the Commonwealth period, much copyhold land was transferred to other family members, mostly sons of the copyholder then returned sometime later, in most cases after the restoration. This was probably to avoid some kind of confiscation by Parliament if a copyholder was seen to be showing support for the crown.

In January 1657, court records list that the ownership of Grindley Hill had passed into the hands of John Dale who was described as living at one half of a 'capital messuage' (this is now the Greyhound Inn) for he surrendered Grindley Field to Richard Fenton. *And a certain parcel of land commonly called Grindley field adjoining the same messuage, containing by estimation six acres of land, more or less, and all the ways, watercourses, easements and appurtenances whatsoever belonging to the same premises, or used or enjoyed with them, All and singular which aforesaid premises lie and are in Penckhull within the aforesaid Manor, and they are now in the tenure or occupation of the aforesaid Richard Mutchell, or of his assign.*

However, the entry on the court roll does not indicate a mortgage on the property. The roll begins with the name Roger Townsend, which is struck through, and that of Richard Fenton inserted, which could either mean an administrative error or else that Townsend changed his mind after the document had been drawn up.

It is, therefore, surprising to find that in the next court entry Roger Townsend was listed as the copyholder but the property was described as being in the occupation of Richard Slaney. It was later transferred back into the use of Richard Mutchell. It would appear that Townsend was just the lender, enabling Mutchell to purchase.

By 1703, Mutchell had surrendered Grindley Hill to Anne Cooke, the wife of Thomas Cooke. The next entry dated 4th April 1706 provides further details of the estate which includes *a messuage all that parcel of pasture land called Grindley Field containing one messuage and various meadow pasture.* Six years later the land was sold again, this time to John Tittensor who took a mortgage from John Terrick for the sum of £24 3s to be paid back by 1710, otherwise the surrender would be void.

Once more Terrick loaned money on the property as by April 1713, Tittensor had died and the property surrendered to Thomas Baker, but this time the mortgage was £67 4s. In 1738, a fuller description is given: *all those houses, outbuildings, barns, stables, garden and orchard.* Two years later, 1740 Thomas Fenton signed a lease for the use of the farm to James Lovatt, yeoman from Bucknall at a rental of £27 p.a.

Looking at the census return of 1841 we read that the farm was occupied by John Edwards, aged 30, his wife Mary of the same age along with their daughters Emma 12 and Ann 6 and three sons John, aged 15, Josiah, aged 5, and Henry, aged 2. They employed a young lad, John Smith, as a servant in the house, not as a farm labourer. He was born at Wolstanton. For some reason a trade directory dated 1846 lists a Charles Stevenson as being the farmer but there is no other confirmation of this. By 1851, wife and children had left the farm, leaving only John Edwards and Elizabeth Roberts, aged 40, whose occupation was described as adulteress. She was born at Cadshall, Staffs. There was just one young lad, recorded as living on the farm, James Cliff, aged 17, who was employed as a farm servant. The census entry also gives its size at thirty acres. In 1861, Edwards was still at the farm then listed as consisting of 27 acres and Eliza Roberts previously recorded as an adulteress, but by 1871 was recorded as a widow, occupation, house keeper. Edwards died in 1863, aged 58, and was buried in Penkhull churchyard on the 25th October that year.

The 1871 census makes no reference to Grindley Hill Farm, but there is a property simply referred to as Grindley Hill. William Goodall, aged 35, lived there with his wife Jane, aged 38, along with their seven children. His occupation was listed as a wheelwright. It may be that Goodall was trading as a wheelwright as his first occupation whilst farming as a second. Having two occupations was not unusual during this period.

By 1891, the farm was occupied by Charles Turnock, aged 66, who ten years earlier lived at 8 Vale Road, Shelton. He was previously employed as a contractor, probably a carrier of goods and keeper of horses. Whilst Charles originated from Biddulph, his wife Martha came from Swinnerton. They had three sons living at home and the eldest, John, aged 30, lived there with his wife Jane and their four children. Charles also employed a local lad, John Machin, aged 18, who was listed as an agricultural labourer.

At some time during the following ten years the farm changed hands, for in 1901, it is recorded as occupied by Henry Mountford, aged 52, who was born in Tunstall. Although he was married, his wife was not in residence when the census was taken. He had two boys of school age and employed Sarah Astbury, aged 44 as a domestic servant. In 1900, a plot of land adjacent to Grindley Hill farm, which was previously owned by Elizabeth Coombe, was sold to the Guardians of the Poor for the building of Penkhull Cottage Homes. There were only six dwellings shown on the plans for the cottage homes.

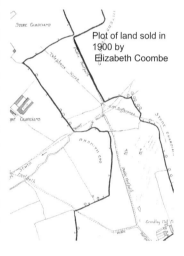

Plot of land sold in 1900 by Elizabeth Coombe

Turning the pages of an Indenture dated June 1830, we find Sir Thomas Fletcher Fenton Boughey on the one part and Mr Lawrence Armistead on the other listed with regard to the sale of the farm. In the will of Sir Thomas, dated the 8th June 1877; he left the estate or one part of it to Sir George Boughey for life and also the power to sell the estate if desired. A further Indenture, dated 3rd September 1878, was signed, this time between the Boughey family on one side and John Richard Armitstead on the other. This agreement did not last long for in December 1880 by Deed Poll the Boughey part of the estate was surrendered into the hands of Robert Fenton Fletcher Boughey. However, the following year it was transferred to a trust. The trust consisted of the Boughey and the Armitstead family.

It must be remembered that during this period, the poor of the parish were maintained in a workhouse. The current City General Hospital was erected as such an institution. The increase in industrialisation in the Potteries bought with it a corresponding increase of the poor. The Guardians of the Poor for Stoke-upon-Trent were conscious of the necessity to increase the amount of land needed to enable sufficient produce to be cultivated and to provide work for inmates as the expanded population of the workhouse required. As a result, the Guardians of the Poor and the trustees of the Grindley Farm estate signed an indenture dated the 31st July 1907 for the transfer of both farm and land. It was described as follows: *All that messuage or farm house with the outbuildings and cottage and the several closes or pieces of land known as the Grindley Hill Farm situated in Penkhull comprising of twenty seven acres, twenty seven roods and twenty seven perches which are now in the occupation of Henry Mountford and the cottage in the occupation of Mr W Roberts. The sale value of this copyhold estate amounted to £1,195.*

In the Duchy of Lancaster Office in London the minute books of the Privy Council reveals a number of documents, one of which was headed *The King to The Guardians of the Poor of the Stoke-upon-Trent Union dated 8th July 1908.* Between *The King's Most Excellent Majesty and the Guardians of the Poor* and deals with the purchase of land from the Duchy which would have the effect of transferring the land from that of copyhold tenure to that of freehold tenure, *common socage freed and discharged.* For this, a charge of £116 16s was made by the Duchy of Lancaster. The document continued at great length to explain that the Duchy still withheld the mineral rights.

Frankland's Farm and Pool Hough

Further up Newcastle Lane in the 19th century the next farm to be found would be Frankland's Farm, a name that continues today, with a different spelling. The farm occupied land where St. Peter's High School now stands between Lodge and Franklin Road, but its history only commences at the beginning of the 19th century. The land belonged to Mr John Harrison of Beech Grove. We shall discuss elsewhere his significant influence in Penkhull during the 18th century as well as his pottery works that once stood at the bottom of Honeywall.

There are a number of early references to the names of mill and pool. The first is dated 18th October 1604 when Randall Bothes mortgages a pasture called Mill field, lying between Harriesfield and the Poole Haugh, between the Stubbs and the Painters paddock. This land was transferred to Richard Hunt. The next entry for this name comes in 1711 when an area called Pool Hough was recorded in the court rolls as being in the possession of Joseph Lovatt. Lovatt lived at what is now the Greyhound Inn, although Thomas Allen, Rector

of Stoke, held a mortgage for his considerable estate. By May 1789 Beech Grove had been built by Thomas Ward and was that year acquired by John Harrison being described as

Franklin's Farm

Out Lane, now Franklin Road leading into Newcastle Lane

follows: *All that messuage or tenement, together with the several closes of land to the same belonging containing forty two acres or thereabouts, situate in Penkhull now in the holding of John Harrison, potter and all barns, stables, gardens, yards, outbuildings, ways, watercourses and appurtenances to the same belonging. Included Pool Hough and Frankland's field nearby.*

Within the manufacture of pottery there was a requirement for the grinding of colours and flint. The landscape of Harrison's estate drops considerably from St. Thomas Place to the area of Lodge Road. There were a number of springs that must have emitted a considerable amount of water, even though there were near to the top of the hill. From this point, water cascaded down into at least two or even three pools giving names to fields in that area; Far Pool Leasow; Lower Spring Meadow; Near Field and Pool Hough. It is not unusual to have abundant water on such a piece of high land. Harrison decided to harness this power to work mills for the grinding of colours and flint for his manufactory.

In May 1802, John Harrison was declared a bankrupt and his entire estate was put up for auction. An advertisement appeared in the Staffordshire Advertiser on the 3rd July the same year. 'To be sold by Auction under the direction of the Assignees of John Harrison, a bankrupt by Thomas Shorthouse of Hanley, at the Marquis of Granby Public House, in Penkhull on Tuesday 20th July, 1802'. Lot 8 read: *a substantial water mill lately erected on a piece of land called the Near Pool Hough, adjoining Lot 7, for grinding colours and other materials for Potters' use, but easily convertible to other purposes; with pools and so much of the land as is now marked out to go with this lot containing in the whole 1 acre, 3 roods and 32 perches.*

The next reference to the mill is dated the 12th September 1803. It refers to the land and a mill lately erected adjacent to Beech Grove in the occupation of Joseph Booth. Just over two weeks later on the 28th September it was a different picture as Frankland's Farm was included in an auction for the disposal of the assets of bankrupt John Harrison: *comes to the Court John Baddeley, Miles Mason and William Boothen (the assignees of the estate of John Harrison, Bankrupt) and surrenders all that close situate in Penkhull called Upper Frank Land, next to Lower Frank Land containing 6 acres to the use and behoof of David Bostock and other parts of lower Frankland* to *Joseph Walley of Hartshill Mill, miller.* Walley, it would appear, also obtained the right to the water to drive the mill from Joseph Booth.

The entry above could mean that either Hartshill Mill was unable to cope with the volume of work and additional capacity was required, or that Walley expanded his business to include the grinding of other materials. A further entry, dated 1806, states *that the purchaser could take the water coming down the gutter or watercourse across the field called Near Pool Hough.* These few

Hartshill Windmill

facts certainly make interesting reading, linking together the windmill at Hartshill, Beech Grove and the pottery industry. The Land Tax record of 1806 records that the land was in the ownership of David Bostock, who paid tax amounting to 6s 4½d.

If we now examine the census returns for Frankland's Farm commencing with 1841, we are first informed that the farm was called Bostocks Farm consisting of sixty-two acres. From the title it is clear that Joseph Bostock must have farmed the land prior to 1841 or tenanted it out. In the census of 1841, ages were recorded to the nearest five years and are therefore unreliable. John Ryder, aged 30, lived with his wife Susanna, ten years his senior together with their six children. By 1851, the farm continued to be run by Ryder born in Wolstanton, aged 44, who by this date had become a widower. He had three sons living with him at the farm, Samuel, aged 20, John, aged 12 and James, aged 11. None of the young boys were in education as they were listed as farm servants. In addition to family members Ryder also employed three others the first of which was named Hannah Steele, aged 48. The census entry makes an interesting reference, stating that *Hannah Steele is his housekeeper and has left her husband to live with Mr Ryder.* However, alongside her name, are those two other servants, husband and wife Michael and Mary McDougherty, both aged 38, from Ireland. All are recorded as sleeping in the outbuildings, and not living in the farmhouse.

The Tithe Schedule of 1849 confirms that the land remained in the ownership of Samuel Bostock but occupied by John Rider. The description then recorded is as follows: *Part of upper Frankland, House and buildings, lower Frankland, Near Field and pool, Far Field* the total acreage amounted to just over twenty acres. Ten years later, in 1861, the farm remained known as Bostock's Farm but occupied by a new tenant, Gifford, a named until recently still found in Penkhull. Henry Gifford was then aged 46 and originated from Newcastle. He was married to Ann, ten years his senior who came from Newport in Shropshire. The land attached to the farm had been reduced from 60 to 21 acres, a size

Franklands Farm

insufficient to support a family. Gifford did not employ anyone but had a full time occupation as a painter in the pottery industry, no doubt to supplement his income.

There is a possible explanation for this, as the majority of the adjoining land formed part of the Mount estate, belonging to Mary Spode. In all probability the shortfall of nearly forty acres would be accounted for by the fact that it had become part of the land associated with the Mount Farm that we shall discuss later. On the 3rd October 1856, the Mount and land was sold to Frederick Bishop. From then until February 1902 the land was passed to a number of people until the final transfer that year, to the Guardians of the Poor as part of their attempt to secure further lands for expansion of the workhouse, as demand dictated.

Gifford had two sons; Frederick, aged 21 who followed in his father's footsteps as a painter and Henry, aged 11, who helped on the farm. Eliza, aged 19, daughter, was listed as a house servant. A nephew, Thomas Bradley, aged 20, also lived at the farm but was employed as a potter's turner elsewhere and not at the farm

By 1871, the name had changed to that of Mill Farm, suggesting that perhaps parts of the building were still being used for their original purpose. There still remained only twenty acres of land, but Gifford was now working full time at the farm. There was no mention of Frederick but Henry and Eliza were still at home with Jane Gifford, aged 18, listed as a servant, originating from Crewe. In a trade directory of the same date Henry Gifford was described both as a butcher and a farmer.

Fortunes would appear to have changed by 1881, as the acreage of the farm had reverted to in excess of 62 acres. Henry by this time was 65 and his wife Ann, 78. Henry junior, now aged 32, had married Mary, a local girl, who had given birth to three children, James, aged 7; Frederick, aged 5; and Maud, aged 2. Henry also employed two servants, Thomas Flanagan, aged 30, and Thomas James, aged 14 years. On the night of the census, they had a visitor staying with them, Ann Bearcroft, aged seventy.

If we move on twenty years to 1901, Henry Gifford had died and his son Henry junior farmed the estate with Mary Elizabeth, his wife, aged 47. Henry

Members of the Gifford family c1925

had also a son called Henry working on the farm who later in life married Alice, and it is they who were the parents of my good friend Norman Gifford who resided until his dealth in 2010 in the same house as his parents, Pear Tree Cottage, in Newcastle Lane. Other children were Frederick, aged 24, farm worker, Maud, aged 23, John, aged 19 who worked in industry, Ann, aged 11; and Edward, aged 9. They employed one servant aged 14 years, named Elizabeth Marrow who came from Penkhull.

The last census available of 1911 lists that Henry and Mary Elizabeth his wife remained as farmers. Their son, Henry, aged 39, was still single and worked within the pottery industry, whereas their daughter, Ann worked as a dairy maid, but still, like her brother remained unmarried. Edward was also still at home and working on the farm. The brother of Mary Elizabeth, John Bayley was living there, aged 60, a farm carter along with George Stacy, a single man, aged 20, from Hartshill.

Norman recalled Frankland's Farm with pleasure as somewhere he used to visit his grand parents. *It was not a very large farm, probably three reception rooms with a large kitchen with red quarry floor,* and then continues. *There were three bedrooms and running water was laid on. However, there was no mains drainage and the outside lavatory consisted of one large double seat, the contents of which were used to manure the land.* Then describing the farm buildings, Norman continues *there was a stable for four horses, a cow shed for twenty cows as it was a dairy farm and other outbuildings.* Norman knows nothing of a water mill although he did recall the pond which was situated around where the school lodge now stands in Lodge Road. Frankland's Farm ceased functioning in the mid 1920s, when Norman's grandfather died. For a short time, a joiner from the workhouse occupied it who both lived there and used the outbuildings as a workshop. Finally, the site was cleared in the early 30s to make way for council house building.

Norman Gifford, July 1936

The Windmill

Further evidence in the mid eighteenth century of Penkhull as a thriving agricultural community is to be found in the building of a windmill. It was situated a few yards down the hill from the centre of the village via Penkhull New Road; just around the corner in what is now Kirkland Lane, but which was known formerly as Mill Street. Before the mill was erected, farmers from Penkhull would have to take their corn to nearby Stoke Glebe mills, just over half a mile away. Additional demand for food from the expanding industrial town of

The site of Penkhull Windmill in Mill Street, just off Penkhull New Road

Stoke prompted local landowner, John Chapman, to invest in a new mill at Penkhull. Chapman was the brother-in-law to Joseph Bourne who owned land called *(The area covering Kirkland Lane down to West Bank.)* After his death, he left his estate to his sister, Chapman's wife Margery. In a copyhold transfer between Margery Chapman and her husband, dated October 1792, the entry included reference to the newly erected windmill. *And also on the land called Hassell's Croft, stands a windmill, lately erected and built by John Chapman together with the road or way leading to the windmill.* In a trade directory dated 1800, Chapman is listed as a corn miller of Penkhull.

The following month saw two new tenants take over the mill, James Caird and Thomas Smith. By December 1814 it was back in the hands of John Chapman who in consideration of £650, sold the windmill to John Cope of Derford in the parish of Cheddleton, who had been the tenant of the mill for some time. The description reads: *All that croft, close or piece of land being the upper part of the close of land called Hassell's Croft, as the same now fenced off by a quick set hedge, and part thereof used and occupied as a garden together with Wind Mill, stable and cow house thereto belonging all of which land contains one acre and the same premises are now in the tenure or occupation of the said John Cope.* It would appear that Cope took out a mortgage from Chapman at the time of purchase for the sum of £450.

By May 1820, Cope had failed to repay his mortgage and it would appear that the mill had been in the occupation of John Broadhurst for a period, but was then in the occupation of James Sutton. Sutton took on the mortgage owing by Cope to the sum of £450. A further transaction dated February 1823 points once more to the fact that the debt continued and interest mounted, and this time Sutton attends court with the executors of Chapman, Messrs Lawton and Lunt and surrenders his interest in the property. In consideration of the sum of £597, including interest. The mill, outbuildings and land was then sold to Josiah Spode. It was recorded in 1831 as still in the ownership of the Spode family but let to a tenant farmer, Michael Baxter. The first record of Michael Baxter as miller is found in a trade directory of 1822 listed as miller, maltster and corn dealer.

As a maltster he occupied property at the rear of Manor Court Street. There is a record prior to this in 1818 which records Baxter as a grocer and flour dealer, but no mention of a mill. The Land Tax records of 1823 confirm Baxter as paying the sum of 10d tax on the mill. In January 1831, the windmill was placed on the open market to let. *For Let – and may be entered into upon immediately. Very advantageously situated at Penkhull now in the holding of Michael Baxter. The tenant may also be accommodated with several pieces of land lying near to the mill. Application to be made to Mr Tomlinson, Solicitor, Cliff-Ville.* Three years later, in 1834, Baxter was listed as a maltster only, there being no mention of the wind mill.

From other records it is noted that Michael Baxter at the same time as being the miller at Penkhull also ran the mill at Hartshill, as he took on a mortgage from Charles Whalley of Knutton for the purchase of Hartshill Windmill. The first note of the windmill appears in a manor court entry dated 5th April 1780 when Jonathan Shelly of Penkhull, gent paid an annual rent of £3 to Edward Bennett for the *recently erected windmill* at Lower Hartshill. Edward Bennett of Stoke was an established miller at the Glebe mills who in June 1780 borrowed £100 from Henry Hatrell of Doddlespool to make improvements. It was then described as: *All that parcel of land, part of a certain close called Lower Hartshill in Penkhull, now marked out, containing one acre wherein a windmill is lately erected subject to a ground rent of 20s per year for a term of ninety nine years.*

Following Jonathan Bennett came Peter Jackson, then Joseph Whalley, followed by Michael Baxter and in November 1824, Daniel Brayford later surrendered the windmill. In 1841 the windmill was in the occupation of one John Walker but Charles Whalley of Knutton held the mortgage. A court entry dated 8th January 1841 shows that the mill and land was sold to Herbert Minton. *Comes to this court Charles Whalley of Knutton, mortgagee and trustee for the sale of a windmill. In consideration of the sum of £250 paid by Herbert Minton of Longfield Cottage, surrendered all that piece of land part of a close called the Lower Harts Hill (formerly Stoke Lane) containing one acre of land with the windmill, mill dwelling house and other outbuildings.*

Penkhull windmill was still in use and recorded in July 1874 was occupied by Joseph Walley although owned by Mary Chatterley. The land passed to Arthur Burrow but the sale was subject to the satisfactory completion of a lease for the mill itself. By 1891 Penkhull windmill had been demolished as it was reported that the spindle had been standing for a long time in the stable at the end of Penkhull Terrace.

Penkhull Farm

Returning to the agrarian history of the village we move on to that of Penkhull Farm situated in Garden Street, listed as one of the ancient messuages in 1714. It went then by the name of Drarwell and was occupied by the Dale family. The Hearth Tax returns of 1665 refer to a Roger Dale, having property with five hearths. Roger died the same year, leaving the farm to his son, Thomas, a bachelor, aged thirty-two. He later married Margeria Townsend, daughter of a wealthy local farming family, in 1672. The parish listings of 1701 confirm a Thomas Dale, yeoman, as living in Penkhull aged sixty-nine. In the list of 1714, his son, also named Thomas, occupied the farm but died four years later in 1719, aged forty-five. His estate was left to his sisters, Elizabeth and Maria. Between the years 1720 and 1781, the farm and considerable copyhold land attached passed to the Alsager family of Alsager Hall, near to Congleton.

It is sad to view the farm today in a poor state of repair, with its buildings having to be shored up at several points. Penkhull Farm stands alone as the last witness to a once thriving industry which had been the mainstay of the village life for over one thousand years or even longer.

Although it is impossible to prove that the origins of this farm lie in the pre-Domesday era, it would reasonable on the basis of the historical information to make such an assumption. For Penkhull, it would reflect

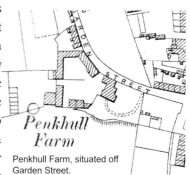

Penkhull Farm, situated off Garden Street.

the same farming structure of other open field farming communities of the mediaeval period. Small farm holdings would be gathered in close proximity for both security and social cohesion. In the first instance they would be just huts encircling a central village space with fenced off smallholdings for the safe keeping of animals. For hundreds of years there would be little or no change until the next phase of development that of the 15th century, when the open fields started to be enclosed into sections.

The first document to consider is the 1414 survey that has already been discussed in detail. Little can be gleaned from that alone but it does present the first piece of the jigsaw. The second piece is found in a later document referring to Elm Tree House, which names the lane Tittensor's Lane on the simple basis that at one time a family called Tittensor once occupied a property in the lane. The 1414 list two Tydensor's, John and, William as holding half a messuage each and various lands or strips of lands within the open fields. Both John and William's property is referred to as being previously held by William. This could suggest that one messuage, once belonging to William, their father and had been divided into two halves for his sons upon his death.

It is unfortunate that we can not be more precise, but this issue is mudded by the fact that further down Garden Street, at No. 16, the old parchment deeds dated 1827 refers to the property as being in the ownership of Ralph Tittensor for many years. Viewing the cottage from the inside it is clear that it is several hundred years old, probably from late 17th or early 18th century, but the period under discussion is over five hundred year period. However, the intervening four hundred years would have seen many changes.

The water is further muddied by the fact that a Tittensor owned at one time Elm Tree House, and so the documents relating to No.16 actually refer to Elm Tree house? It could simply be that a Tittensor owned them all and rented all but one out to tenants. Nevertheless, even with these complications it still remains that the Tittensor's would have been farmers, and the smallholding would have been situated at the time of Domesday in Garden Street, formerly Farm Lane. There are a number of court roll references, which confirm the names: *28th November 1416 Agnes Tetensor wife of William Tetensor came to court and obtained the agreement etc.* Again on the 13th March 1417 were read that *John Sharpcliff is excused by William Tetensore from the action for debt of 13s 4d which he had contested before.* John Tetensore is recorded in a court roll dated 24th April 1417 when *Henry de Mer fined 4d as he assaulted William son of John Tetensor.*

To move the issue further, one needs to view the known facts and, if possible, then work both backwards and forwards. The Copyholders Court of 1714 gives exact information with regards, to Penkhull Farm. *A messuage formerly belonging to John Dale and now belonging to Joseph Bourne.* The corresponding entry for the Reeve Book gives the precise location, *an ancient messuage called Drawwell formerly Dales now Mr Alsager's.* This was Harvey Boulton's now held by Mr Spode. The Dales also first appear in the manorial survey of 1414 when Roger Dale is listed as holding half an acre of waste in Clayton, and charged 3d in rent. The manor courts list John Dale in 1509 as acting as a frankpledge. In the same year, however, he was in court, charged with a debt of 18d. John Dale was further listed in a survey of 1516 paying rental to the Lord of 7s 10d. In a wide-ranging survey of the manor in 1615, Roger Dale is listed as having considerable property and land in Penkhull. *Roger Dale to him and his heirs by Copie of Courte Rolle and payeth 13s 8d for 23 acres a rent of 13s 10d. One messuage and one cottage with appurtenances rent 10d. The two hobcrofts, the waste, the two waste medowes, the wheat waste, the parkes and the riddinge conteyning in arable and pasture 4 acres nyne buttes and a pitt in Hugh Dodyes Longoe, one little croft on ye backside the cottage and 2 croftes on backside*

the messuage in arable 2 acres, one close called the over flatt, & one called great cliff being 4 acres 25 acres. The spittle hay and platt hill conteyning in arable and pasture 2 acres. The 2 new leasowes in arable 2 acres, the two highomes, and Ackford medo in arable and pasture 2 acres. The new piece and further flatt, and 3 buttes in high croft head a butt in Collinsmore and two cliffes together conteyning arable and pasture 4 acres. The haugh in arable 2 acres. The little Grindle Hill and the ground in Great Grindle Hill conteyning arable 1 acre. The little medow, the Rid medow, and half-day math (work) in doles conteyning in medow 2 acres.

This was a considerable holding, and clearly identified the Dale family as wealthy landowners. In a list of rental charges made in 1618, 1650 and 1653, there are two Roger Dales recorded, probably father and son but because Stoke Church registers do not commence until 1630, the exact dates cannot be obtained. The first Roger is listed as holding land amounting to 23½ acres; the second is listed as holding just a quarter of an acre. One Roger was holding the first, the second holding Greenhead House. The Hearth Tax of 1666 lists Roger as holding property with five hearths whilst the 1672 return list John with only four. This could be easily accounted for by the fact that often householders bricked one or more up to avoid paying the tax. In January 1669, Joan Dale died. Her will dated 24th November 1668 points clearly to the family connections and how the farm later became the property of the Bourne family. *Joan to Ann my sister the sum of £400. To my brother John £25 and the £52 he already owes me. To Alice Dale my sister in law, £6. To Elizabeth Bourne daughter of William Bourne of Cheshire and others.* The families of Dales and Bourne had come together as the court entry of listed below confirms.

After a transfer of land from Roger Dale to William Selman, the following entry dated the 20th February 1606 appears and explains the relationship between the two families: *Note: the aforesaid lands are now the inheritance of Ralph Bourne who is one of the Bournes of Little Chell, by the gift of John Dale*

View of Penkhull Farm from the south.

who married the said Bourne's sister, and the said Bourne married to his second wife the said John Dale's sister, but neither of them had any issue by the said wives. There are also other documents that link together the two families. The birth of Ralph Bourne of Little Chell, in 1647 and Ann Dale of Penkhull, born 1651, the daughter of John, on the 3rd June 1672, at Wolstanton are recorded in the baptism registers. Again at Wolstanton, in October 1693, Johannes Dale and Alice Bourne of Wolstanton were married.

John Dale presumably had no issue as his estate following his death went to his sister Ann and her husband, Ralph Bourne. In an attempt to clarify this we next turn to the parish listing of 1701 where it is recorded: *Ralph Bourne yeoman, aged 70, Ann Bourne, his wife aged 72, Alice aged 80, widow along with three children and two servants.* Seven years after this parish listing, Ralph Bourne died, aged 77 years. He was buried in Stoke churchyard on the 8th November 1707, his wife was buried at his side on the 9th May 1711. At some time, Joseph who was the nephew of Ralph, must have acquired lands some before 1700 in several stages amounting to 36 customary acres. Two further acquisitions after 1700 dated 21st April 1708 and 9th November 1721. One year later the property was transferred to his nephew Joseph for we read that on the 13th March 1722/3: *Joseph Bourne of Penkhull to Joseph Bourne of Chell, son of William Bourne of Chell, gent. All his messuage cottages land and tenements in Penkhull.* Nine years later the estate in Penkhull was handed down to yet another generation as the court record for 2nd June 1731 indicates: *Joseph Bourne of Little Chell, gent to William Bourne Jun. of Little Chell, gent, all those messuages lands and tenements in Penkhull now in the holding of Thomas Picken as subtenant and all barns, outhouses, stables, gardens etc. belonging. Fine paid 17s 3½d.*

Just around the corner from Penkhull Farm stood what was Green Head House, known today as The Greyhound Inn where Thomas Dale lived. It is interesting to read in his will, dated 1719, that the following items were itemised as being in the possession of Mr John Bourne: *three barrels, one iron kettle, two little pots, one warming pan, three brass pans, skillets, one saucepan, three blankets and one bolster to the value of £3 15s.*

It is fortunate that the will of Ralph has survived alongside an inventory of his goods and chattels. In his will, he leaves the farm to his nephew, Joseph Bourne, son of William Bourne. By 1738, William Bourne had died and the farm and lands passed over to the Alsager's of Alsager Hall in Cheshire. At the court held at Penkhull on the 26th day of October 1738: *To this court comes John Alsager of Alsager in the County of Chester, gent and prays to be admitted tenant to all the copy hold lands containing 36 acres and tenements with their appurtenances whereof William Bourne, late of Little Chell to*

the use and to hold the premises aforesaid with the appurtenances to the said John Alsager, his heirs and assigns for ever at the will of the Lord etc. Admitted fined 17s 3½d. It is known that John Alsager married Elizabeth Sidebottom of Little Chell on the 5th June 1701 so there must have been a family connection somewhere along the way, which it has not been possible to ascertain.

John Alsager in his will dated the 19th May 1729 bequeathed to Thomas Bourne of Burslem and Joseph Bourne of Little Chell as Trustees, all his property in Cheshire and Staffordshire, to be divided amongst his six daughters. To his wife and son, he first bequeathed his home and other possessions. The rest was to be divided equally between the six daughters. It is interesting that the Swan Inn, Burslem which Thomas Bourne owned, was recorded as being in *possession of Randle Dale and Thomas Bowyer,* two important family names in Penkhull. In a codicil dated September 1740, it would appear that both Thomas and Joseph Bourne were deceased and therefore John Alsager appointed his wife Elizabeth and son John to be his new executors. The court records dated the 1st April 1741 confirm that Ann, Elizabeth, Sarah, Mary, Margaret and Judith Alsager, all spinsters were admitted to the Penkhull estate upon the death of their father John.

By the time Spode acquired Penkhull Farm as a tenant [part of its land remained in the hands of Judith and Mary Alsager, the last remaining daughters of John Alsager. Mary Alsager was born 1712, died March, 23rd, 1795, aged 82 whilst Judith Alsager, aged 75, died in the February, one month earlier the same year. Both sisters made out their wills jointly on the 20th June 1792 which included the legal transfer of the estate from Mary Alsager to trustees, Thomas Rowley, James Twemlow and the Rev. Jonathan Clarke. The court record dated 27th June 1795 reads: *All my copyhold messuages, tenements and lands with their respective appurtenances situated in and near Penkhull in the County of Staffordshire, now in the several possessions of Harvey Boulton and John Smith as farmers and after their decease to be placed into the hands of Trustees, Thomas Rowley, The Rev Jonathan Wilson and James Twemlow.*

An interesting court entry dated October 1701 refers to a garden or orchard adjoining the fold of Roger Tittensor attached to his house and lying next to a barn belonging to Ralph Bourne which had been recently purchased from Roger Tittensor. This confirms that both properties were situated together in Garden Street.

John Alsager never occupied the farm, but let it to tenant farmers. In 1764, the farm and lands were surrendered to Thomas Ward, probably in connection with a mortgage and was recorded as being in the occupation of John Godwyn.

Records for this period are difficult to find. The first is the Land Tax account of 1783, listing Alsager's as owners and Harvey Boulton as tenant farmer, paying £7 12s 4d in land tax. The same amount of tax was again paid in 1789, 1792 and 1796. Harvey Boulton was the son of William and Mary, and baptised at St. John's church, Burslem, on 1st December 1728. He died in 1799, and was buried in Stoke churchyard on the 23rd November that year.

The manor court rolls give further information regarding Harvey Boulton. In July 1756, Boulton provided a loan of £6 to Ralph Tittensor with a security of a *newly erected cottage adjoining the garden of Joseph Bourne.* The same cottage and land were again referred to at a court held at Penkhull on the 7th October 1778, when Jane, the widow of Ralph Tittensor, took possession of the cottage and land from Harvey Boulton, probably upon the re-payment of the loan, and surrendered the same to her son Benjamin. *All that house now in the possession of Jane Tittensor, together with a small parcel of land adjoining.*

Addition to Penkhull Farm built c1800 by Josiah Spode

But Penkhull was not the only place where Harvey Boulton held land. One entry dated the 29th May 1800 lists that he was the occupier of a plot of land in Stoke called Big Stoke Meadow, probably off London Road, the site of the late Minton Hollins factory. *All that close of meadow in Penkhull, called the over part of Big Stoke Meadow, late in the holding of Harvey Boulton but now of Thomas Minton and Joseph Poulson.*

The Will of Harvey Boulton dated the 17th November 1799 has survived and makes interesting reading. He employed three servants: George Gallimore who received the sum of £20, Margaret Goodfellow, and Martha Bloor, who received the sum of £10 each, on condition that they were at the time of his death his house servants. He also bequeathed one guinea to John Smith commonly called Old Blind Jack, (the word blind being inserted at a later date) for tolling the bell rope at his funeral at Stoke old church. It seems as though Boulton did not trust Old Jack, as the sum was only to be paid the day after his funeral. A further sum of 10s 6d was left to twenty poor persons of the village of Penkhull. Most of his property went to his nephew, Samuel Boulton. It is clear that the will was not drawn up until his death was

imminent and his signature points to someone having difficulty in writing his name.

One month following his death, farming stock and contents were to be sold at auction by Cooks of Newcastle. The following notice appeared in the Staffordshire Advertiser on the 30th November 1799.

On the premises at Penkhull, on Tuesday the 3rd December, 1799, and the following days; All the capital farming stock, dairy vessels and household furniture of the late Mr Harvey Boulton; the farming stock consists of 15 in-calf cows, 4 heifers, 4 twinters, 4 stirks, 1 bull, 1 fat pig, 3 strong draught mares, 1 colt, gearing for 4 horses, 1 wagon, 3 carts, 1 plough and a pair of harrows, about 20 bushels of potatoes, a quantity of unthrashed oats, a small wheat stack, 3 . . . of fine old wheat, 20 tons of excellent hay and clover, about 2 tons of cheese of a remarkable quality.

The household furniture and dairy vessels comprise of 4 post and half setter bedsteads with check, home made and other furniture, feather beds, bolsters and pillows, blankets and bed covers, bed and table linen, oak chests, desk and chests of draws, chairs of various sorts, oak dresser, tables and stands, 30 hour clock, iron boilers, grates, fenders and fire irons, cheese presses, cheese-vats and brass milking-pans, battles, mash tubs, coolers, salting tubs, pails and a variety of other useful articles too numerous for mention.

The Auctioneer recommends this Sale to the attention of the public as the cattle are well selected and in high condition, the corn and hay well got and the cheese of quality which does great credit to the dairy maid. The farming stock will be sold on the first day, and the Sale will commence each morning punctually at 11 o'clock.

This impressive list of the contents, animals, furniture and farming equipment reflects a well-managed and thriving business. So much so that it attracted probably the most eminent landowner and pottery manufacturer in the district, Josiah Spode. Spode wanted this farm to prove himself not just as a potter, but also, like many of his contemporaries, a Gentleman Farmer. The situation of Penkhull Farm was ideal for this purpose as it was facing south, towards the estate of the Duke of Sutherland at Trentham and overlooking from the rear the town of Stoke to his pottery manufactory.

Spode acquired the farm and lands with the exclusion of certain fields called Grindley at a court held on the 29th May 1800, which reads *All that that customary messuage, farm or tenement late in the holding of Harvey Boulton deceased with the outbuildings and appurtenances belonging and several fields under the names of Long Croft, Little Croft, White Hough, Bowyers Hough, Thistley Hough, The Plate, The Cliffe, The Wheat Cliff, The Clover Cliff and Rough Cliff, The Little Hardern, The Great Hardern, The Grindley Field, The Townsend,*

The Bent Dole, Two Doles and Red Meadow, except a certain piece of land called Grindley Hill which is now taken and let off from the said farm to the use of Josiah Spode of Little Fenton.

As to the meadow lands usually mown from the 20th day of February last. As to all other lands, except that piece of land called Field at the back of the house which is intended for a Boosy pasture from the 25th of March last as to the messuage and outbuilding and Boosy Pasture from the 1st day of May for a term of twenty one years. At the yearly rent of £140. (Boosy Pasture: An area where fertilizers are added to the soil to assist in the growing of a winter and spring pasture for the use of animals).

Side view showing the old section to the left of c1730

Lease to Josiah Spode from the Alsager's for Penkhull Farm. *That entire Messuage farm house, situate and being at Penkhull late in the possession of Harvey Boulton deceased. Together with the barns, stables, cowhouses, outbuildings and other conveniences. And also the further and additional rent or sum of ten pounds of like lawful money for each and every tree which the said Josiah Spode shall at any time fell, cut down, grub up or lop or crop except timber in the rough for the necessary repairs of the said premises. And further that Josiah Spode shall during the said term maintain and keep the farm house and all buildings belonging to the same (except such of the said buildings as are hereinafter permitted to be taken down) and all new erections that may be erected and also the pump gates, stiles, hedges, ditches, drains and fences of the farm and premises in good and tenantable repair. And also shall farm and use the farm and lands in a husbandlike manner during all the term and not at any time plough, break up or convert into tillage any meadow lands or land usually mown belonging to the farm and shall not during the last three years of the said term have in tillage more than one fourth of the whole quantity of the tillage of the farm in any one year and during such last three years shall and will eat and consume upon the premises all the hay and straw and fodder which shall grow or arise during that period and spread and bestow in husbandlike manner upon the grass lands of the farm all the muck, dung, manure and compost which shall be made or gathered during such last three years of the lease in the Middingshead of fold yard such part as shall be unspent or un-spread at the expiration thereof . . . And whereas the farm is now considerably reduced in size several pieces of land originally held therewith having been let off and in consequence the whole of the buildings standing are now become unnecessary and it would be* a benefit to the owners of the farm if such unnecessary buildings as are now in ruinous state were wholly taken down and Josiah Spode upon Treaty for the Lease so as intended to be granted to him expressed, a wish to be at liberty to remove and take down at his own expense the cowhides standing behind the house and also a shore at the end of the house and to make various alterations and improvements for the purpose of rendering the same more comfortable and convenient residence. Now the said.... do hereby fully authorise and empower Josiah Spode his executors, administrators and assigns in case he or they shall think proper to remove and take down the said cowhides and shore hereby mentioned the materials being used on some part of the said premises and also to alter and improve the said dwelling house and offices in such manner as he may think proper for rendering the same a more convenient and comfortable habitations.*

The lease point to a number of buildings being in a poor state of repair, and the need for partial demolition, as some were recalled as being in a ruinous state. Parts of the farmlands had been let off to others, and permission was given to improve the living accommodation. In fact, it is understood that Spode built the cemented additional residence facing south which has stood for nearly half a century uninhabited, and remains today in its original unaltered state without any mod-cons.

It would appear that the lease was renewed in 1816, rent being increased to £150. The executors of the Misses Alsager again renewed it in 1825 with a further increase to £210 per annum. The property and lands remained in the possession of the Alsager executors until 1850. The Land Tax Records from 1806 to 1819 confirm that Spode was still the tenant of Penkhull Farm, paying a reduced sum of £6 19 4½d, reflecting a reduction of land attached to the farm.

The following is taken from Heaton's Survey and Valuation of landed property in the parish of Stoke-upon-Trent dated 1827. Proprietor: the late Misses Alsager and lists all the land and property occupied by Josiah Spode.

No.	Description of Property	Quantity			Yearly value		
		A	R	P	£	s	d
381	Homestead etc	2	4		11	0	0
383	Stackyard and Croft	1	3	20	4	13	9
382	Barnfield and Little Croft	4	1	15	9	11	1
54	Townsend	3	1	15	8	7	2
386	Flat	4	3	38	9	9	6
385	Thistley or White Hough	5	1	24			
373	Eight Acre Field	9	0	9	28	18	3
385	Little Cliff	4	3	5			
394	Long Wheat Cliff	7	2	26	38	19	0
391	Broomy or Clover Cliff	5	2	36			
392	Cliff Meadow or Rough Cliff	4	2	39			
393	Slang or Little Meadow	1	0	30			

413	Great and Little Hordern	12	0	25		13	6	10
436	Brook or Red Meadow	3	2	15		8	19	8
		----------				-------		
	Totals	69	1	21		133	5	3

This survey was taken following the death of Josiah Spode II in July 1827.

The contents of Penkhull Farm were auctioned off in 1833 although the exact reason for this is not known. However, in all probability it was when there was restructuring of finances for the Spode works and estates through William Baker of Fenton, reached its conclusion in 1833.

TO BE SOLD BY AUCTION BY W. & J. AUDLEY.
On the premises on Tuesday and Wednesday, the 2nd. and 3rd. day of March, 1830

All the prime Dairy Cows, fat Bull, two teams of superior Wagon Horses, a pair of Carriage Horses, Grey Pony, Sheep, Goats, Pigs of excellent breed, valuable implements and carriages, four-horse power Threshing Machine, Stack Frames, with Stone and Iron Pillars, Dairy Vessels, Household Furniture, and other Effects, the property of the late JOSIAH SPODE, Esq. Consisting of twenty prime in-calf dairy Cows, on good note, one fat bull, eight superior wagon horses, one pair of excellent carriage horses, one grey pony twelve hands one inch high, fifty-nine ewes in lamb, one ram, two goats, two high bred brawns, one sow with eight pigs, three in-pig sows, six stores, three broad and narrow-wheeled wagons, three broad-wheeled carts, one small cart, four wheelbarrows, two land rollers, one knife roller and cart, one ox harrow, one under draining plough, one double plough with wheels, four single ploughs, one potato plough, straw engine, straw cutter, capital machine fan, pair twins and shafts, turnip drill, potato scuffle, one capital four-power threshing machine complete in high preservation, a large number of excellent field, barn and garden tools of every description, two sets of ploughing tackle, gearing for ten horses, bends and chains, batch pad, a large number of sacks, beam scales and weights, four wagon ropes, measures, grindstone, sheep cratch, wood and stone pig troughs, corn chests and coffers, potato washers, steaming boiler, turkey and chicken pens, cow trusses, two turnip unchoakers, one set of four-horse harness, one set of pair-horse harness, one set of gig harness, a number of saddles, bridles, &c., &c., too numerous to insert.

The Dairy Vessels - Consist of two excellent stone cheese presses (quite new), one wood cheese press, two dash churns, cheese tubs, vats, ladders and boards, milk coolers, salting tubs and breakers, large brass pan, small brass pan, cheese binders, milk pails, gawns, pans and cans, cream cheese vats and frame, two drying cheese shelves, butter scales and weights, butter tubs and prints, bowls, four iron furnaces complete, benches, harvest bottles, twenty-four milk and cream earthenware vessels.

The Furniture - Comprises bedsteads and furniture, feather beds, blankets, sheets, quilts and covers, deal chest, eight days' clock in oak case, weather glass, tables, stands and stools, oak dresser and shelves, cupboards, chairs, bacon rack, spinning wheel, grates, fenders and fire-irons, pots, kettles and pans, wash tubs, buckets, stillages and benches, pump cistern, meat safe, mortar and pestle, quantity of earthenware, trowels, cleaver, clothes horse. &c, &c.

Once more Penkhull Farm appears to be well established and productive with an excellent stock of animals, farm equipment, dairy equipment and household goods. Even

though the farm was worked by sub-tenants it remained in the hands of the Trustees to the Alsager's until 1850, when the farm and lands were sold. It would seem that John Smith of Springfields House had succeeded Spode as tenant from 1830 but in 1850 purchased the farm from the trusters to the Alsagers.

20th June 1850 To this court comes The Trustees of the Misses Alsager and surrenders the farmhouse, closes, or parcels of land and in consideration of the several sums of £780 and £5,070 making together the sum of £5,850 and also in consideration of a further sum of £1,950 paid by John Smith in full and absolute purchase of the entirety of all and singular the copyhold or customary Messuage Farm house lands and hereditaments Firstly - all that copyhold customary messuage Farmhouse standing and being in the Village and Township of Penkhull formerly in the occupation of Thomas Pickin, afterwards of Harvey Boulton subsequently of Josiah Spode Esquire and after his decease of his son Josiah Spode the younger and since down to the present time of the said John Smith or his under tenants And All those the barns, stables and other outbuildings, fields, yards and other yards, orchards and gardens of and belonging to the said farm house or tenement and usually occupied therewith the sites of which premises are computed to contain one acre and twenty-seven perches or thereabouts. (The document continues to list all the fields and appurtenances attached to the farm.)

And afterwards to the same court comes the said John Smith. To whom the Lord of the said Manor by the Steward aforesaid grants seizing thereof by the rod according to the custom of the Manor and John Smith pays fourteen shillings as a fine and is admitted tenant of the premises.

A general view of the farm courtyard

John Smith was already an established owner of the land at the bottom of Newcastle Lane together with land at Springfields, Seabridge and Clayton. His estate was valued on the 2nd August 1853 at £39,630, including Penkhull Farm, which he had acquired three years earlier. He sold it to Thomas Fletcher Twemlow of Betley Court and George Leeke Baker of Lincoln's Inn, in the County of Middlesex. Smith's estate then included in total two hundred and sixty one acres, three roods and thirty eight perches and all other copyhold lands, farms, lands situate in the townships of Penkhull, Clayton and Seabridge.

It was less than two years following this settlement when the Penkhull section of this sale was sold again to Sir W.M.M. Swinnerton Pilkington on the 23rd July 1855. At various times since this date various plots were sold. One such large plot was for the creation of Penkhull Garden Village, but the farm and what little land surrounded it remained in the Swinnerton Pilkington family until 7th May 1934, when Arthur William Milborn Swinnerton Pilkington sold it to Mrs Alice Jervis, the mother of the last farmer in Penkhull, Doug Jervis. Doug's father, Arthur Jervis came from Betley, the son of a tenant farmer, farming land under the ownership of Sir Thomas Swinnerton Pilkington who originally had found a farm for Arthur to rent. Arthur and Alice were married within one month of coming to Penkhull.

After the death of Doug Jervis in October 2000, the property transferred by gift to Christopher Jones, who in turn sold the farm to David Bagshaw Homes in May 2004. At the time of writing, the farm remains closed behind steel gates and in a serious state of decline. It awaits permission to both restore the old property and to develop the site. Fortunately Grade II listing was obtained from English Heritage to protect the buildings from demolition.

Apart from the census returns there is little information regarding the names of tenant farmers. Trade Directories offer limited details, as it seems that farmers either did not value this means of advertising, or did not wish to pay the fees. Such information as can be obtained is as follows: In 1818 Thomas Sutton is listed as the farmer. By 1834, George Hemmings had taken over. It is quite unusual to find in the newspapers of the period a form of an apology to prevent a course of libel being taken. In June 1830 a short public acknowledgement was printed in the *Potteries Mercury* which read: *Thomas Sutton, farmer having circulated reports injurious to the character of Ann, the wife of George Hemmings of Penkhull for which proceedings in Law were to be taken against me, but*

Early 18 century buildings. Hay loft at the top. Roof timbers 17th century

in consideration of my making this acknowledgement and paying all expenses and donating £1 to the N.S. Hospital Mr Hemmings has consented to forgo such proceedings. I do hereby express my regret at having used the expressions which I did in

regard to Ann Hemmings and which I believe to be utterly false. Signed X (Thomas Sutton).

In 1841, the occupants were Thomas Headman, aged 60, and Susannah Jackson, aged 30, listed as a farm servant. The tenancy situation remains unclear until the Trade Directory of 1869, when William Scales is listed as farmer. This is confirmed in the census return two years later, when William is recorded, aged 63, farming 56 acres. He came from Lancaster. His wife Elizabeth was aged 59. They employed one man, but were assisted by their daughter and her husband in addition to their son William, aged 22, four grand children and a servant.

Between 1871 and the next census of 1881, Penkhull Farm had a new tenant, John Foster. Foster was born at Hill Field House, Wetton, nr. Stafford, the son of a farmer. By at least 1867 he had been farming just below the hill of Penkhull at Springfields farm. The 1871 census lists John Foster, aged 50, farmer of 175 acres employing seven men. He was married to Hannah, aged 52, also from Wetton. They had one son Thomas, aged 18, living at home. His occupation was listed as Brick and Tile manufacturer employing thirteen men. John also employed two agricultural labourers living at the farm and a servant. There is also two farm servants listed, Benjamin Baker, aged 70, who also came from Wetton, and Emma Oakley, aged 35, born at Longton.

At some time before 1876, the family had moved to Penkhull Farm, a much smaller farm consisting of only sixty acres. By this time their son, Thomas had married Fanny Lloyd of Newcastle, and may have been living at the farm. Penkhull church records that three of their children were baptised at Penkhull Church, George and Hannah Margaret on the 21st May 1876, and then Thomas on 16th October 1879. The 1881 census lists John Foster, aged 60, assisted by his wife Hannah, 62 years. By this time their son, Thomas and his wife Fanny were no longer living at the farm as they were managing Fanny's family confectionery business at 13 Red Lion Square, Newcastle. They had six children, four of which were born at the farm.

The 1881 census also shows that the servant Emma Oakley was still living with the family as a general servant, and Frank Sweatman, a farm servant, aged 45, who originated from Swincoe. It is interesting that at the same time there were two other dwellings listed at the farm. In one lived Eliza Roberts, a washerwoman, aged 60, and in the other Susan Leese, a laundress, aged 76, who lived with her daughter and granddaughter.

Hannah Foster died early in April 1882 at the age of 63, and was interred at Wetton cemetery. Widowed John re-married at Penkhull Church in May 1885 to Elizabeth Robinson, a widow from Stone. The marriage lasted for just over ten years until John died in September 1893, aged 72. The 1891 census lists that John was aged 70, and Elizabeth his wife was aged 69. Also living at the farm was their grandchildren; Hannah Margaret, aged 15, a farm servant, Thomas Lloyd, aged 10, a scholar, Colin, aged 9 and John, aged 8. In addition there was a cousin born at Longton named Charles, aged 46, and Joseph Bowyers, aged 22, both employed as farm servants. Finally, Emma Oakley was still working at the farm, aged 58, but this time employed as a general servant and not a farm servant probably with fewer duties to perform because of her age.

The milking parlour

One of their grandchildren, George died an infant in a tragic accident when playing in a hayloft at the farm when he fell from the loft, broke his neck and died instantly. George's father, Thomas, died aged 34, also at the farm on New Year's Eve, 1886 in a riding accident. He had been drinking and was thrown from his horse. It was only three years later when his widow, Fanny, died on the 20th April 1889, aged 33 years. The grandfather, John, took four of the surviving grandchildren to live at the farm whilst granddaughter, Ada, then 11 years, went to live with Fanny's family in Newcastle. It was one of the grandchildren, Thomas Lloyd Foster, who was sent to Paris to learn the art of patisserie. Thomas Lloyd emigrated to Canada and it is his granddaughter, Barbara Hughes, who has assisted with some of the details of the Foster family.

Chickens around the farm yard

By 1901, Elizabeth Foster was still at the farm. Hannah Margaret, the granddaughter of John had married although there was no mention of her husband. Colin was then now 19 and Emma Oakley, aged 68, who remained in service with the family at the farm. No doubt because of her age and being not as active there was a new addition to the household, Sarah Myatt, aged 16, employed as a housemaid who came from Newcastle, probably on the understanding that she would relieve Emma of some of the more difficult tasks within the house.

Doug Jervis, the last farmer of Penkhull

Elizabeth Foster died in June 1901. Emma, the servant to the family for over forty years, went to live at Newcastle, probably with the family at Red Lion Square. She died in the spring of 1907, aged 70 years.

Soon after the death of Elizabeth Foster, a new tenant farmer came to life there, Arthur Jervis. He was a farm hand on the estate of Sir Thomas Pilkington at Betley. Wanting a farm of his own to manage so he could marry, Sir Thomas offered him Penkhull Farm where he married, bought up a family and died. The farm remained in the same family, one hundred years. Although it closed as a dairy farm in the late 1960s, Doug and Betty, his wife continued to serve the district with milk for a further thirty years. A full account of their lives and a full history of Penkhull Farm are covered in an historical documentary, produced two years before Doug and Betty died.

Doug and Betty Jervis 1998

Chapter 10

The Greyhound Inn: Greenhead House.

The present Greyhound Inn, formerly known as Penkhull Hall then later Greenhead House, stands opposite what is now the west door of the parish church, but before the church was built here was a large open space of common manorial waste where the village pinfold was situated. The old building, originally a farmhouse, would be constructed of timber, wattle and daub with one large room, the large parlour, which was used for the Customary Court Baron and Court Leet. This section of the building now forms the public bar section of the Inn. The building still retains its original form, although largely reconstructed in 1936.

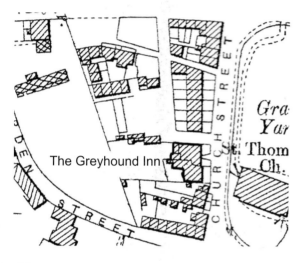

Early 19th century trade directories identify this old building as previously being the place where manor courts were held every three weeks. The manor court records contain much evidence of its transition through the centuries but the first record that can be identified is dated 1536. It refers to the building itself as *being recently built.* Unfortunately the word *recently* cannot be relied upon to mean what it says nor can the limited description of the property with certainty identify the property now known by the name The Greyhound Inn. In many cases, a description such as *'recently built'* can be carried forward within court documents for years, as any previous reference would be copied to the next court

The Greyhound Inn 1928

reference without change. One thing is for certain, the old farmhouse was standing in 1536, but it could date from a much earlier period and may even have been the location for the manorial courts since the need arose to vacate the castle at Newcastle-under-Lyme, probably in the early 15th century or late 14th century.

Much has been written of its history, but regrettably, in most cases, it been a case where *fools rush in where angels fear to tread,* little if anything is accurate. There are stories of tunnels, which pass under the highway to the church through which prisoners escaped, and the appearance of ghosts. Even Stoke-on-Trent official publications list it as being burnt down in 1936. One local historian even wrote that prisoners were bought out screaming from its doors to be hanged on the nearest tree in the churchyard. Sheer fantasy on his part, and a great pity that such romanticism is peddled as fact.

Early records are difficult to come by, apart from the manor court minutes supplemented by manorial surveys, parish and poor law records, land tax returns, tithe schedules and wills etc. Little else of anything has survived.

It has been suggested that The Greyhound Inn can be associated with the property known as Penkhull Hall. A building under that name is recorded not once, but twice, as there were two buildings that were so titled, although not at the same time. The first is recorded in 1581, when Stephen Crompton and his wife surrendered Penkhull Hall recorded as *being recently built by Thomas Crompton Esq.* The estate attached to the hall consisted of barns, stables, yards, gardens and numerous plots of land including Collins Wood. Upon the surrender of the Hall in 1581, it passed into the hands of Thomas Smyth who surrendered it at a court, held in April 1632, probably as security for a mortgage to the value of £150 received from Mary Sprint, a widow from Newcastle. In September the same year, Smyth then transferred Penkhull Hall, with stable, garden and meadow to Mary Prince, widow to secure a mortgage. It would seem that Smyth was an absentee landlord as the property was described as in the occupation of William Brereton.

In the manorial survey of 1615, Thomas Crompton was the owner of a property called Penkhull Hall and the estate with land called Collins Wood. Crompton was listed as an Armager, a person entitled to a Coat of Arms. The name of Collins Wood has survived for nearly four hundred years and is retained today in the name of Collingswood Grove, an elevated tract of land overlooking the Etruria valley and an ideal situation to build a large house or hall. Remember at this time, there was no Hartshill by name; the area was a part of Penkhull. In reality, this property can be discounted as ever being the Penkhull Hall, in Penkhull itself.

A later entry court record notes that the hall had been taken down by Thomas Baddeley and carted by him and *re-erected up in Penkhull Street, Newcastle, where he now resides.* The barn is listed again in 1618, when it was purchased by Mr Roger Margen and re-erected at Batelake House. A further court entry of 1637 states that Penkhull Hall was in the possession of Mr Thomas Baddeley and situated in the horse market at Newcastle. These follow-up entries are sufficient to dismiss any argument that the Penkhull Hall owned by Crompton is The Greyhound Inn of today.

For several decades the origins of The Greyhound Inn has remained a mystery. The question first arose with a reference by Mr Robert Nicholls in his small booklet *Penkhull cum Boothen* published in 1929. Nicholls quotes a court record dated 25th April 1662 whereby *John Lovatt and Joan Dale surrendered to the King one messuage called Penkhull Hall with its buildings, orchards, gardens and pasture into the hands of Ralph Keeling, gent.* No doubt Mr Nicholls would have obtained this reference from the Historical Collections of Staffordshire, and for years it was considered to be the only reference to Penkhull Hall.

This is not the case. I for one wrongly believed that the name of Penkhull Hall was the forerunner of the house later named Greenhead House. The problem we have in the first place is the word 'hall' itself. Far too often this word is perceived wrongly as representing a large black and white Elizabethan House where titled people once lived. Unfortunately this is romanticism! Although this perception can have a place in historical novels, it has no place in historical works like this. The word 'hall' could simply mean a large room where meetings or gatherings were held. This is probably the case with Penkhull Hall.

So what of the entry for Penkhull Hall in 1662, and when does the name appear of Greenhead House? The answer I have come to is that these are separate buildings, for both names appear in court records during the early 17th century. There is, however, a clear explanation as to why the matter has been so confusing. Records have never previously been studied in any detail. One line that occurs in a number of court minutes, and previously not quite understood, is found in later descriptions of Greenhead House. The first reference is in a court minute dated 15th May 1700 when Thomas Dale surrendered *the lower part of a messuage or tenement of Greenhead House.* Once more in 1704, a part of Greenhead house is described as the *lower end of a messuage or tenement called Greenhead House.* It was described as in the holding or occupation of Thomas Dale. The last description found in the manor court records is dated July 1711, when the house was described *a below mentioned part of a messuage or tenement called the Greenhead House.* This 'lower end' could well be the part of the building previously known by the name of Penkhull Hall.

Returning to the court entries of Penkhull Hall and a court entry dated 20th December 1650, which refers to Philip Young, gent, through his attorneys John Lovatt and Joshua Hill, was admitted *to a capital messuage called Penkhull Hall, stable, garden, a meadow called Penkhull Meadow and two closes of pasture called Middle and Lower moor.* At the same court, Young surrendered the hall to Ralph Keeling. The next court entry, dated 1657, refers to the fact that Keeling surrendered it on the 8th June 1654 to Dorothy Machen. Dorothy then surrenders the hall in 1657 to her daughters Jane and Margaret Machen. One year later, on the 7th July 1658, Jane Machen returned the property to Ralph Keeling, no doubt on the discharge of a mortgage. In a survey dated 1618 Roger Machen owned a considerable estate in Penkhull consisting of ninety acres, the largest recorded in that year.

It was the following year, 18th July 1659, when again Keeling surrendered Penkhull Hall after adding various other lands to the package, including the Middle and Lower Moor, the Bearshill waste and the Hole House waste to Joan Dale, on condition *that do well and truly pay unto the said Joan Dale the sum of £106 in the church porch of Stoke otherwise the surrender shall be void.*

Joan Dale was the daughter of John Dale of Penkhull. His last Will and Testament is dated 10th June 1664. He leaves the sum of £100 to his eldest daughter Margaret, and the same sum to his two youngest daughters Joan and Ann. Dale and also three beds and their furnishings to be divided equally between his three daughters at the discretion of *my loving wife Joan.* There was no bequest to his only son John.

The next entry relating to Penkhull Hall is dated 25th April 1662, the entry that Robert Nicholls records in 1929. Unfortunately Nicholls had only half the story, as the court minute continued to add further information not mentioned in his 1929 account. *John Lovatt and Joan Dale surrendered to the Lord King one messuage called Penkhull Hall with all its buildings, orchards and gardens to the use of Ralph Keeling.* It is clear at this point that the mortgage of £106 had not been returned. The next section of the minute then describes at the same court that William Wedgwood was granted seizen (ownership) of the premises and the mortgage of £106 was reassigned to him on condition that Keeling pay this off by the 26th April 1663. There are no further entries found in the manor court records under the name of Penkhull Hall.

From this point in it was originally assumed that the name was changed to Green Head House soon after 1662. This is not the case. The records for Greenhead House date prior to 1662, with an entry in April 1579, in a surrender of property that once stood where now Jeremy Close just off Trent Valley Road. The property was occupied by William Turner and Roger Hutchens and referred to as the inheritance of

Thomas Dale who lives at the *Green Head*. This confirms that not only did the house exist in 1579 but the Dale family also held it.

So where does all this leave the debate as to what stood where? Something that has been pondered over hard and long. There is significant evidence to prove that both existed side by side. Penkhull Hall, containing a large parlour, would be used once, every three weeks for manor court transactions as well as living accommodation. This is the old section of The Greyhound Inn, largely re-constructed in 1936, because of its decayed condition. Greenhead House, on the other hand, was the other section of the Inn.

As the court records have shown already, the name of Dale is significant in the ownership of each, and it is probable that after the last entry for Penkhull Hall in 1663, it all became one property called Greenhead House. During the occupation of the Lovatt family in the early 1700s, the current lounge area and the small room off, would, I am confident, have been rebuilt. Greenhead House simply means the house at the head of the green, which reflects an accurate picture for the term.

From later records when the property was in the occupation and ownership of John Townsend it was described as having had been divided into three separate dwellings, two of which retained their individual status until being sold to Parkers Brewery in 1936.

The following entry dated 26th June 1672, points to the future history of Greenhead House in as much it was surrendered by Thomas Dale, and then described as *in his own possession and various lands to Thomas Dale his son. And to this court comes Thomas Dale (the son) and Margaret his wife and took from the King all and singular the premises aforesaid.*

Joan Dale remained a spinster all her life. She was buried in Stoke churchyard on the 13th January 1669. Her will and inventory of goods has survived. The will is dated 24th November 1669, (Julian calender) written almost on her deathbed (which was often the practice in those days).

To my sister Ann to which I have security of land in Penkhull	£100
To John my brother a fourth of the £52 he oweth me	£ 13
To Alice Dale my sister in law	£ 5
And to my sister Ann the balance of my estate	£ 5

A further four small bequests are made to distant relatives.

The inventory of all goods and chattels of Joan Dale was taken by her brother John and a relative John Bourne on the 25th January 1669.

One trunk with linen in it	£3 13s 4d
Debts upon specialty	
Mr Wedgwood	£100
William Bourne	£ 10
Thomas Dale	£ 10
Debts without specialty	
John Dale	£ 22
John Bourne	£ 10
William Webb	£ 1
Wearing apparel and money in her purse	£ 20
Total value	**£176 13s 4d**

Looking at early manorial surveys and ecclesiastical accounts, more evidence comes to light to further identify the Dale family, as one of the most important families in Penkhull in addition to holding significant property and land. A survey dated 1516/7 lists John Dale as paying 12s 4d in rent to the Lord of the Manor. A further survey of 1618, lists Roger Dale as holding 23½ acres of land. John Dale is listed along with William Turner and Thomas Barnett as holding 49 acres. The figures are also replicated in a survey dated 1650.

A list of parishioners recorded in the churchwarden's accounts for Stoke Church dated 1595, lists Roger and John Dale as church wardens. For whatever reason in the later accounts of 1601, a number of residents were listed as *payeth noe dutye to the churche*. This list included the same Roger Dale twice, and was informed that from that date he must pay for two. *(the two properties are probably Penkhull Farm and Greenhead House)*. A later list of parishioners dated 1616 those paying church lunes included Roger Dale as again of holding two properties one paying 3s 4d on the first, and 2s for the second.

At a copyhold court held at Penkhull in September 1657, the copyhold jury listed both Thomas Lovatt and John Dale. At the same court John Dale and Thomas Dale were sworn in as headborrrows, an important official of the manor court system reflecting their status within the community. By November 1667, Thomas Dale had been elected to the senior position of Chief Bailiff of the district Penkhull with Boothen, within the Manor of Newcastle.

The relationship of family members is made a little clearer in the next document dated 20th January 1657 (note this would be in the Julian calendar until 1753 when dates assumed the Gregorian calendar). It was a court held under the direction of Maj. Gen. Thomas Harrison who had been gifted the Manor of Newcastle by Cromwell. The entry reads: *to this court comes Roger Dale and Thomas Dale, son and heir apparent to the said Roger and release unto John Dale all their rights of either estates including One Capital Messuage now in the peaceable occupation of the same John Dale.* It is not clear if this refers to the Greenhead House or another large old property that once stood in Trent Valley Road. The addition of the word 'peaceable' is interesting and one wonders if this refers in someway to the turbulent times of the civil war.

Thomas Dale married Margery Townsend on the 16th April 1672 at Stoke Church. The union produced four children. Thomas 13th March 1672/3, Elizabeth, 23rd January 1675/6, Maria 10th April 1679 and Margery 23rd May 1683. All were baptised at Stoke old church.

The Hearth Tax record for 1662, lists Roger Dale as holding property with five hearths while the 1672 Hearth Tax return shows that a property held by Thomas Dale had four hearths. This is accountable by the fact that Roger Dale junior died in April 1665, being buried in Stoke churchyard on the 25th. The reduction of one hearth can be explained by the fact that it was common practice to brick up one fireplace to avoid payment of the tax.

A further entry dated the 26th June 1672 refers to Thomas Dale surrendering Greenhead House, described as in his own possession with its appurtenances and lands, to his son Thomas for the period of his natural life and after to the use of Margery his wife and then after her death to their son also known as Thomas. The court record then continued with a further surrender by Thomas Dale called 'Oulde House' and all the lands attached. This property stood in Trent Valley Road and like the first entry was transferred to his son on payment of a fine of 5s. This 'Oulde House' will again be referred to when discussing Penkhull Square, now Jeremy Close.

Roger had two sons, Roger and Thomas. Both names appear at a court held in November 1662. *They surrender to the King one close called Platthill meadow adjoining Boden meadow lying in Penkhull.* In 1672, Thomas Dale, as joint copyhold tenant with his widowed mother, Dorothy, surrendered an estate comprising thirteen parcels of land to Thomas and Richard Lovatt and Richard and John Boughey, both well known local land owners. It would appear that this was to secure a mortgage to enable Thomas Dale to purchase outright the part of the estate belonging to his widowed mother. The estate comprised as Bearshill, Naylors Croft, the two Townsends and the Backsides.

Despite Thomas Dale being a considerable landowner and described as a yeoman, he appears to be short of ready money. For on the 15th May 1700, he took out a loan against his property as security to provide annuities of £12 during their joint lives with his wife, later to be rephrased as £7 for a widow and £5 for a widower. The entry reads *surrendered to Thomas and Grace Harrison the lower part of Green Head House containing two bays, a barn consisting of two and a half bays, one structure called 'vain' house together with various plots*

of land adjoining that of Roger Machin and Thomas Doody. This was the section of Greenhead House known previously as Penkhull Hall.

By 1711, six years following the death of his father at a court held on the 30th July, Thomas Dale junior, received the estate back into his possession from William Harrison, the heir of Thomas Harrison then described as deceased. The court records continue with a further surrender by Thomas Dale of a property called Oulde House and all the land attached. This entry, like previous entries hands over the property to his son.

On the 3rd May 1704, Thomas Dale senior transferred Green Head House which he occupied, and also a part of Oulde House in Trent Valley Road, then in the occupation of William Shaw, together with a significant amount of land including the area now known as the Garden Village, Thistley Hough, the Croft and land in Boothen and Clayton. This transaction was made to enable Mr T D Turner to service a £300 loan to provide the three sisters of Thomas Dale with sufficient beneficiaries. The property was surrendered to Thomas Townsend.

By October 1706, Thomas Dale junior recovered all the estates previously used as security to obtain yet a further loan, this time amounting to £300. He mortgaged the property and part of the lands to Thomas Townsend and Thomas Sutton. The total amount received in loans amounted to £336 which included £36 accumulated interest.

Thomas Dale was buried in Stoke Church yard on the 28th January 1720. Both his will and inventory of goods have survived. His will is dated 16th December 1719, and was drawn-up knowing that he had not long to live.

An indication of the wealth and lifestyle of Thomas Dale can be formed from the contents of the inventory of his goods and shackles, taken by appraisers Thomas Sutton and Thomas Proctor on the 28th April 1720.

One Mare	£ 3 0 0d
Twenty three sheep	£12 0 0d
Hay in Hassall's Barn	£ 4 0 0d
Eight planks	14 0d
In the stable, chains and other goods with two ladders.	£ 1 5 0d
In the corn chamber & cart house sawn and cleaved timber.	£ 1 0 0d
Two tumbrels, two pair of harrows, one plough, two coulters one pair of draughts,	£ 1 5 0d
Four stone troughs, one gate in the fold.	14 0d
In the malthouse	
Two tubs, 6 harrs, 8 heads, 9 boards, 2 sides for ladders. 1 trye, 1 short ladder.	£ 2 0 0d
Hard corn in Clays barn	£11 0 0d
In the large parlour	
One long table, two forms, small table, one joined chair, one folding screen,	

One square table, one cupboard, one chaff bed and bedsteads, one grate, one fire shovel, tongs and fender six silver spoons, six escutcheons.

£ 4 10 0d

In the house place
One table two forms, two arm chairs, one clock, one jack, one gun, three pistols, four spits, two pair of candle sticks, two iron dripping pans, one brass pot, one stew pan. one egg slice, one iron plate.   £ 5 0 0d

In the parlour next to the house
Three bedsteads and hangings, three coverlids, three
feather beds, five bolsters, three chaff beds two pillows   £ 5 10 0d

In the chamber over the house
Three feather beds, two bolsters, two pair bedsteads
and hangings, four blankets, three coffers, one
cupboard, one board, one close stoole and pan, 4 weights.   £4 10s 0d

In the chamber over the parlour two bedsteads, one coffer,
one cord, in the kitchen chamber odd things.   £ 3 0 0d
Cheese press, mall and wedges   19 0d

In the kitchen
One furnace, one pot, one pan, kettle, two benches, one grate   £ 2 10 0d

In the best chamber
Two chests   £ 1 5 0d
One bedstead and hangings, two feather beds one bolster,
two pillows, three blankets, one quilt, one arm chair,
one cupboard, one hanging press, one square table, one small
looking glass, one flock bed, seventeen pair of sheets,
twenty four napkins, seven table cloths, and pieces of
cloth linen, one coverlid.   £16 7 0d

The little chamber
Five chairs, feather bed, two bolsters one stand.   £2 0 0d

In the garrets
One coffer, with thirty two pounds of hemp,
One coffer two blankets and the coffer at the stairs head.   £1 4 0d
In the cellar
Three Barrels, two turnells.   £1 5 0d
In the pantry one table, two chairs, one coffer.   10 0d
133 pieces of pewter, at 8d per piece.   £ 4 8 0d

At old Robert Tittensor's.
One table, one form, one coffer of oats,
One spreading rake, one shovel, two bags.   £1 0 0d
At Mr John Bourne's
Three barrels, one iron kettle, two little pots, one warming pan, three brass pans, skillets, one saucepan, one cleaver, two tubs, one feather bed, three blankets, one bolster.   £3 15 0d
                                        £94 11 8d

This inventory gives not only the contents of the house but also a description of the property, listing each room individually. The document also includes items in both Tittensor's and Bourne's houses. Thomas Dale owned these at the time. If a comparison is made between the list of accommodation in 1719 against a corresponding list of rooms recorded at the time of the reconstruction of The Greyhound in 1936, they replicate exactly only with different names.

The Malthouse	Listed as behind The Greyhound now demolished.
The Large Parlour	The Smoke Room
The House Place	The public bar area of The Greyhound
The chamber over the parlour	Bedroom over the parlour
The chamber over hse' place	Bedroom over the public bar.
The best chamber	Bedroom over the central bar area
The little chamber	Bedroom over the far end of the public bar to the rear

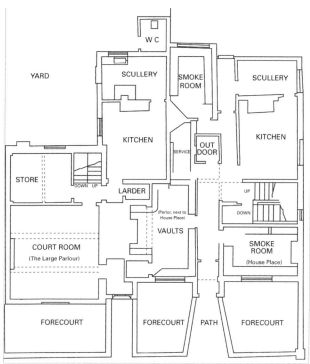
Plan of The Greyhound at the time of its reconstruction, 1936

The transfer of the estate to the executors reads as follows: *And as concerning that messuage Greenhead House in which Mr Joseph Lovatt now lives and all malthouses, barns, stables, gardens, orchards, and various lands belonging to the said Mary Lovatt.* The entry also refers to an additional property called *Tittensor's House in the holding of Robert Tittensor with barns, stables, gardens, orchards etc.* This was left to his sister Margaret Bourne and refers to: *The large house which was later purchased by Josiah Spode, promptly demolished and replaced by a large mansion called The Mount.*

The third sister, Elizabeth, married James Bromfield, a curate of Stoke Church. She inherited an un-named property, which was described as *in the occupation of Richard Heath with barns, stables, gardens etc.* as well as the land off Trent Valley Road, Hunters Way and in Boothen. It was probably the Oulde House previously mentioned. Elizabeth immediately used this security to obtain a loan from Thomas Sutton for the sum of £200. The loan was cleared by 1725.

The following year, 1726, Elizabeth was widowed and once more obtained a mortgage to the value of £220 from Edward Smith using property as security. It would appear that life did not improve greatly for Elizabeth as four years later; in April 1730 the debt had been taken over by her brother Joseph Lovatt. She died the following year.

The parish registers for St. Peter-ad-Vincula in Stoke record from the 2nd quarter of the seventeenth century that the family of Lovatt was already established in the area. The first recorded entry is the burial of Richard Lovatt in 1638. There may have been entries prior to this but the registers only commence in 1629. There are no early entries for a Dale/Lovatt marriage at Stoke or Newcastle, but a search in the Wolstanton parish registers does produce the union of Randle Dale and Elizabeth Lovatt, married 24th February 1686. A further union of the two names comes on the 17th June 1704 when Joseph Lovatt of Mount Sorrel, described as a yeoman with considerable estates in Leicestershire, married Mary Dale of Penkhull. Rev J Bromfield, Vicar of Wybunbury, who later married Elizabeth the sister of Mary, conducted the ceremony.

The will of Richard Lovatt dated 30th May 1687, points to an incentive for the two families to be linked. Lovatt left various lands and property to Thomas Dale and John Cradock in trust. The will then referred to the right of inheritance in as much that any of his daughters must take a husband whose surname is Lovatt without any additional surname. A letter dated 14th April 1704 to Mr John Cheshyre; a solicitor as for a legal opinion with regard to this section of the will.

The document continues to explain the reason for the enquiry: *Some months ago a young man who wrote his name Lovett came a courting to one of the Dales daughters and immediately heard that in the will the surname required of any suitor would have to be spelt with a 'a' and not an 'e' and has since written his name Lovatt. The question arises that if he marries Dales daughter with the consent of her father as the will dictates, is he not entitled to the estate not withstanding he formerly spelt Lovatt with an 'e'?* The reply from Mr Cheshyre stated that *either spelling would not affect the sound and pronunciation of the name although the written name would be.* Mr Cheshyre agreed that if the surname was spelt with an 'a' he considered the marriage would conform to the conditions set in the will.

The marriage of Joseph Lovatt of Mount Sorrel to Mary Dale took place at Stoke on the 17th June 1704, two months following the legal opinion offered by Mr Cheshyre.

Within the Shrewsbury archives, under the heading of the Henlle Hall Collection there are masses of legal documents relating to the Lovatt family estates as well as those of the Dale family. The reason for this is that the last of the Lovatts resided at Henlle Hall in Shropshire; therefore, regardless of the origin of the documents, all were placed into the archives for that county. One such document refers to the genealogy of the two families.

Thomas Dale, born Monday 17th March 1672 at 5 o'clock in the afternoon and baptised the same day.
Elizabeth Dale, born Friday 21st January 1675 about 2 of the clock in the forenoon and baptised Sunday after.
Mary Dale, born on Saturday 5th April 1679 about one of the clock on that day and baptised April 10th 1679
June ye 17th 1704.
On Saturday the day and year above Joseph Lovatt of Mt.

Sorrel, yeoman and Mary Dale of Penkhull were married.
Mary Lovatt died 1st June 1754 at Penkhull.
Joseph Lovatt died 17th March 1754 at Penkhull.
Richard Lovatt, born 16th January 1767. Died as a student at Magdalen Hall, Oxford on the 7th June 1787 and buried there. He was of four years standing at the university.
Joseph Lovatt, born September 18th 1714.
Sarah Lovatt, born 24th July 1717.
Ann Lovatt, born 15th May 1719.
Dale Lovatt *(combination of both surnames)* born, 2nd January 1721. Dale Lovatt attended Balliol College. Matric 26th March 1743.

Joseph Lovatt, the son of Joseph and Mary married Ann the only daughter of William and Margaret Sherman of Newcastle on the 11th July 1743 at St Giles, Newcastle but only after several months of legal disputes regarding a complicated marriage settlement. It is interesting that when considering writing his will in 1771, he wrote to his solicitor expressing his concern using the words: *I feel so strangely fettered that I am almost lost about it, and I desire you will endeavour to show me in what manner we shall be able to raise the money for the use of our children.* Joseph was in his 29th year and Ann in her 33rd year. It was not long after their marriage that they were blessed with a daughter Margaret born at Newcastle on Saturday 14th April 1744. Margaret received a private baptism on the Wednesday following. She died on the 31st January the following year.

William and Ann Lovatt, twins were born at Penkhull on Friday August 7th, 1747. William at about 6 o'clock, Ann about one hour later. Mr Ward, curate of Stoke gave them baptism that evening.

The main theme of Greenhead House continues looking at the Last Will and Testament of Thomas Dale who died in January 1717. The will was presented to the manor court on the 21st April 1720. It was not until the 30th December the same year that the manor court dealt with the implications of surrender by the executors of the will and the admittance of new tenants to the copyhold estate. Dale's three daughters and their respective husbands were admitted. Mary Lovatt to Greenhead House, Elizabeth Bromfield, to a property with considerable land described as being in the occupation of Richard Heath and lastly Margery Bourne to the large property known as Tittensor's House, described as in the occupation of Robert Tittensor, again with considerable appurtenances.

With their new found status, that of some considerable wealth, the story unfolds on the trials and tribulations, mortgages and loans that transpired over the next two decades as the three separate families continued on their separate ways as wealthy property and land owners.

From the date of her father's death in 1717, Mary and her husband Joseph were described as being in occupation of Greenhead House. In 1742/3 they transferred the estate and property to Joseph their son known as Joseph the younger. By this time Elizabeth, Mary's sister, had become a widow and her estates were transferred to Joseph the younger.

On the 1st February 1750, Joseph Lovatt senior was appointed by Mr Richard Myddleton of Chirk Castle, Denbighshire as steward of his estates on an annual salary of £1,000. His duties were to receive rents, let and repair properties, see to the domestic affairs and pay tradesmen's and workmen's bills and generally carry out all business that fell within the duties of provincial land and house steward.

Lovatt senior, then residing at Chirk, asked his friend John Terrick, who lived in an old house which stood where the The Views is now located to over-see his land and property in Penkhull. Two letters from Terrick to Lovatt dated March and June 1753 have survived and are preserved in the National Archives for Wales at the University of Aberystwyth where many years ago I studied the Lovatt file. Both letters present an insight into the social life of the period as well as the structure of Greenhead House.

March 17th 1753.
Sir, Malkin promised the payment of a trifling debt of his father's, but since he hath disputed the matter. Then the charges relating to his father's death they say amounts to about £20 and the bailiffs, about ten days ago took the few goods he had. At present I think he is not very fond of that sort of physical treatment. John Slaney and him are just as you left them as to their affairs, but John hath closed his condition; he married his cousin Whitehurst's daughter and the promise of a considerable fortune. He goes on in the farm according to his promise and I wish his cousin made good his debt. There are some other matters of no great moment that I can mention to you when I see you as well as now.
Your servant, John Terrick.

June 26th 1753
John Reeves will finish that part of the house you ordered to be taken off first this week. He thinks it will not continue long for the other side with mending part of it. The ridge must all be taken off again. Boards for the gable ends I have paid for and John Reeve's sum of money to Bloor it will be a good deal of expense to complete the matter so I intend to stop Reeves until I hear from you.
I think it will be the best time now to do it all. Father and sister give their services to you and your family.
Yours John Terrick
Received by the hands of John Bloor – 29th June 1753

In the following year, 1754 an agreement was drawn up between Joseph Lovatt and John Slaney in which Lovatt surrendered to Slaney, Greenhead House and the malt house except two chambers (bedrooms) over the cart house with ingress and regress for a term of seven years and at annual rent of £80, on proviso that if himself or his wife, after either death, are minded to reside again at the house and give notice in writing requiring possession of the premises then Slaney would have a reduction in the rent. The terms of the lease stated that Slaney would keep the draw well clean in the yard and the buckets, ropes, chains, cords and gearing in good repair.

The Last Will and Testament of Joseph Lovatt is dated 16th April 1773, and appoints his son Thomas and his son-in-law as executors. After the usual payments of debts he left all his copyhold estates in Penkhull to his eldest son William, his household furniture and any books she may choose to his *good wife*. To his other son, Thomas he left all his books of arithmetic, geometry and the like in addition to his mathematical instruments and manuscripts. The will also referred to Articles of Indenture entered into in the year 1771.

Thomas Lovatt married Mary Jones of Plasnewydd, Anglesey. His will is dated 17th April 1780, and refers in the first instance to a marriage settlement whereby: *in consideration of my marriage with the said Mary Jones, now my wife, then Mary, the said sum of £2,000 agreed to be paid by Thomas Jones (father of Mary) as the portion of his said daughter, together with my contribution of £2,000 making a total of £4,000 to be laid out in a purchase of lands and tenements for his own use for life then immediately after my decease to the intent of the said Mary thereafter to have an annuity of £80 p.a. for her natural life.* The marriage produced one son, Richard. After the death of Thomas, John Jones named in the Will as trustee was admitted tenant to the copyhold estates in Penkhull as trustee on the 25th October 1802.

Between these dates William the elder brother of Thomas died on the 31st January 1788 at Chirk, a bachelor and is buried there. By this time much of the copyhold land in Penkhull had been leased out. One such lessee was John Townsend, who acquired land from William Lovatt. Thomas acquired the estates in Penkhull including Greenhead House upon the death of his elder brother William in July 1788, six months after his brother's death. His will dated 18th May 1782, leaving his estates to his young brother Thomas. He also leaves the sum of £500 to his other brother John in addition to shares in mines. To his sister-in-law the sum of five guineas, and also to his nephews Richard, the only son of Thomas, and to John, his nephew, the son of his brother John, the same amount. William also made other bequests. To his male servant the annual payment for life of £5 and to his maidservant the sum of £2 annually, also for life on condition *that they had both stayed with me for five years.*

Thomas Lovatt continued to rent his estates in Penkhull to a number of tenants including John Townsend. Townsend leased out the large farmhouse, Greenhead House, and the farmland for a period of fourteen years from July 1788, at an annual rent of £130 p.a. The land tax assessment confirms that Townsend took possession of the property in 1787 and paid tax for that year amounting to £6 14 6d. At the expiry of the lease in 1802, it was surrendered from the estate of Thomas Lovatt *together with certain plots of land . . . for several years past in the holding of John Townsend.* Thomas Lovatt died on the 5th May 1801. On the 25th October 1802, a series of transactions took place in the manor court that in effect split up most of the Penkhull copyhold estate. Richard Lovatt, the son of Thomas, took possession from the trustees *all and singular those messuages land and property in Penkhull or elsewhere in the Manor, which were the estate of Thomas Lovatt, deceased, previously of William Lovatt deceased and formerly of Joseph Lovatt, with the appurtenances and to which the said John Jones on the 13th October 1801 was admitted tenant in trust.*

The Staffordshire Advertiser, dated the 14th November, carried the advertisement for a forthcoming auction to sell the estate of Lovatt.

To be sold by Auction at the Roebuck Inn in Newcastle-under-Lyme on 21st December 1801. A very valuable Copyhold Estate of Inheritance, called Penkhull, situated in the parish of Stoke in several eligible lots, consisting of two dwelling houses, a malt kiln, and other buildings and 85 acres of excellent land, now in the holding of Mr John Townsend. The premises are situate within a small distance from the populous towns of Newcastle and Stoke, and of the Grand Junction Canal, The canal between Newcastle and Stoke runs through part of the land; many of the fields contain clay fit for manufactory carried on in the neighbourhood.

Following the auction on the 2nd October 1802, the estate was sold, and the manor courts record reveal that Josiah Spode acquired all that copyhold dwelling house and barn and lands called the *Three Hough's of which only one remains in name, that of Thistley Hough.* This land contained over eleven acres. The second section to be sold was to Thomas Minton, potter of Stoke, which included the area formerly called Bearshill on the opposite side of Trent Valley Road from what is now Jeremy Close, containing over seven acres. The third section was to John Davies, shoemaker of Stoke, and was land situated of the south side of the Newcastle canal containing one acre.

The final section was sold to John Townsend, yeoman who used to farm much of the land previously recorded. The minute continues: *all that copyhold messuage with malt kiln, gardens orchard belonging containing one acre or thereabouts,* now and for several years past in the holding of John Townsend, together with the seats or pews and sittings in the parish church of Stoke belonging to the said messuage. The measurements point to the conclusion that the property and land formed the island bounded by what are now Garden Street, Newcastle Lane and Manor Court Street.

Townsend

The first mention of the name Townsend found within the manor court rolls appears as early as May 1565, when Nicholas Townsend was tenant of land at the bottom of Newcastle Lane. There are quite a few accounts listed in the courts when *Roger Townsend held of Newcastle manor a copyhold messuage and lands in Penkhull called Spittal Houses* in 1714.

Townsend mortgaged the property, Greenhead House in April 1806, in consideration of a loan amounting to £350 from William Adams of Cobridge, earthenware manufacturer. Again in June 1813, Townsend borrowed a further sum of £150 from John Brown of Knutton. Until 1812, the farm house and land attached was bounded by three roads with only the village green in front which had seen no changes for over four hundred years. This all changed as Townsend sold off three plots of land, a decision that had the effect of changing the medieval agrarian village centre of Penkhull forever.

To John Burgess, gardener, he sold 1144 square yards for £382, the sale being described as: *all that close of land, croft or orchard adjoining the dwelling house of the said John Townsend late in his holding, abutting north to the road leading from Newcastle to Penkhull, and on the west to the lane called Tittensors Lane and enjoying exclusive rights to the fence or hedge separating the property to Michael Baxter and Thomas Bird.*

To Thomas Bird, bricklayer, Townsend sold a further 550 sq yards for £103 recorded as: *all that plot of land adjoining the dwelling house of John Townsend to the south, together with the brick wall to the front.* At this time Townsend retained the land to the north of his home bordering on to the narrow pathway leading to the malthouse buildings and cottages. He also used the ground beyond this pathway to its junction with Newcastle Street as a garden without formal admittance for it still remained listed by the Duchy of Lancaster as a part of the manorial waste.

In 1827 Joseph Mountford offered to purchase this plot of land for building purposes from John Townsend. Mountford was then described as a farmer living at Croxton in Staffordshire. It was confirmed that Townsend was not the copyhold tenant of the land as the sale was the subject of a presentation by the Duchy of Lancaster.

At a special court held on 14th April 1827 to this court comes John Townsend of Penkhull and in consideration of seven guineas of lawful English money paid by him to the Lord of the Manor, doth grant to the said John Townsend a plot of land now enclosed and used as a garden, bounded on the north by the road leading to Knappers Gate, on the east by the road leading from Penkhull to the lodge turnpike gate and on the west by a private road leading to Michael Baxter's malt kiln and houses being part of waste land in the village of Penkhull.

Townsend was now in a position to purchase the plot consisting of 487 square yards as occupier from the Lord of the Manor. Once completed he proceeded to sell the land to Joseph Mountford in consideration of £60.

Townsend died the same year and his Last Will dated 21st July 1828 was presented to the court on the 2nd October 1828. After his funeral expenses and debts he leaves the residue of his estate to his two daughters Mrs Hannah Hall and Mrs Martha Yale. He bequeaths to Hannah the bed and bedding, and all other items found in the bedroom to his other daughter Martha. A condition of the will was that the effects left to Martha should be put out to interest and not to be at the control of her husband, and then upon her death to Elizabeth the daughter of Martha. John Townsend appointed Joseph Townsend a bookkeeper of Kingsley, who was no doubt a relative, and his own daughter Martha, as his sole executors.

The executors of his estate placed it up for auction in November as the following advertisement in the Staffordshire Advertiser: *Those three newly erected brick and tile dwelling houses pleasantly situated in the centre of Penkhull, with garden containing 150 square yards adjoining, well adapted for building purposes, occupying a front of thirty eight feet. Also, an old respectable Farm House, contiguous to the above, now occupied in three dwellings, commanding an extent of fifty eight feet in front, with a back yard, in which is a stable for two horses, pigsty, coal house and other conveniences and an excellent garden of about eight roods adjoining at the back of the same, all in a ring fence, the whole late the property of John Townsend, deceased.*

It is interesting to note that in a previous advertisement for the sale of the house, dated 1801, the property was listed as *divided into two dwellings*. This gives authority to the assumption that the property of today was originally two, Penkhull Hall and Greenhead House.

A manor court document dated the 5th February 1829 itemizes both property and the outstanding debts of Townsend. It further indicates the results of the auction and how the finances were sorted to accommodate the sale. Firstly his two daughters were admitted tenants to the copyhold estate consisting of four dwelling houses and two

gardens but subject to a mortgage held by John Brown of Knutton Heath. To settle the outstanding mortgage to John Brown, William Bagnall paid the sum of £280 in part payment and discharge of the principal money and interest due. The daughters of Townsend then surrendered all those three dwelling houses described as in the occupations of William Parky, Joseph Dishley and Ralph Pennington, in addition to the land attached to the dwellings to Mr Bagnall. There was also a condition that Bagnall would have the use of the water pump at the side of the other property along with the Malt House.

Regarding the property sold to Bagnall the sale was on condition that the purchase price included the balance of the mortgage to Brown of £36 14s in full payment of the debt, and the sum of £183 6s to the daughters Martha and Hannah. Next, having agreed on these terms, the sisters proceeded to surrender: Greenhead House, *divided into three dwellings with the land adjoining previously occupied by John Townsend, William Hewitt and Thomas Green along with the use of the water pump. And also all those stables, piggeries, outhouses, and the pew seats in the parish church of Stoke. The property was surrendered to Mr George Thomas Taylor, overseer of the poor for Stoke.*

George Thomas Taylor

The remainder of the estate was sold to George Thomas Taylor, assistant overseer of the poor for the parish of Stoke, and an important figure in the community.

Two important events in 1828 had a significant bearing on the future of Greenhead House. On the 25th August, George Thomas Taylor applied to the Justices of the Peace acting in the Hundred of Pirehill North for permission to open an alehouse. The document, after the formal introduction continues: *That your petitioner is the proprietor of a commodious dwelling house with stable yard and other conveniences in Penkhull and which has for some time past been used by Mr George Marlow as a Retail Brewery. Currently the population of Penkhull has very much increased within the last few years, and that it now contains upwards of seven hundred persons.*

There is only one Public House in the place for which a licence was granted when there was not more than one quarter of the present number. In all probability the new Ale House Act of 1828 (9 George IV c61) would have influenced Taylor to obtain a licence to sell ale. He also saw the opportunity for business from the increase in population of Penkhull, as there was only one inn in the centre of the village, being the Marquis of Granby. The Act however failed to make provision for the keeping of licensing records by the Clerk of the Peace, so the discovery of the original application to the Justices of Pirehill North to sell ale just a few years ago in the possession of his great, great grand-daughter Mrs Betty Wildblood makes it even more important.

Your petitioner sincerely believes that an additional Public House in Penkhull is wanted and would be an accommodation and convenience to the inhabitants. This is borne out in such his belief by the testimony of a great number of respectable inhabitants of Penkhull and others.

I beg to leave to draw your Worships' attention to the fact that the present occupier of these premises has sold upwards of thirty barrels of ale off the premises within the last six months. Therefore, I pray your worships to grant a licence to open the said house as a Public and Victualling House and your petitioner will every pray.

George T. Taylor, Stoke-upon-Trent, 25th August 1829

The document included the signatures of thirty-seven names, mostly local businessmen, traders and manufacturers as well as the churchwardens of Stoke Church. The significance of this document cannot be under estimated. Firstly, it tells us that ale had been sold from the house for six months, which takes that date back to the date the property was sold to Taylor. It further informs us that a local brewer was selling ale. Would it be the malt kiln to the rear of Greenhead House produced that the ale?

Taylor emphasizes the increase in the population, giving approximate figures but fails to indicate that this expansion was due to the fact that Josiah Spode had provided housing in the village for his workers. There is also only one other retailer of ale quoted. This would be the Marquis of Granby. However, it is surprising that he did not include The White Lion in Honeywall as part of Penkhull. This was probably because it was considered at that time a hamlet with its own identity.

Part of the application by Mr. George Thomas Taylor.
Below - the names supporting the application

The Greyhound Inn c1930

106

The Penkhull Lock-up

There is only a single reference of a lock-up at Penkhull. But first what is the definition of this term? They were often used for the confinement of drunks who were usually released the next day, or to hold people being brought before the local magistrate the following morning. A typical village lock-up is a small structure with a single door and a narrow slit window or opening. Lock-ups were not a gaol; they were only a temporary place to secure prisoners.

The Staffordshire Advertiser dated the 10th October 1829 refers to the Lock-Up at Penkhull in a press report of the activities of the General Court Leet and Court Baron held at the Wheatsheaf in Stoke. In attendance was the Chief Constable for Stoke-upon-Trent Mr John Davis. Mention was made to the Court of the *necessity, which existed for a lock-up in the town of Stoke - prisoners sometimes escaping from the custody of the constables whilst being taken to that at Penkhull. The Court stated that it had no funds available for such a purpose; and recommended to the inhabitants to erect the building, and defray the cost by public subscription.*

The Penkhull lock-up was situated beneath the old courtroom in what is now The Greyhound Inn. Some forty-five years ago, I recall my visit to Bert Pattinson and his wife Nora who lived at No 27 Penkhull Terrace. He was then aged seventy-two years and could well remember living in that section of the inn, which, at that time was next door to The Greyhound, and a separate dwelling house. Bert continues: *I went to live there in March 1932; my mother purchased it for me. I left in August 1934. It was later purchased by Parkers Brewery. The door to the cellar was very thick and was designed with a little hatch and a slide across so the jailer could see the prisoners.*

The cellar was approached through this door and down the stairs that curved around. Up the far corner were a large wooden stump and a chain fastened to it. There were also shackles fastened to chains into the brickwork. As money was short then I pulled them out and sold the metal to the rag and bone man for a few pence.

The main room that you entered from the front was large with seating all around, the seat parts had been removed but the back panels were still in place, fixed to the walls. In the centre of the main wall the large wooden panel back of the central chair was set into the wall and partly plastered over. At the back of the room was a small room off used as a kitchen followed by a back kitchen and a small yard.

Following on from this interview with Bert and Nora, I then asked my good friend Ken Nutt who knew Bert well. Ken confirmed exactly how Bert had described the cellar, stating that as a young boy he would often be shown the old lock-up and be quite frightened by the whole experience. A

further friend of mine, Mrs Taylor who used to live in Rothwell Street, talked to me, some years ago, describing the old court room as a general merchant's shop where you could purchase items ranging from buckets to paraffin. She confirmed the description of the benches and the wooden paneling and the old cellar.

For many years the old building was used as Ellis' Oatcake Shop. William Ellis and his family lived there during the 1920s and his wife ran the shop. William had returned from the First World War with honour. He died in June 1956, and was brought back to Penkhull Church for his final service.

Conveyance documents, dated 1920, refer to No 5 Church Street, the old courthouse being sold by Mr R G Eabrey to Mr E Forshaw, Junior. It was then conveyed again to Parkers Burslem Brewery on the 30th April 1936.

If we return once more to the general theme of the history of the building, the census returns from 1841 to 1901, give a good insight into who occupied The Greyhound Inn. The 1841 census is not an ideal place to start as it contains only limited information. But here we can read that Elizabeth Taylor, aged 74, a widow was living there with Sarah, her grand daughter. There is no mention of the parents of the children. To clarify the situation, a trade directory, dated 1850, confirms that the landlord was John Taylor, perhaps a relative of Mr George Thomas Taylor, who purchased the property from John Townsend in 1829. There occurs in Whites Directory of 1834, just a short reference to the old building in a brief description of Penkhull. *Among a few ancient buildings still standing in the village is one in which was formerly held the copyhold court of the Manor of Newcastle.* It was also recorded that the courts were then being held at the Wheatsheaf in Stoke on the first Thursday of every month.

By April 1841 Mr Taylor having serious financial problems decided to sell off the inn by auction. This was held at The Wheatsheaf in Stoke on Monday 19th April 1841. He had purchased this along with the old parish workhouse, in December 1834 borrowing the sum of £800 from John Wickes Tomlinson and Frederick Wright Tomlinson of Cliffe Ville. By this time he had also taken out a second mortgage of £500 from Mr William Baker, pottery manufacturer of Fenton.

The arrears amounted to £885 16s 11d, including interest charges and was paid to John Wikes Tomlinson and Frederick Wright Tomlinson by William Baker and also in consideration of the further sum of £564 11s 8d retained by William Baker, being the amount already due and owning from George Taylor to Baker. The court record dated the 29th September continues with a full description of the premises: *All that ancient tenement or Farmhouse heretofore divided into three but now consisting of two dwelling houses with land thereto adjoining situate at Penkhull and for many years in the possession of John Townsend a former owner thereof but after its division into three tenements in the holding of William Warrilow, George Hewitt and Thomas Green but now in the possession or occupation of John Cooper and Thomas Tatton, butcher. Together with the slaughterhouse or butchers shop and the brew house, stable, cow house, piggeries, yard and garden thereto belonging and the concurrent right of using the well of water and the pump in the yard behind the premises to which George Thomas Taylor was admitted tenant to him and his heirs upon surrender of George Yale and Martha his wife, William Hall and Hannah his wife, Joseph Townsend and John Brown at a court held on the 5th February 1829.*

By 1851 more details become available of Mr John Taylor from the census return. He was aged 31, and described as a potter and beerhouse keeper, originating from Liverpool. His wife Ann, aged 28, was born in Shelton. They had two children and a house servant who came from Shropshire. The fact that they had a servant signifies that although Taylor had two jobs, which was quite common as the beerhouse would only be open during the evenings and the weekends; he had sufficient funds and status to afford a servant. The servant could possibly have lived there rent-free in consideration of services in the beer house.

The census return of 1861 lists the beerhouse for the first time under the sign of 'The Greyhound'. Charles Kirkham was head of the family, and like his predecessor was employed locally as well as at the beerhouse in the evenings. He was married to Jane, aged 36. Both were born in Penkhull. They had two daughters, one of which was aged 15, and whose occupation was listed as a servant. There were also four boys, with ages ranging between 4 to 10 years. At the old courthouse next door lived Richard Edge, a labourer, aged 44, and Ann his wife of the same age and both from Penkhull. They had six children aged from 3 to 25 years. In addition to this there were two lodgers living in the house, William and Sarah Brindley from Hanley. Manor Court Street then went by the name of *West side of church*.

The following census of 1871 shows that the premises supported a new occupier, George Chell, who came from Hixon Churtley and recorded as an Inn Keeper/Beer seller with no reference to any additional occupation. He was 38 years of age and his wife Mary was one year older. They had one son, John, aged 6 years, and a lodger Benjamin Blackburn, aged 50. Mary died in January 1880. Three years later on the 3rd May 1883, George remarried to Fanny Degg, a widow and the sister-in-law of Thomas Mayor who lived next door to the inn. Fanny lived there also. Together they ran the inn until George died in November 1891. He had been the landlord for over twenty years and is buried in Penkhull churchyard.

The title documents date from only 1873, and commence with the surrender by William Baker the younger to George Chell. The court minute gives quite an insight to the property. William Baker the younger was an eminent architect of Highfields, Audlem, Cheshire. His name is associated with numerous prestigious buildings throughout the country. The surrender and admittance is dated the 24th April 1873, and revolves around the payment by George Chell of £460 for the purchase of The Greyhound Inn, a number of years earlier. The court minutes give valuable information regarding the old building. *All that ancient tenement farmhouse heretofore divided into three then into two dwelling houses, and now consisting of a dwelling house and Beer house in the occupation of George Chell under the sign of 'The Greyhound', situate at Penkhull together with all outbuildings, yards and appurtenances to the same belonging.*

After the death of his wife Mary and before he remarried, George Chell transferred the ownership of The Greyhound Inn to his son John, on the 26th May 1892. In September 1896, five years after the death of his father. John Chell sold the copyhold property to Messrs Beech and Pakeman. In 1909, Mr E Forsham took over the property for a further eleven years, for in 1920 it was sold to Mr R G Eabry. Eabry then on the 29th September 1925 sold The Greyhound Inn, No. 6 Church Street, to Parkers Burslem Brewery Ltd.

In 1901, just after the turn of the century there was a different tenant of 'The Greyhound Inn', Mr Joseph Webster who was listed as a publican and potters earthenware painter. He was 31 years of age; his wife Sarah Ann was 32 and both originated from the town of Newcastle. They had three daughters and also maintained a servant, Elizabeth Edwards, aged 21. In 1907, the landlord was Alfred Simcock but by 1911, Mr George Henley, aged 29, a joiner's labourer was the head of the family and his wife, Maud, aged 31, was listed as the publican. Next door at No.4 Church Street, the old court houses, was occupied by Henry Ball, aged 60, a tile fixer, his wife Harriett aged 47, and their five children ranging from 6 to 23 years of age.

George Henley and his wife Maud retained the inn until September 1927. An inventory and valuation of fixtures, fittings and stock was taken as part of the handover to the new landlord Mr Harry Tildesley. The document is a snapshot of the time, set over eighty years ago, when public houses were very different from today. It is a social document, itemising both rooms and contents. There would be little purpose served in reproducing the whole document, but a list of each room and any special features is interesting.

The list commences with the front smoke room where there were to be found three cast iron spittoons, an old oil painting and painted panelled windscreen. The old oak panelling on the walls is also noted. The tap room contained, amongst other items, a further three cast iron spittoons; a baize covered board for cards with two peg boards; stone hearth kerb as fixed; a gas regulator on meter in recess. From here, we move to the bar where there was to be found a three-pull beer engine encased in pewter, practically worn out with piping and unions to cellar; three pewter beer measures; 17 earthenware pint jugs; two prints frames, one without glass and a three legged Boston stool.

The next room is the back smoke room that contained only one copper spittoon; a large and a small case of stuffed birds. In the kitchen there was just a small painted table and a Windsor chair with a fractured arm and three shelves in the recess. There is also a scullery with a portable gas washing machine boiler and connections together with a slop stone. Outside at the back is an old stone roller and a set of 18 old

Two photographs taken during the time of the restoration, 1936

iron quoits, which are used in a traditional lawn game involving the throwing of a metal or rubber ring over a set distance to land over a pin (called a hob or mott) in the centre of a patch of clay.

No.5 Church Street was placed on the market for sale in 1935 as a derelict old timber building. Correspondence that I received some thirty years ago from Mrs Aston reveals that Rev V G Aston wanted Penkhull church to purchase this old building to use for church activities and meetings. Serious enquiries were made and an architect employed to view the property. Unfortunately the structural report confirmed that it was in such a poor state of repair that it virtually needed rebuilding. The church did not pursue enquiries any further.

Rev V G Aston later wrote in the parish magazine in 1936, about the part of the building which now forms the public bar that was found to be in a dangerous state with beams rotting. It was purchased by Parkers' Brewery, who undertook the reconstruction of the whole building, and intended to retain every possible part of the old courthouse. *When the front was taken down it was found that such was the state of ruin that little could be rebuilt into the new structure. Thankfully, builders and architects, R Scrivener & Sons, worked marvellously with what they had, and today we see the shape and form of the old court house as it was.*

Such were the concerns of Mr Aston, he wrote directly to Parker's Brewery at Burslem in March of that year:

Sirs, I understand that you have purchased the property adjoining The Greyhound Inn, and that you are contemplating combining the two in order to improve the Inn. I know that I have no right to ask, but might I respectfully submit that any alterations you make will not interfere with the characteristics of this ancient property. You will be aware that it was the old Manor Court House.

A change in its appearance would destroy what is to all intents and purposes a national asset which cannot be replaced. May I also ask that the inn should be called "The Court House", or some such name, to preserve the original title as well as its appearance? Yours very truly, V G Aston (Vicar).

Parkers Brewery responded in the positive, but there was no mention of a change of name for the inn. *Dear Mr Aston, Many thanks for your letter. It has been our intention and endeavour to preserve the characteristics of the Old Court House if at all possible.*

As soon as the draft plans are prepared I shall be pleased to come over and have a talk with you. Yours sincerely, W E Cowlishaw.

Much of the oak inside is preserved for future generations, the old fire place still stands and the oak that was over the Steward's chair forms a lintel over the door. The panelling

17th century Oak Panneling

Oak panneling remains 2010

16th century fireplace removed from an upper room in 1936

which once adorned the courtroom walls was removed and refitted into the small room of the original Greyhound which displays the sign George Thomas Taylor, Alehouse 1829 today.

The longest serving landlord of The Greyhound Inn was Dick Pattinson, 1933-1963, and no pub is complete without its characters and its old stories handed down from one generation to the next. I recall, years ago, my good friend Frank Walker, now deceased, telling stories of people and times relating to The Greyhound.

Dick Pattinson, a short and powerful man was landlord for more than thirty years. He was once referred to by a local worthy as the last yeoman of Penkhull, and I consider that title suited him well. Many will remember him, shirt sleeves rolled up above the elbow, arms thick as young oak trees, resting on the bar top greeting a

Dick and Alice Pattinson with their two sons, Richard and Dennis.

customer with a cheery smile and asking 'How are you'? Anything to report was his favourite question. Dick's forebears were farmers, but his father was a coachman working at The Mount and for years lived at the small lodge at the corner of Greatbatch Avenue.

To the rear of The Greyhound was like a farm yard. There were stables, a row of pigsties full of fat sows and piglets, numerous hens and chickens. One could always tell when Dick had killed a pig as the intricate procedure was always performed in the cellars beneath the Inn by a customer who had been trained in the art. The rasping of knife of steel on the cellar steps would be heard even in the bar. From time to time Dick would replenish the 'surgeons' needs with a free pint from the pumps. On many occasions it would take several pints to see the job complete. I do think that the poor pig could have been drowned in the amount consumed on some occasions.

Many stories have been told about Dick, but the one I like best and know it to be true was when a stranger entered the Smoke Room one snowy winter's day and remarked that the roads were very bad. "Ast cum uptha bonk then" enquired Dick. The stranger, not a local, managed to understand and said that indeed he had come up the hill. "And thee grogged it yet?" asked Dick. The stranger's face registered his bewilderment. "Ah", said Dick, "tha wutna know wot grot is wut? Well it's owd saggers grun up".

The Greyhound in years past was the social centre of village life. This was due to the close association between the church and the Inn. Two of the most memorable vicars of Penkhull, The Reverend V G Aston and Preb. Arthur Perry, had a great affection for Dick Pattinson and his wife Alice. V G in part often sat at the kitchen table sharing a meal with them. A large upstairs room was often used to accommodate weddings, funerals, parties and meetings of all kinds. One of the most popular functions held there was the 'rabbit pie suppers' organised by the church choir. The pie would be prepared by Alice in huge enamel washing up bowl requiring two men to carry it from the kitchen to the upper room. In those days the rabbits would be purchased from 'Pop Holts', that little wooden shop that stood on the corner of Eardley Street. 'Pop' also helped by preparing the rabbits into suitable portions before delivery. One morning after a particularly successful pie supper, Pop Holt called at The Greyhound and remarked on the quality of the rabbits that he

The Greyhound Inn during the 2nd World War. Notice the black-outs and the painted street lamp.

had supplied. *"Tha wun oreyt", said Dick, "but wanna thee supposed ta bey a dozen on'em?" Pop replied that there was a dozen. "Well ar dust thee mak that ite when thee wuz ony eleven pairs o' back legs?" Pop Holt had his leg pulled many times over only supplying eleven pairs of legs to a dozen rabbits.*

I recall, probably around 1971, doing a series of interviews with Mrs Alice Pattinson, then retired and living with her sister in Corporation Street, Stoke. By this time Dick had died some years previous, but Alice was still bounding with energy and eager to share her memories of her time at The Greyhound Inn. These tapes take pride of place in my archives. *One particular person that stands out in my mind was dear old Charlie Alcock who lived in Gladstone Row. He had a shaking of the hands complaint. So much so he always had a half pint in a pint mug so not to spill any. After the alterations in 1936 we had a raised hearth in the snug and Charlie could not carry his drink as his hands were shaking a lot and I or another person would carry over and place it on the mantle above the fire so that Charlie could drink out of it.*

Well this night, I had just cleaned up the hearth and Charlie spit and instead of it going where it should have gone, it landed on the hearth. Well I said "You dirty bugger, now get it up, I don't employ servants to get that up for you or anyone else". Just as I was telling him, and he was about to give me some lip in return,

father (Dick Pattinson) came in, I said "well look what he's done, and he told me to get the servant to clean it up". After a few more words, Charlie left not returning for several months.

Another time, Charlie Alcock would come in thinking he knew everything. I would fill him a quart of beer in a bottle to take out. On this occasion I said to him "this is a bit fuller that it ought to be, av a little drink first before you put in the cork". He replied in his usual slow style "it'al bey oreyt!". I said, "don't push the cork in too far, av a drink first".

Anyhow Charlie pushed in the cork in and put the bottle in his jacket pocket. He then started walking down the passage to the back door where, I heard a loud explosion and the bottle burst, glass and beer flying everywhere. I had told him not to put in the cork too far, but he wudna be told, he was a bigheaded devil.

At a further interview Alice spoke amusingly about the activities of the Home Guard during the war. *I shall never forget one night during the war; Dick said "Don't open the pub until 8 o'clock" when he would be home from Home Guard duty. Well, I got one of the lads with me, Dennis, at the time and he was pretty good at serving, but there was a shortage of beer everywhere and the locals did not know which pub was going to open and who wasn't.*

The news got around that we were opening that night and locals kept coming and knocking on the door and windows. 'Open the door, when are you going to open this door' came the cry. I said to Dennis, 'do you think we could manage on our own?' He said 'Dad said we mustn't open till 8 o'clock'. I replied 'do you think we could manage?' So we decided to have a go and when the door was opened, what a flock. I shouted, 'Look, don't give me pound notes; just give me the right money so we can serve you quicker, because we can't mess around with change tonight'. The locals, desperate for a drink were not having one, but two or even three pints at a time; of course we did not know they weren't for other customers.

Anyway, we soon ran out of glasses, and then old Sam Smith who lived near to Charlie Alcock came in through the door. He stood waiting and he could see that we were being rushed off our feet. Charlie piped up in his usual slow speech 'we've time to go to the Marquis Sam, these people ought not to keep a pub; they're too slow to carry hot dinners'. Anyhow, I didn't say now't; we just finished what we were doing. Then Dennis took the order and I shouted, 'Ay, next time you want a pint carrying across there, you can bloody well carry it yourself, don't ask me'. He replied 'wot's up Alice?' I said 'nothing only that we're too slow to carry hot dinners'.

The last event worthy of recording was a celebration of The Greyhound's being used as a Manor Court in 2005. There were on display a number of copies of the original parchment court rolls. One document showed the attendance of Major General Thomas Harrison at the court and this was read to all. Harrison was second in command to Cromwell and was hung, drawn and quartered for treason against the crown after the restoration of Charles II. The evening was in the form of a specially prepared meal using a typical mid 17th century menu. The event was set in costume from the period.

An old view from the rear of Greenhead House c1850 with the malthouse to the right of the picture

Chapter 11
Church, Chapel - and people of the time.

The Reverend V.G. Aston, in his small centenary history booklet of Penkhull published in 1942 refers to the centre of Penkhull being used by Druids for early religious ceremonies, a not unreasonable assumption. Druids were often described as being addicted to human sacrifices and we can almost see the centre of our village as a place for such ritual surrounded by dense forests and undergrowth that existed four or five thousand years ago. It is also recognised that Penkhull would be a likely location for a Hill Fort, even though all evidence of such has long been washed away.

The ritual worship of Paganism and later that of Christianity drew people from most of what is now the North Staffordshire conurbation, but in particular that of Penkhull as this was both the earliest and the most populous settlement in the area. With the coming of Christianity to Mercia and the work of St Chad, there is no doubt he would have visited Stoke where the old church arches are situated. As the community lived in Penkhull and not in Stoke, it is a reasonable assumption that this first known Christian preacher of the region would walk across what is now the village green to proclaim Christ crucified and to greet his congregation.

Until 1832, the site for religious worship for the villagers of Penkhull was situated nearly one mile away in the town of Stoke. The early parish church of St Peter-ad-Vincula dating from the 7th century was situated there to replace a Druid circle that once occupied such an important junction of two rivers, *from two, one is made stronger*. The site was also chosen for its location nearby the ford over the River Trent, which travellers would aim for, and therefore would make an ideal

12th century Stoke Church

location for early Christian evangelists spreading the good news of Jesus Christ. From this simple form of evangelism with a preaching cross came an Anglo Saxon wooden church to be replaced by that of stone in the 12th century, of which there still remains a token gesture in the form of two arches.

The size of Stoke ancient parish at one time stretched from Norton-in-the-Moors to Caverswall and included Newcastle, Shelton, Hanley, Fenton Vivian, Fenton Culvert, Longton, Meir Lane End, Botteslow, Clayton, Seabridge and Whitmore until the first Rectory Act of 1807. The Act transferred Tithes to each of the five new advowsons. In Pope Nicholas's Taxation of 1291, Stoke parish was valued along with its various Chapels of Ease at 60 marks (or £40) per annum, the largest revenue of any church in the country, except that of Stone, which was charged at the same amount. The outlying areas of the parish had separate chapels, but continued to be dependent upon the mother church of Stoke. For centuries, this church carried out its priestly functions until the early nineteenth century, when the demands upon staff and administration outstripped its resources. Subsequently various Acts of Parliament from 1807 divided and sub-divided the once substantial parish, leaving Penkhull remaining in Stoke Parish until 1853, when it was discovered quite by chance that it had not been legally constituted at the earlier date of 1842, when the church was built.

As Penkhull developed as a working-class suburb of Stoke, the need for a place of worship in the village to cater for the growing population became evident. Not only was there a demand for religious worship but also an urgent need for the secular education of the young and the care of souls. The beginning of the nineteenth century, however, saw a move away from the established church to Methodism, which, at its peak was a serious challenge to the dominance of the established church. The most serious criticism of the established church was its neglect of pastoral responsibilities, especially to the poor. Partly as a result of the void between the poor and the established church, working-class potters and miners turned to Methodism and other nonconformist churches. The Methodist movement grew fast throughout the country recording 89,528 members by 1801, increasing to 249,119 thirty years later, a growth unequalled in any other nonconformist church.

The Methodist movement, founded by John Wesley, became the impetus for many social movements of the day including prison reform. Wesley's contribution as a theologian was to propose a system opposing theological stances. His greatest theological achievement was his promotion of what is termed *Christian Perfection*, or holiness of heart and life. Wesley insisted that in this life, the Christian could come to a state where the love of God, or perfect love, reigned supreme in one's heart.

Wesley believed that the Established Church had failed in its duty to call sinners to repentance; that many of the clergymen were corrupt; and that souls were perishing in their sins. Wesley regarded himself as being called by God to bring about revival in the church, and no opposition, or persecution, or obstacles could prevail against the divine urgency and authority of his commission.

Much of the theology of Methodism is found in the hymns written by his brother Charles that reflects redemption by grace, words such as: *Our hearts are open wide, to make the saviour room, And lo, the Lamb of God, the crucified, the sinner's friend has come.* For the first time the working classes could relate to a faith, a faith based upon a personal message of salvation through the coming of the Holy Spirit into one's life. This was almost in direct opposition to the teachings of established church religion, with little commitment of the Church of England to save souls.

Probably one of the most famous hymns that Charles Wesley wrote sums up this need for the grace of God and the urgency, because of sin, to save every soul. *O for a thousand tongues to sing, My great Redeemer's praise, The glories of my God and King, The triumphs of His grace.* The culmination of this new found relationship with God is summarised in the final verse. *See all your sins on Jesus laid: The Lamb of God was slain; His soul was once an offering made, For every soul of man.* If we reflect upon the traditional hymns of the day such as Reginald Heber's *Holy, Holy, Holy, Lord God Almighty,* the contrast between the two points, to almost exclusion of the working classes from the Church of England becomes clear. Although written in 1826 for Trinity Sunday, the words praise the supremacy of God and the line *Though the eye of sinful man, Thy glory may not see* only serves to separate those in need of repentance.

After Wesley's death in 1791, the Wesleyan Methodists, as they were then known, became divided. The argument being either to remain within the established church, or to act as a supplementary society to the Established Church with no sacrament of its own and debarred from duplicating the times of the services of the parish church and those who wished to recognise that in fact they were already a separate denomination having their own sacraments. As dissent grew, the 1795 conference sought an agreed way forward with a Plan of Pacification. Conference would continue to appoint preachers and would publish formal accounts. Further disputes followed with Alexander Kilham who led the first rebellion by demanding that Methodists should administer the sacraments in their own chapels and laymen should share in the government of the church. At this time Methodists still attended the Anglican Church to receive the sacraments. Representatives from Manchester, Huddersfield, Stockport and Sheffield supported Kilham, upon expulsion. Totally isolated from the Wesleyan movement they met in Leeds and formed a breakaway church - the Methodist New Connexion.

Open-air revival meetings, later known as camp meetings, were organised a few years later at Mow Cop, nearly eight miles to the north of Penkhull. The first was held on May 31st 1807, followed by further meetings, even though they were done without the authority of the Wesleyan Conference. Both Hugh Bourne and William Clowes, joint organisers, were expelled from the mother connexion in 1808 and 1810 respectively. As a result of this action, a further breakaway movement was established known as the Primitive Methodists, who established their first chapel in Tunstall.

The early nineteenth century seemed to muster that concern at the death of the spirit within the established churches. The Anglican Church, conscious of its serious decline following the rise of Methodism, made stringent efforts to reverse the situation by the provision of new churches. The urban working classes, largely alienated, became increasingly apathetic to church going. In many cases, people who had been uprooted from their country parishes, by finding employment in new urban centres, became indifferent to religion. Social mobility and demographical increase often left them outside the scope of the established church, a situation made worse by the emergence of the dissenting sects.

After the war with France and the defeat of Napoleon at Waterloo in 1815, the British people of all classes expected a period of prosperity. But in fact times were hard, and there was little or no improvement in living conditions or employment prospects for the next seven years. National figures made clear as early as 1798 the urgent need to build new churches and to send more preachers where the lower classes were thickest, as a precaution against the growth of Jacobinism. By the year 1827, nearly half out of 10,500 beneficed clergy nationally were absent from the livings, which supported them. Many incumbents of rectories received large stipends from glebe, tithes, pew rents, and Easter offerings and lived in the style of the gentry whilst they often left ill-paid curates to perform duties, with an income barely enough to ward off poverty. The situation was ripe for growth in a new enthusiastic Methodist movement where the preaching of John Wesley and his successors fell upon the open minds and the ardent hopes of the under-privileged working classes. This was the situation in Penkhull and the surrounding Pottery districts.

Dissenters were often regarded as second-class citizens and suffered considerable discrimination. They were not, for example, allowed to marry in their own place of worship but had to use the parish church until Lord John Russell presented in 1835 his second Bill to Parliament. Until this Bill became law in January 1836, Dissenters were obliged to pay church rates towards the upkeep of the Established Church buildings, churchyards and burial grounds. A rate, decided upon by churchwardens through vestry meetings, was imposed upon all inhabitants of the parish, Anglican and Dissenters alike. In January 1834, a poll was taken in the several quarters of Stoke parish, where a considerable majority defeated the proposal. Gladstone abolished Church rates nationally in 1868, following thirty years of agitation. After 1837, five Dissenters' Chapels were licensed within Stoke parish for marriages.

In the disturbed years after the war with France, the Church of England came under fire from the radical press. Rapid deflation of the economy and cyclical depressions meant that the church was seen as an institution unwilling to attend to the people's welfare. The state of the country as a whole was greatly affected by the 1815 Corn Laws, which prohibited the import of foreign wheat until the price of homegrown had reached 80/- per quarter. The purpose of this law was to protect the farmers and landowners against the fall in prices if foreign-grown grains were allowed to enter freely into Britain. The poor suffered greatly for the law kept the price of bread artificially high whilst the agricultural labourer's wages was not raised, their employers pocketing the benefit.

In 1809, the government sought to supplement religious provision in urban districts by making the first of eleven annual grants of £100,000 to make possible an increase in stipends for the poorer livings via what was known as Queen Anne's Bounty. It was a time when state leaders were becoming apprehensive about the problems associated with the sudden increase of population in industrial towns, and the possibility of civil unrest a plan to build more churches, and therefore, hopefully to present Christian principles to the working classes, became of paramount importance. It was essential to contain a situation already experienced in France. The Establishment feared a revolution.

In this context, the Reverend Richard Yates produced his decisive works in 1815 in support of church extension, publishing *The Church in Danger* followed by *The Basis of National Welfare* two years later. Yates categorically affirmed that the state had a responsibility to foster religion amongst the working classes as a matter of importance for the continued stability and prosperity of constitutional government. Both publications listed numerous statistics about the conditions of society, arguing that the appalling environments of the working classes were consequences, not causes of spiritual decline. It was considered that proper Christian instruction would elicit the virtues of Christianity and eliminate misery. Yates' work and recommendations achieved their objectives in 1818, for the government introduced a 'New Church Bill', allocating one million pounds for new church building and appointing a body of commissioners to administer the provision of the Act. A further half million pounds was granted in 1824. By 1830,

one hundred and thirty-four new churches had been built and fifty more were in construction. These national figures included the rebuilding of St Peter-ad-Vincula at Stoke, subsequently followed by St Mark's, Shelton; St Paul's Burslem and St James', Longton.

The Established Church was soon to discover that the population increase was not a temporary phenomenon. It struggled to keep up with the pace of change but never quite succeeded in meeting the needs of the existing population however it tackled the problem. But the increase in population was not the only obstacle. With the rise of the Oxford Movement, the church itself was becoming more divided, with increasing pressure for change. There were also the effects of the growing Chartist movement, which campaigned for political reform, seeking to pressurise government for improvements by actions of civil unrest. It was certainly considered at this time by many academics that the Methodist Revival in the early part of the 19th century helped to condition the English people to accept the prevailing social attitudes and conditions, which certainly would have caused considerable civil unrest in most European countries. Wesley clearly taught the masses to be less concerned with the miserable life on earth, as victims of the industrial revolution, than with the life to come.

Upon reflection, the 1818 Act looked backwards as well as forwards. Its authors were clearly convinced that the ministers of new churches could, in the main, be paid out of pew rents, but short-sightedly provided less than a fifth of all sittings for the poor who were thus restricted to the sides, rear, or the gallery of the church. It was into this national picture that Primitive Methodism developed and became influential. Both Bourne and Clowes made impressive use of field preaching and camp meetings as means of increasing membership. By 1815 Penkhull became a part of this religious fervour, for Ward (1843) records a chapel in Penkhull as follows: *The first Primitive Methodists Chapel in Stoke-upon-Trent was built in Penkhull in 1815 and holds upwards of one hundred persons.* Later in 1834, a second Primitive Chapel was built in Leese Street, Stoke, off Liverpool Road but only seated forty.

It was in 1799, at the age of twenty-nine that Bourne was presented by his mother with an anthology of Christian writings. Until then he lived with a rather morbid fear of being condemned to Hell and spent much time in pursuit of salvation. Through the anthology, a message of salvation really began to resonate. Bourne, so moved wrote: *I believe in my heart, grace descended and Jesus Christ manifested himself to me, my sins were taken away in an instant, and I was filled with all joy and peace in believing.*

Bourne, with Clowes expressed concern for the spiritual salvation and social welfare of ordinary working people. Bourne understood that drunkenness was a major factor that kept working class people down in base conditions. Also, in the face of establishment opposition, Bourne promoted working class education, including instruction in reading, writing and arithmetic, in addition to religious teaching. Many early trade union pioneers were drawn from the ranks of the Primitive Methodist Preachers.

Primitive Methodist hymns reflect his teaching, like those of Charles Wesley. In a small compact Primitive Methodist hymn book dated 1843, most reflect the teaching of Bourne, that of sinners repenting to receive salvation with words like: *Come, ye sinners! Christ has suffered, You from every sin to free, Life eternal now is offered, Through his death upon the tree. Christ will give you consolation; from sin you will refrain; O repent, and seek salvation! Christ the Lord is come to reign.*

The first documented evidence of a place of worship in Penkhull to serve the growing population of working-class people was in 1819, when Hugh Bourne applied for the registration of a dwelling house for divine worship. At that time any nonconformist wishing to have a building licensed for Divine Worship had to apply to an Anglican Bishop for approval. The application reads: *To the Right Rev the Lord Bishop of Lichfield and Coventry and to His Registrar: I Hugh Bourne of Bemersley in the Parish of Norton in the Moors, in the County of Staffordshire, do hereby Certify that a dwelling house and premises situated in Penkhull in the Parish of Stoke-upon-Trent, and now in the holding and occupation of Anthony Athersmith of the same place are intended to be used as a place of Religious Worship by an assembly of Protestants and I hereby request you to register the same, according to The provision of King George the Third entitled 'An Act to repeal certain Acts and amend other Acts, relating to Religious Worship and Assemblies and persons teaching and preaching therein', and I hereby request a certificate thereof.*

Witness my hand, this eighth day of September in the year of our Lord, one thousand, eight hundred and nineteen.
Signed - Hugh Bourne.

William Athersmith is recorded in the Land Tax records of 1806. Unfortunately the address in Penkhull is not given.

From these registrations, the course of the Primitive Methodist Movement can be traced through the many petitions made by Hugh Bourne and other early Primitive leaders. The fact that Bourne was the petitioner of the Penkhull entry is not significant in itself for he also registered chapels in all parts of the country. Registration of the Primitive Methodists was centralised. Observations from the entries indicate that the applications for registration were made in multiples: for example, in the years 1807 and 1811, Hugh Bourne petitioned for four places to be registered. A licence for religious worship by nonconformists could be obtained from either the bishop of the diocese or a justice of the peace. The registration records confirm that registration was infrequent. In 1818 only ten chapels were registered in the Lichfield diocese, in 1819 there were a total of thirty-two, whereas the following year only fifteen were registered. It may have been that the church authorities treated the registration of chapels lightly. It was only when enough chapels were up and running was registration enforced. Therefore Ward's note of 1815 may be correct but the meetinghouse remained un-registered until Hugh Bourne deemed it necessary to register it in 1819.

Methodism in the Potteries was, at its height, a serious challenge to the established church. The first chapel to meet the needs of the Penkhull villagers was erected in 1799, only half a mile away in what is now Epworth Street, Stoke, in the Wesleyan tradition It was replaced in 1801, with a new larger chapel built to accommodate one thousand people. The New Methodist Connexion followed in 1806 with Mount Zion in Hill Street situated only around the corner from the Wesleyan Chapel in Epworth Street, itself being replaced in 1816, by a new chapel offering accommodation for three hundred persons.

These two chapels must have caused considerable embarrassment for the Anglican Church in Stoke, since the inhabitants of Penkhull, having no place of worship in the village had to pass the doors of either chapel on the way to the parish church. In 1851, the attendance at the Wesleyan Chapel exceeded the parish church at Stoke by eighteen.

The following list provides a snap shot of the sudden growth experienced by the non-conformist churches. In 1830 these included in the Potteries: Primitive Methodists 5, New Connexion 10, Wesleyan 12, Congregational 2, Baptist 2, Unitarian 1 or 2, Presbyterian 1. Against the impressive thirty-three or thirty-four non-conformist chapels, the Primitive Methodists took third place with five, as against the Anglican churches only having four churches, while the Roman Catholics had two.

By 1830, a replacement for the 1819 Primitive Methodist dwelling house at Penkhull was found, for the Bishop's Registers record that on the 5th November 1830, Joseph Gallimore of Newcastle registered a chapel at Penkhull, in the occupation of William Sutton. From the tithe return of 1850, William Sutton was the occupier of four cottages in Brisley Hill, just off Trent Valley Road, to the south of the village centre which may well have been the location for the 1830 place of worship. *White's Trade Directory* of 1834 records: *A Dissenting Chapel to the Primitive Methodists in Penkhull.* Even so it was clear as early as 1832 that with the increasing population, this building failed to meet the community needs. As a direct result ten members of the Primitive Methodist Church from different occupations and parts of the Potteries formed a Trust to purchase a site upon which a new chapel would be built. The plot, a part of Green Croft containing four hundred and forty two superficial yards was purchased from Robert Archer, yeoman of Beech Grove, in consideration of £88 8 0d. It is the land where the building is now used as an annexe to Penkhull Christian Fellowship stands at the top of Newcastle Lane.

Penkhull Primitive Chapel built, 1836

Congregations for Primitive Chapels were, in the vast majority, drawn from the lower working classes so funds were limited. It took three years until from 1833 to 1836 to raise sufficient funds to ensure the building of the new chapel which opened that year, no doubt causing some concern to the Anglican Church at Stoke, as they only had a small school situated in what was then the village green. So much so, that it was considered important for this small school to be licensed by the Bishop for Divine Worship, no doubt to offset the challenge from non-conformity.

View from a distrance. Note the state of the roads in the 1950's and the old Police box to the right of the picture

Until the recent restoration of the old chapel by the new owners, Penkhull Christian Fellowship, it was always thought that in the early years the Sunday School was held in the cellar of the chapel. This seems a mistaken view for whilst all the plaster and floors were removed and external walls stripped of cement, what was revealed showed the construction of the first chapel. The floor level in the original 1836 chapel was one meter higher than the present floor. The joist holes of the first floor showed this. On the external wall, situated in the centre of the front, between windows, the brickwork gave away its secrets to show where the original entrance was located in addition to markings being found to show that a number of steps would have led up to a floor level much higher than the existing one.

Inside the Chapel c1953

The design was typical for the period, two floors, with the lower floor being used for weekly meetings and the Sunday School, whilst the upper floor is retained for worship. The entrance to the lower floor was to the side.

Concerns were expressed as early as 1859 about the restricted accommodation for the Sunday school and the sum of £75 was paid to Benjamin Boothroyd, a surgeon from Hanley for the house and garden below the chapel in Newcastle Lane. The following year a new trust was formed, but it took a further eighteen years to raise sufficient funds to pay for a new Sunday School. By 1878, the new building was opened to accommodate both church activities and an expanding Sunday School. As to the two cottages to the east of the chapel, there is no documented evidence to show when they were built or by whom. As it was usual for early chapels to retain a resident caretaker with accommodation, it would be reasonable to assume that they would be built at the same time as the chapel in 1836.

The existing baptismal registers date from 27th August 1879. During the period 1880 to 1890 there were remarkably 236 baptisms, a great number compared with those seeking this sacrament today. Candles first lighted the chapel, followed by gas, and finally electricity. Mr Harry Clay, an old member of the congregation recalled some thirty years ago that the chapel used to be heated by old stove pots and gas lighting, which sometimes failed during a service, so that candles had to be hastily found. He also recalls at one time there was a string band, probably to accompany hymn singing before an organ was installed. There was also open air preaching around the 'Big Lamp', in St.Thomas Place, then called Victoria Place, following a parade with the choir around the village at 5.30 p.m., no doubt to attract a congregation for a visiting preacher.

In the latter part of the 19th century, 'the chapel' was the focus of activity for village life with both men's and ladies groups, youth work and the continued growth of its Sunday School drawing many of its converts from the disenchanted members of the Anglican churches. In 1929, at the height of the depression, it was decided to reconstruct the chapel from the existing central porch entrance to one entrance via the new Sunday School. The chapel floor was lowered and great improvements were made. The chapel men folk, and volunteers did much of the work, and it was recorded at the time that saved it in excess of £300. Sadly, throughout its history, finance was frequently a major problem. The congregation was always struggling to keep the bailiffs away.

The new owners of the old chapel, Penkhull Christian Fellowship discovered a time capsule whilst restoration work was taking place in 1998. It contained a number of items commemorating the work done in 1929/30. One item was a ticket to the opening service. One shilling was charged for the tea afterwards.

Many non-conformist churches and chapels held Sunday School anniversaries during the month of May. Congregation, children and pupils, headed by a small brass band, all suitably dressed but often out of tune, paraded the streets with collection boxes. This was followed by both an afternoon and an evening service when the children would be paraded out, boys in their newly-pressed grey short trousers and white shirts, and girls in pretty white party frocks, many purchased by the use of a 'divi' received from the Co-op. No coloured fabrics, trousers or jeans in those days! Additional chairs would be gathered from all available nearby houses to pack gangways, with total disregard to safety, while staging, in tiers, rose steadily (and un-firmly) to the ceiling. Here would sit row upon row of young, bright faces, smiles beaming almost doll-like across to parents and relatives sitting cramped almost two to a seat, to hear their beloved-ones sing and recite Bible passages and pass along the collection plate with the largest denomination being a very generous six pence, or a shilling at the most.

Sunday School Anniversary c1953

The anniversary was the highlight of the year, the most important date in the calendar when the whole village would

RENOVATING A CHURCH.

Penkhull Methodist Volunteers.

SAVING OF £300.

An enthusiastic group of churchmen are voluntarily undertaking part of the renovations of the Primitive Methodist Church at Penkhull, and, as a result of their labours, it is anticipated that the estimated cost of the work will be reduced by half.

The work, which is under the supervision of Mr. J. Johnson (Secretary for the Church Renovation Scheme), the Rev. T. W. Morgan (Minister) and Mr. T. Chadwick (Treasurer), was started last June, and it is hoped that it will be completed by October.

The chapel itself is nearly a hundred years old and badly needed renovating. The entrance was at the front by the pulpit, and a gallery occupied half the building. The gallery has now been removed and a door constructed at the rear of the chapel. Five small windows on the south side of the chapel have been enlarged and are being reglazed. The walls have been panelled with the old pews, and new seats are being installed.

A new pulpit, given by Mr. J. Johnson, senr., and family, is to be erected to the memory of the late Mrs. J. Johnson, senior, who was a member of the church for over 50 years. Electric lighting and heating apparatus have also been installed.

£300 SAVED.

The front of the church is to be concreted and the fore court covered with tarmac.

The schoolroom where the services are being held during the renovations, has been completely redecorated, while a preachers' vestry and conveniences are being made at the back.

It was anticipated that the renovations would cost £600, but voluntary help has reduced the estimated figure to just over £300.

The work began when eight members of the church gave up their evenings to the task. Since then three members have devoted all their time to the work. The following are the members who have assisted, Mr. T. Chadwick, Mr. A. Deakin, Mr. J. Stanton, Mr. F. Adams, Mr. R. Adams, Mr. H. Harvey, Mr. H. Clay, Mr. T. Davies and Mr. T. Rowley. Lady members, who are anxious to do their share, have promised to clean and polish the woodwork.

Sentinel press report

Primitive Methodist Church,
— PENKHULL. —

Re-opening Services & Tea
THURSDAY, OCTOBER 23rd.

Re-opening Ceremony 3-15 p.m.
Tea at 5-15 p.m.

Tickets for the Tea 1/- each.

somehow get involved. In addition to this there was the Sunday School Queen effort, organised each year from 1953 by Mrs Marjorie Prophett. Under her leadership

Marjorie Prophett   First Producer, Ethel Buxton

many thousands of pounds for the chapel was raised. Another activity that became almost an institution was the Annual Methodist Church Pantomime. Mrs Ethel Buxton started this series of shows that lasted for nearly twenty-five years as a fund-raising effort that lasted for nearly twenty-five years.

The first production entitled Snow White and the Seven Dwarfs was staged in 1958, and was presented almost in a makeshift theatre in the upper schoolroom of the Sunday School. Because of its huge success and public praise, it was decided to present the panto in what was then called Penkhull Senior School the following year. The new venue had a large stage and many schoolrooms that could be used for dressing and props. The next production, Cinderella, surpassed all expectations and the mould was set for an annual pantomime to be presented the week after Christmas. Mrs Buxton continued to produce for three years and was followed in that important role in 1962 by Mrs Betty Powell, by which time the organisation drew in many helpers to build the props, install the lighting and paint the scenery from both chapel members and the local community. My mother-in-law, Meg Palmer, took charge of the costumes; Dennis Cotterill the lighting and electrics. Other helpers in those early days were Mrs Marjorie Prophett; Mr and Mrs Tom Rowley; Frank Adams; and Jim Powell who helped to produce the props.

Red Riding Hood 1966

After a few years at the Senior School, it became necessary for the company to move and the old infant school became available to them. Once more the building had to be adapted for the production, the sides of the stage being built up to form wings and storage space. Electrics had to be added and school classrooms adapted to accommodate a huge cast and

what appeared to be hundreds of mums as dressers. Rehearsals for the children commenced early in September and often the dress rehearsal would be held on Boxing Day ready for the opening performance the following day. I myself became involved in 1963, when asked to assist with the theatrical make-up for the production of Aladdin.

Ali Baba 1972

Mother Goose 1968

Penkhull Pantomime productions over the years

For a short period the production was taken over by Mrs Grace Roberts. The leading role of Aladdin in 1963 was played by Susan Palmer, who was, a number of years later to become my wife. For many years Susan would play the lead whilst her father, local grocer Cyril, would play the part of Dame, a part which he played for nearly all the pantomimes. After finishing her education at Manchester Royal College of Music, Susan took over the important roles of producer, musical director and choreographer, positions that she held until 1991/2.

Sleeping Beauty 1962

Goodie Twoshoes 1973

The Methodists Women's Fellowship were the backbone of the refreshments, bringing trays of tea or orange juice to over two hundred patrons seated either on benches, chairs or even window ledges to get a better view. After the last performance many of the parents would assist in carrying most of the chairs back across the village square to the chapel at the top of Newcastle Lane.

Susan Talbot with her father Cyril Palmer 1963

At its height, the company would consist of nearly a hundred. Around forty to fifty children from 4 years upwards both from the Sunday School and the wider area of Penkhull would be trained to perfection, whilst teenagers took smaller roles and adults took the senior parts. In addition there were around twenty back-stage crew to ensure the show went on without a hitch. Coach loads of parents and children would travel from all over North Staffordshire to see the annual show, which would run for a full week, or even eight performances. Over nearly thirty years probably in excess of £50,000 was raised for the benefit of chapel funds, a remarkable achievement. Unfortunately, Susan was struck down with glandular fever in 1992 and was unwell for some time. As a result the following pantomime was cancelled, and like so many other things it never gathered the momentum to commence again.

One fact is certain, that chapel people gave their all. Battles would be fought, won and lost for chapels and the opportunity to be of service. Lives of both individual and families were dedicated to local chapels in the Potteries and Penkhull was no exception. Both husbands in the men's group and wives in the women's fellowship gave all. The people I remember with such fondness I am sure are today Saints in Heaven, people like Marjorie Prophett, Frank Adams, Tom Hewitt and local cobbler, Jack Burton and many others. God bless them all.

Throughout almost its entire existence, Penkhull Methodist Chapel had one mortgage or another. Like many other churches and chapels it experienced serious decline in membership from the 1970s, and with a decline in membership came a corresponding decline in its weekly income. The remaining, small, faithful, but ageing congregation could not meet the never-ending cost of repairs, nor had it the energy to raise the necessary funds to maintain the old building. Architects came and architects went, their fees seeing off such funds as had been raised to rebuild the old chapel. Plans were replaced by more plans and yet nothing materialised, and hopes were continually dashed, only to be uplifted, and then dashed again. Despite good intentions nothing concrete materialised, leaving the only decision to be made, that of closure, and to place the premises on the market for sale and for its membership to remove to Wesley Church in Epworth Street. The last service was held in October 1996.

Restored Chapel by Penkhull Christian Fellowship

Prospective buyers came, prospective buyers went until Penkhull Christian Fellowship, who had their church in Franklin Road, an expanding church with an emphasis on youth and community, decided to purchase the old building as an annexe to their own. With considerable energy, a willing workforce, good fundraising and a few benefactors, this once old and tired building was regenerated and injected with new vibrant life. What we have today seems almost like a miracle considering the structural state of the building when vacated by the Methodist Church.

Primitive Methodists were called Ranters, and associated with those early camp meetings at Mow Cop. They were filled with the Holy Spirit, often said to almost intoxication.

The new owners, Penkhull Christian Fellowship, follow similar traditions in their worship to the Ranters of nearly two hundred years ago. Upon reflection, what better way to end the chapel's history, where it continues its work in keeping with the same ideals of those first called by God to have a place of witness on this site in the village of Penkhull.

History recalls that relationships between Anglican and Methodists were at best, strained. To meet this challenge from the Primitive Methodists and not to be outdone in its outreach, the parish church in Stoke erected a Sunday school in the centre of the village green, the present churchyard. Information is sketchy, but the minute book of the Privy Council to the Duchy of Lancaster, dated 23rd September 1834 points firmly to its establishment: *Read a petition from the inhabitants of the Parish of Stoke-upon-Trent, praying for a waste hold grant for the erection of a school for the religious instruction of the children residing in Penkhull. The piece of land comprises of about twenty-two yards in front by thirty in depth.* The outcome of this minute was: *let the petition be complied with.* The application was made by Sir. William Dunbar, Curate of Stoke Church.

In 1841, the Government set up a commission to enquire into the state of children employed in the Potteries. Mr Samuel Scriven, a Government Inspector came to the borough to investigate working conditions in the pottery factories. Scriven also undertook, as part of his brief, to enquire about schools and Sunday schools. Mr James Irvine, the Superintendent of the Primitive Methodist Sunday School at Penkhull was interviewed and stated that it had been established for seventeen years beginning in 1824. This confirmed that it pre-dated the present chapel building. The report continues: *I am the superintendent teacher, have attended this school in this capacity for two years. We have 64 boys and 56 girls. There are 16 teachers, nine males and seven females. The nature of the instruction is religious, in no instance secular, except writing. The books used are the Bible, Testament, 'Reading made Easy', work bearing on religion. They attend the religious worship of the chapel in the afternoon, and are instructed in the morning. Think they improve by their attendance. Most of them are children of factors; are well conducted and respectful to us teachers. We do not see much difference between children of potters and others. I think, however, as compared with other places, not manufacturing, that they are not so good. When boys are taken young to work, they associate with men of bad habits and acquire them. Think that by coming to school they lose evil habits and we endeavour by all the means in our power to instill good ones. The room (a chapel) is large, airy, and well ventilated, capable of containing 150 on the girl's side and eighty on the boy's side.* – Signed James Irvine

It is not clear by this entry if in fact there are two groups of children. Those 'of factors', meaning small shopkeepers or business people, and those 'of potters'. The word 'factors', however, may be an abbreviated word for 'factory workers'.

Ann Taylor makes the Anglican entry, aged 34, who recalls that she had been a Sunday school teacher for six years. This confirms that the Parish Church of Stoke established a Sunday school in Penkhull in 1835, Ann Taylor had apparently taught there since its inception. *I am one of the teachers of this establishment; have been a teacher six years; have 48 girls on the books and 46 boys. The system of teaching is the National System, or Bell's. The books used are of a religious character, such as the Bible, Testament, and Prayer. Mr Godfrey, the curate, attends on Sunday mornings, and reads to them. The youngest child at present is four years, the oldest 16. They all go with the teachers to church service; they return to school in the afternoon, and are examined in their catechism. No secular instruction of any kind is imparted. Think they make progress. I do not think that there is any perceptible difference between those who work in factories, and those who do not. They are well conducted, cleanly, and respectful to us as teachers; there are some exceptions. They are regular in their attendance; frequently absent themselves on account of want of shoes and clothing. We have altogether nine teachers, male and female. The room is commodious, airy, well ventilated, and of containing comfortably 150 pupils.* – Signed Ann Taylor

Both reports provide considerable insight into religious instruction for the children of Penkhull, and the priority that parents placed upon its importance. The census returns for 1841 records that there were 258 children between the age of four and sixteen living in Penkhull. Scriven reported that 214 (83%) attended Sunday school regularly. For most children this was the only 'schooling' they received. Day schools, where they existed, were on a daily 'school pence' basis, and although only costing one or two pence a week, that was still beyond the reach of most working-class families. Many working people, however, who themselves failed to attend church on a regular basis, dispatched their offspring to Sunday Schools. Of course, in crowded homes, in the days before compulsory education, there may be a simple explanation for this, for with children at Sunday school, parents were allowed a brief and precious time to themselves.

The teacher-pupil ratio in the two schools is of interest. At the Anglican Sunday School there was a ratio of 10.44 children per teacher, against a ratio of 7.5 in the Methodist Sunday School. Further down the hill in Stoke, a town were to be found manufacturers and trades-people who were often better educated and philanthropic, in comparison with the more rural and working class Penkhull. The ratio of the Anglican Church of St Peter's was 5.76 against the Wesleyan Chapel of 5.5. The New Connexion in Hill Street, Stoke, recorded an attendance of three hundred and eighty-eight, eighteen more than the Wesleyan Chapel, but claimed only fifteen teachers, producing a ratio of 22.5. The total number of children attending Sunday School, derived from the Scriven report, confirms that religious instruction was dominated by nonconformity, pointing to the high number of working-class people who chose Methodism rather than the middle-class Established Church.

Sunday School attendance and teacher figures in 1841 within the district of Stoke-upon-Trent (based on a typical Sunday return) show the attendance for Anglican churches was 4,240; Nonconformist 13,588; Anglican Sunday School teachers 371; nonconformist Sunday School teachers 1,956; Anglican Places of Worship 14; and nonconformist places of worship 48.

In the early part of the 1840s, the Church of England boasted a promotional movement entitled 'The Diocesan Church Building Association'. One of its leaders and prominent speakers was Archdeacon Hodson, who gave an address at Christ Church, Fenton, on the subject of new church building, where, Mr Herbert Minton, a devout Christian, was in the congregation. Minton was so impressed with Hodson's address, that at the close of the meeting he spoke with Hodson and announced his intention of building a church at Hartshill, half a mile to the north of Penkhull at his own expense. Following this announcement, the Rev Thomas Webb Minton, brother of Herbert, promptly intimated his intention of donating substantial funds towards the building of a church for the *populous suburb of Penkhull*. In addition to this generous offer, Thomas Webb Minton provided the sum of £2,000 to be invested with the Church Commissioners, the interest from which was to be used towards the salary of the incumbent. Both Herbert and Thomas Webb Minton were sons of Thomas Minton, a prominent potter.

Thomas Minton was born in Shrewsbury in 1765, and after his apprenticeship as an engraver, migrated to London to seek commissions for his skills. It was there he met and married Sarah Webb, shortly afterwards moving to Stoke to become a master engraver for the pottery industry. Realising that there was plenty of scope for increasing the production of earthenware, Thomas Minton decided to manufacture his own products in 1793. As a consequence he purchased a plot of land in the town, on which he built a home and a small factory with two bottle ovens.

Their first son was Thomas Webb, born in 1791, and educated at Audlem Grammar School where he received a classical education under the headship of Nicholas Breakspear. It was here that he was later joined by his younger brother Herbert. After their education at Audlem, they both joined the family firm at the age of fourteen years. Thomas Webb was quiet and retiring by nature, and benevolent to others, often assisting the poor out of his modest salary. His heart was not in potting, and he persuaded his father to dissolve the family partnership so that he might take Holy Orders in the Church of England.

He was subsequently admitted as a sizar at Queen's College, Cambridge on October 3rd, 1823 as a 'Ten Year Man', he was then aged thirty-two. In 1825, he was ordained priest and at the time Penkhull church was being built was the incumbent of Holy Trinity, Darlington. He married Jane, the third daughter of Joseph Hoskins of Weston, at St George's, Everton.

Herbert Minton was born in 1793, and after his father's death in 1836 became the sole proprietor of the company until the time of his death in 1858. Despite having left the business some twelve years previously, Thomas Webb was left the bulk of his father's estate. Concerned about the injustice towards his brother, Herbert, and the family, Thomas Webb tried to have the will amended but the Lord Chancellor ruled that the will was legal. As a way of compensation, Thomas Webb gave £23,000 to his mother and family, and his younger brother, Herbert, who had been a partner with his father. Herbert then started up a new business with John Boyle, also at a later date taking into the business a nephew.

Penkhull church remains the dominant feature of the village, situated in the centre where from the late seventeenth century stone quarrying had taken place. It is from this quarry that stone for the repair of Stoke Bridge came in c1671 in addition to the buildings and stonewalls in the district. Subsequently the quarry filled with water and thereby a large pond formed which is shown on early maps of the village, to the north of the church. In 1777 the area in the centre of the village was described as 'copyhold waste', belonging to the Duchy of Lancaster. On one old plan of the area a house and garden can be found in the occupation of Joseph Botham.

By June 1811, Samuel Steele of Stoke had erected three cottages on the site. The Manorial records record: *All those several dwelling houses, gardens and tenements, late parcel of waste hold within the manor, lying near the old stone pit hole, situated in Penkhull with stables adjoining.* Around the year 1995, there suddenly appeared a large hole in the churchyard, roughly in front of the flagpole. Here exposed were to be seen the basements to these three cottages with stone steps going down and cold concrete slabs for storage still in situ. In July 1835, an additional grant of copyhold waste was conferred at a Special Court Baron, held at Stoke, which reads as follows: *containing 660 square yards, situated at Penkhull Green surrounded by common highways, extending opposite the old workhouse, upon which piece of land a school is erected.*

The three cottages of 1811 are shown on a Duchy plan dated June 1834, drawn up for the purpose of the grant. The plot forms only the central section of the present churchyard, and is contained in a further grant between Queen Victoria in her position as the Duchy of Lancaster on the one part and John Smith, Herbert Minton and John Godwin on the other. *Read a petition from the inhabitants of the Parish of Stoke-upon-Trent, praying for a 'wastehold grant' for the erection of a school for the Religious Instruction of the children residing in Penkhull. The piece of land comprises of about 22 yards in front and about 30 yards in depth.* The outcome of this minute was *let the petition be complied with.*

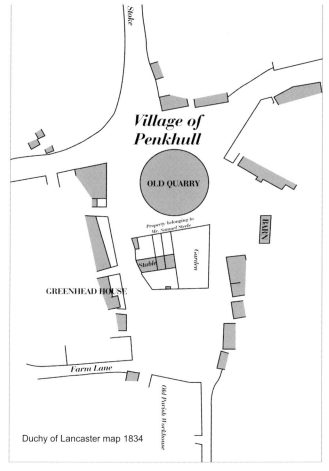

Duchy of Lancaster map 1834

It would appear that the area of churchyard upon which the parish church was built was surrendered in parcels because a further grant, which followed a year later states that during which time the small school had been erected: *At a Special Court of our Sovereign Lord King, held at Stoke-upon-Trent on Thursday, 2nd July 1835 before Thomas Hudson, deputy steward came Rev John Wickes Tomlinson of Stoke Hall, Clerk (Rector of Stoke), John Tomlinson (Patron) Solicitor, of The Cliffe, William Taylor Copeland, Alderman of the City of London, Thomas Fenton of Stoke Lodge, John Smith of Springfields and Arthur Minton of Oakhill, in their proper person and behalf of the Trustees - That in consideration of a peppercorn paid it is Granted: All that plot or piece of land situated in Penkhull Green within the Manor surrounded by common highways, extending opposite the old workhouse of the said parish, 22 yards in depth and 33 yards wide, and containing in the whole 660 yards, being parcel of the waste lands upon which piece of land a school is erected for the religious instruction of children residing in the immediate vicinity.*

The first correspondence relating to the present parish church is dated December 1840, when Thomas Webb Minton wrote to the Church Commissioners, informing them of his intentions of endowing the new parish with £2,000. It was the interest from this investment that provided an income for the vicar in addition to the receipt of pew rents. To enable any plan to proceed, submission had first to be made to the Duchy of Lancaster to approve such a building on copyhold land. The responsibility for this lay with Mr Fenton, solicitor of Newcastle who was Clerk to the Duke of Sutherland as lessee of the Manor of Newcastle-under-Lyme. It was Mr Fenton who communicated with the Duchy Office with regard to land matters. A letter dated Saturday, 19 June 1841, reads: *read a letter from Mr Fenton, dated 31st May 1841, containing an application for a Grant and Enfranchisement of waste land in the Township of Penkhull for the site of a Church and National School.*

At the same Duchy Court, a copy of a letter from the Duchy Office to Mr Fenton, dated the 9 June 1841, was referred to in rather uncomplimentary terms as it would appear that Mr Fenton was slow in replying to correspondence: *Ordered that Mr Fenton be informed that, in the absence of any answer to the letter addressed to him by the Clerk of the Council on the 9th inst, the Council have considered the application in order that he should be appraised of their determination by the time he wished to have it and that supposing there should be legal power to make the demised grant the application will be complied with as in the cases referred to in Mr Fenton's letter.*

The legal implications of Duchy grants can be complicated and long. To enable the new church to be built on the same land, which was granted for the purposes of the school on the 2nd July 1835, that agreement was subject to surrender back to the Duchy and a new admittance secured. This is recorded in the *'wastehold book'* of the manor on the 9th September 1842.

Minutes of the court record show that there were ten trustees, seven of which were new. It was also agreed that the grant was subject to a peppercorn rent, which has never been paid, or new trustees to the land appointed since 1842 by the church. The assent came from the Chancellor and Council of Her Majesty's Duchy of Lancaster. The document itself is worthy of note as although the plot of land contained the same measurement, 660 sq. yards, the boundary to the south had changed because of the position of the village water pump. Also the position of the already established school, determined where on the plot the new church was to be erected. The Duchy Court did not approve the final draft for the Deed of Conveyance until the 30th September 1842, by which time the church had been erected.

Before the consecration of the new church at Penkhull, Thomas Webb Minton had to petition the bishop of the diocese with an application, stating his intentions and an explanation of how funding was to be met. A full transcription can be read under Appendix iv.

After the petition was approved by the bishop, the benefactor was then formally acknowledged as having the 'Right of Presentation'. In the title of this document, dated October 1842 the dedication was not to 'Saint Thomas the Apostle', as the present title, but to 'Saint James'.

Penkhull, Saint James, Declaration of the Right of Nomination

Whereas the Reverend Thomas Webb Minton of Darlington hath erected a church in the Township of Penkhull with Boothen, within the Manor of Newcastle-under-Lyme, and in compliance with a certain Act of Parliament hath endowed the same with the sum of one thousand pounds and now invested in the names of certain Trustees and hath also provided a sum of ninety pounds sterling in the purchase of ninety pounds, seven shillings Capital Stock in the three per cent consolidated Bank as a fund for the repairs of the same Church being a sum equal in amount to five pounds for every one hundred pounds of the original cost of erecting and fitting up the same, And hath also set about the appropriation of one third at least of the sittings in the said church to be and to continue hereafter free and open sittings for the use of the poor.

Now Know All Men, by these presents that we James by Divine Permission Lord Bishop of Lichfield under the authority passed and provided of the said recited Act of Parliament, and in consideration that the several conditions therein required, have been fully and satisfactory performed by the said Thomas Webb Minton, Clerk, do hereby declare that the right of nominating to the Church or Chapel when Consecrated, shall be for ever and hereafter in the said Thomas Webb Minton, the person building and endowing the same his heirs and assigns being members of the United Church of England and Ireland.

In Witness thereof, we have set our Hands and Seal this third day of October, in the year of Our Lord, One thousand eight hundred and forty two and in the third year of our translation.

*Signed sealed and delivered by
the within names James Lord*   *J. LICHFIELD*
*Bishop of Lichfield, being first
duly stamped in the presence of
J.L.Bowstead,*

From correspondence, it appears that the actual consecration date was in doubt, as Mr Fenton, the steward of the Manor, wrote to Lichfield on the 15th September, stating that as steward he had not yet arranged for the grant document. He was waiting for the surveyor to provide a map of the site to enable a Deed of Enfranchisement and Grant to be sent to the Duchy of Lancaster for approval. Two weeks later, on 29th September 1841, a draft grant was submitted by Fenton to Lichfield, asking for a number of alterations, and concluding *I will obtain the Duke of Sutherland's signature as soon as His Grace returns from Scotland.* Just eight days before the consecration date, Mr Fenton submitted the corrected Deed of Enfranchisement and Grant for the signatures of Smith, Minton and Goodwin as Trustees.

A document, dated July 1840, describes the proposed church accommodation at Hartshill, Penkhull and Trent Vale. It records the proposal: *At Penkhull, it is proposed to erect a Church by subscription, which the Rev Thomas Webb Minton has consented to endow £1,000, and thus another step will be made towards the completion of the great design of building five additional churches in the Potteries. The sum of £1,350 is required for the church and churchyard at Penkhull.* The Subscription list was also published to date. Diocesan Church Building Society £350; Jesse Watts Russell Esq. £100; W T Copeland Esq., M.P. £50; Robert Smith £50; Rev Mr Edwards £25; Rev Mr Whieldon £20; Mr John Burgess £20; Mr Daniel Greatbatch £10; Thomas Dimmock Esq. £10; Mrs Arthur Minton £10; Rev Mr Butt £5; T B Rose Esq. £5 and Mr Wm Astbury £5.

Building commenced in 1842 to the design of George Gilbert Scott (later Sir. George Gilbert Scott, R.A.) in the Early English Style and originally consisted of a nave, chancel and west tower, surmounted by a broach spire which contains one bell dated one year later, 1843. It is not known what kind of floor the original chancel had at its time of consecration. It must have been plain for in 1845 Herbert Minton the uncle of Samuel, donated an ornate chancel floor and also paid off the debt still remaining on the church. The beautiful tiled floor remains today as a magnificent tribute to the craftsmanship of those early potters.

Quite by chance whilst researching at the National Archives, I came across the original grant of land for the proposed parish church of St John at Trent Vale dated 26th August 1841; *Thomas Fenton of Stoke Lodge in Penkhull one of the copyhold tenants came before Robert Fenton, gent, the deputy steward of the manor and surrendered into the hands of the Lord a certain plot of land containing one hundred and thirty eight square yards and six square feet situated near a place called Trent Vale in Penkhull to the use of the Venerable and Reverend George Hudson and the Reverend Clement Leigh, John Hutchinson, Edward James, George Edwards and Francis Foreman, Clerk and the said Thomas Fenton and John Smith, Herbert Minton and John Godwin, Thomas Kirkham and Robert Smith Esquire for ever.*
Whereas the said Thomas Fenton seized according to the custom of the manor tenant of the inheritance as of the land next after mentioned under one and the same title did on the 26th day of

July last surrender out of court into the hands of the lord a plot of copyhold land at Trent Vale in such last mentioned surrender now and particularly described by its boundaries and particular dimensions and containing in the whole six hundred and thirty five yds. and 6 inches to the use of the said George Hodson (and all the others listed) upon Trust as in the said surrender are expressed with the view and intentions of erecting, establishing and maintaining upon the site a building to be used for the performance of divine worship and the celebration of religious offices therein according to the doctrine rites and ceremonies of the protestant established Church of Great Britain and Ireland and in such surrender are contained certain provisions and declarations and furtherance's of the Trust aforesaid. And which before mentioned surrender (being also an Indenture) has been duly presented at a court held on the 26th July last and the same have since been enrolled in her majesty's high court of chancery.

In keeping with other lands granted by the Duchy of Lancaster (the Crown) such as for Penkhull Church and the old school, all will revert to the Duchy of Lancaster if the current users cease to have any use for them under the terms of the initial grants.

The Parish of Penkhull was formed in 1843, the year following the Consecration to become known as the District Church of Penkhull. Even though the original area of the proposed ecclesiastical parish is clearly defined on an existing plan the boundary has changed over the years as development of housing and requirements of neighbouring parishes have subsequently changed these. The proposed parish of 1843 is described giving the original field names. This description using a correct street map may be found in *Appendix v.*

The *Staffordshire Advertiser* records the opening of the church at Penkhull in the context of an earlier consecration of the new church at Hartshill on Monday, 10th October. *Two days after the consecration of the church at Hartshill, the new church at Penkhull is also to be consecrated. This, though a much plainer structure is no less a creditable work of the same architects, Messrs Scott and Moffatt of London. We hear the funds for this last named church are much in arrears; but we have no doubt that the collection in aid of them to be made there and in the more favoured sister church of Hartshill, will be such as the occasion demands.*

The *Potteries Mercury* also refers to the opening in its newspaper of the 22nd October: *The edifice occupies a commanding site of the summit of the hill, overlooking a bold and extensive landscape to the south and west. It is built in the early English style in form of a Latin cross. The parish is computed to contain about 800 persons. On Wednesday, October 12th it was consecrated by the Bishop of Hereford before a full congregation. There was a large attendance of clerical gentlemen – and many of the gentry of the neighbourhood. The Rev T.*

Redall read the liturgy; the Bishop officiated during the communion service, and the Rev W Coldwell, Rector of Stafford, preached a powerful and impressive sermon, Psalm 84, verses 9-10. The singing was performed in a very effective manner by the Harts-Hill choir. The sum of £35 was collected after the service.

Samuel Minton

The first incumbent was Samuel Minton, (1820-1893) son of Rev Thomas Webb Minton, the patron, who was licensed on the 10 May 1844. Samuel Minton was born in Stoke-on-Trent on March 16th, 1820 and educated at a private school in Lancashire, followed by Rugby and Oxford. The importance attached to his 'scholarship' had a bearing upon his clerical fortunes in the Church of England, as it enabled him to take a 'title' at his ordination, without having to go through the preliminary process of a curacy.

He was married to Cecil Mary Rosser, daughter of William Henry Rosser, in 1843, by which he fathered six sons and four daughters. The first two, Mary, born March 1844, and Herbert, born July 1848, were baptised in Penkhull Church. Samuel Minton stood out amongst his contemporaries for his determination to recognise the Christian standing of his non-conformist associates and to preach in their pulpits when invited. He stood almost alone in his support of other Christians, but suffered the penalty of being classed as an eccentric by his academic friends. (Sadly, this same attitude was adopted when my good friend Arnold Wain, a lay preacher in the Church of England and well-known evangelist and dentist started to preach in the 1960s in Methodist Churches in support of Christian moderation. It was not long after this that Arnold Wain found all pulpits of the Church of England were closed to him. He took the pain of this rejection with him to the grave).

During his active clerical career Samuel Minton obtained an M.A. in 1848, the same year he resigned his living at Penkhull. From then until he took up a new position in 1851 at St Silas's, Liverpool, he had no other incumbency. Six years later he became the incumbent of Percy Chapel, London. By 1867, Minton, to the great astonishment of many friends because of the previous rejection by the church, became incumbent of Eaton Chapel, a position held until 1874 when he retired on health grounds. During his active preaching career Mr Minton also published over sixty separate books, pamphlets and sermons described as unquestionably above the average of other publications of their type. In later years, Samuel Minton assumed the name of Minton-Stenhouse. This was done as a condition of his eligibility to inherit, through the Hoskins line of his mother, Calder Abbey, built in 1130, which had been in the Stenhouse name since 1730, leaving no male heir in a direct line.

His father, Rev Thomas Webb Minton died in 1868 leaving the Patronage of Penkhull to him. His first appointment thereafter was of Rupert James Rowson M.A. on the 20th May 1876 at a stipend of £150 p.a. In 1892, Samuel Minton offered the Patronage of the living to Frederick Bishop, a solicitor living at The Mount on condition that he should donate the sum of £600 to the parish church. Bishop did not continue to hold the position very long as by March the following year the Parish Magazine reported: *we are happy to announce that the patronage will be transferred to the Rector of Stoke. Mr Bishop, it seems made his offer to accept it under the mistaken notion as to the probable value of the benefice and he no longer desires the patronage. Mr Minton has consented to the transfer.* The benefice was thereby transferred to the Rector of Stoke, where it still remains.

Sir Lovelace Stamer

The poor salary received by vicars and curates was the common rule within the established church; only Rectors with glebe, tithes, offerings and other endowments were reasonably wealthy. The value of the living at Penkhull was of serious concern to Sir Lovelace Stamer, Rector of Stoke when he became the patron of the living. This caused him to sign an Indenture in February 1884 to transfer the sum of £25.00 p.a. from his Glebe rents at Nobies Moore, Moat Meadow, Upper Mill Field, and Stoke Hall Farm to the stipend of the Vicar of Penkhull.

This documents is worthy of reproduction as it contains further historical information which will probably be of interest to the reader regarding Stoke and Boothen: *This Indenture made the 16th Day of February 1884 between the Rector of Stoke and the Patrons of the Parish of Stoke-upon-Trent on one part and the Rev John James Brown of Penkhull. Whereas the said Sir Lovelace Stamer is in right of the same Rectory entitled to the pieces or parcels of land within the said parish of Stoke-upon-Trent, which are mentioned in the Schedule to these presents, and he is desirous of changing the said Rectory for the benefit and support of the Church of the said district of Penkhull.*

Now this Indenture, witness thereto that in pursuance and in exercise of the powers in his behalf given by 'An Act of Parliament' with the consent of the Patrons, doth hereby grant to the said John James Brown, Vicar of Penkhull and his successors, the annual sum of £25 payable by equal quarterly payments each year from the 25th March next from the lands mentioned in the Schedule following: A freehold messuage with garden yard and outbuildings thereto known as Stoke Hall Farm situated at Stoke occupied by John Pool at a yearly rent of £16. A freehold messuage with garden and outbuildings thereto and several closes

of land situated at Penkhull and Boothen called Nobies Moor, part of Moat Meadow, part of Lower Mill field, part of Upper Mill Field and Mill Slang, situated at Boothen now occupied by William and James Cooke at a yearly rent of £72.

A close of land thereto in two parts called the Upper and Lower Mill Field, situated in Stoke now in the occupation of the Victoria Athletic Club at the yearly rent of £30. (This refers to the old Victoria ground).

The stipend of a resident curate seconded from Stoke Church received funds from Queen Anne's Bounty, in addition to fees from pew rents. It was a system dating back several hundreds of years, whereby a class structure dominated the seating arrangements of a church. The pews nearer to the front of the church were allocated to the local nobility in status order, e.g. the Lord of the Manor, the local Squire, Doctor, and Solicitor. Free seats, for the poor were often situated at the sides of the church and often only a small percentage of seats were free. The system caused much dissatisfaction and was said to be a major cause of poor church attendance at the beginning of the 19th century.

From the Consecration deed it is clear that the situation had changed at Penkhull, where only 20% of the total was to be free. It was recorded: *102 sittings on the ground floor and 170 in the gallery are to be set apart as free seats, making a total of 272 and that three pews in the body of the church containing twelve sittings are to be set apart for the use of the Minister, his servants and the Churchwardens respectfully and that the remainder of the pews being 55 in number and containing 216 seats are to be let as part as a stipend for the maintenance of the Minister of the church.* This reflected a percentage of 55.7% but it had to be noted that 62.5% of the free seats were in the gallery away from the main body of the church.

No documented evidence remains as to the influential occupiers of the pews rented. Only the isolated reference to the total benefit to the minister remains. A Primary Visitation held on the 21st August, 1845 lists all the buildings, fees, emoluments belonging to the perpetual curacy of St Thomas, Penkhull which are indicated below:

Firstly, the churchwardens were Daniel Greatbatch of The Views, and John Burgess of Elm Tree House. The parsonage was described as having three sitting rooms and eight bedrooms standing on half an acre of land with garden.

The income was describes as: fees, burials £3 p.a.; pew rents £65; interest on £1,100 in the hands of Queen Anne's Bounty. Interest on £75 repair fund and £5 p.a. from pew rents goes on repairs.

FEES: Clergyman		Parish Clerk	
Marriage by Licence	5s	Marriage by Licence	2s 6d
Asking of Banns	1s	Asking of Banns	1s 0d

| Headstone | 21s | Churchings | 6d |
| Flatstone | 42s | | |

The Clerk was also the Parish Sexton. He received 2s for each burial and had in addition a salary of £5 p.a.

The opposition to private pews complicated the case for church extension and further encouraged the growth of nonconformity. Most bishops condemned excessive pew renting. There can be no doubt that the appropriation of seats, resulting as it did in visible class segregation, kept many working class people from the church. There were those, however, in the Church of England who defended pew rents. In 1842, Samuel Wilberforce supported the convenient separation of worshippers of different statuses for reasons derived from a critical view of social class. Wilberforce maintained the opinion that rank and station were inseparable. *They are evidently part of God's appointment for maintaining quick and real mutual charity,* wrote Wilberforce. Most church leaders opposed his view and pew rents were slowly phased out, becoming extinct by the 1890s.

In the new church of Penkhull, 62.5% of the seating was allocated as Free, against that of 37.5% rented. The high percentage of free seats represented a challenge to the already established Primitive Methodist Chapel. The first declaration of income to the Church Commissioners was made by Samuel Minton in February 1845, who noted his income as follows: Interest on Investments £70 0s 0d; Pew Rents £25 0s 0d; Fees £2 10s 0d. Total Income of Incumbent £97 10s 0d. By May 1851 the total stipend had increased to £102 12s 2d including the amount of £58 0s 0d for pew rents. At a further inquisition into the benefice of Penkhull in 1883, a return to the Governors of the Bounty of Queen Anne stated that the annual income consisted of: Interest on Investments £70 0s 0d; Queen Anne's Bounty grant £62 0s 0d; Fees £10 0 0d; Pew Rents £35 0s 0d. Total Income of Incumbent £177 0s 0d.

During the incumbency of William Moreton (1853-1860), approaches were made to the Church Commissioners requesting the abolition of pew rents. In a letter dated 12th September 1860, Moreton asked the commissioners if the stipend could be increased, to replace the value of the pew rents. The reply on the 17th, informed Moreton that the Commissioners were not prepared to consider his application.

In 1844, a licence was obtained by Samuel Minton for the solemnization of marriages at Penkhull Church under the Act of 1 and 2 William IV c.38, allocating a district to the church. In the original declaration, no allocation of fees was made to the incumbent of St Thomas's and therefore, by neglect, these remained a part of the income to the Rector of Stoke, as the Mother Church. It was not until August 1856 that the oversight was discovered by Moreton, and as a consequence correspondence continued between the Patron and the Church Commissioners until 1863 when the allocation of fees was finally resolved, and a district confirmed.

The fortunes of the Primitive Methodists and the Anglican churches had reversed by 1851 as seen in attendance figures for the Sunday school compared with those of a decade earlier:

Sunday School Attendance
| Primitive Methodist | 1841 | 94 | 1851 | 64 |
| Anglican Church | 1841 | 110 | 1851 | 108 |

There is no obvious reason for the change in the Sunday School attendance figures. It may be that since 1841, a new parish church had been erected within Penkhull and therefore a resident clergyman with time to spare to encourage parishioners had reversed the balance. To many, the Established Church, with its formal traditions was still a better place to educate children in religious matters than any dissenting church, and any future employer in the town of Stoke, if an applicant attended such a Sunday School would certainly be looked upon with favour for job prospects.

The true nature of early and mid 19th century religious practice was revealed in the first and only Religious Census, conducted on March 30th 1851. The first half of the 19th century was a time of considerable concern for the established church. Until the 1840s, working class areas like the Potteries and other northern towns and villages grew at an unprecedented pace. This new industrial base was the nucleus for the massive expansion of nonconformity. It was among such people that Wesley and his followers made conscious and effective inroads. The breakdown of the old parochial system became a matter of concern. And when, in 1828 and 1829 Parliament removed disabilities against dissenters and Catholics, it seemed that many of that former hegemony of the established church were threatened with destruction. Where it failed to apply its authority to the reform of social or economic evils, its failure can usually be explained, not by its adhesion to reactionary politics or class selfishness, but by the considered application of what were supposed to be the most enlightened social theories.

The view was taken that to solve the growing national problem of the increase of dissenting churches it was agreed to build more Anglican churches. This policy was given higher priority than social reform, thus widening further the divide between the working classes and the church. It was thought that the provision of worship was, for those of convinced Christian beliefs, the first essential condition for the creation of a better society. From the beginning of the century to 1851, the Church of England had built 2,529 new churches, at a cost of £9 million. But new churches were usually more than half empty, and those who did attend were more likely to be drawn from the lower-middle class than from the working-class.

It was against this background of events, conjecture and concern of the growth of non-conformity that the first and last religious census was taken. The underlying reasons were twofold; to discover how many people were outside the institutional church; and to show that the Church of England was still the church of the majority. A census return was sent to the clergyman, minister or pastor in charge of every place of worship in England and Wales. The count was taken mid-Lent, alias Mothering Sunday, listing all those of ten years of age and over who attended a place of worship. Attendance on this Sunday may have also been affected by a period of unusually severe weather and widespread illness.

The basis for the census had methodological flaws and statistical weaknesses and the disputes and quarrels about its reliability, were at the time heated and formed the major reason why no further subsequent census was attempted. A balanced and thorough examination of the uses and limitations of the census figures were given by *The Times* and other writers, who took the contrary view that the result may be taken as substantially accurate and trustworthy. This was done probably in an attempt not to be seen to criticize the established church.

The final count, a humiliating result by the expectations of the Victorians, revealed, to their surprise, that no fewer than 47%, but certainly no more that 54%, of the population attended church. It showed that 66% of available seats in the Established Church were unoccupied, disproving the view that more places of worship were needed. Furthermore the final assessment of the figures showed that out of those who did attend worship on census day, slightly below 50% were Church of England, dispelling the myth that the Anglican Church was the church of the overwhelming majority of Englishmen.

Thomas Owen, the steward of the trustees, who resided at Boothen, compiled the Primitive Methodist return for Penkhull. The Vicar, the Rev J C T Stretch, compiled the parish church return. There is a notable difference in the times of the Sunday services; the Primitive Methodists have an afternoon and evening service, while the Anglican Church preferred a morning and afternoon pattern of worship.

The census return lists the number of attendances at the morning, afternoon and evening services, but no attempt was made to establish how many people actually attended church more than once on a Sunday. It is suggested that

Dissenters attended more often, probably two or even three services more than Anglicans. If double counting occurred the total of attendants would certainly exaggerate the real strength of Dissenting churchs at the expense of the Anglican Church. To obtain accurate numbers of people who actually attended, as opposite to recorded attendances is impossible. It is estimated that 50% of those attending in the afternoon had not been to church in the morning, and 33% of those at an evening service had not attended either in the morning or the evening. This formula, although biased in favour of the Church of England, in fact confirmed that the Anglican Church had their largest attendances in the morning.

From the third quarter of the nineteenth century, the population of Penkhull increased considerably, to such an extent that both the Primitive Methodist Chapel and the Anglican Church sought additional accommodation to seat their expanding congregations. The Methodists were in the forefront, for as early as 1859 the need for additional seating was expressed. It was not until 1878, however, that the suggestion became a reality with the building of a new Sunday school next to the 1836 Chapel. Funds were inadequate, so a loan of £300 was obtained from Mr John Leigh, a Trustee, to settle the account.

Information with regard to Anglican Church activities is scant. Early weekly service books do not exist and later books give little indication of parish life in the nineteenth century. Stoke church however, commenced its publication of a monthly magazine in 1880. The Rector in an attempt to obtain a wide circulation within the area encouraged neighbouring smaller parishes to include a page of local intelligence each month. From this valuable contribution to social history, lasting six years, a rare snapshot of the spiritual and social life of Penkhull can be obtained.

Under the leadership of Rev G Molynuex in 1880, great support were made to increase the vicar's stipend. With the efforts of local people, the sum of £250 was raised, which when added to a grant from the diocese and the Ecclesiastical Commissioners, amounted to £550. The *Parish Magazine* of March 1880 concluded: *It is hoped that this sum will augment the value of the living by £36 a year.* The weekly church collections stand as a perfect example of the underlying poverty of the working classes of Penkhull, for in December 1881 an attendance of one hundred and forty in the morning and two hundred and twenty in the evening, produced collections of only £1 2s 5d.

During the latter years of Mr Molyneux's incumbency, two church societies were recorded, the Girl's Friendly Society, whose prime objectives appear to be either organised sewing classes or to take tea at the vicarage! The life of the G.F.S. like most church activities had its good years as well as bad. In

August 1882 the *Parish Magazine* reported: *we have no lady in the parish willing to undertake the duties connected with the G.F.S.* Four months later, Miss Booth of Richmond Villa, and principal of a Dame School *offered to open her home to the G.F.S. sewing class each Monday evening.*

In November 1881, Rev J J Brown, MA, sometime scholar and theological exhibitionist at Trinity College Dublin, was installed vicar of Penkhull. It became clear to Brown that the parish was in urgent need of spiritual and moral guidance. One month after his institution he commenced preparation classes on a Thursday evening at 8.00 p.m. for Sunday school teachers. Here he would teach the collects, Gospels, catechism and the book of the Acts of the Apostles. Brown's concern for the Christian upbringing of children was further expressed by his sermons, teaching and magazine editorial on the need and necessity of family prayer. By May 1882, his concern centred on the apathy of some Sunday school teachers as he wrote: *we are sorry that the preparation class held every Thursday for Sunday school teachers is not well attended. As so often the case, those who attend most regularly are those who are most occupied by the day.*

Brown turned to other activities once more to improve the moral welfare of the young, most of who were working in the rough and tumble of the pottery industry by day, with little or no stimulation or encouragement to seek a wider vision of life or spiritual matters in the evenings. The *Parish Magazine* of April 1882 explains his intentions: *We are glad to announce the formation of a new institution in Penkhull called Penkhull Young Men's Institution and Mutual Improvement Society. This is to promote the reading of papers and holding of discussions on subjects of general interest meeting fortnightly in the schoolroom.*

By June it was reported that the new initiative was making good progress with large attendances whenever an interesting subject was on the agenda. In December, Rev Brown comments: *after a magic lantern show on the magnificence and misery of London the sum of £2. 5s 0d was collected and donated to the Church Missionary Society - a much larger sum than contributed after a sermon in church.* Following the failure of the preparation classes for Sunday school teachers, Brown in October 1882, set about forming a new Union or Guild of Penkhull, whereby it was *intended to unite together teachers of the Sunday School and other communicants of the parish in a bond of union and common interest of some kind of church work.* In November it was reported that *a goodly number attended.* The Guild was still in existence in 1885.

Brown's deep concern for the young was displayed further with the formation of a Penkhull branch of a 'Band of Hope' in July 1883. Under the care of Mr Evans and Mr Brassington, the new group *showed signs of vitality.* Many

concerts, to the high acclaim of the parish, were presented in the schoolroom over the following years. The *Parish Magazine* reported in December that the Band of Hope was *flourishing.* This was a temperance organisation for working-class children and founded in Leeds in 1847. All members took a pledge of total abstinence and were taught the 'evils of drink'. Members were enrolled from the age of six and met once a week to listen to lectures and participate in activities. Music played an important role and competitions were held between different Band of Hope choirs. Members of the local Temperance Societies also organised outings for the children and with the growth of the railways, trips were arranged to the nearest coastal resorts.

By June 1885, the leaders of the group were appealing for funds to enable a *trip to the countryside to be undertaken.* These efforts were rewarded by a trip to Barlaston, six miles to the south of Penkhull by canal from Sideway.

It was during the incumbency of Rev Inglis C R Scott that the Penkhull Church was enlarged in 1892 by the addition of two side aisles and a baptistery to accommodate the growing congregation, drawn from extensive housing developments in the district. This was accomplished to celebrate the 50th anniversary of its opening. The gallery, previously used to seat the poor of the district was removed and internal arrangements changed. After the alterations, all seats were declared free. Miss Stamer, daughter of the Bishop of Shrewsbury and former Rector of Stoke, executed the cornerstone laying ceremony in May. The total cost of the alterations, refurbishment and the provision of an additional 166 seats amounted to £1,600. By December of the same year, work was completed and the church rededicated.

The Staffordshire Advertiser records the event as follows:
> On Saturday afternoon, Miss Stamer, daughter of the Bishop of Shrewsbury Sir Lovelace Stamer, Bart. laid the corner stone for the enlargement of St Thomas Church in the presence of a large company.
>
> The proceedings commenced with a procession from the schools amongst those present were the Bishop of Shrewsbury, Miss Stamer, the Rev H C Turner, the Rev I C R Scott vicar and a large number of local clergy. In the ceremony the diocesan office was used and Miss Stamer laid the corner stone bearing a suitable inscription with a silver trowel presented to her by the church authorities. The extension provides an additional 166 for worshippers.
>
> The total cost would be around £1,600, towards which they had already raised about £1,150 including various grants of £150 from the Diocesan Church Extension Society. In addition a donation of £50 was received from the Incorporated Church Building Society and further donations of £50 each from the Bishop of Shrewsbury (Patron) and Messrs W Tomlinson and F Bishop.

The Bishop said that it was a joyful day for all those who loved the church, and desired to see it growing and extending itself to meet the needs of an ever-increasing population. There was a great need for the work they had undertaken and the wide interest, which has been taken in the church, was a matter of devout thankfulness.

The proposed extension was not all they could desire, but considering the nature of the site, the alterations were well designed and provided additional accommodation that was required.

An offertory was taken at the close, which realised £11.14s 6d. Mr E P Warren of Westminster is the architect and Mr T P Yoxall builder of Stoke has been entrusted with the execution of the work.

Shortly after Rev Samuel Minton became incumbent, the need for a parsonage house became important for there was nowhere for him to reside. In July 1844, Minton wrote to the Ecclesiastical Commissioners asking if they would contribute towards the cost of such a parsonage, placing a value of £500 on the building. It appears that Minton had already a house in mind, converted from either two or three cottages in Doncaster Lane.

In an Ecclesiastical return of December 1882, the vicarage was described by James Brown the incumbent as follows: *There is a house of residence in a terrible state of repair considering its nature, and wholly unsuited for a parsonage formed out of two or more cottages. The Diocesan Architect has condemned it as a parsonage.* Brown also wrote a letter in the *Parish Magazine* stating: *if a new parsonage could be built and the church is made free and open without loss of income, the parish would be in a more favourable position than at present.*

Several gentlemen have kindly promised to support the movement. It seems likely that something may be done with the help of friends, but Penkhull is certainly not a wealthy place and will require an effort to raise even £180 that is required to obtain grants from the Diocesan Association and the Ecclesiastical Commissioners of £400.

By October 1883, £800 of the £1,000 required had been raised by donations from local businesses, individual donations and grants. It was then reported: *the present vicarage had long been a burden upon the parish.* It was the original intention to build the vicarage on a different site, but because of legal difficulties and increasing expense it was decided to build on the existing site after the demolition of the old vicarage. In April of the following year the *Parish Magazine* records: *Steps are being taken to commence the building of the new parsonage, and the first was to pull down the old parsonage house, which although it had proven an expensive and uncomfortable shelter, one could not feel some regrets at its demolition.*

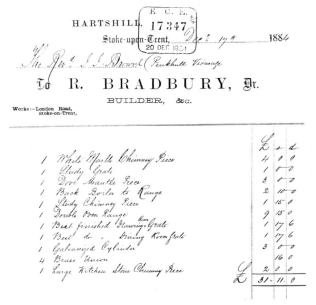

The architect was Mr Charles Lynam, who intended to complete the parsonage with a luxurious interior containing a white marble chimney piece; dove mantelpiece and best finished grates in the drawing and dining rooms, all supplied and fitted by Mr Bradbury the contractor. The total cost of the parsonage amounted to £1,072 9s 3d.

An assessment of the assets of the parish in 1884 reported that the parsonage was new and of a moderate size of red brick situated in Doncaster Lane, built in 1884 from £1,220 raised by subscriptions and grants from the Church Extension Society and Poor Benefice Fund of Lichfield diocese. It has 3 sitting rooms, 6 bedrooms, dressing room, bathroom, closet, washhouse and coalhouse, but no stable, and a small pleasure ground on a site of half an acre. The house was substituted for an old, dilapidated building unsuited for a parsonage.

The parish intended to acquire the plot of land in front of the new parsonage at the time of rebuilding, but cost prohibited this. Six years

Penkhull Parsonage, Doncaster Lane

later, on the 5th August 1890, Mr Frederick Bishop of The Mount, sold the land to the Diocese for the sum of £174 3s 0d for use as the vicarage garden. By June 1884 the *Parish Magazine* reported that the building was making *satisfactory progress, though some objections has been made by those interested in it to the quality of some of the materials being used.* Following this intermediate report on the progress it was a further four months before the work was completed as the Vicar announced in the Parish Magazine: *The Vicar is glad to be able to announce that the new vicarage house is now completed by the contractor, he has pleasure in expressing his satisfaction, and that of the committee with the general result. The house is likely to be most comfortable and convenient in its arrangements inside, and the builder has done his work well.*

Inside Penkhull Church c1900

Parish Records

Information of any significance regarding important events of the parish is hard to find, let alone documented. The first baptism recorded in the parish registers is of John Wareham of Honeywall on the 1st January 1843. The first burial took place on 1st April 1844 and was that of Elizabeth Cartlidge, a young girl aged 14 years. The average age of death for the first five years of the registers was just forty-three years. There are no preachers books earlier than 1875, so what better place to start than in that year.

3rd January 1875. Alec Smith, then Vicar wrote: Services were held in the schoolroom, the boiler to the church having burst. This continued for two weeks. Holy Communion was only held twice a month.
4th April 1876. Rev R J Rowson took his first service in Penkhull.
26th March 1876. Rev Samuel Minton returned to preach for that day.
26th November 1876. £1 5s 8d was collected for the retiring organist.

1st April 1878. There were 35 at Easter Communion.
2nd April 1879. Sir Lovelace Stamer installed the Rev G Molyneux as vicar. £1 4s 9d collected. He commenced his incumbency with meetings on instruction for communicants in church and also instigated the 8.00a.m. service.
21st April 1879. there were 17 only at Easter Communion.
Easter 1880, there were 61 communicants.
5th October 1881. The last service for Rev G Molyneux.
9th October 1881. The first service by Rev J Brown. Services were then held at 8.00a.m. 10.45 a.m. 6.30p.m. and 7.30p.m. However attendances dropped dramatically to an average of only ten.
13th August 1883. No communion held today, only one person present besides the clergyman.
12th August 1883. No one present for Communion.
25th December 1883. Total of 35 for communion.
2nd June 1889 Rev Brown's last service.
3rd July 1889. Institution of Rev Inglis C R Scott by the Bishop of Shrewsbury.
2nd October 1889. First Collection for church enlargement.
10th December 1892. Dedication of additions to church.
14th February 1897. Collection for Indian famine relief raised £2 11s 8½d.
25th December 1898. Nearly 200 hundred communicants.
22nd January 1901. Her Majesty Queen Victoria departed this life at 6.30p.m. R.I.P.
26th January 1901. After having been previously proclaimed in London, His Majesty King Edward VII was proclaimed in Stoke-on-Trent. The vicar and choir attended the service for the purpose at St Peter's in Stoke.
2nd February 1901. Memorial Service for Queen Victoria.
4th June 1908. Dedication of organ.
20th May 1910. Funeral of Edward VII.
5th May 1912. Rev Scott's last service.
18th May 1912. Rev William Duke-Baker admitted to the benefice.
10th October 1920. Dedication of War Memorial Screen and choir stalls by the Bishop of Stafford.
24th December 1912. First midnight Mass held.
27th March 1927 Rev V G Aston invited to preach at Penkhull.
19th May 1928. Institution of Rev F Rothwell by Bishop of Lichfield.
11th May 1930. Rev A. Perry preached at Penkhull.
14th December 1930. Rev Rothwell's last Sunday.
18th April 1931. Institution of Rev Vernon Gladstone Aston by Archdeacon.
15th August 1934. Dedication of Lady Chapel.
20th January 1936. King died at midnight.
29th September 1938. Dedication of Lady Chapel in memory of Mr Harold Steele and Ada Noke by Bishop of Stafford.

It is always interesting to find what is hidden away for years in my own archives. The first church magazine I came across is dated 1906 when Rev Inglis C R Scott was vicar. There are only two pages of 'church news' the rest is summed up as nationally published material, stories and examples of witness. At that time the activities of the church included: The Girl's Friendly Society; boy's practice; weekly Sunday School teacher's class; men's union and choir practice. The weekly offertory averaged around £4. The next magazine is dated 1909 which informs us that at the Christmas services consisted of three communion services at 7.00a.m., 8.00a.m. and 12 noon. The traditional service of Matins was held at 11.00a.m. In this issue there is a summary of statistics for the parish for baptisms, confirmed, communicants and collections from 1887 to 1908. The number baptised in 1887 was 30 increasing to 82 by 1908. The number of confirmed varied considerably, the lowest being nil, the maximum 56 followed by 49. Communicants commenced in 1887 at 75, whilst by 1908 they had increased to 176. Weekly collections varied no doubt in relation to the un-predictability of regular employment. In 1887 the total annual collections amounted to £73 4s 7d but twenty years later had increased to £140 19s 1d. by 1908.

The next set of church magazines relate to the last three months of 1917 by which time activities in the church had increased to include Church Lad's Brigade, Mother's Union and a Girl's Bible reading class. Mr Duke-Baker had become the vicar. The same year saw the church saved from serious fire damage when in January a resident of the Garden Village saw smoke coming from a beam adjacent to the furnace chimney. Mr Alldis, the caretaker of the church was immediately called, who with the aid of a bucket of damp sand quickly extinguished the fire, thereby saving the church from serious damage. Other references which reflect upon the Great War are found in the December issue when the writer comments: *The list of men from our parish now in khaki is too long to read right through and unfortunately at the present moment our list is by no means complete, because the names of many who have gone recently have not yet been handed to the vicar or placed in the box for that purpose.* The article went on to state that those who value prayer may wish to recall their names at the communion service on Christmas day.

The Rood Screen in memory of those who lost their lives 1914-18 war.

However, in the September 1919 issue, sold at a war time price of 1½d, the vicar talks about a war memorial, and the need to raise the sum of £950 to provide the necessary funds for the plan in recognition of those lives lost It reads: *This is the next big piece of work we have to undertake. We want it to be in some degree worthy of the sacrifice made and we want it to be a memorial to everyone in the parish and those connected with the church that live outside our parish boundaries. The members of the church council desire that our War Memorial should express our thankfulness to Almighty God for allowing us to achieve victory and also to perpetuate the memory of those who gave their lives in obtaining it. £950 seems a large amount of money for the scheme but if every house will contribute liberally there ought to be no difficulty at all.*

First World War memorial service conducted by Rev. W. Duke-Baker

The war memorial took the form of a Rood Screen and choir stalls. The two central figures of Mary and John were added in December 1958 in memory of Harold Bennett and his wife Beatrice.

The annual garden fete was held in the grounds of the parsonage in Doncaster Lane. In July 1930, a live fowl was offered as a prize in the raffle. Something, which would not be allowed today! The church magazine has an interesting entry for August: *the fowl drawn at the fete still remains at the vicarage waiting to be claimed. It has laid many eggs and so has paid for its keep but the vicarage people will be glad to hand it over to its rightful owner on production of the winning ticket, otherwise it will be sold.* Unfortunately, there is no record of how the fowl was disposed of.

Vicarage Garden Party - late 1930's

Until the mid 20s Trent Valley Road, formerly, Trentham Road was bounded on either side by fields with the exception of Penkhull Square and Brisley Hill. This changed in 1926 as we read that the properties on the left had been built and become occupied. *We extend a very hearty welcome to all our new parishioners in Trentham Road and we hope they*

Choir outing 1928

will very soon feel quite at home among us. The new homes with their gardens in front area are a great improvement to Trentham Road.

Vicars of Penkhull

S Minton	1843 – 1848
I C R Scott	1849 – 1853
W Moreton	1853 – 1860
E N Jones	1861 – 1868
A Smith	1868 – 1875
R G Rowson	1875 – 1879
G Molyneux	1897 – 1881
J J Brown	1881 – 1889
I C R Scott	1889 – 1912
W Duke-Baker	1912 – 1928
F Rothwell	1928 – 1930
V G Aston	1931 – 1956
A Perry	1956 – 1967
J D Andrews	1968 – 1980
I Maiten	1981 – 2006

There are no further vicars, as the parish became a united Benefice with the parishes of Hartshill and Trent Vale.

Rev Vernon Gladstone Aston
Vicar of Penkhull

The longest serving vicar by just a few months is the The Reverend Vernon Gladstone Aston; 'VG', as he was affectionately called. He came to Penkhull after serving as vicar at Onecote, Nr. Leek for a short period. Born at Stourbridge in 1893 he was educated at King Edward VI Grammar School. After taking Mods in mathematics, he graduated BA of St David's College, Lampeter, for Holy Orders. His first appointment was as curate in Burslem and St Luke's, Florence, Longton, having a special calling to the ministry to actors as they visited the theatres in the town.

In 1931, Penkhull was a very different place from the village of today. It remained just as it had been for several hundred years a rural community with fields stretching over a wide area, mostly down Newcastle Lane and Trentham Road. Around the village's central area were little cottages with long narrow gardens, old shops, beer houses and pubs.

The majority of the population were working class with the exception of those occupiers of Princes and Queens Road and a few in the new larger properties in Trentham Road. It is to this setting that VG arrived in 1931 to become a parish priest respected by all. He enjoyed socialising and held the record among the clergy of the parish for being the fastest to shake hands at the church door after the evening service and yet still the first to be at the bar in The Marquis or The Greyhound. VG was a familiar face in all the local hostelries, for he considered *his flock* were to be found everywhere and, as priest he should meet them where they were comfortable. Many a free half was gained with the tale of *so much per yard of bell rope to be pulled at ones funeral to be purchased in advance from the public bar.*

VG was very much an intellectual. He gave regular monthly talks on a wide range of topics to the men's group who used to meet in an old building situated next to the bowling green at The Marquis. To celebrate the churches centenary in 1942, he published his little book on the *History of Penkhull.* In 1946 he published a further book entitled *A Vicar's Anthology of Verse*, containing many poems he had compiled about people of the village, situations or replies to his critics when he wrote to *The Sentinel.* In addition to this he penned an unpublished manuscript entitled *Thirty years in the Potteries*, in about 1948/9, which his son Dennis gave to me some forty years ago. It is full of anecdote, characters, places and people who influenced his life in the Potteries. It is a piece of local history one seldom comes across and it is a great pity it has never been published. He also composed church music, two settings to the Communion Service and many hymn tunes and chants. For years he studied the origins of hymns and hymn-melodies but never published the work. He also had a talent for lighter music.

Penkhull Belles

A further talent that VG used in his ministry was that of music. He compiled incidental music, the Penkhull Anthem and other songs for that series of Parish Revues entitled Penkhull Belles, a name that became associated with Penkhull for many years. The first revue took place in January 1932 under the title of Penkhull Beaux-Belles as a way of raising funds for the parish church. VG was no stranger both to script writing, compilation of music and producing. In total VG wrote the music, and words, for ten pantomimes of which five were produced at Penkhull. They consisted of appropriate sketches for the time, singing, both choral by adults and children as well as a team of outstanding soloists.

For many years, men, women and children of Penkhull presented these revues in the church hall to the great delight of people from both Penkhull and the wider area of the Potteries. Indeed they were so successful, financially and artistically, that, the name of Penkhull Belles became a household word through the district and even reached the national press.

SECOND ANNUAL REVUE

PENKHULL

BEAUX-BELLES

By the REV. V. G. ASTON, B.A.

PRESENTED BY

The Penkhull Revue Company.

No records have survived for the first revue, but the second performed in January 1933 was to established the annual productions as a real community event. There were a number of men whose roll was to play comedy, Colin Simpson, John Mackensie and William Bishop.

The sketch that year was based upon The Forty Thieves as seen through the eyes of an ABC reporter. The chorus of robbers consisted of eight men, whilst that of the ladies and dancers totalled twenty. There were speciality dances by Vera Hassall and children and singing by Hilda Hesbrook and Bunty Phillips whilst Mrs Aston was in charge of training the young children for a children's ballet.

Sketch 'The Forty Thieves' 1933

So professional, the whole evening as supported by no less than a ten-piece orchestra and on each evening a different local dignitary would act as Chairman including the Lord Mayor of Stoke, Mr. Louis Taylor, The Arch-Deacon of Stoke, Mrs Ronald Copeland and Dr A P Spark.

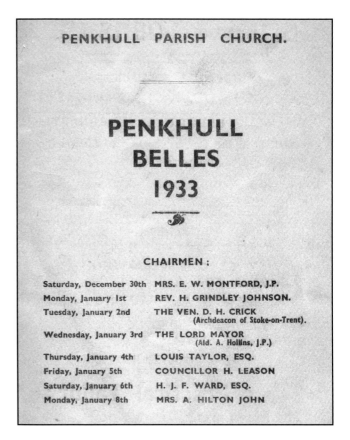

PENKHULL PARISH CHURCH.

PENKHULL BELLES 1933

CHAIRMEN:

Saturday, December 30th	MRS. E. W. MONTFORD, J.P.
Monday, January 1st	REV. H. GRINDLEY JOHNSON.
Tuesday, January 2nd	THE VEN. D. H. CRICK (Archdeacon of Stoke-on-Trent).
Wednesday, January 3rd	THE LORD MAYOR (Ald. A. Hollins, J.P.)
Thursday, January 4th	LOUIS TAYLOR, ESQ.
Friday, January 5th	COUNCILLOR H. LEASON
Saturday, January 6th	H. J. F. WARD, ESQ.
Monday, January 8th	MRS. A. HILTON JOHN

THE VICAR—REV. V. G. ASTON.

THE NAME "Penkhull Belles" has become something of a household word in the Potteries and even much further afield. Most of our great daily Newspapers have written of it in their columns, and we feel that such mention is not unmerited in view of the great number who have witnessed the "Revues" under that title.

Three years ago we felt that there was need for a complete breakaway from the ordinary Church Concert or Children's Pantomime, while still retaining the Christmas atmosphere which centres around children. Thus the Parish Revue was "born" and at our first effort we made over £50, at our second, the "Beaux-Belles" we made over £100, and this year we wish to realize £150. Whether we do this depends upon you, good reader, for your advertisement will help us much. This year great alterations have taken place to give a more spectacular effect, but these have cost a great deal of money, well spent if it enables you to witness a better show in greater comfort than hitherto, for there is now much more room.

We have to cover all expenses by gifts and subscriptions to enable us to save entertainment tax, so we solicit your kind help also in this way.

After the first two productions, they were considered an established tradition with its own Revue committee. As soon as the curtain came down on one-production rehearsals commenced for the next. Their success inspired VG and his more than willing assistants to think big and to improve the venue. As a result in 1933 the rear of the hall was opened into the room behind the hall to create a permanent proscenium arch and the room made higher to accommodate flies. Local builder and close friend of VG, Tom Meiklejohn and his helpers transformed the hall into a mini-theatre. The stage itself was semi-permanent being removable so the room could be quickly transformed back to use for educational purposes. A stone plaque on the gable end of this extension forms a permanent memorial to this fact.

Work backstage August 1933

In 1933 VG wrote: *The name of Penkhull Belles has become something of a household word in the Potteries and even much further afield. Most of our great daily newspapers have written of it in their columns, and we feel that such a mention is not unmerited in view of the great number of people who have witnessed the Revues.*

The press report for the following year referred in its headline to being *'up-to-date and gay and witty'* and continued: *With the polish and finesse of a professional show, the third revue by the Vicar of Penkhull made its bow to the public on Saturday evening. The Revues have earned a wide reputation and this year's production not only lives up to the high standard but surpasses them.*

Revue 1938

VG was assisted by his wife Lily who helped to train the children taking part. The January 1938 Review was based upon the Coronation of the previous year with many

sketches and national songs such as *Land of Hope and Glory*. One dance was a Children's Ballet with speciality dancers Joan Meiklejohn (now Reid) and Beryl Lawton. VG wrote in the introduction that any money raised would help to provide funds to provide the church organ with electrical apparatus for blowing. Each revue was more ambitious and impressive than the previous one described by the press in 1939 *as a show of superb quality, which moves with scintillating vitality and vigour from the joyous opening chorus to the spectacular finale.* The accompanist was

Vicar's Third Revue Success

"PENKHULL BELLES" UP-TO-DATE

GAY AND WITTY SHOW

With the polish and finesse of a professional show, the third revue by the Vicar of Penkhull (the Rev. V. G. Aston), entitled, "Penkhull Belles, 1933" made its bow to the public on Saturday evening.

The Rev. V. G. Aston's revues have earned a wide reputation, and this year's production not only lives up to the high standard set by its predecessors, but surpasses them in every respect. Two years ago Mr. Aston set out with two objectives—to provide an entertainment worthy of the name, and to raise money for the Church funds. He succeeded in both, realising more than £50. But that did not finish the matter. He found talent among his congregation, support from the district and an eagerness for more. The result was the production of "Beaux Belles," which realised more than £100, with a run of six nights, early in January last year. With that, such ventures were not going to be allowed to lapse, and so the Vicar was urged to compile his third revue, and "Penkhull Belles, 1933" was launched on a run of eight nights, with the object of being able to hand over the sum of £150 to the Church funds.

PENKHULL BELLES

ANOTHER EXCELLENT SHOW BY CHURCH MEMBERS

ORIGINALITY AND SPECTACLE

"Penkhull Belles, 1939," an addition to the series of revues staged by members of Penkhull Parish Church, opened a run of six performances in the Penkhull Church Schools last night. It is an excellent show that worthily upholds the reputation established in recent years.

Last night was principally a children's night, and a host of youngsters gave the show a hearty send-off.

In past shows, thousands of North Staffordshire people have seen and praised the originality and attractiveness of "Penkhull Belles," and several

Miss Winnie Hesbrook, while her sister Hilda, (later to become Littler) was one of the many star performers often singled out by the press for her outstanding singing.

This Coronation Revue was set apart by its staging with a running illuminated fountain in the middle of the stage whilst singers and children danced and sang around to the changing colours of the leaping water, a scene reported as being of *real beauty* all designed and built by Mr. Tom Meiklejohn and his team.

Another highlight was singing and dancing by Joan Meiklejohn and Beryl Lawton and sketches of George Formby's 'Cleaning Windows', and four Belles, Peggy Skellen, the Phillips sisters and I Lawton performed the 'Balloon Dance'.

C A S T

Children :

A. Arnold	B. Groves	M. Lawton	K. Snape
A. Barker	V. Grundy	J. Lovatt	J. Tansley
M. Corbishley	D. Henson	Billy	R. Thomas
A. Cotgreave	M. Hill	Meiklejohn	M. Till
J. Davies	I. Johnson	J. Meiklejohn	M. Tyldesley
J. Floyd	M. Keeling	H. Myatt	B. Underwood
D. Gould	M. Kelter	B. Phillips	B. Weston
D. Greenoff	B. Lawton	D. Ryder	

The " Belles " :

L. Beech	L. Corbishley	C. Holmes	M. Rodgers
F. Bishop	J. Dobson	I. Lawton	J. Simpson
H. Brereton	P. Dobson	B. Lee	P. Skellern
L. Cope	F. Ellis	I. Phillips	M. Taylor
	G. Ellis	P. Rawlins	

Ladies :

Mrs. Aston	Mrs. Powell	Mrs. Phillips	Mrs. Rigby
	Miss E. Ball	Miss H. Hesbrook	

Men :

W. Bishop	F. Fradley	J. Mackenzie	C. Simpson
P. Evans	L. Griffin	W. Marlow	A. Taylor
S. Evans	B. Groves	J. Poole	J. Taylor
	F. Harvey	C. P. Powell	

The company 1938

The end, like so many shows of the period was patriotic with songs like 'Britannia' with a miniature king and queen in the middle and led by Mrs Aston concluding with first an anthem written by VG 'Penkhull Forever' which has pride of place in my archives followed finally with the National Anthem.

Like so many groups the onset of war in 1939 brought the revue to an end. The props and costumes were retained optimistically for a number of years and then, with no hope of the revues returning they were finally sold.

As a final *encore,* I was delighted to be associated with Mrs Winnie Wys, (now Mrs Roberts) in arranging in May 1975 a reunion of sixteen former Belles and helpers. Over sixty attended the event in the church hall including Bunty Philips, now Mrs Long, who in 1945, left the UK for America as a GI bride but returned for the event. The highlight of the evening was the playing of a taped interview I took some years previously with Mrs Lily Aston at her home in Worcester. Dennis Aston, her son, also wrote a letter dictated to him by his mother after I had invited them both to attend. It makes interesting reading and is found in *Appendix vi.*

PENKHULL BELLES

Amid the grim, forbidding aspect of our times, when every day well-nigh a sign compels,
One bright sound's emitted from the chimes, of **Penkhull Belles.**
If you're 'fed-up' since modern drama palls, or bored by prophecies of HG Wells,
Or worried by the pace Stoke City falls, See **Penkhull Belles.**
If you have had your share of winter's ill, And still you suffer 'epiglottic spells',
The one sure cure, eclipsing doctor's pills, is **Penkhull Belles.**
If 'fore your income-tax your courage fails, And if the bank your latest cheque expels
If 'last demand' stands topmost in your mails,
See **Penkhull Belles.**
In short, if for an hour or two you'd see, a different show that all the rest excels.
Hail '34 and laugh out '33, See **Penkhull Belles.**

Probably the last enduring memorial to VG was the creation of the Garden of Rest as a memorial to those from Penkhull who sacrificed their lives during the Second World War. For some time following the end of hostilities the question of a suitable war memorial was on the local agenda.

The last regular burials in new graves were in 1901 after which the churchyard was by Act of Parliament closed. There are a total of 1,797 burials from the first burial of Herbert Bailey on the 16th October 1844 aged three months to its closure in 1901. After this date there were only a few additional burials allowed and these were into existing graves. The last was of Arthur Bell in February 1939, aged 74. Even so, the churchyard was allowed to become un-kept, overgrown and neglected. During the 1920s sheep were allowed to graze whilst awaiting 'execution' by Mr Berrisford the butcher. Doug Jervis was also encouraged to put a few cows inside the boundaries to keep the grass down. From time to time, he would cut the grass for silage as he did for both the hospital grounds and parts of Stoke churchyard.

Penkhull churchyard has been the focal point for celebration at various important dates in recent history. Still within memory was the occasion when a new curate from Europe came to work for a period at Penkhull Church. It was his custom in the village of his birth, once a year to light up to all the windows with candles, and have no street lighting. VG took the challenge and shared his vision with all, so much so that the cottages around the churchyard took part, in addition to what appeared to be hundreds of lights strung around the churchyard trees. As expected, villagers turned out in there thousands to witness the sight of Penkhull being transformed to that of a continental view for one night.

Candel lighting around the churchyard 1935

Churchyard 1935

On two occasions there was tree planting, first to commemorate the Jubilee of King George V on May 6th, 1935 and then the Coronation of King George VI on the 12th May 1937. On each of these occasions, six saplings were planted around the churchyard and remain today as a witness to that event together with a remaining few nameplates of the children appointed to the task. The churchyard was bursting with parishioners, civic dignitaries to overflowing point as photographs of the event display. The children involved were Margaret Berrisford, Michael Holt, Mavis Lawton, Kenneth Cheadle, Betty Rowlands, Barbara Holbrook, Stuart Gittins, Freda Hawkins, Beryl Turnock, James Grundy, Ruth Bardell, and William Meiklejohn. Many others such occasions have followed since then but are far too numerous to record here in any detail.

Tree planting May 1937

VG first mooted the thought to transfer the neglected churchyard to the city council in 1950, writing in May of that year, asking for the council to consider taking over the churchyard under the 1906 Open Spaces Act. Unfortunately VG did not consider the unusually high objections to the scheme from both members of the PCC and parishioners. These were strong and vibrant. In correspondence from the city council as late as September 1953, there was talk of the matter even going to a Consistory Court if all the objections were made formal and in writing, so concerned, even at the plans for the Garden of Rest, let alone the re-siting of seventy seven tombstones to the south section of the churchyard. Mr Francs from Wain Drive became instrumental in drawing up an alternative set of plans, subsequently dismissed. The opposition mounted from a group who just did not wish to have the graves of their loved ones changed. Though leaving their mortal remains in situ, the headstone would be relocated under VG's plan.

Correspondence came and went from the vicarage. One rather objectionable person, Mr Guy Jones from Ashby-de-la-Zouch hounded VG with his complaints about the removal of the tomb of his grandparents Mr and Mrs James Robinson and even demanded that once removed, the tomb be repainted in the colour of his own choice. In addition to this were the complexities of planning law and also the Diocese to deal with.

The total cost of the project amounted to £2,800. At last a way forward through the quagmire of issues was found. Firstly a Faculty had to be obtained from the Diocese followed by an Agreement document with the city council. *In the Consistory Court of Lichfield to all Christian People to whom these presents shall come, we John Percy Ashworth, Vicar General of the Rt.Rev Father in God Arthur Stretton, Lord Bishop of Lichfield, sends greetings.* This document deals with the Diocesan legal requirements of the faculty. The second is the Agreement between the PCC of St Thomas and the Lord Mayor and Citizens of Stoke-on-Trent. It is headed the Rev Vernon Gladstone Aston, Clerk in Holy Orders, the Parochial Church Council of St Thomas and the city council and dated the 27th May 1954.

In view of the current long-standing misuse of the churchyard, the conditions laid down in the agreement are interesting as follows: *The Corporation shall undertake forever the upkeep, maintenance, care, management, control and supervision of the churchyard and will indemnify the Vicar and church council from all claims in respect of. The Corporation shall take steps necessary to prevent abuse and damage. The grounds shall be only used as a Garden of Rest for the quiet enjoyment and use thereof by the general public and the playing of games therein shall be forbidden. Cycling and all unauthorised vehicular traffic shall be strictly prohibited and notices to that effect shall be erected. The corporation shall re-site the existing tombstones and memorials.* The council were also to lay new paths as part of the scheme. Permission would be granted to the church for any future maintenance of cables, sewers etc. but the church would be responsible for their reinstatement. The council did not at any point take over the responsibility of the Church or the churchyard boundary wall. These remain as always the responsibility of the parish church.

It is indeed a pity that this Garden of Rest, in memory of those who died during the war, is abused being used as

Church Choir 1939

Church Choir 1957. Rev. Arthur Perry central when he was the Lord Mayor of Stoke-on-Trent.

Minton Hollins tile floor in the Chancel.

recreation ground for games, alcohol consumption and general anti-social behaviour, particularly as there are still the remains of all those that have been buried there lying just beneath the surface and the ground is a consecrated area. There are many people still living in the village whose family members are buried in the churchyard including five of my own, the Underwood's. The sign restricting Ball Games, was removed, damaged or lost many years ago. There is now little or no concern expressed by the Church at any of the activities that take place in the churchyard or of its original purpose as a garden of rest.

VG had for many years struggled against illness. His health was failing whilst working for his last project for his beloved Penkhull. He was able to dedicate the new Garden of Rest in July 1955, just over a year before he resigned the living. The notice appeared of his ill health in the magazine. The mid-week services of communion were suspended. Reluctantly, VG had to resign his living and took his last service at Penkhull at the Harvest Festival on Sunday 28th October 1956. VG died at his home in Worcester in September 1962 following a long illness. His family and friends gathered together to purchase the highest tribute to a past servant of the parish in the form of a new High Altar in his memory and celebration of his witness and services in Penkhull for over 25 years.

At a meeting of the PCC held in April 1963, it was reported that a faculty had been applied for and the new altar to the design of Turnercraft Ltd. of Burslem at a cost of £300 of which £200 was by personal gift of Mrs Aston. The Bishop of Lichfield performed the dedication on Sunday 29th September 1963. A long and valued friend of VG, Dr. Mrs Ramage, wrote in the *Parish Magazine* for November 1962.

May I add a word in appreciation of our late Vicar, the Rev V G Aston, B.A. He was a man of remarkable gifts as shown by his ability to make rhymes out of any special topical event. Many of these were published in the Evening Sentinel. In the world of music VG composed two settings for the Sung Eucharist, one of which was used in our Church until recently. In addition to this he wrote songs, and music and words for his revues such as the Penkhull Belles. He compiled a commentary on all the hymns in Ancient and Modern; A history of Penkhull and at least one novel also flowed from his pen.

Having a degree in mathematics he delighted in proving the existence of eternity by a mathematic formula! It was his dearest wish in later life to see Penkhull churchyard turned into a

Annual Church Walk around the parish c1930's

Annual Church Walk around the parish 1933. Here along Greatbatch Avenue

garden of rest and he was delighted when at the last the City Council decided to do it. VG was ill for six years before he died but never forgot his beloved Penkhull. It is true to say that he thought of his old parish daily. Mrs Aston nursed him with devotion and he could not have lived so long without her loving care.

View of Penkhull from the top of Trentham Road c1950
by E.D.J. Warrilow

It was only a short time following the resignation of VG before the Rev Arthur Perry was installed vicar later the same year. The following year Arthur became involved in the major work of church restoration, mostly in faith. The work commenced on the roof followed by the restoration and resurfacing of the external stonework including the gables, an enormous task. The estimated cost for the project was £22,000 and yet Arthur commenced the project whilst there remained a shortfall of £6,000. In 1957/8 Arthur Perry became the first clergyman in the country to hold the office

of Lord Mayor but continued throughout his calling of parish priest. Ten years later, Arthur died suddenly on the 17th August 1967 at the age of 67. His good friend, Sir Albert Bennett, continued the work of restoration and raised the necessary funds to complete the work. It is fitting that the great work of restoration is attributed to Prebendary Arthur Perry in the form of a memorial which stands above the vestry door on the south gable: *In Memory. The restoration of this church was inspired by the faith and dedicated service of Prebendary Arthur Perry, Vicar of Penkhull, 1956-1967.*

After the unveiling of the plaque to Prebendary Perry, Mrs Perry, the Rev. Andrews, the Bishop of Stafford, the Rt.Rev. R.C.Clitherow, The Lord Mayor and Lady Mayoress and Sir Albert Bennett..

Rev VG Aston with his son Dennis c1948

YOUR OLD VICAR'S GOOD-BYE

O my dear Penkhull Church where good people search
From shop, street and mart for Christ's Sacred Heart,
Through gardens sunkissed or wintery mist;
To kneel at God's Altar, sing praise from the Psalter,
With choir's noble paean to the Great Galilean,
That flies Heavenward on deep organ chord;
A collect, a prayer, mourners' sorrow to share;
With the East Window above me and those who still love me;
Heartache for the crying, a prayer for the dying;
Or a quiet hour to spend in talk with a friend;
A joke with the glad, a sigh with the sad;
O what beautiful things on memory's wings
To remember for years, to remember with tears!

V. G. *(Harvest, 1956)*

Chapter 12
Education

Early Christian philanthropists founded institutions for the education of the young in Penkhull. Benefactors often endowed or financed religious education, followed by secular instruction for a limited number of children. One such benefactor was Dr John Weston, Rector of Stoke (1604-1618), who maintained two schools at his own expense. One of these schools at Stoke, accommodating forty boys was opened by 1604 teaching reading, writing and the catechism.

A specific reference to Penkhull was made as early as 1623. In the Presentments at the visitation of Thomas, Bishop of Coventry and Lichfield, held at Stafford on 25 August, the question was asked: *Mr Taylor teaches boys at Penkhull, is he licensed?* Upon checking the facts the parish records for Stoke confirm a Richard Taylor and his wife Margarita lived in the parish of Stoke at that time.

For the working classes, who represented the overwhelming majority at the end of the eighteenth century, little instruction existed, except that which was provided either by the parish church in Stoke for older children, or Dame schools for young children. The expanding role of commerce in the growing towns of the Potteries accentuated and extended the demands for a rudimentary education, and Dame Schools became fashionable to meet this demand.

Dame schools were places not so much of instruction as of 'periodical confinement' where children were looked after generally by old women, but sometimes by old men whose only qualifications for the job, according to a contemporary report, was their unfitness for every other.

The earliest record of a Dame School in Penkhull dates from 1818, established in Honeywall under the principalship of Ann Pinhorne. The next stage of elementary education, mainly for the poor, was made by early advancements of the Sunday School Movement.

The employment of children in factories was condoned and even welcomed because of the current laissez-faire theories, and demands by manufacturers for child labour. For parents their children's earnings were needed to support the family. Working on a factory left only one day a week free, and this made it possible to learn to read and write through the Sunday School Movement. This movement was associated with Robert Raikes, who founded the first Sunday School in 1780. By 1785, the Sunday School Union began to spread over the whole of England. By 1787, Burslem, the mother town of The Potteries, boasted 'The Burslem Sunday School', established under the Wesleyan Connection. The Wesleyan Chapel in Cross Street, now Epworth Street, Stoke, founded a Sunday School in 1805. Many other churches followed

this initiative during the early years of the nineteenth century. Stoke parish church held a Sunday School in the National School, adjoining the churchyard where 230 boys and 215 girls attended in 1842.

Occasionally evidence can be found of the establishment of a private school. One such school, opened in 1808 by Mr Hutchin, was a school for boys situated just below the hill of Penkhull at Boothen. An advertisement of that year continued to describe the school at Boothen Villa. *J. Hitchin begs leave respectfully to inform the inhabitants of Stoke-upon-Trent that he is about to relinquish the Market Hall at Stoke* (this would be an upper room in the old market situated in what is now Hill Street) *and to enter upon a new and commodious house at Boothen Villa, where he intends to educate a select number of pupils in the necessary and useful branches of learning and he trusts that the eligibility of the situation, as possessing a pure air and being more retired, will be generally approved of. He has no doubt but, by a conscientious and unremitting attention to the best interests of those committed to his care, he shall continue to enjoy the confidence and support of his numerous friends. Terms*

Reading 10 6d per quarter
Reading, writing and grammar 15 0d per quarter
Reading, writing, grammar and arithmetic, including merchants Accompts, Algebra etc. £1 1s 0d per quarter

The number of Day Students not to exceed thirty. Tuition to commence on Monday 5th July next. Mr Huchin will undertake to board and lodge six young gentlemen, who will be kindly and liberally treated.

Penkhull Primitive Methodists had established a Sunday School by 1824. It was reported that *no secular instruction was given except writing and the books used were the 'Bible' and 'Reading made Easy'.* It was not until 1834 that the parish church of Stoke decided to provide a Sunday School in Penkhull, probably as a result of children attending a non-conformist church, as the Anglican Church in those days strongly opposed the expanding Methodist Church and saw its growth not only as a threat to its own teachings, but also feared a revolution in the country in an attempt to destroy the corrupt Established Church.

These deeply and widely held concerns led to St. Peter's Church in Stoke erecting a Sunday School in the centre of the village green in 1834, and gave secular instruction whereas the Methodists gave no secular instruction of any kind. By 1841 the Methodists boasted an attendance of 150 children while the Anglican Sunday School nearby fell short of this number at 75. In comparison, the Wesleyan Chapel in Cross Street, now Epworth Street, just down the hill from Penkhull held a Sunday School for 393 children and the Methodist New Connexion Chapel in Hill Street, held a

Sunday School for 336 children. The increasing success of the Sunday School Movement in the Pottery towns reflects the working-class background of the district. As for the town of Stoke and the village of Penkhull, in excess of thirteen hundred children attended Sunday School, reflecting the deprivation of the times.

The first Anglican Day School in Penkhull originated from the already established Sunday School, situated in the centre of the village green. In 1834, the land became the subject of a Copyhold Grant from the Duchy of Lancaster for the religious instruction of the poor children in the area. When this had been approved, the Rector of Stoke applied to the Duchy for financial support towards the building of the school. Upon the receipt of the request, the Chancellor to the Duchy asked for information regarding a list of subscribers and subscriptions already raised towards the object. The Rector of Stoke Rev J W Tomlinson complied with the request as the Duchy minutes confirm *a list of subscriptions, for the building of a schoolhouse for the education of the poor at Penkhull amounted to £119, against the estimated cost of £200*. It was ordered *that a warrant be prepared for a grant from the Duchy revenues of £50 towards the object*. In December 1836, the school was licensed for Divine Worship in the name of Rev. Sir William Dunbar as Curate of Stoke (1832-1839). Dunbar later became Rector of Welwyn Castle in Pembroke, followed by All Saints, Dumper, Hants, where he died in 1885. There is a memorial tile in Stoke Parish Church to his memory.

Entry from the Manorial Wastehold Book dated 7th December 1836

Little is known of this school. Apart from a government report, no documents have survived, if they ever existed. A government inspector into Child Labour, Mr Samuel Scriven prepared his report in 1841. For the district of Penkhull the report lists a school as an 'infants' school' caring for forty children, with one female teacher, E J Bentley, who stated: *I am teacher of this school; have had no previous education to fit me for it. The instruction is very simple, as reading, writing, exercises, and singing. We have thirty boys and fifty girls on the*

books, but owing to the badness of the times have only sixty altogether attending. The girls are taught to knit and work; they come as young as four or five, and continue sometimes until they are eight or nine. A few are as young as two; they do not do anything. The expenses of the school are defrayed by voluntary contributions, and partly by payments of the children. The amount is two pence each weekly, if we have three of one family, four pence will defray the amount for all. The rewards for good conduct are small books and occasional holidays; we give them other holidays at Christmas for fourteen days. The punishments are trifling, and are left to the discretion of myself as their mistress. There is no other governess or monitor.

Scriven sums up his feelings on the subject of education within The Potteries:
I almost tremble, however, when I contemplate the fearful deficiency of knowledge existing throughout the district, and the consequences likely to result to this increased and increasing population, and would willingly leave the evidence to speak for itself, did I feel that I should ill discharge my duty were I to shrink from the task. . . . It will appear that more than three fourths of the persons therein named can neither read nor write. An inference may be possibly drawn that I have been partial in my selection of them, but I beg distinctly to be understood as having on all occasions chosen those irrespectively of any educational competency. . . I conceive to be that of sending children at too early a period of life to labour from morning till night, in hundreds of cases for fifteen or sixteen hours consecutively, with the intermission of only a few minutes to eat their humble food of 'taters' and 'stir pudding', and where they acquire little else than vice, for the wages of one or two shillings per week, whereby they are deprived of every opportunity of attending a day or evening school. In all the schools two pence a week is required from every pupil, which although trifling in amount, is beyond the reach of many.

The following entry taken from the manorial waste hold book unfolds the origins of the school in detail. Firstly it refers to the school granted to Sir William Dunbar in 1835 but, interestingly, the same site appears to have been used for the building of the current parish church as the words used are *lately built and ready for consecration* appear in 1841. It was agreed by the Duchy that an additional plot of ground on the village green be used for the building of a new school, which, like the church, had already been built. The minute seems to be retrospective permission being granted. The following is taken from the Manor wastehold book.

At a Special Court Baron held on the 29th September 1841 before Thomas Fenton Esq.

Whereas a court held on the 21st July 1835 for a certain plot of land on Penkhull Green containing 660 yards for a nominal consideration granted to trustees W Taylor Copeland, John Smith etc. (as listed in previous document) *together with John Tomlinson and Arthur Minton (both now deceased) and also Rev John Wickes Tomlinson, Thomas Fenton trustees for the said school for religious instruction for children.*

And whereas the plot of land so granted as aforesaid having been deemed an eligible site for the erection of a church or chapel lately built and forthwith intended to be consecrated for the celebration and performance of Divine Worship of the established church. Surrender was agreed to be made only upon the understanding that another plot of land on Penkhull Green shall be granted for the purpose of the said school to ten persons nominated as trustees and a new building intended to be appropriated to the purpose of a Sunday school before mentioned has recently been erected by voluntary subscriptions upon the plot hereafter mentioned and granted.

And in consideration of a peppercorn, paid by the Trustees a grant from the Chancellor and Council of Her Majesty's Duchy of Lancaster.

The grant entered in the wastehold Book of the Manor continues to describe the plot of land and why it is shaped the way it is today, especially at the southern end as it needed to take into account a public water pump and secondly the recently erected church school adjacent to the church itself.

All that plot of manor waster delineated upon the original minute of this grant containing 600 sq. yards, bounded northward, eastward and westward by public highways and southward by the new boundary of the water pump on Penkhull Green and partly by the public approach to the water pump from its eastern and western sides. And also all those buildings, which have been erected upon the plot for the purpose of a school.

From 1841, until the building of the present school four years later in 1845, the combination of events and scattered references has confused to some extent the known educational pattern in Penkhull. Examination once more of the Duchy minute book provides the answer with an entry made on the 24 May 1845, referring to correspondence dated the 22nd May received from Mr Fenton, the steward of the Manor.

A school has been lately built in substitution for and only a few yards distant from that mentioned in Mr Fenton's of May 1841, which school was demolished and on the same site, a new church had been built. On the demolition of the original school, another was built upon a plot of land adjoining the church. However, this school was found inconveniently situated with regard to the position of the church. As a consequence it was removed and its site added to the churchyard. Therefore a new school, for which enfranchisement is asked, in now being built upon Copyhold land purchased and situated only a few yards from the original school.

For many years I was confused by the account John Ward gives in his book of 1843 with regard to the school at Penkhull when he writes *A school house has for a few years been maintained here in connection with the church at Stoke* (referring to the 1836 school), *and a neat school house has lately been built near to the site of the church.*

The explanation obtained from the Duchy minute book makes sense of Ward's reference to the school. Ward is referring to the second school erected in 1841 after the 1836 school was demolished, but before the 1845 school was built.

The first intimation of a third new school appears in an application to the National Society, (a division of the Church of England which dealt with Anglican Church Schools) on the 22nd December 1843. Samuel Minton, the priest in charge of the new parish church applied for financial aid to assist with the building costs. The original estimate was £230, of which £84 5 4d had either been promised or raised, suggesting a possible grant from the Committee of Council for £185. On 7th March 1844, the Committee agreed to offer to pay half of the Master's salary amounting to £70 per annum for two years, *to enable the applicant to obtain assistance from the Committee of Council towards the building of a school.*

The first grant towards the Master's salary was paid on 27th February 1845, but at a reduced figure of £25, which was decided upon at a council meeting held in October 1844. In October 1846, Minton applied to the council for the second year's grant, stating a schoolmistress had been employed to take charge of the infants. Since the original grant had been reduced by £20 over the two years, Minton asked for an additional grant of £300 to assist with her salary. By June a revaluation of the situation, estimated the cost of building the school and the master's house had risen to £704 6s 0d, leaving a shortfall of £156 4s 0d after all grants and donations had been taken into account. Nine months later, Minton again refers to the additional expense of a movable

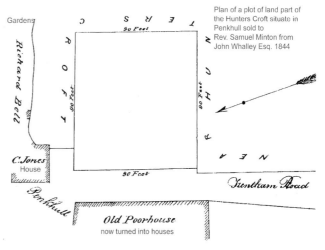

Plan to the original plot of land for the proposed new National School

143

Application for Aid towards { building, enlarging, } of { one, &c. } School-room*s* for { Boys, Girls, } to go
fitting up,   { two, &c. }   { Infants, }
with a Residence for a Teacher *or Teachers*, at *Penkhull* { near the } *Newcastle und*
                                                            { Post-town of }
The Schools { are to be } United to the National Society { state } *when built* — A.D. 18 *44*
            { or more }   { when }

If it is intended to purchase a house to be converted into a School-room, instead of building a new one, the circumstance must be clearly stated, and a Surveyor's certificate be forwarded, which may shew the actual condition of the building, and what its state will be when the undertaking is accomplished. The date of erection must be also mentioned, and the purpose to which the building was originally applied.

1. The Population of the *district* for } *1250* and now is about *1300*
   which the Schools are intended, as } was
   taken in the year 1841 . . . .
   State whether it is manufacturing, mining, agricultural, or commercial. — *Manufacturing* —

2. Existing Provision for Education gratuitously or at a very small charge
   in Schools connected with the Church is as follows :

		ACTUAL ATTENDANCE.			ACCOMMODATION.		
Sunday or Daily.		Number of Boys.	Number of Girls.	Number of Infants.	Number of Boys.	Number of Girls.	Number of Infants.
the School No. 1	*Sunday*	*100*	*110*		*50*	*50*	
No. 2	*Daiy*	*20*	*30*	*20*			
No. 3							

Be pleased to state whether one, and which, *of the above existing Church of England Schools is* to be merged in the School for which aid is now solicited.

and in Schools not connected with the Church is understood to be
Two dame Schools which have about 40 scholars between them
A Primitive Methodist Sunday School: attendance 80. last year 170.

3. The new Schools, allowing an area of six square feet for each child, will accommodate *120* Boys, *120* Girls, and— Infants,
   in *two* room*s*, to be Sunday and *Day* Schools.

4. The instruction in the Schools is to be afforded at the rate of *2nd* a week, or— *quarter, from each Child.*

5. The estimated annual charge for Master and Mistress, Books, &c. is about £ *105* ; and the means by which that annual charge is to be
   met are *Children payment Collection & Subscription.*
   so that there is a reasonable prospect of the Schools being permanently carried on.

6. There is accommodation provided for *720* Children in the *Gallery, or body* of the { parish } Church.
                                                                                  { district }

7. The Boys' School-room is to be internally *44* long, *22* wide, and *14* high, to the *wall plate* ; making an area of *748* or *6* to each Boy.
   The Girls'   ditto   ditto   *44* do. *22* do. and *14* do. *748* or *6* to each Girl.
   The Infants' ditto   ditto   do. do. and do. or to each Infant.
   State whether the height is measured to a flat ceiling, or to the wall-plate and spring of a sloped ceiling.
   If it is intended to add a Teacher's residence, state the number and size of the rooms. *Kitchen 13 ft × 12 — master room 12 ft × 11 — bedroom 12 ft × 9 — 7 ft 6 in —*

8. The materials are to be as follows : foundation *brick upon natural rubble* floor *earthen* the walls of *brick* ; roof *Slate*
   and the property is to be held on the following legal tenure, viz. *...*
   and it, or has been, conveyed to the following Trustees, viz.
   ...
   so that it will be legally secured for the purpose of educating the Poor in the principles of the Established Church.
   In specifying trusts, it should be directed that " The Trustees shall hold for the use of the Managers for the time being of a School at which shall always be united to the National Society for Promoting the Education of the Poor in the Principles of the Established Church throughout England and Wales, and shall be conducted in conformity with the principles of that Institution, and towards the advancement of its ends and designs."

9. The entire estimated Cost of the undertaking is £ *769 6 —* ; which sum includes the expense of conveyance, the value of any ground, labour, or
   materials given, viz. conveyance, £ *20* ; ground, £ *90* ; building, labour, and materials, £ *560 6* ; fittings-up, £ *35*—
   State, if possible, the separate cost of the residence.

10. The exertions that have been made to }   { by Subscriptions in money . . . . £ *90 0 0*
    provide means to meet the estimated } viz.   { by Collections after Sermon . . . . £ *9 0 4*
    cost, actually raised or promised, are }   { by Donations of ground, materials, cartage, labour, &c. valued at . £ *162 16 0*

11. So that the total means already provided or promised to meet the cost are . . . . £ *548 4 4*

12. The only further local source of funds is }
    which is expected to produce about . . . . £
                                              Total means raised or promised . . . £ *548 4 4*

To be signed by the Incumbent, as well } (Signed) *Saml Minton*
as the Applicant or Secretary of the }   *William Leam*
School Committee.   }   *Applicant*

To be transmitted through the Bishop of }
the Diocese, for his Lordship's approval } Approved by me, *J. Lichfield*
and counter-signature.   }

This *31st* day of *May* 18 *44*

N.B.—It is particularly requested that a copy may be preserved of the Application, and also a copy of any further correspondence that may take place relating to it.

A Draft of the Conveyance should be sent to the National Society before the Deed is engrossed.

Original Grant Application dated 1844

gallery, fireplace, well pump and washhouse in the Master's house, amounting to £47. The total cost by now appears to have peaked at £977 7s 5d. A Certificate of Completion, dated the 13 March 1845, brought an additional £100 grant from the National Society, leaving a £278 7s 1d, deficit on the account.

Making a joint bid from the church and the National Society, Minton applied to the Privy Council for assistance in building. In his application dated 30th May 1844, Minton reflects upon the change of fortunes of the village, from that of a small agricultural setting, to the demands of an expanding industrial suburb: *the present school is not half large enough for our Sunday School, and is badly built, designed and situated to render it almost impossible to carry on a good day school in it, and now we are to establish a Master in it, we shall have considerably more than the school will hold.*

In the same application, Minton refers to the numbers attending as twenty boys, thirty girls, and twenty infants, in addition to the two Dame Schools which totals combined added to a further forty scholars receiving education in Penkhull.

One month later on the 20th June, Minton and his churchwardens, Burgess and Smith, signed a building contract, with John Bryan and Son, to erect the new school to the design of George Lynam for the sum of £400. George Lynam was the father of Charles Lynam who later became one of the Potteries leading architects. The new school was built to accommodate up to 240 children in two rooms, one for either gender. The floor was of ornamented earthen tiles, and the Master's residence included his room, kitchen, and two bedrooms. The proceeds of the sale of materials from the previous school adjacent to the church amounted to £50, the sum being used to defray costs for the building of the new school.

But what about the land upon which the school was built, a subject still being debated today. Minton acquired the copyhold land, upon which the new school was built, upon the surrender of George Taylor of Threadneedle Street, London on the 29 May 1845, on a lease for thirty-one years. The land was listed in the Copyhold Court as 'Customary inheritance of John Whalley Esq.' and it was to Whalley that Minton paid the sum of £90 for the land. It appears almost certain that Taylor was Whalley's mortgagee who had been admitted tenant to strengthen his security. Until this time the land was being farmed by John Rider who also was the tenant farmer at Franklins Farm just off Newcastle Lane. The land consisted of part of the croft *Near Hunters Croft*, and measured some ninety feet square.

A Grant Deed dated the 9th July 1845 was executed between the Duke of Sutherland as lessee of the Manor and Samuel Minton as Incumbent. The Chancellor of the Duchy of Lancaster granted the land upon the surrender of Herbert Minton to William Leman, a Solicitor of Newcastle, who was to hold upon trust, to the proper use of the Minister and his Wardens for the purpose of the Act. This Act was to provide land from the Duchy for the sole purpose of a school for the education of children and adults of the labouring, manufacturing and poorer classes in Penkhull. Copyhold (a feudal system of land tenure) is not freehold, and as it was granted under this Act of William and Mary the land is only held by the trustees as part of the terms of the Act, and reverts back to the Duchy of Lancaster when it ceases to be used for its original purpose.

Despite the attempts to provide an education for the poor of the district by the church, there were just the odd schools that provided a private education to those that could afford it. One such school was the subject of a court transaction held on the 21st August 1841, which refers to three cottages, which had been taken down, and a new one erected which was to be used for a school for boys. It recorded the fact that Arthur Minton, the brother of Herbert and Thomas Webb, had acquired the property in 1832. This stood on land near to The Cottage Inn at Oakhill.

The growth of Penkhull as a residential suburb increased in line with the pottery trade of Stoke. With an expansion in population, came the need for additional school accommodation. To meet this demand, additional ground on two sides of the existing school site was conveyed on the 7th June 1873 to the *Vicar and Church Wardens* from Frederick Bishop of The Mount, by the Chancellor of the Duchy of Lancaster, in addition to making a grant of £150 11s 3d towards the building costs. These additions consisted of one large and two smaller rooms at the far end of the existing building to comply with Foster's Education Act 1870, upon which, parliament took on the responsibility of securing that every child had the opportunity of attending school. As a consequence of this Act the school was transferred from The National Society, to Stoke-upon-Trent School Board in December 1876. The school was further enlarged under the Education Acts of 1876 and 1880.

Grant by the Rev. Samuel Minton dated 9th July 1845 of the school site to the minister and churchwardens of St.Thomas Church, Penkhull. (3 pages long)

The original application form for funding has survived and gives a snapshot of the school at that time. The application was to secure funding for an extension to the building for the education of infants. Figures are shown that the attendance at the schools within Stoke Parish totalled 1280, those at Hartshill, 230 and at Trent Vale 150. Attendance for the National School at Penkhull amounted to 300 although accommodation was only provided for 200 insufficient for the population of the village creating serious overcrowding. The number of children classified as 'infants' were in excess of 100 daily. The object of the extension was to provide separate rooms for the infants and to allow boys and girls to be taught separately in line with Her Majesty's Inspectors.

In financial terms, the following incomes supported the school: donations, £25, collections, £12, school pence, £170, government grant, £200, other sources, £150. A total of £420 was secured to run the school on an annual basis. The initial request for funding was dated 31st October 1870.

Further questions were asked about the freehold of the land to be acquired for the extension. This was Copyhold to the Duchy of Lancaster, and occupied as tenant by Mr Frederick Bishop of The Mount. The costs for the extension was as follows: building £400, boundary wall, £100, desks, benches etc. £30, Architects commission £26 10s and other expenses £5. The total amounted to £561 10s. Mr Charles Lynam of Penkhull was the appointed architect. In his submission for funding, Rev. Smith, the Vicar, stated that following donations there remained a shortfall of £287.

Mr Bishop, in addition of the transfer of the land valued at £62 10s gave a further donation of £50. Finally the application stated that the National School had previously granted £350 in 1845 towards the original building costs and £35 10s in 1856 towards laying a boarded floor.

School Log Books of any school provide an amazing insight into both educational traditions and social patterns of the day. Penkhull is no exception. By 1850, the headmaster, James Horne ran the school on what was known as 'the monitories' or 'Bell's system'. By this method one teacher could adequately cope with at least one hundred pupils, with a hierarchy of monitors including a monitor-in-chief to take charge of the other monitors.

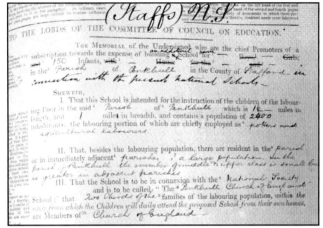
Application for funding dated 1870

As early as 1841, the system then used for teaching was condemned by a local Anglican clergyman. Writing to Mr S. Scriven, a government inspector appointed to report on the working conditions of children in the Potteries. *I believe Dr Bell's system of teaching to be essentially and radically bad. Its principal defects I conceive to be these; firstly, the assembly of a great number of children under one teacher; second, the employment of monitors, who generally are unfit either to teach or to rule, third; the waste of time in matters of mere parade and show; fourth, the want of sufficient grammatical instruction.*

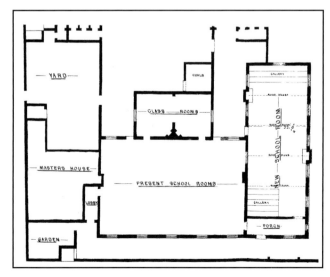
Plan by Charles Lynam showing the extension 1870

What I have said accounts for the thin attendance in large schools, will explain my views. In the first place a school ought never to exceed what one teacher or one assistant can instruct, or at the very least personally superintend. Not mere literary education is to be imparted, but manners and morals are to be formed, and not least, a deference to authority is to be inculcated; this last point especially cannot be safely overlooked in the present day, and none of these objects can be attained if the number of scholars be so great that the master's eye cannot be constantly on every one.

Penkhull School built 1845

The school minute book dated January 1865, recorded that Mr Lynam, the architect was asked to look at the current dimensions of the schoolhouse to prepare an estimate for making the premises habitable. However, little appears to have happened, as the school manager's report of June 1865 in a reply to the question *if the master lived in the house* was as follows, *that he does not as the residence is un-inhabitable.* Their Lordships were unable to reconcile this with the statement that the managers received £6 rent for the house. *My Lord requests to be furnished with an explanation on this point.* The last occupant of the schoolhouse was Mr William Alldis, who became caretaker in 1895. He was caretaker for thirty-eight years and lived in the schoolhouse until 1910. From then onwards it was used as the head teacher's room and to provide additional cloakroom space for children.

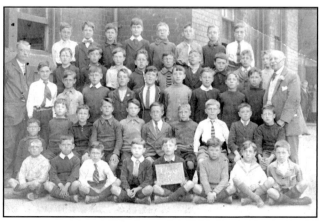
School Class c1900

During most of his working life Mr Alldis was caretaker at both the school and the church. It was a double appointment with huge responsibility. After the First World War the two positions were separated.

How appropriate that his daughter Winnie, now Mrs Roberts, carried on the family tradition of school caretaker.

Winnie Roberts

Winnie was a faithful and conscientious worker, who looked upon her task as a pleasure to complete over thirty-five year's service. I recall her having to move several tons of coke at a time years ago for the old heating boiler after deliveries. This was before gas was laid on to the school. What young lady would undertake such at task today? Before central heating, Winnie had to light eleven fires and stoves each morning before school opened, not forgetting cleaning out the ashes first.

Penkhull Infants School c1925

Fortunately the Log Books written by the head teacher for Penkhull School are complete from 1862 onwards. They are an invaluable source for social and education students. The first entry is dated the 1st October that year and refers to the school inspection by Rev A J Bonner, H.M.I.S. After the inspection the children had the afternoon off. Very different from the inspections of today. There was clearly a shortage of desks in the area as it was recorded two days later that the school had to close as the desks were removed to Stoke for a Prize Scheme Examination.

In those early days of general education there was a need for children to commence work at an early age, as shown by the following entry. This points to the need for a child to learn a trade rather than to go on to further education.

7th October - *Bailey left us by mutual consent - his father thinking that all things considered, it would be injudicious to send him to college and therefore that he had better be set to a trade at once.*

I list just a few of the hundreds of entries that give an insight to life in school during the 19th century.

8th March 1864 - *Mrs Cliff came to complain to Mr Salmon about him striking John on the head - I could do nothing in the matter as I have several times remonstrated to Mr Salmon on this point.*

13th March 1864 - *A complaint from Mrs Wainscott that Ralph Jackson has struck Harry - it seems to have been an accident in that Wainscott was at fault if either was!*
At this time open fires heated the school and the next entry shows that parents were concerned about the cold conditions for their children.

8th January, 1864 - *Punished S. Brunt for spreading an untrue report that we have no fires in the infant's school, as I found out from one or two parents that it had caused them to keep their children away - only 30 here this morning.*

21st December 1864 - *Simpson (monitor) found striking a boy - gave him a caution and warned him that if it happens again he would be instantly dismissed.* (Monitors in those days assisted in the teaching, and are not to be confused with a student monitor of today)

6th January, 1865 - *Received a message from Mr Wainwright complaining that Mr Tomlinson had struck Emma on the head - these complaints are getting more frequent and I must take the matter before the next committee meeting.*

11th April, 1865 - *Kept Henry Keeling in to do his work at dinner time for he was idle all morning, he went away leaving it undone and to make it worse told his mother that he had done it - she gave him a good thrashing.*

All these examples could imply that the teaching standards at Penkhull National School were poor. A report from the School's Inspector dated October 1865 indicates that the standard of teaching at the school was at best, mixed.

Pleased with order and intelligence of the children. Reading very free from monotony but too low and not sufficiently animated. Writing and spelling very fair in two first classes. Arithmetic generally accurate but not very far advanced - Holy Scripture - good as far as it went - catechism imperfect.
Infant's School Report - well taught and orderly. Needlework unusually good especially one of the young girls.
Results for Mrs Peake's work are very creditable to her. The school has increased considerably since Mrs Corn took charge of it.

In June the following year the report continued more favourably: *The school is in a very satisfactory state as to the construction. The groundwork is well taught and the children very fairly accurate. The discipline is very fair on the whole, but the large numbers require energy and skill on the part of the teachers to keep the children in good order. The evening scholars are doing well and will, I hope, make satisfactory progress.*

Penkhull Infants School c1932

The large numbers mentioned continued to grow, for in 1867, we read that the school had increased on the corresponding quarter from an average of 144 to 212, and more than 80 had been admitted to the school since Lady Day.

No doubt the teaching staff would welcome school holidays as a time free from the tribulations of work. The following entry emphasises this point.

June 1867 - *Glad to finish work this week - there has been an average of 233 pupils for the week and I have been compelled to place classes in the yard for reading and arithmetic lessons.*
Other entries may be gleaned to give just a glimpse at the social life of the village.

Infant School c1932

Friday 21st October 1862 - *Mrs Stanway sent word that she has taken her boy away because we would not give him a ticket for a tea party - he never asked for one!*

It must be remembered that education was at this time not free, and parents had to pay the *school pence* for children to be educated. The following entry emphasises the poverty being experienced in the working class towns of the Potteries.

Tuesday 7th January 1863 - *Joseph Collis absent because his parents unable to pay the school pence.* Another entry later the

same year refers to the fact that two boys had to remain in the 3rd class, although fit for promotion, because their parents could not afford to pay the additional 1d per week.

Thursday 3rd March 1864 - *Night school very thin last night, many of the men who attend are riflemen and were at a volunteer practice.*

Monday 29th February 1864 - *Mrs Smith called with John, bringing a ½d. She thought he had got from school - found that it was the change from 1d. he had taken from home and spent. Sent word to his mother by Mrs Salmon, leaving the mother to settle about it.*

30th August 1864 - *Sent a note to Mr Sutherland saying that William would be expelled unless his clothes were kept clean. They are well-to-do people and need not, at any rate, send him dirty and ragged.*

Friday 20th January 1865 - *Snow so deep that very few children came - so few indeed as not to be worth keeping the school open.*

Tuesday 2nd May 1865 - *Many late comers as the school bell was broken down – kept school open after time for two hours so late comers could make up their time.*

Young infant children leaving school

Friday 14th July 1865 - *Mr Tomlinson went to look after absentees, found most of them nursing while mothers were at work during the busy time before 'The Wakes'.* (Remember there was no holiday pay in those days)

Wednesday 28th July 1865 - *Saw Mrs Willott about George who has been truant playing - left her to settle with him. As we dare not punish the boy as he is suffering from an injury to his head and the young rogue seems to be aware of this and is taking advantage of the fact.*

The logbooks also reveal numerous appointments of monitors. One such appointment was recorded on the 28th August 1865 as a result of an accident: *William Walker of Newcastle came on trial as monitor in place of John Carpmail,*

Coronation school concert 1953

who was drowned during the holidays while swimming. The wages of monitors was dismal, as we read a note made on the 26 September 1864: *Henry Simpson commenced as pre-monitor at the rate of one farthing per week to begin with.* Three months later, Wednesday, 21 December, Simpson was the subject again of an entry in the school logbook: *Simpson, found striking a boy, gave him a caution and warned him that if it happened again, he would be instantly dismissed.*

By September 1873 the school unsuccessfully advertised three times for pupil teachers the head teacher writing *I am doing with an average of 170 and only one pupil teacher. I have accepted the services of John Boulton from Trent Vale School as a monitor to sit as a candidate next April. He will be thirteen years of age on the 11th October and promises to make a good teacher.* Regrettably, only two weeks later it was recorded that *John Boulton only here for two weeks. Tells me that his parents have changed their minds and intend that he should become an apprentice joiner.*

The new Penkhull Senior School built 1896

The following year it became clear that finance was the important factor in the employment of staff as a boy only aged thirteen years was employed. September 1874, *William Rhead, aged thirteen on the 4th inst. Commences duties as paid monitor at 2/- per week. Comes from Orme School at Newcastle but was formally a scholar in this school.*

January 1874 witnessed an exceptionally cold winter. There was no coal to be obtained, no fires. A similar picture was recorded three years later in October 1877: *no fires allowed till further order. By the 19th fires were only allowed in the mornings and children suffering colds.*

By 1876 the school was overflowing with children as can be seen from the following entry dated 25th May. *124 boys present this afternoon. As I have but two young pupil teachers now, the work is heavy and the discipline unsatisfactory. There is little chance of any success at the next examination unless more help is given.*

Although the National School should have been taken over as a Board School in 1876, by September it still remained under the control of the National School. The head wrote on the 4th September 1876, *The pupil teachers have received no pay for five months. We are without pens, ink and chalk and in altogether a very unsatisfactory state.*

18th June 1877 *I cannot succeed in getting a pupil teacher. I employ two 1st class boys as monitors and giving them a gratuity of 6d each per week.*

The annual salary for a teacher in 1881 was £35.

The social deprivation of Penkhull appears to have affected school attendance. There are numerous accounts of poor attendance as parents were unable to afford the school fees of 2d per week. Also, many children could not attend, as they had *no proper clothes to wear.* Poverty also affected upon the health of the children as an entry in July 1867 reads: *I find several of the infants have been taken ill with whooping cough, which is likely to prove very serious in the district.*

Following a rather poor report for the school, the headmaster and head mistress were dismissed on the 9th September 1878 to be followed by a new appointment of Mr Samuel Steven on the following 23rd. It is recorded here that music was being taught and the popular National song of the period, 'God Bless our Sailor Prince' to the words of Tennyson, was being taught.

In addition to public education, private education was becoming popular. By 1879 three schools for girls were listed in the local trade directories; Miss Burrows, West Bank, Ellen Greatbatch, 14, Penkhull New Road; and Miss Poulson, James Street.

Senior School c1910. Mr. A.T.Wood Headteacher to the right.

From the tables on illiteracy, an improvement on the previous year is evident in 1879, although some decline in reading and writing standards had been experienced from 1859 to 1869. The change in 1879 coincides with the improvements established by the 1876 Act. It may be concluded from the Stoke figures however, that illiteracy in the high density housing of Stoke is reasonably balanced between gender. No doubt this reflects large immigration in the growing and expanding economy of the pottery industry. Here, past traditions which affected social attitudes within family structure, were held to be less important than each member of the family being taught to read. With urban development and the rise in population, came the demand for additional school places.

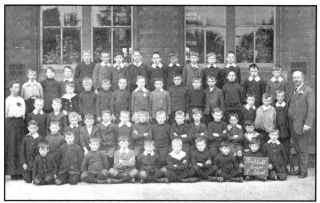

Children of the Senior School c1915

It was not until the commencement of the new term of 1891 that education became free to all children and it was recorded that there were 237 present on that day to celebrate. As a result accommodation at the school became an increasing problem with no immediate sign of it being resolved. As we move on to nearly the end of the 19th century other concerns, not previously mentioned were expressed in the logbooks. Perhaps these reflect the first signs of the permissive society arriving at Penkhull.

2nd October 1895 - *Found girls talking indecently in the playground, saw their mothers.* Then in May the following year the situation had become worse *John Cole from Penkhull New Road wrote indecent words and passed them to girls - saw his father and other parents. The Chairman of the Board ruled that the attendance officer was to see that the boy had a good flogging from his father. The next time the Board will summons and ask for a birching.* How things have changed!

It took nearly three years of struggles with overcrowding in the school before finally in 1894 the issue was raised with the School Board over the size of the school and the ever-increasing number of children wanting to attend. Many new children were from the new housing development in Princes Road and the Allotments estate. The head wrote in May: *I suggested breaking down the walls of the schoolhouse to create a little more space. The numbers at present exceed 332. There were 65 children in the west classroom built for only 40 and 73 in the east classroom built for only 50 pupils.*

The following year it was reported that the 'Cooking Classes' were suspended as there was no room to hold them, and that new admissions were being refused. The School Board rejected this and instructed that the school must admit those children from the district - attendance was then recorded as 602.

With urban development of the 'Allotments Estate', the Rector of Stoke Sir. Lovelace Stamer, an established advocate for improved education in the city, purchased a number of plots of land at the end of what is now Greatbatch Avenue from the Stoke Workingmen's Dwelling Association for the purpose of erecting a new school.

The old National School in the centre of the village was overcrowded and no further land was available for expansion. In February 1896 Mr. Wood wrote in the log book referring to the problems with the old school and the hopes for the new one.

As a result of the serious overcrowding the United District School Board decided to build a new 'Senior School' at the junction of Princes Road then called Penkhull Street just north of the village. This was completed under the provision of Sandon's Act of 1876 and Mundella's Act of 1880 that finally made elementary education compulsory. The site for the new school was purchased by Stoke-upon-Trent School Board from Robert Clement Clive of The Mount on the 31st October 1895 for the sum of £955 13s and described as:

The year has been a trying one on account of the overcrowding.

The 2 or 3 classes occupying the N. end of the main Room and facing each other ("double banked" desks) with very little space between, form a problem as regards satisfactory arrangement which I have never been able to surmount. It is almost impossible to maintain good order and instruction in that part and I am afraid it has a little effect on the other classes.

I have taught there repeatedly and have to give it up.

The next year will apparently be no better until the New Schools (for the Mixed Dept.) are entered. Digging commenced a week ago about and the block may be ready before Xmas — September says the Chairman of the

Acc*is to be provided for 470 capable of extension to 660, Central Hall system. (H the Inf.ts to occupy all old premises.

All that plot of land situate at Penkhull and part of the Mount Estate and which plot of land contains by recent measurement, including the footpath to a proposed new street and half of the back road six thousand, three hundred and seventy one square yards.

The School Board also agreed to pay half the cost of constructing curbing, channelling and sewers of the proposed new street. One interesting item, which reflects the period, is that occupants of The Mount would always have access through the new proposed street with or without horses, carts and carriages.

The school was built to the design of architects Messrs R Scrivener & Sons, a local company and was officially opened on Monday, 3 May 1897 by Sir Lovelace Stamer Bart, who by this time had become the Bishop of Shrewsbury. As a result of educational classification, the new school became known as the 'senior school', catering for children over ten years of age, while the old village National School concentrated on the education of younger children.

Once more Mr. Wood reflects in the school log book on his time in the old building and the opening ceremony. The first notes is dated 30th April 1897, the second on the opening day of the new school, May 3rd 1897.

Friday   The last day in these old premises. After 17 years in them one cannot leave even one's prison without regret and retrospective affection

New schools opened – Public ceremony – Bishop Shrewsbury: who as Sir Lovelace showed me many kindnesses.

The logbooks at the new school continue to be a great source for social history, and begin with the illness of boys from the Spittals Workhouse, with fifteen cases of diphtheria. The boys were off school for a period of six weeks. Once more health issues are recorded in 1927: *scarlet fever had reached epidemic proportions at the Cottage Homes and all the children from there were away either ill or being kept away.*

Children from Penkhull Cottage Homes attended the new school as well as Cross Street School, (now Epworth Street). By 1909 the school at Penkhull recorded 32 boys and 24 girls attending from the Cottage Homes.

It was not long before this new senior school became overcrowded as population increase bringing with it further demands on space. By 1912 a new north wing was reported as *progressing slowly* and that there were *'now five classes held*

in the hall containing between 200-260 children alone. The new wing was opened on the 13th June 1913. Only ten days later, after a tea party and a concert for parents to celebrate the opening, the head wrote: *there still remains dreadful overcrowding!*

It was decided at this point that the Committee of the Board of Education should visit the school and witness for themselves the severe overcrowding. At the time of it's opening, the new s c h o o l accommodated 470 pupils on a central hall system. As well as local children, a number of children from Penkhull

PENKHULL COUNCIL SCHOOLS.

Opening of New Wing.

Although there is grumbling at times on the part of many ratepayers over the expenditure on the education of the children, there is no-one who is concerned with the welfare, physical and mental, of the young people who does not like to see them occupying buildings of the very best type that it is possible to provide for them. In this respect there is a great contrast between the school buildings of a generation ago and those of to-day. The modern schools are often among the most imposing erections in a town. Prominent among the elementary schools of the Potteries is the Penkhull Senior Council School, which occupies an excellent site at the Penkhull end of Princes-road. These premises were opened in May, 1897, by the Stoke-upon-Trent School Board, the education of the senior scholars having to be carried on prior to that time in a building erected near the church about 1850. That, added to from time to time, was, as a senior school, transferred in 1876 to the School Board. About four years ago the Stoke-upon-Trent Education Com- mittee decided to extend the new Council school, but there was considerable discussion over details, and the work has only now been carried through by the Stoke-on-Trent Educa- tion Committee.

Cottage Homes in Newcastle Lane were accommodated, being transferred from Cross Street School in Stoke, thus relieving the pressure for places there.

The first headmaster appointed was Mr Arthur Thomas Wood, a native of Keighley, Yorkshire who was the current head of the old National School. He continued in that position until he retired in 1922 at the age of sixty-five. He survived until December 1943, and after his death a moving tribute was paid by the Chairman of the Education Board for his services to education, followed by a period of silence in his memory. Such was his contribution to education that the Education Committee paid tribute to him and condolences are sent to his family and stood for one minute in silence to pay a silent tribute. In 1913, an additional north wing was erected to accommodate the increasing numbers of children requiring places, as further working-class housing development in the immediate area brought the need for extra school places.

Senior School camp 1932

Logbooks continue to reflect the important events of the period. Each year Empire Day was celebrated with patriotic songs and the National Anthem. The occasion of listening to the first radio in the school hall is recorded and royal visits such as that by the King and Queen to the North Staffs Hospital on the 23rd April 1913. The day before, it is recorded that the teachers were decorating the school with flags and preparing for a huge school party to celebrate. In the afternoon the children marched to Hanley Park to sing before the King. No doubt this important Royal occasion bought about the desire for a flagpole to be placed in the grounds of the school. On November 7th it was recorded that *flag hoisted for the first time by Alderman Elliott, Chair of the Education Committee.*

Other national events are recorded, such as the declaration of war on the 4th August 1914: *12 noon England declares war on Germany.* This was followed by a national campaign to produce our own food, and having their own allotments at the bottom of Richmond Street encouraged children.

STOKE ORGAN RECITAL.

Penkhull School Choir's Fine Singing,

The feature of the weekly organ recital at the King's Hall, Stoke, on Tuesday night was the appearance of Penkhull Council School Choir, which assisted at one of these series of recitals for a second time this season. There was again a very large audience, who listened with genuine appreciation to a very delightful programme by Mr. S. H. Weale, Mus.Bac., on the organ, and to the children's choir.

The choir, composed of about 40 children. principally girls, was conducted by Mr. E. J. Bridgewater, who deserves to be highly complimented on the efficient state of the choir and the finish of their singing. Their voices were not only of a sweetness which was a delight to the ear, but the blend and the delicate balance as well as the expression, all call for warm praise. The audience were obviously charmed and encored the children vociferously. During an interval Mr. Weale expressed the feelings of all present in thanking the headmaster of the school (Mr. A. T. Wood), the conductor (Mr. Bridgewater), the accompanist (Miss Russell) and the choir for their excellent singing. He said they sang in a manner that an adult choir might be proud of

Mr. Bridgewater, in reply, said the choir deemed it an honour to sing in the King's Hall under such circumstances. He remarked that the object of the teachers was to inculcate in the children a love for the highest class of music.

The organ recital programme was of an interesting and varied character. There will be no recital next Tuesday, but on the following Tuesday, April 5th. Mr. Herbert F. Ellingford, organist to the Liverpool Corporation, has kindly consented to pay a visit and give a recital. Vocal numbers will be given Mr. W. A. Dudley-Baker, tenor, of the London and provincial concerts. A splendid concert is anticipated.

Penkhull School Choir sing at the Kings Hall, Stoke,
Tuesday 22nd March 1921

One event, probably nearly equal to seeing the King and Queen was recorded on the 9th July 1921. The excitement must have been overpowering. *The new largest airship R36 flew over the school - sounded the fire alarm and managed to get all the children out quickly for a good view - a fine sight.*

The events of the Second World War are widely recorded in a further chapter. The first reference is written for the school was in October 1938 when the troubles in Europe were being reported in the UK. *Our new head Mr Banks away attending a course for instruction on Air Raid precautions.* The next entry is made on the 4th September the following year *Owing to the outbreak of war the school did not open.* The school remained closed until the following 15th when it opened again for children to attend but restricted to only 1½ hours on alternate days.

By December 1939 things had not returned to normal, as we read *This morning about forty children whose parents had signed a form expressing willingness to allow their children to attend school although there are no shelters here. Using the facilities at the Children's Homes to the full will enable us to give each child half a day's instruction on alternate days.* Matters had not improved by the beginning the new term in 1940 as it was reported that the new shelters promised had not been built. It was not until the 12th February that full time education resumed at the school.

Other events in the school in the early years of the war are recorded: June 25th 1940 - *Last night the district had its first air-raid warning of the war but there were no planes over.* It was not until Monday the 1st July that we read about bombing in Penkhull *Monday - many children absent today owing to the Air Raid in this immediate district. Many thousands of people spent their Sunday viewing the damage.* The school, like many other buildings suffered damage during the war albeit very limited January 16th 1941 - *an incendiary bomb was dropped on the school last night doing a certain amount of damage to the roof.*

But probably the most memorable thing for children during the war years was having to carry gas masks with them even though many of them were defective 21st April 1942 - *The usual beginning of term inspection of gas masks revealed that one hundred children have defective masks, mostly broken eye pieces and punctured face sections. Asked for replacement glasses - told could have only 24 at a time. Will take five weeks to arrive.*

Finally, the war ended the school celebrated in the National Celebrations VE celebration on May 8th 1945.

Chapter 13
The Kingdom of Spode

The name Spode is synonymous with Penkhull. Spode became the largest land owner and occupier ever recorded for the district apart that is from the Duchy of Lancaster. The title of this chapter reflects the influence of Spode on Penkhull during the 19th century and later the 20th century. But this relationship with Penkhull does not commence with the building of The Mount, it starts years earlier.

Josiah Spode 2nd (1757-1827) was the son of Josiah Spode 1st (1733-1797) and founder of the Spode manufactory in the town of Stoke and known as Josiah Spode 1st, even though his father went also by the name Josiah.

Josiah Spode 1st was born in a village that is now part of Stoke-on-Trent. He was the son of a pauper and also a pauper's orphan at the age of six. He was apprenticed to potter Thomas Whieldon in November 1749 and remained with Whieldon at least until 1754, the year in which Josiah Wedgwood became Whieldon's business partner. Wedgwood stayed with Whieldon until 1759. Spode worked alongside Wedgwood and with the celebrated potter Aaron Wood (father of Enoch Wood) under Whieldon's tuition, and was with Whieldon at the high point of production. Whieldon Road, Fenton is named after the potter and his works were situated off City Road, Fenton.

The current site, until recently occupied by the Spode works from 1776-2009 was once called Madeley Meadow. The first record of the site is dated 1725 when Benjamin Lewis, a yeoman bought a substantial piece of land consisting of 42 customary acres. This probably comprised land on either side of what was to become High Street, now Church Street, Stoke.

The first reference to a potworks occurs in May 1751 when Lewis transferred the site to his son Taylor Lewis: *All those newly erected workhouses, potoven, warehouse, formerly a barn, in Penkhull with the yard to the same belonging.* On the 22nd August 1753, Taylor Lewis mortgaged the property for £150 to Thomas Heath a carrier of Newcastle, but three years later on the 18th August 1756, he and his mortgagee sold this property to William Clerk of Caverswall, gent who in turn sold the investment on 7th November 1759 to William Bankes and John Turner.

Serious financial problems followed, a mortgage was raised and on the 7th December 1763, Turner sold his investment to Bankes. Bankes then purchased more of Madeley Meadow from Benjamin Lewis to add to the site on the 18th January 1764. A few more turbulent financial years followed until the property and mortgage was acquired by Jeremiah Smith. After the formal admittance to the copyhold estate through the manorial courts, Smith then sold the estate to Josiah Spode on the 29th February 1776, with the help of a £1,000 mortgage from Smith. A complete list of all the transactions can be found in *'Copyhold Potworks and Housing in the Staffordshire Potteries'* by Peter Roden.

Josiah I married Ellen Findley on the 8th September 1754. She ran a haberdashery business in addition to bringing up eight children. She died in 1802, aged 76. They had three sons, Josiah II (1755-1827); Samuel (1757-1817) and William (1770-1773) and daughters Mary; Ellen; Sarah; Anne and Elizabeth.

Josiah Spode II (1755-1827) succeeded to the business in 1797. He was magnificently prepared for the role, an experienced salesman as well as a potter, having gained an invaluable knowledge of marketing in fashionable London. He was also a flautist, and was father of Josiah III, and grandfather of Josiah IV, a convert to Roman Catholicism, who founded Hawkesyard Priory near Rugeley.

Josiah II married the daughter of John Barker, a manufacturing potter of Fenton, in 1775 at Stoke. Between that year and the death of his wife in London in 1782, he had moved between Longton and Cripplegate, where he was doubtless manager of the Fore Street warehouse under the guidance of William Copeland, his father's friend and London partner. Spode became head of the business following his father's sudden death in 1797. He became Captain of the 'Pottery Troop' Cavalry Division affiliated to the Staffordshire Yeomanry, at its foundation in 1798 and remained so until its disbandment in 1805.

The second son, Samuel, for whom Josiah I erected the Foley factory at Lane End, produced salt-glazed wares up to the end of the eighteenth century. Samuel's son Samuel emigrated to Tasmania and afterwards to Queensland, where his descendants held positions in Government.

Josiah Spode II acquired much land in the area of Stoke around the Liverpool Road, Berry Street and Hill Street area. He also extended his holding beside the Newcastle canal as it travelled along London Road, Stoke including what became known as Commercial Buildings and Penkhull New Road. The Commercial Inn still retains the name today. Spode also purchased much land in the hamlet and district of Boothen.

In keeping with his financial success, Spode, like many of his contemporaries, wished to reflect his position in society by becoming a country landowner. What better situation in which to establish himself than the hill of Penkhull which overlooked his factory in the town of Stoke below. It was this symbolic aspect that encouraged Spode to acquire the largest farm available, Penkhull Farm, when it came up for auction.

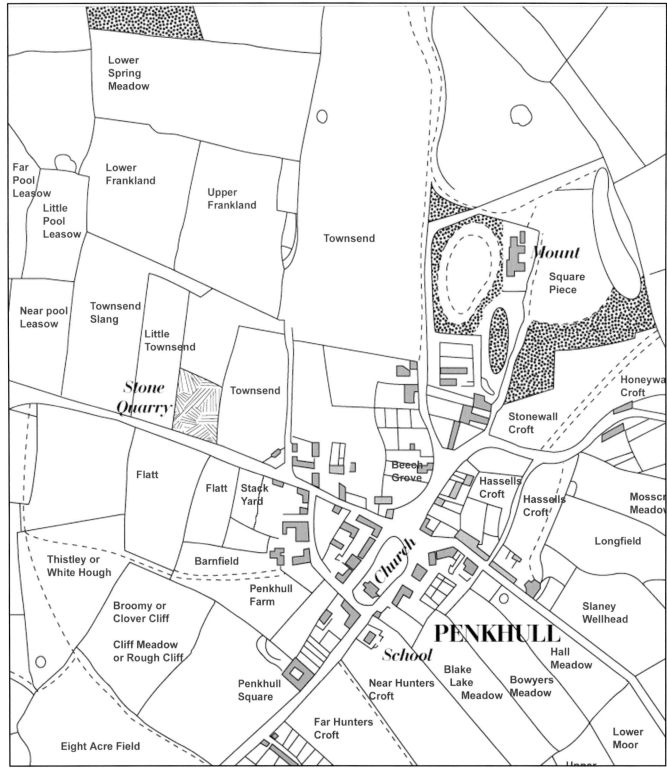

Map of Penkhull with field names based upon Lynam map 1848

He signed the lease on the 7th December 1799 from the trustees of the will of Judith and Mary Alsager spinsters, both late of Congleton. The lease was for a period of 21 years, at a rent of £140 p.a., and consisted of not only the farm, but also a considerable amount of farm lands belonging to the Alsagers of Congleton. At this time Spode lived at Little Fenton. Although there is no direct evidence to support the theory he once lived at the farm, documents however point to the fact that the living accommodation at the farm was *not being in a good condition*, and Spode promptly built a new addition which faced the south overlooking Trentham Hall, something that would have impressed visitors to the new

house if Spode actually resided there.

The initial thoughts are that it was Spode's intention to live at the farm himself but just before he was to move into residence, a large estate of John Harrison, a bankrupt, was about to come up for auction which included the site where Spode built The Mount. Penkhull Farm site was both copyhold and on lease whereas the land belonging to Harrison could be purchased with no lease which in all probability was the deciding factor.

In March 1800 Spode, elder, purchased five dwelling houses from Samuel Turner of Newcastle. By 1831, these five were extended to eight and situated on the South East side on Honeywall. A further seventeen dwellings were purchased by Spode on the 12th September 1803 from the assignees of John Harrison, potter, bankrupt. They were originally purchased in May 1790 from an earlier potter Ephram Booth. By 1831 these seventeen, had a further three added making twenty for workers. There were other land and property acquisitions in many other areas too, outside Penkhull.

The potworks at the bottom of what is now Honeywall (where a number of new three storey houses have recently been built 2008) belonged to John Harrison and were called Harrison's Works. This also was purchased by Spode on the 10th December 1807. *All that dwelling house with outbuildings at Cliffe Bank and afterwards used as a warehouse and manufactory thereto adjoining in the possession of John Harrison and also those pot works, workhouses and warehouses and all other erections contiguous to the dwelling house.* A part of this land was occupied as gardens by various tenants. On the 27th March 1824, Spode sold this plot for the sum of £35 to Hugh Booth of Clayton, but it was recorded as in the holding of Messrs Ward and Co.

Reference has already been made to the purchase of a potworks and buildings from John Harrison declared a bankrupt in May 1802. It was from the estate of Harrison that Spode made the largest of his acquisitions of land in Penkhull. The following advertisement appeared in the Staffordshire Advertiser, 3rd July 1802 listing Lots up for auction. *To be sold by Auction under the direction of the Assignees of John Harrison, a bankrupt, by Thomas Shorthouse, of Hanley at the Marquis of Granby Public House, in Penkhull near Newcastle-under-Lyme, on Tuesday 20th July, 1802. A valuable copyhold estate, situate at Penkhull late belonging to, and principally in the possession of John Harrison, and which will be divided and put up in the following, or such other Lots as shall be pointed out at the time of sale.*

Lot 1. *A handsome modern built dwelling-house, with convenient offices and outbuildings, all of recent erection, garden part walled-in, and croft adjoining, pleasantly situated at Penkhull Green, about one mile from Newcastle-under-Lyme and a short distance from the great north road and now in the occupation of Mrs Haywood; the whole containing 1a 1r 23p and forming a most delightful residence for a small genteel family.* (This Lot refers to the property known as Beech Grove, just off St. Thomas Place)

Lot 2. *The Homestead, to consist of a Messuage or Farm House, near Lot 1, with barns, stables and other outbuildings to the same. Two gardens and an orchard; two crofts adjoining, and such parts of the large piece of land lying at the back of the small messuage (now called Brick-kiln Field, but formerly in several pieces, and then called the Barnfield, the Pear field, and Lamb field) as is*

staked out to go with this Lot, being the upper part, and what lies next the lower croft, on a line with the outer garden hedge, the whole containing 12a 3r 19p. This is also an excellent situation for a country retreat.

Lot 3. *The remainder of the said piece of land called the Brick-kiln piece, being the lower part thereof, adjoining the road, the same containing 4a 0r 14p.*

Lot 4. *An excellent piece of grass land called the Little Townsend containing 2a 0r 22p*

Lot 5. *A piece of land called the Big Townsend, now held with Lot 1, containing 3a 2r 6p*

Lot 6. *A piece of land called the Upper Frankland, adjoining Lot 5, containing 6a 3r 30p.*

Lot 7. *An adjoining piece of land called the Lower Frankland containing 5a 3r 36p.*

Lot 8. *A substantial Water Mill lately erected on a piece of land called the Near pool Hough, adjoining Lot 7, for grinding colours and other materials for Potters' use, but easily convertible to other purposes, with Pools and so much of the said piece of land, as now marked out to go with this lot containing in the whole 1a 3r 32p.*

Lot 9. *The remainder of the said piece of land called the Near pool Hough, with the adjoining piece of land called the far Pool Hough, containing together 6a 2r 12p.*

The Road with Lot 7 will be let through Lot 6 as now used, and thence continuing through Lot 7 to Lots 8 and 9.

Penkhull is one of the pleasantest villages in that part of the country; the land is of the first quality, adjoining to the premises of Sir Thomas Fletcher, Bart., Miss Terrick, Daniel Whalley Esq., Messes Walker and Ward, and other respectable owners, and the different Lots command very extensive and diversified prospects. The whole of the Estate is copyhold of inheritance within the manor of Newcastle and subject only to a nominal fine.

Lot 1. 'The Grove', or by its correct title 'Beech Grove' was bought by Joseph Booth. Other parts of the former Harrison estate were purchased by Samuel Doncaster, David Bostock, Joseph Walley, William Johnson and William Booth. The largest acquisition was made by Josiah Spode II, commencing with what was to become a little empire where the name of Spode would become synonymous with Penkhull for centuries to come.

Spode also purchased Lot 2 which was described as an old farm house called 'Tittensor's House'. This property stood where 'The Mount' now stands. The site was copyhold and the court records the transaction:

September 12th 1803 The assignees in Bankruptcy of John Harrison, to Josiah Spode of Stoke upon Trent, Esquire. All that messuage or farm house formerly called Tittensor's house, situate at or near Penkhull Green, with the barns stables and other outbuildings gardens and orchard to the same belonging, and also all those two crofts or small pieces or parcels of land adjoining, formerly called the Barn Croft, and all that large close piece or parcel of land lying at the back of the said messuage now called the Brick Kiln piece but formerly in several parts and then called the Calf or Cade Croft, the Pease Field, the Over Field, the Pit Croft and the Lamb sich, or by whatsoever other name or names the same are or have been called, the whole of the said premises, including the sites of the said buildings, containing together 16ᵃ 3ʳ 33ᵖ or thereabouts, and late in the possession of the said John Harrison, and were surrendered to him by Thomas Ward and William Ward, with other lands, on 1 May 1789, and afterwards surrendered by him, on 20ᵗʰ December 1800, to the use of Charles Hassell's and William Hassell's (since dec'd) as Co-partners, for the intents and purposes therein mentioned, and by the said Charles Hassell's this day surrendered to the 'said assignees, together with all and every houses outhouses edifices buildings ways waters watercourses timber and other tree conveniences etc.; fine 2ˢ 6ᵈ.

Tittensor's house and its estate were of some substance and we shall refer back to this later. The name Thomas Ward is also mentioned, a name which was given to the new development in the grounds of Beech Grove.

The lot which was sold to Samuel Doncaster at the same auction was purchased by Spode in 1810, extending further his ownership of property of Penkhull. 16th October 1813: The court entry reads *Samuel Doncaster of Penkhull, Engraver, and Richard Timmis of Crewe, yeoman, (a mortgagee), for £360 to said Richard Timmis, (in full for all monies owing to him), and also £665 to the said Samuel Doncaster, making together the sum of £1025, to Josiah Spode*; No admittance is recorded which was unusual but was rectified later after Spode II's death.

All that piece or parcel of land in Penkhull called or known by the name of the Little Townsend, which was surrendered by the assignees of the estate and effects of John Harrison, a bankrupt, to the use of the said Samuel Doncaster on the 12ᵗʰ September 1803, save and except such part thereof containing 512 superficial yards as was surrendered by the said Samuel Doncaster to the use of William Adams of Cobridge in trust, on 1ˢᵗ June 1810, and also all that messuage or dwelling house and all buildings thereon erected and now or late in the tenure of, Samuel Doncaster.

The formal admittance did not come about until the 13ᵗʰ May 1831 when the executors of Josiah Spode III's estate, after the presentation on the 7ᵗʰ January 1830 of his last will took formal admission through the copyhold court when record is made of the *land and dwelling houses, which were surrendered by Samuel Doncaster and Richard Timmis to the use of Josiah Spode the elder on the 16th October 1813.*

Probably one of the most significant talking points for decades was Penkhull Square, situated off Trent Valley Road, where now stands Jeremy Close. The land was purchased by Josiah Spode II in 1802 only a few months after purchasing substantial property from the estate of John Harrison. *October 25th 1802, John Jones, (Trustee for Lovatt as in preceding Recovery), to Josiah Spode of Stoke upon Trent, Esq. All that copyhold dwelling house and barn, and all those pieces or parcels of land commonly called or known by the names of the Great Hough and Far Hough containing by measurement 11ᵃ 1ʳ 31ᵖ or thereabouts, in Penkhull, which said pieces of land were formerly in three parts and then called the Three Houghs, and with the said messuage or dwelling house were formerly in the holding of Richard Heath, afterwards of John Slaney, but late of John Townsend and were late the estate of Thomas Lovett dec'd, previous of William Lovett, dec'd, and formerly of Joseph Lovett otherwise Lovatt the younger; fine 1ˢ 5d.*

In a schedule of the property belonging to Josiah Spode IV dated 31ˢᵗ May 1831 the property is described: *All that close piece or parcel of land, lying at Penkhull adjacent to the garden of the parish workhouse, now usually occupied as garden ground by sundry tenants, late of the said Josiah Spode the elder, and commonly called the Hempbutt containing 1 rood and 35 perches, which close of land was formerly occupied as the garden and fold of a dwelling. And also all those 20 other messuages or dwelling houses, standing and being at a place usually called The Square, near the South end of the village of Penkhull, now or lately in the several holdings of Anne Shore, John Pugh, Samuel Harding, Jane Tams, the widow of William Shore, John Steele, Samuel Davis, Thomas Underwood, Robert Hollinshead, Richard Pye, Joseph Bird, Thomas Ridgway, Samuel Laynton, Thomas Crutchley, William Robinson, Thomas Forrester, Richard Ball, Myatt Brookes, William Spooner and John Ridgway, or their under tenants, which were built by the said Josiah Spode the elder.*

A further eighteen acres were added to Spode's kingdom on the 24ᵗʰ May 1809 when he acquired land previously owned by John Chapman. *All those three several closes pieces or parcels of land adjoining or lying near to each other and now in the possession of the said John Chapman, of Penkhull, and containing by estimation 18ᵃ 1ʳ 34ᵖ and which was formerly the estate and inheritance of Joseph Bourne of Penkhull, gent, deceased, and upon his death intestate descended to and vested in Margery Bourne, now his sister also deceased, who afterwards intermarried with the John Chapman.*

It was just twelve months later when Josiah Spode II purchased a substantial estate in Penkhull, one which included one of the earliest known sites of a potworks in the area, that of Thomas Doody. Simeon Shaw in 1829 records this as one of three producing coarse brown pottery in 1660, and once stood on the site of the present Victoria House in

St Thomas Place. The purchase included land which now form a section of Penkhull New Road and also land in the London Road area of Stoke. Spode purchased the property from Richard Lovatt on the 2nd May 1810 for the sum of £6,860. *All that messuage tenement or dwelling house in Penkhull, called or known by the name of Doody's messuage, formerly in the holding of Thomas Whitehurst, afterwards of Sampson Bagnall since in the possession of Joseph Bourne, and now of John Chapman, and all barns stables outbuildings folds yards gardens orchards crofts and all those several pieces of land meadow or pasture ground, now and for a long time past and called by the several names The Backsides, into four parts divided and then called The Meadow, The Lane, and the two Wastes which were afterwards laid together, the Hall Croft, the Hall Meadow, Middle Moor, Lower Moor, the two Long Fields, the Hassell's Croft, with the barn standing thereon, and the Boothen Heath, but which lands and premises are now called by the several names and consist as follows:*

• *the Hall or House Croft, containing with the dwelling and outbuildings and the garden to the same, 1ª 1ʳ 20ᵖ;*
• *Doody's Meadow, including what was formerly called the Lane, containing together 3ª 3ʳ 14ᵖ;*
• *the Upper Waste, as separated by the Turnpike Road, (London Road, Stoke) containing 2ª 3ʳ 36ᵖ;*
• *the Lower Waste, as separated by the Newcastle under Lyme canal, containing 1ª 0ʳ 33ᵖ, and which three last mentioned closes or pieces of land, of the lower waste was used in the making of the canal.*
• *The Hall Meadow, containing two acres one rood and eight perches 2ª 1ʳ 8ᵖ;*
• *The Middle Moor, containing four acres two roods and nineteen perches 4ª 2ʳ 19ᵖ;*
• *the upper part of Lower Moor, containing 1ª 2ʳ 29ᵖ, and the lower part of Lower Moor, with such part of the said Lower Waste containing together 1ª 3ʳ 15ᵖ, and which said three last mentioned closes or pieces of land comprise of the Middle Moor and Lower Moor, the same having been separated when the new turnpike road and canal were created.*
• *The Long Field, formerly in two parts containing 4ª 0ʳ 15ᵖ, and comprising both closes of land formerly called the two long fields;*
• *Hassell's Croft, containing 2ª 0ʳ 7ᵖ, as the same now consists (about one acre thereof having been some time being fenced off and were surrendered to the said John Chapman)*
• *the Boothen Heath, containing 3ª 1ʳ 20ᵖ; and also all those five several dwelling houses, in Penkhull, situate standing and being near to the said messuage called Doody's messuage, with the gardens and appurtenances to the same respectively belonging, part comprising of formerly a barn standing on a croft called Hassell's Croft, these many years ago converted into dwelling houses and which are now in the respective occupations of Thomas Evans, John Jordan, John Fox, Thomas Baddeley and Margaret Smith; and also all those two other messuages tenements or dwelling houses, in Penkhull, near the Poor House, formerly in one dwelling and then called or known by the name*

of Turner's otherwise Ingram's with the garden and now in the several occupations of Sampson Butterton and Samuel Leigh; and also all those five several other dwelling houses in Penkhull, near to a certain messuage and premises called Green Head House, now belonging to John Townsend, with the gardens which are now in the respective holdings of Mary Bird, John Tunstall, Peter Bird, Ann Barker and Thomas Allcock, and which were formerly the inheritance of Joseph Bourne of Penkhull, Gent. dec'd, and afterwards of his sister and heir at law Margery Bourne, also deceased, who intermarried with the said John Chapman, and on 30th October 1792, surrendered the same, with other premises, to the use of the said Margery Chapman for life and the remainder to the use of the said John Chapman for his life.

Doody's messuage was later demolished by Spode and replaced by Victoria House which still stands today. The five cottages referred to adjacent to Doody's house, were originally considered to be those set back from the road in St Thomas Place. However, this is not the case, but was, it seems the origins of what was to become known locally as Ten Row, that neat parade of elevated terraced cottages which stood at the top of Penkhull New Road. The survey of Spode's estate in 1831 confirms this as the same tenants can be identified. *All those 10 other dwelling houses, with the outbuilding gardens situated in the village of Penkhull near to a messuage formerly called Doody's Messuage, which said 10 dwellings are now or lately were in the several holdings of Joseph Blackburn, William Hamersley, George Hulme, James Davenport, John Sutton, Ralph Myatt, Thomas Plant, Thomas Brunt, James Grocott and Joseph Lycett, or their under tenants, and the same 10 messuages have been newly erected on the sites of or otherwise converted or altered out of 5 messuages, formerly in the holdings of Thomas Evans, John Jordan, John Fox, Thomas Baddeley and Margaret Smith.*

Turner and Ingram's was a large medieval house which occupied the site of the current Jeremy Close. Hall meadow refers to the land which stands in front of The Views, just off Penkhull New Road and the Moors is land found further down the hill along with those with the name Wastes.

The 1810 copyhold transfer refers to a further five cottages. These same cottages can be identified as Garden Street, formerly Farm Lane. By 1831 they had been demolished and replaced by six as the following entry confirms: *And also all those 6 other dwelling houses, with the outbuilding gardens situated in Penkhull near to a dwelling formerly called Greenhead House, which said six dwellings are now or lately were in the several holdings of William Bratton, John Smith, Ralph Jackson, Thomas Shore, John Lees and Robert Harriman, or their under tenants, and the same six messuages have been newly erected on the site of five messuages, formerly in the holdings of Mary Bird, John Tunstall, Peter Bird, Anne Barker and Thomas Alcock,*

For the sum of £65 12 6d, on the 12th March 1814, Josiah Spode, sold a strip of land, probably where the present Donald Bates home stands to the Guardians of the Poor for Stoke-upon-Trent. The court record states: *All that plot of land, situate at Penkhull, adjoining and lying up to the Poor House there, on the West side thereof, and containing 375 superficial yards of land, the said piece of land comprising the site of two tenements now taken down, formerly in one messuage, and then called or known by the name of Turner's otherwise Ingram's.*

The history of Penkhull Windmill is recorded elsewhere, but Spode II purchased this from James Sutton and others on the 8th February 1823: *James Sutton of Penkhull, and Joseph Lawton and Thomas Lunt, both of Barthomly, yeomen, (ex'ors of*

Location of Penkhull windmill, Mill Street, off Penkhull New Road

John Chapman, late of Penkhull, gent. dec'd, who was a mortgagee), for £550, (£505 3 6d paid to said Joseph Lawton and Thomas Lunt, and £44 16 6d paid to James Sutton), to Josiah Spode of the Mount, Esq. All that croft close or piece land in Penkhull, being the upper part of the close of land there called Hassell's Croft, as now fenced off by a quick set hedge, and part used and occupied as a garden, together with the windmill stable and cow house, all which land in the tenure or occupation of John Cope, afterwards of John Broadhurst, and now of the said James Sutton. All which said premises were on 3rd December 1814, surrendered by John Cope of Penford in the parish of Cheddleton, miller, owner and proprietor to the use of the said John Chapman subject to redemption on payment of the sum of £450 and interest, now satisfied and paid.

The tradition of acquiring more lands established by Josiah Spode II was continued after his death (1827) by Josiah Spode III (1777-1839) with further acquisitions. They commenced on the 8th October 1814 with a purchase from Charles Hassalls and Elizabeth Jones, to Josiah Spode III for the sum of £3,925 7 6d: *All those five several plots of land, called the Leasows, and called the Great Leasow, situated at Penkhull, formerly in the occupation of ... and containing together 25a. 1r. 12p., and which said lands are bounded on the north and North West sides by lands belonging to Sir John Fenton Boughey & Daniel Whalley Esquire, on the west side by lands belonging to Mr Joseph Booth, on the south side by lands belonging to the said Joseph Booth, David Bostock and the said Josiah Spode, and on the east side by lands belonging to the said Daniel Whalley Esquire and the said Josiah Spode, and were formerly the inheritance of John Terrick.*

On the same date Josiah Spode III also acquired land upon lease from Elizabeth Jones and Terrick Jones for the annual payment of £20. *All that cottage or tenement, situate in Penkhull, now and for some time past in the holding of Amy Machin, widow, and also all that adjoining piece or parcel of*

land called the Orchard, formerly in three pieces and then called the House Orchard, the Orchard, and Blakeman's Croft, and with power to take down and remove the said cottage and buildings and the materials thereof, and to convert any part of the said land, except the Blakeman's Croft, into gardens not exceeding one statute acre in the whole and with an optional power on the part of the lessee to erect any buildings on the said premises. Blakeman's Croft forms a part of the Penkhull end of Queens Road.

Josiah Spode III continued to acquire more land, this time a further substantial addition, comprising a total of seventy acres and reaching out to cover the area of Hartshill down to the Lyme Brook with its boundary with Newcastle-under-Lyme. It was purchased from the Reverend John Whalley (as in Whalley Avenue) and his sons John and Daniel, and John Stow, for the sum of £13,500 on the 2nd April 1829. Nine months later Spode died, in December, aged 52. The land consisted of: *All those copyhold messuages dwelling houses or tenements, and other buildings closes pieces or parcels of land meadow and pasture, situated in Penkhull particularly described as a dwelling house standing in the village of Penkhull formerly in the occupation of Thomas Moss and afterwards in the successive occupations of Thomas Atherton, Benjamin Burbridge, and Sarah Maskery respectively which dwelling house has for many years been subdivided into and occupied as four dwelling houses, which have been inhabited by servants belonging to the family of Josiah Spode and his late father now deceased.*

A close formerly in several parts and then called the Bear Yard and Crofts, but now called by the names of the Honey Wall Croft and Bears Yard, or one of them. Also another close, usually called the Great Longoe or Longhough, together with the slip of land lying between the said two last mentioned closes and belonging to one or both of them, and which during the life time of the said late father of the said Josiah Spode was used by him as part of the private carriage road leading from Stoke-upon-Trent to the Mount.

The list of field names is extensive but includes such names as Doody's Longway, Pit Close, Square Piece, Cooper's Leasow, Upper Slang, Great Stone Pit Field, Far Stone Pit Field and land lying at the south end of a meadow adjacent to the Brook running from the town of Newcastle-under-Lyme to the River Trent, usually called Newcastle Brook. The list continues to include fields in the Hartshill area such as The Brick Kiln Leasow, otherwise the Upper Harthill Field, Lower Hartshill Field.

The next court record refers to a mortgage taken by Josiah Spode III to finance the purchase of land. He now surrendered back to Daniel Whalley and John Stow the land as security for a mortgage to the value of £8,500.

Josiah Spode III was born in 1777, and little is recorded of him within the pottery business. A report in the Staffordshire Advertiser published after his death in December 1829 refers to a terrible accident that befell Josiah III in 1803. *After the completion of the installation of a steam engine for mill work for the grinding of materials he was inspecting the operations when a crown wheel struck his hat, and in lifting his arm to protect himself the hand passed between the cogs of the wheels and immediately amputation became indispensable.*

At the time of his marriage, at the age of 38, he moved to an estate at Great Fenton provided by his father and retired from the business. However twelve years later he returned, after death of his father, and lived at The Mount. His estate valued three years after his death amounted to £162,576.

Tittensor's House

Spode's acquisition of Lot 2 at the auction of the estate belonging to John Harrison included an old farmhouse called Tittensor's House. This was promptly demolished by Spode who erected a new mansion house called The Mount on the site in c1803/4.

Tittensor is a very old Penkhull name, and the earliest record in the district was recorded in a Subsidy Roll, dated 1327, introduced by King Edward III to meet the expenses of the war with Scotland. The names of John de Tytensore who pays xiid and Willmo de Tytensore who pays xvd. A William de Tytensore appears in a further roll dated 1350. By the mid 15th century the spelling had changed to Tetenshire, later to become Tytensore. The name is consistent throughout the manorial court records from the 14th century later to become altered into what it known as Tittensor. It could well be that the family was one of the 17 farmers listed in Penkhull in the Domesday record of 1086, but unfortunately no names are given.

The extent of the land belonging to the Tittensor family is recorded in the first survey of the manor in 1414 with two entries under the names of John and William, perhaps father and son. *John Tydensore holds half a messuage [4½d] 20 lands of socage [22d] two acres [2s] and one part of an acre of land of demesne [2d] formerly held by William Tydensore and pays per annum at the terms of Saint Andrew the Apostle, the Annunciation of the Blessed Mary and the Nativity of Saint John the Baptist and St. Michael equally: 4½d.*

William Tydensore holds half a messuage [2½d] 8 lands of socage [5¾d] 3 lands of demesne [6d] and the third part of an acre called Holeplane [9d] 4½ acres and one rood of land of waste [2s 3½d] formerly held by the aforesaid William and pays per annum at the same terms. 4s 3¾d.

In a survey dated 1516, the name of William Tyttensor is listed as having lands and paying an annual rent to the Duchy of Lancaster of 12s 4d. Again in a further survey of 1615, the name Thomas Tyttensor appears. In 1618, Thomas Tyttensor the younger, is listed as holding 17 acres, and later in a 1650 survey a Thomas is also listed, probably his son as he is addressed as Thomas junior, holding 17 acres at a rental of 3s 4d. In the Staffordshire Hearth Tax of 1660, the name William Tittensor appears as living in Penkhull. By 1714, it was recorded that the land was owned formerly by Thomas Tittensor, and again another plot of land was described as formerly owned by Roger and John Tittensor.

The use of property names or addresses in rural areas like Penkhull did not exist until the latter part of the 19th century. Only a few dwellings in the court records are identifiable, most being referred to as '*a messuage, tenement or dwelling belonging to*'. Therefore it was unusual to have the name of Tittensor's House from early records even though the property could have existed from several hundred years before the first record appeared. The first reference to Tittensor's House found in the manor court rolls does not appear until the 27th February 1716, when Roger Tittensor, son and heir of John Tittensor, transferred the property to Thomas Lovatt to secure a mortgage for the sum of £6 6s. The next reference is dated December 1720 when the house is referred to as *now in the holding of Robert Tittensor, with all barns, stables, outhouses and orchards.* Again the copyhold records refer to the property in October 1792: *all that dwelling called 'Tittensor's House' together with stables, barns, orchards etc. and the other dwellings in the several holdings of Sarah Tittensor, Sarah Dishley and George Hudson.*

Other documents in addition to court records, such as wills and inventories can assist in building up snap-shot of properties, ownership and wealth. The first document the last will and testament of Thomas Tyttensor, the elder is dated the 17th July 1588, the time of Queen Elizabeth 1st. First reference is made to the messuage where he lives with all its lands, meadows, pastures which was formerly in the hands of his father John Tyttensor. He continues to make a number of bequests but leaves the property to his second son Thomas, although one third is reserved for his wife Elizabeth and his money to his two daughters Agnes and Ellen. Unfortunately the inventory fails to list items on a room by room basis, (or these may not have survived) but lists steers, bullocks, cows, calves, a mare and colt, sheep and swine. It continues to list a number of husbandry items consistent with this being a farm.

The next Tittensor document is an inventory dated the 17th May 1632. It is consistent with that of 1588 in listing husbandry ware and animals but here the numbers of animals represented a much lower farm stock with only one swine, one horse and two calves. There is no mention of cows or bullocks for example. However, the inventory of his goods and chattels more than compensates with the listing of household items such as, 3 featherbeds and 4 bolsters to the value of £1 6 8d, 1 chaff beds and 2 chaff bolsters at 6s 8d. There is also pewter listed at 11d and brass at £1 followed by 7 chairs and 5 pairs of bed socks, a long table, one short table and cupboard at £2.

The circumstances causing the decline in the farm are not known. There could be a number of reasons such as poor weather, poor harvests or even disease or plague. Whatever the reason Tyttensor had serious financial problems as his total assets arrived at by the appraisers amounted to only £20 13 8d, whereas his debts owing to his relative Thomas Tyttensor at the time of his death amounted to well in excess of £100.

The next inventory dated 23rd May 1701, lists Thomas Tyttensor, probably the grandson of the above Thomas. By now events had changed: the inventory includes; five cows to the value of £18; 2 stirks, 6 pigs, 15 sheep and 2 calves and 7 bales of oats. The document continues to list the various rooms of the house the appraisers calculating the total value for each room. This gives the first indication of the size of the property: middle chamber (bedroom), store chamber, little chamber, chamber over the house place, the parlour and the house place. This inventory does not give the impression of a large house although it does list four bedrooms which are significant for the period. This conclusion is confirmed by the hearth tax records which list only one hearth, although others could have been bricked up.

The Reeve Book refers to the dwelling as formerly belonging to Thomas Tyttensor, later belonging to Mr Lovatt of Fulford, and afterwards Peggy Ward, before it was purchased by John Harrison. The house was surrendered to John Harrison by William Ward, with other lands at a court held on the 1st May 1789.

The copyhold court records from 1720 to 1792 often refers to property which was not changing hands but was security for loans. By 1721 it is recorded that Tittensor's House was still in the occupation of Robert Tittensor, but a mortgage was held by John and Margery Bourne to the value of £62 10s only to be transferred to Thomas Fenton as trustee for Joyce Lloyd, heir of her late father Marmaduke Buckley. Again the assets of the property were used in 1728 and 1739, when Thomas Lovatt secured a mortgage for the sum of £800 from John Allen, gent. By December 1742, Allen returned the estate back to Lovatt, probably on the basis that the mortgagee was to be changed again as the estate was transferred to Henry Dolphin, gent for the sum of £800. The 1729 transaction refers to the fact that Robert Tittensor was no longer in occupation of Tittensor's House.

On the 21st March 1749/50 Tittensor's House and land was being rented to John Godwyn at an annual rent of £42 with a 21-year lease, but on the 11th April 1764, the Devisees in trust of Thomas Lovatt, late of Fulford transferred the house and lands to Thomas Ward. It was the sons of Thomas Ward, Thomas and William, potters of Lane End, who in turn sold the estate on the 1st day of May 1789 to John Harrison subject to an annuity of £10 a year to Margaret Unett, who could well have been the remarried widow of Thomas Ward, then deceased. (This is the same Thomas Ward as in Thomas Ward Place.)

Harrison also owned a pottery works at the bottom of Honeywall and was for a short period in partnership with Josiah Wedgwood. However, because of the lack of business experience he went bankrupt and had to sell his home, factory and huge estate. This was done as previously recorded at an auction held at The Marquis of Granby on Tuesday 20th July, 1802.

The Mount
Before coming to Penkhull, Josiah Spode was renting Fenton Hall, which hardly reflected his growing importance in the district. Like many industrialists of the period, Spode wanted to be within a short distance of his factory. In was not until the 12th September 1803 that the manorial courts record the transaction twelve months earlier. Tittensor's House by this time had been demolished by Spode and the present building commenced. Building work progressed quickly, for it would appear that The Mount was ready for occupation the following year.

What is it that made this splendid mansion pre-eminent in the entire borough? The first account of it from Simeon Shaw (Staffordshire Potteries 1829). *In one part of Penkhull, is the Mount; one of the best mansions in the district, a spacious and elegant square edifice, with suitable attached offices, surrounded by extensive gardens and pleasure grounds, and enjoying a prospect almost unbounded over the vicinity and the adjacent counties.* John Ward later wrote: (The Borough of Stoke-upon-Trent 1843) *of the mansions within the Township of Penkhull, we may say, indeed within the compass of the Borough, The Mount erected by the late Josiah Spode, Esq., bears acknowledged pre-eminence. It stands near the village, and is surrounded by plantations and a highly ornamented domain. The house is an oblong building of brick and stone with a semi-circular entrance on the west front with an elegant and lofty dome which lights the staircase and gives an exterior air of grandeur to the structure.*

Even today, The Mount remains an imposing structure, built to impress upon visitors the commercial success, wealth and status of its owner. Spode wanted to be seen not as a potter with the basic materials of clay, but as a successful businessman and landowner. The house comprises mainly of brick with stone used to emphasise its architectural features. It was built in two sections; the larger part is rectangular in shape and two storeys stores high. The front elevation is symmetrical, of seven bays, dominated by a large bow in the middle of ashlar with adjacent Roman Doric columns.

Hargreaves Map 1832 showing the extent of The Mount

To further his status in the locality and with an aim to impress his friends, the Mount was designed to face south west, away from Spode's factory and the town of Stoke with all its pollution and humble workers dwellings, but towards the estates of Clayton Lodge and Trentham Hall, a significant talking point to his guests and visitors. The rear elevation is of a simpler design, also of seven bays with a slightly projecting central section which originally contained the rear entrance. Internally, two halls lead from the main entrance to the principal staircase with its iron handrail, balusters, and trellis panels. All this is illuminated by a circular skylight. The smaller, plainer structure to

The main stairway of The Mount

the northwest is the service wing which contains a separate staircase for the servants.

The house and its contents were shown off to visitors who were entertained in a lavish style. One large party was held in November 1809, to celebrate the marriage of Josiah

Spode's daughter to George Whieldon, of the Inner Temple, London. Enoch Wood, the potter, who was present on a later occasion the following year records in his diary: November 23rd 1810. *Dined at the Mount at Mr Spode's, the most splendid and sumptuous entertainment I ever attended. No intoxication.* Thomas Caldwell, a solicitor, who was also in attendance writes: *November 23rd, 1810. Dined at Mr Spode's with a large party where we partook of the most sumptuous entertainment accompanied with every mark of kindness and hospitality.*

In addition to the parties for friends, the working classes of his factory in Stoke were allowed in on special occasions. One such occasion was the 50th anniversary of the accession of George III which was celebrated in style by Josiah Spode II. The Staffordshire Advertiser reported on the 28th of October 1809 under the headline 'The Jubilee in Staffordshire'. *At no place in the Kingdom could the jubilee be celebrated with more demonstration of joy, than it was by Josiah Spode, Esq., China Manufacturer to His Royal Highness the Prince of Wales, at Stoke-upon-Trent, in the Staffordshire Potteries. Before the time of divine service, the servants began to muster at the works, and being collected together, walked in procession to*

George III

the church, where a most appropriate and impressive sermon was preached by the Rev. William Robinson, Rector to a very crowded congregation. The servants afterwards were drawn up at his manufactory, headed by a band of music, chosen out of his own servants. Mr Spode, attended by about thirty gentlemen of the neighbourhood and the servants two by two, to the number of near 600, paraded up to the Mount, an elegant mansion, recently built by Mr Spode; the music playing 'God save the King.' The line of servants extended a long way, and the fineness of the day, with the great number of spectators attending, all dressed in their Sunday clothes, together with the happy countenances of the whole, rendered it a most pleasing sight. When they arrived at the Mount, they were marched round the lawn in front of the house, when the skies resounded with three times three. They afterwards paraded as before, close to the house, where each person drank the good Old King in half a pint of good Staffordshire Ale. They were then formed three deep round the Bowling Green where 'God save the King' was sung in full chorus, the whole of the spectators, not less than three thousand joining heartily in the song. Two additional verses, written by one of Mr Spode's servants, were sung and received with the loudest plaudits. The gentlemen who attended, were regaled with a most elegant cold collation in the house, good Staffordshire ale, and choice wines – here the good Old King's health was drunk with a large number of loyal and appropriate toasts were drank together with the health of the hospitable and worthy host with the loudest acclamations - some elegant lines, written by the Rev. W. Fernyhough, on the memorable occasion, were recited in a very energetic manner, by Mr Tomlinson, of Hanley, and received with much applause. Afterwards each servant drank Mr Spode's health in half a pint of more ale, and each of them received a good loaf of bread and one shilling in money. They then paraded as before down to the manufactory, and sang 'God save the King' with the two additional verses as before. Mr Spode's and family's health was proposed in a very handsome manner by a gentleman, and followed by nine times nine. These exclamations must have been heard at an immense distance. Mr Spode then claimed silence, and in a very handsome manner thanked his servants and the spectators for their attendance, and the good order they had preserved. They then dispersed, each going comfortably, and happy to their own home.

The sense of patronism towards King and Country was distinctively different from that of today. Every opportunity was taken to celebrate and therefore a further occasion held in 1821, although not directly at The Mount, represented a further example of the generosity of Mr Spode to his workers.

George Augustus Frederick became King George IV on the death of his father George III on January 29th 1820. His coronation was not held until July 19th 1821 probably because George IV greatly enjoyed planning a ceremony down to the very last detail. Once more Mr Spode took the lead in organising the local celebrations. The Staffordshire Advertiser reported the event on the 21st July.

The inhabitants of Stoke-upon-Trent were awakened by the merry peal, and pleasure took place of business. The shops and manufactories were closed, and the inhabitants were general in their expression of zealous loyalty. A large procession of Freemasons made their appearance about 12 o'clock, and soon afterwards the principal Gentlemen and Tradesmen assembled at the Talbot Inn. After waiting a short time, these together with all the servants of Mr Spode, comprising men, women and children, and the scholars belonging to the National School, went in procession to the Mount. At their head were an excellent band of music, flags, garlands &c. On their arrival at Mr Spode's residence, they formed a circle on the lawn, and sang the National Anthem of 'God Save the King' and 'Rule Britannia,' which has a most pleasing effect. The wealthy owner then joined the procession, which moved on through Penkhull, and along the new road to the Talbot Inn, where a circle was again formed, and 'God Save the King', sung. The whole of Mr Spode's servants were then most liberally treated, the men and boys with an excellent dinner, and plenty of ale, at the Talbot and King's Arms; the women and girls with tea at the manufactory. A numerous party of gentlemen sat down to a sumptuous dinner at the Wheatsheaf, Josiah Spode, Esq. in the chair. Loyal toasts and suitable songs were not wanting, and the utmost unanimity accompanied the festive scene.

The Land Tax Assessments of 1825 confirm that Josiah Spode was paying the sum of 5s 2d assessed for The Mount.

The majority of his workers' dwellings were assessed at just 3d, while his manufactory in the town of Stoke was assessed at 16s 8d. Spode was also involved in the building of the new parish church in Stoke. In 1826, he compelled his men to give a week's wages towards the rebuilding of the new church. He urged Mr Minton to do the same; but he, Minton declined exercising any compulsion and left the workpeople to obey their inclinations. Some gave, but the majority did not. Some of Mr Spode's workers left his employment rather than submit.

The Mount c1870

Charles Heaton, surveyor of Endon, prepared a survey and valuation of Landed Property for the Parish of Stoke-upon-Trent in 1827. The results of this survey are listed showing the extent of the land attached to Penkhull Farm that was in occupation of Josiah Spode. The ownership was held by the estate of the late Misses Alsagers.

The following schedule lists the field names together with the measurement in acres, roods and perches.

No's	Description of Property Quantity	A	R	P	£	s	d
381	Homestead &c.		2	4	11	0	0
383	Stackyard and Croft	1	3	20	4	13	9
382	Barnfield and Little Croft	4	1	15	9	11	1
54	Townsend	3	1	38	8	7	2
386	Flat	4	3	38	9	9	6
385	Thistley or White Hough	5	1	24)	28	18	3
373	Eight Acre Field	9	0	9)			
395	Little Cliff	4	3	5)	38	19	0
394	Long Wheat Cliff	7	2	26)			
391	Broomy or Clover Cliff	5	2	36)			
392	Cliff Meadow or Rough Cliff	4	2	39)			
393	Slang or Little Meadow	1	0	30)	13	6	10
413	Great and Little Hordern	12	0	25)			
436	Brook or Red Meadow	3	2	15	8	19	8
	Total	69	1	21	£133	5	3d

The whole estate, either occupied or owned by Spode II is well documented. It contains all the properties in Stoke Town and Boothen as well as Honeywall and the village of Penkhull. The following is the section that refers only to The Mount: *All that Mansion House situated in the Township of*

Penkhull with Boothen late in the possession of the late Josiah Spode the elder deceased. Together with the stables, coach houses, offices and other outbuildings, hothouses, greenhouses, gardens, orchards, pleasure grounds, plantations, shrubberies, paddocks, pools, roads, walks and avenues thereto belonging. All which mansion house buildings and premises contain according to a survey 17a 0r 34p.

During the period when Josiah Spode occupied The Mount he must have lived like the Lord of the Manor, for, apart from living in the largest house in the district, he was in fact the landlord and employer of a good number of its inhabitants. One can imagine when his carriage passed on its way to and from the pottery works in Stoke people would stop and address him as 'Sir'. He presumably had absolute authority of all things.

By the early 1800s it was reckoned that there were about 670,000 people employed in domestic labour throughout Britain. It was a fact that during this period the typical English worker was not the factory worker but a domestic servant. As servants received low wages in the 19th century, Josiah Spode could employ servants by the score. Cooks and kitchen maids would look after the food, and stillroom maids would prepare the jams and bottle the garden produce from The Mount vegetable gardens. Housemaids kept the rooms neat and tidy, footmen waited at the table. Here the housekeeper and butler ruled in state and the rest sat in order of importance from cook right down to the little boy who washed the dishes in his first job. The footmen were usually chosen for youth, size and handsome appearance, so that they could set off to the best advantage their liveries of gold laced, long tailed coats, white silk breeches and long silk stockings. It takes little to imagine Spode in his coach, with footmen to the rear, perhaps going down Trent Valley Road to Trentham to visit the Sutherlands or to Clayton Hall, or Mr Tomlinson's home at Cliffe Ville. The housekeeper would have her own room and the butler would reign like a king over those underlings. The servants had their own servant's hall where meals would be taken. Outside in the gardens and plantations of the estate, men and boys laboured under the head gardener. Others worked in the great stables where the coachmen, grooms and stable boys kept the horses for driving and riding immaculate.

On the16th July, 1827, Josiah Spode II, (1755-1827) died at the age of 72 years leaving his son Josiah Spode III (1777-1829) to take over the business. Sadly he died only two years later on the 6th October 1829, aged 52. His widow Mary and his young son Josiah IV continued to live at The Mount for ten years, until 1839 when they moved to their new home at Armitage Park near Rugeley. A number of years ago I had occasion to stay at Spode House, Armitage Park where Mary and Josiah IV lived. It was strange as it was from this address

that many letters were despatched to prospective tenants of The Mount all of which I have handled.

In 1831, a survey of the estate of the late Josiah Spode III was conducted to secure a mortgage amounting to the sum of £10,000 from William Baker of Fenton. The Mount was described as follows, *The Mount stands together with stables, coach houses, offices and other buildings, hothouses, greenhouses, gardens, orchards, pleasure grounds, plantations, shrubberies, paddocks, pools, roads, walks and avenues thereto belonging. Also those several closes or parcels of land, lying together in a ring fence near The Mount, containing in the whole over 150 acres.* These 150 acres acquired between 1803 and 1827 covered the area from Stone Street, down Honeywall to Hartshill Road, up this road to The Avenue at Hartshill, down and across in a line where now Lodge Road lies to Newcastle Lane, then along Queens Road to the end of Doncaster Lane and back to The Mount.

In 1838 Mary Spode, widow of Josiah III, decided to leave Penkhull and placed The Mount on the market 'To Let'.

The advertisement in the Staffordshire Advertiser is dated the 24th November 1838.

TO BE LET
For a term four of years (furnished or unfurnished) and to be entered upon at Lady-day Next Year
A Capital first rate Mansion called The Mount, eligibly situated in Staffordshire with a handsome entrance lodge.

This most desirable residence is spacious and convenient as may be seen from the following brief statement. It comprises excellent cellars of good temperature for wine, ground floor spacious double entrance hall with handsome staircase, dining room, 27 feet by eighteen, drawing room 26 feet by 24 feet, billiard room and library 24 feet by 18 feet and breakfast room 18 feet x 18 feet all 12' 6" high.
The bedroom floor contains a delightful morning room, with bow window, seven principal bedrooms to several of which dressing rooms are attached and a suitable number of convenient sleeping rooms for servants. The domestic offices, which are quite commensurate, adjoin the house, and are equally well built. The stable, coach house and harness room form two sides of a well-paved and enclosed yard. Large walled garden, stocked with choice fruit trees, in full bearing, hothouse, pinery, green-houses, and excellent ice-house. The pleasure grounds are extensive, and tastefully laid out, and include an ornamental sheet of water.
This delightful abode, replete with every convenience is fully adapted to the accommodation of a high respectable family. It stands upon an eminence and commands views, including the park, woods and ornamental grounds of Trentham, Butterton and Keele.
The roads are good in every direction; situated within two miles of Newcastle-under-Lyme; 150 miles from London and 6 from

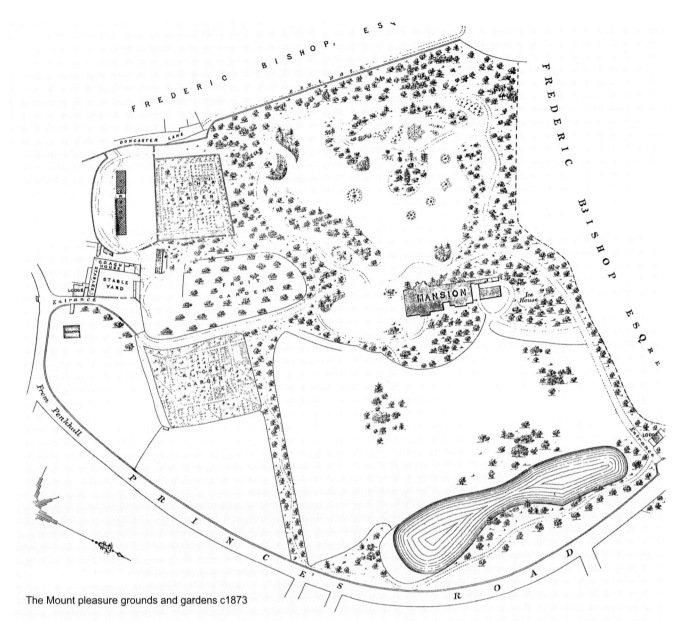

The Mount pleasure grounds and gardens c1873

the Grand Junction Railway station at Whitmore. About 120 acres of land together with 9 labourer's cottages and convenient farm buildings will be let, if desirable, to tenants.

From a schedule dated 1839, indications are that certain repairs were necessary, probably caused through the lack of maintenance after the death of Josiah III. For example, in the cellar the boiler which provided hot water for the bathrooms *was out of repairs for want of use.*

The only information there is regarding the furnishings in the house comes from the sale of part of the contents which took place in 1839 on the departure of Mary Spode. Some of the items listed below were probably originally purchased by Josiah Spode II and inherited by Josiah Spode III on the death of his father.

On the premises, at THE MOUNT, on Tuesday, Wednesday and Thursday (if necessary), the 10th, 11th and 12th days of December, 1839.

Part of the elegant and valuable HOUSEHOLD FURNITURE, and other effects, the property of Mrs Spode, who is changing her residence, - comprising a beautiful Rosewood Drawing Room Suite, consisting of 12 rosewood chairs, covered with crimson velvet, an elegant sofa couch, richly carved drawing room commode, with crimson silk doors and glass back, rosewood chiffonier, ditto fire screens, with crimson silk, a beautiful rosewood loo table, pair of card tables, rosewood work table, with crimson bag, set of quartette tables (en suite.) The Dining Room consisting of handsome mirror, in gilt frame, three sets of moveen window curtains, mahogany chairs, large folding screen, handsome pedestal sideboard, mahogany slide screen, covered with damask, two mahogany couches, pair of footstools, &c, &c. A powerful rich-toned Cottage Piano-Forte, by Clementi. The Sitting Rooms comprise several mahogany Pembroke and other tables, neatly painted chairs with cane seats, backs, and hair cushions, Venetian blinds, handsome chimney glass, in gilt frame, 5 feet 2 inches by 2 feet 2 inches, various steel and other fenders, fire irons, window curtains and gilt cornice, carpets, mahogany chairs, mahogany chiffoniers, two sets of book shelves, &c, &c.

The Bedrooms consist of handsome four-post bedsteads, with dimity and chintz hangings, mattresses, bed steps, dressing glasses in handsome mahogany frames, chests of drawers, dressing and wash tables, carpets, window curtains and cornice, chairs, fenders, &c, &c. Also an excellent barrel organ, large-sized desk, with drawers, suitable for an office, upwards of 40 glass bottles, a very handsome grate, with steel front, steel fenders and dust pan, a capital mash tub, capable of mashing 36 bushels, in good condition, with sundry kitchen requisites.

The Sale to commence each day at 12 o'clock.
The Auctioneer begs to observe that the furniture is in very high preservation, and may be viewed on Monday, the 9th instant, by ticket only, which may be had on application to M. JOHNSON, Auctioneer, Synch House, Burslem, Staffordshire Potteries.

The first lease following the departure of Mrs Spode and young Josiah IV was for a period of 4½ years designed to take the date up to the period when Josiah became of age at 21. The new tenant, Mr Lewis Adams was born at Bagnall in 1805, and the son of William Adams, a pottery manufactory in Stoke. After his father's death in 1829, Adams continued to live with his mother and unmarried sisters at Fenton Hall until he took possession of The Mount in 1839 the same year that he was appointed to the important position of chief bailiff for the town of Stoke-upon-Trent, a position he held for two years. Mr Adams remained single throughout his life and in 1841 was listed as 36 years of age, living with his mother Sarah, and his two sisters Elizabeth and Fanny.

The lease to Lewis Adams is dated 10th day of December 1839 from Mrs Mary Spode to William Adams. By this time Mrs Spode had moved to Armitage Park.

Between Mary Spode of Armitage Park in the County of Stafford and widow of Josiah Spode Esq. and guardian of the estate of Josiah Spode her son and an infant of the age of 16 years, and Mr Lewis Adams of Stoke-upon-Trent in the said county Merchant. That in consideration of the rents and covenants agreed Mary Spode as such guardian leased unto Lewis Adams all that newly erected messuage or dwelling house being of Freehold Tenure standing near Hartshill in the township of Penkhull in the said county now used as the North Entrance Lodge to the mansion house. Together with such part or parts of the pleasure grounds, shrubberies, plantations and carriage roads immediately adjoining to the said entrance lodge as is or now Freehold Tenure and all the fixtures and fittings in premises which are mentioned in the schedule written or hereupon enclosed.
To have and hold from the 25th day of December for the term of four years and half to be complete and ended if the said Josiah Spode the son shall so long live yielding and paying therefore during the term until the said Josiah Spode the son the clear

yearly sum of Five Pounds of lawful English money, equal half yearly payments on every 24th day of June and the 25th day of December during the said term.

And this Indenture also witness and agree that the said Mary Spode lease All that copyhold capital Mansion House called the Mount and the south entrance lodge and all the stables, coach houses, hothouses, offices, out houses, gardens, lawns, pleasure grounds, shrubberies, plantations, yards, avenues, walks and pools of water adjoining and belong thereto and all so much and such part or parts of the carriage road leading from the mansion to the north lodge.

To the use of the said Lewis Adams from the 25th day of December for the term of four years and one half and paying during the said term the yearly rent of fifty seven pounds by equal half yearly payments.

And also shall and sufficiently repair maintain amend, scour, cleanse, preserve and keep in good repair and order the said Mansion House and Lodges and all the outhouses, edifices and buildings aforesaid and all the glazed windows, sashes and fences thereof and all the iron and other gates, iron and other fences, rails, pales, grates, spouts, sewers, drains, hedges, ditches, mounds, walls, carriage and other roads, avenue, walks, gardens, shrubberies, plantations and pools belonging to the premises and the same premises so separated and kept in repair as aforesaid at the end or together determination of the said respective terms shall and will yield and deliver up to the person or persons for the time being entitled to the revision of the same premises expectant on the determination of the aforesaid terms.

And also that Lewis Adams, his executors etc, shall and will once at least during the continuation of the said terms cause all such parts of the said Mansion House and offices adjoining as well inside as outside as have been painted to be effectually painted with a good coat of oil paint.

Following on from this lease, a schedule of fixtures and fittings was executed on the 23rd and 24th December 1839 by Mr Henry Ward of Stoke, Surveyor. The schedule provides a unique insight to The Mount and the lavish proportions of its rooms and contents.

Ground Floor: Principal Entrance Hall: Lock and four bolts and one chain bolt on front door.
Four shutter latches and two bars. Two sash fasteners.
***Billiard Room:** Four shutter latches and two bars. Two door locks and four finger plates. Two sash fasteners. Bell with two leaver pulls. Grate, and marble chimney piece and hearth.*
***Drawing Room:** Four shutter latches and two bars. Two door locks and four finger plates. Two sash fasteners. Grate, and marble chimney piece and hearth. Bell with two leaver pulls.*
***Staircase:** Two door locks and four finger plates. Large flush bolt on folding doors. Stove grate.*

Entrance Hall (East): Two shutter latches and one bar. Front door lock and four flush bolts.

Dining Room: Marble Chimney piece and hearth. Lock and bolts to folding doors. Six shutter latches and three bars. Three sash fasteners. Bell with two leaver pulls.

Breakfast Room: Door lock and three finger plates. Four shutter latches and two bars. Two sash fasteners. Marble chimney piece and hearth. Bell with two lever pulls.

Closet in Breakfast Room: Door lock and one finger plate. Two shutter latches and one bar. Cupboard divided in two. Two cupboard locks and three bolts and two brass hooks. Six drawers with a lock and two handles to each.

Butler's Pantry: Door lock and one finger plate. Two shutter latches and one bar. Grate. Cupboard divided into three in height with turnbuckle fasteners, two locks and two small bolts. Lead cistern with water pipe and tap and waste pipe. A small cupboard at the end of the cistern (quite decayed). Dresser with six drawers, ring handles, and four locks. Cupboard over the dresser with lock and one bolt. Another cupboard with two locks, (one without key) and two bolts.

Lobby leading from Best Staircase to Offices: Two pin rails. Closet with small pin rail and spring latch fastening to door. Door lock and two finger plates.

Water Closets: Three door locks and small brass bolt. Out door lock and iron chain bolt. Two shutter latches and one bar. Two water closets complete.

Servants Hall: Grate. Two shutter latches and one bar. Cupboard divided into two in height, two locks (one without a key) and two bolts. Two pin rails with seven cloak pins. Sash fastener.

House Keepers Room: Door lock. Four shutter latches and two bars. Two sash fasteners. A cupboard on each side of the fire place divided into two in height, four cupboard locks and one bolt. A range of cupboards occupying one entire side of the room and divided into four separate cupboards or presses - four locks and three bolts. Eight drawers under cupboards with a lock and two handles to each. Small drawer with lock and partitioned off inside.

Kitchen: Two door locks. Two shutter bars. Kitchen grate with two creepers, oven and boiler. Smoke jack stove, shelf over fire place and two closets (without either locks or bolts) corner buffet with one lock. Kitchen dresser with three drawers and four drawer handles. Three cupboards under drawers in dresser, with two twin buckle fasteners and two small bolts. Eight rails, with hooks for hanging covers etc. on. Sixty three beef hooks in ceiling. Two coffee mills.

Larder: Door lock. Four shutter latches and two bars. Two wire lattice windows, three shelves and one pin rail. Small wood lattice safe with lock. Round table in the centre, and table fixed to the wall all round. Proper frame with meat hooks and labelled.

Lower Larder or Dairy: Two bar lattice windows. Two shutter bars, door lock and thumb latch. Brick stillage on three sides.

Scullery: Grate. Two boilers with water pipe and taps. Two shelves. Cupboard divided into two (without locks or bolts). Door lock with thumb latch. Brick sink with wood kerb. Lead pump.

Store Room: (Door lock taken off) One shutter bar. Small dresser. Five tiers of shelves supported on timber uprights and bearers. (N.B. The uprights fixed to the walls and the skirting is entirely decayed.)

Back Entrance Porch: Door lock, two thumb latches, two bolts, one chain bolt and a knocker.

Cellar No.1 - Boiler and piping to supply bath (all out of repair for want of usage).

Cellar No.2 (ale) Wood stillage on three sides. Thumb latch on door.

Cellar No.3 (ale) Wood stillage on three sides. Door lock. Entrance door to wine vaults with lock (one inner door quite decayed) one vault fitted up with two tiers of wine bins on each side, built of brick.

Basement: Apple Room - Two heights of shelves on two sides. Thumb latch and two sash fasteners. Trap door in cellar lobby (the door itself wants repairing and the frame is quite decayed) Cellar stairs door spring latch. Two bolts and a bar.

Chamber Floor: Bow Room- Bell with one leaver pull. Grate. Marble chimney piece and hearth. Door and two finger plates. Six shutter latches and three bars. Three sash fasteners.

Bedroom over Drawing Room: Two shutter latches and one bar. Two door locks. Two finger plates and one night bolt. Grate. Marble chimney piece and hearth. Bell (without any pull affixed) One sash fastener. Dressing Room attached to the above Bedroom. Two shutter latches and one bar. One sash fastener. Door lock. Bell (without pull) Grate.

Bedroom over Dining Room: Grate. Bell (without pull) Four shutter latches and two bars. Three door locks and one night bolt. Two sash fasteners. Dressing Room attached to the last mentioned Bedroom. Two shutter latches and one bar. Grate. Bell without pull. One sash fastener.

Bedroom over breakfast room: Grate. Two door locks and one night bolt. Two shutter latches and one bar. Bell (without pull). One sash fastener. Dressing Room attached to the above (and over East Entrance Hall). Grate. Bell (without pull) Door lock. Two shutter latches and one bar. One sash fastener.

Bedroom over Billiard Room: Grate. Bell. Two shutter latches and one bar. Two door locks and one night bolt. One sash fastener. Dressing Room attached to the last mentioned Bedroom. Door lock. Two shutter latches and one bar. One sash fastener. Grate and Bell (without pull).

Lobby: leading to Bedroom also Closet in the same. Two door locks and one small bolt.

Bedroom over the Butlers Pantry: Grate. Door lock and night bolt. Bell. Two shutter latches and one bar.

Bathroom and Water Closet: Two door locks and one bolt. Water closet complete. Bath (pipes etc. out of repair for the want of usage.) Two sash fasteners (one of them broken).

Bedroom over Servant's Hall: Grate. Bell. Door lock and sash fasteners.

Bedroom over House Keeper's Room: Grate. Bell. Door lock and two sash fasteners.

Bedroom over the Larder: Grate. Door lock, two sash fasteners and small pin rail.

Closet at the end of Lobby: Spring latch and two shelves.

Two servants Bedroom: One grate, two door locks and three sash fasteners.

Ground Floor Kitchen Yard: Cleaning room: Three shelves, boot rack, door lock and thumb latch.

Entrance door, Lock, bolt and thumb latch.

Pump in Yard: Laundry: Two door locks, two thumb latches and water tap (fast).

Brew house: One boiler, two water taps (one out of repair) old (parlour) grate, stone table, door lock and thumb latch.

Carriage doors: Bolt, bar and padlock. Water tap in yard (fast).

North Lodge: Front door lock, three sets of movable shutters, three sash fasteners, two spring latches, two thumb latches and bolt.

South Lodge: Door lock, five thumb latches, two sash fasteners, one bolt and two shelves in pantry.

Stables: Four stalled stable - four harness pins, door lock and thumb latch. Hay Barn (Wants repairing) Two – two stalled stables. Two door locks, two thumb latches and five small harness pins.

Harness Room: Twenty nine harness pins, three saddle trees, table and shelf. Stove pot. Door lock and two thumb catches.

Carriage Houses: One door lock (no key) thumb latch and two bolts. Loose Box - Thumb latch.

Garden etc: Door near stable yard - Lock, thumb latch and bell.
Dutch pit – *Old boiler for cistern. Thumb latch. Two furnaces.*
Garden House: *Small cupboard with lock (no key) Door lock and thumb latch.*
Chamber over the above – Two grates, door lock and latch.
Door leading from orchard to Dutch pit. Lock and thumb latch.
Green House: *Old boiler for cistern, and two door locks.*
Vinery: Two door locks and water pot. Middle Vinery two door locks.
Lowe Vinery: *Large zinc cistern (out of repair) and two door locks.*
Gardens and Pleasure Grounds: *Two trellis gates (one of them broken off the hinges and without lock) one lock, two door locks to garden doors. Lock and latch to door in outer wall. Lock to orchard door. Two thumb latches. Seat on pleasure grounds enclosed with lattice work.*
Lists of Furniture: *Fourteen sets of Venetian window blinds. Billiard Table with cues, maces and marking board complete. Dining Room - Grate and four tables fitted in niches. Breakfast Room – Grate.*

Dated this 30th December 1839
Henry Ward, Surveyor of Stoke

There were three entrances to the estate and at different times, three lodges. The first front entrance was from Honeywall where it joined just below what is now Stone Street and then called Old Coach Road. From this junction, the road ran through what is now the Allotments Estate to The Mount.

The Mount c1920

The rear entrance to The Mount was via what is now the end of Greatbatch Avenue, where until just a few years ago stood the giant pillar which supported the gate. The stables and coach houses associated with Mount farm were adjacent. There was a cobbled courtyard in earlier days, with a fountain in the middle, where tired horses, after their climb up Honeywall would take a welcome drink. Behind these buildings was Mount Farm which was later converted into three cottages. Here also stood south lodge overlooking the corner of Greatbatch Avenue where a school playground still remains. This lodge was built prior to The Mount for it was described in 1839 as *a dwelling now used as the south lodge' containing in fixtures a door lock five spring latches, two sash fasteners, one bolt and two shelves in the pantry.*

The Lodge was occupied by various tenants including the father of Mrs Winnie Roberts, Mr Alldis, and later the late Burt Pattinson. I understand that when these cottages were

demolished, there were found walls made of wattle and daub which indicates that they were well over three or four hundred years old and a part of the original Tittensor's House estate.

The old coach road became unused when a new splendid drive was laid by February 1831. The cost of constructing this new carriage drive across this land north to Hartshill. amounted to £406 6s. The entrance to this new prestigious drive was near to the junction of what are now Queens Road and Princes Road and the long drive to The Mount was bordered by a fine line of trees. In the triangular section at the road junction, there are still visible the remaining few trees marking the driveThe northern exit was fronted with iron gates set in iron railings and by a *handsome stone Lodge* which is recorded in the advertisement dated 1838 *To Let.* The new tree-lined drive can be seen on early maps of the area. The old drive from Honeywall was cleared away although a short section survived at its junction from Honeywall continued to be called The Old Coach Road until the end of the 19th century. The cottages here remained in occupation until the early part of the 20th century and the road was replaced by an electricity sub-station in the 1950s.

The only lodge remaining today was built by Frederick Bishop in 1861 and is located near to the entrance of what is now Mount Avenue. It was built of a cream brick with classical stone portico entrance. At some time, either late 19th century or early 20th century, the building was enlarged to accommodate a kitchen and an additional bedroom. It was re-roofed in the early 1970s and has undergone extensive interior repairs and modernisation by the owner Mr George Bowden. The lodge is now listed by English Heritage. The Coach Road passed right in front of the lodge, not up Mount Avenue as it does today. No doubt the path was re-routed when the site was sold off in plots and housing developments progressed. Just a few yards in front of the lodge, under the garage floor of the house called Doon Ville on the corner of Mount Avenue, there is a deep well supplied with fresh running water.

Mount Lodge in Princes Road

Lewis Adams vacated The Mount at the expiry of the lease in 1844 and moved to The Watlands, Wolstanton where he died on the 24th September 1850. From the following it would seem that his new intended abode at Wolstanton would not contain all the furniture he had acquired for The Mount, and so decided to sell off a number of the larger items. The first advertisement appeared in the *Potteries Mercury* dated the 8th June 1844 which places certain items up for auction that Adams did not wish to take with him to The Watlands. *Mr Johnson has been favoured with instructions to sell by auction at The Mount in the course of the present month a portion of household furniture and miscellaneous property belonging to Mr Lewis Adams, Esq., who is changing his residence. Descriptive particulars will appear in the catalogue in due time.*

The following week a second advertisement contained more details. The auction was to be held on the 20th June at 12 noon. After the initial introduction various items are listed. *Comprising of a fine-tuned grand piano by Clementi* (Clementi born Rome 1752 was first a world class composer of piano sonatas and accomplished recitalist. He later gave up this work to produce pianos, mainly of the square piano-forte design but also the Grand. The instrument would be valued highly and may well have been restored at some time and even be in use today) *two sets of drawing room curtains with guilt cornices, painted and mahogany chairs, couch to correspond, card tables, mahogany book shelves, handsome mahogany sideboard, an excellent set of Spanish mahogany dining tables in four compartments.* The last item was a very superior Iron Chest Barouche for one or two horses *with German shutters, a handsome Gig, nearly new, a set of double harnesses, London made &c.*

Mount Lodge c1910

The lease for The Mount stated that Adams should maintain the mansion in a good state of repair and decoration. However, it is apparent that it was not in such a good condition when he took possession and was in an even worse condition when he left in 1844. A report on the state of The Mount was submitted to Josiah Spode IV by Henry Wood, architect and surveyor on 1st July, 1844:

Sir,

I have surveyed the Mansion, out-offices, garden, grounds and lodges, to The Mount, late in the occupation of Louis Adams Esquire, and have estimated the cost of repair and painting.

There were neither repairs carried out nor painting done to the premises before Mr Adams entered upon them. He took to them in the state they were and consequently I have not estimated the repairs of such things as were not of repair when he took possession. It appears to me the more necessary to state this to you because you made some observations on the state of the trellis gates etc., in the pleasure grounds near the gardens, when I saw you at Newcastle and which observations led me to think you were not at the time aware of the fact. Moreover, on looking into the schedule of fixtures, you will find it there noted as being out of repair at the time the schedule was taken, as also many other things which show that no repairs were done, or intended to be done.

In preparing this estimate, I have given each room separately, and have also kept the woodwork distinct from the walls and fixtures in order that it might be in a more convenient form for your proceedings with Mr Adams. In the first place, if Mr Adams objects that he has painted any part of the interior of the mansion during his tenancy, he must specifically state what room he has painted, the amount of which he will readily be able to take from the estimate.

I have examined the glass in the greenhouses and vinery and pits, and believe it to be in a similar condition to what it was when Mr Adams took possession. Whatever amount you may think proper to claim from Mr Adams, I would suggest you claim all in one sum, not separately, for painting, fixtures and repairs, for it is probable that he may be apt to take exception to some part of the cost and thereby cause you much unnecessary trouble.

Signed: Henry Ward, Hanley,   1st July, 1844.

In a further letter from Mr Ward to young Josiah dated the 3rd August 1844; dry rot had been discovered and described in the following extract.

The repairs were commenced the first day after I received your instructions for them to be done. The inside work is in a forward state and would have been finished but that I have found more trouble in eradicating the dry rot than I first anticipated. It has spread considerably to the billiard room, drawing room, dining room, and bow room. The woodwork round the bottom of these rooms and also the windows is nearly all destroyed by it. The paint has preserved the outer face but the timber, as far as fungus is concerned, is entirely destroyed. Although the cost of repairing it and stopping its progress now will not be serious had it gone six months longer without being noticed the floors of these rooms would have been entirely destroyed by it. At present but little mischief has been done to the floors but to stop more serious damage I would suggest some ventilation in the outer walls, to allow a current of pure air under them. *This and this alone can preserve them from the effects of this destructive vegetable, which is generated and kept alive solely by the confined and foul air under the floors.*

The next occupant of The Mount was William Allbut. Allbut was the Editor of the *North Staffs Mercury* and at the time living at Northwood, Hanley. He apparently wanted to tenant the mansion so his wife could transfer to the Mount an already established ladies' school from their home at Northwood. However, Josiah Spode IV at the same time became of age and in doing so, took over the management of his estates from the trustees of his late father. In his new role he wanted to view the property before all future contracts were signed.

The original contract drawn up for the rental of The Mount to Allbut was for the sum of £60 per year, on a lease for seven years up to 1852, but Spode decided to hold up the lease until he had visited the property. The following letters will explain this and also the reader can see how concerned Allbut became over the delay involved. The following letter dated 21ˢᵗ June 1844, was thus to Josiah Spode:

Sir,

I have arranged with Mr Keary for entering upon 'The Mount on 26ᵗʰ instant, immediately after Mr Adams leaves but I have just had a note from him this morning, instructing that as business is not out of the hands of Mr Williamson for whom he acted, I had better receive your direct sanction before taking possession and signing the execution of the lease. I shall be obliged if you will favour me with this per return of post as I have my furniture packed and I leave my present residence on 24ᵗʰ to make room for the new tenants. I am ready to execute the lease at any time, according to the terms agreed upon.

I shall feel obliged by your giving instructions which will ensure the speedy completion of the painting and repairs. You will excuse me for being urgent on this point when I tell you that Mrs Allbut's school will re-open on about 2ⁿᵈ July and it will be desirable that the paint be dry and free from unpleasant smell before that time.
I am sir,
Yours obediently,
Wm. Allbut.

Josiah Spode gave this letter to his solicitor, Mr F Green, to respond and the reply dated 22ⁿᵈ June, 1844, is reproduced.

Sir,
Mr Spode has handed your letter on 21ˢᵗ yesterday, to me as his solicitor. Having recently attained his majority, Mr Spode is anxious to inspect his property before he can sanction any arrangements which his trustees have entered into.
On Tuesday next, 25ᵗʰ he will accompany me to Stoke and most probably he will call at The Mount between 1 and 2 o'clock on

that date. He will then be happy to meet you there, when I trust, arrangements may be made satisfactorily both to Mr Spode and yourself.
I am sir,
Your old friend,
Fred. K. Green.

William Allbut replies to this letter on the following day, 23ʳᵈ June, 1844:

Sir,
I will not fail to be at The Mount at 1 o'clock on Tuesday to meet Mr Spode and yourself. But not being able to take my family and furniture there tomorrow, will I fear, is of great inconvenience and expense. All my arrangements have been made unto the expedition of leaving my present residence on 24ᵗʰ and my business is of a description that requires all my attention at the close of the week.
In other respects, I am glad that Mr Spode will inspect the premises himself before I enter them.
I am sir,
Yours affectionately,
Wm. Allbut.

After his visit, Josiah Spode decided to issue a new lease with a number of new terms to the increase of rental. This indenture is dated 26ᵗʰ June, 1844, and is listed as follows:

Between Josiah Spode of Armitage Park, on one part and William Allbut of Hanley on the other part, printer and publisher. That in consideration of a yearly rent of £75 doth hereby lease unto William Allbut, that entire capital mansion house called The Mount, late in the occupation of Louis Adams and continues. . .
Permit the premises to be made into or used for the purpose of trade, business of for any other purpose whatsoever than that of a private residence and that if he, that is, William Allbut, thinks fit to use the premises as a school for the education of ladies, but this exception is not to be deemed as permission to use the mansion house as a school for the education of boys or boys and girls together.

William Allbut signed the contract and returned it to Spode with the following letter which brings out a few points of interest:

28ᵗʰ June 1844 Northwood, Hanley
With this is returned the draft of the lease, my signature being added to the agreement on the last page. There are a few points however, that I wish to mention, but are not as conditions but for some favourable consideration and therefore they need not cause any delay in my receiving permission on Monday. Indeed, I trust to your writing to that effect by return.

1. You have not made it clear the words 'natural decay' in the exceptions to my liability, I think you should arrange that the expense of replacing some gates, which are not likely to hold together the whole term of the lease.

2. You appear to have over looked the position that the outside of the house should be painted in the fourth year of my tenancy. This was one of the objects for which the additional rent was to be paid. It will be of importance to me that the external appearance of the mansion should be maintained.

3. I have never contemplated having a boys school or boys and girls school, but I have a son about six years of age who will remain home for a few years. I hope that having one young gentleman of his own age as his companion to study and play will not be objected to if named at any time to you. (This was not agreed to by Mr Spode).

4. Allow me to say that in conclusion, that I have no intention to express myself discourteously in my last letter. It is true I was most vexed that I was not informed of the objections to the original agreement before I prepared to leave my present residence because the delay exposed me to much inconvenience and might have placed me at a serious disadvantage. I have no hesitation in asking you to accept my apology if my letter has the appearance of want of courtesy.
I am sir, Yours obediently,
Wm. Allbut

As a result of all these problems over the terms of the lease, the commencement of the painting and repairs to the property was delayed. Mr Allbut wrote to Mr Green on the 6th July asking for the commencement of the work as agreed. This work is listed in Mr Ward's report dated July 1st for which the estimate amounted to the sum of £132 16s 4d.

The correspondence points to the fact that The Mount was to be used as a residential school for girls by Mrs Allbut. Unfortunately, little documentation has survived. *The Potteries Mercury* was carrying advertisements from December 1840 advertising a Ladies School at Northwood. *Mrs William Allbut and Miss Mort's School will re-open after the Christmas vacation on Tuesday 19th January 1841. Terms: Board and Instruction in the usual branches of English Education, Needlework etc. - 30 guineas per annum. Day scholars 8 guineas per annum. The accomplishments are taught by highly qualified Masters; but they are considered subordinate to the acquition of useful knowledge and correct principles of conduct.*
The first reference to the new establishment at The Mount appeared in the *Potteries Mercury* on the 13th July 1844 (shortly following the sale on site for the former tenant Mr Lewis Adams) stating that the Ladies School had already removed from Northwood to its new premises at Penkhull described as *being near to Stoke-upon-Trent and Newcastle-under-Lyme.* The advertisement is minimal considering that her husband was the proprietor of the newspaper. It therefore

could be assumed that the school was already well established and required little else but a formal acknowledgement to a change of circumstances.

Six months later in January 1845, the newspaper ran a larger advert setting out what the school for young ladies had to offer. Firstly, the district of Stoke-upon-Trent has been dropped, reference being made only to that of Newcastle-under-Lyme, no doubt in an attempt to reduce its association with the industrial scars and habitations of that town in favour of the more genteel market town of Newcastle on the other side of the hill.

January 11th 1845 *Potteries Mercury.*

Establishment for Young Ladies, conducted by Mrs William Allbut and assistants.

The system pursued is as much on the domestic plan as possible, combining the advantages of home and school training. The aim of the Principal is to educate, not merely to instruct her pupils.

The course of study includes the usual branches of a polite English education. The French language is taught by a Lady who has resided some years in Paris. Physical education is regarded as one of the first importance; and in this respect The Mount possesses peculiar

advantages the situation being salubrious, the house large, airy, and commodious, and the pleasure grounds extensive.
TERMS; Borders 30 guineas per annum. Day Scholars 8 guineas per annum. The school will re-open after the Christmas vacation of Monday, January 27th 1845.

Two and a half years later, 17th July 1847, an advertisement for the commencement of the new term points to a considerable increase in fees, reflecting perhaps the more genteel and wealthy families that attended the school.
Mrs William Allbut respectfully intimates that the duties of her school will resume after the summer vacation, on Tuesday, the 27th of July.
Terms: Under twelve years of age, 40 guineas per annum. Above twelve, 50 guineas per annum.
These terms include all branches of a thorough English education;

also French by a resident Governess. In the domestic arrangements of the establishment, an attempt is made to combine the comforts and enjoyments of home with careful school trainings, while the delightful situation of The Mount, and the extent of the pleasure grounds, afford every facility for healthy recreation. Prospectuses may be had on application.

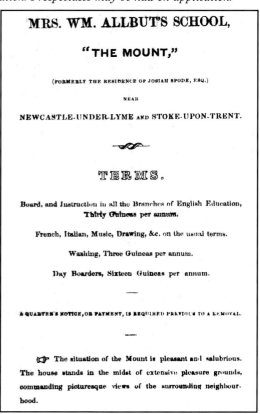

The census return for 1851 presents a well established school whose reputation stretched to almost the other side of the world. A full list of people attending the school gives an insight as to who attended, from which many conclusions can be drawn.

Name	Age.	Occupation	Place of Birth
William Allbut - Head. & Farmer of 43 acres	41	Newspaper Editor	Hanley
Sophia Allbut - Wife.	40	Principal of Ladies School.	Norton
Elizabeth Ann Allbut - Daughter.	11	Scholar.	Hanley
Thomas Henry Allbut - Son.	8	Scholar.	Hanley
Sophia Jane Allbut - Daughter.	6		Penkhull
Mary Dorothea Allbut - Daughter	3		Penkhull
Elizabeth Mort - Sister-in-law.	35	English Teacher	Kingston-upon-Hull
Amee Alexis Samson.	29	French Teacher	Native of France
Helen Mayer Ridgway.	29	Teacher of Music	Hanley
Ellen Allin.	45	Cook & Hse keeper	Stafford
Eliza Withinshaw.	18	Kitchen Maid	Norton
Catherine Ault.	30	Servant	Mar ton, Derby
Eliza Hoult.	18	Servant	Derby
Elizabeth Griffiths.	18	Servant	North Wales
Anne Jackson.	20	Nursery Maid	Eastwood, Staffs.
Mary Ann Southern - Visitor.	21		Manchester
Harriet Bancroft - Visitor.	20		Manchester
Sarah Allden.	15	Scholar	Birmingham
Mary Allden.	13	Scholar	Birmingham
Frances Allden.	11	Scholar	Birmingham
Agnes Allden.	9	Scholar	Birmingham
Jeanette Adshead.	11	Scholar	Staleybridge, Lancs.
Mary Bancroft.	14	Scholar	Manchester
Emily Carlton.	13	Scholar	Manchester
Hannah Carlton.	11	Scholar	Manchester
Fanny Cartwright.	14	Scholar	Birmingham
Elizabeth Cartwright.	12	Scholar	Birmingham
Edna Crabtree.	12	Scholar	Macclesfield
Caroline Dubel.	17	Scholar	Switzerland
Matilda Farraday.	17	Scholar	Birmingham
Eliza Ann*Gibbs.	15	Scholar	Manchester
Mary Rawson Hollins.	15	Scholar	Sheffield
Mary Sadler Kennedy.	16	Scholar	Burslem
Mary Kendall.	14	Scholar	Liverpool
Evelyn Macintyre.	13	Scholar	Longport, Staffs.
Margaret Mayall.	16	Scholar	Morphley, Lanes.
Isabella Metcalf.	15	Scholar	Keighley, Yorks .
Emily Oxenbould.	12	Scholar	Birmingham
Harriet Parks.	13	Scholar	Bury, Lancs
Harriet Rowbotham.	11	Scholar	Bedworth, Warks.
Eleanor Redfern.	15	Scholar	Oldham, Lancs.
Elizabeth Southern.	12	Scholar	Manchester.
Ann Maria Simmons.	17	Scholar	Oldham, Lancs.
Catherine Taylor.	17	Scholar	Oldham, Lancs.
Elizabeth Wilson.	13	Scholar	Liverpool
Eliza Wood.	14	Scholar	Ramsbottom, Lancs.
Alice Howarth.	9	Scholar	East Indies, Calcutta

At the same time as Wm. Allbut took possession, Mr Spode decided to rent out the produce section of garden occupying the area of the current Tilson Avenue, to local gardeners Burgess and Kent who were the former owners of what remains today as Lewis' Nursery in Newcastle Lane.

Lease dated 24th June 1844.

This indenture between the Trustees of Josiah Spode IV and John Burgess and Joseph Kent of Penkhull of Gardeners. And in consideration of a yearly rent of £25.

All those two pieces or parcels of garden ground adjoining each other adjacent to the mansion called The Mount surrounded by back walls including the hot houses green houses walls and other erections and carriage ways. Trees shrubberies and plants standing in place together with a road or carriageway from South Lodge and the mansion called The Mount to the use of John Burgess and Joseph Kent there from the 24th day of June instant for a term of seven years paying by equal payments half yearly on the 25th day of December and the 24th day of June in each year.

And also shall and will and sufficiently repair, maintain his garden, cleanse preserve and keep in good and tenantable order the green houses hot houses, walls and other erections and buildings now standing and being in and upon the premises and all the gates, rails, fences, ditches belonging to the same premises having, being first put into good and tenantable repair by the said Leasers at the commencement of the said term. And also shall and will at least during the continuance of the said term cause all such part of the green houses and other buildings gates, rail fences in or belonging to said premises with good oil paint it as and also shall at all times during the continuance of the said term keep the said gardens and orchard well cropped and manured and managed to the approved methods of gardening.

William Allbut left The Mount in 1853, it was let to Frederick Bishop, a solicitor. In 1855 Josiah Spode IV decided to sell, not only the mansion but the whole of his land in the area. The Staffordshire Advertiser dated the 19th May 1855 contained the following advertisement.

The Staffordshire Advertiser 19th May 1855.

This very choice and compact estate, situated at Penkhull, in the Parish of Stoke upon Trent in the County of Stafford, and within a mile of Stoke station on the North Staffordshire Railway, will shortly be offered for sale by auction, unless previously disposed of by private contract.

The estate, as it exists, offers a most desirable investment for a person having any business connection with the district, being a residence sufficiently in the country, beautifully situated, and yet within a convenient distance of the Pottery towns. It consists of a Mansion House, erected at a very large outlay; and about 130 acres of excellent land, having dry subsoil; with farmstead complete, and a lodge.

The mansion has a varied and extensive prospect looking across the valley towards the picturesque village of Clayton, and also, towards Trentham, so as to command a view of the hall, monument, etc. Its principal aspects are to the south and west, and it is well sheltered from the north and east. It comprises on the ground floor, three halls of the entrance, opening one into another, with handsome stone staircase; dining room, drawing room, and billiard room, all of ample size, Butler's pantry, two water closets, kitchen, servants hall, storeroom, scullery, wash house, back staircase, and large and excellent cellars. On the upper floor are eight best bedrooms, one of which serves either as a bedroom or dressing room, bathroom, water closet, four servants bedrooms laundry etc. The rooms are all large and have good proportions and the condition of the house is excellent.

In the stable yard, coach house, harness room, and stabling for ten horses. The pleasure grounds and gardens including green houses etc. are extensive and are all in good order and condition.

To capitalists and of those inclined to speculate, the estate offers advantages rarely to be met with for disposing of it in blocks for the building of villa residences, for which it unquestionably fully presents some of the most charming sights to

be found within many miles around; and its being offered for sale at this particular junction will supply the wants so much and so long felt in the district. Indeed the whole estate may be fairly considered to be building land.

A plan of the estate, carefully laid out so as to show its capability and how it may be most advantageously divided into building blocks for houses of all classes, has been prepared, and may be seen on application at the offices of Messrs Ward and Son, architects, of Hanley, in the Staffordshire Potteries; or of Messrs Landon and Gardner, solicitors, Rugeley, to whom parties are referred for permission to inspect the property, and for all further information relating thereto.

The estate was offered for sale by auction by Messrs Edwards but bids fell well below the reserve price of £15,000, the highest being £13,500 and consequently the property was withdrawn from sale. Twelve months later, Mr Bishop agreed to purchase the house and land from Spode. The Copyhold court records dated the 3rd October 1856 record the transaction.

To this court came George Barlow, representing Josiah Spode of Armitage Park, Esquire and Mary Spode of Brereton Lodge, widow, and in consideration of £15,500 paid to the said Josiah Spode by Frederick Bishop, surrendered to the Lord of the Manor according to custom; all that mansion house called The Mount together with the out buildings, pleasure grounds, gardens and avenues belonging to it. And all pieces of ground near The Mount called The Little Townsend, part of which is the site of three dwellings and The Large Close or Big Townsend formerly in several parts, Lower Spring Meadow, the Clover Leasow, the New Leasow, the boundaries of all of which have been much changed. The total contains in all 126 acres and 14 perches. And afterwards came the said Frederick Bishop and prays to be admitted to all the above premises and he pays the Lord one pound one shilling and one penny and is admitted according to the custom of the manor.

Following on from this court entry a further entry records the mortgage which Bishop undertook to complete the purchase of The Mount. The sum of £4,000 from Thomas and Abraham Beever; £3,000 from Robert Sutton; and £3,000 from Grosvenor, Frederick and Percival Hodgkinson.

While living at Penkhull, Mr Bishop was active and well admired in the village. He often allowed the church Sunday school to use the grounds of The Mount for the annual Sunday outing. He was a regular attendee of

Inside of the dome

the parish church, but seemed to have his children baptized equally between Penkhull and Hartshill churches and two of his children who died in infancy are buried in Penkhull churchyard. In addition, Bishop became patron of the living from 1870 to 1883, and during this time gave a piece of land for the extension of the church school in Penkhull, a fact already recorded in the chapter covering that subject.

The census return of 1861 gives an insight to the occupation of The Mount. Mr Frederick Bishop was aged 45 and his wife Eliza, four years his junior. He had nine children, from William, aged 17, and Caroline his sister, aged 16, down to Emily, aged 3, and Charles, aged 3 months. Mr Bishop employed a footman, Charles Capewell, aged 21, a cook, a nurse, a housemaid and an under nurse. Living there also was his sister-in-law, Penelope Bakers, aged 41. Considering the size of the mansion, there would be employed a number of local daily staff as servants and grounds men.

The Mount in recent times (2007)

When Bishop bought The Mount estate it was copyhold, and as such a less attractive proposition to a buyer than land held in freehold. Bishop intended to develop part of the estate for building. To increase the value of the land and the desirability of the area, he paid a nominal sum to the Duchy of Lancaster to have the former copyhold land made freehold.

Princes Road
Bishop then proceeded to lay out new roads across the estate, Princes Road being the most important. The maintenance of roads was the responsibility of the Stoke Highways Board until 1874 and then of the Borough of Stoke-upon-Trent.

Plots of building land for larger houses on the best sites were advertised. Land for smaller houses was sold to the Workmen's Land Society the development of which is covered in a further chapter. As the Workmen's Land Society had only a small frontage to Princes Road, most was retained for large house plots. Bishop's professional adviser was Charles Lynam, an established surveyor and architect of Stoke-upon-Trent.

For many years, there had been a footpath between Penkhull and the district which later become known as Hartshill. This crossed the land owned by Bishop who realised the importance of that area for development. His first intention was to close off that footpath as the Annual Minutes of the Stoke Highway Board dated 31st March 1860 record:

Mr R Steele said that he understood that Mr Bishop intended to stop up a footway leading from Hartshill to Penkhull. He would do his utmost to prevent this way being stopped up. The footways were constructed before the ownership of Mr Bishop. He (Mr Steele) considered that it was wrong for any man to stop up a road unless he first obtained the unanimous sanction of the parishioners to do so. (Hear, Hear). Mr T Oakden said that Mr Bishop had informed him that morning that he intended obtaining an Act of Parliament to construct a new road and that he would meet the Board on the subject. The Chairman intimated that a similar intention was entertained about the footpath from Hartshill to Newcastle.

Mr R Leason thought that as a body it was not the duty of the Board to prevent the stopping up of the road in question, but that as ratepayers they ought to be jealous when such a step was contemplated by anyone. Mr Oakden said he was sure Mr Bishop did not want to do anything by a "side wind". The effect of making a new road would be to make a wider way to Penkhull. Mr Leason had no doubt that the wider road would be an improvement, but the ratepayers must not forget that Mr Bishop was actuated by a desire to make a good road to his own property. To stop up the footways across the fields was to rob the poor man of the opportunity of leaving the highways for the purpose of having a pleasant walk. The Chairman expressed a strong feeling that the footway in question ought not to be stopped.

The following resolution was passed, *That if any attempt is made to close or interfere with the footpaths, the Board is requested to call a meeting of ratepayers to take this into consideration.*

Bishop had second thoughts, probably because he realised he needed only the infrastructure to be laid across his land for development to commence.

The next Annual Meeting of the Stoke Highway Board held on the 12th April 1862 reflect this change.

The Chairman, Mr R Leason, read a letter from Mr Bishop, of The Mount, dated December 17, 1861, giving note of his intention to dedicate to the public the new road recently made by him across The Mount estate from Penkhull to Hartshill. The Chairman read the clause of the Highways Act specifying the conditions under which a private road should be dedicated to the use of the public. The persons offering such a road to the public were required to give three months notice of their intention, to describe the situation and extent of such road, to make it in a substantial manner to the satisfaction of the Surveyor and of two Justices of the Peace, and to keep it in repair for twelve months, after which time it should be kept in repair by the Board of Highways.

After some conversation, in the course of which it was suggested that a public meeting might accept the road without applying to the Justices, Mr Bishop stated he did not pretend to know much of the Highway Act, which was very complicated, but it seemed to him that where the Highways Board thought it desirable to have such a road, there was no objection to their making it a public highway if they thought proper. With respect to the road in question, of course every ratepayer could judge whether it was a matter of sufficient importance to be made a highway. He might just say he had heard several persons express the opinion that it would be a great public convenience, and one gentleman had said that ever since he was a boy there had been a wish that there should be a road from Penkhull to Hartshill, and expressed his thanks to him (Mr Bishop) as had several others, for what they considered a matter of public advantage.

Mr Bishop did not claim any merit. He did not say he had made the road for public advantage. He had made it because he believed that he should at some future time receive the benefit of it in the increased value of his property, but at the same time the public would have the advantage of it. The road had cost him something like £1,000, and had taken up several acres of land, for which he asked nothing, and if the public thought it of sufficient importance to take it as a highway they were welcome to it.

The Chairman said that everybody admitted that the road was a great public convenience, and it was very much used. He thought it would be a great boon to the whole neighbourhood, and his thanks were due to Mr Bishop for his gift. Mr Lovatt proposed that Mr Bishop's offer be accepted, and the proposition was seconded by Mr Hulme, and carried unanimously. The Chairman, on behalf of the Board and the public, thanked Mr Bishop, who, after acknowledging the compliment, expressed a wish to consult the ratepayers in reference to laying out the footpaths etc.

Ten years later, the new road had fallen into disrepair. It would not have had a hard surface as roads do today, it would be made up of broken stones and lacked drainage at least on one side. Again the Stoke Highways Board met to debate the issue on the 3ʳᵈ August 1872.

There was another long discussion as to the unsatisfactory state of Princes Road, leading from Hartshill to Penkhull. A deputation from the Board had been appointed to wait upon Mr Bishop, of The Mount, and to consult as to the best course to pursue to effect an improvement. Mr Bishop had made an offer to contribute a certain sum if both sides of the road were paved, kerbed and channelled by the Board. The Highways Board felt they could not entertain this, in the first place because it was

contrary to their custom to pave both sides of such long roads, and in the next place, the funds would not admit of so large an outlay as would be required. The Board, however, decided that they should drain, pave, curb and channel one side of the road if Mr Bishop would contribute a fair amount towards the cost.

At a meeting held the following month on the 7ᵗʰ September 1872 the Stoke Highways Board decided to address the issue. *It was decided to proceed at once to put Princes Road from Hartshill to Penkhull in repair. The work will include the laying down of a drain and the construction of a footpath on one side with proper kerbing and channelling. Mr Bishop of The Mount has agreed to give £50 towards the expense. (The cost of the work was £280).*

It was suggested in 1860 that a park be established for the new Workingmen's estate on the Allotments. Mr Bishop gave ten acres of land for the park to become known as Penkhull Park. Donations were promised from Mr Colin Minton Campbell £500; Sir Lovelace Stamer, Rector of Stoke £100, Mr W Keary £100; Mr C Dickinson £100; Mr Richard Copeland £10 and Mr J. Dimmock £50. There were other small amounts donated together with a number of collections at nearby factories. Altogether several thousands of pounds were promised the scheme fell through, simply because a sufficient number of gentlemen could not be obtained to become trustees.

The Hartshill – Penkhull footpath

Mr Bishop was also involved in another issue at the same time, that of creating Quarry Road, again discussed by the Stoke Highways Board in April 1871.

1ˢᵗ April – Mr Nixon called attention to the threatened alteration in the footway leading from Stoke to Hartshill through the formation of a new road by Mr Bishop. After considerable discussion it was agreed that the public footpath, which was of a very great use by foot passengers ought not to be interfered with.

15ᵗʰ April – Mr Leason alluded to the attempt made to tamper with an ancient and very pleasant footpath at Hartshill. He was glad to see the Board make a stand against the rights of the people being tampered with impunity by people for their own convenience.

29ᵗʰ April – A letter was received from Mr Bishop relating to accusations made about the alterations of footpaths. A letter from Mr Leason was also read explaining that he had not intended to accuse Mr Bishop of having tampered with footpaths, he was solely concerned about the effect the new Quarry Road now being cut by that gentleman might have on public paths. The Highways Board disclaimed any intention of charging Mr Bishop with interfering with public paths.

Building Plots

It was the original intention of Bishop to sell off plots of land bordering the new Princes Road for the building of Villa Residences maintaining the prestige position they would have in relation to The Mount. He decided to advertise in the *Staffordshire Advertiser* on the 14th May 1859. The first sale was secured by the end of the year, but unfortunately for Bishop there were no further sales of building plots for nearly fifteen years. In the meantime Bishop decided to build a group of smaller dwellings consisting of a row of eleven terraced dwellings on the edge of The Mount estate at the top of Honeywall in 1861. As these dwellings were situated at the top end of Honeywall overlooking Penkhull Terrace and therefore because of their nearness to this earlier development, Bishop took the initiative to call this group of houses *North Terrace.* The site is now occupied by a small number of bungalows. The second section in the advertisement refers to land available in Princes Road.

To be sold, in large or small lots, to suit the convenience of purchasers, and at a moderate price, several plots of desirable building land, part of The Mount estate, fronting to the road from Penkhull to Stoke-upon-Trent. Also several lots laid out as sites for Villa Residences, in healthy and agreeable situations between Penkhull and Hartshill, with southern and western aspects, commanding beautiful and extensive scenery, entirely free from the smoke of the pottery and iron manufacturers, and within about a mile from Stoke railway station. The above land has been recently enfranchised by the Duchy of Lancaster, and purchasers will have the benefit of the cheapness, facility, and privacy of transfer, of having votes for the country, and other advantages of freehold tenure; and they may be accommodated with advances on deposit of their title deeds without the expense of mortgage. Apply Mr Lynam, Surveyor Stoke-upon-Trent or Messrs Bishop and Blakiston, Solicitors, Shelton.

During his time at Penkhull, Bishop sold a number of larger plots of land from the estate, including a ten acre site for the present North Staffordshire Royal Infirmary in 1864, the site of the present cemetery, and most of the land which extends from Princes Road down to Honeywall, although in individual plots.

Finally, Bishop decided to sell off The Mount and it was advertised for auction to be held on Tuesday, July 1st, 1873 at the North Staffordshire Hotel. The Sale document, prepared of the auctioneers Messrs Edwards describes The Mount as follows: *Situate at Penkhull comprising Mansion with offices, entrance lodge, stabling, coach-houses and coachman's dwelling, lawns, pleasure grounds and ornamental planting, flower gardens, walled kitchen gardens, conservatory, vineries, pasture land, fish pond &c. &c. measuring altogether 20 acres. The Mount was built by the late Josiah Spode, Esq., for*

his own residence, at a cost exceeding £20,000. The excellence of its design, the character of the materials and workmanship employed in it, and the completeness of its arrangements will appear from the accompanying plan, and a report submitted by Mr Lynam on the structural details.

On 30th October, 1875, the remainder of the estate including the mansion house was sold to Mr John Bromley for the sum of £8,000, a mortgage for which was held by Mr John Adams. One interesting fact is that while Mr Bromley lived at The Mount, he married at the age of 45, Louisa Jackson, aged 21, of Penkhull Terrace in February 1880.

"The Mount," near Stoke-upon-Trent,
STAFFORDSHIRE.

TO BE SOLD BY AUCTION,
BY

MESSRS. EDWARDS,
AT THE

North Staffordshire Hotel,
STOKE-UPON-TRENT,

ON TUESDAY, JULY 1ST, 1873,
At Four o'clock in the Afternoon (for Five punctually),

SUBJECT TO CONDITIONS TO BE THEN PRODUCED:

THE IMPORTANT FREEHOLD

RESIDENTIAL PROPERTY,
Called "THE MOUNT,"

SITUATE AT PENKHULL, STOKE-UPON-TRENT, IN THE COUNTY OF STAFFORD,

Comprising MANSION with Offices, Entrance Lodge, Stabling, Coach-houses and Coachman's Dwelling, Lawns, Pleasure Grounds, and Ornamental Planting, Flower Gardens, Walled Kitchen Gardens, Conservatory, Vineries, Pasture Land, Fish-pond, &c., &c., as shown on the accompanying Plan, measuring altogether **20a. 1r. 33p.** ; and with the option to the Purchaser of taking any portion of the surrounding Turf Land at a valuation.

The Bromley family took an active part in the life of the village, and like their predecessors, allowed the church to use the grounds of The Mount for various activities. The mortgage was held by different people until 1889 when it passed to Warwick Savage and Robert Clement Clive. By 1891, Warwick Savage had died and in March 1896, Clement Clive, who was a colliery proprietor, decided to further split up the estate and sell The Mount.

Old entrance to The Mount Blind and Deaf School

The mansion was then left with 17 acres, the same amount as when Josiah Spode II purchased it in 1803. It was sold to the North Staffordshire Joint School Authority for the sum of £3,606 on the condition that The Mount should not be used for any other purpose other than for public elementary education. It also stated that the School Authority should pay half the cost of constructing sewers, curbing and laying of footpaths on one side of Greatbatch Avenue. The site was purchased in 1896 and after considerable extensions the school was formally opened on the 3rd May 1897 by Mr Godfrey Wedgwood.

The Staffordshire Advertiser covered the opening and reported the following on Monday, 8th May 1897.
The scheme is the outcome of the Elementary Education Act of 1893, which threw upon school authorities the responsibility of educating the blind and deaf children in their districts. Mainly by the efforts of Mr Godfrey Wedgwood and Mr W H Bishop, both of whom have devoted much attention to the welfare of the children afflicted by the deprivation of sight or hearing, the School Boards of the district were brought into line on this subject, and a joint authority was formed for providing and carrying on a blind and deaf school for North Staffordshire.

An eligible situation was acquired at The Mount, Penkhull, the mansion being designed to furnish part of the school accommodation required but as the project developed, one of the Boards that of Newcastle demurred to the increased estimates and withdrew from the scheme leaving the joint authority to be composed of representatives of Hanley, Wolstanton, Longton, Burslem, Stoke, and Norton School Boards.

The house is an oblong building with a semicircular entrance of stone on its west front. An elegant and lofty dome gives an interior grandeur to the structure. This latter feature, and indeed the whole of the principal facade of the mansion, has been preserved, and converted into the administrative department. The plans of Messrs. Scrivener and Son, of Hanley, for the adaptation of the old building to its new purpose and the extensive additions thereto were adopted by the authority and approved of by the Education Department, the total cost of the undertaking reaching the sum of £20,000.

The exterior is of simple character, to harmonize with the old part, except that two towers have been added for ventilating purpose. Within them are placed water storage tanks. The fittings are of the most modern type especially suited to the special class of teaching required in such an institution, and the central hall is fitted with gymnastic appliances so as to serve a dual purpose as assembling and teaching hall and gymnasium. Asphalted playgrounds for each department are provided and the 7 acres of grounds provide football field and gardens, where gardening may be taught and recreation obtained. Care has been taken to provide against panic from fire, as there are in all six staircases in the building, and fire hydrants at various points outside, together with hose to attach to them, and fire buckets are placed at convenient places inside. There is accommodation for 139 children and the necessary teaching and servant staff.

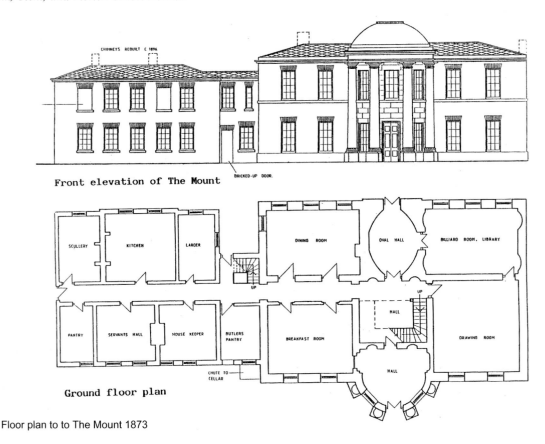

Front elevation of The Mount

Ground floor plan

Floor plan to to The Mount 1873

Chapter 14
Law, Order and Social Concern.

The Penkhull Association of the Prosecution of Felons

In England, well down to the middle of the nineteenth century, the responsibility for the initiation of criminal prosecution in the courts rested on the victim, who was also usually left to decide on the severity and nature of the charges. Criminal prosecution was, in other words, rather more like civil litigation. Private prosecution, however, was expensive. Only wealthy people could afford to pay for a lengthy court trial. The practice of paying magistrates to issue arrest warrants was common. Often the threat of prosecution was hung over someone's head as a guarantee of future good behaviour. During the 18th century it was not just for assaults but also for all thefts and even for some murders that it was left to the general public to bring a prosecution. Therefore the responsibility for the initial expense and the entire conduct of bringing someone to justice was thrown on the victim or their family. As late as the mid 19th century no public official was responsible for ensuring that even the most serious offences were prosecuted.

The difficulties of private prosecution were compounded by the absence of an effective police force capable of tracking down offenders. In cases of burglary, it was difficult for victims to trace those responsible. The growth of newspapers in the latter half of the eighteenth century aided the process as people would advertise and offer a reward for information. As a direct consequence of an inappropriate legal system, wealthy people in a defined district would form themselves into Associations for the Prosecution of Felons. These organisations took subscriptions, much like an insurance company and could hire 'thief takers', who today would be called private detectives, to seek out the criminals on their behalf.

The magnitude of the problem of public disorder grew at an alarming rate as the population in towns increased to satisfy the demands of the industrial revolution. For the period covering the late 18th and early 19th centuries, the severity of the problem may be appreciated from the fact that the number of Associations for the Prosecution of Felons, founded in Staffordshire alone, amounted to between 130 and 140.

The associations were formed as a means of mutual protection for communities in a period between the disappearance of the manorial courts, the hue and cry pursuit, and the introduction of a civil police force and a publicly funded prosecution service.

The district of Penkhull was first included in the Stoke-upon-Trent Association for the Prosecution of Felons founded in 1798. By 1806, the residents of Penkhull formed their own entitled the Penkhull Association for the Prosecution of Felons with fourteen members. John Townsend was the first treasurer and other members included were John Burgess, Michael Baxter, James Finney and Thomas Harrison. A member from the town of Stoke was Thomas Highfield and those of Penkhull Lane were represented by George Fitchett, Thomas Austin, James Warner, Thomas Knight, William Austin, Robert Stevenson, John Chapman, and for Clayton by Richard Bill.

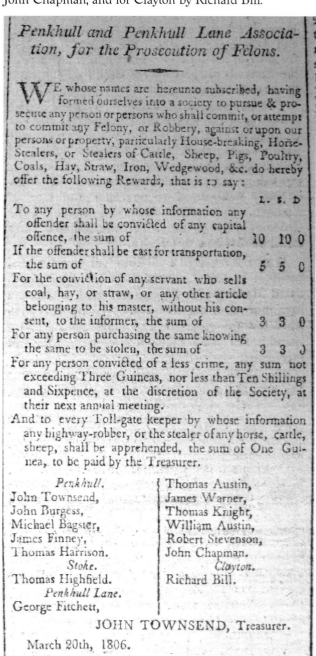

The Staffordshire Advertiser April 1806

The first advertisement for this new association appeared in the Staffordshire Advertiser in 1806 and opens with the familiar introduction used by all Associations for the Prosecution of Felons. *We whose names are hereto subscribed, having formed ourselves into a society to pursue and prosecute any person who shall commit, or attempt to commit any Felony, or Robbery, against or upon our persons or property, particularly House-breaking, Horse-stealers, or Stealers of Cattle, Sheep, Pigs,*

Poultry, Coals, Hay, Straw, Iron, Hedge-wood &c. do hereby offer the following Rewards, that is to say.

To any person whose information any offender shall be convicted of any capital offence, the sum of £10 10s. If the offender shall be cast for transportation the sum of £5 5s. For the conviction of any servant who sells coal, hay, or straw, or any other article belonging to his master, without his consent, to the informer, the sum of £3 3s.

For any person convicted of a lesser crime, any sum not exceeding Three Guineas, nor less than Ten Shillings and six pence, at the discretion of the Society, at their next annual meeting. And to every Toll-gate keeper by whose information any highway-robbery, or the stealer of hay horse, cattle, sheep, shall be apprehended, the sum of One Guinea, to be paid by the Treasurer. Signed John Townsend, March 20th, 1806.

Many societies throughout the country were formed in a similar way to that of Penkhull with the objects of securing a conviction. Locally the first association of its kind was formed in 1694 as an association for the discovery and prosecution of horse stealers for the Parish of Stoke with sixteen members. The first Association for Hanley, an Association that still meets today under that name but restricts itself to that of a Gentleman's Dining Club came later in 1762.

Other local villages and towns commenced their Associations. Endon and Stoke in 1805, Seaford, Stableford and Trentham 1806; Burslem, Cobridge, Longport, Tunstall and Uttoxeter 1808; Caverswall, Barlaston, Bradeley, Gnosall, Knutton and Wolstanton 1808. Even in the small village of Ashley an association was deemed necessary, theirs being formed in 1812. The association for Burslem town only was formed later in 1821, and like that of Hanley, still meets today.

By May 1807, the Penkhull association boasted sixteen members, all from within the Penkhull area. The rewards offered were reduced. The previous rewards of £10 10s and £5 5s being dropped. Also the list of offences of included is more specific. *Murder, burglary, highway-robbery or foot pad robbery, or stealing any horse, mare, gelding, cattle, or sheep, or setting fire to any building, corn, grain, or hay, or straw, or other offences, whereof the offenders shall be capitally convicted, the sum of £3 3s. For stealing pigs, geese, or any kind of fowls. £1 1s. For robbing any garden, orchard or fishpond, stealing hay, straw, turnips, potatoes, or corn; stealing, or wilfully destroying any grass mowed or un-mowed, or corn in the fields; for stealing, cutting down or destroying any tree, under wood, gates, stiles, walls, pales, hedges, posts, wagons, carts or any implements of husbandry, or any iron, wood, bricks, stones, or thing or things, affixed or belonging to any messuage or outhouse, gate or otherwise, upon conviction for the same £1 1s.*

A new crime was also introduced, no doubt where the members of an association were in all probability producers or dealers in coal. *For selling coals from wagons and carts. For the information of the buyer or seller of coals, on conviction, the sum of £1 1s. And for any offence not being specified, a reward will be given according to the atrociousness of the crime.*

In this advertisement just about every eventuality had been covered. This was unusual at the time in its format. However, it does itemise the type of crimes that may be associated with those living in agricultural areas. For many of the offences the courts would have issued the death sentence or transportation.

PENKHULL ASSOCIATION
For prosecution of Felons and other Offences.

We those whose names are hereinafter mentioned, inhabitants of the Township of Penkhull, in the County of Stafford, having entered into an Association for the prosecution of any persons or persons who shall commit any murder, burglary, highway robbery, felony, larceny, or other offence, of upon, or against any of our persons or properties; do hereby offer the following rewards for the detection and apprehension of such offender or offenders, to be paid upon conviction, by the Treasurer, viz.
For murder, burglary, highway robbery, or foot pad robbery, or stealing any horse, mare, gelding, cattle, or sheep, or setting fire to any building, corn, grain, or hay, or straw, or other offences, whereof the offenders or offender shall be capitally convicted, the sum of   £3 3 0d

For stealing, pigs, geese, or any kind of fowls. For robbing any garden, orchard, or fishpond, stealing hay straw, turnips, potatoes, or grass mowed or un-mowed, or corn in the field, for stealing, cutting down, or destroying any tree or trees, under-wood, gates, stiles, walls, pales, rails, hedges, posts, wagons, carts, or any implements of husbandry, or any iron, wood, bricks, stones, or thing or things, affixed or belonging to any messuage, outhouse, gate or otherwise, upon conviction for the same.   £1 1 0d
For selling coals from wagons and carts. For the informer of the buyer or seller of coal, on conviction, the sum of.   £1 1 0d

And any offence not before specified, a reward will be given according to the atrociousness of the crime.

John Chapman	William Austin
George Fitchett	John Burgess
Thomas Knight	Thomas Austin
Thomas Harrison	Michael Baxter
Mr. Hughfield	John Finney
Robert Stevenson	James Warner
Richard Bill	William Houlden
John Townsend	Samuel Nicklins

JOHN TOWNSEND, Treasurer and Secretary
March 3, 1807

The following year, 1808, the Annual Meeting of the association was held on the 2nd March at the home of Thomas Knight, The Black Lion, Penkhull Lane. On this occasion the financial rewards of £10 10s and £5 5s were reintroduced with the additional reward of 5s for any person convicted of a less crime not exceeding three guineas.

In 1810, a notice of an Association for the Prosecution of Felons for the town of Stoke-upon-Trent appeared. The meeting of its members was to be held at the home of Mrs Johnson, The King's Arms, in what was then Market Street, but now Hill Street, Stoke, *on Wednesday the 25th April at ten o'clock in the forenoon to transact the necessary business of the society.*

As the notice refers to existing members of the Association it would appear that the association was founded earlier than this date as in its conclusion there is also reference to any previous members, who were also invited to attend the meeting. The only conclusion that can be drawn from this press announcement and based upon the fact that no advertisement had appeared in the press for the previous four or five years, infers that the association had ceased to function. New members were being encouraged to join in the form of a revival.

The objects of the Stoke association appear from the introduction to be more stringent than the Penkhull association. This probably reflects the frustration of the pottery manufacturers and trades people at the lack of any pursuit of criminals. *We, the Members of the Association call for the more effectual and expeditious pursuit, apprehension and vigorous prosecution of all offenders against our persons or property, do hereby offer the following rewards to be paid on the conviction of highway robbers or foot pads, stealers of horses, cattle or sheep, persons trespassing on our lands, or destroying or pilfering the fences thereof, suffering their pigs to go astray, stealers of pigs, poultry, coals, hay, straw or iron, or offenders of any other indiscretion, cognizable before the civil magistrates.*

Members of the Stoke association numbering nineteen were listed as follows: Josiah Spode, William Kenwright, Richard Shaw, Thomas Allen, Samuel Spode, Jacob Marsh, William Bagnall, Thomas Poulson, William Johnson, Thomas Broade, Thomas Minton, Hugh Booth, Robert Bill, Daniel Whalley, James Greaves, Joseph Booth, Joseph Whalley, John Tomlinson and John Kirkham.

The following year, the Penkhull Association saw an increase in membership to nineteen and for the first time included the names: William Glover, Francis Bill, Richard Butters, William Houlding, Samuel Nickling, J Davis, James Cash and Thomas Gething. The meeting, like the previous meeting was to be held at the home of Mr Thomas Knight, The Black Lion in Penkhull Lane on Wednesday 6th March. The rewards for information remained the same as the previous year.

In 1815, the association continued to thrive and offered substantial rewards for information. £10 was offered for information leading to a capital offence. There were changes in its membership. John Townsend was no longer listed and the position of treasurer was held by Mr William Glover and the following new names appeared on the list: J E Pool, John Boot, Samuel Kirkham, John Salmon, Samuel Doncaster, Francis Mole, Richard Turnock, Daniel Cotton and William Swetmore.

The last advertisement for the Penkhull association was in 1820. There after it would appear that it became absorbed in the Stoke-upon-Trent association, as in 1834 four of its residents are listed as living in Penkhull. From the end of this decade there was a considerable reduction in press notices advertising the activities of associations, a clear indication of their demise probably because policing powers were given to the Commissioners for the Stoke district by an Act of 1839, and the appointment of a Chief Bailiff, watchmen and beadles.

Police Force and Punishments

From 1839, the organisation of the police became the responsibility of the Chief Bailiff. He appointed a single superintendent of police. In August of that year, a superintendent and two policemen were appointed for the town of Stoke-upon-Trent and district and a house in Liverpool Road was leased for three months as a temporary station. Concerns caused by the Chartist riots in August 1842 which aroused fears that the size of the police force was inadequate, which led to the establishment of a County force in Stoke the following year, a measure which had been firmly opposed in 1839, and again the following year, on the ground of expense.

These early years of the 19th century were difficult times for the manufacturing classes. The need for some form of law and order cannot be underestimated. Living conditions along with poverty forced many desperate people into crime. The punishments were severe, many being sentenced to death or to a period of transportation. But those in employment fared little better, for the treatment by many employers could be referred to as barbaric. Young boys were beaten across their backs with a clay cutting wire for simple things such as not having lit the stove early enough in the morning. Many young children were found by the inspectors to be living on the premises where they worked and having to find a small corner in the workshop, along with a bundle of straw, which would provide some comfort at night.

The *Potteries Mercury* reports contain many examples.
In April 1830, one young boy, William Rowley, aged 14, pleaded guilty at a court held locally to stealing an ass, the property of Ann Boulton. The chairman of the juvenile court stated that because Rowley had become associated with evil people this was taken into consideration and that he (the chairman) wished to restore the young man to virtuous habits and remove him from such bad influences. It was therefore decided not to have the young lad executed but that his sentence be commuted to confinement in one of his Majesty's hulks (ships) where pains would be taken to instil principles of a different kind to those which were now so firmly fixed in the lad's mind: *seven years transportation.*

Thomas Finny, aged 19, appeared at the same court charged with stealing a quantity of earthenware from Mr George

Collins of Stoke. Finny pleaded guilty. He was sentenced to transportation for the term of seven years.

Philip Jones, aged 16, was charged with stealing one rasp from John Meacham, in addition to two other rasps from Mr James Meacham at a court held in 1827. Jones was transported for seven years.

In January 1830, Job Morris, John Williams, Thomas Privatt and Josh Johnson of Hanley and Shelton were found guilty of having on Sunday night, 22nd November, stolen from a cart in the gig house of the New Inn, Hanley £1 18s in copper, the property of a pot seller Wm. Lewis. They were sentenced to be further imprisoned for one month and to be whipped.

On the 20th March 1830, William Darby was charged with stealing a sheep, the property of George Stronhitharm, was found guilty and sentenced to death. At a further court held on the 7th August 1830 the following appeared and were sentenced. James Harrison for stealing from the home of William Leek of Newcastle, three £20 notes of the Stafford Old Bank. Pleaded guilty and sentenced to death. John Bayley who was tried and convicted for receiving them knowing they were stolen was sentenced to gaol for one year.

Joseph Mellor and Isaac Mellor for breaking into the house of Samuel Smith at Cheadle, and stealing a silk handkerchief and money. Sentence of death recorded.

Joseph Middleton, Richard Lymer and Richard Beard for breaking into the shop of John Durose and stealing a quantity of leather shoes and boots. A sentence of death recorded.

The press cuttings for 1842 show similar sentences were being administered by other courts. *Potteries Mercury* 9th April 1842; Eli Cooper, aged 15 years, for stealing one pair of stockings, the property of James Saville & Co. of Longton. Two months imprisonment.

No doubt because of the extreme poverty when shoes for many were considered a luxury and many would go bare-foot it was not un-common for shoes and boots to be stolen. William Osborne, 15 and Joseph Worthington, 13, for stealing one pair of cloth boots, the property of Henry Plant, seven years transportation each.

Absalom Nixon, 42, for stealing one duck, the property of Richard Shirley of Stoke-upon-Trent, two months imprisonment.

Ralph Brammer, 25, for feloniously embezzling a quantity of eggs to the value of £3 and upwards, the property of his master, Richard Kelsall. Three months' hard labour.

James Davenport, 20, for stealing a piece of beef, the property of Mary Thorpe, six months imprisonment.

We conclude with an unusual case heard at Stafford, of William White, a surgeon of West Bromwich. White was found guilty, on two separate indictments. The first was that of stealing an ivory case, a shirt-pin, a neckerchief, and a handkerchief. The second charge was of stealing a Queen Ann's sixpence. The press was informed that the prisoner, who occupied a respectable position in society, was on the point of marriage with a lady of considerable fortune; and so confident was she of his innocence, that she attended his trial with the expectation of their reunion under happier circumstances. The result, however, proved the futility of some of the most cherished expectations of hope, for he was found guilty, and sentenced to be transported for seven years.

In many cases where the verdict was *sentence of death recorded* the punishment was commuted to being transported to the colonies for either seven or fourteen years. Most never returned.

Those who were sentenced to death endured one of the most horrific punishments, as it was then considered a public amusement. One such execution was that of George Jackson, convicted for what was to become known as the Abbots Bromley Murder. Jackson was executed at Stafford on Saturday 8th August 1857 at 10.00 a.m. Such was the known hunger for the sordid details of the event, that the Staffordshire Sentinel published a one-page supplement to the edition of that day. The pictorial account is typical of the period.

Hanging

The story reproduced here is picked up when the correspondent commences with the events of the day, beginning on the Friday night.

At length the night preceding the fatal morning came; and never did more dismal night precede more dismal morning. The rain came on heavily with midnight, and lent additional horrors to the contemplation of the scene that was about to be taking place. Cold, cheerless, dismal, drooping, the most depressing was Stafford at midnight on Friday, for unlike the hours preceding the execution of Palmer, there were not the galleries and platforms, the windows, commanding a full view of the scaffold, filled with 'fashionable parties', nor the crowd, the muster, and the excitement which prevailed on that occasion.

While the convict waited in dread the arrival of the fatal hour every highway was being travelled by persons hastening to see the sight; and as we passed along we overtook crowds hastening along in sullen, drenching rain, and passed others seeking shelter under trees or in hovels by the road side. On reaching Stafford, we found the public houses full, owing to the same cause, and as day dawned and broke crowds continued to arrive on foot, on horseback, and in vehicles. The avenues to the gaol became thronged; and we have never heard more ribaldry, or witnessed more levity in the anticipation of such a scene, then were presented on this occasion.

The anticipation of the officials that the courage of the wretched culprit would be completely destroyed ere the fatal hour came was terribly realised, and the scene within the goal was one of the most fearful character. About three o'clock in the morning, the Rev R H Goodacre, the chaplain and his assistant, the Rev J Bowden, visited Jackson in the condemned cell, and found him in a state of terror, and unable to reply to the questions which they put to him. Then came the officials with the terrible summons to prepare for death, when he became terribly excited, and fell into a most pitiful paroxysm of tears, sobs, and groans, and continued in this state until brought out of the condemned cell to be pinioned.

In vain the Chaplain and the Assistant Chaplain told him of hope and mercy beyond the grave; the contemplation of the grave; and the ignominious road he must travel to it, absorbed all his shattered faculties; and "Oh dear," "Oh dear," was the continuous sound, uttered in a tone of anguish, which escaped his lips. When the fatal knell tolled his paroxysms considerably increased, he sobbed and groaned with increased intensity, and struggled so violently, that it was only with great effort that four stout warders could bear him to the scaffold, sobbing, groaning, struggling, and exclaiming piously, "Lord, have mercy upon me!" "Lord, have mercy upon me!" At length the procession, headed by Mr Hand, the Acting Sheriff; Col. Hogg, the Chief Constable accompanied by the Chaplain, and the Assistant Chaplain, reached the scaffold.

The scene on the drop was of a most sickening character. Bore thither as he was, and seated in a chair which had been prepared for him, tied and struggling, his whole frame was convulsed; his eyes expressed the most alarmed anxiety; the movements of his hands corresponded; his sighs, his exclamations were most harrowing. The rope was, however, speedily placed around his neck by the hangman, the fatal noose adjusted, the cap drawn over his eyes, when as if by a mixture of premeditation and spasmodic terror, he raised his hand, bent his head, and grasped and removed the cap. Again was the cap adjusted, and he was kept by main force from repeating that effort; but working himself with terrible muscular violence, and in the agonies of anticipated death, had not the drop instantly fallen, he would have overcome hempen ropes and human sinews, and thrown himself from the chair.

An audible murmur was expressed, a felt horror pervaded the crowd while this was going on; but, a short struggle, a few liftings, heavings, and shuddering of the frame and he swung a lifeless corpse in the murky air and under the sullen rain. Accustomed as are the officers of the gaol to witnessing painful scenes, they declared this to have surpassed everything which they ever witnessed, a scene so strongly contrasting with that presented on the occasion of the execution of Palmer, as to suggest whether they could have been creatures of the same order and kind.

The crowd was variously affected; but we question if any were beneficially influenced. Three or four thousand gazers

gradually and quietly withdrew. The body, after hanging the legal time, being cut away, was buried within the prison.

Climbing Boys

This report is just one aspect of life both nationally and locally during this period. A further example which sadly portrays the working conditions under which young boys were expected to work and the value placed upon a young life is conveyed by an article in the *Potteries Mercury* on the 24th April 1830, under the heading 'Climbing Boys'.

On Friday morning the chimney of a government building took fire, and burnt with fury upwards of an hour, when, by covering the top with mats &c., it was subdued, if not extinguished. The sweep was on the spot, and sent a boy down the chimney. He dropped himself through it almost at once, and cried when he came out, having it is said, hurt his foot. He was again sent down, crying, from the top of the chimney, a hammock having fallen, or been thrown before him. Soon after cries of distress were heard, and a rope was let down, which he grasped two or three times, but could not hold fast. A loop was then made at the end of the rope, and he was told to put it over his head, but replied that he could not. His voice was heard no more.

After a delay of some time in an attempt to find the right chimney it was finally broken into in several places before the young boy was found, head downwards, completely roasted from the waist upwards, the scull being bared. The hammock under him had taken fire. He was an interesting boy about ten years of age. Whether coercion was sued or not will appear at the inquest. The master appeared, on ordinary occasions, kind to his boys, but the horrors of a system, from which such a catastrophe can result, must be great. The boy was an illegitimate child, fondly loved by his mother, and, but for this, would not have been a parish apprentice and a sweep.

In 1841 Mr Samuel Scriven, a Government Inspector was sent to Stoke-on-Trent to report on the serious issue of the employment of child labour in the pottery industry. Scriven also recorded how many scholars were receiving an education, both within the Sunday school system and the day schools and the relationship between the numbers of children and teachers. For example whilst Penkhull was teaching 40 infants with one teacher, Kidsgrove was teaching 292 with 3 teachers, Tunstall 402 with 4 and Burslem 429 also with four teachers.

Mr Scriven commences his extensive report with the following introduction: *I have the honour to lay before you the evidence that I have collected relating to the physical and moral condition of the children labouring in the important district of the Staffordshire Potteries, which comprise the parishes and townships of Stoke-upon-Trent, Longton, Fenton, Lane Delph, Hanley, Shelton, Cobridge, Burslem, Longport, and Tunstall, extending from north to south, a distance of nine miles, of unequal breadth of from one to three miles, and having a population of 70,000 souls, chiefly of the working classes.*

The reports of child labour are numerous so only a small number of examples have been chosen to enable the reader to have an understanding of the period being addressed. The first is taken from Benjamin Taylor, aged 12 years who worked for Messrs Minton and Boyle in Stoke.

I have worked in the pressroom 2 years; I come at half past 6 in the morning, and leave at 6 at night. I have half hour for breakfast, 1 hour for dinner. I make cockspurs to place ware upon when it is baked; have one brother working in the same room. It is 4 shillings a week; don't know what brother gets, he is older; got a mother, but no father: father has been dead 10 years; he was a presser; working here; he died of consumption; he was 49, when he died. I give my money to my mother; get nothing for myself; never work more hours. I go to Sunday-school down to Methody's; can read, can write, can cipher a little; can tell how much 3 times 7 is, 21; 4 times 9 is 36; my health is pretty good; can eat, drink; and sleep pretty well. I find it very hot in the workroom and very cold when I go out. I make no difference in clothing, summer or winter; believe there are no boys or girls in the works who do night-work. I get meat for dinner three or four times a-week; other day's milk and tatoes. Some times open the window, but can't stand the draught.

The next entry is from George Burton, aged 9 years. He works also at Messrs Minton and Boyle of Stoke.

I work in the oven as stoker, and carry coal to the fires; begin work at 6 o'clock and leave at 5; I do not attend at night; the oven-man, Henry Reach, does that from 9 o'clock at night to 5 in the morning; he then goes home. He's the fireman; there are 6 as takes it in their turn, so that one man only sits up two nights a-week. His father does the same work as him.

I don't know how much wages I get a week; all goes to father; he sometimes gives me a penny, sometime two pence. I can't read, can't write. I went to Sunday school; don't go now; there is no school belonging to the works. I am in good health; I have a good appetite; I get bread and cheese for dinner, sometimes tatoes and bacon; never get ale. I feel the cold on coming out of oven, 'tis very hot there; I get very thirsty there. This is all the clothes I got; I have no change at home for Sunday. Overseer is kind to me, so is master. I never get a strapping, except sometimes from father.

For years arsenic was used in the mixture of colours. Glaze included lead and although it was known to be dangerous to health, manufacturers still used lead in glaze to give whiteness and high quality sheen. Dippers, because of the dangerous nature of the job were the highest paid workers in the factory. A dipper had a life expectancy of about 40 years but in many cases workers were susceptible to lead poisoning and therefore many died within 12 months of starting work. Women and children were more susceptible than men. It was not until 1898 that any restriction on age was introduced into the industry. The workers were willing to work with lead because it was highly paid and perhaps thought wrongly, that they would be one of the lucky ones not to suffer as a result. These precious examples convey a picture of the social working conditions found in the pottery industry.

Social unrest, the Chartist Riots.

Chartism was the greatest working-class movement in nineteenth-century Britain. It was a movement for democracy: The Chartist Movement had at its core the so-called 'People's Charter' of 1838. This document, created for the London Working

Chartists Riots

Men's Association, was primarily the work of William Lovett. The charter was a public petition aimed at redressing omissions from the electoral Reform Act of 1832. It quickly became a rallying point for working class agitators for social reform who saw in it a 'cure-all' for all sorts of social ills. The early supporters this Charter saw it as an initial step towards a social and economic revolution.

The Chartists believed that only through a working class representation would the House of Commons become thoroughly democratic and take action to improve the condition of their class and remedy the appalling problems of poverty, misery and deprivation, which were associated with the Industrial Revolution. The movement reached its highest peak of mass support in the severe years of early Victorian depression, unemployment and hunger.

It was possibly because its demands were deemed excessive by its supporters that it eventually faded out. The large number of demands probably diluted support for any one single objective.

The People's Charter outlined 6 major demands for reform.
These were:
Institution of a secret ballot
General elections be held annually
Members of Parliament not be required to own property
MPs be paid a salary
Electoral districts of equal size
Universal male suffrage

The first gathering of Chartist delegates took place in London on the 4th February 1839. As the law stipulated that no public gathering of over 50 men were forbidden they took care that the number present at any one time did not exceed this amount. At this gathering some delegates favoured violence if necessary, some favoured a general strike, and there was even talk of electing a 'people's parliament'. The Convention finally adopted the motto 'peaceably if we may, forcibly if we must'. This, by its very nature, probably frightened a number of the more moderate middle-class members who might have been persuaded to support their cause.

The Chartists' demands were of long standing. In 1815, following the Napoleonic war popular radicalism had surfaced. The Act of 1832 brought change only on a very modest scale. Industrial towns, like the new Parliamentary Borough of Stoke-on-Trent, gained representation at last with elected two M.P.s. The new voters however, were almost all middle-class and only one adult male in seven had the vote. Working-class radicals saw the 1832 Act as a betrayal; while most middle-class reformers gratefully accepted the small gains achieved.

Locally, the colliers were aggrieved because their wages were being reduced. They also had long-standing complaints with regards to the exploitative habits of colliery charter-masters (the middle men) and the profiteering of those who ran the company owned stores. *(Truck method of payment)* At Westminster, the government was so panicked at the possibility of full-blown national revolution that they ordered what was as yet an infant police force to keep a close eye on any Chartist activity, and to record it diligently. There were many disturbances throughout the country with processions, petitions and strikes for better pay.

At its height, the General Strike of 1842 involved up to half a million workers and covered an area which stretched from Dundee and the Scottish coalfields to South Wales and Cornwall. It lasted twice the length of the 1926 General Strike, and was the most massive industrial action to take place in Britain - and probably anywhere - in the nineteenth century.

At the root of the strike were the swingeing wage cuts that accompanied a downturn in trade. The economy had been in desperate straits for a full five years since the end of the war. But the strike grew into something far more than a strike for wages as workers took up the political demands espoused by Chartism. This led to confrontation, not just with employers but also with the state.

William Benbow, a self-educated Lancashire radical, had worked out the idea for a general strike in detail more than a decade before the events of 1842. Benbow had published

his proposals in a pamphlet entitled *Grand National Holiday and Congress of the Productive Classes*. Over the same period, the unions were also developing - changing in kind from secretive brotherhoods with pseudo-masonic rituals into early industry-wide organisations of the sort that would, despite the setbacks of the early 1830s, become commonplace in mid and late Victorian Britain.

During the summer of 1842, colliers in Staffordshire walked out over proposals to reduce their wages, and for the first time demands for shorter hours and better pay began to be linked with a demand that the People's Charter be made the law of the land. The unrest spread, and in July began to centre on South East Lancashire, where, in response to demands for a wage cut of 25% the mill workers of Ashton, Stalybridge, Dukinfield and Hyde called meetings to formulate their demands for a return to the wage levels of earlier years and to plan their next move.

August 7th was a crucial day: two mass meetings of workers from Ashton and Stalybridge were held on Mottram Moor, and support was given for a *Grand National Turn-Out* to begin the following day. Support for the Charter was incorporated into the resolutions passed. The next day, the turnout began as workers left their factories and began to move from workplace to workplace, turning out other workers to join them. Most of the northern industrial towns came out in support, not only in Manchester but in the towns around it Preston, Burnley, Blackburn, Chorley, Todmorden, Bacup, Stockport, Macclesfield, Leek, Congleton, Oldham, Glossop, Dukinfield, Wigan, Bolton and St. Helens.

In June, three hundred Longton colliers came out on strike against a cut in wages. By mid-July the strike had widened to include all the North Staffordshire pits. As a result of the extreme poverty experienced by the strikers hundreds were walking the streets asking for money. As a result of the strike the potteries had to close there being no coal to fire the kilns. Disorder was on the cards and therefore troops were sent to the district to keep order, and camped for a number of days at the Hanley racecourse.

By early August, the colliers were slowly drifting back to work, driven by hunger, many living at almost starvation level. The troops were withdrawn. On Saturday, the 6th August, three men, carrying a begging-box through the alleys of the shambles in Burslem Market, were taken into custody by the police constables on a charge of vagrancy and placed in the lock-up beneath the Town Hall. Their incarceration became known to their Hanley comrades who then assembled numbering around 200. Then towards midnight, proceeded from Hanley to Burslem, broke open the Police Station and carried off their friends in triumph. Along the way they committed other mischief by the demolition of windows, and the illuminated dial of the Town Hall clock, before retiring before dawn of day. The miners' situation looked to the Chartists to be the opportunity they wanted to enforce the Chartists' movement. The Chartists were sympathetic to the colliers' demands and a number of local Chartist leaders addressed miners at open-air meetings.

On Sunday August 14th, Thomas Cooper, the Leicester Chartist leader arrived in Hanley and preached a brilliant *Chartist sermon* to an immense crowd of disillusioned strikers at Crown Bank. This stirred desperate men to boiling point, and when the news arrived that the Manchester Trades Conference had called a strike for the Charter, the Potteries Chartists and miners united the next day in calling on all workers to follow suit.

The following day, Monday 15th August a further meeting was held at Crown Bank in Hanley at seven o'clock in the morning and once again Cooper addressed a crowd estimated to be around eight to ten thousand. He told them that *peace; law and order* must be their motto and if they kept their strike peacefully they had nothing to fear from the law. A proposal by John Richards, an elder statesman of radical politics in North Staffordshire, then followed: *That all labour cease until the People's Charter becomes the law.* It was seconded and no one opposed it. The meeting broke up, seemingly as a great success but the crowd had been inflamed by the words of Cooper and were hell bent on the revenge and destruction of the employers and of the society they believed responsible for their plight.

The dry tinderbox had been lit and led to two days of destructive rioting in all the Potteries towns except Tunstall and neighbouring Newcastle. The first move after the Crown Bank meeting was made by a large group who went to Earl Granville's Shelton colliery, raked out the fires and pulled the plugs of the engine, thus bringing to a halt any chance of coal being bought to the surface. From here the mob then proceeded to Hanley and broke open the Police Office, also a print-works, a principal pawnbroker's shop and the house of the tax collector before proceeding to Stoke. Here, despite the station being ready for the rioters with windows and doors secured, men soon broke in, and they armed themselves, with cutlasses. Stonier, the chief of police, who lived in the building, managed to escape, leaving his wife behind to face the mob. One of the rioters cut the head off a cat, and threatened to do the same to her but she managed to escape to an upstairs room. The house of Mr T Allen, Esq., at Great Fenton was also attacked and wrecked on the excuse that there was a large quantity of arms belonging to a corps of volunteers on the premises.

The rioters then proceeded across the fields in the direction of Fenton police station, but a company of the 12th infantry accompanied by Mr T B Rose, and Mr W Parker arrived and took possession of the Court House. The presence of the military brought the rioters to a temporary stand, and after about half an hour a group of them proceeded to Penkhull to the home of Mr Thomas Bailey Rose and the larger section went on to Longton. The military remained at Fenton police station.

Riot at Beech Grove

Beech Grove, site fof the Chartists Riots

The *Potteries Mercury* records in great detail the events that followed at Beech Grove, Penkhull, the home of Mr Thomas Bailey Rose: *Following the appearance of the military, after the assault on Mr Allen's house at Fenton, a section of the mob retraced their steps as quickly as possible, passing through Stoke up to Penkhull, their avowed object being an attack on Mr Rose's House. On the way, however, they practiced intimidation in begging from various parties, and where they were not speedily and profusely supplied, they helped themselves.*

A gentleman on horseback having learnt the intention of the mob, had outstripped them on the road, and informed Mrs Rose of the pending danger. Accordingly she removed herself from the house with her family before the arrival of the mob. In a short time afterwards they arrived, and in the most tumultuous manner took possession of the law and commenced an attack upon the premises. Just at this time another gentleman on horseback, with great courage rode among them, his object being to ascertain if Mrs Rose and family were safe. The reins of his bridle were immediately seized by one man; two others seized hold of the gentleman's feet and stirrup-irons, in order to pitch him from his seat; whilst a fourth drew a sword and used the most threatening language. They, however, did not harm the gentleman, but ultimately suffered him to retire.

In the meantime the work of demolition had gone on; the door and windows were dashed in; the furniture broken to pieces, the valuable law library completely destroyed, and the house thoroughly ransacked and plundered. One fellow, with a large dung hook (which there seems little doubt but he had carried away from Mr Allen's) made a dreadful havoc with every article of furniture that came within his reach. Several of the mob had appropriated to themselves wearing apparel, indeed one man unblushingly appeared clad in one of Mr Rose's surtouts, (a great coat or frock coat) and over that a shooting jacket. After the mob had been engaged here a short time, an alarm was given that the military were coming, when they scampered off in every direction, but it proving only an alarm, many of them returned to the premises and completed the wreck, only three articles of furniture having escaped whole, and every portable article having been carried away.

Shortly afterwards it was ascertained that the military were really approaching, and the mob took to their heels; the greater part of them down the new road to Stoke (Penkhull New Road), and the other portion in the direction of the Spittals workhouse, which it was given out they meant to attack. In this direction the military followed; but no attack on the workhouse was made, and this portion of the mob dispersed themselves. Their object however was gained, in having drawn the attention of the magistrates and the military from the other part of their body, which again returned through Stoke and Great Fenton, to engage in other work.

It was reported later, that in fact, the family silver had been removed for safety by Mary Steele, aged around 15, who lived just around the corner in Doncaster Lane. Quickly with some initiative, young Mary hid the contents in a pigsty at the bottom of her garden until it was safe to return them to Mrs Rose. The 1841 census confirms that Mary Steele did live in Doncaster Lane with her parents William and Hannah along with her two sisters and a brother, which leaves little doubt that this story is true.

On Tuesday morning the 16th of August, the crowds began to assemble in Burslem and in the town of Hanley. William Ellis continued to encourage the people to continue until the Charter became law. At a further meeting in the town John Richards called on the crowd, now that the parson's house was down, that they must now go for the churches. The crowds decided to move on to Burslem to join the crowds there to the cry 'Now to business'.

The crowd joined many others in Chapel Square where trouble soon broke out as the mob broke into the George Inn stealing £14 from the till and alcohol. By ten o'clock word was sent to Major Trench, the commander of the fifty or so 2nd Dragoons who had been stationed in the town

following the previous troubles. By chance Captain Powys, a magistrate, was talking with Major Trench when the news of the incident at The George arrived and instantly asked the Major to assemble his troops and proceed to the Market Place. The situation at the George Inn was rectified quickly but Captain Powys being aware of the imminent arrival of a mob, numbering four to five thousand from Leek; decided it was time to halt the current trouble in the town.

Powys positioned himself in full sight of the crowd in Market Place and *read the Riot Act in the loudest tone of voice.* Behind the troops gathered two hundred Special Constables and a few Metropolitan Police Officers, many of whom were the worse for drink in an attempt to sustain courage. The order came from Powys to *Clear the Streets*, and then *Charge*. Despite all efforts, the mob gained the upper hand.

At around noon, the sound of the huge mob from Leek could be heard as they marched down Smallthorne Road accompanied by a brass band to the tune of *See the conquering hero comes*. Despite attempts by Captain Powys to secure a peaceful end to the events, the mob rejected all his requests with threats of violence and one could see they carried a large amount of stones ready for battle. Further reasoning was thought pointless so Captain Powys called on Major Trench to prepare his men to open fire. The troops were now placed at the entrance into Market Place from Leek, opposite the Big House, prepared to shoot directly into the crowd. The shout *Fire* came and in the first volley, Josiah Heapy, a young shoemaker from Leek, was killed outright. He had been standing on the steps of the Big House throwing stones at the troops. He was hit in the head, and his brains were scattered across the pavement below.

The crowd felt for the first time opposition to their riots and terrified, fled the scene. As a result many were kicked and trampled upon by the now fleeing masses of humanity. Other reports stated that up to three, five or six were killed that day and many with serious gunshot wounds. Many later reports carry conflicting stories of events.

Arrests followed including those responsible for the attack on the home of Mr Thomas Bailey Rose. The case was heard on Monday 22nd August 1842. *The Potteries Mercury* reports the court appearance on Saturday, 27th August 1842.

John Johnson was charged with riotously assembling and demolishing property, at the house of Mr Rose, and at Mr Forrester's and with stealing part of a side of bacon from the former. Elizabeth Sawyer, about 12 years of age, living at Northwood, saw the prisoner at Mr Rose's, on Monday, the 15th instant, breaking the goods from the house with a stick, and also thrashing them against the wall, and heard the prisoner express a wish to set the house on fire; but one of

The Chartists Riots

the colliers said, *No, I think we have done enough.* The mob said they would not touch Mrs Rose, but they would kill Mr Rose if they could catch him. They broke open a money drawer, but witness did not see any money taken out, and they threw a chest of drawers out of the window from upstairs. The prisoner brought a side of bacon out of the house on his back, and put it on the grass; it was then cut up, and she saw him carry some of it away. On the same night she saw the prisoner at Mr Forrester's, and he helped to set the office on fire, and to demolish the furniture. Eliza Barrett corroborated the evidence touching the prisoner being among the rioters at Mr Forrester's. Mr Johnson was committed for trial.

At the same court Thomas Lee, a Chartist residing in Stoke, was brought up on a charge of assisting a rioter to conceal a weapon, immediately after the attack on Mr Rose's home at Penkhull. Mr Thomas Gribbin, draper of Newcastle, who arrived at Penkhull just as the mob were leaving Mr Rose's, said he saw many of them with cutlasses and other weapons in their hands. Witness saw the prisoner between Mr Holroyd's (This refers to the old 'Marquis of Granby') and Mr Harrison's shop (Mr Harrison held a slaughter house and a butcher's shop next to the old 'Marquis of Granby') and at that time he was assisting a collier looking man, who appeared to be drunk, to conceal a sword or cutlass in his trousers; and after he had done so, he pushed the man off, and told him the soldiers were coming, and he would be taken prisoner.

Mr Williams appeared for the defendant, and in answer to his questions, witness said he did not see any respectable females near; nor did he hear prisoner say he was sorry to see anyone with such an unlawful weapon. John Hassalls, an engraver residing at Penkhull, confirmed Mr Gribbin's evidence, except as to the words spoken by prisoner, which he did not hear. Samuel Woodhouse, of Hart's Hill, a china painter at Messrs Minton and Hollins', (where the prisoner also worked) said the prisoner had since told witness that he arrived at Mr Rose's about five minutes before the soldiers, and called out to the people in the house to come out, as the soldiers were within a yard or two of them. He likewise remarked to witness how the mob stared at him when he told them. In reply to Mr Williams, witness said that some time ago he and a prisoner had a quarrel about the principles of the Charter, but they agreed not to mention the subject again. Prisoner was committed for trial, but bailed out the following day.

The Potteries Mercury reported in the same edition the results of the trials that were held the previous week.

Charged with beginning to demolish the house of Mr T B Rose, Penkhull: John Johnson, John Neile, John Ashley, jun.

all acquitted as the evidence not being sufficient to sustain the charge. Lawrence Simpson pleaded guilty.

Charged with Riot at Penkhull and an attack on Mr Rose's house: The same Lawrence Simpson pleaded guilty sentenced to 18 months in gaol. John Johnson pleaded guilty, sentenced to 2 years in gaol. John Neile 2 years, John Ashley 12 months, John Evans, 18 months.

Thomas Lee was found not guilty. Lawrence Simpson was allowed to withdraw his plea of guilty, on a charge of beginning to demolish the home of Mr Rose, and to plead guilty on this charge of riot and attack. Neile was Secretary of the Chartists in Hanley, and is understood to have made some disclosures while in gaol.

The question remains. Were the Potteries workers foremost interested in political change or were they used, manipulated, engineered and coursed into a frenzied mob by those outsiders bent on national political change and using whatever means they could to bring the matter to ahead and to the wider attention of the public?

Ringleaders of the Chartists used the sad state of affairs in the six towns and brought about industrial strife, which led to almost abstract poverty in many households to forward their campaign for change. It is doubtful if the riots of 1842 would have taken place if the colliers were not driven to such lengths in an attempt to provide for their families if the coal mine proprietors were more amenable to the needs of their workers.

Thomas Bailey Rose was born in Kentish Town, North London in 1805. After Parliament sanctioned the establishment of a stipendiary magistrate for the Potteries area he was appointed to that position in 1839. Rose strongly believed that the liberal manufacturers in the area were to blame for the troubles amongst the working classes and rapidly acquired a reputation for severity and prejudice in the courts against Chartists and trade unionists. He was responsible for making a decision to withdraw all troops from the area during the night of 15th August, thus giving over the area to the rioters. The Home Office for this action subsequently censured him. He continued to serve as a magistrate until 1864 at which time an inquiry into his conduct on the bench was under consideration.

Chapter 15
Homes for the Working Classes.

The first large scale housing developments in Penkhull arose out of two differing influences. The wish of Frederick Bishop to sell a part of the Mount estate and secondly from a political desire to secure more Liberal Members of Parliament.

A previous development of smaller terraced properties at the top of Honeywall by Bishop was followed in the same year by a deal resulting in Bishop laying a road called Stone Street from Honeywall to the new road, Princes Road. This was in agreement with Richard Stone, owner of the White Lion and the land upon which the road was laid, hence the name Stone Street. By 1865 houses were occupied on the east side of Stone Street. Unfortunately there was little interest shown in the plots for villa residences in Princes Road, so by way of compensation, Bishop promoted as an alternative the formation of a Workingmen's Freehold Land Society in the mid 1860s.

The concept of a Freehold Land Society was not new. Freehold land societies arose in the 1840s as part of a politically inspired movement organised by Liberal radicals to effect Parliamentary reform. These societies were initiated and encouraged as messianism by which the supporters of reform could become enfranchised within the existing system, and thereby change the balance of political power, and ultimately the system itself.

Following the Reform Act of 1832, the two most important voting qualifications were: the ownership of freehold with a minimum annual value of forty shillings, and the occupation of a house worth at least £10 a year. Neither of these qualifications were easily obtainable, not least by the 'industrious' classes. But there was obviously a limit upon the number of houses with a £10 annual value, and this was probably one important reason why reformers chose to concentrate their efforts on an expansion in the number of forty-shilling freeholders.

The first to implement the idea of a land society was the Birmingham Freehold Land Society in 1848. The first Freehold land society in Stoke-on-Trent was formed in Hanley in 1849, followed by a further nine between the years 1850-1856. By the late 1850s, most of the activity of local Freehold Land Societies had subsided and the political fervour of the movement had become dissipated and replaced by a more calculated business consideration.

After the first flush of societies, which had produced sufficient house plots to more than absorb the demand for years ahead, revival commenced locally in 1864. The following year saw Bishop's suggestion taking hold as a

meeting of interested parties held at Stoke Town Hall on the 13th of March 1869, to consider forming a Workingmen's Land Society. The Staffordshire Sentinel reported the meeting: *On Monday evening a public meeting was held in the Town Hall to consider forming a Workmen's Land Society. It may be stated that this scheme has originated with a few residents in the town who have been desirous of meeting a want which Stoke has long felt, that of a decent kind of residence for the workmen's families of the town. In consequence of the want of this accommodation very many men who labour in Stoke have residences some distance away from the town, and one result of this has been that other places have had the benefit of the money earned in Stoke by such workmen. Places for employment are said to have greatly increased in Stoke during the last few years; in fact that the town can now employ 2,000 more hands than it could a few years back. The growth of household property has not proportionately increased, and the result is that rents have risen by 10% to 15% per cent. The purchase of ten acres of The Mount from Mr Bishop having been provisionally arranged for upon very advantageous terms a committee was appointed. It was proposed to lay out the land in about 300 allotments of 100 sq. yards each; and the cost of each allotment being established at about from £10 to £12.*

The Chief Bailiff of Stoke, as Chair, remarked that in the morning and he had seen crowds of working men going to and from Stoke, and although a short walk might be beneficial, he thought: *for working men to go so far as Newcastle, Trent Vale, Hanley, or elsewhere after, perhaps, being confined during the day in a close room, was not so desirable.* It was proposed to erect suitable dwelling houses on the brow of the hill at The Mount, a place which to him seemed very suitable. The society would have its advantages in promoting habits of saving. *When a working man had a few shillings to spare at the weekend it was better that he should invest them in a savings bank or society like the one proposed, than spend them in a public-house. By saving a little money, and making such an investment as the one proposed, he might get a house of his own, and then he would feel in a more independent position. (Hear, hear). Under good management this society might be made as successful as the one established at California, Fenton.* He wished the society every success.

Mr T Smith reported to the meeting that when he saw about Mr Bishop about two months ago, Mr Bishop said that there was an urgent need of houses for working men in that locality. He further added that he would be glad to sell 8 or 10 acres of his land at a reasonable price, with a view to the erection of houses to meet that need. This matter he brought before the committee and at the first meeting it was reported that there were in excess of 150 shares applied for than could be offered. The addition of more land, he understood, could, however, be obtained. In the proposal, it was intended that every member should receive equal benefit, and that no

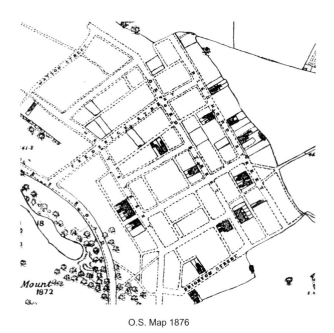

O.S. Map 1876

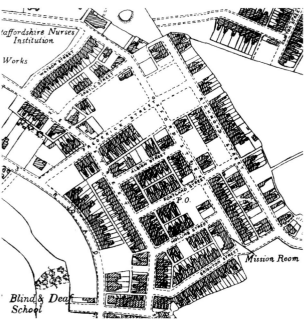

Above O.S. Map 1900   Below OS Map 1924

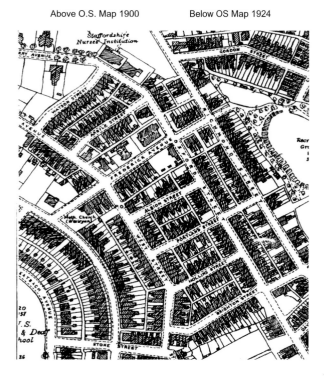

person should get special and prominent gain over the others. The land would be sold for £400 per acre although £350 was the final price paid. Mr Turner stated that it was proposed to borrow £1,000 to pay Mr Bishop as the first instalment. After the roads had been laid and the drainage complete, Mr Bishop at that juncture would be willing to receive the remaining money as and when the society could pay it. A depositor might pay for his allotment at once, and therefore avoid the liability of interest on the borrowed money.

Mr Lynam, surveyor, produced plans of the land proposed to be allotted, and explained that there would be 291 allotments, about 11 of the number having a little more than 100 sq. yards. It was suggested to reserve a portion of the frontage of the site in Princes Road and Frederick Avenue. It was also suggested that some of the corner allotments should be reserved, thinking that they might be ideal locations for shops. It was decided that the twenty corner allotments should not be reserved for this purpose.

The legal process of setting up the Freehold Land Society and the purchase of the land from Mr Bishop took nearly six months. The Staffordshire Sentinel dated 25th September 1869 reported: *Nineteen acres of land which the Workmen's Land Society has purchased from Mr F Bishop, especially for the erection of a respectable class of workmen's houses, was formally conveyed to members at a meeting held on Thursday evening, Mr T Smith was in the chair. The Rev Sir T L Stamer, Rector of Stoke, with his usual anxiety to promote educational progress, secured six allotments suitable for a site for new schools. The Rector, we note would be willing to give this land for the building of a school. A new, and probably populous, district will arise here, and a school will, of course, become a necessity.*

Mr Lynam, as surveyor, received his instructions to stake out the land but it was six months later that his report dated the 30th April 1870 confirms: *Agreed that Mr Lynam, the Society's surveyor stake out the allotments drawn in the ballot so that members might take possession of them for gardening purposes.* It would appear that this was the general use of the land in the first instance, hence the name Allotments.

It was a further twelve months before any building work took place as the following press report dated the 29th April 1871 reads: *At the annual meeting of the Workmen's Land Society, the secretary reported that a considerable number of houses were likely to be built upon the allotments during the coming year. He explained that Mr T. Smith had been asked to retire as a trustee because of his connection as agent for Mr Bishop. A letter was read from Mr Bishop stating that Mr Smith had never been his agent in this matter and that the remuneration paid to Mr Smith was commission on the shares taken by the Society. A considerable expression of personal feeling was called forth in the discussion that followed.*

From the deeds to No.103 and 105 Oxford Street, dated the 2nd September 1871, two plots were conveyed to Mr James Robinson, a draper from the town of Stoke. *That in consideration of the sum of £14 9s 4d paid by the purchaser All that plot of freehold land situated near to the Mount having a frontage of thirty feet.* Ten years later the plot remained undeveloped and was sold to Mr John Wood of Richmond Street, a stone mason and John Shortland, a builder of Stoke for the sum of £32 10s

In 1872 the Stoke Highway Board agreed at their August meeting to accept the liability of the new streets for the Allotments estate on condition that they would first keep them in good repair for a period of twelve months. But the formation of streets was only one issue for the residents to cope with as properties started to spring up, albeit slowly. In June 1874, it was reported that a further forty-five houses would be built but the problem lay with the fact that the only available water supply was via a small pump and that was more sewage than anything else. The minute of the meeting dated the 5th June continued: *The Town Mayor said the waterworks company was bound to carry the water to The Mount estate if the inhabitants would guarantee a consumption which would be equal to ten per cent upon carrying the main there. All that was wanted was for the inhabitants to combine. Considering the close proximity of the Penkhull reservoir he should think that a main would succeed in paying for itself.*

In November 1877 the Stoke Town Council agreed that ten street lamps should be erected on the Allotments estate and that the gas company be requested to lay a new main. But street lighting was only one issue that plagued the new development the other was direct road access to the town of Stoke. In December 1880 one resident took it upon himself to write to the Staffordshire Sentinel.

To the Editor. *Sir, The Mount estate is partly covered with new houses, of the value of about £31,000. There is not a single cart-road leading direct from Stoke to it, while the two foot roads, which are largely used by residents of Penkhull, Hartshill, Newcastle, &c., as well as by ourselves, are in a highly dangerous and disgraceful dirty condition. If the Aldermen and Councillors of the West Ward would venture to ascend by one of the paths and descend by the other, after dark, they would more fully experience the truth of the above assertion.*
I am, yours, &c., ANOTHER RESIDENT.

The inconvenience of inaccessibility from the Allotments Estate continued for a further seven years before the Town Council decided to rectify the situation. This was dependent upon the owner of the land at Upper Cliff Bank giving the required section of land. The report of the Highway and Lighting Committee explains all. *Stoke Town Council, The Mayor read a memorial, which had been received from a hundred ratepayers and owners of property on The Mount estate. The memorialists called attention to the fact that there was no direct communication with the town from The Mount estate, except for foot passengers. This was not only a cause of great inconvenience and loss to the residents of this estate, but was also detrimental to the trade of the town. Understanding that plans were to be laid before the Council that was calculated to meet the requirements of the district, the memorialists expressed a hope that such plans would meet with the best consideration of the members of the Council.*

Alderman Faram moved the following recommendation *that if the owner of the property between Upper Cliff Bank and Richmond Street is willing to give the required quantity of land necessary for a new street between the two points, the Corporation will undertake to construct the same at an estimated cost of £300. In support of the motion, the speaker said opposition might be raised to the proposition on the grounds that this land belonged to a private individual, and he, and not the Council, ought to be prepared to make and pay for the making of the road. (Hear, hear).*

Mr Bromley was entirely against spending ratepayers' money in opening up anyone's estate. It was the duty of the landowner to make the street and put it in proper order before the council had anything to do with it. Mr Mellor seconded the motion. From what he could learn the owner of the estate was not desirous of opening up the property for building purposes; that, in fact, it would be more to his interest to keep it as it was. When they came to consider the great advantage to a large quantity of ratepayers living on this estate the opening out of the road would be, he thought they ought to do something to assist. What was proposed to be done could not be looked upon as a precedent, because they had done something like it before.

Mr Boulton supported the proposition. He did not agree that the work if done by the Corporation would be for the benefit of the owner. It would be principally for the benefit of the present inhabitants residing there. At the present time, the market and shopkeepers of the town suffered considerably from the fact that there was no road to The Mount. The motion was carried by 10 votes to 8. This street was first called Jubilee Road but in the 1950s became part of the existing Richmond Street.

The local press does not include any reference to society transactions after the previous one. Once the society had achieved its objectives, the society ceased to function. Although the development remained slow, only sixty houses being built during the 1870s, the remaining plots being used as garden 'allotments'. By 1899 there were 326 houses on the estate and by 1914 the number had been increased to 460 virtually completing the development.

Penkhull Garden Village

In December 1907 an interest was expressed in establishing a suburban garden village on the outskirts of the Stoke town, to improve the health and living conditions of the working classes. The concept of country suburbs was nothing new. The introduction of suburban railway services made it easy to combine the pleasures of a rural retreat with a place of work situated in the town. The last quarter of the nineteenth century saw an increase in railway commuter services to Richmond and Hounslow and to the west and southwest of the metropolis. There were other examples of modern housing estates erected by private enterprise, such as those built by Cadbury at Bourneville from 1879 and by William Lever at Port Sunlight from 1888.

The founder of the Garden Cities movement was the pioneer sociologist Ebenezer Howard. In a series of influential works between 1890 and 1902 he associated an alternative vision of an urban city-scape in which the main priority was provision of healthy surroundings for a new generation of industrial workers. His model in urban development emphasised such features of town-planning as widely spaced houses with broad thoroughfares and extensive recreational and play areas for children and adults alike. His schemes, not unsurprisingly attracted the support of philanthropists and social reformers committed to reversing the historical dispossession by re-housing the poor in cheap accommodation. After 1902, Howard's project was put into practice by Co-Partnership Tenants Ltd., which grew out of the Garden Cities Association he established in 1898. The Co-Partnership Tenants was influential in inspiring developments at Hammersmith and Ealing in London, Harborne in Birmingham, Fallings Park in Wolverhampton and ultimately, Penkhull in Stoke. These, however, are more properly 'garden suburbs' or 'villages' rather than the full-scale cities Howard had envisaged.

The preferred choice by a group of interested parties, who in 1908 established themselves into the Trentham Garden Village Tenants Ltd, was a six and a half acre site at Trentham. The position of the site, stood at a height of 450 feet on a southward-facing plateau. Here, the prevailing winds would disperse the smoke from the Potteries and harmonise with the pastoral image of the scheme. Accordingly in June of that year the project managers obtained a two-month option to purchase land situated at Northwood from the landowner, George Peake. However, advisers from the Co-Partnership Tenants were unhappy with the location for the project. Thomas Adams, who was closely involved in the 'Garden Village' developments at Fallings Park, Wolverhampton and Accrington in Lancashire criticised the smallness of the site and its poor communications with the town centre of Stoke.

Had there been a direct road between Stoke and the proposed site there would probably not have been an issue, but the only road leading from Stoke is a circuitous one that would turn around at Trentham and therefore would have meant a two miles journey from the trams for the residents. A pathway could obtain a short cut across the fields, but this would prove difficult in winter and might even have been inaccessible during frosts and heavy rains.

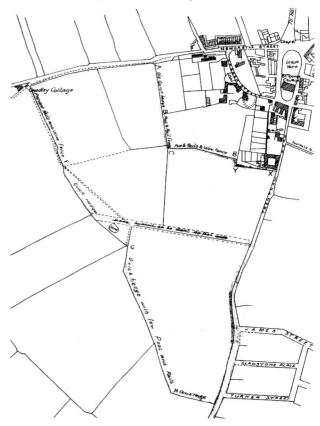

New site for the Garden Village, off Trentham Road Penkhull

Following consideration of these concerns the committee surveyed an alternative site at Penkhull comprising an area of thirty-eight acres belonging to Sir Thomas Pilkington. The site combined the advantages of proximity to Stoke (it was only a mile from the town centre) with a southward-facing plateau similar to that at Trentham and swept by the same prevailing winds. Spectacular views of the surrounding countryside reinforced the rustic environment that the architects of the scheme would seek to create for the tenants.

The views of the beautiful open countryside include the well-wooded districts of Keele, Clayton, Hanchurch, and Trentham, whilst Mow Cop, the Wrekin and Cannock Chase in the far distance may easily be seen on a clear day.

The ideals of the association broadened in view of this new location and interest turned from Trentham to the purchase of a thirty-eight acre site adjacent to Penkhull Square, to the south of Penkhull village, a move that would complete the transformation of a rural village into that of an industrial suburb. In January 1910 following negotiations with the owners of the land, plans for its development were agreed. As a result of the pending move to the Penkhull site, the name of the association changed to 'Stoke-on-Trent Tenants Ltd.' A private meeting of a few leading people of the district was held on the 15th February at the North Stafford Hotel, at which the Rt. Hon. the Earl of Harrowby presided. Dr G Petgrave Johnson (Chairman of the new Stoke-on-Trent Tenants Society) explained the proposals and Mr Bryce Leicester, the Assistant Secretary of the Co-partnership Tenants Ltd outlined the financial aspect. As a result of the initial interest it was agreed to hold a public meeting ten days later.

At that meeting held at Stoke Town Hall, the scheme for the laying out of a garden village suburb of the Potteries was put to a well attended meeting where it was proposed and agreed upon to commence with fifty houses at a total cost of £14,000, the sum estimated to develop the whole scheme would be £100,000.

My good friend, the late Arnold A Wain, who once lived in the largest house in the Garden Village, recalls:

Arnold A. Wain

I remember the Garden Village being built and going to see the show-house, how small it was I thought. It was, I think, the corner house of Barnfield. As a very poor lad at the age of 14, I attended a meeting that was convened at Stoke Town Hall, at which the subject of the Garden Village was being discussed. To think that I was at that inaugural meeting just having started work at the Minton's Factory, without a halfpenny to my name listening to the wonders of bathrooms, gardens, space and fresh air. If someone had come up to me at that meeting and told me that one day I would own a house in that Garden Village, in fact, the largest house, I would have thought they were mad.

Arnold Wain in later life became, despite his initial upbringing in abject poverty, a well-known local dentist, a member of the city council and a respected Lay Reader within the Church of England. Mr Wain was an outstanding orator, and during the 2nd World War regularly filled the Victoria Hall, Hanley as people came to listen to his speeches on behalf of the Anglo-Soviet Friendship Committee. He was also actively involved in the promotion of the benefits of growing your own food as part of the war effort and the creation of allotments throughout the city.

In its conception, the scheme followed directly the principles of a national movement, which had been established as a reaction against the crowded, polluted industrial towns of the country, in favour of the rural idyll. Co-partnerships

Tenants Ltd. had been consulted from the outset and with their expertise and cooperation they oversaw the preliminary work of the Penkhull scheme involving locally W Campbell & Sons, a firm of architects from Hanley, to design the houses.

The Penkhull scheme at Stoke-on-Trent was typical of the ad-hoc and improvised nature of Garden City organisation at local level and illustrated the limitations of the association's projects at the turn of the century. Such bodies brought together disparate groups of local philanthropists, pastoral idealists, and utopian reformers. The example of Penkhull provides a model of the uneasy partnership existing between these various groups. In its preliminary stages a committee of working-class enthusiasts energetically promoted the scheme. Its most active supporter was a local artist and engraver, J P Steele, who was associated with the project from the beginning. The utopian nature of the scheme and the radical politics of some of those who endorsed it, fuelled rumours in Stoke that socialists were behind the project. The Earl of Harrowby, who became the estate's patron, at a public meeting in Stoke town hall, addressed such concerns: He had heard a criticism hostile to the society. He was told that it was run and supported by leaders of the Radical Party. He did not know whether it was so or not and he did not care and concluded. *The objects are good, the scheme was good, and it should be supported by all who were keenly anxious for the social welfare of our teeming population in the country.*

Lord Harrowby

The objects of the society to which Lord Harrowby referred at the opening of the meeting, *were radical for the time.* Plans were based upon on a co-partnership principle that had already proved its success nationally. Co-partnership Tenants Ltd. had considerable expertise with nine other projects throughout the country comprising of a total of nearly three thousand houses.

The site chosen was of thirty-eight acres of copyhold farmland situated on an elevated rural plot bordered by Trentham Road to the east and Newcastle Street to the north. Sir Thomas Edward Milbourn Swinnerton Pilkington of Wakefield owned it. Sir Thomas purchased the land from The Hon Edward Parker Jervis in June 1894. The copyhold site became freehold on 23rd March 1910 in consideration of £328 14s 6d paid to the 'King's Most Excellent Majesty'.

Stamp £1.15.

This Indenture

made the *23rd* day of *March* 19*10*

BETWEEN THE KING'S MOST EXCELLENT MAJESTY of the one part and *Sir Thomas Edward Melborne Swinnerton Pilkington of Chevet Park near Wakefield in the County of York Baronet* one of the copyhold or customary tenants of the Manor of Newcastle under Lyme of the other part WITNESSETH that in consideration of the sum of *Three hundred and twenty eight* pounds *fourteen* shillings and *six* pence of lawful money of Great Britain paid into the hands of the Receiver General of the Revenues of the Duchy of Lancaster by the said *Sir Thomas Edward Melborne Swinnerton Pilkington* (as appears by the receipt of the Deputy to the said Receiver General indorsed on these Presents) His said Majesty by and with the advice and consent of His Chancellor and Council of His said Duchy and upon the acceptance of the said *Sir Thomas Edward Melborne Swinnerton Pilkington* (testified by *his* execution of these Presents) DOTH hereby release and confirm unto the said *Sir Thomas Edward Melborne Swinnerton Pilkington* and *his* heirs for ever ALL *those pieces or parcels of land containing 38 acres and 24 perches or thereabouts situate in the Parish of Stoke on Trent in the County of Stafford as the same are more particularly described and delineated on the map or plan drawn hereon and thereon edged with a pink verge line and comprise the fields Numbered 262, 263, 270 and 272 and part of the field Numbered 269 on the 25 inch Ordnance Survey of the said Parish 1900 Edition and to which said premises together with other premises the said Sir Thomas Edward Melborne Swinnerton Pilkington was admitted tenant by the description following videlicet*

Indenture dated 23rd March 1910 confirming the transfer from copyhold land to that of freehold

The membership of the management committee was mixed, attracting both artisans and white-collar professionals. From an early stage, it was linked very closely to the building work of the local council. During preliminary discussions in 1907-1908, the Garden Village project was embraced by council officers as a way of providing cheap, affordable housing for the labouring poor. The Housing and Town Planning Act of 1909, which established rudimentary town planning guidelines and empowered councils to oversee work by private developers, strengthened this collaboration.

Stoke council had a great deal to gain from this legislation; it became the responsibility of the developer to build roads, sewers and other basic amenities at such developments. Once built to the required standard they were turned over to the council for maintenance. In Stoke, as elsewhere, the Penkhull scheme was therefore incorporated into council planning policy. The project was monitored by council officials and use was made of council sub-contractors.

An emphasis was placed in the Penkhull development on the communal, in arrangements and facilities. The site can be thought of and planned as a whole, and the certainty of some degree of co-operation would enable spots and natural beauty with distant views of hills and dales to be preserved for common enjoyment it was considered. In this way, instead of the building being mere endless rows, or the repetition of isolated houses having no connection one with another, they would naturally gather themselves into groups and the group clustered around the greens will form larger units.

The original plans were impressive extending from Trentham Road across farmland to the far fence of what is now Thistley Hough School. From the current Thistley Hough, other roads would lead off, the first after The Croft would be the extended Bromley Hough along which would be an outstanding 'view point'. A large open space would have occupied the area now taken up by the allotments in Bromley Hough.

The next road to the left would have been 'West Point' leading down the current playing fields. 'The Ridge' would have followed linking up to 'The Flat', which extended and making its exit into Newcastle Lane about where Marchwood Court now stands. Off this would have been a small road, 'The Green' linking back into Thistley Hough with a large open space created around which houses would have been built. Finally, a smaller road, with its junction opposite Barnfield would have joined 'The Ridge' at the bottom of the field. There was proposed an impressive Institute for the exclusive use of residents of the garden village to be built before the war where Lowndes Close now stands.

Ten or twelve houses per acre was the proposal, ninety-five

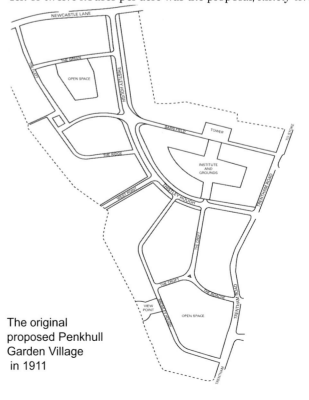

The original proposed Penkhull Garden Village in 1911

houses in all, *varying in size and design all with large gardens so that the people will develop a sense of home life and interest in nature and obtain security against the evil arising through living in unhealthy and crowded areas,* continued the report.

On the 7th April, 1910, the purchase of the site was completed. To enable the project to get underway the sum of £6,000 was loaned from Mr Frederick George Johnson, earthenware manufacturer, of nearby Clayton Hall. On the 9th April two days after the signing of the documents, the inaugural ceremony took place at which the Countess of Harrowby, after being presented with a silver spade, cut the first sod. There were in excess of five hundred people who had come to see this event, no doubt with high aspirations to become a tenant in the future. In an effort to maximise publicity, the ceremony was timed to coincide with a window-dressing competition held by the shopkeepers of Stoke and judged by the town's civic dignitaries. The workmen employed on the site were unemployed Staffordshire miners hired by Stoke-on-Trent council.

By autumn 1910, a total of ten cottages on the west side of Trentham Road were completed and ready for occupation. For this occasion there were upwards of five thousand people who attended the ceremony, as well as civic heads and local dignitaries. Such was its uniqueness to the district. The first houses were completed on the 24th September 1910, and officially opened at a ceremony by the Mayoress of Stoke-on-Trent, Mrs Cecil Wedgwood.

Opening Ceremony Mrs Cecil Wedgwood unlocks the door of the first cottage 24th September, 1910

The design of the estate incorporated classic Garden City features. The houses were constructed not in lines of tenements as in most urban estates, but in separate clusters, each group differing slightly in architectural style. There were to be only ten houses per acre rather than the standard forty houses per acre common in the majority of industrial towns. All were to be southward facing where possible *thus allowing them to glean every shred of sunlight.* The construction of outbuildings was also avoided to prevent 'the formation of narrow enclosed courts'. Each house was to be provided with a garden, an eighth of an acre in extent, for the tenants to cultivate. It was hoped that this would both improve the appearance of the village and allow the tenants to augment their income through the sale of produce.

The first six cottages completed

To further enhance the pastoral image of the scheme, existing trees were to be retained and more planted, whilst garden boundaries were to be marked by lines of bushes, not by walls so that *with them will also disappear the mortar, dust, cobwebs and rubbish corners that they cause.* Tenants were encouraged to keep window boxes. Facilities such as electric light, gas for heating and cooking, a good water supply, a bath and an inside toilet were included in every cottage.

The first six cottages built at the top of Trentham Road

Roads were wider than fifty feet on average, with grass verges where possible and common road frontage pathways serving some of the houses. Each group of houses was planned as a cluster surrounding a series of greens, open spaces and viewing points, intended to provide extensive and picturesque playing areas for the tenants' children and to give the estate overall coherence. The society's promotional literature explained the thinking behind the estate's layout in the following terms:

Play places and shelters for the children, greens for tennis, bowls or croquet can be arranged with the houses so grouped around them that while they provide the occupants with ample recreation ground, they also both afford more pleasant prospects from the street. In this way, instead of the buildings being mere endless rows, or the repetition of isolated houses having no connection one with the other, they will naturally gather themselves into groups and the groups again clustered round the greens will form larger units and the interest and beauty of grouping will at once arise.

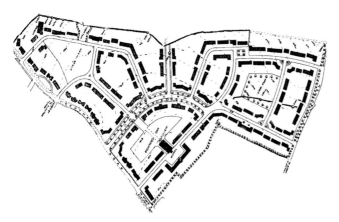

Proposed development with not more than ten houses to the acre.

It was one year later in July 1911 that Lord Harrowby visited the Garden Village, this time to open the new bowling green and tennis courts along with Col W W Dobson. Lord Harrowby, who by way of Chairman of the Stoke-on-Trent Tenants Ltd, referred to the debt of gratitude to the gentlemen who had first put their heads together to start the Garden Village. He then referred to 'there being nothing like an English village' and hoped that the Penkhull site would soon have its own institute and village club and looked forward to the time when the 38 acres of the estate would be covered with houses.

At present, he stated, there were only 39 houses occupied and 11 were ready for occupation. There were also 24 partially-built and it was intended to build a further 26 before the end of the year commenting that he hoped they would endeavour to build them more cheaply, so that they could be rented out at a rent of 4s per week *('Here, Here',* the audience responded).

Lord Harrowby concluded by suggesting that many may consider investing £2,000 or £3,000 in £5 shares, which would help to forward the movement.

The Annual General Meeting of the shareholders of Penkhull Garden Villages was held in March 1912 at which Lord Harrowby was the chairman. Among those present were the Rev I C R Scott, vicar of Penkhull, Dr Petgrave Johnson, Messrs F Parry, G Ridgeway, J. Wadsworth and Mr R J Bell (Secretary).

The first item discussed referred to the fact that the corporation had agreed to improve the frontage to Trentham Road and referred to the position that at the end of 1910 there had only been 20 houses completed but was now pleased to report that there were now 70 and seven more in the process of being completed. Lord Harrowby then reported that there were near 200 people living on the estate enjoying the privilege of living in substantially built sanitary dwellings.

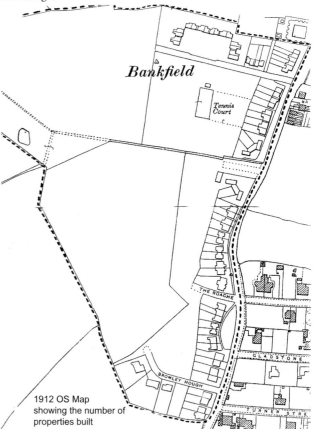

1912 OS Map showing the number of properties built

The Annual Report for 1913 makes reference that the houses in Thistley Hough and The Croft had been completed and thereby bringing the total houses into occupation to 95, increasing the total assets to the society's property to £43,438. Plans had also been completed for the building of a number of cottages fronting what is now Newcastle Lane of such a size and type that would meet the requirements of the waiting list of applicants. (These were never built and for years the land was used for allotments).

The committee agreed to pay a dividend of 5% on the paid-up share capital and a further 2½% dividend to be credited against the rents of investing tenants. The report concluded that *the Movement was still in popularity and more appreciated by residents as a healthy and sociable life could be enjoyed in the garden village away from the town.*

Barnfield, designed with open space to the front

The history of the estate constructed by this partnership at Penkhull reflects many of the problems Garden City developments of this type experienced in the years before the 1st World War. In a flush of early enthusiasm for the project, ninety-five houses were built at the confluence of Newcastle Lane and Trentham Road, Penkhull. By 1914, however, the momentum had almost disappeared from the movement, only to come to a halt after 1919 when a more vigorous programme of state-sponsored council house building superseded the activities of private developers and tenants' associations. In the 1920s a number of the properties were being sold off.

The Green, Barnfield in its better days

To further the aim of re-housing the poor, the society was organised around a popular share-holding scheme intended to broaden the basis of its membership and involve working people in the project. The constitution was drawn up in accordance with the Provident and Friendly Societies Act. Under its terms tenants were required to buy shares in the society, up to and exceeding the value of £50 per tenant, and paid either in instalments or all at once. These shareholders' investments provided the building capital and entitled each investor to a tenancy. A moderate interest was paid on each share by the society and any surplus profits were divided amongst the members in proportion to the rent they paid. For those tenants who did not have £50 in the society, no dividend was paid until they had accrued £50 worth of shares.

This system was intended to be mutually advantageous to both the society and the tenants. The society could draw upon each individual tenant's share if necessary for arrears. Rent-loss by non-payment was thus rendered impossible. It was also able to subtract from the £50 the cost of any repairs needed to a property should the tenant wish to vacate. For his part the tenant was entitled to receive a dividend on the rent paid out of the profits of the society. It was reported at the time that this was to the advantage of the tenant members who receive the surplus profit. They had an incentive to make these profits as large as possible by taking care of the property, by helping to find tenants for empty houses, and by the punctual payment of rent. Tenants were entitled to the return of their £50 share, less any deductions for dilapidation, after leaving the scheme. The society also undertook to keep rents stable and as low as possible. Despite the resonances of co-operation and radical land colonies in the project, the society's constitution made no provision for the democratic participation of investors in the overall management of the estate. A self-perpetuating elite, not answerable to the tenants, managed the Stoke-on-Trent Tenants. Moreover, from an early stage the project was taken out of the hands of those it was notionally intended to help. The Committee of Management was entirely made up of local businessmen and council officials.

The first chairman of the Stoke-on-Trent Tenants was Dr G. Petgrave Johnson, the Medical Officer of Health for the Borough of Stoke. Surprisingly, the member's list shows that he held only one share. In addition, the Co-Partnership Tenants became actively involved after the scheme's launch. Although the houses themselves were designed

Dr. G. Petgrave Johnson

by a local firm of architects, W Campbell and Sons of Hanley, a Birmingham builder, Frank Williams, who had worked on other Garden Suburbs projects in the West Midlands, was also brought in to act as site manager and became a member of the Committee of Management on the estate between 1914 and 1929. This liaison with the Co-Partnership Tenants allowed those involved in the Penkhull scheme to buy tools and building materials cheaply through the society. Moreover, the scheme gained the patronage of the town's civic dignitaries. The Earl of Harrowby, one of the largest landowners in North Staffordshire, gave it his support and the Mayor of Stoke presided at its inaugural meetings. A project that had begun as a local initiative was therefore rapidly subsumed within the broader structure of the Garden Cities Movement and began to change its character as it developed into an extension of the management structure of Stoke Town Council.

A typical picture of 'respectability' in the Garden Village

occupants of the six terrace cottages, numbers 50-60 Trentham Road, at the northern extremity of the estate, the smallest of the houses on the site, paid the lowest weekly rental of only 5s. 6d in 1911. The rateable value of the properties amounted to £11 per annum in 1914. The tenants of the two larger groups of houses, numbers 130, 132 and 134, and 136 Trentham Road, midway along the Trentham Road frontage, paid a higher rental of 7s. 9d per week and having a rateable value of £16 10s per annum. Equally, the larger size of the rooms in numbers 92 and 94 Trentham Road and number 2 The Roche was mirrored by the houses' slightly higher weekly rental of 8s 5d, the rateable value being £17 per annum. The tenants of the largest houses on the Trentham Road frontage, numbers 168-196, paid a much

New houses facing Trentham Road

Control by a benevolent autocracy of paternalists had important consequences for the development of the estate. The scheme was underpinned by notions of respectability, and sought to bring out the correct moral values and appropriate community loyalty in its occupiers. A visit by George V and Queen Mary to the site in 1913 reinforced this vision of the tenants as an ordered, loyal, deferential community as well as making the estate a fashionable and desirable place to live. The original ideology for the estate had gone. The strict paternalism governing the project was reflected by the determination to keep unsightly industry and manufacture that might mar the appearance of the village off the estate; the covenants of each property stipulated that no industry or business of any sort should be carried on from any of the rented accommodation on the site. A similar desire to ensure correct standards of behaviour is apparent in the society's stipulation that there should be no public houses on the estate and that recreational facilities were to be used only for improving pastimes such as lectures and concerts. As with other developments of this type the main concern here was to reduce the incidence of drunkenness and unruly behaviour.

The marked variance in the size of the individual houses in the scheme was reflected in the large variations in both rents and rates paid by the tenants of the properties. The

higher rental of 10s. per week. The rateable value of the houses was also much higher than that of the others along the road at just over £3 per month. The occupants of the large detached residences on Bromley Hough (numbers 3, 5, 7 and 9) paid the highest rental of any of the tenants on the estate at £5 per month. As tenants of considerable social standing and financial means it appears that, unlike other tenants, they were allowed the privilege of paying their rents weekly, rather than monthly. The rateable value of the four houses on Bromley Hough reflected their large size. The rateable value of number seven Bromley Hough was £49 per annum and that of number 9, £44 10s in 1914. By 1952 only two, No's 2 and 4 remained in the ownership of the company. Mr Bell at No. 2 was paying £16 5s per month rent and Mr Parry at No.4 was paying £12 10s 6d which for both properties included the rental for their garages. In December Mr Perry at No. 4 died and the house was then sold. The last house belonging to the society No. 2 remained in their possession until 1957 the rent charged being £18 5s per month. It was sold in the November of that year. Against the address in the ledger is marked *ask for £4,000.*

When Stoke-on-Trent Tenants Ltd vacated the rent collection office at 10a Thistley Hough they left the old account ledgers and share holding book. Mr John Bullock, then living at No. 10 managed to retrieve these and kept them for all these years. The information from this collection of old legers has provided many facts and figures for this chapter.

The occupants in 1912 are recorded as Frank A Bell at No. 3 who held 69 shares; Mr Edward E Parry, at No. 5 was a director of Stoke-on-Trent Tenants Ltd and ceramic designer who held only 5 shares; Dr Gilbert Petgrave Johnson, Medical Officer for Health and also Director of Stoke-on-Trent Tenants Ltd. held only one share and Mr John W. Wadsworth, Art Director of Minton's factory living at No. 9 held only five shares.

The Estate Office on the corner of Trentham Road
and Thistley Hough

As the Penkhull scheme developed, many of the stated aims of those who had initiated the venture were discarded. The rhetoric surrounding the inauguration of the project had conveyed the concern felt by respectable Edwardians at the conditions in which urban workers lived. The society's promotional material stated that the scheme was intended to re-house Stokes manual workers. In reality admission to the estate was stringently policed. The Stoke-on-Trent Tenants reported in 1913 that medical practitioners involved in the scheme would recommend some of their patients (but not others) to apply, indicating that an informal screening of candidates was already in operation, even before the official admission procedure. By the autumn of 1910 the society was openly seeking to attract a more prosperous class of tenants. The Staffordshire Sentinel for 26th September 1910 reported: *The intention is to care for the artisans and clerk classes, but the estate offers an ideal home for other people as well–young married*

people, quiet bachelors or spinsters, old couples and in fact quiet and nice people of all classes. As a matter of fact the Medical Officer of Health for the Potteries, Dr Petgrave Johnson, who is one of the principal promoters of the scheme, is building himself a house there.

The society's attempts to cater for a new class of residents led to a corresponding increase in the size of the accommodation they furnished for their tenants. This was in accordance with a line of policy reported in the Staffordshire Sentinel of the same date: *of course, those in authority will be guided in regard to the class of residences which will be most numerously represented by the responses on the part of prospective tenants.* Overall the provisions of the scheme were sufficiently stringent to provide a barrier to the large-scale involvement of working families in Stoke. This was highlighted in a series of letters published in the Staffordshire Sentinel, one of which read: *I was present at the meeting held a few weeks ago explaining the formation of the Stoke-on-Trent Tenants Ltd. Whilst agreeing to some of the principles of the same I can only come to one conclusion and that is, strictly speaking, it is not a workingman's scheme. The rent of a house is 5s. rates would come to about 2s. 6d. a week and the share outlay about 1s. 3d. a week, making a total of nearly 9s. a week. Now sir, trade as it stands at the present, will not warrant the outlay from the wage of the average man and, to one willing to better himself, the hardship. There again, to expect one to do his own inside decorations and repairs (repairs to come out of the bonus if pressed by the committee) seems to me to be rather too much to expect of anyone. What we want is not a scheme like this, but one in which the investor may see his thrift increase. Could not a scheme be devised such that at the end of a certain number of years the cottages may become the property of the tenant?*

From 1914 onwards, rents were increased annually so that total revenue from rent income increased from £1,877 19s. 2d at the end of 1914 to £1,950 13s. 3d. at the end of 1915. There were further steep rent increases in the aftermath of the First World War; the society's revenue from rents jumped from £1,986 14s 5d. in 1918, to £2,209 1s. 3d in 1920.

Analysis of the occupations of those who became tenants on the Penkhull estate confirms that, despite the original good intentions surrounding the project, it did not serve to re-house slum citizens from the centre of Stoke. The occupations of 65 tenants are listed in the Potteries and District Directory for 1912. Skilled craftsmen from respectable artisan trades were the lowest status group amongst the tenants. There were only eleven in this category, five of whom were employed in the pottery industry. The majority of these craftsmen occupied the first group of houses on the site, numbers 60-70 Trentham Road, including the show-house, number 70. The occupants were respectively a carpenter, a pottery decorator, a pottery engraver, a potter, an engraver and a brakesman. Only one of these craftsmen, an engraver, R. J. Ridgway, attained a position on the estate's Management Committee; he acted as the society's rent collector from 1910. The remaining tenants at the Penkhull Garden Village were from salaried clerical or middle-class occupations.

The Estate Office to the left and showing Trentham Road as a narrow country lane c1920

A significant proportion came from white-collar council employees who had played a prominent part in inaugurating the venture. Eleven of the 65 tenants on the estate in 1912 were council officials, directly or indirectly involved in the project. They included Edwin Carratt, a chief sanitary inspector; he held only 65 shares. Matthew Piercey, an engineer and surveyor holding only 60 shares; and Thomas Stake, the sanitary inspector held only 11 shares who had been active in local Garden Cities projects since the turn of the century. Petgrave Johnson, chairman of the Stoke-on-Trent Tenants, had a spacious residence built to his specifications at No. 7 Bromley Hough, which he rented, rather than owned. He held the lowest number of shares at only one. From 1920, the borough surveyor, Amos Burton holding a respectable amount of shares 178, occupied this house.

Council officials involved in the project also occupied the three other large residences on Bromley Hough. John Wadsworth, art director to the council and adviser to the Stoke-on-Trent Tenants, lived in the largest house on the estate at number 9. The house is equipped throughout with bell pushes, indicating the presence of servants and stressing the difference in status between this occupier and the respectable working class at whom the project was ostensibly aimed. Edwin Parry, a designer in the employ of the council and a member of the Committee of Management, occupied the third of the large houses in the Hough, now No. 5. Also well represented amongst the remaining tenants were sales representatives (seven) and school teachers (six). In addition there were four clerks, four agents, three clergymen, and two secretaries of local societies resident on the site and connected with the running of the estate. The occupations of

the remaining seventeen tenants spanned the full range of middle-class professions from a solicitor and an N.S.P.C.A. inspector to a draper and a barber. The predominantly middle-class/shopkeeper status of the tenants at Penkhull is further demonstrated by their recreational pastimes. The Stoke-on-Trent Tenants' annual report contained a detailed summary of the Athletic and Social Club's activities for the year.

In 1912 the Staffordshire Sentinel produced a directory of each address in the city listing the head of the family and their occupation. This list has been a valuable resource for historians over the years. In addition the Rate Books for Stoke have survived for 1914; the information contained produces a further dimension to the amount of information, which further expands the knowledge of the Garden Village in its early years. All the evidence produced indicates how the committee sought from the beginning to promote an elite establishment of residents at the expense of the initial concept of better housing for the working classes of the town of Stoke.

The residents included at least seven officers of the newly federated county borough of Stoke-on-Trent. Dr G Petgrave Johnson, Edwin Carratt and Thomas Stake. Others included. Edward Barratt Lee, Solicitor, living at 114 Trentham Road, who was the deputy town clerk of Stoke-on-Trent; Frank Pugh Sissions, Civil Engineer in No 174 Trentham Road, was the deputy borough engineer and surveyor by 1916, and Samuel Johnson, Sanitary Inspector, 112 Trentham Road, was Inspector of factories, workshops and smoke. At least seven other residents were teachers in various educational establishments. William Henry Warburton jr., for example in 40 Barnfield, was the Head Teacher at the Central Boys' Evening Technical School in Stoke and F R Woldridge, 8 Thistley Hough, taught at Stoke Art and Technical School. Several other residents were also employees of public bodies such as William Halliwell, 6 Barnfield, who worked in the Weights and Measures Department for Staffordshire County Council, and Frederick John Little, Relieving Officer, who worked for the Stoke-upon-Trent Poor Law Union.

There were also people who worked in the pottery industry. They included John William Wadsworth, 9 Bromley Hough, who was Art Director at Minton's in Stoke. A very high proportion of potters on the estate were designers, decorators and engravers who were paid comparatively high wages. At least three residents - Josiah Ward, John Henry Latchford and E F Latchford, worked for one company, Latchford & Ward, designers and engravers, based in Corporation Street, Stoke. Another indicator of the residents' social status was the preparatory school run by Miss M E Bamber at No 110 Trentham Road which also served as the estate office.

Using this information, alongside the shares held by those considered wealthy, the results are alarming and therefore throw doubts, even at this early stage in the development of the Garden Village on the integrity of the Directors and management committee. To place the following into context, the person holding the highest number of shares was Mr J B Hackney at 253.

The Share Book, unfortunately undated, lists a total of 254 shareholders holding a total of over 30,000 shares. The numbers of Shares allocated are divided as follows:

1 - 25	38 share holders	15%
26 - 50	24 share holders	9%
51 - 100	44 share holders	17%
101 - 150	56 share holders	21%
151 - 200	51 share holders	20%
Over 201	45 share holders	17%

Trentham Road (now Trent Valley Road).
Those marked 0 The share book pages are torn.

House Held	Tenants	Occupation	Weekly Rent	Shares
No. 60	Frederick Ridkin Allen	Carpenter	5s 6d	53
No. 62	Wm. A. Hancock	Potter Decorator	5s 6d	55
No. 64	John George Stanway	Pottery Engraver	5s 6d	nil
No. 66	John George Stuart	Potter	5s 6d	25
No. 68	George Mason	Engraver	5s 6d	17
No. 70	Alfred Abbott	Brakesman	5s 6d	26
No. 76	Josiah Ward	Engraver	6s 6d	125
No. 78	Rev. Robert B. Ashley	Minister	6s 6d	4
No. 80	William Millard	Railway Agent	6s 6d	240
No. 82	E.F. Latchford	Director	6s 6d	135
No. 84	Charles Redfern	Electrical Engineer	7s 6d	0
No. 86	Rev. David Di Menna	Minister	7s 6d	5
No. 88	Francis Smith	Clerk in Hold Orders	7s 6d	73
No. 90	Benjamin Arthur Leech	Commercial Traveller	7s 6d	48
No. 92	Jams Waters	Inspector N.S.P.C.A.	8s 0d	87
No. 94	William Turnbull	Electrical Engineers	8s 0d	58
No. 110	Miss M.E. Bamber	Teacher Prep. School	8s 0d	0
No. 112	Samuel Jackson	Sanitary Inspector	8s 0d	62
No. 114	Edward Barratt Lee	Solicitor	7s 6d	94
No. 116	Edgar Harry Pearce	Agent	7s 6d	60
No. 118	Miss A. Shufflebotham	Asst. Schoolmistress	7s 6d	149
No. 120	William H. Boulton	Railway Clerk	7s 6d	0
No. 122	Miss Edith Turner	High Schoolmistress	7s 3d	77
No. 124	Miss Marian Watkins		7s 3d	146
No. 126	Wm Swetnam Dale	Class Master	7s 3d	14
No. 128	Edward J. Bridgewater	Schoolmaster	7s 3d	0
No. 130	Mrs Sarah Hargreaves	Widow	7s 9d	28
No. 132	Benjamin Joseph Bell	Sec. SOT Tenants	7s 9d	2
No. 134	Edwin Carratt	Chief Sanitary Insp.	7s 9d	63
No. 136	George Ridgway	Engraver	7s 9d	195
No. 154	Frederick John Littler	Relieving Officer	9s 0d	65
No. 156	Henry George Martin	Draper	9s 0d	93
No. 158	David Henry Grenaway	Typewriter Agent	9s 0d	82
No. 160	Matthew A Piercy	Eng & Surveyor	7s 6d	188
No. 163	Joseph James Barber	Hairdresser	7s 6d	98
No. 164	Bertrand Rhead	Dealer office Equip.	9s 0d	0
No. 166	John Phillip Steele	Engraver	9s 0d	16
No. 168	Thomas Coulton	Agent	10s 6d	88
No. 170	Francis Stephen Bell	Commercial Clerk	10s 6d	69
No. 172	Mrs Theodosia Carter	Widow	10s 6d	31
No. 174	Frank Pugh Sissons	Civil Engineer	10s 6d	70
No. 190	William Bruce Bell	Commercial Traveller	10s 6d	0
No. 192	Thomas Stake	Sanitary Inspector	10s 6d	11
No. 194	Joseph Barber	Commercial Traveller	10s 6d	98
No. 196	Walter Harold Watton	Commercial Rep.	10s 6d	66

Barnfield

No. 1	N.G.T. Ward	No occupations or rents	
No. 3	William Evans	available	101
No. 5	Sarah Sturge		0
No.7	B. Holt		223
No. 9	John H. Latchford	Engraver	135
No. 11	George S. Crosby		210
No. 2	John S. Smitten	Plumber	74
No. 4	Ralph Cowell	Railway Clerk	18
No. 6	William Halliwell	Weights & Measures	85
No. 8	William J. Dawson	Potters' Secretary	83
No. 10	Miss Mary Brian	Teach of Music	95
No. 12	Joseph Poole	Manufacturer	90
No. 14	John A Jones		0
No. 16	William Thomas Evans	Engineer	97
No. 18	Caroline Watford		138
No. 20	Alice Faith		0
No. 22	William Warburton, sen	Commercial Traveller	76
No. 24	Herbert J. Glover	Photographic Artist	0
No. 26	Stephen B. Hartley	Pottery Designer	15
No. 28	Henry Charles Faram	Assistant Schoolmaster	20
No. 30	Herbert Jones	Postal Clerk	96
No. 32	M.M. Smith & Annie Saunders		0
No. 34	F. C. Rhodes		130
No. 36	H. Jones		96
No. 38	Mrs Annie Goldstraw		217
No. 40	Wm Henry Warburton	Teacher	59

Thistley Hough

No. 1	Stanley Powell	Traveller	74
No. 3	R. J. Campbell		0
No. 5	W.R. White		0
No. 7	Vacant		
No. 9	J. J. Barber		98
No. 2	Henry Broughton	Clerk	61
No. 4	W. H. Taylor		143
No. 6	Lawrence A. Banks	Clerk	0
No. 8	F.R. Woldridge		145

The Croft

No. 1			
No. 3	T. J. Dowswell		0
No. 5	A. B. Davis		140
No. 7	George E. Harding	Accountant	159
No. 9	Thomas Hassall		75
No. 11	A. Alcock		106
No. 13	H. H. Closeley		0
No. 15	J. W. Twyford		127

The Roche (Now part of The Croft)

No. 2	George Townsend		12
No. 4	N. French		0

Bromley Hough

No.3	Frank A. Bell		69
No.5	Edward E. Parry	Director	5
No.7	Dr. Gilbert P. Johnson	Medical Officer of Health	1
No.9	John W. Wadsworth	Art Director	6

The total share issue for the properties recorded amounts to 5994. Those with 0 against their names are not listed in the Share Register. As a proportion of the total number, the Share issue to the residents represents around 20% leaving investors to purchase the remaining 80%.

The following table represents how the Shares were allocated in various quantities to each household, the representation of this is set in percent and the total number of Shares by this group, again in percentages.

Number of shares

held by house holders			Represented by %	Shares held by share holders
1	-	25	15	21%	15%
26	-	50	4	5%	9%
51	-	100	34	47%	17%
101	-	150	12	16%	21%
151	-	200	5	5%	20%
Over		201	4	5%	17%

These figures show a considerable discrepancy in percentage figures reflecting the fact that occupants held a smaller number of shares than investors. The largest ratio differential is in the top three of share numbers, proving the hypothesis that those occupants on the whole, but in particular those best placed financially to purchase more shares than others abused the system, especially those holding high positions within the Society to their own benefit and personal gain.

Unfortunately, there is a problem with the data; as it is not dated. Therefore even though 98% is written in the same hand, facts point to the likelihood that it was written sometime after 1911 as the odd entry refers to that fact that a shareholder is the executive of a previous shareholder deceased. Making use of the Register of Electors for 1919, further names appear as residents, which confirm the fact that the Share Register was written sometime after that date.

The results are quite remarkable as only 35 of the residents listed in 1912 remained in occupation to just after the 1st World War. The occupiers of 60 houses had left and were replaced by other tenants. A further analysis shows a much larger share allocation to these new residents, probably a requirement introduced to attract only those with both social and financial status. Next is listed those properties which had changed hands and the share holding of each.

Trentham Road.		Shares held
No. 60	Frances Coldrick	172
No. 84	Charles Beates	89
No. 88	John Patterson	92

The Croft c1930

No. 92	John Henry Dickins	173
No. 94	Charles Cuthbertson	147
No. 112	Harret Brookfield	152
No. 116	Joseph Bernard Shemilt	183
No. 122	Joseph Edward Finney	181
No. 124	Bessie Maria Stephens	156
No. 132	John Henry Scott	187
No. 154	Frederick John Littler	65
No. 162	Agnes May Hamilton	182
No. 164	Charles Arthur Rigby	192
No. 166	Harry Taylor Haselgrave	212
No. 170	Rose Edgar Waller	123
No. 172	John Wildig	78
No. 192	Thomas Edward Dale	171
No. 194	Frederick William Carder	142

Barnfield

No. 1	Henry Hinde Stanford	196
No. 5	Annie Octavia Stringer	117

Bowls and Tennis Club members 1911

Garden Village Tennis Club late1920's

No. 11	William Silvers Creswell	190
No. 2	Albert Percy Dobson	120
No. 6	William Herbert Millard	169
No. 12	Hugh Davis	124
No. 20	William Warburton	109
No. 24	Frederick James Ridgway	90
No. 30	Edith Alice Goldstraw	104
No. 38	Daniel Hallam	213

Thistley Hough

No. 3	Ernest Everard Wilshaw	24
No. 7	Arthur Manchester	191
No. 4	William Harley Grocott	216

The Croft

No. 6	William Quinney	160
No. 7	Henry Crinean	185
No. 13	Emma Kemp	179

Bromley Hough

| No. 7 | Edwin James Browne | 215 |
| No. 9 | Amos Burton | 178 |

The total number of shares issued above amounts to 5,609 giving an average of 156 shares per occupier compared with 119 per occupier in 1912 representing an increase of 31%. Further examination of the Share Register shows that 16 names had no shares allocated to them, further suggesting that they had vacated the properties before the Share Register was compiled, probably sometime in the 1920s.

Following the end of the First World War, Stoke-on-Trent Tenants once more turned its efforts to the development of Penkhull Garden Village estate. In 1919 plans were at last prepared to construct a further 320 houses on the land that had not yet been developed. The Committee made application to Stoke-on-Trent Council for assistance with the infrastructure needed, as well as the provision for gas and electricity hoping that the council would meet part of the cost. Unfortunately, the council's view had changed from that in the early stages of the site development for at a planning committee held on the 10th April 1919 the plans were rejected. However, just one year later because of generous government subsidies being given to private builders to stimulate the construction industry, the council reversed its decision in the summer of 1920 and agreed to invest £25,000 in order for the society to commence work on a further 300 houses.

Researching the press reports of the period, a tragic incident happened in the early 1920's when the Deputy Coroner Mr E Hollinshead returned a verdict

STOKE TRAGEDY.

COLLIERY ACCOUNTANT'S SUICIDE.

The Deputy Coroner for North Staffordshire (Mr. E. Hollinshead), at Stoke, on the 4th inst., returned a verdict of suicide during a fit of temporary insanity at an inquest on the body of Lawrence Alboine Banks, colliery accountant, of 6, Thistleyhough, Garden Village, Stoke-on-Trent, who, on the previous Wednesday evening, was discovered in his bath with his throat cut. He died the following day at the North Staffordshire Infirmary from heart failure, arising from shock.

The evidence showed that the deceased had been overworked for two years, and owing to the last coal strike had not had a holiday during that time. For a few weeks he had been depressed because of the large amount of work he had to do, but deceased had no financial or other worries.

Mrs. Marion D. Banks, the widow, stated that the deceased went to have a bath, and a few minutes later she heard a noise. The bathroom door was forced open by a next-door neighbour, Mr. William Grocott, a schoolmaster.

Mr. Grocott, in evidence, stated that when he opened the door he saw the deceased lying in the bath, which was three-quarters full of water, with his throat cut. There was no evidence that he had been shaving, but close to was a blood-stained razor. The deceased was lying full length in the water, but was not under the water. He was unconscious, and was later removed to the Infirmary.

Dr. Edgar C. Myatt, who conducted the post-mortem examination, said the cause of death was heart failure, from shock arising from the injury. There was a deep incision in the neck reaching to the spinal column.

The Deputy Coroner, in returning the verdict, said he had been informed by the colliery company that all the deceased's accounts were perfectly correct; he was a man in whom the company had the greatest confidence, and everything he had done for them had been done in a perfectly creditable and proper manner.

Lord and Lady Harrowby at the 'Coming of Age' gala held in July 1912

The bowling green. Loundes Close now occupies the site

of suicide at an inquest on the body of Lawrence Banks, colliery accountant of No. 6 Thistley Hough. He was discovered in his bath with his throat cut and died the following day at the North Staffs Royal Infirmary. It was reported that evidence showed that he had been overworked for two years and owing to the last coal strike had not had a holiday during that time. He had been depressed but had no financial worries. His widow, Mrs Marion Banks, stated that her husband retired to have a bath and a few minutes later heard a noise. The bathroom door had to be forced open by a neighbour Mr Grocott, a schoolmaster. Mr Banks was found lying in the bath, which was three quarters full of water and his throat cut. The post-mortem examination revealed that the cause of death was heart failure from the shock arising from the injury.

Gilbert Richards cultivates the old bowling green as part of the war effort

As with most generous awards, such as the £25,000 council grant, there are always strings attached. Stoke-on-Trent Council agreed but there were conditions that were outlined in the minutes of the Housing Scheme Committee for May 1920.

That the new proposal submitted be approved subject to Stoke-on-Trent Tenants Ltd. amending their rules and regulations to the satisfaction of the council; especially the appointment of two representatives of the council upon the Board of Management of the Society and the approval of the Ministry of Health. That subject to approval being obtained, application be made to the Ministry of Health for sanction to the borrowing of the sum of £25,000 to be invested at 5% in Loan Stock of the Stoke-on-Trent Tenants Ltd. Under section 18(2) of the Housing, Town Planning Act, 1919.

The society rejected this offer and cited the rise in building costs, which followed the ending of the First World War as a barrier to development at that time. High building costs of the immediate post-war period were a disincentive to any further development. The society's annual report for 1921 commented: *No opportunity has presented itself during the year for dealing with the society's undeveloped land.*

The failure of the 1919-1920 attempts to resuscitate the venture led to the abandonment of the Garden Village scheme and the eventual break-up of the Penkhull estate. Apart from the construction of a series of 91 allotments abutting Newcastle Lane, the surplus acreage of the estate remained undeveloped. From the end of 1910 it was let on a short tenancy to Mr Arthur Jervis of Penkhull Farm as agricultural land. In November 1920, the Stoke-on-Trent Tenants Ltd. offered to sell to Stoke council the 95 houses in

Tennis players 1930's

Tennis players mid 1930's

the Garden Village scheme for use in its housing programme. Although the council declined the offer, in 1929 it purchased the undeveloped land at Penkhull as the site for new girls' grammar school, Thistley Hough.

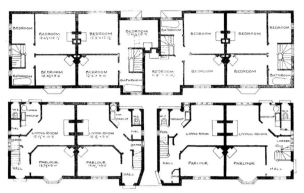

Group of four houses. The arched way gives access to the rear garden

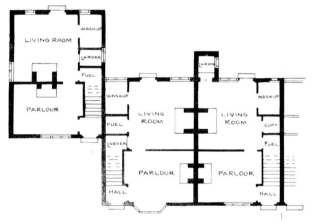

Ground floor plan of the first group of six houses

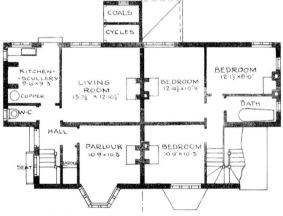

Semi-detatched house with entrance at the side

From 1921 onwards, the annual reports of the Stoke-on-Trent Tenants record revenue derived from the sale of houses on the estate to their occupants. Number 7 Bromley Hough was sold in 1921; numbers 122 and 92 Trentham Road were sold in 1929 and 1932 respectively. As the sale of these houses took place, so the features that had been incorporated into the scheme to create a harmony of design were allowed to lapse. The common road frontage pathways and shrubberies that characterised the houses along Trentham Road were steadily broken up as many tenants constructed individual paths and gateways to their homes.

By the 1930s the Penkhull estate was almost indistinguishable from any other development on the margins of industrial towns in both its occupancy and its position in an increasingly undifferentiated suburbia. The Stoke-on-Trent Tenants Association survived the dismantling of the estate and in 1939 retained sufficient reserves to begin the construction of 22 semi-detached houses along the west side of Thistley Hough. These, however, were functional and conventional in design and bore no real relationship to those in the earlier Garden Village scheme.

Recent photographs of Penkhull Garden Village 2010

Despite these difficulties, at the time all was considered well at the Garden Village as it continued to promote itself as an elitist residential area, especially by contrast with the adjacent Penkhull Square, which was occupied, in the majority, by the poor labouring classes.

In July 1932, Lord and Lady Harrowby attended a 'Coming of Age' gala and exhibition at the Garden Village to celebrate the 21st anniversary of its inception. The Garden Village, then described as one of the most delectable spots in Stoke-on-Trent held the event within the grounds of its social club. The Earl and Countess of Harrowby both expressed pleasure at the progress and prosperity of the village and the remarkable fine arts and crafts exhibition and the excellent horticultural show. *The club grounds at Barnfield were gaily decorated and the weather at its best. There was a full attendance of members of the club to welcome the Earl and his wife. On the platform were Mr E E Parry (President and Chairman of the Club) and Mrs Parry, Mr G C Crosby (Hon. Secretary), Mr G Ridgeway, senior, Mr Spencer Smith, Mr J H Latchford, Mr J W Wadsworth, Mr J Ward, and Mrs H C Faram. Glancing through the handicraft section, which The Countess had the honour to open she was struck with the number of model ships on display and wondered why was this? At the conclusion of the events a bouquet of spirea and pink carnations was presented to Lady Harrowby by Miss Jean Latchford, the little daughter of Mr E. Latchford one of the foundation members of the Club.*

Ten years after the end of the 2nd World War, when house building was on the move again and materials obtainable it was decided in 1955 to extend Thistley Hough with a number of new properties designed as flats. They were built by Joseph Jones of Newcastle and between December 1955 and December 1956, £24,300 was paid for building work followed by a further payment of nearly £19,000 in 1957.

The war also extinguished any possibility of the re-establishment of the bowling green and tennis courts, as they were found almost unrecognisable to their pre-war conditions. There was no maintenance to the grounds. With the need for allotments as part of the war effort the bowling green finally gave way to the needs of the times. After the war, the area became residential as Lowndes close flats were built in 1958 following on from the new flats built in the previous year in Thistley Hough. The old pavilion and meeting room were lost and any sense of community cohesion for the Garden Village for the future was at an end. Indeed the original concept for the Garden Village included a large community facility for library and recreation and meeting room.

To finance these extensions and to complete the flats in Thistley Hough, the committee took out loans in 1957 amounting to over £37,000, followed by additional loans amounting to £20,500 in 1959, £35,000 in 1960, £90,000 in 1960 and a further two loans from a shareholder Mr H.W. Pier who owned 244 shares of £5,000 in the January and March of 1962.

The rental charges for the new flats in Thistley Hough Nos. 12 to 50 in 1956 varied between £15 3s 4d and £16 5s 0d per month. Residents in the first group of cottages built at the top of Trent Valley Road were paying a rent of £3 2s per month in 1954 which by 1961 had increased to £7 3s 4d. The new tenants in the flats in Lowndes Close were paying in December 1958 the same as those in Thistley Hough; either £15 3s 4d or £16 5s per month. In comparison No's 2 to No. 8 Thistley Hough were paying between £3 11s 4d per month to the most expensive No.10 at £4 6s 8d in 1955, increasing to £7 3s 4d and £6 respectively in 1959.

In 1964, the Stoke-on-Trent Tenants Ltd. became a wholly owned subsidiary of Bradford Properties Trust, which owned part of the site of the Hull Garden Village at Ealing, and properties at Titus Salt's industrial village of Saltaire. In recent years Bradford Properties Trust has been taken over by a foreign investor.

The first promoters of the Penkhull Garden Village scheme inaugurated an ambitious and imaginative project in line with the visionary housing schemes of the late Edwardian period promoted by Ebenezer Howard. They could rightly congratulate themselves on the construction of a series of spacious, well-designed residences at Penkhull displaying such innovative features as indoor toilets, electric lighting and ample kitchen and bathroom facilities. In most respects, however, they failed to accomplish the overall objectives they had set themselves. In that sense the Penkhull scheme was typical of many other Garden City schemes throughout Britain during these years. Less than a third of the development, barely 95 houses were ever completed and the end product bore no relation to the original designs devised by the society's planners. Instead of a harmonious cluster of buildings with a central focal point, it comprised merely a truncated ribbon development on the west side of Trentham Road. Nor did the scheme serve to re-house working men from Stoke-on-Trent.

On the contrary, in 1912 the tenants on the estate were predominantly salaried or clerical middle-class occupations, and entry by any other class was effectively blocked. Above all the scheme did not act as the hoped-for spur stimulating the building of other 'Garden Villages' in the North Staffordshire area. The building of Welwyn Garden City in 1919 and the construction of Wythenshawe in Manchester in the 1930s demonstrated that the Garden Cities movement was very much alive elsewhere after the 1st World War, but the failure of the Penkhull scheme by 1919, despite limited attempts to enlarge the estate, meant the end of the project in the Potteries.

The author acknowledges the use of account and share books in the possession of Mr John Bullock and also acknowledges part of the work carried out by Mr Anthony Taylor and published in *The Local Historian* 1973. Town Planning, Urban Stoke-upon-rent 1902-1939 together with material from his own archives.

Chapter 16
Properties of Note.

Although there remains in Penkhull only a handful of properties, which are sufficiently interesting, they are worth recording. Penkhull was an ancient agricultural community and contained a number of properties dating from the 14th and 15th centuries which survived until the early years of the industrial revolution. However, only The Greyhound Inn remains from such an early period but those long past which were representative of a period of Penkhull's history reflect upon its once importance. Elsewherein this book there are additional accounts of three properties, the Greyhound Inn; The Views; Tittensor's House and The Mount.

A starting point here is the Reeve's Book that covers ancient messuages from the 16th to the 20th century. There are a total of seventeen ancient messuages listed. This information creates the all-important link between the past and the present.

The Views

Under the single title of The Views, is a property which holds a position of regard. There are two properties No.1 and No.2 and are found down a short drive off Penkhull New Road, next to the Terrace Inn. The Reeve Book records: *The Ancient Messuage, formerly Bower's, now Mr Terrick's. This is taken down; it was in the meadow where Mr Henny's house stands. Several houses on the meadow. Daniel Greatbatch's house stands on the site of the old messuage.*

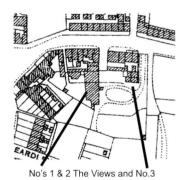

No's 1 & 2 The Views and No.3

The immediate link to this property is Daniel Greatbatch. There is mention of him in the deeds to both No.1 and No.2 The Views. His occupation was as an upholsterer. On the basis of this information from the Reeve Book it would seem that there was a much older property that once stood on this same site, the field name of which was Bowyer's or Bower's Meadow. This meadow stretched from Penkhull Village to roughly just below what is now Hunters Way. Below this was Upper Vine Meadow, which continued down to London Road. A small narrow meadow did stretch over from Bowyer's as far as Penkhull New Road, under the name of Halls Meadow, which again flowed down to approximately Hunters Way followed on by Lower Moore that broadened out covering an area now occupied by Penkhull New Road. It was across Lower Moor that Josiah Spode laid the final section of Penkhull New Road from West Bank into London Road in around the year 1812.

The name of Bowyer or Bower has been connected with Penkhull from the early 16th century. The name is not just confined to Penkhull as the manor records refer to Bower or Boyer as having land in Clayton, Boothen, Knutton, Shelton, Hanley, Wolstanton and Whitmore. The court records contain references to numerous plots of land being rented by Bowyer as the main tenant of copyhold land.

The first references to Bowyer's Meadow is found in the last will and testament of Thomas Bowyer dated 17th February 1536. His first request is that his body be buried in the chancel of St Peter's Church, Stoke, which immediately suggests his status and wealth. Not only this, but his will was drawn up by Sir Thomas Campston, curate of St Peter's Church from 1533-36, a further indication of his circle of acquaintances.

From the inventory of *all goods and chattels* compiled upon his death, we note that his debts owing to numerous people amount to £5 12s 9d, whereas the debts owed to him amounted to only 7s 0d. The inventory taken by John Bowyer, points to a small farm holding including items: *2 bullocks 26s 8d; 3 cows 34s; 1 young mare 15s; 3 pigs 6s; 4 geese 6d; corn in the field 16s 8d; corn in the barn 20s; bedding 30s; brass and pewter 23s 4d; 1 wagon; plough; harrow and other husbandry utensils 7s. The total value of goods and chattels amounted to £10 4s 6d.*

In 1568, Bartholomew Bowyer's land described as *now enclosed in the Haugh* was leased to Thomas Machin for 21 years. In the following year, 1569, he surrendered three-quarters of a day's math (work) in Honeywall Meadow to Thomas Turner. By April 1579, Bartholomew Bowyer was acting as a thirdborough for the township of Penkhull. By 1595, a Thomas Bowyer was appointed churchwarden for St Peter's Church in Stoke, and in the same year he was paying church lunes to the value of xiid *(1shilling)* charging the parish for *wrytinge my accompts vid.* (6 pence) as churchwarden.

A survey of the manor, dated 1615, lists in *Penckle* a property called Bowyer's house. The land consisted of 1¼ acres, and one croft called Grindle field, consisting of 2¼ acres. The same survey lists *William Bowyer junior by copy of court roll and paying iiijs ixd (3s 9d) in rent to the lord for two tenements and land* consisting of over nine acres.

The office of Reeve for the manor in 1672 was served by John Bowyer junior. The position was laid upon his father's property for that year but John his son undertook the position on behalf of his father. In 1703, John Bowyer died. His Last Will and Testament dated the 30th January, 1702/3 recites that he left to his wife an annuity of £30 p.a. from the rentals of all his lands. To his daughter, Anne, the sum of £500, and to his son John *all my goods and chattels and personal estate*. In June 1706, John Bowyer junior mortgaged the property for the sum of £505 to Randle Baddeley. The property was described as: *all that messuage, cartilages, barns, stables, orchards, gardens, meadows and pastures now in the holding of John Bowyer*. There is no reason to doubt that this is the property referred to in the Reeve Book.

An inventory taken on the 9th March 1702/3 includes the contents of the house in the rooms where they were held. From this information it can be established that the house contained a parlour, house place, kitchen and four bedrooms. In addition, his total estate consisted of items such as six oxen and two bullocks to the value of £37; seven cows, three twinters and a bull calf and four yearling colts to the value of £36 10s; two mares, one gelding, one three year old colt and two yearling colts valued at £27 10s. There were also pigs and sheep listed.

In the adjacent barn, there was hay and corn, some threshed, some not, to the value of £6, and the husbandry ware amounted to £9 15s. Typically for the period, a holding would support such items to produce beer, cheese, weaving etc. The inventory also includes haircloth sacks; winnow sheets, three ladders, one shovel and muck fork, axes, a mattock and iron vice. Wooden ware included looms, three spinning wheels, cheese tubs, churns, butter basins, one kymnell, barrels, cheese fats, hair sieves, one counting reel, a nager or norger a form of carpenter's tool and one hopper.

In the house place - a large room for the day to day activities of the family - there was one table and two forms, one screen, one clock, five chairs, a salt coffer, one mortar and pessal and one fender. Other items included an iron kettle, five spits, two pairs of tongs, two smoothing irons, one pair of bellows, two dripping pans, five candle sticks and many other items to the value of £6 14s.

The room set aside for special occasions was the parlour. Here was found one table with three forms, one joined bed, one chest, five joined chairs, one grate and fire shovel, a warming pan and one looking glass. As a wealthy family this room boasted a carpet and books to read. It is reasonable to assume that the traditional use of the room had given way to that of an additional bedroom, as a bed and warming pan were itemised.

In the kitchen were to be found brass, pewter, iron pots, cheese press, 28 measures of malt, two dressers and other items to the value of £9 12s 6d.

Lastly, the bedrooms or 'the chambers' as they were then called were listed; the little chamber contained one bed, one chest of draws and six thrown chairs; the chamber over the

parlour contained one bed, six thrown chairs, a wing chair, basket and six turkey cushions; the chamber over the kitchen contained two coffers and one feather bed, a prize possession in any family. In a further chamber were to be found two chaff beds, five blankets and one set of curtains, two little chairs, cheese, beef and bacon. Finally the chamber over the house place was the largest and contained two beds, two chairs, one cloth basket, a chest and two coffers. The total value of goods for the three chambers amounted to £26 12s.

Unlike his father, John Bowyer had no creditors or debtors listed, but in addition to extensive lands in Penkhull, John Bowyer owned land and property in Shelton and Hanley.

On the 14th October 1712, the son, John Bowyer, sold the land and property to John Terrick described as: *all those lands on which a certain messuage of John Bowyer stands in Penkhull with barns, outbuildings belonging with all folds, gardens, orchards and all pieces or parcels of land, meadow or pasture below the house, the Duncott Lee and the Haugh, all which were formerly the inheritance of John Bowyer*. This is later confirmed, for John Terrick was serving the office of Reeve for the manor for this ancient messuage in 1725, described as *lately purchased by him from off John Bowyer*.

In October 1764, John Terrick, gent, sold to John Slaney part of Bowyer's Meadow, measuring 20 yards in length and four yards in breadth. It was over thirty years later when we read that Samuel Slaney, bricklayer of Manchester, a relation of John Slaney, together with Ann Carter and her sister Elizabeth Barlow, his daughters and son-in-law James Carter all came to court held on the 30th December 1801 and surrendered the land, then measuring eight yards in length and just over five in depth, described as in the occupation of Samuel Doncaster.

From the above two entries, it is possible to assume that Bowyer's old house had by 1764 been demolished. Little or no evidence has survived except in the garden of No.2 The Views where a large number of sandstone blocks, cut and shaped, were discovered by Deaconess Smee who lived there from around the late 1950s. These could well have been part

The Views, Penkhull c1920's

of the old property that stood previously to the site. The Terricks sold off a section of Bowyers Meadow in 1783 to Michael Henny. The property described in the Reeve book as *where Michael Henny's house stands,* could well form the old section to the south gable end of what is now No.1. Michael Henny also held land at the top of Penkhull New Road and was the owner of The Marquis of Granby at a later date.

To put the documented evidence together, it is necessary also to view the present physical structure. Firstly, looking from the front of No.1 and No.2 The Views, it is obvious that they were built at different times. There is a join in the brickwork and although both are of the same height, No.2 has lower lintels and windows and dates from an earlier period than that of No.1. Also at No.2, whilst plastering was in progress on a side bedroom wall some years ago, the remains of a window was discovered. This at one time would have looked out across an open space to a small brick cottage, that now is incorporated into the structure of No.1 The Views.

The gable end of No.1 also gives away its secrets, so do old plans of the property. Further examination of this section from the front shows the old door, now bricked up. An old small window remains to the right of the door, and the brickwork is not as high as the remainder of the house, and the windows are positioned differently. Inside, features remain unaltered from their original positions; there is a staircase behind the main room at the front of the building and the ceilings are much lower than those in the rest of the property. All these are giveaways to its past secrets.

Although it is difficult to prove or disprove, this old section of No.1 could well have been a remaining brick section of Bowyer's old messuage, which later was converted into a separate single dwelling when the old mediaeval house was demolished. It pre-dates The Views being built probably c1720.

Next door, at No.2, there are differences from No.1. The chimney pots are not the same. The room ceilings are lower and the exposed gable end overlooking Penkhull New Road bears the give-away scars of past buildings. The old chimneystack of the once adjacent property stands proud. To the right of the stack at a height of the first floor there remains an old door lintel, although the door itself has long gone. This would have led directly into a bedroom or the landing of the attached property known as No.1 Commercial Row. At a later date, this large substantial property was divided into two smaller properties.

In all probability No.2 The Views was the last in a row of three houses, the first two being situated to the north; these became known as No. 1 and 2 Commercial Row. The

property attached to the now exposed gable end of No.2 may have been built shortly after 1764 by John Slaney, who purchased that section of Bowyer's Meadow from the Misses Terrick. The court transaction refers to a partly built house on the land forming No.2 The Views or nearby. The Views only became separated from the remainder of Commercial Row when a brick garden wall was erected. Later a carriageway entrance formed to separate the properties known as The Views, from those in Commercial Row and the old gateway bricked up.

The Misses Terrick sold a section of the land now occupied by The Views to William Hulse in 1801 described as *marked out from a meadow called Bowyers containing 54 feet from that part remaining unsold.* A further plot was sold to Daniel Greatbatch on the 2nd April 1803, adjacent to that plot sold to William Hulse, with the freedom to use the new street. Greatbatch, at a later court held on January 1805, sold a section of this land to John Eardley containing 92 sq yards of the 399 sq yards to which Greatbatch was admitted. Further plots were later added in March 1810 *part of Bowyer' Meadow, lying between that purchased by William Hulse and a further plot belonging to William Lea, together with the pump thereon standing and the full use for the said Daniel Greatbatch of the public street adjoining the plot.*

The Views c1930

Hulse already had property and land in Penkhull although it is almost impossible to identify which from the court records but it could well have been property at the top of Penkhull New Road, *To this court held on the 28th June 1780 comes Richard Ball of Trentham and Samuel Taberner of Hilderstone and surrender to William Hulse, all that dwelling house, with two shops adjoining, one of them formerly a butchers shop, together with garden belonging and now marked out and in possession of Wm. Hulse.*

Other sections of Bowyer's Meadow were sold off by the Terrick sisters, one being on the 14th February 1800 to Samuel Doncaster, engraver, recorded as within *one foot of Michael Henny's garden now in the holding of Samuel Doncaster.* In other words, Doncaster had been the tenant of the land before he purchased it.

From the following surrender and admittance at a court held on the 26th March 1811, the answer becomes clear as to who built at least No.2 The Views. *Comes to this court William Hulse, late of Penkhull but now of Tunstall, Nailor and in consideration of £120 paid by Daniel Greatbatch for the purchase of all that land marked out from Bowyer's Meadow within one foot of the hedge of Michael Henny and from the street up to the hedge of Samuel Doncaster together with the dwelling house thereon erected by the said William Hulse and now in the use of Thomas Laker to the use of Daniel Greatbatch.*

From the Land Tax records of 1823, it would appear that although William Hulse still owned a plot of land called Bowyer's Meadow, it was tenanted out to Daniel Greatbatch, confirming that although Hulse had acquired a plot in the first place, he gained access to that plot via a new road from Commercial Street (now Penkhull New Road) across Halls Meadow, the land itself was in the occupation of Greatbatch.

Daniel Greatbatch died on the 21st June 1866 at the age of 85. At some time after 1861, he moved to Blandford Forum, Dorset. In his will he left all his estate to his wife Mary Anna in trust, on condition that she did not remarry. Upon her death, the estate would then go to his daughters equally. If however, one had died before the death of Daniel Greatbatch, the estate would go to the remaining daughter and, if she had died, to be divided equally between his two sons Edward and William.

Further information comes to light from a document dated July 1866 which states firstly that Greatbatch owned: *All those two messuages with yards and gardens situate in Penkhull and then known as No.1 and No.2 The Views.* This fact qualifies the earlier assumption that he first lived in one, being No.2 The Views, built by Hulse who then built what is now No.1 between that property and the small 18th century dwelling a little distance away, shortly after 1811, when he had purchased No.2 from Hulse, and additional land from Doncaster. It is further qualified by the next statement *that since he came to live in Penkhull wherein he then resided with the two adjoining houses then occupied by his mother and his sisters.* Could this mean the property No.2 and the old 18th century cottage not yet incorporated into No.1?

The documents at this point are not quite clear. They refer to two cottages adjoining, in the occupations of Messrs Harding and Lewis but late of Fitzjohns and Deacon. I suggest that these would be the last two cottages in Commercial Row before reaching Penkhull New Road. The document then continues to recite a further two cottages nearby in the occupation of Messrs Vann and Hume, but since converted into one, now known as No.3 The Views. Part of this building remains today and forms the rear section of the garage adjacent to the west side of the drive. Miss Fanny Swetnam then occupied it. The document then mentions three other dwellings, known as No's 106, 108 and 110 Penkhull New Road.

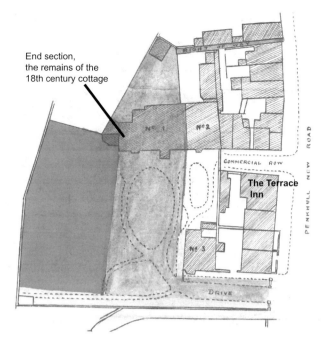

Site plan of No.1, 2 & No.3 The Views c1900

After the death of Daniel Greatbatch, his daughters married, Marion to Andrew McCreery in 1881, and Frances to William F Drew in 1899. The combined property was finally sold for the sum of £550 to be divided equally between the two sisters. All the property, Nos. 1, 2, and No.3 The Views, together with the additional cottages in Penkhull New Road were sold to Edwin Brett, a timber merchant who had already been living at The Views as tenant since Daniel Greatbatch moved to Dorset.

A further source of information to assist in identifying the occupation of properties can be found in the census returns. The available dates are from 1841-1911. For the first three returns, 1841, 1851 and 1861 no addresses are given although in the 1841, the enumerator identifies firstly the road as being Commercial Road *comprising the houses opposite Ten Row.* No additional information is given, or reference to any property set back from the road such as The Views. The 1851 census gives even less. It itemises properties in Honeywall, but lists together all the properties in the centre of the villages under one heading, Penkhull. The 1861 census identify the addresses as only Commercial Street.

Probably for over a hundred years, the famous physicist of the second half of the 19th Century, Sir Oliver Lodge has been recorded as being born at The Views, although the exact house has never been established. The census return dated 31st March 1851 gives no address details, except that of Penkhull and the names of his parents. Lodge was born just over three months after the census was taken. It was not until the 1871 census return that the name of 'The Views' appears.

The parents of Oliver Lodge are listed in the 1851 census. Oliver Lodge, head, aged 25, railway writing clerk and his wife Grace, also aged 25. Oliver senior, was the twenty-third of twenty-five children, and had to make his own way in the world. Living at the same address was Samuel Lodge, aged 22; brother of Oliver, an under-graduate at Oxford, and their house servant Elizabeth Brough, aged 21. No attempt has even been made by the Lodge family or past historians to prove, or otherwise, the assumed birthplace of Sir Oliver Lodge was The Views.

Tomb situated in Penkhull Church graveyard where the parents of Sir Oliver Lodge, Oliver and Grace are buried.

To follow any line of research, commencement is always made with the known facts. It is a known fact that Daniel Greatbatch built both No.1 and No.2 The Views. The 1841 census lists Daniel Greatbatch, although as stated no actual address is given, only that of Commercial Street. Both Daniel junior, aged 30, and Daniel senior, aged 60, are listed. The properties are six properties in number from each other in the census listing. The entry for either side of Daniel Greatbatch senior is John Rose, and the other Mary Bloor.

The 1851 return again lists Greatbatch, senior, aged 70. The listings either side are those of Henry Lawton and Jervis Platt. The entry for Oliver Lodge and his family is located five property entries before that of Greatbatch. If, therefore, Lodge was in occupation of a property which twenty years later was to become known as The Views, next to that of Daniel Greatbatch, it would have been listed in 1851 as being the entry either before or after that of Greatbatch.

Further evidence of the ownership of both properties can be found in a general valuation of properties by Stoke-upon-Trent Corporation in the 1870s. The valuation lists both the occupiers and the owners. Daniel Greatbatch both owned and occupied No.1 The Views, was valued for rateable assessments at £34, and No.2 at £19, which reflects the size of properties. No.1 was described as house, stable, garden and yard.

Sir Oliver Lodge

It therefore can be now established that Sir Oliver was not born at either property known as The Views, but at a far more undistinguished and humble property nearby in Commercial Street. Reflection on the period explains why the wrong address was given.

When a person rises through social ranks of that period, he needs to promote his standing in society by allowing it to be thought that he was born into a certain social level as it was considered at that period that *one should not rise above his station*.

Oliver Lodge went on to become one of the most important physicists of his time and to whom credit is given as the first person to transmit radio waves through the atmosphere. This is attributed to a live demonstration given at a meeting of the British Association for the advancement of science at Oxford held on the 14th August 1894, in the form of Morse code, one year before Marconi. This started the worldwide development of radio technology which was used in the first non-stop flight to Australia by Charles Kingsland in 1929. Four years following this demonstration in 1898, Lodge developed the moving-coil loudspeaker.

Lodge made a major contribution to motoring when he patented a form of electric spark ignition for the internal combustion engine. Later, his two sons developed his ideas and in 1903 founding Lodge Bros, which eventually became known as the Lodge Plug Ltd., the largest spark plug manufacturer of its time. It was a later version of the original, which operated four times faster, that was used in the Spitfire in the Battle of Britain.

Throughout his career, Lodge viewed electricity as a clean power and worked to promote this concept, and later saw the potential for nuclear power years before anyone else. He went on to write over forty books, published worldwide.

Lodge became a Doctor of Science in 1877 at the age of 26. Membership of the Royal Society in 1893, and President of the Physical Society in 1899 was followed by the 1st Principal of the new Birmingham University in 1900, a position he held until he retired in 1919, at the age of 68. And, at the age of 69, he undertook a lecture tour of America commencing with the first at Carnegie Hall in January 1920, followed by more than a further forty major USA cities.

He became a Knight Batchelor in 1902 and awarded the freedom of Stoke-on-Trent in 1928. Lodge died on the 22nd August 1940. Despite the massive contribution to the world of wireless and electrical technology at a critical period in history and acclaimed throughout the world, Stoke-on-Trent City Council have only recognised Lodge by a street name on a mid-wars council estate in the village of his birth. It would have been more fitting to have a University or at least a prominent 6th form college named after him.

The top of Commercial Street, now known by the name Penkhull New Road was statistically one of the poorer streets in the village as figures from the Stoke valuation show. The following are the average rateable values based upon streets. The value in pounds, shillings and pence has been converted into decimal amounts.

Eardley Street	£4.93
East Street	£4.87
Penkhull Square	£4.86
Brisley Hill	£5.81
St. Thomas Place	£12.93
Garden Row	£5.22
Manor Court Street	£10.50
Newcastle Lane	£4.33
Doncaster Lane	£7.75
Princes Road	£27.75
Penkhull Terrace	£9.69
Richmond Terrace	£13.25
Commercial Street	£5.50

These figures support the occupations listed in the 1881 census, identified as non-manual, skilled manual and others. The above list of streets are covered in the study so a comparison between the two sets of figures can be analysed to confirm or otherwise that the lower working classes lived in poorer properties identified by lower rateable value. The occupations for these three streets are: for the male non-manual 19%. The results for female non-manual are 8%. In comparison, Richmond Terrace, just below The Views, have different figures, male non-manual 49%, and female non-manual 32%.

It could be assumed that because Oliver Lodge and Grace his wife employed a servant as listed in the census of 1851 that they would have been reasonably wealthy. This may not have been the case. Many entries in census returns list a servant. A servant could be a member of the family, younger or elder sister, a distant relative living with the family free in return for domestic duties, or even a lodger taking on duties as a form of rent. There is no way of knowing the circumstances.

Other comparisons locally can be found to substantiate the point that a person's lower social status would impede their attempts to make their way in the world. These are several cases in which places of birth have been exaggerated so as to give someone credibility as they climbed the social ladder. For example, Dinah Craik, the author of, ' *John Halifax, Gentleman'* and other Victorian novels born Dinah Mullock, the daughter of a fire-brand Irish preacher, who thought himself God, and the grand-daughter of Jane Mellard, a tanner from the Lower Street area of Newcastle. In her biography and all other references to her early life, she is recorded as being born at Longfield Cottage, at Hartshill, a substantial residence. In reality Herbert Minton, a well

established and important potter from Stoke resided there, at the same time as Dinah Mullock is supposed to have lived there as a child. The Mullock's lived in a small nearby cottage. Another example is Sydney Malkin (1865-1953) who became a well-known local tile manufacturer in Burslem. His biography states that he was born at The Mount in Penkhull, no doubt to impress his contemporaries of the period, but in fact at that time The Mount was firmly in the occupation of Mr Frederick Bishop.

The debate caused by this revelation about Lodge will no doubt continue for years to come. Society has since changed in this respect. Nowadays those who have done well for themselves sometimes reflect upon their humble beginnings, which in most cases helps to promote their status in life.

The 1871 census firmly places The Views as an important residence, reflecting the wealth and occupations of its occupiers. Living at No.1 was John Turner, aged 44, a retired surveyor of tax who originated from Surrey along with his second wife Mary, aged 25. He has a son Edward by his first wife, aged 17, described as a *scholar at home* followed by younger children Mary, aged 2, John, aged 1, and Clement aged 8 months. In addition was their servant, Catherine Rogers, aged 15.

Next door lived Charles Tebbs, aged 30. He was a solicitor's clerk who was born in Middlesex. His wife was Lillian, aged 25. They had one child; Charles, aged 1, but also had a ward

Inside rooms of No.2 The Views c1950

Lillian, aged 4. Mary George, aged 22, was resident cook and servant.

The 1881 census shows that at No.1, Frederick Charles Painter, aged 47, a commercial pottery traveller resided with his wife Emily, just one year younger. They had a total of seven children from the ages of 24, to Edwin the youngest at 3 years. They employed two servants Mary and Emily Lightfoot, aged 18 and 15, and a children's nurse, Mary Hazelwood, aged 33.

In 1901 Edwin Brett, a timber merchant, aged 42, and bachelor, born in Sydney, Australia lived at No.1 along with his cook and housemaid, whilst at No.2 lived William Whittaker, a widower, aged 70, a retired head gardener together with his son William, aged 41, a bank clerk, and his wife Ann, also aged 41. They employed one servant aged 16.

The last census currently available is 1911. Humphrey Gamon, a solicitor, occupied No.1, aged 30, and his wife Alice, aged 31. They employed three servants. William Whittaker senior had died leaving William his son, aged 51, a bank accountant, and his wife Ann of the same age living in the house. They employed two servants. At No.3, Fanny Swetnam, aged 31, and single, a boarding house helper, lived alone.

At the time of his death in 1866, Daniel Greatbatch owned *the house wherein he then resided with the two adjoining houses, gardens and premises then occupied by his mother and sisters. In addition they owned a further nine cottages in Penkhull.*

Edwin Brett purchased these properties from the daughters of Daniel Greatbatch for the sum of £550. The sale took place on the 26th July 1898, one year after the death of his widow Mary. The above description is unclear when it speaks of *the two adjoining houses.* However a later conveyance for the property helps to clarify the situation: *All those messuages with yards, gardens and outbuildings known as No.1 and No.2 The Views the same formerly in the respective occupations of Edwin Brett and Basilla de Clare, painter but now that of Edwin Brett and the other void. Also those two cottages adjoining in the occupation of Messrs Harding and Lewis. Also those two other cottages near thereto occupied by Messrs Vann and Hulme and those three other cottages Numbered 106, 108 and 110 in Penkhull New Road in the occupation of Messrs Worthen, Cope, and Rhodes.*

Following the death of Edwin Brett, his estate was placed into the hands of his sole trustee and executor, Frank Thomas of 18 Bedford Circus, Exeter, solicitor. A document which has survived, dated the 25th November 1909, helps to clarify unanswered questions as it itemises the property by occupiers. *All those two messuages, yards, gardens and outbuildings known as No.1 and No.2 The Views and now in the*

respective occupations of Humphrey Gamon and William Whittaker, and also those two cottages adjoining now in the occupation of Mrs Deacon and Mr B. Fitzjohns. The property known as No.3 The Views now occupied as one property by Miss Fanny Swetnam. Those three other cottages known as Nos.106, 108 and 110 Penkhull New Road. After dealing with other matters the document continues: *And thirdly all those four, now occupied as three cottages being No.1 and No.2 Commercial Row and Nos.102 and 104 Penkhull New Road which were subsequently converted into two houses by Edwin Brett in the occupations of Messrs J. Dooly and M. Bellingham.*

Until the 27th February 1901, the entrance to The Views was via Commercial Row, which ran directly into a private driveway. The outline of the entrance, now bricked up, remains behind the current overgrowth and in all probability there would have been iron gates to add to the importance of the properties and their occupants. The current driveway, together with the land to the south of No.1, was at one time the property of Josiah Spode, later to be purchased by Frederick Bishop of The Mount. After the death of Bishop in October 1891 at Cannes, the property was left to his sons, who sold the land adjoining the south of No.1 to Edwin Brett. The area consisted of 845 square yards. In addition to this plot, the land that now forms the current driveway was added to the sale. *All that piece of copyhold land abutting on the Penkhull New Road and partly adjoining the garden of the dwelling house occupied and belonging to Edwin Brett, which plot of land, contained by estimate 210 square yards.* Both were sold for the sum of £141 4s 6d. Both Gamon and Whittaker were still residents in 1907 and 1912. By 1914, No.1 is listed as void, Mr Arthur Piercy occupied No.2 and No.3 by Fanny Swetnam.

Both properties remained in the hands of Frank Thomas, solicitor as trustee of the estate until the sale of No.1 The Views including the additional land to the south and the new access drive to Miss Beatrice Mary Lowe on the 25th

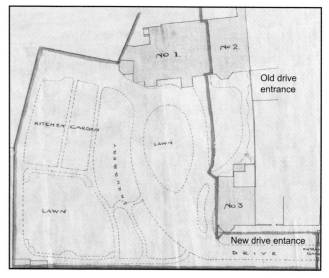

Plan of the site showing the original size of the plot and the new drive created in 1891

June 1924. Miss Lowe was then residing at No. 20 Penkhull Terrace. The property was then described as previously occupied by Frederick Septimus Stinger, but at the time of the sale, void. The total value amounted to £850.

Miss Lowe married John Townsend in September 1942 and died on the 11th March 1988, appointing Barclays Bank to administer her estate. The property was subsequently sold to Sir Stanley and Lady Matthews on the 7th October 1988 for the sum of £112,000. Following the death of Sir Stanley Matthews, aged 85 on the 23rd February 2000, the property was sold in August 2001 to its present owner, Dr Charles Pantin.

Sir Stanley Matthews

Mr Thomas did not sell No.2 until the 31st December 1925. It was purchased for the sum of £425 by Mr Ernest Carr, a motor engineer then residing at Clifton Street, Hartshill for £275. The sale was restricted to what is known as No.2 The Views; those properties in Commercial Row and Penkhull New Road were sold separately. Twenty years after its purchase, Carr went to live in Franklin Road and sold the property on the 13th June 1945, for the sum of £875 to Mr Frank Smee of St Albans, a retired provisions dealer.

Frank Smee died in January 1946, and the property was inherited by Victor Smee, who, two years later, gifted the house to his sister, Deaconess Miss Beatrice Irene Smee. Miss Smee was a deaconess in the Church of England and on the staff at St Peter's Church in Stoke. She died on the 23rd November 1971. Miss Smee remains today a well-remembered and valued figure in North Staffordshire. Upon the death of Miss Smee the house was passed into the ownership of Mr Richard and Mrs Elaine Holland. Mrs Holland still resides in the property.

Penkhull Square.

An ancient messuage called Turner's in the Lane, now Mr Joseph Lovatt's, Mr Spode has purchased and pulled down this messuage and built 20 houses upon the site.

In a number of documents this property is referred to as Turner's and Ingram's in the Lane, the lane being Trent Valley Road. In some instances it is recorded as Turner's, formerly Ingram's which suggests that it may have been one property. It stood on the site of what was formerly Penkhull Square, now Jeremy Close. Little if anything is known of this but it is worth recording for it occupied a significant site within the village. The name of Ingrum or Ingram first recorded in the Rolls of the manor from 1649 when Joan Ingrum, widow was fined 2d for brewing ale. She appeared again in 1654 charged with the same offence. It was not until

Penkhull Square was demolished in the 1960s, that while excavating for new development, foundations were exposed of a much older property.

I was then employed by the contractor who was installing electrical heating systems and was told about the find and its extent, which indicated a large property. Phone calls were made to the contractors and architects for permission to view the site, but I was warned at this stage by my employer that I faced dismissal if I pursued my line of inquiry. This was to prevent a team of archaeologists holding up the work on the site whilst investigations were made. As a result nothing was recorded.

Many of the old mediaeval properties in Penkhull, as acquired by Spode, promptly demolished them making way for new cottages for his workers.

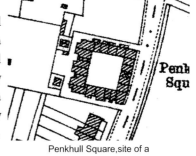
Penkhull Square, site of a previous ancient messuage

The earliest reference in the name Turner is found in 1450 when William Turner was fined 2d for possession of land for which he was not the tenant. A Roger Turner is recorded in the 1516 survey of the manor paying 10s 10d rent. In April 1589, it is recorded that William Turner senior, married Agnes Huchens the daughter and heir of Roger Huchens, who held property in the Lane. This could well have become known as Turner's at a later date.

The copyhold court minutes of 5th November 1612, record that William and Agnes Turner surrendered a cottage and land to Thomas Rawlins on condition that they would pay 8d a year at the usual feast days to the King which was part of the rent due. The Last Will and Testament has survived for William Turner dated June 1613, presents a wealthy yeoman farmer. Included in the inventory is corn to the value of £15 10s, hay £3 6s 8d; butter and cheese £3 4s; bedding; sheets and napery ware £10 6s 8d; pewter at £20; and brass at £2. He left all his goods and chattels, moveable and unmoveable, to his son William junior. By the survey of 1615, the rental had been increased to 17s 6d, but there are two messuages listed and several pieces of land of arable and pasture. By 1650, William Turner was paying rent for a total of 49 acres.

Each year, the manor court officers were appointed for the position of Reeve, a position that few would undertake because of the responsibilities of ensuring that all were called to court attended on the right day and the responsibility for the administration of governance of the manor. In May 1621, after the death of his father, the court ordered William Turner junior that he ought to serve the office of Reeve for the following year for *the house called oulde Turners house in the lane.*

Occasionally the manor court rolls record events that give a snapshot of life at the time. One such record is dated 6th October 1625 when Agnes Turner, the widow of William was fined 40s. Her crime that *she caused certain old timber and stones, which has been for the foundations for a previous old part of her premises to be set at another copyhold premises in Penkhull and that Margaret her daughter, now the wife of William Hunt, cut down various trees and two crab-apple trees - fined 20s.*

On the 13th December 1638, the property was surrendered court by William Turner, junior and his wife Anne to Roger Dale, owner of Greenhead House for the sum of £486. The transfer of property and land included, *one messuage with all buildings, one field, one hamlet, three crofts called Nealers or le Hough together with the enclosure called le Slade, a field called Bearshill and land called le Waste.* A survey of the manor shows that Thomas Dale occupied the property in 1714 and recorded as *formerly Turners and Ingram's, now in the holding of Thomas Dale.*

The land and property were later transferred to Thomas Lovatt then to William and lastly Joseph Lovatt, all of whom lived at Chirk in Denbighshire. Upon the death of Joseph Lovatt, his trustee, John Jones was admitted tenant at a manor court held in October 1801. The following year, 1802, John Jones surrendered the land to Josiah Spode by which time Turner's old property had been demolished, but recorded as *lastly in the occupations of Sampson Butterton and Samuel Leigh.* Spode then set about building twenty workers dwellings on the site, which became known as Penkhull Square.

No. 16 Garden Street.

The next property worthy of mention is hidden away in Garden Street behind a brick wall. In fact it was built gable-end on to the old lane, a feature often used for building. Number 16 has held the secrets of its past from the early 17th century. Garden Street was formerly called Farm Lane, but prior to this went by the name Tittensor's Lane, reflecting no doubt an important resident of a property in the lane at an earlier date. Garden Street remains almost suspended in time and part of the ancient village of Penkhull from mediaeval times, with its dry stonewalls and no footpaths.

Although the present owners Paul and Janet Kelly have allowed me access to their property deeds, these unfortunately fail to mention any owner or occupant prior to 1821. The reason for this is that the cottage was at that time classed as enfeoffed. This term dates from the feudal system; enfeoffment was the deed by which a person was given land in exchange for a pledge or service. It can also mean to put

No.16 Garden Street

a tenant legally in possession of a property. This is a most unusual term but it is found in Penkhull where the land was copyhold to the Duchy of Lancaster. Further research was needed to unravel this complicated legal issue.

Old section of No.16 with original features

For whatever reason, that former copyhold land was granted to William Davies on the 20th July 1822 and the transaction is recorded in the Wastehold book for the manor. The document recites that Davies paid to The Special Court of the Sovereign King, Lord of the Manor held at Penkhull the sum of £2 and that the deputy steward of the manor *Granted to William Davis All that small cottage situate in Penkhull adjoining on the north side a dwelling house in the holding of Margaret Tittensor, late in the holding of Thomas Alcock and now of the said William Davis. And the Lord of the manor granted sezin thereof to William Davis.*

We conclude from such a grant that the person who previously held this cottage had died intestate, and Davis being the owner of the property next door asked the court for himself to be entered upon the court rolls as tenant of the manor and on a payment of £2.

A cottage or a number of cottages are shown on Yates map of 1775, and again on Hargreaves' map of 1832. There are no maps or plans earlier than this date. The first document available for research is the Last Will and Testament of Jacob Tittensor, potter dated 21st October 1821. It recites that after his death his estate would go to his wife Elizabeth and after her death to his son Jacob, then a soldier but not knowing if he was still alive, passed it on to his grandson, James Chalton followed by his daughters Ellen Chalton and Margaret, known as Peggy. Other records available identify at least the existence of the cottage at a much earlier date.

In a survey dated 1654, two properties can be identified as in the ownership of persons of the name Tittensor, one named Roger, the other Thomas. Roger is known to have owned Tittensor's House which was demolished by Josiah Spode to make way for The Mount. The rentals due to the lord of the manor itemised in this survey reflect the size of property and land, Roger's being £1 and that of Thomas much smaller at 2s 6d. The Hearth Tax records of 1662 and 1666 also identify two properties in the name of Tittensor, William with two hearths and Thomas with one.

The first indenture, which legally binds both parties to a sale of No.16, is dated 3rd July 1827 between Peggy (Margaret) Tittensor and William Davis, labourer of the same place. The cottage with its land was sold to Davis for the sum of £30 and listed as *unoccupied but for many years occupied by Ralph Tittensor, deceased.* The Indenture continues to inform the reader that it was next to a cottage, also owned by Peggy Tittensor, but in the occupation of William Davis.

There are no copyhold court transactions for this property after it was granted to Davis in 1822 but the name of Ralph Tittensor identified in the Indenture dated 1827 provides the necessary link to take the cottage back to its origins. The cottage had been passed down, from one generation to the next, back to a court record dated 14th March 1723 which refers to *all that newly erected cottage, standing in Penkhull, adjoining the garden of Thomas Pickin and land adjoining together with the liberty to come across the adjacent land to building the new building upon the premises and to repair the said cottage and all the new building as necessary.*

From this short account it would seem that in addition to the new build that was ongoing, the old cottage still formed a part of it as access was required to maintain the property in good repair. Could this old section of the new building therefore be the property listed in the survey of the manor dated 1654?

In April 1730, Thomas Tittensor, the son of Ann, deceased, transferred the cottage to John Terrick, probably on the condition of a loan from Joseph Tittensor. It was Joseph who sold the cottage to Ralph Tittensor who either rebuilt the cottage or added new sections to it. In 1756, Ralph mortgaged the cottage to his neighbour Harvey Boulton,

tenant of Penkhull farm, for the sum of £6. Later in 1772, Ralph sold the cottage to John Tittensor, potter subject to 8d a week, given to his mother Sarah for life, but in October the following year, the cottage was returned into the ownership of Ralph who mortgaged it for the sum of £12.

Following on from 1772, the cottage remained in the hands of the Tittensor family until 1778, when Jane the widow of Ralph Tittensor took possession, it was held on security for a mortgage. The property is not recorded again until October 1792, when Margery Chapman, late Margery Bourne the only sister of the late Joseph Bourne, is holding Tittensor's cottage as part of a substantial inheritance. From Margery Chapman, by whatever means it returns to the Tittensor family in October 1821 when it is listed in the Last Will of Jacob Tittensor.

Returning once more to the documents in hand, it appears that first one cottage is sold and then another, but at different times. After July 1827, the next document is dated 22nd November 1827 and covers the transfer of property from William Davis to James Yates and William Machin of Swinnerton. What complicates research further is that there were four cottages adjacent to each other, not just one, but this will become clear as the story unfolds. The indenture dated the 22nd of November 1827 included: *whereas Yates and Machin acquire two cottages all those two cottages situate in Penkhull adjoining each other and bounded on one side a cottage belonging to and in the occupation of Ellen Chalton and which cottages are intended to be conveyed, previously belonging to Peggy Tittensor and have lately been conveyed by her to William Davies and William Machin.* The purchase price for these two cottages was £67.

At a further copyhold court held on the 4th February 1830, William Davies sold one of the cottages for £45 to George Bagnall, a farmer. The record reads: *all that cottage adjoining north of the dwelling house formerly occupied by Margaret Tittensor, but now of William Leese belonging to William Davis as granted to him of the 20th July 1822.*

In March 1831, William Yates as trustee of George Bagnall sold two cottages to Job Bagnall for the sum of £60. By November 1838, Jacob Tittensor had returned from the army and reclaims his rightful inheritance of the cottages. *Jacob Tittensor, late a private in the Fourth Regiment of Foot but now residing at Lane End and George Bagnall, yeoman of Penkhull and Job Bagnall of Tittensor, miller his Trustee. Whereas Jacob Tittensor is entitled to the fee simple* (the freehold which passes to the lawful heir without restriction) *and inheritance has agreed to sell the said dwelling houses and land for the sum of £12. All those dwelling houses situate in Penkhull many years previously occupied by Jacob Tittensor deceased, father of the said Jacob Tittensor and afterwards of his widow late Ellen Banks and now un-tenanted.*

At this point, the line of ownership becomes confused for there is no documentation after 1838 until 1909, when Daniel Cotton made a statutory declaration before a Commissioner of Oaths on the 7th June as to its ownership. But it is not this document that tells the whole story, but one that comes all the way from Philadelphia, North America which explains how the property came into the ownership of Mr Daniel Cotton of Clyde Street, Hartshill.

So what do we know of Jacob Tittensor junior who returned from the army? His army record has survived and is quite revealing. He was born in Echertean, Staffordshire c1796 and at the age of seventeen enrolled in the 4th Foot Regiment, London on the 6th December 1813. Why it is not known, his occupation was that of labourer and probably was attracted by a sense of adventure for it was a time of heroism against Bonaparte. Jacob never passed the rank of Private. He deserted on the 28th December 1818, but was returned on the 13th January the following year. Following corporal punishment by the birch, he was pardoned and reinstated afterwards to the position of Private.

From the 11th July 1829 to the 22nd of July, he was imprisoned but no reason was given. During his service he was a foot soldier at the Battle of Waterloo on the 18th June 1815 and also the Battle of Bladensburg, just a few miles from Washington D.C. He was one of three thousand foot soldiers from England fighting that day.

Private Tittensor spent three years in France, seven in the West Indies, one in Portugal, five in New South Wales and a period on the East Indies, quite an outstanding period in the army until he was discharged in January 1838 on medical grounds at the age of nearly 42 years. The reason was given as: *a consequence of a broken constitution from Rheumatism and long service in different climates, especially at Coxs' River in New South Wales.* General John Hodgson in his report on Tittensor's service wrote, *Jacob bears the character of an 'indifferent' soldier in the Regiment but his conduct whilst in hospital has been always very good and contributed every thing in his power to accelerate his cure.* By this time Jacob had completed 25 years service as a foot soldier and considering the conflicts he was involved in, it remains remarkable that he survived.

The following year he married Sarah Hudson at Wolstanton. By 1841, he had returned to Penkhull living at the lower section of Honeywall. His wife died in 1848 and is buried in Stoke Churchyard. The following year he was remarried to Thirza Lythgrove at Wolstanton. By 1851, he was back living at Penkhull where he died in 1867. His widow was still living at Penkhull in 1871. She died in 1876.

Thomas Haywood was the grandson of Job Bagnall and the property in Penkhull and a one half share of the estate passed down to him. The other name recited in the document was Thomas Deaville who died and his estate divided between his wife Mary Elizabeth Deaville and his two daughters, Ella Ann Fanny Bullock, Dora Hilda Beverage. Under the terms of the will, dated 22nd February 1840, Daniel Cotton was to receive the share passed down to Thomas Haywood although under the terms of the Will of Job Bagnall, Cotton was to inherit three cottages.

The Tithe Map and Schedule dated 1849 lists the four cottages, in the ownership of late George Bagnall, executor of John Bagnall in the occupation of Susannah Lees and others.

By 1909, three of the four original cottages had been demolished and the sites have been added to and formed a part of the garden of the one remaining, then identified as No.16, which was previously held by Arthur Shenton, but in 1909 of Thomas Bardell. On the 10th June 1918, Mary Deaville, her daughters and Daniel Cotton sold the remaining cottage to Henry Hind of May Bank, general builder, for the sum of £85.

Eighteen years passed before the property was sold again. Mr Hind had died and his widow Mary Elizabeth sold the property to Mrs Elsie Taylor, wife of Louis Taylor of Elm Tree House, for the sum of £90. The cottage was purchased to house their driver and odd job man. In 1937, the Taylor's sold Elm Tree House and No.16 Garden Street to Mr Frederick Watson Duthie, surgeon, for the sum of £1,450.

It was three years later in 1940, that Mr Duthie sold both properties to Dr Richard Gamble, a local physician from Stoke, for the sum of £1,550. In December 1949, Dr Gamble sold No.16 Garden Street to Mr Roger Shewring of 11 Bath Street, Stoke, for the sum of £300. In 1956 he mortgaged the property to gain a loan for the sum of £1,485 from Stoke-on-Trent City Council for improvements and extensions. This work included replacing most of the external walls and the construction of an additional living room, dining room, landing, kitchen and bathroom.

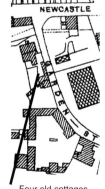

Four old cottages

In February 1963, Shewring sold the greatly improved and altered cottage to Mr Charles Shaw of Oxford Street, Penkhull, for the sum of £3,400, and Mr Shaw went on to sell it again in July 1969 to Mr and Mrs R Sharratt for the sum of £6,000. The present owners, Paul and Janet Kelly, purchased the cottage from the Sharratt's in 1999.

Elm Tree House.

This property, found at the junction of Garden Street and Newcastle Lane is probably the oldest and largest of the houses still remaining in Penkhull. The current name did not appear until early in the 20th century which considerably hinders the tracing of its history.

The property was for centuries known as Tittensor's Messuage, differing from a further property under the title of Tittensor's House which previously stood on the site of The Mount. The name of Tittensor was also given to the lane where Elm Tree House stands. Before being called by its present name, Garden Street, it was appropriately called Farm Lane, but in mediaeval times went by the name of Tittensor on the basis that Tittensor's Messuage (dwelling) was situated there.

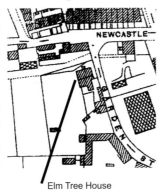
Elm Tree House

In a survey of the manor, dated 1414, two Tyttensor's are listed as holding land within Penkhull. John held half a messuage and various strips of lands within the open fields of the village. William held also half a messuage and lands within the open fields. In the description it is said that a William formerly held both the properties and land. It could be assumed therefore that the earlier William was the father, and John and William were brothers.

Throughout the court records and surveys of the manor, the names of the two families remain consistent. However, it is almost impossible to distinguish which family held what until the 17th century, when we read in the copyhold records of March 1608 of the death of Robert Tittensor and that his messuage and land were transferred to Thomas Tittensor, his son, at a following court dated the 15th May 1608. In this entry there is a description of the property, *Tittensor down in the town of Penkhull* sometimes referred to as *'down in the Town of Penkhull'*. An unusual description and it has proved difficult to identify what it means. Perhaps it referred to the town of Stoke being situated in the Township of Penkhull. However, other documents confirm without doubt that it is referring to the centre of the village of Penkhull. The reason is explained further by property known by the name of Tittensor's, was located a little distance from the village where The Mount now stands. To separate the two properties, both owned by a Tittensor, the wording was used *Tittensor's up in the town of Penkhull,* referring to the village as we would know it today.

Thomas died in 1631, and the copyhold court record gives a further description in the amount of land attached: *Thomas*

Tittensor has died since the last court seized of a messuage and lands belonging in Penkhull. A heriot of 17s is due (implying a customary acreage of 17 acres) and that Roger is his son and next heir and of full age. The writer of the entry, John Fenton added, *"This was Tittensor's land down in the town of Penkhull."* In a survey of the manor taken in 1650, Thomas Tittensor, jun. is listed as having 17 acres of land.

The Manor Reeve Book, undoubtedly one of the most important documents for the period, helps to identify ancient messuages and their occupancy in considerable detail. Robert Tittensor is listed in one of the very first entries in a record of 1585, confirming the copyhold account dated 1608. In reality, his son Thomas may well have taken over the running of his affairs before this date, as in 1606, he is listed as being appointed to the office of Reeve for the year 1606.

The following entry of 1684 shows that father and son, Roger and John were living at the old house, but the office of Reeve was performed by Richard Cartwright for which a payment would have been made for this service.

In an attempt to unfold the mystery of this house, and in particular the initials on the cast-iron plaque dated 1694 situated high on the wall overlooking Newcastle Lane it was necessary to visit the National Archives at Kew. The answer was discovered in a court roll dated 22nd October 1693 towards the end of the reign of King William and Mary, when John Tittensor and Elizabeth surrendered the copyhold land and property to Daniel Edwards.

The court record, written in Latin, commences with John and Elizabeth attending the court and a third person by the name of James Heath. Elizabeth was first examined secretly to show that she was not under any coercion from her husband to surrender the property she had an established interest in.

It was described as in the occupation of John Tittensor and John Spencer listing barns, stables, cowsheds, bake house etc. Then followed an unusual condition that the sale of the property did not include the whole of the building as all the constituent materials of the south part of the messuage containing *about 33½ feet in length on the south side of the common passage exclusive of the street and crocks standing on and making up the south part or side of the entry.* It further itemised the building and its materials on the east part of the barn being one bay of building, which was adjacent to a further bay used for threshing.

There are two properties listed here, a farmhouse and farm buildings. From this court record it would appear that John and Elizabeth were selling only half of the property, which was to be demolished but the building materials retained.

Hence the detailed exception to the surrender. The farmhouse was to remain occupied by John Spencer. The court record also listed a number of fields including *Minorsley, alias Milnersley, meadow.*

This additional wording helps to confirm that the property being discussed is Elm Tree House and the following two records further confirm. The first is from a survey of the manor dated 1615 which lists the property of Thomas Tyttensor: *one little medo called miln[er]sley medo.* The second confirmation comes from a further survey dated 1714 where the property is described as: *the ancient messuage as formerly in the ownership Roger and John Tittensor as being re-edifyed by and belonging to Daniel Edwards.* The word re-edifying means to re-build which would be the appropriate description following the re-building in 1694.

The plaque reads from the top the letter 'E', for Edwards followed underneath by the letters 'D J' for Daniel and his wife Jane, followed by the date 1694. From this, the picture comes into focus as the building today is made up of two parts, the front dating 1694 and a small section to the rear of the property dating

Plaque dated 1694

from an earlier date. Inside the house there are two staircases, adding further to the conclusion that Edwards, upon purchasing the old Tittensor's Messuage in 1693, either demolished part of this for a new section, or just added on to the side of it. Whichever, the facts have been discovered, but even this older section would have replaced a much earlier property which stood on the same site from the time of the Domesday inquisition.

The parish listing of 1701 includes the name of Daniel Edwards; yeoman, aged 44, wife Jane, aged 42, and ten children from the ages of 2 years to that of 16. A further plaque which once appeared on an adjacent barn contained the initials D.L. under which are the initials of W.R.T.G., and again followed by the date 1694. These initials could well represent the initials of other family members.

A few words noted in a copyhold record dated the 30th December 1713 refer to a large estate including land and property in Hartshill and Clayton in addition to Penkhull, being mortgaged by Daniel Edwards, but points to an earlier transfer of ownership of Elm Tree House. It states *'which premises were purchased by the said Daniel Edwards of John Tittensor'.*

It was twelve years later in January 1725/6 that Daniel Edwards sold the house and land to Margery Bourne, widow

Elm Tree House, front section built 1694, rear section is much older

and it is through marriage probably of her granddaughter also named Margery, and described as the sister of Joseph Bourne, late of Penkhull, gent, deceased, that the property passed. Although the formal admittance was not until the 3rd September 1792, the property was leased out to John Burgess, gardener in October 1790 by which time Margery had married John Chapman, yeoman.

The copyhold entry is worth recording: *renting for 21 years at £12 p.a. The property now made into two and previously in the holding of John Wagg and Joseph Sharlott with all stables, outbuildings, garden and large orchard.* Further information of the admittance lists the various lands attached to the property including the field on the other side of Newcastle Lane, Little Townsend and three other small messuages in the occupations of Sarah Tittensor, Sarah Dishley and George Hudson. The wider inheritance also included Penkhull windmill.

John Chapman died on the 26th May 1821. In his Last Will and Testament dated 1st December 1818, Chapman leaves it to: *my affectionate wife Elizabeth a life annuity of £25 p.a. to be charged to his copyhold estate in the holding of John Burgess.* Personal bequests amounted to the sum of £280 and his estate he left to his nephew William Chapman, farmer of Stockton, Shropshire. In addition he directed that one of his

Back view of Elm Tree House showing the two styles of building

tenants, George Hudson should enjoy tenants' rights and continue to live there free of rent until his death. William Chapman was formally admitted as tenant of the manor at a court held at Penkhull on the 18th September 1821.

Side elevation of Elm Tree House

In December 1829, John Burgess, the son of William Burgess, borrowed from his mother Margaret, the sum of £200 to pay William Chapman as a surety for the property. This was held over until June 1836 when Margaret Burgess paid a further sum of £600 to complete the purchase and was admitted tenant to: *All that messuage standing in Penkhull with garden, orchard and dwelling house formerly called Tittensor's Messuage and also those three other cottages with barn adjoining standing nearby. And also all those copyhold lands called Little Townsend which are now in the occupation of John and Margaret Burgess and other lands of which John Chapman died seized* (in occupation of) *which were the inheritance of William Chapman.*

The next document dated 2nd December 1839, is a pre-nuptial agreement explaining in detail what was to happen to her estate when she married Joseph Kent, a partner in the nursery business. It firstly lists Peggy Burgess (Margaret) the widow of William Burgess, who was intending to marry a once business partner of her late husband, Joseph Kent. Reference is made first of all to a previous court held in June 1836 whereby Peggy Burgess was admitted tenant upon the surrender of William Chapman and his mortgagee. It then continues with a brief description and a reference to the name by which the house was formally known: *All that customary messuage situate in Penkhull with the garden, orchard belonging formerly called Tittensor's Messuage, and also all those three other dwelling houses with the barn belonging and standing near the first mentioned messuage but which three dwelling houses and barn are now converted into a store room or warehouse, cart house and stable, and all that close of land called Little Townsend all of which are now in the occupation of Peggy Burgess.*

Peggy Kent died on the 25th September 1866, her daughter Mary Ann Burgess, who was married to Mr Stephen Astbury

Hughes, had died before her mother, leaving four children, George Burgess Hughes, Annie Hughes, Stephen Astbury Hughes and Elizabeth Walmsley Hughes. Under the terms of the surrender to her trustees in 1836, the estate was sold and the assets divided either after her death or once Mary Ann had reached the age of 21 years. The estate was surrendered at a court held on the 2nd March 1872 to Mr George Henry Jones, pottery manufacturer of Stoke as trustee and husband of Elizabeth Walmsley Jones (formerly Hughes) of Stoke for the sum of £450. After the death of Mr George Henry Jones it passed to George Jones, being a settlement made on the marriage of George Henry and Elizabeth Walmsley. George Henry died 1st October 1916.

Although the property was transferred by the copyhold court to George Jones, it was described as recently in the occupation of Basil Frederick Blois, and now of Louis George Taylor, auctioneer and brother-in-law to Sarah Hollinshead. In 1919, Mrs Elizabeth Walmsley Jones sold the property to Mrs Sarah Hollinshead of The Elms, Penkhull, wife of John Hollinshead, earthenware manufacturer. Sarah Hollinshead died on the 27th March 1920 several years after the death of her husband John who died in December 1912. Her executors sold the property to Mrs Elsie Taylor, wife of Louis George Taylor, on the 25th April 1923 for the sum of £650. It is interesting to note that in April the following year Mrs Taylor took out a mortgage on the property from The Leek United and Midlands Building Society for the sum of £900.

In 1937, Mrs Taylor sold Elm Tree House to Mr Frederick W. Duthie, surgeon for £1,450, and also the old cottage next door No.16 Garden Street to be followed shortly after by Dr Richard R. Gamble, a general practitioner in the town of Stoke in February 1940. Dr Gamble paid the sum of £1,550 for both the properties. Dr Gamble died in the June of 1955. He was a much respected and admired resident and G.P. His widow Dr Mrs Annie Gamble, herself a local G.P. continued to live in the house until 1989 when it was sold to Mr and Mrs J Brightmore for the sum of £130,000. The property is currently owned by Mr Gus Hills.

W. Lewis's old nursery shop
On the corner of Garden Street opposite to Elm Tree House stands a modern flower shop trading under the name of W Lewis. The whole area at one time was previously run by Burgess later to become Burgess and Kent. The property lay on the south side of Newcastle Lane and butted out into the road. The front of the house was at right angles to the road facing up the lane. The the rear of the house was used for the retail of flowers via access along a path to its junction to Garden Street after the old barn was demolished. Following the demolition of the old barn on the other side of Garden Street for road widening flowers were kept cool in a large cellar beneath the shop.

Despite major difficulties in tracing the history of previous properties and sorting the many pieces of the jigsaw to enable their stories to be told, the history of this property has been relatively easy to unravel.

Old Barn   Penkhull Nursery

The original documents to the property are now in the hands of Nick Plant of Garden Street. Through these documents a link from those dating from the middle of the 19th century to earlier records within the copyhold court archives was established, the link name being Edge.

The first mention of Thomas Edge is found in 1656 when he acquired, for the sum of £4 4s 8d, one close of land called Bearshill from Roger Machin. Bearshill is the area now known as Brisley Hill and Hunters Way. The next reference comes in 1682 when he was fined 2d for erecting a property on the wasteland of the manor. Could this be the property later to become used as both the home and flower shop of William Lewis? Thomas Edge died in 1705 and his son

Lewis's old house jutting out at right angles into Newcastle Lane

Hugh inherited the old cottage. There are no further references in court records until October 1717 when John Cooper is admitted tenant, probably a distant relative of Edge. Cooper acquires additional land across the road by the name of 'Townsend' in 1741 from John Alsager, owner of Penkhull Farm and a cottage which Cooper already occupied on a 99 year lease for one penny from John Terrick. Sometimes the name of Cooper is spelt as Cowper.

Following the death of John, his widow Margaret was formally admitted tenant in October 1778, but in the following year she died. Her son George Cooper, yeoman of Penkhull, was admitted at a court held on the 27th October 1779.

The next transaction of importance was on the 24th April 1808. Following the death of George Cooper, John his son, described as a potter, inherited the property, but this time the estate contained a further cottage. *All that small house, late in the occupation of George Cooper, deceased but now of William Brunt, and all gardens. And also that other small house, heretofore in the holding of Mary Cooper, afterwards of Samuel Alcock and now of the said John Cooper.*

This additional property referred to stood a little distance down Newcastle Lane opposite to what is Franklin Road, almost cut out of the embankment. In fact this was a typical encroachment onto the Lord's waste and as such was referred to in a survey of the manor in 1777 as being in the occupation of George Cowper.

View of the front of Penkhull Nursery from Newcastle Lane c1960

In May 1812, John Cooper transferred the property to John Burgess for a mortgage of £100, only to have to borrow a further £50 in May the following year. The mortgage then passed to a number of people. Although we are dealing with the ownership of the old property in Newcastle Lane, the occupation may well be different. In this case there are signs to suggest that Burgess was the occupier. The land to the rear of the house was formerly a part of the land attached to 'Greenhead House', (The Greyhound Inn). The owner in 1812 was John Townsend who divided up the of land into three. One of the purchasers was John Burgess who purchased on the 21st April 1812 *All that close or piece of land or ground of croft or orchard adjoining the dwelling house of John Townsend marked out by a quick set hedge and containing three thousand, one hundred and forty four square yards late in the holding of John Townsend but now of John Burgess his assigns or under-tenants abutting to the north of the road leading from Newcastle to Penkhull and on the west to the Lane or road called Tittensor's Lane there John Burgess for ever enjoying the rights to the fence separating the respective properties now sold.*

The Tithe map and schedule dated 1849 states that it was owned by John Burgess, senior, and in the occupation of Burgess and Thomas Kent.

Entrance to the retail flower shop to the rear of the house

From the ownership of John Burgess it passed through the family to Peggy Burgess and to other family members, including her granddaughter Elizabeth Walmsley Hughes, who took the name of Burgess until her marriage to George Jones. From Elizabeth Walmsley Jones and others it was sold to William Lewis on the 30th January 1919 for the sum of £600 and described as: *All that plot of copyhold land situate at Penkhull with messuage erected and called Penkhull Nursery and the seed house, greenhouses and other buildings also erected on parts of the plot and now or lately in the occupation of William Lewis and Arthur Sproston. And also that other plot of land but divided there from by a lane called Garden Lane with the messuage erected on the said plot now being described as with yard, stables and other buildings and the nurseries thereto belonging and now known as No.26 Newcastle Street and now in the occupation of Mr Alcock. To the use of William Lewis.*

William Lewis died on the 20th May 1943, leaving the nursery, house and land to his son William Lewis, junior. He died on the 23rd December 1960, leaving all to his wife Lily Lewis. It was Lily, who under a plan to widen Newcastle Lane subsequently had to demolish the old premises and sell two strips of land to Stoke-on-Trent city council in October 1973. The City Council paid the sum of £5,000 for the land, and was responsible for the demolition of the old house and for rebuilding a stone wall on the new line with Newcastle Lane. The plot of land remaining and facing Newcastle Lane, bordering Elm Tree House, to the west was sold to the city council in December the same year for the sum of £29,000.

Beech Grove, St. Thomas Place.

Beech Grove, which later became known as The Grove, was a substantial Georgian, gentleman's property. It became a children's nursery residential home run by the city council taking in the very young from the Cottage Homes in St Christopher's Avenue in the 1950s. Following the closure of the residential nursery, The Grove finally became an old people's home, before its closure just a few years ago. It was then purchased and completely restored to its original form and the grounds redeveloped into what we have today.

Before restoration, the building was in two parts, an old section to the rear and side used as the kitchens for the residential home, and the Georgian section that remains. The old section was demolished at the time of re-development to leave just the original Georgian detached residence standing. The house stood on a plot of land called Green Croft once described as *with extensive pleasure grounds attached.* It had a garden lodge, which was later to become known as Grove Cottage. A bricked up window and door to this remain visible in the wall to the left, at the top of Doncaster Lane. This old cottage later became known as Doncaster Works that was occupied for a number of years by ceramic engraver Henry

Beech Grove 1882

Doncaster. A further corner section of Green Croft land bordering Newcastle Lane was sold to Penkhull Primitive Methodists for the building of a new chapel in 1836.

The first record which identifies the property is dated 5th June 1700 when John Woodcock sold a *messuage with all buildings, barns, stables, cowsheds, garden, orchard, all parts of Green Croft together with another piece of land called Townsend and Little Townsend* which were occupied by John Philips to John Bowyer, the same Bowyer who owned the site where The Views now stand.

Beech Grove c1960 showing the old section to the right of the picture

In March 1711, Bowyer sold the land to Thomas Doody. The court records help to clarify further the estate that was transferred. It was adjacent to land belonging to Thomas Blakeman. Blakeman's Croft was situated where Queens Road now stands. In fact, the name is retained in the title deeds of the property, 227 Queens Road with a nameplate over the front door. The document dates the old section of Beech Grove referring to a new property of Thomas Doody on which is now building a certain dwelling house now inhabited by John Phillips. There is also reference to the attached field, named Pool Hough. This was where St Peter's High School now stands. A further section of the estate went by the name Little Townsend, the area from the top of Newcastle Lane to its junction with Franklin Road.

Thomas Doody mortgaged the dwelling and land from Ralph Sneyd of Byshton for the loan of £630 10d in May 1719. It was then described as being in the occupation of John Baddeley. By September 1726, Thomas Doody had died and his son John had inherited it. John then sold the land and property in the occupation of John Jenkinson, gent, to Thomas Lovatt of Cotwalton, Nr. Stone.

View showing the first cottage on the site

The estate and property remained in the hand of Thomas Lovatt until the next entry dated the 21st March 1749/50. The entry states that Lovatt was renting out the house to John Godwyn for the sum of £42 p.a. After the death of Thomas Lovatt, the property was held in Trust by Wm. Armishawe and John Walker. A court held on the 11th April 1764 was sold to Thomas Ward. It is this name that gives The Grove its current name, Thomas Ward Place, and with whom the present house must be first associated. The house was described then as being in the occupation of John Godwyn. In 1786, Margaret Ward the widow of Thomas surrendered 42 acres of land in Penkhull, which was already in the occupation of John Harrison the younger on a rental basis, Harrison paying the sum of £70 p.a.

In May 1789, brothers Thomas and William Ward, potters and sons of Thomas Ward senior, then deceased sold Green Croft and the old house to John Harrison, the younger, subject to an annuity of £10 p.a. to Margaret Unett for the term of her natural life. The witness was Wm. Unett and in all probability Margaret had become remarried to William Unett after the death of her husband Thomas Ward. It was under the terms of the will of Thomas, that his widow would only hold the estate if she remained unmarried, hence this transaction. The manor court records the property: *all that messuage together with several closes of land belonging containing*

42 acres of land in Penkhull, with barns, stables, yards and outbuildings.

The building of Beech Grove which remains today was built soon after this by Harrison as it was from this date onwards referred to *as recently built.* The court records however adds that it was previously in the occupation of Thomas Haywood, deceased but then of his widow. This reference refers to the old section of the house, which remained until the property was reconstructed in 2004.

In May 1802, Harrison was declared bankrupt and his assets and property were auctioned. Two months later, on the 3rd July the auction was held at The Marquis of Granby. The house, Beech Grove was Lot. 1 which read: *A handsome modern-built dwelling-house, with convenient offices and outbuildings, all of recent erection, garden part walled in, and croft adjoining, pleasantly situated at Penkhull Green, about one mile from the borough of Newcastle-under-Lyme, and a short distance from the great north road, and now in the occupation of Mrs Haywood; the whole containing 1 a 1r 23p and forming a most delightful residence for a small genteel family.*

Joseph Booth purchased the property. He and his brother Hugh were in partnership and traded under the name of Booth and Sons. Their business stood opposite Mr Harrison's potworks called Cliff Bank Works, which was situated on the corner of Shelton Old Road and Hartshill Road. They inherited the business from their father Ephraim, who in turn obtained a life interest in the business from his brother Hugh who died in 1789. Hugh and Joseph traded until around 1808.

It is not certain whether Joseph Booth left Beech Grove in 1812 to live at Whitchurch permanently, or somewhere else first. The house was not sold by auction for a further two years. When he left Penkhull, he generously donated a quantity of bread to the needy of the village, as the Staffordshire Advertiser reported on the 23rd May 1812.

View from the side showing the extended bay to the lounge

On Friday last, the 15th inst. Joseph Booth, Esq., of The Grove, on leaving his residence for another situation, very handsomely distributed a large quantity of bread to the poor families of that neighbourhood, 80 families receiving this donation. The partakers of this seasonable relief expressed themselves highly thankful on this occasion and the beneficent act reflects much credit to the donor.

The Land Tax records confirm that he was in occupation both in 1805 and 1806. The records for 1818 show that although he retained the ownership of the shop it was in the occupation of Mrs Mary Tilstone, gentlewoman. A Trade Directory of the same year lists Mr and Mrs Joseph Tilstone, of Beech Grove, Penkhull.

For whatever reason, Joseph Booth put Beech Grove up for sale in 1814. Details of the forthcoming auction were recorded in the Staffordshire Gazette on the 19th July 1814. The auction was to be held at The Wheatsheaf in Stoke, on the 28th July. However, either Booth decided not to sell, or the bids did not reach the reserve price for it remained in his ownership until 27th March 1824.

'The Grove', situated at Penkhull late the residence of Joseph Booth, Esq., together with about 8 acres of land attached, and a fulling Mill erected thereof, which at a trifling expense be fitted for the purpose of grinding colours and glazes, for use in the potteries, the necessary machinery being upon the spot; or with a small additional power, be converted into a Forge having a reservoir of nearly 100 yards in length supplied by natural springs. The village of Penkhull is situated on an eminence, remarkable for the salubrity of its air affords many picturesque views and is embellished by a sprinkling of wood and pleasant walks. The house, which is replete with every convenience for the reception of a genteel family, has the advantage of a productive garden, and is ornamented by a shrubbery and lawn with appropriate decorations; to it are attached outbuildings, consisting of stable, coach-house, cow-house, piggeries &c.

The vicinity is most respectable, and the house is little more than half a mile from the opulent and well-supplied market town of Newcastle. (No mention of Stoke!) The purchaser may be accommodated with the whole of the purchase money on satisfactory security being given to the vendor of the premises.

The 'fulling process' was the scouring, cleansing and thickening of raw cloth by beating it in water. The earliest method was by men trampling upon the cloth in a trough, which led to the task being called 'walking.' During the thirteenth century the cloth was beaten by large wooden mallets, which were worked by a water wheel. Why such a mill should be situated in Penkhull is not known, but its location at a spring and pool would be appropriate. Perhaps this was some remains from the medieval period?

The next record in the manor rolls, which refer to Beech Grove, is dated 27th March 1824. Joseph Booth, then of Oak Cottage, Whitchurch, sells the house and land to Robert

Archer, yeoman for the sum of £800. In May of the same year Archer sells a small plot to the south west of Beech Grove to Michael Baxter, miller for the sum of £9 6s 6d. It is on this land that Baxter built a row of cottages of which one was called Canada Cottage. A further plot of land from Green Croft was sold for the sum of £88 8s. to the trustees of Penkhull Primitive Methodist Church for the building of a new chapel.

Robert Archer looked upon his purchase as an investment for a return, not as a residence for himself, as he almost immediately placed an advertisement in the Staffordshire Advertiser dated the 29th May 1824 under the heading 'To Let'. *To be Let and entered upon immediately. Grove House, situated in Penkhull within about two miles of Newcastle, formerly the residence of Joseph Booth, Esq., consisting of entrance hall, dining room, drawing room, kitchen, pantries, cellars, six bedrooms, brew-house and stables, coach houses, lofts over, pig-sty, and other conveniences with a good garden walled on both sides, cropped and stocked with choice fruit trees, pleasure grounds and shrubberies. The House is in complete repair, and had just been painted throughout. Eight acres of old pastureland may be had if wanted. Refer to Mr Archer, of Penkhull, who will show the same.*

Trade Directories show that Archer did reside in the house for a period. However the house was again advertised To Let in 1838 listing also the tenant: To be let, *The Grove House, situate at Penkhull now held by the Rev. William Ford. The house contains an entrance hall, dining room, study, and sitting*

Above the old lounge - below the newly restored lounge of Beech Grove

room, two kitchens, pantry, two cellars, eight bedrooms, brewhouse, large garden, and pleasure ground, and pump of good water. The house is quite dry and in good repair. Stable for two horses, with a loft over, and a gig house may be had if wanted. There was no mention of the 8 acres of land previously attached.

The Grove Nursery c1960

In all probability it was this advertisement that attracted the new tenant in 1839 when Thomas Bailey Rose was appointed the first Stipendiary Magistrate for Stoke, who needed a property to reflect his status in the town. The 1841 census lists the family living at Grove House, Penkhull; Thomas Bailey Rose, aged 35; his wife Arabella, aged 30; their three children Thomas George, aged 6, Arabella, aged 5 and Lucy, aged 1. They also employed a cook, Mary Hand, aged 30; Martha Murray, aged 20, female servant; Samuel Hammersley, aged 20, groom; and Ann Harrison, aged 20, nurse. The family was also recorded in the 1851 census but appears that Thomas Bailey and his wife and older children were not at home the night when the census was taken. By this time, the family had increased and three new names were listed, William, aged 10, Roslin, aged 7; and Charles, aged 4. There were now five servants, one from Worcester, three from Trentham and one from Maer. Their titles included housemaid, nursery maid, cook, scullery girl and John Sutton, aged 39, for whom no occupation was given.

Beech Grove today, restored to its former glory

During this time the property remained in the ownership of Robert Archer. By January 1850, Archer had died. The estate was held in trust to John Ward, gent and Ephraim Edwards, Solicitors clerk, both of Newcastle. At a manor court held on the 13th January 1850, Beech Grove was sold to Robert Kidd for the sum of £875.

It was nearly twelve months following the move to Penkhull the wife of Robert Kidd, Rose, aged 45, died in December 1852 and is buried on Stoke Churchyard.

The 1861 census lists Kidd as the occupier, a retired grocer from Yorkshire. The property remained as Grove House. Kidd lived with his son Robert, aged 24, and his daughter Claire, aged 23. There were two servants employed; Margaret Coates, aged 30, from Yorkshire, and Emma Simpson, aged 15, from Hanchurch. By 1864, the house was used as a ladies' boarding and day school run by Jane Bradshaw, followed by a number of tenants. In 1869, Mr William Jones, brick and tile maker of Springfield's occupied it. Jones was previously living at Hawthorn Cottage, Trent Vale and was employer of 38 men and 21 boys at his works. Jones was probably the son-in-law of Robert Kidd. Later in 1871, Grove House was occupied by Christopher Dickenson, aged 52, a miller, employing 19 men. He lived with his wife Sophie, aged 55; his children Alfred, aged 26, also a miller working with his father; Annie, aged 21, of no occupation; William, aged 20, also working for his father; and two servants Sarah Finney, aged 30, from Stoke, and Emma Brassington, aged 35, from Lichfield. By 1879, Dickenson had moved to No.25 Hartshill Road.

Grove House remained in the ownership of Robert Kidd until his death on the 18th June 1866. Under the terms of his will dated the 19th September 1857, he appointed his children Rose, Alice and Elizabeth as his trustees. As he did not leave the estate to be sold, application was made by his two remaining descendants, Alice Whittaker and William Jones under the 1882 Land Act. With the legal position then established, the house and estate was sold to Mr Michael Hoole Ashwell on the 25th June 1885 for the sum of £1,625. It was described as follows: *The Grove, situated at Penkhull with garden lodge, wash-house, stable, coach-house, cow-house, potting house and other outbuildings.*

Mr Ashwell was born at Coddington Manor near Newark, in 1825. He qualified at University College Hospital, London after which he became house surgeon at Newark Infirmary. He came to the Potteries in 1852 and entered into a partnership with Dr Robert Garner, which lasted until 1879. On the incorporation of the Borough of Stoke-upon-Trent in 1874, he was appointed medical officer of health. He died on the 13th July 1891.

After his death, the property was transferred to his eldest son John Blow Ashwell upon trust. John was born in Stoke-upon-Trent in 1855. After his education in Malvern and then at the Royal Medical College at Eton, he was articled to Keary and Marshall, solicitors, being admitted a solicitor in 1878. Later on in 1884, he became a city councillor only to resign five years later to become the town clerk of Stoke-upon-Trent, a position he held until Federation in 1910. John did not live at Beech Grove but at The Quarry, Hartshill. He died on the 19th October 1910.

For a short period the house was tenanted. In 1901, Mr Waltser Copeland, aged 34, a solicitor born in Hanley occupied it. Copeland was not married but retained a resident housemaid Fanny Middleton, aged 20, from Newcastle, and Laura Viggars, aged 28, as cook, originating from Leek. As the period of occupation by Copeland coincided with that of the ownership by John Blow Ashwell, it may be that Copeland was a friend or colleague of his. By 1907, it was occupied by Robert Jamieson, a china manufacturer. It was shortly after this date that the Ashwell family moved into Beech Grove as they are recorded at that address by 1912.

The property remained in the hands of the Ashwell family until the 27th January 1950, when the descendants of Michael Hoole Ashwell sold it to Stoke-on-Trent City Council to be converted into an extension of Penkhull Cottage Homes for the care of very young children. The sale price was £2,985. The corner plot, formerly Swinnerton Works, facing St Thomas Place and Doncaster Lane had for some years been in the ownership of Benjamin Nicholls but he sold this to Mary Edith Ashwell in 1935. A conveyance for this small plot is dated the 15th February 1950, when for the sum of £15, it was also sold to Stoke-on-Trent Council.

It must have been around 1968 when I visited a Miss Phyllis Ashwell, then retired to a nursing home in Rhyl with tape recorder and note book in hand. Miss Ashwell was, I recall, 92 years of age, frail but with perfect recall. *When we first went to The Grove in 1911, we kept chickens and hens and lived there for nearly 39 years until mother died in 1949. My father made a number of alterations to the house and removed some very old oak beams when the roof was retiled in the 1920s. He was so thrilled with the quality of the timber he made a model of the house as a kind of dolls house for us children. There remained at the back one or two old cottages that were attached and formed the kitchen and pantry for the Georgian house. Near to the back door, our gardener discovered a well when his foot went through some rotten old timbers. It had brick walls, below which was cut out of sandstone and very deep. Father got Dean and Lowe Iron Foundry from Stoke to come and fill it in with clinker from their iron foundry. I recall also the need to replace some old cast-iron spouting and down spouts.*

After the property had been converted for suitable accommodation for children from Penkhull Cottage Homes, it was handed for use by the council on the 13th July 1953. After it had ceased being used for young children, it was adapted into an old people's home by extending the existing home and building additional accommodation in the former pleasure grounds. In the year 2000 the city council decided to close the home and a few years later in 2003 sold it to property developer Andrew Plant who demolished all the extensions and additional buildings, renovated the house throughout and developed the site into what we have today.

Grindley House.

Grindley House was called after the name of the adjacent area, Grindley Hill, at the lower reaches of Newcastle Lane. The house was situated on the site of the present St John's C of E Primary School. Although no accurate date can be found of its building, it did not appear on Hargreaves' map of 1832 but the property was listed on the 1841 census and is illustrated on Lynam's map of 1848 as Grindley House. The census of 1841 lists Robert Smith, aged 41, a pottery manufacturer; his wife Sarah, aged 32; together with four children, Sarah, aged 7; Robert, aged 5; John, aged 2; and James, aged 7 months. Smith was also named as a trustee in August 1841 for the land upon which St John's Church was erected.

To research the name of Smith can be difficult, but we first pick up two names, Thomas and John Smith. They were born in Kingsley, Thomas in August 1721, and John in December 1725. They were the sons of Robert Smith. Together they began to purchase numerous plots of land from early to the mid 18th century in an area now called Springfield's but at this time the area went by the name of Penkhull, as it formed part of that Township. The land purchased was mostly to the west of the turnpike road from Newcastle to Trentham. It was the Smith family that built Springfield's House, a large mansion with extensive pleasure grounds and gardens in the third quarter of the 18th century. This later become the Springfield Hotel, but now goes by the name of The Orange Tree.

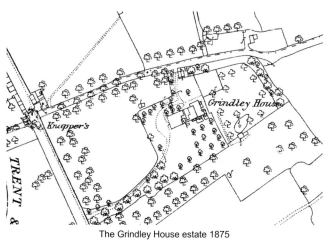

The Grindley House estate 1875

John Smith died in 1795, (1725-1795), followed by his brother, Thomas in 1803 (1721-1803). Thomas is buried in Stoke Churchyard. It appears that John Smith left the estate to Thomas Smith. Thomas had no issue and in the terms of his will dated 13th December 1798, left two small dwelling houses to his niece Mary and the remainder of his estate to his nephew, Robert Smith (1761-1812) Robert died in 1812 at the age of 51 years, leaving his estate to his son Robert, aged ten years (1802-1866). His first wife Sarah, died, aged 45 years, in 1854 but he re-married in 1855 to Ann Hallam of Newcastle.

Grindley House and its approch from the drive

Grindley House was subsequently described as: *All that messuage known as Grindley House with orchards, plantations, pleasure gardens, tennis and other lawns, kitchen garden and closes.* In 1841 there were three servants employed at the house. At the same time John Smith, a cousin of Robert, was living at Springfield's House together with two servants. He was then aged 45, a farmer.

The 1851 census records as follows; Robert Smith, aged 49, pottery manufacturer; Sarah his wife, aged 42; William, his son, aged 19; followed by Robert, aged 15; James, 12; and Mary Jane, aged 10. They employed three servants. In the same year Robert Smith was listed as a trustee of the proposed new church at Trent Vale.

Grindley House from the front showing the extensive pleasure grounds

The union of Robert and his new wife Ann produced a further son, Richard Hallam, born two years after the marriage in 1857. The 1861 census lists Robert, aged 59 years, his second wife, Anne and their son Richard Hallam, aged 3. For whatever reason, none of the children by the first marriage of Robert were resident at Grindley House when the census was taken. A nephew, Henry Rawson, aged 12, was living there as well as two servants.

By this time Grindley Lodge had been built at the entrance to the drive from Newcastle Lane. It was a single story, red sandstone building, situated to the left just inside the entrance gates. Henry Brassington, aged 64, the gardener, his wife Judith and son, aged 27 occupied it. Robert Smith died in June 1866. The following census of 1871, recorded Anne Smith, widow, living on an income received from property and land. Her son, Richard Hallam, was aged 13. In addition to one domestic servant, who came from Flintshire, a gardener Samuel Bates was employed living with his wife and two sons at the Lodge.

Anne Smith died on the 19th October 1874 aged 54. Her will is dated August 1866. It appointed her brother Henry and sister Martha and a friend as executors leaving Grindley House and an extensive land portfolio in Penkhull and Springfield's to her son, Richard Hallam. There was no mention of any of the children of the first marriage of Robert. Four years later in 1879, Richard Hallam married Martha Jane Webber of Whitchurch. She was aged 17, he was 21. Her father was George Webber, a bank accountant. They were married St Peter's Church in Stoke.

The census of 1881 does not record them at Grindley House; only the brother of Martha, George Webber, aged 11, in addition

Springfields House c1900

Richard Hallam Smith, his family and staff. c1918

Mrs Hallam Smith in her pony and trap

John Myatt, and his family outside Grindley Lodge
situated just off Newcastle Lane

to two domestic servants. Richard Hallam and Martha were both staying with her parents in High Street, Whitchurch. Richard Hallam was described as a land proprietor. The interesting thing is that whilst visiting the in-laws, a servant from Grindley House, Georgina Goodall, aged 19, travelled with them to Whitchurch, no doubt to attend to the needs of Martha Smith.

Ten years later in 1891, the Smiths are recorded at Grindley House along with two servants. Living at the lodge at the entrance of the driveway was John Myatt, aged 42, employed as the gardener. In this small single story building the situation must have been very cramped as there is also recorded his wife Caroline, two sons and four daughters.

In 1901, Richard Hallam and his wife and servants were not living at Grindley House. They were residing at Chapel House, Sandon, Staffs, along with their cook and kitchen maid. Grindley House was let out to Mr John Tomlinson, aged 37, a biscuit tile manufacturer with his wife Edith, their one-month-old son, a hospital nurse and two domestic servants. In all probability Mr Tomlinson owned Springfield Tileries just around the corner. In September the same year, the house was let for a period of seven years to Mr Herbert Darby Minton Stenhouse, on the terms of £93 p.a.

Due to health, the Smiths decided to relocate to Colwyn Bay. In July 1921, the house was sold to Mr M E Dickson who subsequently died. In April 1935, by which time his widow Mrs Dickson, sold the house to Mr Charles Walley for the sum of £4,500. Upon his death in January 1942, the property went to his sister Sarah Jane Whalley, who, being unable to keep up the mortgage payments, saw the house repossessed by the building society and sold for the sum of £1,073 9s 8d in September 1943 to Harpfield's Estates. After being left for a number of years to decay, Grindley House was finally sold to Stoke-on-Trent Corporation for the sum of £2,250 in February 1950. It was then demolished to make way for the building of Springfield's Primary School.

Newcastle Lane c1918

Canada Cottage

The first record of Michael Baxter in Penkhull is to be found in the trade directory of 1802 where he is listed as a 'huxter' *(a peddler of wares).* By 1818, the name appears as a grocer and flower dealer. Shortly afterwards Baxter increased his business interests in the village, for by 1822, he had his own malt house and windmill as well being a corn dealer. In 1834, Baxter had given up other business interests concentrating on the production of ale at his malt house, situated to the rear of what is now Manor Court Street.

During the early working years of Michael Baxter, no indication is given as to where he lived. The name of Canada Cottage in Queens Road has always fascinated, wondering how it obtained its name. Early records indicate that it was built in 1824 on land purchased

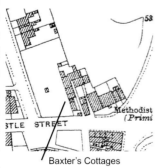

Baxter's Cottages

from Robert Archer of Beech Grove: *To this court comes Robert Archer of Penkhull, yeoman, and in consideration of the sum of nine pounds, six shillings and six pence paid by Michael Baxter of Penkhull, miller in full purchase of a plot or piece of land. All that plot piece of land being a parcel of copyhold land called the Green Croft as the same is now marked out of the southwest corner thereof.*

Michael Baxter was, at his height, one of the most important persons living in Penkhull. He owned the local windmill, malthouse and numerous plots of land and premises. Married to Mary they had four children, Mary, born 1794; Margaret 1796; John 1799 and Michael in 1802. One of the early trustees of the Primitive Methodists Chapel was Michael Baxter, but whether father or son it is not known. What is known is that Michael, junior (1802-1889) emigrated to Canada and was received on trial by the Methodist Church there in 1843 to be ordained minister three years later in 1846. Baxter ministered in many districts of Canada including St. Andrews, Elizabethtown, Demorestville and Welland, his last appointment was to Pelham in 1871. He died in Welland, Ontario in 1889, aged 87. His first home in Canada was called Penkhull Cottage, and his old home in Penkhull became Canada Cottage.

Michael Baxter senior built three cottages on the land that he purchased from Robert Archer in 1824. They were approached via a narrow path leading from Newcastle Lane, as Queens Road was not laid until much later. Baxter lived in the largest cottage, the last in the row; the first two were subsequently converted into one and then later demolished under an order from the city council. The cottages went by the name of Baxter Row Nos 1, 2 and 3. The address in the early census returns was Baxter's Row off the Newcastle Street. Canada Cottage was No.3 and the house number still remains today on an inner door of the last remaining cottage as a witness to this fact.

Canada Cottage c1971

In his will dated 11th January 1881, John left his estate after the death of his wife Ellen to his son, Edward John, earthenware manufacturer living at The Brampton, Newcastle. The estate consisted not only of the cottages but a further strip of land described as *recently purchased* from Frederick Bishop. Edward John died, aged 21, on the 17th February 1889, leaving his estate to his wife Lucy, and after her death to his son, John Edward Joseph Baxter.

Canada Cottage was then tenanted out, so too was the cottages next door. In 1901 they were occupied by James Rowley, aged 61, from Fenton, a potter and his wife Sarah, and in Canada Cottage lived Alice Barlow, a widow, aged 87, her daughter, son-in-law and grandchildren. In May 1917 the cottages were sold to Mrs Eliza Tatton. In 1933 the property again changed hands for the sum of £450, to Henry Bertram Owen. The property was then described as follows: *All those three cottages, formerly consisting of their outbuildings, situate in Newcastle Street, Penkhull, one of which cottages is known by the name of Canada Cottage and the other two as No.4 and 5 Baxter's Row in the occupation of Parton and Bosley respectively adjoining buildings formerly belonging to Mary Broad, deceased.*

It would appear that Henry Owen changed the name of Canada Cottage during his ownership, for when it was sold again in 1935, it went by the name of Burlesdon House. After then the name of the cottage reverted back to its original. It was purchased by Mrs Hill. In October 1971 the cottage was

Canada Cottage after restoration

In 1871 Mary Whitehall occupied No.1; a widow, aged 70, and her son. No.2 by Jonah Leigh, a potter, aged 25, and his wife Sarah. One of the sons of Michael senior occupied No. 3, John, aged 71, and Ellen his wife, aged 64. John was listed as a retired timber merchant. The strange thing is that in 1881 it would appear that they were living apart; John remained at No.3, while Ellen was at No.2 sharing the house with Eliza Ridgway, a visitor, aged 48; Elizabeth Hipkiss, a widow, aged 36; employed as a nurse; and one servant, Emily Leadbeater, aged 16. Both are however buried in Penkhull churchyard, John on the 31st August 1881, and Ellen, who survived her husband by six years, on the 24th May 1887.

conveyed to Mr and Mrs Leighton of West Avenue, Penkhull in whose ownership it remained, until the present owner Caroline and Barry Steele purchased the cottage in 1981.

Chapter 17
Business and Trade.

Penkhull throughout history has been set apart from the rest of the city as a rural agricultural community. Even so within such a setting, business can thrive. Local farms all continued successfully until the war years, then with demand for housing and improvements to transport they all but one disappeared. In addition to these farms, Penkhull boasted a thriving a garden nursery business that continued from the beginning of the 19th century for over a hundred years, the remains of which are encompassed in the retail outlet of flowers, Penkhull Nurseries in Newcastle Lane. During its hay-day most of its production would have gone to market at Newcastle and other markets throughout N. Staffordshire.

In contrast to this, I have recorded the account of a small cobbling business run by the late Jack Burton. It is edited from his autobiography written over thirty years ago.

Penkhull Nurseries - The Burgess family

John Burgess, nurseryman, had commenced business by 1790 as the copyhold court records dated the 7th October that year records: *John Chapman, yeoman, and his wife Margery renting out for a period of 21 years at £12 p.a. all that dwelling house late made into two and in the holding of Jonathan Wagg and Joseph Sharlott and all stables, outbuildings and a large orchard belonging.* The building described here refers to Elm Tree House. By 1802 a local Trade Directory was advertising Burgess as a sole trader. Other land situated across road called Townsend, where the newsagent's shop stands reaching down to Lodge Road was all part of the nursery business.

In April 1812, more land was added to the business of Burgess when John Townsend decided to sell off parts of his estate belonging to Greenhead House, now the Greyhound Inn and bounded by Garden Street and Manor Court Street because of financial difficulties. The court entry reads: *All that parcel of land adjoining the dwelling house of John Townsend as the same is marked out and containing 3,144 sq. yards now in the holding of John Burgess, abutting on the North to the road leading from Newcastle to Penkhull, and on the West to the lane called Tittensor's Lane (now Garden Street).* By 1818, the business was recorded as *gardener and seeds man.* The owner of the house and land was Chapman who died in 1821 and left Elm Tree House together with other cottages and land called Townsend to his nephew William Chapman, a farmer living in Shropshire.

At this time Elm Tree House was called *Tittensor's messuage* which in 1821 was described: *All that customary messuage situate in Penkhull with garden, orchard belonging now in the occupation of John Burgess. Also all those other dwelling houses adjoining standing near the said last mentioned messuage and a parcel of land called the Little Townsend.*

In 1827, still tenanted from Chapman, the estate comprised of two acres. Allbut's directory of 1822 lists both John Burgess, senior, and thirty-six year old John Burgess, junior, as *gardeners and seeds men.* In January 1828 John Burgess purchased the freehold for the sum of £4 5s from the Duchy of Lancaster *for a cottage erected on the waste land of the manor, then described as in the occupation of John Burgess together with the garden lying at the back adjoining on one side the dwelling house late in the possession of Anne, the widow of Thomas Moore and the other side of the dwelling house of Edward Broad.* In all probability these three cottages were to become the old shop cum garage and store which once stood to the front of 'Elm Tree House' but were demolished for road widening in the 1970s.

Old barn that stood in front of Elm Tree House
previously three cottages

As the problem of crime grew so did the need for Associations for the Prosecution of Felons in proportion to the demand. Penkhull had an association, so did the town of Stoke. John Burgess became the treasurer for the Penkhull Association in 1835 and was also listed as a member of the Stoke Association.

Mr George Thomas Taylor

In the years 1827 and 1829, both John Burgess, senior and John Burgess, junior, agreed to finance a £500 Bond of Security to the Churchwardens of St Peter's Church, Stoke-upon-Trent for Mr George Thomas Taylor. This was for the purpose of a guarantee as he was elected by the parishioners to be the Assistant Overseer of the Poor with the responsibility of collecting and administering the parish poor rate collections and expenditure.

He married Sarah Burgess at Stoke Parish Church on the 1st March 1815. Taylor was 25 years of age and became the son-in-law of John Burgess senior. He was born at Leith in Scotland but by 1814 was living in Kensington, Middlesex. It is from here that he commenced corresponding with Sarah having being introduced to her by a friend whilst visiting a relative in the area. The union produced eight children, of whom one died aged six months and another at fourteen months.

Remarkably, letters have survived from George Thomas Taylor to Miss Sarah Burgess. These were sent from

Kensington. The correspondence between them is a welcome contribution to an understanding of love letters of the period both in language and protocol.

Kensington January 18th 1814
Dear Sarah,

This is to inform you that I am well thank God and I hope he will give you the same. I received your kind and welcome letter and I thought myself highly honoured by your kind congratulations. Therefore I sit down with the greatest of pleasure to write you an answer, which I hope you will be pleased to accept. I am extremely sorry for the my conduct for addressing part of your fathers letter to you but as it was a misunderstanding of mine I earnestly hope you will excuse me for the first time and I will do better for the future.

When I was at Liverpool I was often asked by the old lady and my mother when I would come down to Stoke and I told them as soon as possible. But since then I have taken a second thought and I know several places, which is more likely to suit than Stoke. So I shall continue on in an industrious line for a short time and when you have got the principal it is easy getting a shop and the principal thing of all is to look out for a partner for life for which I am completely un-provided at present. The girls in London do not take my fancy at all so therefore I must make application elsewhere and I know not where unless less I come down to Staffordshire which you may depend will be the case when I want a wife.

And in that county I do not know any that would give me more pleasure than yourself and though far distant apart as we may be there is time for all things. If you will accept of my hand and heart you may depend they are at your pleasure and I will forever remain your true and constant admirer. Should you at this time be disengaged, I hope my pen may have the desired effect or should it be to the contrary. By favouring me with an answer I shall for ever respect you and the rest of your family and if I should succeed in my proposal, and please God to give us health and strength I have not doubt we may be crowned with success. You may think that flattery dwells upon my tongue, but believe me my dear these are the sentiments of my mind and might I perish if I plant in thy bosom a thorn, a later communication might be carried on very early.

When I read that part of your letter, which informed me of the indisposition of poor Mary I was unhappy and was a good deal surprised as I had a letter about a fortnight ago and all was well. So I hope to God she will have a speedy recovery and I should be very glad to hear it, as I am sure it must make your father and mother very uneasy. Now if you please, I will trouble you for a few lines when you're at leisure as Valentines Day draws nigh.

So I remain and hope I shall have the pleasure of remaining your constant admirer.
Geo. T. Taylor.

The next letter makes reference to celebrations to follow in London following the end of the 22-year war with France when the British and their allies captured Bordeaux at the battle of Laon in March 1814 and the allies entered Paris. As a result Napoleon abdicated and was exiled on the island of Elba, off the Tuscan coast in Italy.

Kensington, April 14th 1814
Dear Sarah,

It now becomes my pleasing sensation to acknowledge the contents in your last letter saying that you and your sisters had some hopes of coming to town, which gave me great consolation. I flatter myself with the expectation of seeing you in a short time that is the only object of my youthful fancy. I give you my dear and your sister and whosoever may be in company a most kind invitation and shall be exceeding glad to have the pleasure of your company in London when I shall think myself highly honoured in conducting you to the most fashionable parts of London and at that time when it is supposes a general peace will be proclaimed which will be the grandest sight you and I have witnessed.

The illuminations have been very great for this three nights past and general one is going to take place we expect in the month of May.

Should you come as I hope, you may depend that the old lady of Fulham has every thing fit for your reception and I hope Miss Sarah, you will let me know in time that I make it my duty to be at the Inn to receive you. Let me know what coach you will arrive as you may rely on my attendance. I hope you will send me a line or two as at the time I shall expect either to see or have something from you. But the sight will be most gratifying.

By this time I hope you will bring me word of Joseph's recovery as I think the weather is in his favour and I hope your next letter will say all friends are well which will give me great happiness as I feel for any of the family. I hear today that the Stafford Militia is to be discharged on the 1st June according to an order from the war office; it will give me an opportunity of specifying to you every particular that our circumstances may require.
Yours affectionately.
G.T. Taylor

The final letter is to Mr John Burgess, the father of Sarah. It was the accepted practice that a suitor should ask a father for his daughter's hand in marriage and the following is a typical example.

September 15th 1814, High Street, Kensington.

To Mr John Burgess, Gardeners, Penkhull, Staffordshire.
Dear Friend.
By this you will find that I am in good health and I sincerely hope that this will find you the same. At the same time it will serve to inform you of my correspondence, which for some time past has been carried on between myself George Taylor and your daughter, Miss Sarah which I trust has been agreeable to you and all the family. At various times I have such a thorough knowledge of Miss Sarah's abilities and out of the love and universal respect that I always had for her ever since the first time I saw her has induced me to make this application to you. Indeed as I have the desired effect to accomplish the object of my fancy by obtaining her most mutual consent I now must humbly solicit your approbation to that intended union.

I hope you will excuse me should I be guilty of doing wrong in not communicating it to you before, but the distance from you must make up that deficiency as it is a delicate matter to write. A few weeks ago when I had the pleasure of Miss Sarah's company, I several times communicated my future intentions to her in respect to the time when I thought that a matrimonial ceremony would take place. But as an affectionate dutiful daughter to her parents she refused anything that she thought would not be agreeable to the family at large.

Therefore, it was not by any means my intention to make her endure the displeasure of her parents or draw down any unpleasing sentiments of any branch of the family upon her.

I am pleased to mention to Miss Sarah and Miss Mary that Mrs Paxton received their kind present and her favours daily came to hand and Mr and Mrs Paxton return their most hearty thanks for a present of such a rarity in London at this time of the year. They arrived very safe and was extremely good and they acknowledge them the best peas they ever had tasted. But the rascal of a carrier did not deliver them all on the Monday morning when I should have done myself the pleasure of inviting your cousin Barnett to be a partaker of the game.

I always made it my study to act upon those honourable principles are no disgrace to no man. Now Mr Burgess, my intention is that I intend coming down to Penkhull about the month of February should it be agreeable as under other circumstance than a universal approbation it would be a folly that during my stay in the Potteries which would not exceed a few weeks, I must shelter under your roof.

After performing that part of solemnisation we should go to Liverpool and then to embark in the business of my profession which I am fully assured would answer the purpose well and by my industry and care and devoting my time to my business which I have received a thorough knowledge and by my future attention I make no doubt. But I should give satisfaction to those who might honour me with this command.

And should God please to give us both health and strength to execute the duties of our profession and by our industry we must increase our wealth as you may depend for the love and esteem she holds in my breast that I shall for ever continue a true and faithful husband until God is pleased to separate us.

Now should you approve of the above both in respect of time and place you will greatly oblige your humble servant by favouring me with a few lines to that effect in a week or two or when you are most at leisure and I conclude at present with the greatest respect.

Yours George Taylor.

After their marriage the Taylor family settled in Shelton where George set up business as a baker having his own shop. It is the same George Thomas Taylor who later purchased 'Greenhead House' (now the Greyhound Inn) and the old parish poor house, Victoria Buildings in Penkhull. During this period Taylor was probably one of the most influential people in the town. In October 1830 he went on to purchase his own pew in Stoke old church at a cost of £45. Fortunately many documents, original letters and family heirlooms such as the wedding ring of Miss Sarah have been passed down to Mrs Betty Wildblood of Seabridge and are now secure in the City Museum and Archives in Hanley.

It is not known why or how Taylor fell from his important role in the community. He lost his position as Assistant Overseer of the Poor in 1835, continuing in a limited public life after this date as well as running his shop in Shelton. By 1851 he was living at a small house, No.73 Mill Street, Etruria, his occupation being a watchman at an Iron Furnace, no doubt at Shelton Bar. By 1861, he had moved to No.95 Granville Street, Burslem and described as a Gas Weighing Machine Clark at the age of 69. His wife Sarah was still recorded at the age of 71. She died in 1869, aged 80 whilst George Thomas survived until early in 1871 when he died aged 79.

Back to Burgess

By 1834, John Burgess senior had retired and the business was run by his son John Burgess junior and his brother William. William married a relative, Margaret *(known as Peggy)* Burgess of Caverswall. The marriage was only to last for twelve years for on Thursday, 16th August 1834 William died aged thirty-nine. By this time Peggy, had three children Margaret, aged twelve, John, aged eight and Elizabeth aged five. In the same year her father-in-law, John Burgess senior died at the age of eighty-five.

As a result of the death of William her husband, it was necessary for Peggy to attend the copyhold court to formally record the decease of her husband and for herself to be admitted tenant to the property. *At a copyhold court held June, 1836, Peggy Burgess admitted copyhold tenant to her husband's estate comprising: All that messuage with garden, orchard called Tittensor's Messuage and also those three other houses and barns now converted into a cart-house and stable and land called Little Townsend and all premises occupied by Peggy Burgess.*

After five years as a widow, Peggy remarried to Joseph Kent in December 1839. Kent originated from Barthomley, just across the Cheshire border and fifteen years her senior.

It was not the first union of the same name as on the 2nd August 1807, Ann Burgess, the daughter of John Burgess senior married James Kent, farmer also of Barthomley; and again on the 7th February 1837, Thomas Kent, the son of James married Ann Burgess with the consent of his father as he was under the age of 21. Eight months after the marriage Ann gave birth to a daughter, Martha, who was baptised at Stoke Church on the 9th November 1837. The marriage produced eight children, the last being James in January 1857.

Prior to her marriage to Joseph Kent, Peggy Burgess decided to safeguard the estate before the marriage for her son, John by her first marriage, and transferred her copyhold estate at a court held on 2nd December 1839 in trust to her brother-in-law, John Burgess, and Michael Baxter, until her son John, Burgess, then aged thirteen, reached his maturity.

The Special Court Baron and customary court held at Stoke Lodge the second day of December in the year of our Lord 1839 before Thomas Fenton Esquire Steward of the manor. Whereas at a court held for this at manor on the second day of June 1836. Now to this court comes the said Peggy Burgess and Joseph Kent in their proper persons and she the said Peggy Burgess surrenders into the hands of the Lord all that dwelling house situated standing and being in Penkhull with the garden orchard there to belonging formerly called Tittensor's messuage and also all those other dwelling houses with the barn there unto belonging and standing next to the said first mentioned messuage which the former three dwelling houses and barns are now converted into a storeroom or warehouse, cart-house and stable and also all that close peace or parcel of customary land in Penkhull called the Little Townsend which are now in the occupation of the said Peggy Burgess. And all other copyhold lands within this manor to which she, Peggy Burgess by the name of Margaret Burgess was admitted tenant at a court held on the second day of June 1836.

To the use and the behoof of John Burgess of Penkhull, gardener, nursery and seeds man and John Baxter of Shelton for ever entrust for the said Peggy Burgess her heirs and assigns until the solemnisation of the said intended marriage.

And immediately after such marriage entrust to pay up and apply the rents or profits of the said surrender shall be paid to Peggy Burgess for her sole separate use until such period as John Burgess, the son of Peggy Burgess, by her late husband William Burgess now an infant at the age of 13 years or thereabouts shall obtain the age of 21 years or shall depart his life without having to attain such change.

And from and immediately after his reaching the age of 21 years then and from during at the remainder of his natural life but during the remainder of the natural life of Peggy Burgess to raise and levy out from the rents and profits of the said premises annually the sum of £30 to be paid to Peggy Burgess for her own use.

By 1841 the Burgess Nursery business had grown and covered an area amounting to forty acres, employing seven men. After the marriage of Peggy to Joseph Kent the name changed its title to Burgess and Kent. Shortly after this in June 1844 the partnership took on a seven-year lease of the former kitchen garden and orchard of The Mount, from the trustees of Josiah Spode. The land covered by this garden forms the area now known as Tilson Avenue.

It was not until 1850 that a local trade directory listed the partnership but from the following Indenture dated 1844 it would appear that a partnership had already been established between Burgess and Kent for some time.

Indenture, dated 24th June 1844. All those two pieces or parcels of garden ground adjoining each other adjacent to the mansion called the Mount. The above parcels of land usually occupied as a garden and are surrounded by back walls including the hot houses, green houses and other erections and carriageways trees shrubberies and plants standing together with a carriageway from South Lodge. To the use of the said John Burgess and Joseph Kent from the 24th day of June instant for a term of seven years thence next ensuing and fully to be complete and paying therefore yearly and every year during the continuance of the said term unto the said trustees the clear yearly rent of £25 by equal payments half yearly on the 25th day of December and the 24th day of June in each year.

And also shall sufficiently repair, maintain, cleanse, preserve and keep in good and tenantable order the green houses, walls and other erections and building, the gates, rails, fences and ditches to having, being first put into good and tenantable repair by the said Leasers at the commencement of the said term. And also shall at least during the continuance of the term cause all such part of the green houses and other buildings gates, rail fences to be well and effectually painted as well inside and outside with good oil paint.

Also shall at all times during the term keep the gardens and orchard well cropped and manured and managed to the approved methods of gardening, and shall not nor will cause or destroy any of the fruit trees in the same garden and orchard except the lilac trees growing near the south wall of the garden which they shall be at liberty to cut down and remove and except such trees as shall be decaying or shall cease to be productive of fruit would benefit if properly pruned at seasonable times of the year. And will plant in the place of such fruit trees as shall be decayed or become unproductive.

The 1841 census return makes interesting reading and goes part way in explaining the different families. Ages in the 1841 census were rounded up to the nearest five and are therefore not accurate. Thomas Kent, aged 25, gardener. Ann Kent his wife, aged 25, Martha Kent, daughter, aged 4, and Benjamin Kent, aged 2.

The following court entry refers to the old Penkhull Nursery house situated to the left on the corner just before Garden Street reads: Joseph Kent, aged 35, nurseryman, Margaret Kent, aged 45, (this would be Peggy the widow of William Burgess) Ann Burgess, aged 50, independent, John Burgess, aged 15, (the son of Peggy) and Mary Burgess, aged 8, her daughter. At the same house there was also Mary Bolas, aged 35, and her two children, Jane, aged 10 weeks and George, aged 10 years. It is not known if she had any family connection, perhaps a sister? Also Emma Harvey, aged 25, a servant and Henry Allen, aged 11, an apprentice potter.

Finally, 'Elm Tree House', where residing was John Burgess, aged 55, nurseryman and his wife Mary, aged 59 years.

The 1851 census gives no addresses, simply listing all entries as being in Penkhull. The following three entries follow on from each other. *John Burgess, aged 66, Nurseryman, seeds man, farmer of 50 acres, employs 9 labourers.* This entry reflects a thriving business. His wife Mary is listed aged 70.

The next property reads: Joseph Kent, aged 42, nurseryman, in partnership with John Burgess. His wife Margaret (Peggy), aged 58, Mary Ann Burgess, stepdaughter, aged 18, Mary Ann Burgess, aged 27, niece, a visitor. Elizabeth Sherwin, aged 13, also a visitor and three servants, two male, one female.

By 1861 John Burgess formerly of Elm Street House had been widowed and was living with his daughter Margaret (Peggy) and his son-in-law Joseph Kent at what was the old nursery house situated to the east of Garden Street where it joins with Newcastle Lane.

Joseph Kent, aged 52, nurseryman and market gardener occupying 38 acres, employing 16 men and 4 boys. By this time although the land had been reduced by 12 acres there was a considerable increase in staff no doubt reflecting an increase in trade. Margaret his wife, aged 68, John Burgess partner, widower, nurseryman and market gardener and Mary Booth a visitor, single, aged 25. There were also one female servant, aged 25 and a young boy, George Saltner, aged 15, years listed as an assistant gardener who came from Clayton.

No reference is made in the 1871 census of the Burgess or Kent partnership, but only to Thomas Kent, then aged 50 described as a nurseryman and employer. His wife was 59 living with four of his children and William Butler, aged 18 described as a field servant from Stafford. A Joseph Kent was at the same time living in Richmond Hill, that group of houses on the right hand side going down Penkhull New Road, just below The Terrace Inn. Thomas was aged 26 and listed as a nursery and seeds man's son. He was married to Harriet, aged 30, together with their three children, Margaret aged 4, Joseph Kent, aged 2, and Arthur, aged 2. They also took in a boarder; James Middleton, aged 24, listed as the nursery foreman. The marriage produced a total of seven children.

The 1881 census brings a change of circumstances. Number 22 Newcastle Street was uninhabited but at number 24 was Thomas Burgess, aged 33, and then described as a puddler in the iron industry. He lived with his wife Mary, aged 35, and their two children Thomas and Alice aged 8 and 7 respectively and born in Shifnall. There was no mention of Kent of Richmond Hill. Soon after this, David Foulkes, seeds man and florists, occupied No.22.

By 1887, the old partnership of Burgess and Kent and the name of Floulkes had been replaced by Allcock and Gresty. Allcock is listed in the 1891 census as living at No.24 Newcastle Street. James, aged 43, nurseryman, born Penkhull; Joseph, his son, a scholar, and Ann, his daughter, aged 16, a dressmaker. The next entry is that of William Gresty, aged 46, nurseryman and gardener, born in Bowden in Cheshire. His wife Mary, aged 43, was born in Swynnerton, along with their daughter, May, a dressmaker, aged 19. Three years later the names were reversed to Gresty and Allcock, gardeners, seeds men and florists, but by this time sections of the former forty acre holding had been acquired for small urban development. Elm Tree House was occupied by Thomas Williamson, aged 46, and his family.

The first indication of a reduction of the nursery and seed business is found in the 1901 census when James Allcock is referred to as a coal carter. His son, Joseph, was also listed as a coal carter. A boarder lived at the same address, Joseph Bailey whose occupation was that of *domestic gardener,* presumably he was maintaining the greatly reduced nursery business. In 1907, the local *Sentinel* directory lists the business as Lewis and Sproston, nurserymen and florists. The property used for this was the old barn converted from formerly three cottages standing in front of Elm Tree House. In 1912, the business was advertised as Lewis and Sproston, nurserymen and florists, 20 Newcastle Street, Penkhull.

The entry following in the 1907 directory lists again James Allcock at No. 26 Newcastle Street, a coal dealer. The coal yard was situated next to the old flower shop and before an old cottage that stood opposite Franklin Road. By the early 1930's the business had been taken over by Mr John Furber and was subsequently taken over and become known as Masons, coal merchants. This was later left to his nephew Charles Harthern who for many years lived at No.14 Newcastle Lane.

Penkhull churchyard contains the remains of Ann Burgess, aged 26, buried 20th September 1855; Mary, aged 78, buried 4th March 1859; John, aged 85, 27th May 1870; Thomas, aged 67, 14th August 1875; Samuel, 1 day 14th April 1881; and Sarah 7 months, 30th September 1883.

Shops in Penkhull

Some form of shops existed from early times, the first record being in 1737, occupied by William Kearley. The major difficulty in the use of Duchy of Lancaster copyhold records is that they only record the ownership of properties, only infrequently do they record the occupier, and their occupation, namely, baker, maltster, smith etc. thereby limiting their value for this line of research. Because of the nearness of the towns of Stoke and Newcastle, Penkhull never materialised in its own right as a centre where domestic requirements could be obtained. Local shops only catered for general food provision and little else.

The first trade directory for Penkhull of 1800 lists three hucksters (small shop keepers) in Penkhull, Michael Baxter, William Hill and Mary Broad. William Hill commenced business in 1794. After his death in 1805 the shop was taken over by his son William. Later in 1818 he was described as a baker and provision dealer. Michael Baxter was born in 1764 and appears to have been a tenant shopkeeper, corn miller and maltster. He purchased the local malthouse situated to the rear of Manor Court Street in 1824 from John Townsend. By 1831, Baxter had retired and built his house in Queens Road on land purchased from Robert Archer of Beech Grove, and by 1841 he is recorded aged seventy-seven years as living by independent means. Mary Broad retained her shop in Honeywall to at least 1818. There was also a village blacksmith by the name of George Shenton before 1818.

Little change is recorded until 1822, when service shops appear. Two boot and shoemakers were recorded and Samuel Philips had opened up a shop as village baker. But with the increase of working-class properties the demand for daily items by 1834 showed a considerable change to these facilities in Penkhull. There was a boot and shoemaker run by John Heath, a butcher run by Thomas Tatton entered the scene and six corner shops had become established in the ownership of Messrs Lowndes, Mountford, Martin, Nicholls Pickering and Taylor. There was also a village tailor by the name of William Till, probably working from his home and although there were only two Inns listed, The Marquis of Granby and The White Lion there were three beer houses, in addition to the two maltsters brewing the local ale, Mr Baxter and Mr Hill. Ladies had to wait much longer for the first dressmakers as none were listed until 1864 when two were recorded, by which time an additional boot and shoe repair shop had also opened.

Five years later, with a substantial increase in urban development, two butchers were trading and as an indication of better times, two bonnet makers and a similar number of tailors. But Penkhull was nothing more than a small village, where local traders could not compete with the neighbouring towns and markets where domestic goods and equipment, clothes and materials could be purchased at more competitive prices.

The Village Cobbler

One small business that survived for over thirty years was that of the village cobbler. The story of Jack Burton, village cobbler from 1938-1969 is an important one. It represents not an unusual set of circumstances for young men between the two great wars. Life was difficult, almost impossible in comparison with that of today. It is a story, written by himself and circulated amongst the Methodist fellowship in 1993 to raise funds for the chapel. His little cobblers shop was situated to the left of the 'Greyhound Inn', in Manor Court Street.

Life of a 'Cobbler' 1907 – 1993

'I was born into a strong Methodist family on 12th April 1907. My Grandfather and one of his sons were both Methodist Local Preachers and I was taken as a baby in arms to the Primitive Methodist centenary celebrations at Mow Cop, which was held in May 1907. It was reputed that 100,000 people were there. My mother and her sister (my aunt) plus my mother's old aunt, together took me. At this camp meeting a lot of babies were being christened. My mother's aunt wanted my mother to have me christened also. My Mother's sister had got lost in the crowd, she had bought my christening robe but she could not be found. I was since glad she had, because if the old aunt got her way, I should have been christened, *Hugh Bourne Clowes Burton*. Fancy signing your cheques like this!

Jack Burton in his old shop in Manor Court Street

Going to School during the First World War 1914-1918

What I remember most was from say 1916 to 1919. Exercise books and the sheets of paper we used for drawing lessons as we called them were very scarce and the sheets had to be saved and used for other lessons such as sums or composition. Nothing had to be thrown away if it was possible to be used again. The last two years of the war, manpower and workers were in short supply - so much so that in October we were given two weeks holiday to go potato picking. I do not remember how much we were paid but I think it was about 6d an hour. I left School at the age of 14 on July 31st 1921.

My Father was a miner and in 1921 there was a miner's strike, which started in April and lasted till October. Getting a job was impossible, as there were three million out of work in this country and no dole money, as this was not in force or if it was, it was not paid to anyone on strike. How my parents managed I shall never know.

I was two years of age when my sister was born in 1909 and as my mother did not enjoy the best of health they sent me to be with my aunt and uncle who lived two doors away. This was to be for a short while, but I never went back to my parents and lived with my aunt and uncle until I married in 1935. The uncle I lived with was named Albert Eardley and he was the village shoe repairer (cobbler).

I got tired of being unable to get a job, so in desperation, I asked my uncle if he would teach me the trade of shoe repairing and clog making. He said that he would, but as trade was so bad he could not pay me a wage but I could still live with him. Also he said I would have to promise to do one thing. This was to give my mind to learning the job or it was no use starting to work with him.

I worked with my uncle for nine years until I was 23 years of age. Never had any wages, just 2s. 6d. a week pocket money, which today is 12½ pence. My uncle and I had been looking around for some months to find a place where I could start in business on my own. It seemed like an accident that I got a little shop and business.

One morning at the end of August 1930, another uncle of mine asked me, if I would get out my bike and go to Newcastle to deliver a letter for him, which was urgent. As work was slack, my repairer uncle let me have the morning off to deliver this letter. After I had delivered this letter, I remembered reading in the Sentinel the night before 'For Sale – Shoe Repair Business' in Penkhull. I did not know for sure where Penkhull was but was told on enquiry that it was near N.S.R.I. I got on my bike and went towards Hartshill. On my way I saw a railway man delivering parcels. In those days goods were delivered by horse and cart, lorries and vans then were few and far between. I asked him if I was on the right way for Penkhull. He said *Carry on till you get to a Church, and then turn right. You will see two roads - they both take you to Penkhull.*

I rode round Penkhull church and saw this little shop. I did not stop but rode round the church again to see if it was the only shop. I did not see any more cobblers but later found there was another one not far away. I went home and told my uncle I had been to Penkhull and seen this little shop and thought it would be worth a visit to see if it was suitable.

A couple of days later my uncle and I went to Penkhull to visit this little shop. When we went inside we had a shock. The old gentleman was sitting there at his work bench which was about 18" off the floor. For a seat he had a chair, the legs of which were about 12" high. This was because he had been wounded in the First World War and he had his legs blown off, one below the knee and one above. He had two artificial legs which somehow he strapped to what leg he had left. He walked the short distance from home with the help of two sticks.

We had a talk with the old man who told us that he had sold this business to a man from Audley about one month previous. A few days later, this man was taken ill and sent to hospital where he died about three weeks later. As a result to shop was back on the market. The price he wanted for the business was £23, which included the small stock, a few hand tools and a Singer patching machine. I took over the shop on September 16th 1930. Rent was 6s. 0d per week plus rates about 2s. 0d. weekly. All the money I had then was 30s. 0d. (£1.50)

The charge at that time for men's shoes soled and heeled with leather was 4s. 9d. (about 27 pence) and ladies soled and heeled with leather was 3s. 3d. (about 18p). My uncle arranged with his wholesaler to provide me with stock and give me one month's credit. My uncle paid the wholesaler so that he was the owner of the business. (my uncle). I gave my uncle the week's takings each Saturday night, as I still lived with him. He gave me 10s. 0d. (50p) a week pocket money. This went on for about three years. Then I asked him to sell me the business for £36, which was all the money I had saved. From then on I had to pay 25s. a week board but I was anxious to have my own business by this time because I had started to walk out with the sweetest girl in the chapel choir.

We married in June 1935. No honeymoon, as I had to go to work the next day. She received £2 5s. 0d from me to keep house each week. She was a good manager. My wages at that time were about £4 weekly. I gave her more as business increased. If, in 1935 a man earned £5 weekly, he was considered to have a good job. We lived in a terraced house at the time the rent was 6s. 0d. weekly plus rates. This was at Talke and I travelled to Penkhull by cycle in summer and by bus in the winter until I bought a house in Franklin Road in 1947.

In 1936 when we had been married a little over a year we had our first setback. The lady, who owned my little shop and the two cottages next door, gave all three of us notice to quit our premises. She had received an offer to buy the lot from the Silverdale Co-op who wanted to knock the lot down and build a new Co-op shop - but would not buy them until all the three premises were empty.

The landlady offered me the premises if I would buy them. I went to a building society in Newcastle to see if I could get a loan. I paid 30s. 0d. for a survey and they told me the property was too old to lend any money on so I had to forget it. The landlady was unable to get us out and this went on for two more years. I would have bought the lot but still could not raise the money.

Then in September 1938 the landlady got her solicitor to send us all seven days notice to quit and if we were not out we should have to appear in court on a date in November, where we should all get an eviction order. So this was the second time I was almost turned out of Penkhull.

In the meantime the man who collected the rent (He was the landlady's nephew) came to see me to find out if I still could not buy them, because if I could she would sell for £100 less than she asked for in 1936. Still I said that I had not enough money to buy them. So he said did I mind telling him how much I had got. I told him that all I had was £75 as I had only been married for three years and this was all we had been able to save. So he asked me where the £75 was and I told him it was in Barclays Bank in Newcastle. He said that if I would go with him now to Barclays he would introduce me to the Manager, as he knew him very well. This he did and explained the situation I was in and gave me a good reference.

The manager went into his office and returned a few minutes later and said he was sorry but he could not do anything for me. So my friend, the rent man said *Come on across this way to Lloyds, as I know the Manager there.*

Again I was introduced and the situation I was in was explained. Also we told him that the £75 was in an account at Barclays. So he said to me straightaway, without any considering, *go and collect your £75 and with it open a current account here and I will allow you an overdraft of £200 to be paid in two years.*

This was a very kind offer by the Manager of Lloyds Bank because £200 was all the landlady wanted for the property. So a generous bank manager and a rent man, both of who need not have bothered at all, had solved my problem. So, I was sure now that God was on my side. So at the beginning of December 1938 I became a 'PROPERTY OWNER'.

1939

This was when the Second World War started and it was not long before leather was rationed. We were allowed to buy only a percentage of the amount we bought in 1938.

As it happened I had bought more leather than I was using so I had built up a stock. By doing so I was never without leather. We were told to only half heel where possible and to put toe bits on if this could be done. One trick we used to do with the heels was to heel the shoes and then to get a hack knife and cut the heel across using one good blow with a hammer. A hack knife is a knife used by a plumber to cut putty from a window when going to replace the glass. It then looked as it if had been half heeled.

1941

The cottage next door to my shop became empty and I was able to make the two into one shop. In 1941, I had to go for a medical for the army. I passed Grade 2 because of flat feet. Also as shoe repairing was classed as a reserved occupation. I was not called up to join the army. During the war years the shop was always packed with shoes waiting for repair. At any one time there could be well over 200 pairs of shoes or boots waiting to be repaired. This meant two to three weeks work at any one time.

1947

The war being over we moved from Talke as soon as possible. We bought a house in Franklin Road number 16 and we lived in this house for 21 years. Straight away we began to worship at Penkhull Methodist Chapel. Soon I was asked to take a boys class in the Sunday school. At that time we had 300 scholars but we did not have the morning service for adults as we do now. Sunday school began at 10.30 a.m. The senior scholars all met in the chapel for the morning service and the superintendent asked each senior teacher in turn to conduct the service from the pulpit and be responsible for the address.

All Change in Penkhull

In June 1961 I had a visit from one of the city council who asked me to fill in a form and send it back to the office. I looked at it and then said to him *I have already filled one of these forms in before* to which he replied. '*When*' he said. *February last year*, I said. Then he said *Well our boss is on holiday and we have nothing to do in the office, so I have been sent out to deliver these forms.*

So I asked him what did they intend doing in Penkhull because if they want to knock the place about, I have plenty of room behind to put up a new shop. He advised me to go down to the planning office in Stoke and they would tell me what was planned. The man in charge took out a map of Penkhull and then said *shops are planned for Manor Court Street, Penkhull.* He advised me to send in an outline plan of what I wanted and see if the council would pass it. This I did straightaway and at the end of July I received Planning Permission for building two shops on condition that living accommodation was built over them. A few weeks later on September 1st, almost everyone in the older parts of Penkhull received a compulsory purchase order. This meant that the council would buy all the property, demolish and rebuild.

All the shopkeepers in Penkhull went together to the planning office and were shown plans of what was to be done. A church car park was planned in place of my proposed two new shops. So I took from my pocket the planning permission I had already received from the council for the new shops and flats. So I said to the man in charge w*hat about this*. He told me someone in the office had made a mistake and I should never have received it. Then, one of the shopkeepers with us wanted to know to whom I had given a *backhander* to obtain such permission. This you will note was September 1961.

As time went on the council tried to get myself and Norman Hill, who was to have the other shop, to rent one of the shops in the Spar block below, because this block was intended for four shops. I would not agree to this so they made all kinds of excuses about drains not suitable, also there would have to be an exchange of land. This was eventually sorted out and the builders started work on the job 1st July 1968. We were able to move in the shops and flat in April 1969. I now had a very nice shop, workshop and flat. Unfortunately, I was only in this nice new shop eighteen months, when I was forced to retire because of ill health.

Looking back on my life, it has been changed by unexpected happenings and circumstances. Starting from birth - being born two weeks too late caused me turn to shoe repairing.

The uncle sending me to Newcastle with a letter. An advert in the Sentinel the night before, advertising a shoe repair business for sale in Penkhull. The shop being sold one month before and the buyer taken ill and died before he could take over. Being given notice twice to vacate the premises.

The rent collector who had no need to have bothered introduced me to Lloyds Bank. The bank manager who lent me the money without any fuss, to buy my shop and two cottages next door'.

Chapter 18
Pubs and Beer Houses.

The Ale Houses Act 1551 was passed to control the *abuses and disorders as are had and used in common ale-houses*, which laid the foundation of the modern licensing law. It provided that the Justices of the Peace were given powers within their jurisdiction to stop where they felt it to be appropriate and convenient the selling of ale and beer in common ale-houses and tippling-houses. No-one was to be permitted to keep an ale-house without being licensed by the Justices at Quarter Sessions, and the Justices were to take a bond and surety of the keepers of common ale-houses and tippling-houses. This surety was to prevent the playing of unlawful games as well as for the maintenance of public order.

The Act was repealed by Section 35 of the Alehouse Act 1828.

Prior to the 18th century gin craze, English taverns primarily sold beer and ale. As the production of gin rose the country became dangerously lawless, as famously depicted in William Hogarth's Gin Lane, the Government took action. In 1751, The Gin Act put drinking establishments under the control of local magistrates and obliged manufacturers to sell only to licensed premises.

As a consequence in 1830 the Government passed the Beerhouse Act, which aimed to wipe out the re-emerging gin shops and promote the healthier alternative of beer. This Act allowed a householder, assessed to the poor rate, to retail beer and cider from their own premises on payment of two guineas. The purpose of the legislation was to popularise beer at the expense of spirits. The Act was repealed in 1869.

As a result of this new Act the number of the beerhouses exploded, licenses being easily obtainable. Publicans' set up business often in the front parlour of their own homes. By 1869 this growth was checked as the precursors to modern licensing laws were introduced, paving the way for beerhouses to become public houses properly licensed to sell beer, wine and spirits.

The first record of an Inn in Penkhull is dated the 8th March 1607/7 when the Justices of the Peace at Newcastle granted permission for Thomas Tittensor of Penkhull to keep a common victualling house, alehouse or tipplinge house. The permission was granted at a payment of £10.

Penkhull in the early 18th century was an expanding community. One family that came to exploit the possible advantages of an increase in population was Thomas Elkin. Elkin was born in Wolstanton, two miles to the north of Penkhull. His wife came from Trentham, two miles to the south. They were married at Wolstanton church in 1677 and their union produced nine children, all baptised at Stoke Church.

The first record in the copyhold minutes comes in 1720 when Thomas Elkin borrowed the sum of £52 from Thomas Lovatt. This was on the assurity of his property then recorded as a smithy with garden adjoining to the messuage in the lane which ran from Penkhull to Clayton next to a property owned by Robert Smith. This limited description suggests that it could have been situated somewhere half way down the current Newcastle Lane. In a later record the property also contained an alehouse. Elkin died in 1723, his will being written three years earlier. He was then by profession a blacksmith and followed by that of an alehouse keeper. The inventory taken on the 20th November 1723 following his death lists a large property consisting of brew house, barn, smithy and other buildings. There was also land attached, called backfield and one croft called Thornditch. The inventory lists the items found in the alehouse, six barrels, one brewing tub and two dozen bottles in the cellar to the value of fifteen shillings. The total value of his estate including his wearing apparel and money in his purse of £2 10s amounted to £18 7s.

This ale house and brewery were subsequently inherited by his wife. It would appear that the loan from Thomas Lovatt was not paid off until January 1729 when the Alice was readmitted through the court. Alice at the same court surrendered the estate to Edward Smith (her son-in-law) in respect of a loan of £67.

It was seem that this debt was paid off for at the time of her death in 1738 the land was transferred to her son Richard Elkin, a yeoman of Penkhull. Ten years later in December 1749, the land and cottage was sold to Mr John Terrick, the younger, but there was no mention of the smithy or brewhouse.

Apart from the two licenced inns, The White Lion in Honeywall and the Marquis of Granby in the centre of Penkhull village there were no other establishments apart from beer houses which continued until the Act of 1869, when such establishments became public houses. Early records are not only scarce, but also difficult to interpret because names that have survived are often difficult to locate as to whom ran what and where.

The Beehive Inn
The Beehive Inn is located in Honeywall which originated as a separate hamlet. It is formed from three old cottages set in a row of back to back working class terraced houses. In all probability the row of workers cottages, like those in the surrounding area were built by Josiah Spode at the beginning of the 19th century for his workers. The location is shown on Hargreaves' map of 1832.

The census of 1841 does not indicate there being any inn at the site. The 1851 census however does list a Thomas Howell as a greengrocer and beer seller. In simple terms, he would have had a little greengrocer's shop, and at the same time, probably had a couple of hand pumps, one for Mild and the other for Bitter beers, both for consumption off the premises. It is from here that the residents of the nearby houses would fetch the beer in a jug after a day's work to have with their evening meal. The seller would not sell spirits. Thomas was born in Eccleshall, and was married to Hannah, who was recorded in 1851, aged 62, and came from Oldham. They both probably came to Stoke to find work and met locally. They employed a servant, Elizabeth Cook, a local girl, aged 21.

By 1861, Thomas Howell was no longer recorded but his son Enoch Howell, aged 50 was listed as beer seller at the same address but by this time the premises had become a Beer House under the sign of 'The Beehive'. Thomas was married to Sarah and they had four children together with a servant Julie, aged 22, from Silverdale.

The Beehive Inn c1940's

Looking much further into the pages of a trade directory dated 1887 there was no mention of the shop, only the Inn. John Trickett was listed as the landlord. This fact is further endorsed by the 1891 census which confirms John Arthur Trickett, aged 36, as a beer seller, born in Hanley, living at No. 53 Honeywall along with his wife Sarah, aged 34, a local girl together with live-in servant Hannah Beech.

The 1911 census informs us that the inn was held by Albert Beech, aged 36, and his wife Mary, aged 38. John was recorded as both a beer-bottler and a beerhouse manager. John's mother, a widow, aged 67, and a niece, aged 14, working in the pots. They had one child, Albert, aged 4 years. By 1914, the beerhouse remained in the occupation of Albert Beech but owned by the brewery, George Pimm & Co. The annual rental at the time was £35 whilst the rateable value was £30.

One of the most interesting assets of the inn is its cellar, carved out of the native sandstone. This helps to maintain the beers in perfect condition.

So why the name The Beehive? Probably this links with the address in Honeywall. There is no evidence to suggest that it has any direct connection is with bees or honey. However, it is known that, for centuries bees provided the only sweetening agent available, and there are records of beekeepers in Penkhull from medieval times. Therefore, it is not beyond the possibility that beekeepers were active on the lower slopes of Penkhull behind, the inn.

The Beehive Inn, Honeywall 2010

If the visitor may think that once a beekeeper resided at the small cottage just above the inn entitled 'Beekeepers Cottage' they would be mistaken. The cottage had this name given to it by myself when two lads purchased the old cottage some thirty-five years ago to restore it from near dereliction. They asked me what name they could give to it which had an historical connection. In view of the names of Honeywall and the Beehive Inn what better than 'Beekeepers Cottage' by which name it has been known ever since.

The White Lion, Honeywall
The White Lion Inn has at various times in its history has had the name Hotel tagged on. It commenced life as a coaching inn situated on the steep hill called Honeywall commencing from the town of Stoke-upon-Trent, a road which dates from prehistoric times. The inn is shown on Yates's map of 1775, and the 1777 Duchy of Lancaster Map on which it is recorded as in the occupation of Mr Thomas Appleton. Records for the Justices of the Peace at Stafford note the issuing of a licence to sell wines and spirits from the mid 18th century.

It would seem that Thomas Appleton had established himself as a property owner as early as 1762 when the copyhold records list him as renting a property described as: *all that house, shop and chamber over the same and garden and yard in Penkhull currently in the holding of Thomas Appleton.* The annual rental for this amounted to £12.

Appleton was involved in numerous mortgage transactions over the following years, mostly concerning three cottages and stables, two of which were rented out while he occupied the other. Although no direct name is given to the property, I think it safe to assume that these three cottages would be the origins of what is now the White Lion Inn of today. The view from the front of the inn points to the conclusion that this could originally have been three cottages later converted into one.

In May 1764, Appleton rented two crofts situated to the rear of the cottages called Shaws Crofts for the sum of £6 p.a. on the basis that the owner, Edward Shaw was free to continue to access the land *to make and burn brick and do all things necessary for that purpose.* By 1767 and in two further land transactions of 1773 and 1775 Appleton was referred to as an inn holder. The following year he was listed as a Yeoman in a deal to secure a mortgage on five other cottages, three of which were *lately built situated at Cliff Gate Bank.*

In May 1816, Appleton died at the age of 83, but by this time he was recorded as living at Lane Delf. He was buried in Stoke churchyard. Later in the same year on the 30th October 1816, his son, also called Thomas was formally admitted to The White Lion. It was then described as follows: *All that customary dwelling house in Penkhull called The White Lion, and also all those several other dwelling houses or tenements near or adjoining thereto, and which are now in the holding of James Atkin, Richard Brindley and another, and all other copyhold property in Penkhull.* From this point information regarding the inn is thin. . . . In April 1829, James Appleton, one of the grandsons of Thomas Appleton junior surrenders: *All that copyhold messuage situated in Honeywall called the White Lion with buildings, brew-house, gardens occupied by John Biddulph as tenant. And also those four other messuages with outbuildings and gardens belonging situated in Honeywall and now in the occupation of John Biddulph and his under tenants.*

For what ever reason this transaction was not completed because on the 6th March 1834 a Declaration of Trust respecting the purchase of the White Lion was executed. It would appear that the grandchildren of Thomas Appleton agreed to surrender to the legal representatives the inn together with other dwelling houses adjacent for the sum of £650. The document goes on to state that the inn will be held in trust as part of the personal estate of Josiah Spode deceased.

The inn was advertised to be let in the *Potteries Mercury* in April 1839 *And may be entered on immediately, that old established, well known, and well accustomed inn known by the sign of the 'White Lion', with suitable out buildings, and a large excellent garden, situate at the Honeywall, midway between Stoke and Penkhull. The incoming tenant will be expected to take from the present tenant the small stock of ale and spirits, with the household furniture etc. Apply to William Outrim, Stoke-upon-Trent.*

Trade directories throw light on who occupied the White Lion. In 1802, the licensee was Thomas Egerton. For the turbulent years of the early 19th century tenants came and went in rapid succession: 1818, James Atkin, (he was one of the tenants listed in 1816 as living nearby). 1822, William Bird; 1834, Joseph Reeves; 1851, Frederick Poulson; 1864, John Walton; 1887, George Aston; 1907, Harry Howell. The census returns help to identify occupants. In 1841 the inn was held by George Vernon, aged 25 but in October that year the Inn was advertised TO LET and could be entered upon immediately. It was described as: *That old established and well-accustomed public house now in the occupation of Mr George Vernon, who is declining business. There is a three stalled stable and a good garden belonging to this house. Stock and fixtures to be taken at a valuation. Further particulars apply Mr Vernon on the premises.*

The White Lion Inn, Honeywall. Parts date from the 18th century

By 1841, John Walton, a local person is listed, aged 43 as licensee. He was supported by his wife Mary and their daughter, aged 20. John's mother, Ann, aged 83, a widow, was also living with them. The 1851 census lists a different tenant; John Poulson, aged 31 and his wife Ellen, aged 30. John originated from Fenton and his wife from Hanley. They had three children, Joseph, aged 6, Charles, aged 4, and William, aged 1, all born in different towns within the city indicating frequent changes of address. It is interesting that the trade directory lists Frederick Poulson as the landlord, while the census lists him as the brother of John, aged 26, with an occupation of a tailor.

The 1861 and 1871 census returns list John Walton as licensee. The census of 1901 records Earnest Bell, aged 35, a bachelor from Newcastle living with his brother Albert, aged 39, a solicitor and their sister Lillian, aged 26, together with two servants, and John Bromley, aged 26, a visitor.

In 1861 it was owned by Richard Stone who sold the plot of land at the rear of the inn to Frederick Bishop to enable a new road to be built from Honeywall to Princes Road, thereby opening up the area for housing development from 1865. Note the name Stone Street.

Probably as a direct result of the development of the nearby allotments housing estate towards the end of the 18th century, The White Lion was extended as can be seen from the red brick addition. By 1914, the inn was occupied by Harvey Howell, and owned by Burton Brewers, and described as the White Lion Inn with stables and garden. The annual rent paid by Mr Harvey amounted to £60, and the rates amounted to £48. If compared with those of The Beehive, it is obvious that The White Lion was a much more substantial establishment than The Beehive just across the road.

The Terrace Inn, Penkhull New Road

The origins of the old Terrace Inn commences with the building of a row of five terraced properties, just below what was to become known as Commercial Row, the old narrow street leading to The Views. The first deeds to the properties are dated the 29th July 1858, with the transfer of the cottages to Hester Till from her late husband John. By 1870, Hester had died and the property was left to her daughter, Mrs Priscilla Scholes of Derby, and her son William Scholes. The property was then sold to Mary Ann Cliff on the 29th December 1870 for the sun of £451. Mary Cliff, the licensee, was recorded as a widow but later married Mr Thomas Bratt.

Evidence suggests that from the original five houses, three were converted into The Terrace Inn by 1879, when a trade directory confirms it was occupied by Samuel Bowers and Mrs Wolfe. By 1881 William Birch, aged 33, born in Stoke was the licensee. He lived with his wife Emma, aged 36, together with two children William, aged 5, and Albert, aged 3. The following year, 1882, the new husband of Mary Cliff, Thomas Bratt was now listed as the landlord with no mention of William Birch. It is not clear as to why but the Rate Books of 1889, although listing the owner as Mary Ann Bratt; the occupier was Mrs Sarah Kinder. By the time the 1891 census came around, Mary Bratt was the licensee and widowed again.

The old Terrace Inn on the corner of Commercial Row

By 1901 George Radford, aged 32, had become the licensee and shared the business with his wife Sarah, aged 30, both came from Stoke and they employed two servants. By 1907, the inn was run by Frank Radford, probably a close relative.

The old Terrace Inn dating from the late 1800s

For many years the old Terrace Inn was probably the most popular with the locals. Many stories still circulate of the old characters that frequented the pub. I recall my late friend Ernest Tew talking to me some thirty years ago of his memories of the 1930s and 40s when the back room snug was often referred to as 'The Third Programme'. *The highlight of the pub was the little men's smoke room where the conversation was brilliant, debating most things of the day from politics to religion. Sometimes they became very heated, especially after a few pints. Mugs were frequently picked up in anger but never actually thrown. It was here in this little room that everyone was an equal no matter what his position was. All were on Christian name terms and included many high ranking officials from the council. It was truly a remarkable meeting place.*

The new Terrace Inn situated below the old Inn

Another good friend, the late Reg Brunt, who used to live just around the corner in Penkhull Terrace and was known locally as the Mayor of Penkhull, recalls an old chap called Bob Dowie who used to enjoy a few pints at the old Terrace each evening. *Bob, whenever he ordered his pint, would strike a match as if going to light his pipe and threw it into the freshly pulled pint with its head still overflowing the glass. Even though some nights he would stretch out a pint to last some couple of hours, the match would remain, sitting at the top of whatever remained in the glass. One night I asked him why he did that and came the reply 'that with the match on the top, if he had to the need to visit somewhere during the evening, be could be sure that no one would bother to drink his beer with a match on the top'.*

As part of the city council compulsory purchase plan to demolish most of the old village in the early 1960s the old Terrace Inn was purchased by the corporation on the 5th October 1964 for the sum of £550.

The Royal Oak, Manor Court Street

At the corner of Manor Court Street and Newcastle Lane stood for many years, The Royal Oak Inn. The premises were surrendered as mortgagee in default to William Bridgwood in 1860 who converted two cottages out of a row of eight into a beer house. At a copyhold court held on the 13th day of September 1866 the properties were sold to John Royal.

The 1861 census lists the property as The Royal Oak, but then recorded not in Church Street, but at the top of Newcastle Street, numbered 1 and 3. It was occupied by a direct ancestor of mine George Henry Underwood, aged 36, beerseller and potter, born Penkhull. He was married to Eliza, aged 38, of Stoke. They had four children, Henry, aged 16, John, aged 12, and both working as potters' boys, followed by Frank, aged 9 and James, aged 2. James was my great grandfather. His daughter Eliza Ann was my grandmother who married Thomas Talbot in 1908.

George was born in April 1816 not in 1825 as suggested by the census. His parents are listed as Frances and Elizabeth, of Penkhull Lane, labourer. In a surrender dated 1866 from William Bridgwood to John Royal there were eight houses *but two of which have lately been converted into one and used as a beer house occupied by William Benbow.* The trade directories manage to pre-date the court record for in 1864 William Benbow is listed as a beer seller, Royal Oak, Penkhull. The row of cottages and beer house remained in the ownership of Bridgwood until January 1870 when they were sold to William Bradbury for £525.

The 1871 census shows that Benbow, then aged 36, also worked as a *potters colour maker* as well as running the beerhouse, a practice not uncommon for the period. Benbow was not local; he was born at Coalbrookdale and married to Jane, aged 37. She was widowed. Her son, George Willott, aged 13, was working as a turner. Three other children were also living at the house. They took in lodgers; Mary Addison, aged 65, and her son James, and lastly Edward Lewis, aged 28. A total of nine people in such small accommodation, but again a not unusual practice for this period in history.

Ten years later in 1881, The Royal Oak was held by Mr David Shenton, aged 45, and his wife Mary, aged 42, together with their seven children ranging from Albert, aged 20, to Blanch, aged 1. Three years later, in May 1884, his wife Mary died and is buried in Penkhull churchyard. Her gravestone reads *In Loving Memory of Mary Ann, the beloved wife of David Shenton of the Royal Oak Inn.*

By 1891, David Shenton had remarried to Emma, aged 34, eleven years his junior. At the time there remained four children living at home, together with Jane Bryan, a domestic servant. David Shenton died on the 15th March 1900, aged 72. He is buried alongside his first wife Mary. On the gravestone there is no mention of Emma his second wife. The epitaph under his name reads *his end was peace.*

On the 30th June 1898 two years previous he had sold his other property in Penkhull. Shenton had already sold The Royal Oak in 1890 to Parkers Brewery although he continued to run the establishment at least until 1891 on their behalf. The court minute commences by stating that Shenton was formerly of The Royal Oak, licensed victualler but afterwards of No. 14 Church Street, grocer but at the time of the court record living at No. 191 Campbell Road Stoke.

The record continues to list all the property that he owned No's 6, 8 and 10 Newcastle Street, and No's 13, 14 and 15 Church Street, (now Manor Court Street) together with two other dwelling houses converted into one and used as a beerhouse. The document refers to a common ash pit at the rear and reserving to the owners of The Royal Oak the cellar lying under a portion of the dwelling house No.13 next door as it was used and occupied by the inn for the storage of ale. The property was sold to Angelina Reeve of No 20 Penkhull Terrace for the sum of £550.

The former Royal Oak beerhouse to the right of the picture c1910

By 1901 it had ceased being used as a beer house and had become a domestic residence. In 1911 it was occupied by William Woolley, aged 30, a pottery worker and his wife Florence, aged 32, and their three children. By 1912 it was occupied by Walter Roberts whose occupation was a goods porter. Later the same year the premises were purchased by Mr Albert Swetnam who previously held a small shop on the corner of Seven Row in Penkhull New Road. He converted the old Royal Oak Inn into a high class grocer's shop. Two invoices for the work have survived. The first, from Charles White, painter and decorator from Albion Street, Hanley, and dated 5th March 1912 itemises work to be done to the old inn including complete decoration. The second invoice is from Meiklejohn & Son, building contractors from Edwards Street, Stoke. The invoice notes first that the contract was for alterations and building to the former 'Royal Oak Inn'. The amount of work was considerable including work on the roof, chimney, spouting, removing interior walls to make the premises suitable for a shop. The total amount of the invoice came to £79 16s 6d including material and labour. In comparison with today's prices it is interesting to note that the cost of a joiner for five hours work was 4s 2d (21p) and the cost of a bricklayer for 10 hours work amounted to 14s 2d (around 73p). Mr Swetnam continued in business until 1955 when Mr Brunt purchased the shop.

The Marquis of Granby

This old established inn has proved the most difficult to research its early history. I was always of the belief that the original inn would date from the medieval period on the basis that Penkhull was situated on the main highway from the south to the north of Stoke-on-Trent before the current London Road, Stoke was laid.

Here in Penkhull, at the top of a long climb up the hill from the Trent Valley at Hanford before the downward path to the town of Stoke, an inn was listed in the 15th century under the sign of Lord Wagstaff. The court rolls list a *Thomas Bagnall victualler of Penkhull in 1587*. A Thomas Tittensor was licensed to sell spirits in 1606; James Bourne was named a victualler of Penkhull in 1775. Sadly none of these identify the inn by any name.

Some thirty five years ago, I interviewed Miss Maskery of Richmond Hill she was then in her 80s. She had a vivid memory and could recall the *Relief of Mafeking in May 1900* during the second Boer war by the ringing of a hand bell by a young lad as he ran around the village shouting '*Mafeking has been relieved, the siege is over*'. Miss Maskery also remembered the old Marquis, a thatched building standing back from the road followed by the building of a new Marquis. She was able to date this by the fact that the scaffolding once removed was employed in the construction of the new senior school in Princes Road in 1895/6.

The name The Marquis of Granby is interesting as there are so many pubs of that name throughout the country. John Manners, the eldest son of the 3rd Duke of Rutland, and known by his father's subsidiary title of the Marquis of Granby, was a highly distinguished soldier and later a politician. Manners died in 1771 and when his soldiers

retired, John Manners helped financially many of his soldiers to set up public houses who subsequently named those inns *The Marquis of Granby* out of respect and admiration of the former Major General. When he died the Marquis left £60,000 of debts with assets of around £23,000 which could imply that he was most generous during his life time.

The Marquis of Granby built 1896

The Church Lune Book for Penkhull, although not identifying the inn by name, confirms that it was owned by Thomas Gibbs and in the occupation of Robert Archer. The earliest record which mentions the name is in the trade directory dated 1818, when Edward Candland was the licensee. He was married to Ann as the 1841 census confirms. Candland continued in business until the running of the inn was taken over by John Holroyd prior to 1841. It would appear that Holroyd married the widow of Edward Candland by the fact that the census lists as landlord John Holroyd, aged 40, and his wife Ann, aged 45. *(Actual ages for this early census are not guaranteed as accurate and rounded up to the nearest five)* together with her four children from her first marriage, Ann, aged 20; Elizabeth, aged 15; Martha, aged 15; and William, aged 13; all with the surname of Candland. By 1851, Ann Holroyd, then aged 60 years, was widowed again and three of her children, Elizabeth, Martha and William still lived at home. There were two lodgers, William Brown, aged 76, a widower, and his brother Thomas, also a widower, aged 64. In all probability these were related to Ann, perhaps brothers as their birthplace, like hers was listed as Grindon in Warwickshire. A further lodger was Ann Bill, aged 28, a potter's paintress born at Penkhull, and finally Ann Highfield, aged 19 years, a domestic servant from Sandon.

Ten years later in 1861, Charles Simpson, aged 34, and his wife Mary, aged 36, both from Hanley were running the inn and by 1891 George Salt, aged 45, and Sarah his wife, aged 42, were in charge. They had two children, Florence, aged 15, and Eleanor, age 7. Apart from Charles' mother and his sister-in-law living there, they had two male servants John Harris, aged 29, and Alfred Thomas, aged 23.

The census dated 1901 shows a further change in tenancy. Charles Sims, aged 49, from Stoke was the licensee supported by his wife Mary, aged 47. They had five children Maud, aged 20, to Harold, aged 4 at home. Mr Sims was still the landlord in 1914, and the property owned by George Pimm and Co. The annual rental for The Marquis was substantial at £85 which had to be found, in addition to the rates being charged at £65.

Searching the copyhold minutes, the first record which conclusively identifies the site of the inn does not appear until September 1783. The land upon which The Marquis now stands was formerly a part of Bowyers Meadow owned at the time by the Terrick family. There was no Penkhull New Road as we know it today, only a narrow track to where West Bank now stands. The record states: *To this court comes John Plum of Houghton in Lancashire Esq, and his wife Hannah. Hannah was previously living together with her sisters, Elizabeth and Mary Terrick surrendered all that small parcel of land now marked out lying at the top of Bowyers Meadow to be enclosed by a foot set hedge and formerly in the holding of Mr Wm Ford to the use of Michael Henney, wheelwright.*

Michael Henney died at the age of 83, and was buried in Stoke churchyard on the 6th May 1785. The land was then transferred to his widow Elizabeth, who survived a further twelve years after the death of her husband until May1797. In September of the same year, the copyhold court dealt with the transfer of the estate to her son, also called Michael, upon trust. The blacksmith's shop was recorded as being in the *holding of John Gallimore, but now of Thomas Cheadle.* On the 13th May 1802, Michael Henney junior died, leaving his estate to his widow Hannah upon trust.

Under the terms of her will, Hannah Henney put the estate in trust at a court held on the 31st December 1814. At the following court held on the 2nd January 1815, Samuel Spode of the Foley, as the only surviving trustee under the terms of the will, surrendered the estate in consideration of £484 to Henry Brassington, victualler, and William Pratt, grocer, both of Lane Delph *All that copyhold messuage, situate in Penkhull with the malthouse garden and appurtenances formerly in the holding of Michael Henney deceased.*

The next transfer was held on the 2nd April 1829. *To this court comes Henry Brassington of Penkhull and Felix Pratt of Fenton, manufacturer of earthenware which Henry Brassington and Felix Pratt are Devisees in trust for sale of premises listed in the last will and testament of William Pratt late of Lane Delph, maltster and shopkeeper deceased, and of Henry Brassington and in consideration of the sum of £570 paid by William Hill for the absolute purchase for the tenement after mentioned, if not the sum of £585, to the said Henry Brassington and Felix Pratt, as such Devisees in trust, for sale and the sum of £285 to the said Henry Brassington for his own sole use (the receipts acknowledged), surrendered all that copyhold messuage dwelling house in Penkhull with malt house, garden and appurtenances*

thereto adjoining now late in the occupation of Henry Brassington to William Hill, shopkeeper.

By July 1840, William Hill had died and the property passed to his son, Henry. Henry took out a mortgage from John Frost, a farmer from Leek to the value of £450. The next document referring to the Marquis of Granby is dated 1853, and it is this that throws considerable light on to the history of the inn. *To this court comes Samuel Crewe of Stoke-upon-Trent, inn keeper, and Mary Lees of Burslem, widow and Frederick Crewe Lees, solicitor of the will of William Crewe and prays to be admitted tenant to all that dwelling house, garden, outbuildings and estate in the holding of Joseph Pickering, deceased afterwards in the holding of William Kettle since successively of Robert Archer, Edward Candland and Robert Holroyd and now of his widow Ann Holroyd and is now and hath for many years last past been used and occupied as a public house and known by the sign of The Marquis of Granby.*

This part of the court record tells us the name of the property, The Marquis of Granby. It further confirms that the inn was previously in the ownership of William Crewe. His will dated the 26th October 1852, also confirms that he owned The Marquis of Granby as well as The Nantwich Arms situated in the Swine Market, Nantwich, and a large house in Marsh Parade, Wolstanton and several other properties. William Crewe states in his will: *I give and devise all my messuage or public house by the sign of The Marquis of Granby now and for many years past in the occupation of Mrs Holroyd. Together with the malthouse buildings and garden attached at Penkhull to my son Samuel Crewe my daughters Mary Lees and my grandson Frederick Crewe Lees of Burslem, solicitor.*

The documents list the previous occupiers of The Marquis; Joseph Pickering, William Kettle; Robert Archer; Edward Candland; Robert Holroyd then his widow Ann Holroyd. This document gives the first evidence of The Marquis prior to 1818. A trade directory of 1800 lists William Kettle, victualler, Penkhull but no address or the name of business. With the evidence of other documents it is shown that it refers to The Marquis of Granby. Not only this, the previous occupier is also listed, Joseph Pickering. The court records point to the fact that Joseph Pickering acquired property in Penkhull in March 1772, a date which ties in with the assumption that inns, trading under the sign of The Marquis of Granby, followed shortly after the death of John Manners, the Marquis of Granby in 1771. This is conclusive evidence.

With the additional record of Joseph Pickering that the site of the property today originally comprised of two different parcels of land. The first entry lists the building, and the second under the name of Bowyers Meadow dating from 1783. The court records identify Joseph Pickering as being admitted tenant to the copyhold tenement on the 25th March 1772 upon the surrender of John Slaney of Penkhull.

Slaney only acquired this land in October of the previous year from Thomas Astbury, potter of Lane Delph. Thomas Astbury himself had only acquired it following the death of his father Thomas at a copyhold court held in May 1771. The ownership of the tenement goes through family members from the first in line, Joshua Astbury, who acquired it from William Colclough on the 2nd January 1734/5, It was then in the occupation of William. William inherited it from his mother, Anne Colclough, widow on the 6th April 1717.

Unfortunately records for the previous decades are not clear, but working back through the Hearth Tax records pick up the thread with a John Colclough listed in both the 1662 and the 1666 entry as holding property in Penkhull comprising seven hearths, a substantial holding. The number of rooms almost mirror the last entry of 1895 at the time of its auction when it is recorded as having five bedrooms.

The property remained in the hands of Mary Ann Lees, until her death at Southport. She was buried at Hanford on the 19th November 1894. By the terms of her will dated the 16th May 1873, The Marquis of Granby was left in trust to her daughter Annie Crewe Lees and Mr William Challinor of Leek, earthenware manufacturer, *until it should be deemed advisable to convert it into cash but should not be sold during the lives of her three daughters unless the major part of them should consent to such a sale.* After her death it remained in the hands of the trustees.

On the 17th May 1886, the trustees entered into an agreement to lease out the premises to Mr Henry Elshaw for a period of ten years at an annual rent of £82. It was recorded that the property had been in the occupation of Mr George Furnival for some time. The same document refers for the first time to the addition of a bowling green adjacent to the pub. On the same date Mr Elshaw assigned the lease by way of mortgage for security of £306 from Mr John Robinson.

The next we learn of the ownership of The Marquis of Granby is at the time of its sale by auction by Messrs Butters and Pointon of Cheapside, Hanley on Tuesday 23rd April 1895. Lot 4 reads as follows:

The old established, and fully licensed hotel situate in Penkhull in the Parish of Stoke-upon-Trent called The Marquis of Granby, together with a large garden and greenhouse, bowling green, covered skittle alley with billiard room over, all adjoining, and now in the occupation of Mr James Duff. Also the building adjoining occupied as a slaughter house and two stall stable with harness room over now occupied by Mr Arthur Salt.

The hotel contains bar, tap room, snug with bar, kitchen and parlour on the ground floor, and five bedrooms with underground cellar. This lot is pleasantly situated near to Penkhull Church and within a short distance of the new Stoke cemetery and North Stafford Infirmary.

Next to The Marquis of Granby was the old malthouse. This came under the hammer as Lot 5 consisting of *a three storeys high, with building adjoining used as a Loose Horse Box, also two-stalled stable with loft over and coach house now in the occupation of Mr Mountford.*

The property was in the ownership of Mr J W Dunn probably from 1895, but by 1914 it was owned by George Pimm & Co, subsequently being sold to Marston's Ltd.

The final subject of research comes with the opening of retail outdoor beer houses which were popular in working class areas. A pint of bitter or mild could be purchased from the pump and served direct into the customer's own jug. After a working day, beer would often accompany the evening family meal. Out-door beer houses traded from converted front rooms or parlours in terraced rows of houses. They needed very little capital or facilities to make a living, but more often than not, the business supplemented a poor weekly wage from a local potworks.

With the change in the law from the 1970s when supermarkets were allowed to retail alcohol, the business of the 'out-door' has disappeared. Trade directories sometimes list these, but in some cases the references are hard to differentiate from beer houses for consumption on the premises. The following lists those outdoor beer houses found, but many smaller properties did not advertise.

1864
John Boulton, Penkhull Street, Enoch Howell, 56 Honeywall.
1865
Eliza Underwood, Penkhull Street.
1869
Henry Cliff, Samuel Lowndes, Margaret Robinson, all of Penkhull.
1882
Herbert Ball, Edward Heath, Honeywall; Elijah Lea, John Lowe, Richard Parks, John Pritchard.
1887
James Bates, 37 Honeywall; Thomas Parkes, Garden Street; Robert Charles, 19 Honeywall; William Smith, Penkhull.
1896
Robert Hall, East Street; James McPherson, 12 Garden Street; William Smith, East Street; Caroline Stone, Mill Street; Joseph Webb, Church Street.
1907
Henry Robinson, 27 East St.; R. Edwards, 19 Honeywall.

Chapter 19
Concern of the poor.

The great agrarian revolution which began during the 15th century and continued throughout the 16th complicated further an already growing poverty problem. Much land changed to new vigorous men, sensitive to the economic realities of the period. Many converted their holdings from arable to grazing, or reconstituted the wasteful open field system. A number of farmers gained control of the former monastic lands, extending further social dislocation. There were, then, complex economic and demographic forces that were producing, on the one hand periods of agricultural prosperity for the landowners, and, on the other hand, misery and dejection for the marginal elements of the agrarian community.

Government's most pressing concern during this period was vagrancy. Vagabondage was widespread and organised. It flowed across the land, imposing burdens and damage upon rural villages. These rootless beggars were the first social evil, the second a chronic plague. The first Tudor Poor Laws were largely concerned with ways of punishing vagrants and sending them back home, though the second Beggars' Act added that the deserving paupers could be licensed to beg. An Act of 1536, five years later, ordered in its area a parish or municipal authority to assume full responsibility for the impotent poor so that they would not be compelled to wander to other parishes as beggars. This Act marked a shift of emphasis away from Hundreds, Manors and Courts Leet, and began the construction and recognition of the civil parish.

The Bill of 1536 sought to restrict the poor to their own area, where they customarily belonged and where they were known. The children of the poor were to be taught a trade and set to work. Alms were to be raised by voluntary means in each parish for support of the helpless poor. The statute lapsed soon after it was passed, but it began to define the strategy for the future; work, as well as punishment, for the idle and able-bodied poor, cash payments to those who could not work; and, as a consequence, a ban on begging and casual alms-giving.

An Act of 1547 introduced a new determination to discipline the vagrant poor, prescribing servitude for two years upon first conviction and penalties leading to lifelong slavery or a felon's death for those who proved to be intractable. The children of beggars were to be forcibly apprenticed, work provided for the aged poor, and weekly collections sought for the impotent poor who were not to beg. At the same time, the suggestion was expressed that individual communities should erect houses for the reception of the impotent poor.

A subsequent Act of 1550 repealed the Act of 1547 as unworkable and mandated a return to the demands of the 1531 Act. Parliament moved cautiously in this unchartered field of legislation. Public conscience was aroused to undertake the burden of responsibility. Shortly after the 1547 Act, London embraced the principle of a compulsory rate. In 1570, a celebrated assault was made on the complex problem of urban poverty. It is from this date that church lunes, (a method of collection from each householders based upon property size to support the poor of the parish. They were collected monthly, hence the word Lune) were assessed and charged in the parish of Stoke, which included the district of Penkhull, as the churchwardens' accounts for that year show a total of £13 4s 1d was collected from the following townships within the parish.

Bagnall	£1 6s 0d	Longton	£1 2s 0d
Bucknall	£2 12s 0d	Shelton & Hanley	£2 1s 6d
Fenton Culvert	17s 9d	Clayton/Seabridge	£2 1s 3d
Fenton Vivian	£1 0s 10d	Penkhull	£1 12s 7d

This ancient document provides evidence that Stoke parish was in advance of the 1572 Act, which formally established the office of Overseer of the Poor in each parish. Overseers were appointed annually by the justices of the peace from persons having a certain value of property. The justices were empowered to levy rates on all eligible persons in an attempt to raise the funds to meet the needs of the lawful poor. They were also empowered to remand and gaol those, who after due persuasion, declined to pay. In addition, the law also clamped down heavily upon the professional poor, as vagabondage and begging were outlawed under pain of whipping and being burned through the ear for a first offence.

Further action by the Government was inevitable as a result of the devastating poverty experienced by the country as a whole. The direct result led to a period of economic depression starting in 1594. Furthermore, heavy and unseasonable rains, prior to this date, resulted in poor harvests for five consecutive years. These were difficult years for all, and the continuing war with Spain only added to the suffering.

It was in the year 1596, which witnessed the most severe effects of decline, when it seemed certain that the dearth of necessaries was so great, prices so high, and unemployment so general, that numerous regions were threatened by famine. Despite the sternest efforts of Government to control prices and relieve communities where the scarcities were greatest, the prices of bread grain rose wildly. There were cases of outright starvation. Clergy were instructed to preach against hoarding and to encourage almsgiving. The turbulence so feared by the Tudors spread across the realm in the wake of hunger. Bread riots occurred in numerous towns. The problems experienced in 1596 prompted the Government into action, resulting in the great legislative measures of 1597-1601. Recognition of the several kinds of poor was established by this Act. The impotent poor were defined as those who could not support themselves because of age, sickness, bodily injury or extreme youth, all of whom had to be maintained by the parish. The more difficult to assist were the poor who were quite able to work and willing to support themselves but could not find employment, and who, therefore, should be assisted. Beggars, idle wasters and vagabonds were to receive no help and were to be *whipped until bloody,* by order of a Jr or parochial officer and subsequently returned to their native parish. The justices had the power to commit the incorrigible to gaol or a house of correction, to condemn them to banishment from the realm, service in the galleys, or even execution.

The churchwardens' accounts for Stoke Ancient Parish are incomplete. Only a few have survived. For example, the next account following the year 1570 is for 1595. It lists nineteen families in Penkhull, seventeen of whom paid their church lunes for the year, amounting to 10s 6d for half a year. There are two accounts for 1596, the first being submitted by Richard Lovatt, the second by Bartholomew Bowyer, both churchwardens. These accounts reflect financial demands outside the parish, as the sum of £25 was given to maintain maimed soldiers wounded in Brittany, and the sum of £5 8s 0d for gaol money at Stafford. Could this item be for the maintenance of the poor who were sent to gaol under the Poor Laws? For the same year, it would also be prudent to assume a reluctance to pay church lunes for the sum of 1s 0d was paid for a *cytation* for unpaid lunes against Messrs Machin and Hitchin, both of Penkhull. The following year an item was paid to Wm Adams, the churchwarden, for *wrytinge the lune accounte viiid.* (8p) (which means that they kept the records of those paying the church taxes, 'Lunes'.)

The same account gives an insight into how the collection of church lunes was complied: *Received for the half lune for the relief of the poor £6 6s 3d,* and later in the records an insight of the poverty in the area is given, for the parish paid for *the burial of Thomas and Jo Clover. 3s 4d.* By 1600, the sum collected for church lunes by the overseer of the poor for Penkhull amounted to £1 11s 4d, and again the need for parish relief were itemised: *item to Anthone Phillips for keepinge the bastarde 2s 5d.* The same accounts refer to Thomas Turner and John Hutchins, both of Penkhull, who left their lunes unpaid, and accordingly were charged the sum of 1s 11d.

The next churchwardens' accounts presented by Rob Keeling are for the year 1602, they disclose for the first time, efforts to maintain the poor which relate directly to the village of Penkhull:

Item kepeying the lame. . . . old at Penkhull viiis (8 shillings or 40p).

The lack of further supportive evidence or a consistent run of overseers or churchwardens' accounts makes it impossible to assume that this was the first expenditure of its kind within the parish. Some indication however may be obtained in the second half of the year's accounts, whereby an association in terms connect it with two entries: *Whereof, vs. (five shillings) is payed to the land of olde* and *Item payed to Roger Dale for mach...es of old xviiid(18d).*

Both these entries suggest that the parish were making payments to the elderly, and in the first entry land was involved. Furthermore, *a keeper of the old at Penkhull* could have been paid a wage by the following entry: *Item layd out to the clerke of old, iis 0d (10p).*

It is clear that by 1602, the overseers were observing the law, recommending cash to be *doled out* to the *deserving poor,* besides providing a home for the impotent poor. The phraseology of the 1602 entries are identical to the preamble to the 1531 Act, distinguishing the impotent poor as persons *olde, sick, lame and not able to work for their livying,* a quite noteworthy association of issues which should not be under-estimated. In 1570, pressure was placed upon parishes to establish charitable institutions, so it is possible a poor house could have been established in Penkhull by the middle of the sixteenth century.

From these early records of those supporting the poor through church lunes, the practice of distributing a parish dole to people in real need is obvious as the churchwardens' accounts include grants to those in such need: 1605 *Item Paire of shoes for old Boothes xiv,* 1606. *Item Sherrett for keepinge the boy, viis viiid. (28p).*

In the year 1610, the names of Thomas Lovatt . . . viiis, and Wm Bagnall . . . ixs were listed as debtors for both the current year and the previous year. By 1613, Thomas Broade presented those who did not pay their lunes amounting to £ii ixs xid, and again in 1615 when 'two cytations' were issued against Thomas and William Lovatt for *deteyninge their church lunes.* In the same year, seventeen residents of Penkhull paid £i iv xid against fifteen residents of Shelton, who paid a total of £i ix xid. It became evident the following year that the overseers were taking the debts more seriously, for they employed Mr Taylor to represent the parish against Thomas Malpass's deteyninge his lune.

By 1627, Richard Cartwright was charged eight pence for half a year. In 1620, the amount collected in lunes for half a year amounted to £i 0s xd, whereas by 1626, Nicholas Barratt collected for *"Penkhull £iv is 0d" (£4. 5p).*

A most interesting contribution to the income under the collections of church lunes lists many of the former townships, has recently come to light, hidden for many years at the County Archives under a heading, un-related to its contents. The small book was the working notes of Thomas Fenton, in his capacity as the legal representative for the Manor of Newcastle-under-Lyme. A part of his work includes the collection of the church lunes for the year 1672. From the document it would appear that the list was compiled by John Machin of Botteslow for which he was paid the sum of £1 6s 10d. The list contains the occupants paying church lunes in every district and the amount assessed with totals. Unfortunately it does not list those exempt from the tax on account of poverty, therefore will not allow any assessment of population. Below is the entry for Penkhull.

Roger Machin	5s 4d
Boothes lands	4s 0d
Robert Tittensor's land	4s 0d
Thomas Tittensor's	2s 0d
Thomas Barrett	2s 0d
Bradshawe's land	1s 4d
Randall Woodcocke's land	3s 0d
Mr Baddeley	2s 0d
Thomas Turner	2s 0d
John Bowyer	2s 0d
William Turner	2s 0d
John Hutchin's lands	2s 0d
William Machin	1s 8d
Thomas Tagge	1s 8d
Roger Dale	1s 0d
James Hudson	4d
Thomas Fenton of Boothen	1s 8d
John Ames and Randell Pateson	1s 8d
Thomas Bagnald	1s 0d
Roger Dale	1s 8d
Total (twenty names)	**£ 2 2s 4d**

These figures may be compared with the total revenue collected from other parts of Stoke-on-Trent for which they have been summarised.

Longton	value	£1 1s 0d	entries	9
Great Fenton		£0 17s 4d		4
Little Fenton & Botteslow		£1 0s 10d		8
Bagnald		£1 6s 6d		9
Buckenhall		£2 11s 6d		27
Shelton & Hanley		£2 1s 4d		16
Clayton & Seabridge		£1 17s 6d		10
Total amount collected		**£12 18s 4d**		

If placed into context with other townships, Penkhull is seen as a large wealthy community, with 20 people paying church lunes ranging from 5s 4d to 1s 8d amounting to £2 2s 4d. By this date both coal mining and the pottery industry were expanding. The townships of Hanley and Shelton, in addition to Longton would be experiencing the first signs of industrial growth, bringing with it an influx of workers. The vast majority would live in hovels surrounding their places of work. Others would erect small dwellings on the manorial waste. There would be no sanitation and the communal water supply would be via a well or a stand pipe. These properties because of their low rentable value would pay no church lunes.

The figures provided in the return are therefore an unreliable source of information as the results may be influenced by the number of buildings on the sides of roads and upon the manorial waste as described above. The figures both in money terms as well as entries for districts such as Clayton, Seabridge and Bagnall as rural districts would be reasonably accurate as demand was low. However, those districts of limited urban growth such as Little and Great Fenton, and Penkhull, would probably be to some small degree, not suffer a great deal of immigration. Those districts of Hanley, Shelton and Longton, on the other hand would have a greater number of properties than stated in the return, but the overriding fact would be that they were not taxable and therefore distort the any conclusions.

The annual festival of Church Ales was established as a principal source of funding for the relief of the poor. It was not fundamentally a beer festival, but a place of voluntary work where free ale was provided by the church as an incentive. Ward, 1843 describes the organisation of Church Ales for Stoke parish during the mid sixteenth century. Nicholls, 1929, lists in his analysis of Stoke churchwardens' accounts various entries of expenditure in connection with Church Ales, but no income. This may be due to the fact that income was entered into another account directly to support the poor house in Penkhull. By 1633, Penkhull, Boothen, Clayton and Seabridge, quarters of the ancient parish of Stoke, were grouped together for the purpose of church lune collection, where the following figures represent an increasing demand on resources from 1633 to 1831/32, reflecting the large increase in population caused by the growing labour demands of the pottery industry.

Expenditure for the whole Parish of Stoke-upon-Trent on Poor Relief

The parish expenses for the year ending March 1832, had reached the enormous amount of £19,747; but according to John Ward, during the three following years were reduced to £13,429, which was attributed to improved management. This was far from the truth as the management exploited every opportunity to secure for the Select Vestry and the Governor benefits in kind or otherwise.

The reality lay firmly in the fact, that the new Poor Law Act, called a halt to the vast majority of outdoor relief and the draconian treatment of poor people. So bad were conditions that many paupers would attempt, by any means possible, not to seek parish relief in the workhouse, thus reducing the burden of the poor rate on the parish.

1633	£10 5 2d	1794/5	£ 3523 1 7d	1833/4	£15,859 10 2d
1648	£ 8 13 2d	1800/1	£ 4465 6 0d	1837/8	£ 9,564 15 0d
1666	£37 6 7d	1810/1	£ 7904 18 7d	1840/1	£ 10,716 7 0d
1684	£72 13 0d	1820/1	£10,754 19 9d		
1690	£60 4 11d	1830/1	£18,607 13 7d		
1756	£762 6 1d*	1831/2	£19,747 3 2d		
1775/6	£948 2 4d				

This date represents the first available record available since the industrialisation of the Potteries.

Stoke Parish.

ABSTRACT of the PARISH ACCOUNTS,

FROM THE 21ST. OF MARCH, 1823, TO THE 25TH OF MARCH, 1824,

(FIFTY-TWO WEEKS.)

ROBERT HAMILTON, JOHN KIRKHAM, } **Churchwardens.** | WILLIAM RIDGWAY, GEO. FOX, HERBT. MINTON, JAS. MEAKIN, } **Overseers.**

RECEIPTS.

	£.	s.	d.	£.	s.	d.
Balance in hand				132	2	3½
Arrears of Lady-day, 1822—23, collected				1628	10	1

RATES OF 1823—24.

	£. s. d.			£.	s.	d.	£.	s.	d.
First Rate Amt. 2381 15 6½ Deduct Arrears		369	2 9½	2012	12	9			
Second Rate...... Ditto		501 6		7	7	11			
Third Rate....... 2375 4 3 Ditto		584 15							
Fourth Rate...... 2369 13 11 Ditto		1466 13 9		903	0	2			
9505 7 8		2921 18 2½							
Arrears supposed collectable		2018 17 6½							
Loss by void Property and small Houses, ...	903	0	8						
*Bastardy				507	12	1			
Received from other Parishes				70	4	8			
Received from Pensioners				81	13	9½			
Incidental Receipts				46	17	2			
Paupers' Earnings				170	18	6½			

25TH. MARCH, 1824.

	£.	s.	d.	£.	s.	d.
The Parish has to receive Arrears of Rates as above, supposed	2018	17	6½			
Bastardy supposed collectable	350	0	0			
Amount due from other Parishes	87	7	8			
Stock of Clothing, &c. on hand.....................	2450	5	2½			
	50	16	3½			
	2512	1	6¼			

TO PAY.

	£.	s.	d.	£.	s.	d.
Bills for Debts contracted for the Year ending March 25th, 1824.......................	228	19	9			
Amount due to other Parishes	43	0	4			
Take off Stock of Clothing already paid for.......	272	0	1			
Net Amount included in the Expenditure of 1823 and 1824....................	56	16	3¼			
	215	3	9¼			
Balance due to the Overseers.....................	....	147	3	6¼		
	£.	9368	11	7¼		

* In addition to the above, Debts amounting to £ ...... 4d. have been cancelled by persons being sent to

DISBURSEMENTS—*By Order of the Select Vestry.*

	£.	s.	d.	£.	s.	d.
Paid on Account of Debts contracted in the Years 1820—21, and 1821—22.						
Workhouse Repairs, 5s. 6d.—Provisions for the Workhouse, £3 15s. 4d................ ...	4	0	10			
Miscellaneous for the Workhouse..................	4	2	6			
Wheelbarrows, 6s. 6d.—Constables, £2 4s. 6d...	2	11	0			
Apprentices Fees, £2.—Horse & Coach hire, £5.	7	0	0			
Solicitors, £2 9s. 6d.—N.S. Infirmary £80, (two Subscription.)		9	6			
				100	3	1
Paid on Account of Debts contracted in the Years 1822—23.						
Workhouse Clothing, £25 16s. 10¼d.—Miscellaneous for Workhouse, £19 10 2..........	45	7	0½			
Provisions, £23 2 7½—Stationary and Printing, £25 18 9—Constables, £4 17 6—Coals for the Workhouse, £7 9 5......... ...	61	8	3½			
Coffins, £3 19 7—Repairs of Workhouse £33 12 5	37	12	0			
Solicitors, £125 16 2—N. S. Infirmary, £40....	165	16	2			
Incidents, £5 15—Paid to Poor belonging to other Parishes, £49 1 4—County Asylum, £26 14 4—Insurance £1 15—Surgeons £44	127	5	8			
				437	9	2
Paid to Permanent Poor				2774	18	8
Paid to Poor belonging to other Parishes.......................				93	7	6
* Paid on Bastardy Account				933	12	3
Paid to Incidental Poor				1827	9	0
Clothing to Out-Poor, £19 8 11½—Coffins, £74 15 6....				94	4	5½
Stationary and Printing				95	7	2½
Expences of Removing Paupers, £18 16 7—Suspended Orders £6 12—Provisions for the Poor-house, £436 10 10				461	19	5
Clothing and Bedding for the Poor in the House				297	17	5½
Miscellaneous for the Workhouse				92	9	6½
Coals for the Workhouse, £53 2 9—Assessed Taxes,£3 6 2½				56	8	11½
Repairs and Building at the Workhouse.....................				195	10	6½
Paupers in the Lunatic Asylum, £98 15 2—Parish Surgeons £14 14—County Rates, £1075 15 6½				1189	4	8½
N. S. Infirmary, £40—County Infirmary, £10 10				50	10	0
Assistant Overseer's Salary				396	18	3
Assistant Overseer's Expences attending Justices, £25 0 6—Horse-hire, £25 9 5—Toll-Gates, £1 16				52	5	11
Justices Clerks' Fees, £52 7—Constables' Bills, £76 16 8½				129	3	8½
Incidental Expences, £69 19 2—Postage, £6 1 6				76	0	8
Coals & Candles for Vestry, £3 9 8—Plan for ditto, £10 2 6				13	12	2
				£.	9368	11	5¼

* Of the above amount £220 1s. 10d. has been paid on Account of Children whose Fathers are either dead or left the country.

NET RECEIPTS from the **Rates and** INCIDENTS, with the NET EXPENDITURE of the Parish.

Year.	Amount Rates	Loss by void property and Poor.	Collected.	Incidental Receipts.	Net expenditure of the Parish.
	£.	£. s. d.	£. s. d.	£. s. d.	£. s. d.
1819 and 1820. 5 Rates.	11472 6 2	1716 5 7½ or 343 5 1½ per Rate.	9756 0 7	633 8 6	9799 15 8
1820 and 1821. 5 Rates.	11539 5 5	657 15 6 or 331 11 1 per Rate.	9881 9 11	656 12 7½	10930 8 9¼
1821 and 1822. 5 Rates.	11659 3 0	1457 16 7½ or 291 11 3¼ Per Rate.	10201 6 11	608 11 4½	10289 4 8
1822 and 1823. 3 Rates.	7129 0 11	677 5 6 or 225 15 2 Per Rate.	6451 15 5	992 15 9½	8631 4 2
1823 and 1824. 4 Rates.	Amount of Rates 9505 7 8	Supposed loss as 1822-3 £903 0 8 £225 15 2 per Rate.	Supposed collectable upon the same scale as 1822-3 £8602 7	877 6 3	Net expenditure as near as can be ascertained, *£9046 2 4½

ABSTRACT OF THE PARISH ACCOUNTS,

From the 17th of March, 1832, to the 16th of March, 1833.—(52 Weeks.)

JOHN GOODWIN, High Grove, } CHURCHWARDENS.

TIMOTHY DIMMOCK, Shelton,
JOHN BURTON, Hanley,
THOMAS HUSON, Lane-End,
DANIEL COTTON, Stoke, } OVERSEERS.

RECEIPTS.

	£ s. D.	£ s. D.	£ s. D.
1833. March 16. To Arrears of Rates, 1831—2		3185 6 2½	
Amount actually received of First Rate, 1832—3	3308 3 0		
Ditto ditto Second ditto	3193 5 11½		
Ditto ditto Third ditto	2809 19 4½		
Ditto ditto Fourth ditto	2116 8 1		
Ditto ditto Fifth ditto	1033 1 1		
		12460 17 6	
Total Amount of Rates Collected		15646 2 8½	
Sale of Stones broken by Pauper Labourers not in the Workhouse	16 1 1		
County Voters	53 13 0		
Amount of Money raised by Loan....£1811 0 7½			
Deduct Amount Repaid 1311 0 7½			
	500 0 0		
		569 14 1	
		£16215 16 9½	16215 16 9½
Balance due to the Overseers			18 2 1½
			16233 18 11

STATEMENT OF THE RATES, FOR THE YEAR ENDING, MARCH 16, 1833.

	Total Amount.	COLLECTED.	ARREARS.
To First Rate	3965 10 3½	3308 3 0	657 7 3
Second	3975 12 0	3193 5 11½	782 6 0½
Third	3958 18 5½	2809 19 4½	1148 19 1
Fourth	3966 7 8½	2116 8 1	1849 19 7½
Fifth	3072 10 5½	1033 1 1	2039 9 4½
	£ 19838 18 10½	12460 17 6	7378 1 4½

ARREARS SUPPOSED TO BE COLLECTABLE.

Second Rate	150 0 0	
Third Rate	502 0 0	
Fourth Rate	1165 0 0	
Fifth Rate	2290 0 0	
		4117 0 0
Loss on the Year's Rates (Five) by Void Property and Small Houses Uncollectable	£	3261 1 4½
Loss on the Average of each Rate		652 4 3

19th March, 1833, Examined,

Geo. Lynam,
Auditor.

DISBURSEMENTS.

	£ s. D.	£ s. D.	Debts owing March 16th, 1833. £ s. D.	Actual Cost of the Year. £ s. D.
1832. Mar. 17. By Balance due to the late Overseers		93 1 8½		
1833. Mar. 16. Clothing and Bedding for the Workhouse	161 5 8½		245 16 0	407 1 8½
Provisions for the Workhouse.........090 0 3				
Deduct Earnings of Inmates.........134 11 1				
Marbles made by ditto....24 2 7½				
Less Raw Clay.......... 8 8 11				
15 13 8½				
150 4 9½				
	839 15 5½		508 1 3	1347 16 8½
Clay, &c. for making Marbles			6 0 10½	6 0 10½
Miscellanies for the Workhouse	43 10 8		92 19 9	136 10 5
Bread Baker	35 5 0			35 5 0
Barber	15 1 8			15 1 8
Schoolmaster	28 14 0			28 14 0
Schoolmistress	11 10 0			11 10 0
Building and Repairs	43 3 2		9 13 7½	52 16 9½
Coals and Carriage for the Workhouse and Parish Office	22 3 1		145 4 3½	167 7 4½
Insurance of the Workhouse			1 11 6	1 11 6
Assessed Taxes	5 0 5			5 0 5
Governor's Salary of the Workhouse			60 0 0	60 0 0
		1205 9 2	1069 7 4	2274 16 6
Bastardy Payments.........£947 9 3				
Deduct Amount Received 719 8 11½				
		228 0 3½		228 0 3½
Collector's Salary		53 5 9		53 5 9
Constable's Salary		41 12 0		41 12 0
Weekly Payments to Pensioners.........£1119 9 8				
Deduct Amount Received 1071 14 5½				
		47 15 2½		47 15 2½
Weekly Payments to Poor belonging to other Parishes.........£478 0 0				
Deduct Amount Received 318 12 1				
		159 7 11		159 7 11
Weekly Payments to Incidental Poor		5346 16 11½		5346 16 11½
Weekly Payments to Permanent Poor		2761 1 2		2761 1 2
Surgeons		13 15 0	136 1 6	149 16 6
North Staffordshire Infirmary		4 4 0		4 4 0
County Infirmary		10 10 0		10 10 0
Stafford General Lunatic Asylum		88 19 6		68 19 6
Clothing for the Out Poor		26 4 0	41 1 4½	67 5 4½
County Rates		1142 0 4½	378 18 6½	1520 18 11
Constable's Accounts		29 19 1½	47 19 8	77 18 9½
Justice's Clerks' Fees		65 7 4		65 7 4
Assistant Overseer's Expenses at Justice's Meetings		13 13 10½		13 13 10½
Expenses in proving Settlements		24 17 7		24 17 7
Incidental Payments.........£107 11 6½				
Deduct Amount Received 26 16 1½				
		80 15 5	1 4 3	81 19 8
Removal of Paupers		26 2 3		26 2 3
Coffins and Funeral Fees		199 9 4	15 7 8	214 17 0
Tolls and Postages		15 7 11½		15 7 11½
Wheelbarrows, Planks, Hammers, &c.		12 11 3	24 9 1½	37 0 4½
Apprentices' Fees		6 0 0		6 0 0
Horse Hire		6 3 6	11 16 2½	17 19 8½
Appeals		10 11 3		10 11 3
Printing and Stationery		7 10 6	146 10 6	154 1 0
Ditto, &c. the County and Borough List of Voters, including £30 9s. 4d. the Returning Officer's Account			97 8 7½	97 8 7½
Expenses in keeping the Parish Horse and Ass, Repairs of Carts, &c.		43 1 0	14 6 0	57 7 0
Assistant Overseers' Salaries		351 3 4		351 3 4
Superintendent of Pauper Labourers		[illegible]		419 9 8
Stones to be Broken by the Pauper Labourers			5 2 0	5 2 0
Rent, Furniture, Repairs, and other Necessaries for the Parish Office		62 14 4	8 9 5	71 3 9
Rent of Wharf for the purpose of breaking Stones		10 0 0		10 0 0
Auditor of the Parish Accounts		5 0 0	5 10 0	10 10 0
Stamps for the Contractors and Surveyor of the New Workhouse		18 18 5		18 18 5
Ditto for the Assistant Overseers and Collectors' Appointments		58 7 2		58 7 2
Solicitor		99 3 1	19 10 2	118 13 3
Suspended Orders		2 13 6		2 13 6
Old Debts		1257 6 0		
		14054 11 3	2023 2 4½	14727 5 11
CONTINGENCIES.				
Board of Health, including the Erection of the Cholera Hospital, at Lane-End		1051 14 11	98 14 3	1150 9 2
The Committee (appointed the 23rd February, 1832) for the Erection of a New Workhouse at the Spittles		1127 12 9		1127 12 9
Amount of Disbursements for the Year		£16233 18 11		
Amount of Debts Owing and Contracted within the Year			£2121 16 7½	
Actual Cost for the Year				£17005 7 10

RETROSPECT.

To Easter.	Out Poor. £.	s.	d.	House Poor £.	s.	d.	Paup. Earn. £.	s.	d.	Count. Rates £.	s.	d.
1816 ... 53 Weeks.	5087	5	0	634	7	6	88	6	5	279	7	1
1817 ... 52 Weeks.	6692	14	1½	665	14	9	140	5	10½	428	5	1
1818 ... 52 Weeks.	8849	14	8	1076	8	1½	161	10	10½	1087	10	11
1819 ... 52 Weeks.	5896	6	5½	1155	9	11	116	2	7	1252	10	0
1820 ... 53 Weeks.	6679	7	7	806	1	2	118	12	10½	1406	5	6
1821 ... 52 Weeks.	7581	9	5¼	612	17	2¼	86	9	7	1282	17	3
1822 ... 52 Weeks.	6772	9	3½	651	13	4½	92	12	4½	1265	0	10½
1823* ... 52 Weeks.	5547	7	0	358	16	4	108	9	9	1074	3	10½
1824* ... 52 Weeks.	5629	5	7	520	18	0	170	18	6½	1075	15	6½

To Easter.	Law Expen. £.	s.	d.	Med. Assist. £.	s.	d.	Mil. Ex. £.	s.	d.	Salaries. £.	s.	d.	Poundage. £.	s.	d.	Incidents. £.	s.	d.	Building. £.	s.	d.
1816 ... 53 Weeks.	45	0	2	162	15	0				255	13	0	131	9	5	101	13	5			
1817 ... 52 Weeks.	70	5	1	229	0	0				258	3	3	173	16	6	74	4	11			
1818 ... 52 Weeks.	75	7	7	49	10	6				254	12	0	209	5	1	80	13	4			
1819 ... 52 Weeks.	62	10	8	128	6	0				254	12	0	173	9	1½	74	16	0			
1820 ... 53 Weeks.	59	0	4	42	10	6				254	12	0	175	12	8½	73	19	1½			
1821 ... 52 Weeks.	33	2	4	41	14	6				254	12	0	165	13	9	76	3	8½			
1822 ... 52 Weeks.	113	7	10	270	3	6				265	19	7	188	15	5	84	17	6½	15	7	0
1823* ... 52 Weeks.	125	16	2	170	17	0	4	6	0	461	4	11				48	8	4	46	9	11
1824* ... 52 Weeks.	47	3	4	106	3	0				396	18	3				69	19	2	195	10	6½

** Include Arrears which have been Paid during the last Year.*

AVERAGE OF THE WEEKLY EXPENCES OF THE OUT-POOR AND WORKHOUSE.

	OUT POOR. Cost. £.	s.	d.	WORKHOUSE POOR. Wkly. No.	Food. s.	d.	Clothes. s.	d.	Cost. £.	s.	d.
For 1816 ... 53 Weeks.	98	2	7	65	2	5	1	5	13	13	3¾
1817 ... 52 Weeks.	129	5	6¼	91	2	4½	0	6	15	10	0
1818 ... 52 Weeks.	170	3	8	134	2	4	0	5	15	11	0
1819 ... 52 Weeks.	113	7	1½	115	2	10	0	6	22	4	5
1820 ... 53 Weeks.	126	0	0¼	93	2	4	0	6¼	17	5	0
For 1821 ... 52 Weeks.	146	0	0	84	3	0	1	1	17	8	0
1822 ... 52 Weeks.	130	0	3	86	2	7	1	1½	15	18	11
1823 ... 52 Weeks.	106	13	6	72	1	10	0	7½	11	1	11
1824 ... 52 Weeks.	108	5	1¼	88	2	3¼	1	3½	15	14	10¼

Exclusive of Maintenance of Poor in the Lunatic Asylum.

The above retrospective parish accounts dated from 1816-1824 showing the payments made for paupers in-house and those paid as a 'dole' out poor relief

The reasons for increased numbers claiming parish relief are complex, but the main reason can be identified for the period 1800-1830, a period which, for various reasons, was apparently critical. First, the years up to 1815 were largely years of war against revolutionary and Napoleonic France. As a result conscripted militiamen's families received payments, thereby masking the true depth of poverty before 1815. Other years of war during the mid 1790s and again in the early 1800s, were years of high food prices. For example, the price of wheat rose from around 48 shillings and 58 shillings a quarter to 92 shillings and, as a result, the price of bread rose to previously unknown heights. Wages in both agriculture and local industry, failed to match these rises.

Where poor relief records are complete, a clearer picture can be obtained as to the percentage of expenditure which was associated with food price increases, as opposed to population growth. Kinship aid meant that families frequently provided for relatives to prevent them claiming poor relief.

The post-war depression in the pottery industry, with many large employers becoming bankrupt, brought misery, starvation and poverty to unprecedented levels. Circumstances in which parishes found themselves reflected a two fold increase in outdoor relief between the years 1800 and 1820, with a further eighty percent increase during the next decade.

In 1830, economic distress in the Potteries caused concern. The long-continued inclemency of the winter months had almost stopped what little trade there was. Parish authorities undertook to organise collections and to supply soup and bread. A local mine owner gave in excess of eighty tons of coal to those in need. It was reported that in February 1830 there was more suffering from the effects of cold and actual starvation than in any period since the winter of 1826.

Two years later a national epidemic of cholera took hold within the district, especially among those who had little or no resistance as a result of poverty. Subscription lists were published in the local press of donations received from wealthy business people, and concerts were given to raise funds in the town hall in Stoke. The Board of Health took on special powers: *to whitewash any house in which there exists dangerous impurities, to remove any offal or filth from slaughter houses, to engage medical inspectors to visit all lodging houses for the reception of vagrants, to open sewers, or cover drains, ditches and cesspools, the parish undertaking to defray the expenses. To purchase land for burials as no one dying of cholera will be allowed to be buried in a normal burial ground.*
Further distress in the Potteries followed in 1833 as a result of the first strike called by the newly-formed Pottery Workers' Union. In excess of 20,000 operatives withdrew their labour

though they had no other income. Poverty and starvation were so acute that many families were driven to seek help from the Board of Guardians. Those out of work were required to be at The Spittals workhouse from 8.00am to dusk, men worked in the fields and women at housework while children attended the workhouse school. They received just sufficient to keep them from starvation.

The principal mode of poor relief operating for these years both in Stoke and nationally, was by low wages enhanced by either cash handouts (dole) or by the provision of tokens used in local shops for the purchase of food or clothing. Only a small proportion of the money was used for maintenance of people in the parish poor house at Penkhull. The figures for poor relief do not reflect in reality an accurate picture of the extent of poverty in the area. Many factors relevant are not available for a fair evaluation.

Under the 1662 Settlement Act, as subsequently amended in an Act of 1697, rules were laid down for deciding the question as to which parish a person should qualify for poor relief under the terms of the Act. A settlement could be gained in many ways. The most important are listed:

(a) An individual had settlement in the parish where he or she was born but, while a child, settlement was in his or hers father's place of settlement if this was known. Illegitimate children thus had a settlement only where they were born.
(b) A married woman's settlement was in her husband's place of settlement.
(c) An apprentice acquired settlement in the parish where he was apprenticed.
(d) A worker acquired a settlement after being hired to work in a parish for a year without a break.
(e) If an individual owned or rented a house valued at £10 a year or more, a settlement could be acquired in that parish.

During a lifetime, many people acquired more than one settlement; the one most recently acquired being the one that mattered. The Act of Settlement also allowed a parish to remove anyone who had not obtained settlement there, even if no request for poor relief had been made. A conscientious overseer took care to remove from the parish anyone likely to need relief before a settlement was obtained. The law restricted movement of poorer people and was more difficult to enforce in more populous towns like the Potteries, although some factories were known to deposit bonds with neighbouring parishes against claims for relief.

A parish faced with unemployed workers having the right of settlement could let them go elsewhere with a certificate acknowledging that they had settlement in their former parish, and guaranteeing to relieve them unless they acquired settlement elsewhere. This process protected a worker and his family from being removed from another parish while the worker was able to support them.

In numerous 18th century parishes, as many as a fifth of the population might be termed 'unsettled' and labourers were sometimes hired for a period of less than a year, thus preventing them to qualify for parish relief. The chief effect of the law was two-fold: first to deter migrants coming to a parish, and second to deter those migrants already in residence from claiming poor relief for fear of being sent back to their home parish. As a consequence, the depth of poverty experienced by this section of the community was far more severe than found in native-born residents. The desired effect was achieved, limiting the burden on the finances of the parish.

The Poor House

The lack of early records for the Penkhull poor house is mirrored by discrepancies in parish registers. It appears that no policy existed for the writing up of records. As curates came and went, so the policy of recording the address, district, age or occupation of inmates changed. A number of historians suggest that the district poor house, or the workhouse as it was also referred to, has its origins in 1735, probably based upon the burial record of January 1734/5 of Sarah Law, widow, 'out of workhouse', and followed by Ann Cooper in January 1736. The next burial was not until 1738, which recorded Edward Broad, 'out of poor house'. This seems to confirm its use as a place to support the impotent poor under the 1531 Act.

The borough of Newcastle offered relief in numerous small cottage-type corporation-owned alms houses, until a workhouse was built in 1732. However the poor house at Penkhull would appear to be the earliest in the Potteries, followed by Burslem in the 1780s, Norton in 1798 and Trentham in 1809/10.

The poor house at Penkhull was a large three-storey, 'L-shaped' building of an institutional design with a cemented facade. It was situated at the junction of Trent Valley Road, and Manor Court Street, a location illustrated on T. Hargreaves' map of Penkhull 1832.

From the early churchwardens' accounts for the parish it becomes clear that this was not the first workhouse or poor house in Penkhull. The first court reference which names the workhouse is dated 24th May 1754, whereby *John Terrick the elder on behalf of the trustees for the poor of Stoke-upon-Trent namely John Fenton, Thomas Broad, Jeremiah Smith and John Terrick the younger was admitted to all that cottage or tenement in Penckhull, with the outbuildings, gardens to the same belonging, now used for a workhouse and formerly purchased from the executers of Richard Godwyn deceased.* From earlier

records, it is known that Godwyn died at some time between 1721 and 1728, for in 1728 his widow, Jane, surrendered the property to Samuel Tonnycliffe. The property was then described as a blacksmith's shop in the

Hargreaves map 1832 showing the position of Stoke Poor House

holding of Thomas Burton, and the other rented out to Michael Henney, a wheelwright.

In 1732, Jane remarried to Matthew Tatton and was able to regain the property in July the following year. It is difficult to make definite conclusions on the evidence available, but on the facts provided by the burial registers it could be assumed that the property was used as a workhouse from around this date.

The name of Jeremiah Smith, referred to as one of the trustees in 1754, again appears in a further court minute dated 26th October 1768 which refers to two cottages being converted into a workhouse: *To this court comes Eliza Alsager, Sarah Alsager, Margery Alsager, Judith Alsager and others and surrenders all that copyhold pair of buildings forming two cottages now converted into a workhouse for the use of the parish of Stoke-upon-Trent situated at Penkhull to the use of Jeremiah Smith.*

The early eighteenth-century building at Penkhull replaced an earlier poor house referred to in 1662. The exact form it took is not recorded. The new house was built in keeping with the objectives of the 1722 Workhouse Act, *whereby church wardens and overseers could acquire property and contract out with anyone for the maintenance and setting to work of the poor there.* This was confirmed in 1775/6 when just over one thousand pounds was spent to support eighty inmates in the poor house. This figure remained relatively unchanged for nearly ten years as the average expenditure on poor relief for the years 1783-1785 amounted to £1,235 0 7d. What percentage of the population the figure of 80 inmates represents is unknown.

George Hanny was guardian of the poor house from 1784 to 1806, and responsible for the payment of 3s 1d per half year land tax. By the early 19th century the inmates were being employed in the potworks of the area under the supervision of Christopher Preston, guardian of the poor. In 1802/3 government returns list 195 persons as having received workhouse relief, with more than 300 receiving only occasional relief. The total expenditure on poor relief amounted to £5,116 5s 4d, the largest recorded in the Pirehill North Hundred followed by Burslem at £2,141 2 7d.

The next mention of the workhouse, was in March 1814, when Josiah Spode sold a piece of land to the *Visitors and Guardians of the Poor* adjacent to the poor house to the value of £65 12s 6d where once stood a large property which went under the name Turner's, otherwise Ingram's.

At a further court held on October 1827, reference is made to a further plot of land being added to that of Penkhull workhouse. This was part of the land which was associated previously with the large house which stood on the site of the present Jeremy Close which had been purchased by Josiah Spode.

A set of accounts for the poor house reflect the costs to the parish. These are listed below indicating the average weekly expenditure for the parish and the difference between out poor relief and that of the workhouse poor.

Out Relief:
>   1816 £ 98 2s 7d,
>   1817 £129 5s 6d
>   1820 £126 0s 0d
>   1822 £146 0s 0d
>   1824 £108 5s 1d

Workhouse:

Year	No. Inmates	Cost inc. clothes Average Weekly
1816	65	£13 13 3d
1817	91	£15 10 0d
1820	126	£17 5 0d
1822	84	£15 18 11d
1824	88	£15 14 10d

In 1825 other expenditure included: Bedding £161 5s 8d, cost of clay for the manufacture of marbles £6 0s 10d; baker of bread £35 5s 0d; barber £15 1s 8d.

A general vestry meeting of the inhabitants of the parish held on the 26th March 1824, and for which the minutes have survived, covered the re-election of the overseers of the poor and the twenty *substantial householders* of the parish to the position of board members. The position of assistant overseer of the poor and superintendent of the poor house was offered to William Joynson at a yearly salary of £50.

Poor Relief in the Parish of Stoke

Year and amount spent on Penkhull Workhouse poor relief: Annual Average: 1776: £1,006; 1783/5: £1,235; 1803: £1,116; 1814: £98 6,841; 1825: £11,559; 1826: £7,005; 1827: £10,985; 1828: £12,669; 1829: £11,547.

From these figures it would appear that the number of inmates in Penkhull nearly doubled in three years, reflecting the deteriorating local conditions and increasing numbers of the poor in the Potteries. The parish of Stoke did not adopt Gilbert's 1782 Act until 1816, conducting its business by Select Vestry with the authority to appoint paid overseers who would devote their whole time to the collection and doleing out of poor relief. Gilbert's Act enabled parishes to unite for the maintenance of a central poor house, given with the consent of two-thirds of the rate-payers. As Gilbert argued, a union of parishes would facilitate the construction of efficient institutions and the appointment of a higher class of paid and permanent staff.

As the parish of Stoke was large enough to maintain the workhouse at Penkhull, no amalgamation with a neighbouring parish was necessary. The overseer of the poor received only a minimum wage. In 1824/5 the total amounted to £179.18. 9d p.a. which included sums paid to staff for the collection of poor rates. Two years later, with the appointment of the new overseer, Mr George Thomas Taylor, the amount increased to £269 13 3d, followed by a further significant increase in 1827/8 to £451 3 0d. It continued to increase in 1831/2 to £568 15 1d. In 1833, the figure paid was described as 'very great'. After considerable criticism in the local press, Mr Taylor reduced the collectors' wages, saving the parish upwards of £100 during the year 1833/4.

It was the practice of the parish to charge the father where possible for the maintenance of his illegitimate children. Two documents have survived, providing an insight into these activities. Both relate to the same account, whereby George Lynam is charged the sum of 2s 0d per week for maintenance of his illegitimate child, Ann Bradbury.

VESTRY ROOM, STOKE-UPON-TRENT.

Mr. G. Lynam   March 3. 1827

Dᴿ. TO THE CHURCHWARDENS ᴀɴᴅ OVERSEERS
OF THE
Parish of Stoke-upon-Trent.

For support of your Bastard by	from	to	No. of weeks.	per week.	£.	s.	d.
Ann Bradbury		March 22			6	3	—
					6	7	6
Cash	11. 7 6						
	5. 0–0			£			
	16 · 7 · 6						

Sir,

By Order of the Churchwardens and Overseers, I transmit the above statement of your account, which they wish to be fully paid on or before the 25th day of March 1827 else for the recovery thereof, you will be proceeded against, in the manner the Law directs, without further notice or indulgence.

For the Officers,

Sir, I am your obedient Servant,

Invoice to Mr. George Lynam charges for the keep of Ann Bradbury in the Parish Poor House at Penkhull

252

The Select Vestry

Although the day-to-day business of poor relief was undertaken by the Select Vestry, the officials did not have the powers to make important decisions without a general meeting of parishioners. To qualify as a voter, property to the value of £10 per annum or more was necessary. Shortly after 1819, Sturgess Bourne's Act was adopted, whereby the parish could elect a Select Vestry to manage its affairs, but under this Act the wealthier residents of the parish had more votes. The voting system was scaled from six votes for property over the value of £150 to one vote for property under £50.

In 1832, Josiah Wedgwood II, spoke out against the system *whereby a parish the size of Stoke could hold a General Vestry Meeting with so great a number of persons attending who are not rate payers and therefore were not entitled or fit to exercise any influence in the concern of the parish, but who may overpower the actual rate payers by their numbers.*

Under the provision of The Reform Bill of 1832, eleven townships, vills and hamlets were united to form the Borough of Stoke-upon-Trent. The number of qualifying electors paying a minimum annual rent of £10 amounted to between fourteen and fifteen hundred, small compared with the fifty-three thousand head of population of the new borough and thereby reflecting the extent of poverty in the

Stoke first 'Poor House' in Penkhull later known as Victoria Buildings

district. As the towns within the Borough of Stoke grew, so did the provision for paupers became of wider concern to the Select Vestry. Accommodation in the Penkhull poor house proved inadequate to meet the demands of the day.

In 1828, Simeon Shaw wrote of the Penkhull workhouse: *The parish workhouse is on an elevated spot, and will be inspected with pleasure by the philanthropist for the cleanliness and comfort here afforded, to the aged and the infirm, the week minded and the destitute. In fact all the attentions of humanity are supplied to them.* This idyllic summary of the workhouse conflicts wildly with the report of the assistant overseer in 1833, when he refers to the old workhouse in Penkhull: . . . *full of idle and insolent paupers, without the least desire to quit their abode or to amend their condition and there found numerous children running up the same way.*

This local report of 1833 is comparable with the Poor Law Commissions report issued the following year in their general assessment of a parish poorhouse: *A large almshouse, in which the young are trained in idleness, ignorance and vice, the able-bodied maintained in sluggish sensual indolence and the aged and more respectable exposed to all the misery that is incident to dwelling in such a society without government or classification.*

It should be remembered that writers such as Shaw and Ward depicted the treatment of the poor by local manufacturers and Board of Guardians in a far more generous light probably because the sponsors and readers of their work were the very same people.

In November, 1830, Mr G. T. Taylor published a twelve page letter to the rate-payers of the parish entitled 'Causes of the Increase of Pauperism in the parish of Stoke' with remedies for their alleviation, or total prevention. The letter, in itself, is an enormous contribution to the social history of the period. Only parts of this comprehensive insight into the time are reproduced here: *The alarming increase in the expenses and disbursements of this parish induce me to inform you of the principal cause.* Taylor then lists the total disbursements which showed an almost 100% increase from 1825 of £8,981 to 1830 when the amount nearly doubled at £16,537. He then continues to explain the economic situation with regard to employment in the mines and pottery manufacturers: *Numbers of strangers are attracted hither, by the possibility of higher wages for themselves by employment in the manufactories. Although in these works where there are kept regular books for hiring, Sundays and holidays excepted, to prevent strangers gaining settlements.* (Taylor uses the item 'strangers' to refer to those who do not have settlement to live within a parish as stipulated under the Poor Law Act.) *As a result many employers use this cheap labour and* tradesmen and gentlemen employ domestic servants with total disregard to the rights of settlement and as a consequence many are thrown onto the parish for support it cannot afford.

Mr Taylor then continues to explain the current demands upon the parish: *No longer is parochial relief asked, it is demanded, as the person's indisputable freehold right, which, whenever peculiar circumstances induce the overseers to refuse or withhold, causes application to be made immediately, and too often successfully, to some magistrate, whose humanity predominates over his judgement, and whose decision, "that the poor can not starve, and the overseers must find then either work or money", give the pauper the impression that he has gained his point, which is quickly communicated to all his acquaintances, and excites others to pursue the same line of conduct.*

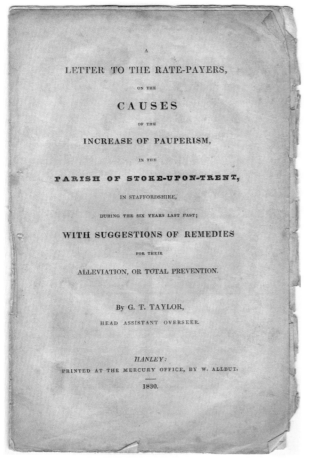

A

LETTER TO THE RATE-PAYERS,

ON THE

CAUSES

OF THE

INCREASE OF PAUPERISM,

IN THE

PARISH OF STOKE-UPON-TRENT,

IN STAFFORDSHIRE,

DURING THE SIX YEARS LAST PAST;

WITH SUGGESTIONS OF REMEDIES

FOR THEIR

ALLEVIATION, OR TOTAL PREVENTION.

By G. T. TAYLOR,

HEAD ASSISTANT OVERSEER.

HANLEY:
PRINTED AT THE MERCURY OFFICE, BY W. ALLBUT.

1830.

Front cover of the report by Mr. G.T. Taylor dated 1830

Bold statements with which many today would concur! Taylor then gives a unique insight into the Penkhull workhouse. However bad the conditions were inside, the reality was that many inmates, once finding employment outside, wanted to return to the better living conditions of the workhouse where they could continue in idleness. The following quotation is a valuable contribution to the social and economic issues of the time.

The smallness of our workhouse, and the difficulty of providing labour, leave numbers of paupers altogether in idleness, who continue so year after year, without evincing the least desire to obtain employment either at home or in other places. Those who have been admitted into the workhouse have, from the small size of the house, so little labour, (for the domestic business is scarcely sufficient exercise to preserve health), that no inclination is manifested to quit its accommodations.

After being there for a while, both boys and girls have such an attachment to it, that though they had been placed apprentice, they seek to return to it; and the utmost caution has been successful in preventing them from communicating to each other schemes how this can be most effectively accomplished. Indeed, such is the wish manifested by the paupers to remain in the workhouse, that two girls, during the last six months, were committed to prison for this offence, and, on being released, have declared that they will rather return to prison, than to their place of servitude.

Taylor continues to state the case against the payment to those who do not qualify for poor relief on the grounds of non-settlement as a serious cause for concern: *The total average amount, exclusive of the expenses of the workhouse, paid to the poor in money, is about £200 weekly or £10,000 yearly; of which, as near as can be ascertained, £100 is paid to paupers not natives of this parish, but settled here in consequence of gaining settlement. The fact remains half of the levies collected are paid to persons really belonging to other parishes.*

Taylor later in the document makes three main recommendations:
Firstly, that the parish is divided into three distinct poor law districts.
Secondly, landlords who prefer to let property to paupers in the knowledge that they will obtain the security of payment from the parish and pay little or no poor rates should be forced to pay the rate.
Thirdly, and this is the most striking of all, although I calculate on great advantage resulting from the proposed division of the parish for the collection of poor rates, I still think that by only a complete reformation of the principle, can there be effected any considerable reduction in the parochial assessments.

Future Proposals

From one to four hundred acres of land, on Wetley Moor, may be purchased for about £10 per acre. Now were a workhouse erected there, sufficiently capacious to accommodate all persons belonging to this parish who receive or require relief, they might be supported by the governor, at a stipulated sum per head according to the respective ages. The non-payment of rates by these persons would be prevented in reference to the houses now occupied by them, and therefore no relief being paid in money.

This arrangement could save the parish at least £3,000 yearly and a sum sufficient to purchase from one or two hundred acres of land, and to erect a commodious workhouse, might be borrowed on security of the poor rates. The governor's interest would be to render the labour of the inmates as productive as possible. For men he provides spade labour, and Wetley Moor would supply sufficient of this for centuries, in fact for ever; like a garden it might be dug over each year. To each of the women is weighed at stated times, a certain number of ounces of worsted for knitting into stockings, bed-rugs, and horse-cloths for sale and the children weave, or make straw hats. They will also have a mill by which their own corn is ground by hand labour, and the whole establishment will form a complete house of industry.

The committee have been informed that provisions may be purchased to most advantage in large quantities, and inclusive of all ages. The expense of maintenance is under two shillings weekly for each person, and it understood that every able person must work before he will be permitted to eat, very seldom indeed does any person go into the workhouse who can by any possible means support himself out of it, or manage to keep away.

An establishment of this kind on Wetley Moor, or on any more approved situation, would resemble a large well-cultivated farm, consuming its own produce. The children as they came of age might be bound out apprentices, and taught habits of industry, instead of being brought up in idleness as on the present plan.

This report has not been previously published. It is indeed explosive material viewed in the light of today. The value of this document to the student of social history is immensurable as well as daunting, and brings sadness to many whose past loved ones experienced such treatment.

The Poor Law Amendment Act 1834

From Tudor times, the categories of impotent poor, the aged, the sick and lame were all accepted as in need of care and assistance. The worsening social conditions of the 1790s, however bought another group into the public eye, namely those in work but unable to earn enough to survive. The problem was first confronted by the magistrates at Speenhamland in Berkshire in 1795, who decided to 'top up' local wages by a supplement, regulated according to the price of bread.

The answer found in Speenhamland to the problem of poverty amongst the working classes was copied in many other places. Many farmers consequently reduced their agricultural labourers' wages to a minimum, thereby pauperising the farm workers. Unrest followed in many rural areas as a direct result of the Speenhamland policy, which brought many families to the poverty level needed for parish relief. If the system had not been implemented, however, poverty would have been more serious, with consequential civil unrest. In 1832 a commission was appointed to investigate the situation and their subsequent report became the basis of the 1834 Poor Law Amendment Act.

Two principles adopted in this Act were the *workhouse test* and *less eligibility*. By the first, all out-relief to able-bodied persons and their families was to be abolished. By the

second, conditions for the inmates were to be more miserable than those of the lowest paid labourer. In the words of the report, *by the workhouse system, is meant having all relief through the workhouse, making this workhouse an uninviting place of wholesome restraint, preventing any of its inmates from going out or receiving visitors, disallowing beer and tobacco and finding them work according to their ability; thus making the parish fund the last resource of a pauper, and rendering the person who administers the relief the hardest taskmaster and the worst paymaster that the idle and dissolute can apply to.*

The commission also concluded that paupers were often responsible for the position in which they found themselves: *one of the most encouraging of the results of our enquiry is the degree to which the existing pauperism arises from fraud, indolence or improvidence.*

The Poor Law Amendment Act and the Poor Law Commissioners went beyond their published ideas. The relief of the able-bodied poor was to be restricted to relief in the workhouse. The Poor Law Commission emphasised the point of absolute destitution as the only grounds for relief in its correspondence with the Board of Guardians at Stoke. It was intended to make relief of the able-bodied poor so undesirable that only those whose need was desperate would take advantage of it.

The logic displayed in the 'workhouse test' cannot be denied. The objective was to deter those with the potential to work. The principal problem was that the Act only specified the less eligible of the able-bodied, but in the event it applied to all. In future, the relief of the able-bodied would not interfere with the labour market, since the workhouse effectively took them out of society altogether. Workhouses were established where the quality of life would be so low that only the genuinely destitute would allow themselves to become a burden on the parish rate.

The Act also simplified the Law of Settlement, but the principle of a settlement was not abolished. All were to have settlement from where they were born, except wives and children under sixteen years who had the same settlement as the husband or father.

The new Act saw the parish system of poor relief with its overseer and select vestry changed to an elected Board of Guardians. One of its objects was to reduce the abuses of local and individual interests. The old system had become inadequate and inefficient, and with national expenditure in 1832 amounting to nearly £7 million, demands for change had to be met.

The Spittals Workhouse

Although the Poor Law Commission initially seems to have favoured the continued use of a number of existing workhouses in each union, they were soon convinced that in most cases the construction of a large new workhouse was essential to the success of the reform. Not only would this be more efficient, argued the commissioners; it would also be a powerful symbol of an entirely new approach to relief provision. According to an assistant commissioner, the forbidding architecture of a new workhouse was intended as a *terror to the able-bodied population* and another remarked that *their prison-like appearance inspires a salutary dread of them.*

The pressing needs of the poor, coupled with the growing importance of the district, led to the Select Vestry's decision to erect a new parish workhouse at what was known as The Spittals, in the north-west extremes of the district of Stoke-upon-Trent on the boundary with Newcastle-under-Lyme, but remaining within Stoke parish. The new workhouse was to be built on the site of Spittals Farm owned by Mr Josiah Wedgwood II and Mr Smith, a site that bordered the town of Newcastle, but within what was later to become the parochial district of Penkhull. Mr Wedgwood had purchased the copyhold estate in 1801 from Messrs Walker and Co. who had converted farm buildings to a manufactory for white lead used for the manufacture of glaze in the pottery industry.

The plan of The Spittals was based upon the design of Thurgarston workhouse, built in 1830, at Southwell, Nottinghamshire. This was a model for the new concept in workhouse design. The general principle behind this design was that not of *keeping the poor in the house, but from keeping them out of it; by constraining the inferior classes to know and feel how demoralising and degrading is the compulsory relief drawn for the parish, to silence the clamour, and to satisfy the cravings of wilful and woeful indigence; but how honourable is that independence, which is earned by preserving and honest industry.*

It was hoped that the plan *would prove beneficial to the industrious poor, operate as a check to those who only used relief because they were too idle to work, and at the same time be the means of greatly reducing the rates.* One commenter of the time placed the establishment of the Union Workhouse into the context of a revolution in moral arithmetic. *The Union Workhouse of the late 1830s was designed to accomplish nothing less than a revolution in the moral arithmetic of pauperism. Through its forbidding appearance and its disciplinary regime, the new institution is intended to impress on the poor the virtues of independent labour.* It has been suggested that the strategy of 1834 was merely one of blind repression, in contrast to the more complex mixture of negative deterrence and positive treatment which characterised policy after 1840.

The overseer of the poor for Stoke, Mr George T. Taylor, visited Southwell in August 1832 with others to view the new design and to ascertain the benefits of the new workhouse. Following the visit, Taylor wrote to the Rev'd J. T. Becher thanking him for his hospitality. He further stated: *our proposed workhouse is isolated from the bulk of the population and capable of containing 500 to 700 inmates. Our Select Vestry for the present year found 1,100 cases or families receiving parish relief in money weekly, many having been permanent for years. The Vestry are resolved to send half of that number to the new establishment but out of the 550 who received Orders of Admission, 50 refused; consequently making a saving of £70 per week.*

The site was advertised for sale by auction in the Staffordshire Mercury. It was described: *A desirable freehold, situated on the road from Trentham, only half a mile from Newcastle, consisting of six to seven acres of land, dwelling house, cottages, stable and garden; together with the buildings, steam engine, machinery lately used as a manufactory of white lead. There are two reservoirs of water. The premises may readily be converted into a flint mill. The timber and gardens having been planted some years ago, and the situation commanding a beautiful view of Trentham wood and the country around render the property worthy of attention as building land.* The auction was to be held at the Roebuck Inn, Newcastle at five o'clock on Monday May 31st.

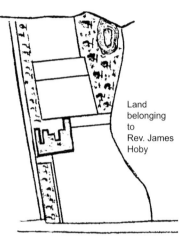

Land belonging to Rev. James Hoby

To Newcastle ——————— To Stone

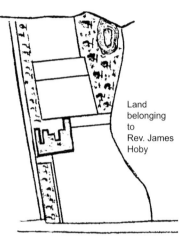

WHITE LEAD WORKS.

TO BE SOLD BY AUCTION,

At the Roe Buck Inn, in Newcastle-under-Lyme, on Monday, May 31, 1830, at Five o'Clock In the Evening ;

A DESIRABLE FREEHOLD, situated on the road to Trentham, only half a mile from Newcastle under Lyme, consisting of Six to Seven Statute Acres of Land, Dwelling House, Cottages, Stable, and Gardens; together with the Buildings Steam Engine, Machinery and Utensils, lately held an a Manufactory of White Lead; There are two Reservoirs of Water.

The Premises may readily be converted into a Flint Mill, on appropriated to other Manufacturing Purposes where Machinery is required.

The Timber and Gardens having been planted some years, and the situation commanding a beautiful view of Trentham Wood and the Country around, render the Property worthy of attention as Building Land.

Different Utensils, of which a List is left on the Premises, may be taken at a Valuation, or permission reserved to remove them.—A person residing will shew the Premises.

In February 1832, a notice for a General Vestry Meeting appeared for the purpose of discussing on the 23rd of that month the outright purchase of the site at The Spittals from Mr Wedgwood. It was pointed out that the costs would be high. Interest was then shown by the parish to lease the site and a four-year period was agreed upon, with the provision to purchase at any time during this period for the sum of £1,350. The Select Vestry decided to buy the estate fourteen months after entering the agreement with Wedgwood. It became obvious that the initial plan of Taylor to build a new workhouse at Wetley Rocks had not received sufficient support probably on the grounds of distance from the parish, and it became the desire of electors to erect one with similar ideals on a site more appropriate.

By April 1832, the plans for the new workhouse were complete and available for tendering, on the condition that the existing buildings at The Spittals would be taken down and where possible, their materials incorporated in the new structure. An advertisement was placed in the N.S. Mercury on the 28th of that month offering to tender the work which would consist of a house, capable of accommodating five hundred inmates. Tenders were to be returned to Mr George Thomas Taylor at the parish office by the 15th May.

The *North Staffs Mercury* presented in its reports an acceptable face of the workhouse system which was far from reality: *The new workhouse was to be an asylum to the infirm poor who are unable to work, to the orphans who have no protection, to the destitute who have no refuge and to the aged who are friendless. . . . the management to be instruction, and the formation of industrious habits for the young, and quiet for those who are past labour, suitable domestic employment for those who are capable of doing indoor work, spade or similar for those who are able to perform out door work and increased comfort for all.* The building contract was awarded to Messrs Ferneyhough and Bramwell for the sum of £2,898 12 0d, which included upwards of £800 for the use of the materials on site. The thought of placing these costs directly on to the rate-payers of the borough concerned the Select Vestry, who believed it would *be unwelcome, unjust and oppressive.* Therefore, a loan

for £2,000 was taken out over three years, the balance being found from Select Vestry funds. The building was completed by the end of March 1833, *with the exception of the garden and roadways.* The committee reported: *they had satisfaction that a plain and substantial and commodious workhouse had been erected, capable of containing four to five hundred inmates and that it will do credit to the parish.*

The following report in the *North Staffs Mercury*, bought discomfort for some parishioners on the subject of the segregation of the sexes and any credit to the parish appears to have fallen by the way-side: *In pursuance of one part of the plan on which the workhouse was constructed viz. the separation of the sexes, the Select Vestry had been obliged to part man and wife, as the workhouse was not intended to be a breeding house. In adopting these and other arrangements, they had drawn down the severe animadversion of some well-intentioned persons, who thought the measure too strict, and also of any anonymous writer in the newspapers; but notwithstanding they had been held up to scorn on account of these arrangement, they had persevered in the plan, from the conviction that the old system of almost promiscuous intercourse had a direct tendency to demoralise the paupers.*

The following letter referred shows that the doctrine of the New Poor Law was not unanimously approved by the public: Sir, *May I, through the medium of your valuable journal, be permitted to inquire from the constituted authorities of the parish of Stoke-upon-Trent whether there is any truth in the widely circulated rumours, that are productive of such prejudice and of such an unwillingness in the minds of the poor to enter into what is called 'The 'Spittals', i.e. the new Poorhouse. I allude to this reported separation of the dearest connections in life, dividing parents from children, and husbands from wives. The propriety of such an injury I think is unquestionable, since the Parish has a right to know, or any lay payer to inquire, into the manner in which the government of the parish is conducted, and a negative answer to the inquiry will remove a great deal of unpleasant feeling that appears to exist. If, however, such is the act, and an affirmative answer is given, it then remains with the voice of the lay payers to decide on the propriety or impropriety of the arrangements. I am etc, A Lay Payer.*

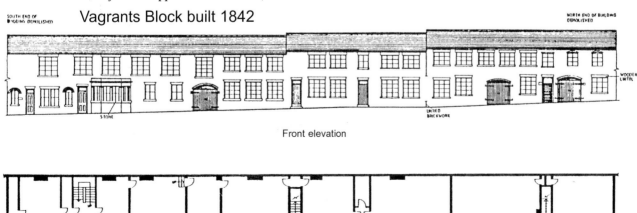

Vagrants Block built 1842

Front elevation

Ground Floor Plan

Segregation not only continued, but was to become an ever-growing obsession. With the completion of the new workhouse, the figure expected from the sale of the Penkhull poor house was in the region of £740. *The committee recommended that the old house be continued for another year and with it the present governor. The youngsters would pay their way and the old ones may be drafted down by degrees to the new premises, so as to fall in better with the system there to be adopted.* In March 1834, the Select Vestry sanctioned the sale of the old Poor House in Penkhull by auction, the proceeds of which were to be used to reduce the debt at the District Bank. The decision prompted an advert in the *North Staffs Mercury.*

Front view of the Vagrants Block built 1842

PENKHULL OLD POOR HOUSE
To be sold by Public Auction at the Wheatsheaf Inn, Stoke on Thursday 1ˢᵗ May 1834

The Poor House at Penkhull with land there belonging containing 2,124 square yards. The premises are situated in the pleasant and healthy village of Penkhull, and may at a moderate cost be converted into dwelling houses for which there is a great demand in the neighbourhood.

The absence of the term 'copyhold' implies that at a previous unknown date, the land was probably granted by the Duchy of Lancaster to the parish for use as a poor house. During the final year of its use as a poor house, marbles are recorded as being manufactured on the premises providing an income of £2 5s 9d. In the same year the total expenditure for the upkeep of the poor house amounted to £1,364 2s 10d.

From press reports of the day, after all the inmates had been transferred to The Spittals the old workhouse in Penkhull was still used as a marble factory. The overseer of the poor, Mr George T. Taylor reported to a meeting held on the 22ⁿᵈ March 1834 that even though a large number of marbles had been made during that year when earnings were high many remained unsold. He noted that many paupers were now working on building roads locally which yielded no profit.

Balancing the Budget

With improved management during the three following years, the figure for maintaining the poor of the parish was gradually reduced. In 1833/34 a total of four parish rates were collected amounting to £14,198 11s. From this sum £6,632 8 2d was paid in out relief showing a reduction of £1,475 over the previous year. Improvement was also being made on the bastardy account, which annually lost on average £500. In 1832/33, the loss was reduced to £221, while in 1833/34 it fell further to £100.

Serious debts had been incurred by the Select Vestry by October 1834. Many tradesmen's bills remained unpaid. A desire to present the parish in the best possible situation concerning the implementation of the new Poor Law Amendment Act prompted the question *how it might be expedient to farm the poor at a certain sum per head.* Poor Law Commission approval was forthwith obtained for the scheme. It would appear this resolution was to rectify an already-established practice as the *North Staffs Mercury* in March of the same year reported that the question was asked at the Annual General Meeting of the Select Vestry, *Why were paupers' earnings so low?* The system of farming was subject to abuse, even by Mr Bagnall, the governor of the old poor house in Penkhull. A case was reported whereby Mr Bagnall had employed up to six inmates on his land, none of whom had been paid. Mr Bagnall replied that *the work done was to no value.* On a further occasion Mr Bagnall paid paupers one shilling a day for their labour, but allowed them to keep a part of this sum and return only six pence to the workhouse.

Due to economic difficulties in 1834, the Select Vestry reduced out relief, which in turn had a beneficial effect on the parish. The report continued: . . . *the idle and able-bodied poor were partially driven back on their own resources and soon found employment, which they had hitherto been so reluctant to seek after.*

By March 1835 the Select Vestry, with careful economy on the cost of food, arrived at a figure for inmates' upkeep of two shillings and ten pence per week. Mr Bagnall offered to farm out paupers at two shillings and five pence per week and to resign his position of governor and with it his salary of £60 per annum. The Select Vestry agreed to the terms, but did not let the matter rest there. At some time after the agreement, ten paupers who worked for Mr Bagnall were examined by the Select Vestry to ascertain any grounds of complaint. The reply was that food was *good in quantity and quality,* and their general treatment *kind, as it was in the workhouse.*

Farming out became the acceptable means whereby additional income reduced the poor rate on the parish, so much so that the *North Staffs Mercury* carried advertisements on behalf of the Select Vestry as to the availability of able bodied paupers and the trades they offered. It became a regular feature by 1837, whereby any local manufacturer or tradesperson who might be in want of hands from the list available should apply to The Spittals workhouse.

The half yearly report and accounts from March to September 1835 were presented to a vestry meeting held on Thursday 29th October. The chief bailiff, Mr John Askey, who was in the chair, gave the report which contained some alarming comments for the inhabitants of the parish: *Although the Select Vestry, in discharge of their public duty, will have to advert in their report for the past half year to circumstances of a painful nature.* After the preamble about how efficient the Board had been in the administration and that they had paid off the debt from the previous year, Mr Askey continued: *the Select Vestry have discovered that Mr Polgrean, the cashier omitted in the statements to give credit for several sums of money he had received and they felt themselves bound to discharge him instantly. It also appears that Mr Splatt, one of the Churchwardens, has received several sums of money from rate-payers amounting to the sum of £35 0s 6d which have not been brought into the accounts and he is now a bankrupt.*

At no time in the report was the name of Mr George Thomas Taylor mentioned. It is, therefore. all the more surprising that a notice appeared in the *North Staffs. Mercury* on the 7th November 1835 from the parish office, signed by its chairman, Mr Thomas Fenton, *that Mr Taylor be discharged from the Office of Head Assistant Overseer for neglect of duty; for carrying on measures in secret to frustrate the designs of the Select Vestry; and for acting, from time to time, in total defiance of the repeated orders and resolutions of this board.* In the following week's edition, Mr Taylor responded: *Sir, The Resolution of the Select Vestry of the Parish of Stoke, which you have published, is too remarkable to escape my attention or the attention of the public, and, least of all, the attention of the Inhabitants of that populous parish. I will lose no time in affording the authors of it a public opportunity to justify their conduct, or, if that cannot be done, to atone for it in a manner becoming to themselves, and satisfactory to.*
Your faithful servant, George Thomas Taylor.

As a response to this request from Mr Taylor, a public meeting was called and held on Thursday 3rd December 1835.

The North Staffs. Mercury reported almost word for word the business of the meeting, commenting in its first paragraph on the scene laid before all to see: *We hoped that the scene of clamour and confusion, which have conferred such unenviable celebrity on Stoke parish meetings, were gone by, and that henceforward the proceedings would be conducted with the calmness, order, and decency, which ought to mark the public affairs of an intelligent people. Such were our hopes, but the reality, as presented can be paralleled only by some of the worst previous meetings in the same place.* The introduction continued in exactly the same mode commenting that it lasted for several hours and were so unpleasant a character, involving so many accusations and recriminations, that we had great distaste for noticing them at more length than is absolutely necessary.

The meeting commenced at the parish office but because of the large number attending moved to the town hall in Hill Street. *First agreed was the desire of the Select Vestry to take legal measures against William Polgrean for the recovery of money due to the parish.*

Mr Green, on behalf of the Select Vestry continued to make out the case against Mr Taylor: *When the Select Vestry entered upon their duties, they found the parish office all in confusion, there being not one person in it who discharged this duty, according to their confession, and no remonstrance, or entreaties, or threats, could induce them to apply to business. It was evident that the affairs would not be attended to, for the precedence was given to breakfasts, differs, and suppers. It was resolved to move the office from Stoke to 'The Spittals', but the paid officers set themselves up to oppose this.*

At the workhouse, affairs were little better; if there was no tavern there, the officers got drunk from those at a distance and actually took paupers from the workhouse to drink with them in the fields.

As a result of this and similar charges, three of the clerks and Polgrean were discharged. Mr Green continued to inform the meeting as a result of such behaviour, much of the poor rate had not been collected. Mr Green had by all accounts previously drawn the attention of this to Mr Taylor some months previously and a request for a report to be made weekly. This weekly report however continued only for only two weeks. Mr Green claimed that if Mr Taylor had carried out his duties correctly, deficiencies in collections, or the wrongs by Polgrean would not have occurred.

Further claims against Mr Taylor continued, including those that he had overpaid himself for the previous two years money which he had refunded, and that he was aware of the activities of Polgrean and Splatt but did not report it to the Select Vestry promptly.

Mr Taylor in his reply stated that *he attributed all the unpleasantness that had arisen between himself and the Select Vestry, to his refusal to concur in plans which he knew was to be illegal, and in the cruel treatment of the poor.* He continued to state that much has been said of the sins of paid officers, but then decided to expose misdeeds of the unpaid officers. *My refusal to sanction the disposal by the Select Vestry of the provisions at the workhouse to the farmer of the poor for £165, when he believed them to be worth £210.* He charges the workhouse Governor as being allowed to benefit from paupers' earnings, while those paupers and their families were chargeable to the parish and that there was more corruption going on between the Select Vestry and the Governor.

A care of a workhouse boy was referred to by Mr Taylor who, was employed by Copeland and Garratt. *He was fed on stinking bacon, and was so severely flogged because he complained to his employer, that Mr Copeland thought it his duty to cause a magisterial investigation, and the case was compromised with costs. Nothing would be said of the Contractor and the Governor, nor would they be complained of while the Select Vestry were fed and feasted at the workhouse.* To which those assembled shouted *(Here Here!).* But Mr Taylor had not finished. The Select Vestry boasted of their eye to business; *a good dinner was sure to procure a good attendance.* (Uproar) *as long as Vestry men were fed on jugged hare at Stoke, and hashed venison at Hanley.*

Further accusations were then placed before Mr Taylor about poor book-keeping in particular regarding the sum of £125, which Mr Taylor had paid to himself on account of some old law proceedings and the interest on the money. Mr Taylor stated that this was in the execution of his duties in 1828 under the Old Poor Law. It was now 1835 when Mr Taylor set aside this amount for himself. The final accusation against Mr Taylor was that of general neglect of his duties, and with endeavouring to make those who looked after the parish affairs appear in an obnoxious light.

In his summary of the proceedings Mr John Boyle, in a dispassionate address listed the charges against Mr Taylor. The excuses by Mr Taylor were not acceptable as he had not maintained a vigilant observation of those underneath him. Mr Boyle continued to press for the resolution of dismissal against Mr Taylor which was upheld.

Looking upon this case in all its ramifications and taking account of familiar cases over the years, especially in the world of high finance and even in the Houses of Lords and Commons at the time of writing, the accusations made by Mr Taylor concerning the workings of the Select Vestry and the conditions at The Spittals were, probably a true reflection of the facts. However, Taylor was to be made an example of to protect the reputation of the Select Vestry, the governor and officers of the workhouse, and he had to go.

Three weeks later dated the 26th December 1835, the *North Staffs. Mercury* published the following notice. Due to its length and general substance of glorification of his superiors it has been substantially edited.

To the Overseers and Select Vestry. Gentlemen,
As you have unanimously expressed a wish, that I should conduct the affairs of this parish, at a time when the whole system is involved in confusion and difficulties; a duty devolves upon me to tender you my thanks for the confidence you have reposed in me. I think I may take credit to myself in saying that the confidence has been made manifest by you from the desire I have always shown to serve the interests of the parish, irrespective of the emolument attending that office.
If this be your conviction, which I am persuaded it is, I can only say, your inference is right, your conclusion just: for it is to be the pride of my heart, that whilst great and mighty minds are employed in eradicating every description of abuses in higher places, that I should contribute my humble mite in destroying the abuses which have crept into smaller institutions; and in none to a greater extent than the poor Law establishments.
I am Gentlemen,
Your faithful servant, John H. Copeland.

No further reference is made to Mr Taylor until the Annual Yearly Report and Accounts for 1835. In its summary, Mr Heathcote, the chairman, referred to Mr Taylor: That the demand on the grounds of him being dismissed from his situation wrongfully, be stated in a case (drawn up for mutual approval) and submitted to the Poor Law Commission for their adjudication, with an agreement that the same shall be final.

Following this meeting The Poor Law Commissioners issued an order for new elections for the Board of Guardians on the 16th April 1836. All residents of the parish could be nominated on condition that they were currently rated to the poor-rate in respect of their property to the value not less than £20 p.a. A new board of seventeen was subsequently elected from the nominations. Its first duty was to appoint those staff at the workhouse which would receive remuneration.

A head clerk, with a salary of	£150
Second ditto	£72
Third	£52
Relieving officer	£120
Relieving officer's Clerk	£52
Governor of Workhouse	£45 *
Matron	£25 *
Auditor	£20
Schoolmaster	£20 *
Schoolmistress	£10 *
Porter	£5

*Those with an asterisk * were to reside in the workhouse and have their maintenance there.*

An acknowledgement of the new Poor Law Amendment Act, 1834, was reported at the Annual Meeting of the Select Vestry held in October of that year. It was noted that it was the last meeting of the Select Vestry, after which it would be placed under the control of the Board of Guardians. It would appear that no action on this resolution was taken for nearly two years. The final report of the Select Vestry was produced in March 1836. Considerable appraisal of the parish affairs and past abuses was itemised. The outcome of the report however, was to present the workings of the Select Vestry over a period of the previous two years in a most favourable light:

It has been thought by some that it would be desirable to get rid at once of the old debt owing by the parish, and for that purpose a fifth rate was intended to be collected; but it appears to have given dissatisfaction, the Select Vestry have abandoned that intention.
When the Select Vestry commenced their duties, which may be said to be two years ago, they found a great accumulation of debt. Accounts for the proceeding year, amounting to a very large sum of money, unpaid - that, the parish expenditure had generally upon an average of proceeding years amounted yearly to £18,000 and upwards, and they very soon discovered that proceedings had been, and were going on in the parish office, which loudly demanded their constant attention.

With a view to remedying the evils surrounding them, they were determined to take nothing for granted, but diligently and perseveringly to apply themselves to the practical details of the parochial business in all its departments. At the conclusion of the report it was stated that all debts had been paid and a credit balance of £106 was returned. The Select Vestry also announced the arrival on the previous Saturday of an assistant Poor Law Commissioner and thought that the transfer of the administration to the new system would commence in about three weeks' time.

In reply to the report, a correspondent in the *North Staffs Mercury* wrote complaining that the Select Vestry had been involved in a cover-up and their report had conflicted wildly from the truth: . . . .*but in every branch of the administration of affairs in Stoke, the hand of reform was wanted; abuses had crept in everywhere, for instance, the governor of the workhouse had long been contractor for the supplies, and was allowed the earnings of the paupers; the consequences of this arrangement were that the governor allowed more able-bodied workers to remain in the workhouse, so their earnings would be increased. When the practice was discontinued the number immediately fell from 210 to 135. The governor also provided a better diet, in the interests of alluring more able-bodied to the establishment.*
The classification in the house was so imperfect, that three unmarried females became pregnant in the last year. The parish accounts, almost defied investigation; two officers were convicted of embezzlement during the last eighteen months. The late cashier absconded, and his successor discovered that there had been no entry of receipts for sixteen weeks. The collection of rates was conducted most fraudulently, thirty percent was usually lost, and no rate had been regularly balanced for many years.

Daily life in the Workhouse
An annual report of 1835 presents the daily timetable for inmates of the workhouse.

25ᵗʰ March – 29ᵗʰ September.
Rise at 5.30a.m. Breakfast 6.30-7.00a.m. Work 7-12 noon. Dinner 12 noon – 1.00 p.m. Work 1.00-6.00p.m. Supper 6.00-7.00p.m. Bed 8.00p.m.

29ᵗʰ September – 25ᵗʰ March.
Rise 6.30a.m. Breakfast 7.30-8.00a.m. Work 8.00-12 noon. Dinner 12 noon – 1.00 p.m. Work 1.00-6.00p.m. Supper 6.00-7.00p.m. Bed 8.00p.m.

The day would begin with a roll-call of all inmates and inspection of all able-bodied over the age of 7 years half an hour after the bell had been rung for rising. Other rules were under the heading of decorum. No able bodied inmates over 7 years were allowed to be in the sleeping rooms during the day without permission. No alcohol or change of diet to be allowed except if recommended by the medical officer, and even then it had to be approved by the board.

Any inmate was at liberty to leave the workhouse after giving reasonable notice to the master on condition that they took the whole family with them. There was also a list of offences for which inmates could be punished. Offenders were divided into two categories. Those deemed to be disorderly might be put on a reduced diet for one or two days. Those committing a second offence or insulted a parish officer, or became drunk or indecent would be called *refectory,* and punished more severely by legal action, confinement or a further reduction in diet.

Offences included. *Making a noise during a period of silence, e.g. meal times. Using bad language, insulting another inmate by words or actions, threatening to assault another inmate, neglecting to duly care for their person, refusing to work or work properly, playing games of chance, attempting to enter the accommodation allocated to another class of inmate, misbehaviour during prayers and worship, disobeying the orders of any workhouse officer.*

Before the new system came into operation, it was obvious from the report that the Select Vestry in charge of the Poor Law was in chaos. Indeed, a major reason for the support of the Poor Law Amendment Act in Stoke was that the Select Vestry believed that to adopt the changes would save the ratepayers money.

During these troubled times staff for the new workhouse were often sought after through advertisements in the *North Staffs Mercury.* One such notice, dated 13ᵗʰ August 1836 read as follows. *Wanted, at The Spittals Workhouse, a Man and his Wife, without incumbrances. The man will be required to attend to the cookery and baking department, also to the management of the cows, and to make himself generally useful. The woman will be required to assist the Matron in the management of the female wards, and generally to fulfil and perform all such Lawful Orders and Regulations as may be required of her. No persons need to apply whose characters will not bear the strictest investigation.*

Six months after the 1834 Act had been in operation, the Clerk to the Stoke Board of Guardians wrote: *I am persuaded when it comes into full operation it cannot fail to produce the most beneficial results in diminishing the rates. . .*

Apart from one ledger-type book nothing of the early years of The Spittals Workhouse has survived. This is the Admittance and Discharge Book dating from January 1836 to the end of March 1838 which provides a unique insight into the names of those admitted and the circumstances together with those discharged and the reason why.

The statistics alone are themselves distressing, and reflect a period of unemployment, poverty and destitution. In 1836 there were 352 admissions compared with 934 the following year. For the first quarter of 1838 there were 449, and if multiplied to gain an annual figure (it is recognised that there may be seasonal differences) this came to around 1,700. The increase in numbers are astronomical, the first year is a 265% increase followed by a 483% increase over the figures for 1836. The discharges in 1836 is 212; 1837, 902; and for the first quarter of 1838, is 342; represented by an annual approximate figure of 1,368. Like the admittance book, the numbers reflect a similar pattern in 1837 with an increase of 425%, and for 1838, 645%.

So what were the reasons for admissions? There were numerous including: *father absconded, mother dead, mother in home, pregnant when admitted, husband unable to maintain wife, very infirm, insane, idiot, cripple, asthmatical, broken arm, re-admitted, destitute, father run away, out of work, parents unable to maintain her, lame with travelling, came in ill and neither friends nor home, old and infirm, neglected by father, imbecile, father dead and orphan.*

The reasons for discharge once more reflect a wide range of reasons, but alongside this there appeared a comment column which is in itself interesting. Discharges: *parish apprentice (means found work), bad behaviour, at her own request, by mother's request, left without leave, husband's request, neglecting work, went over the wall, left with mother, sent to asylum, able to work, removed to his own parish, to get a living,* and the list continues.

Comments at the side of the names of some of the entries are also varied and interesting: *insolent, quiet but disposed to work, not contented, poor helpless creature, quiet and harmless, lazy, imprudent, came in sick, recovered, Mr Boardman's whore, a dangerous bad man, fighting in the house, found fault with the food, a good working girl, a nice boy, behaviour good, discontented and saucy, dissatisfied and lazy, foolish and dishonest, ragged and lousy, indecent behaviour and scandalously abusive.*

The following invitation for traders to tender for goods and services appeared in the *North Staffs Mercury* on the 13th June 1836 and makes interesting reading:

The Board of Guardians for the Parish of Stoke will be ready at their meeting to be held at the Parish Office on Wednesday the 20th inst. At 11.00 o'clock to receive Tenders and to contract for the supply of the under-mentioned articles.
Flour – Best seconds in sacks of 16 stones
Bread – made of best, second's wheaten flour in loaves of 4 lbs, each baked upon the oven bottom
Good Beef, consisting either of Rounds, Beds, Stickling pieces or by the side.
Good Oatmeal in loads of 240 lbs.

Other items included: salt, sugar, tea, good coco, best treacle, candles, starch, soda, vinegar, yellow soap, soft soap, black pepper, brooms, best hair brushes, hearth brushes and scrubbing brushes.

Also required were coffins made of elm, inch thick, wall pitched for persons both adults and those under 14 years and infants.

In a report on the state of finances for the parish in 1838, serious concerns were made with regards to the continued method of payment for out-door relief which, in addition to the cost of running the workhouse, was causing concern to the parishioners who would have to find additional church lunes. As a result, the Board of Guardians made it known that *sending paupers to the workhouse for relief instead of giving them money for food; by which means the inhabitants of this parish may be assured that those who are really destitute will be supplied with lodgings, food and medical assistance if necessary, and that those merely make begging a means of living in idleness, will have the test of work applied to them and be thus driven out of the parish.*

The serious effect of unemployment during the 1830s brought about continued poverty amongst the working classes of Stoke. It appears, however, that the Board of Guardians were concerned, but not those with genuine needs, but for those who used the situation to benefit themselves. Thomas Griffin, clerk to the Board of Guardians, clearly sympathised with this view of undeserved relief. He reported to the Poor Law Commission that the Board of Guardians had found several cases of fraud amongst the poor receiving out relief. He noted: *it is necessary for me to point out the moral degradation induced by such persons having parish relief open to them.*

The following year saw the Board of Guardians sending a petition to the House of Commons, supporting the Poor Law Amendment Act in terms which repeat and epitomise this contemporary moral attitude: *In its general principles the Act is calculated to produce lasting benefits to all classes and to the community at large, by affording relief to the aged and infirm and really necessitous by eradicating from society the influence arising from the habits of the idle, dissolute and able-bodied paupers who can now no longer be supported in their vicious practices, and, moreover, by effecting a great permanent improvement in the moral character of the labouring poor.*

Although the original intention was to build a workhouse with accommodation for 500, the reality provided for 270. This consisted of one long two storey building, one wing for men and another for women, the two sections being divided by the master's and officers' quarters and a dining hall. Further buildings to the front of this block were devoted to the use of boys on one side, and girls on the other. To the rear, there was an additional block for old men, the bake house and nursery.

With the severe trade depression in the early 1840s, and consequent high levels of unemployment and industrial unrest caused by strikes, The Spittals became swollen with those seeking relief. No lessons had been learned of the need for more accommodation from the consequences of the 1836 industrial strikes. The *Staffordshire Advertiser* in a report dated 21st March 1846, clearly apportions blame to the potters' strike as the direct cause of trade depression. Five years of economic depression had followed the great strike and lockout of 1836, which saw social unrest and poverty, culminating in the Chartists riots in the Potteries in 1842. Moreover, trade was badly affected by the collapse of the American markets for nearly one half of local pottery production was exported there. Over capacity in the industry exacerbated the crisis and the high price of corn bought near starvation to many families in North Staffordshire.

The assistant commissioner failed to accept that the main cause of unemployment was trade depression and wrote to the Poor Law Commission: *I learn from the relieving officer, that all men out of work are defective workmen, either from deficient skill or bad character, and that the good men, although at some places working at reduced wages, are generally employed.*

In 1841, The Spittals workhouse accommodated a total of 246 inmates which included 43 girls, 65 boys, all under the age of 15 years representing 44% of the total. When the Poor Law inspector visited the workhouse the following year he submitted a disturbing report of overcrowding. Of the children's department he wrote: *in the room for the class of girls between nine and sixteen of the same measurement as the other rooms (five hundred and fifty square feet), five girls sleep in*

each bed, and there are sixty of these girls sleeping in the room about nine square feet for each person. The boys' schoolroom is by far too much crowded. The girls' schoolroom 33' x 10' with sixty three scholars, about five and three quarter feet square for each. This school was less close and offensive than the boys' school, in consequence of the room's being narrow with large windows on each side opening into court yards. The boys' bedroom is 22' x 25', five hundred and fifty square feet, fifty-six boys sleep there, giving about nine and three quarter feet for each person.*

Assistant Commissioner Gilbert reported to the Poor Law Commissioners on the same subject of overcrowding. His description continues: *there are 350 inmates, but accommodation is only adequate for only half this number. In the women's room there were thirty five adults and thirty children occupying 555 square feet of space. This means each adult female has approximately only four square feet. In the same sized women's bedroom there were thirteen beds, each holding at least two women and one child. The bedroom for girls aged between 9 and 16 holds sixty occupants with five in each bed. In the boys bedroom fifty six boys sleep in a room measuring twenty-two feet by twenty-five feet. The girls' schoolroom measures thirty-three feet by ten feet and holds sixty-three pupils. The boys' schoolroom is even worse.*

The Board of Guardians was unwilling to correct the situation by building additional accommodation because of the depressed state of the economy, but was conscious of the need to provide better conditions for inmates. In an increasingly authoritarian attitude towards classification, the newly established policy of the workhouse made things far worse as the rules meant additional accommodation to satisfy the rules of classification.

As the position was becoming more critical because of the limited accommodation in The Spittals workhouse, the Stoke Guardians persisted and petitioned the House of Commons in 1841, requesting a larger discretion in the application of out-door relief: *The inhabitants of this parish chiefly employed in the manufacture of china and earthenware have of late years suffered from fluctuations of trade which have subjected a considerable portion of the working class to great distress in season. We have found the Poor Law Amendment Act too severe in requiring such persons to pass through the test of going into the workhouse. Many families have suffered the last extremities of wretchedness, rather than submit to such alternatives... Families in this class are at such times in arrears if they consent to go into the workhouse, the landlord takes possessions of the remains of their bedding and furniture and rents the house to others. They are then pauperised for life and sink degraded into hopeless indifference to the future. In many cases the elder children are employed in manufactorys and contribute in part to the substance of the family; if the parents are taken into the workhouse with their infant children the working boys and girls are deprived of parental protection and of home.*

They are thrown on the temptation of the world. . . if they are taken with their parents to the workhouse the burdens of the parish are increased and they are prevented from learning a trade.

A letter to the Poor Law Commissioners dated, 29th April 1842, referred to possible additions needed.

Sir, With reference to your letter dated the 27th, I beg to state that a meeting of the Guardians is called specifically to consider the workhouse accommodation and it very probably will be considerably enlarged.

The following communication from Mr Griffin, dated the 30th April, states the view that a new house should be erected. *I beg to report that the Board of Guardians considered the details of the crowded state of the workhouse and the general defective arrangements. It appears to me as I stated to the Guardians that the most economical course would be to build a new house rather than to make an outlay on the present.*

The new Poor Law and the increase in the number of inmates led the guardians finally to expand the workhouse. In a plan to move the old and children, vagrants and sick away from the able-bodied adult inmates, it was decided to build a new school, hospital and vagrants' block. Again the guardians placed their emphasis *in the whole of the buildings and erections, particular attention to be paid to strict classification and thorough ventilation.* The 1842 additions to The Spittals could then accommodate five hundred paupers and was already regarded as a model workhouse, underlining the success of the new system and, as such, was an encouragement to the neighbouring unions.

The finance required for these improvements were made possible by savings made over the previous six years as stated in a letter to the Poor Law Commission, dated 22nd April that year. *Sir, I have the honour to transmit to you at the request of the Guardians to submit the tables of the receipts and payments for the previous six years.* This amounted to a saving of £14,482 and Mr Griffin continued to explain that this had come about as a result of trade in the potteries flourishing and prosperous as at any known period. This statement is in sharp contrast to that written later in 1841.

In February 1846, the Parish of Stoke-upon-Trent made public the amended dietary schedule order for inmates at the workhouse. For some unknown reason this order was rescinded and replaced by a further dietary order on the 8th March the following year. The introduction makes interesting reading. *We do Order and Direct, that the paupers of the respective sexes described in the table hereunder written, who may be received and maintained in the workhouse of the parish of Stoke-upon-Trent, shall, during the period of their residence be fed, dieted, and maintained with food and in the manner described and set forth in the said table.*

And we hereby empower the Guardians of the Poor to allow to each infirm person resident a sufficient quantity of tea for breakfast and supper, not exceeding one pint per meal sweetened with an allowance of sugar, not exceeding half an ounce to each pint of tea, together with an allowance of butter, not exceeding eight ounces per week, in lieu of the milk porridge for breakfast, and broth, milk porridge, and cheese for supper prescribed in the table.

And we do hereby further Order and Direct, that children under the age of nine years, shall be fed, dieted and maintained with such food and in such manner as the Guardians shall direct; and that the children above the age of nine years, and under the age of thirteen shall be allowed the same quantities as are prescribed for women.

We also Order and Direct that the sick paupers shall be fed, dieted and maintained in such a manner as the Medical Officer shall direct. That this printed Order shall be hung up in such public places in the workhouse and renewed from time to time. Breakfast; Bread for men 8 oz and women 6 oz. Milk porridge, men 2 pints, women 1½pints each day. Dinner: Men 6oz of cooked meat twice a week, women 5oz twice a week. Bread served only three times a week. Boiled rice, men 18oz, women 16oz but only twice a week to which meal was added vegetables. One pint of milk was available just twice a week. For supper the meal consisted of bread each evening supplemented on two days a week with broth, three days milk porridge and two days cheese.

Real Hardship

The intentions of the 1834 Act was to reduce the huge burden of out-door relief on the parishioners of Stoke. Even so, many still received this relief in the form of a small sum

A typical scene in a workhouse

of money, one or two shillings, or income in kind, usually loaves of bread baked at the workhouse bakery. Conditions for this payment were restricted, usually to the death of a husband, sickness, desertion by the husband, and infirmity, and occasionally to able-bodied men out of work.

In the past the Poor Law Commission had different views. They had written to the Stoke Guardians in 1836 stressing that *for all able bodied applicants, relief in the workhouse is most in accordance with the spirit and provisions of the Poor Law Amendment Act; and the commissioners therefore consider that no able applicant should receive out relief so long as there remains room in the workhouse.*

Despite representations and appeal to the House of Commons, the guardians of Stoke continued to give outdoor relief to the able-bodied. However, the pressure against this practice continued, and in 1855, the Stoke Guardians threatened to resign if the Poor Law Board would not allow them to make out-door payments at a time of general distress in the town. An agreement was reached that the heads of families should go to the workhouse, perform a certain amount of work, have their meals at the house, and at night, take home bread in proportion to their families.

The severity of the law continued as the Poor Law Board in 1859 charged the Stoke Guardians with the cost of giving their paupers a treat at the last wakes to the tune of £12 15s 6d reporting: The Guardians considered *that the powers of the Poor Law Board, and the order that the Guardians should not give the paupers a treat out of the funds of the union were oppressive.*

A typical scene at meal times in an early Victorian workhouse

Despite the provision of the workhouse for those unable to care for themselves, there remained many who would not enter the workhouse, no matter how bad things were. The Poor Law Amendment Act was designed to reduce excessive expenditure of the parish on paupers by the illumination of out-door relief, dole. Every effort was made to ensure that conditions were worse in the workhouse than the conditions found outside, even in the most deprived areas of the Potteries, as to dissuade even the most desperate to seek help from the guardians, so reducing the financial burden further.

As a result, some were reluctant to stand the workhouse test for admittance, and as such, many died of destitution. The *Staffordshire Advertiser* reported in January 1856: *an inquest was held into the death of Eliza Holland the wife of Thomas Holland, a labourer living in Longport, who died in the infirmary. The deceased was only brought to the infirmary on the day of her death and she appeared in a very low and exhausted state. Her husband, it seems, had refused to go into the workhouse with his wife and three children for the last week, and that they had nothing but dry bread. His wife had a bad cold, and he considered her illness had been caused from want. Mr. Kolker, the house surgeon of the infirmary, gave it as his opinion that the deceased had died for want of the common necessaries of life. The Jury accordingly returned a verdict to that effect.*

A further case of destitution appeared in the *Staffordshire Advertiser* the following March: *On Saturday W. Harding Esq., coroner held an inquest on the body of Joseph Capper, a child of two years. It appeared that the father was a bricklayer's labourer, and had not worked for several months; but for some reason he and his wife objected to applying for parochial relief or medical assistance from the parish. The deceased child was very ill on the Thursday and the mother hearing that Dr. Moseley had on former occasions given his advise gratuitously to poor people she went to see him and that gentleman promptly attended.*
The doctor, however, found that he had been called in too late, as the child was in a dying state. Dr Moseley, who was admitted as a witness, stated that the child's death had originated from want of proper sustenance, the jury returned a verdict in accordance to that fact. Several of the jury were well acquainted with the father of the deceased and spoke highly of him as a sober and well-behaved father. The coroner and the jury kindly collected nearly 20s to the relief of the family.

But there were different issues, those who always did not accept workhouse discipline. One such case was referred to the police for theft. It appeared in the Staffordshire Advertiser in January 1857. *William Rowley was charged with being a refractory pauper. Mr Brown, the master of The Spittals workhouse, stated that the pauper had twice absconded with his pauper clothes had been placed in the workshop under the overlooker of the tailors, but had been found too incompetent or too lazy to qualify as a member of that craft; had been placed with the able-bodied labourers, with a similar result; had assaulted the master by running violently against him.*
As a climax to his numerous escapades, he led a chorus of some 50 paupers, who had disturbed the peace of the house by singing a number of indecent songs. The chorus was silent at the command of Mr Brown but the incorrigible Rowley continued his unmelodious roar, grinning, to use the novel simile of Mr Brown, 'like an otter with one foot in a trap.' He was committed to twenty-one days for the assault, and ordered to pay a fine of £4 and costs for absconding with clothing; in default two months' imprisonment, the two terms to run consecutively.

Changes to the workhouse

The annual report for 1842/3 has survived. It gives many interesting details, both of the running of the workhouse and of its enlargements and improvements. It also carries an account of the new parish hospital. From its introduction it appears to have been written following the Chartists Riots in August 1842.

Parish of Stoke upon Trent report of the Board of Guardians 1842/43

In giving a summary of the proceedings the board adverts with sorrow to the unprecedented depression of trade throughout the district and the disturbances and other untoward circumstances which have occurred during the year. The circumstances have made it a year of great labour and anxiety, as well as great pressure up on the rate payers, but most of all of suffering amongst the working classes which comprise of the majority of the population.

Happily, the discretion entrusted to the board by the commissioners has enabled it to dispense exclusive relief out of the House, as well as to afford all the relief within as its capabilities would allow. It is its painful duty to require an additional rate for the services of the year, but considering the wide and spreading distress all round, and the unparalleled demand for relief, the board is thankful that the increase has not been far greater and it's the earnest wish that such an improvement may take place in trade, and in the condition of the people which then shall render any further increase not necessary. But that it now proceeds to state:

That the receipts from the first five rates amount to £13,004 9s 7d
That the expenses of maintaining the poor in the workhouse had been £3,010 9s 5d
Relief to the out-door and casual poor £4,813 18 9d
Salaries of the establishment £880 7s 8d
Collector of the rates £397 1s 8d
Medical officers vaccination and Registrar £72 10s 6d.
The County Asylum for lunatics £200
Law Expenses of all kinds £398 19s 4d
Removal of paupers £208 11s.6d
County rate £1,115 4s 2d
First payment to Constable force £450 4s 2d
Miscellaneous expenses £1,792 9s 10d

That the debt now owing amounts to £2,260
The rates collected £3,561
Leaving a balance in favour of the parish £1,301

A principal feature in the proceedings of the year has been the alterations and enlargement of the workhouse. To these or to a new one, the Board has called the Assistant Commissioner for his advice when he comes to look into the crowded state of the House. There now stands 450 inmates being boarded and lodged in quarters only estimated to contain 300. Their consequent exposure to disease and the impossibility of classifying the adults, of giving due comfort to the aged, of separating the young as they ought to be, and of providing suitable means for the recovery of the sick. However, it felt not to build a new House, but at least to make such alterations and additions to the old one as should be consistent with the demands and as should provide the desired ends.

The Board, therefore had the premises surveyed, then obtain plans and estimates and after much deliberation fixed upon one of the best, but adapted to carry out their wishes and wants. Contracts were promptly made for the work, and the amount needed was £2,500. This sum was procured from the Government to be repaid by instalments with interest over a period of 20 years. On 20th August building work commenced, and by the 20th November the whole were erected and covered in.

The Board now has the pleasure to report that the original buildings hitherto appropriated indiscriminately, initially to the reception of the adult of all classes, and of the youth of both sexes, is now set apart for the able-bodied adults, the men in the eastern and the women in the western division with the Governor's House. This is found in the centre, separating and commanding both with suitable arrangements for their classification. The chapel is so improved as to make it an excellent dining room and a commodious place of worship.

The Board has also to report that the schools which have been erected in front of the main building are finished and occupied. The master and mistress would request that their respective charges have apartments and rooms and yards to themselves and for the first time this interesting part of the institution is a credit to the neighbourhood and of benevolent design.

In addition to these the Board has caused the old buildings, joining to the north eastern boundary be converted and adapted into a warehouse and laundry. The board moreover has to report the erection of a large building at the north-west including a lodge and house for the porter and a visiting room for strangers, probationary and tramp wards for both sexes working rooms and water and engine house. Lastly a mill and granary, the former of which is proposed that the able-bodied men should work by hand so that the corn may be ground, and the whole of the bread would be prepared on the spot have been included in the building work. The last of the additions to which the Board request attention is to the Hospital which forms the southern part of the building for, besides providing a reception of the casual sick, it also caters for cases of infection. There are also apartments for the helpless and infirm, for lying in women and for idiots supposed to be harmless with surgery rooms for the nurses, and in short with every accommodation which can be desirable for so useful an establishment. It is true the interior is not finished for in fact, time has not been allowed for the purpose, but the fittings are in preparation, and in less than three months the whole may be occupied. Two things however will be requisite before the hospital will be thoroughly compatible with a resident surgeon and heating by means of steam. The Board shall have no doubt that in addition to the separation of the sexes and yards being set apart for each and the other comforts so liberally provided then two yards will easily be added.

The Board had already reported that the first estimate of contracts were as near as possible to £2,500

School Block built 1842

Further the Board suggests that the same regulations should be adapted in the women's department in attending to the meals, in the charge of bedrooms and in sundry other duties, not forgetting washing and drying, ironing etc. which can never so well be done as by being entrusted into separate hands, thereby creating responsibility and ensuring system, attention and the best results. The infant school, in the opinion of the Board will require a Mistress superior to the ordinary inmates of the House and there is no doubt such a female may be obtained for a small salary added to her board and keep. Such a person shall be looked out for. But a more important question for consideration will be who to place in charge of the infirmary? It is clear that the governor and his wife will be unable to take on that duty and it is quite clear that neither the visiting surgeon nor any nurse can take charge of it. It certainly will be well not to rush into any serious expense without seeing and feeling the necessity of so doing. In the first instance therefore, as the governor will be relieved to some extent in his own house, the Board would suggest that he takes charge of the Infirmary also, with an experienced Matron under him, who shall be placed over the nurses and the stores and that a special weekly return be made from the department, the same as from the others.

The Board takes shame that it has not sooner addressed the legislature for an alteration in that part of the Poor Law which relates to Bastards. The Law, the Board is of the opinion, bears too hard on the female, affords encouragement to reduction, and therefore requires to be amended, as at its last sitting the Board agreed, and to petition for such modification, as will remedy the defect, and do justice to all parties. The Board at the same time expressed its hope that the separation of aged couples may be rendered unnecessary by allowing the practice to be carried out generally that it is now adopted and there by doing away with a reproach and an evil.

It is the opinion of the Board that the Commissioners cannot do better than to give to its successors the same discretion which they have given to it and it believes that the discretion will not be withdrawn, so long as it is necessary and wisely used. In its last expression of its feelings, the Board heartily hoped that its successors will pursue the same discriminating conduct which it has endeavoured to pursue and that they will require their servants to do the same, that whatever may be the events of the year and certainly the proposed in not encouraging the wants of the destitute and are treated with just regard to the right of the rate payers, so that all may be satisfied and the country be grateful for their services.

A further report authorised to look into the working conditions of children in the Potteries was submitted by Samuel Scriven a government inspector appointed to report on child labour in the Potteries and also to the conditions of the poor in 1842. In his report, he quotes Mr William Emery, the relieving officer for the district on the conditions of the poor: I am the relieving officer of Stoke Union. In this capacity I attend families resident in the parish. I find the trade in the area very depressed, and a great number of people thrown out of work, the most of the cases are among the improvident; they are parties who will not keep their credit good when in work. The children are not well educated, although there are good opportunities of being so, there are so many schools. I have often an opportunity of witnessing the sick people in their homes and have seen a great deal of consumption among the females. There is also a good deal of asthma among the elderly people; there are a good number of cripples with palsy. The effects of lead in the dipping department of factories cause consumption and asthma. The children are taken to work too young, some as young as eight. There are a great many applicants made this last month for relief, within the last two weeks, 186 applicants were made from persons out of work. I think the cause of their absenting themselves from Sunday-schools is the want of shoes and clothing.

The parish placed an advertisement in the North Staffs Mercury dated the 10th January 1844, for the following officers for the workhouse:

A Schoolmaster
He must be fully competent to teach boys reading, writing and arithmetic. He must pay particular attention to their religious and moral instruction and endeavour to train them up to industrious habits. He will have to devote the whole of his time to the service of the parish, and assist the master in maintaining due subordination and regularity in the establishment. Salary £30 p.a. with board and lodgings.

An Infant Schoolmistress
She will be required to take charge of the children under the age of six years. To keep them in order, cleanliness, and regularity, to attend to their clothing, and to have the management of them generally, under the superintendence of the matron. Salary, £10 p.a. with board and lodgings.

A Nurse

To attend to sick in the hospital, one having knowledge of midwifery will be preferred. She must be of a kind feeling and disposition, combined with firmness of character. She will have to make herself generally useful in assisting the matron in maintaining order in the establishment, and devote her whole time to the service of the parish. Salary, £15 p.a. with board and lodgings. Testimonials, as to character and ability, for any of the above situations to be sent to the clerk to the guardians.

With the continued increase in inmates, The Spittals adapted to meet demand, but the adaptation brought no change in the harsh policy of deterring all but the neediest, by ensuring that the life of the inmate was physically and functionally repellent. The Spittals became a community in its own right, self-sufficient in every way. The numbers increased in the 1850s and 1860s from 235 to 528, and by 1871 the total inmates numbered 719.

After a few years, the growing population, with an increasing number of child inmates, brought about the necessity for a new and larger school within the workhouse grounds. In 1866, a school was built in Elizabethan style, to a design by Charles Lynam. The building combined the former boys' and girls' school with an infants' school and accommodated 400 children. Teaching rooms were on the ground floor, dormitories above, separated by the apartments of the teaching staff. The cost of this building was £1,400. In 1897, it was decided that the children, where possible should attend local board schools, for which the sum of 6d per week for each child was paid to the county council.

The sick, as always, constituted a considerable proportion of the inmates. Attempts at separating these from the healthy grew increasingly complicated, especially during times when epidemics and seasonal illnesses created serious overcrowding. It was found that many of the people who sought admission to the workhouse were sick, infirm or aged. The necessity to have a separate place for dealing with this particular branch of the guardians' work became obvious. In May 1842, a committee to consider defects in the workhouse reported: *that upon inspection of the premises it is desirable and absolutely necessary to provide additional hospital accommodation both as regards the health of the patients and inmates generally and that the building be separate and distinct from the house.* It was proposed that the site for the hospital be on the side next to the pool between the able-bodied men's yard, leaving a clear space between sufficient for a cart road. It was suggested that accommodation be provided: male and female wards for general cases; male and female wards for old and infirm; male and female fever wards; male and female itch wards; male and female smallpox wards; male and female lunatic wards; midwifery ward; nursing sick ward; bathroom; surgery; shower rooms; water closets; dead

house. The number of beds allocated to each ward is not known but in a further document it is reported that the new hospital would have eighty beds. The front of the building had the following inscription:

STOKE-UPON-TRENT PARISH HOSPITAL
ERECTED 1842.

The Parish Hospital. Erected 1842

The following year a new diet was published for the sick at the hospital. Full diet: *Breakfast, one pint of coffee, 6oz of bread; Dinner, 4oz of meal, 12-14 oz of potatoes, half pint of watered milk; Supper 1 pint of tea, 6 oz of bread.*

Half diet: *Breakfast 1 pint of coffee, 4 oz of bread; Dinner 8-10 oz of cooked potatoes, half pint of milk and water; Supper pint of tea, four oz of bread.*

Low or fever diet: *Breakfast; coffee, bread and butter; Dinner: broth and bread or rice pudding, half pint of milk and water; Supper-tea, bread and butter.*
Toast, water, barley water or linseed tea will be allowed as a general beverage to the sick.

It is difficult to obtain information with regards to the conditions at the hospital. Reports sometimes do not portray the real situation as the truth is often covered up for the benefit of the inspectors. However, on a rare occasion a patient may decide to write a letter of complaint which gives an accurate snapshot of life in the hospital. One such letter was written by William Lambert, who went into the parish hospital in May 1858. Many will find his letter disturbing.

To the Honourable Poor Law Board May 31st 1858
Gentlemen
I feel it my duty to lay before your honourable board the following facts relative to the treatments of the sick poor in the workhouse hospital, Stoke-upon-Trent.
On Monday the 10th May, owing to severe illness I entered Stoke-upon-Trent workhouse. I was not ten minutes in the workhouse till the Master saw me and desired that I should be taken at once to the hospital and was by direction of the nurse placed in the Idiot Ward. I was not two minutes in this ward when one of the

idiots was carried in bleeding profusely from his nose. The effects of a fight during my stay of three days in this ward being preceded by frantic yells were of frequent occurrence. Upon enquiry I found it was quite common for the nurse to place sick patients in the Idiot Ward. I may also state there is no partition to prevent the idiots from rambling into any of the wards to the greater danger of the other patients.

The following day Mr Ashford, the assistant or medical partner of Mr Garner, entered the hospital and left again without seeing me, although I was very ill on the 12ᵗʰ when Mr Ashford again came and again went without seeing me. Upon this occasion I asked the nurse why I was not introduced to the Doctor or the Doctor to me, and was flatly insulted. I requested an interview with the Master but was refused.

On Thursday, the 13ᵗʰ, I was taken from the Idiot Ward and placed in the old men's sick ward when Mr Garner the medical officer visited the hospital and inquired of my complaint. I told him my chest was strangely painful and adding that I had a pain in my right side which was killing me and was also troubled with palpitation. I was asked to strip for an examination when Mr Garner remarked that I must have been ill for a long time.

The new school block built 1866. Designed by Charles Lynam

The Parish Hospital built 1842

I told him I had a continuous pain in my chest and pointed to the place. 'I know you have now can you be otherwise be quiet,' was his reply. After sounding me he pointed to the nurse 'this man wants little or no medicine' and I can positively affirm little or no medicine did I receive with the exception of a large cup full of a dark mixture called opening medicine more adapted for horses than sickly creatures. This opening medicine is nicknamed by the patients 'Blackjack'.

The doctor when prescribing invariably tells the nurse to give this man a little of this or that, or mix a little of so and so with so and so just as the case may be, whether the nurse has a knowledge of dispensing medicines and whether this is a matter deserving attention I will have your Honourable Board to determine.

During my stay in the hospital, I saw every day one or another of the patients comb their heads in pursuit of lice and I noticed particularly in every instance found them some in large numbers. This is not surprising as there are no facilities for personal cleanliness, no basins of any kind to wash in. Nothing save the chamber pots and there is a sad deficiency there. Patients feel a repugnance to wash in a chamber pot not used by themselves in the ward where I slept. There were no towels, no soap and but three chamber pots for seven men. I have seen the old men's ward which was my day ward where for three days successively it was without soap of any kind, hard or soft. In this ward there were but two small towels for 11 or 12 men. I have myself washed these towels several times when they were shamefully filthy and could procure no soap for the purpose.

I may also point to the fact of the sick ward being in close proximity to the old men's ward and the same water closet sufficing for both. I went into this ward and saw two beds in it with very filthy covering, in the bed a man and in the other four boys, two at each end. I asked the man if all the boys had diarrhoea but the nurse took no notice of the boys upon the bed. I was told they were nearly free from it which must be attributed to bad food or filth or perhaps both.

My daily diet of bread, butter and coffee for breakfast and then in the evening make no mistake in stating in addition to the coffee and tea being nearly cold, the bread was insufficiently baked and the butter was rancid. I have seen patients scrape the butter off the bread. My dinner was rice and broth although the rice was musty and inferior being baked or boiled in some watery matter certainly not all milk and insufficiently sweetened. The broth was devoid of any vegetables and owing to the meat being very often over cooked was tough.

If the patients complain of their meat being sprinkled with vinegar I begged a small portion from one of them and found it was so sprinkled, this process I was told most frequent.

In the hospital where the nurse rules supreme no knives, forks nor spoons you must wait and borrow from those that are so fortunate as to possess one. Upon enquiring I was told knives, forks and spoons were allowed in the House and this deprivation to the sick is entirely the work of the nurse, a woman that is paid £20 yearly with rations for attending to the wants of the sick.

I question if any of the patients would have the courage to complain of this state of things lest they should invoke the temper of the nurse. For my own part, I did not manage to get a chance for during my stay in the hospital, I never saw the Master during the whole time nor any of the Guardians.

On Thursday, the 19th Mr Ashford visited the Hospital and prescribed for a time with 'Black Jack' and thank God for giving me strength to crawl away and although I am sensibly convinced my case is entirely hopeless, I feel thoroughly thankful my illness was has been long and heavy is not attributed to my misconduct of my own but a freak of nature as natural defect. I may also add my health is improving every hour, but it will not last long. I am depending for support and the generosity of my trade.

Such a state of things calls loudly for redress and I have no doubt you only require the facts to be laid before you to insure your kindest and vigilant attention.

I am Gentlemen, your very humbly William Lambert.

To the Hon The National Poor Law Board, Whitehall, London. May 26th 1858

So serious was this letter taken, that an immediate response was requested from Mr Garner who pointed the finger of complaint to the staff and workhouse officers. He made no reference whatsoever with regards to the shortages experienced by Mr Lambert.

On the 15th June 1858 the local board met to discuss the complaint with Mr Doyle who was a government poor law inspector of workhouses.

The committee appointed to meet Mr Doyle and investigate the complaint made by Lambert, report that Lambert did not attend

Front Elevation

Stoke-upon-Trent Union Workhouse
Parish Hospital 1842

Ground Floor Plan

the meeting that they considered Mr Garner's reply and explanations he gave satisfactory, but they considered certain alterations need attention requisite:

They recommend that the closet at the end of the passage up stairs in the hospital the female syphilitic ward be converted into two water closets. That doors to stop wandering be fitted and kept locked. That a sufficient number of washing basins and chamber pots be provided in the several wards, that knives and forks also be provided for the use of the sick in the hospital. That nurses do strictly attend to any sick that may be sent to the hospital, going before the medical officer at the first visit after such admission. That the governors do make arrangements for the male sick having the use of the pleasure garden in front of the hospital one portion of the day and the females another portion.

It is agreed that the report of the committee be forthwith carried into effect.

Regardless of the evidence, writers of the period reflect a different view of the conditions in an attempt to present the care and attention shown to inmates by the Board of Guardians in the best possible light: *When a person desires to enter the workhouse as an inmate, having received their proper form of admission, they are taken first of all to the new receiving ward. Here their clothing is taken away, thoroughly disinfected, and stowed away in case they may be required again. Then they are taken to an excellent, warm and comfortable bathroom, where a hot bath is given, after which a nightgown is supplied and the applicant shown to a good bed, in a room where about twelve can be accommodated. First thing in the morning, the doctor examines them, and on that man's certificate is placed in whatever department they are fitted for. They are now on probation, and at the next following meeting of the guardians their case is gone into, and if found deserving, they are allowed to stay; if not an alternative course is taken.*

The overcrowding situation was only temporarily relieved by the new hospital as in 1875 a further attempt to alleviate the increasing problem of the sick was made. With the growing shortage of sick beds a new infirmary, with accommodation for over 145, was erected at the south end of the workhouse.

By 1882, the situation became critical again with serious overcrowding in the infirmary. The guardians agreed, therefore, to spend £13,000 on the provision of additional hospital buildings, to the west of those erected in 1875. As a result of this decision, the old parish hospital was altered to accommodate elderly inmates. By 1900, there were 130 residents, despite limited space described as being designed for only eighty.

Schools within the workhouse

In August 1845 a new set of workhouse rules were agreed upon for the schools.

Boys:

Rise in the summer at 6.00 a.m. Washing and prayers with the governor.

7.00 a.m. Breakfast, play until 8.00 a.m. then wash and get ready for walk.

8.00 - 9.30 a.m. Walk for one and half hours or if the weather is bad, singing; or the master to examine or read to the boys.

    9.30 - 10.00 a.m. Writing.

    10.30 - 11.00 a.m. Arithmetic, written.

    11.00 - 12 noon Reading and spelling.

    12.30 - 1.00 p.m. Wash first and then dine.

    1.00 - 2.00 p.m. One hours play.

    2.00 - 3.00 p.m. Reading and spelling.

    3.00 - 4.00 p.m. Mental arithmetic.

    4.00 - 5.00 p.m. Geography and singing.

    5.00 - 5.30 p.m. Tea.

    6.00 p.m. More play followed by the boys and girls with the master and mistress, the master reads and explains the prayers.

    7.00 p.m. Off to bed.

Sinks used by inmates

The daily programme differs for girls, with the additional subjects such as sewing, knitting, mending and accounts.

It is very easy in the light of social benefits currently enjoyed by the general population in Britain to consider the treatment in workhouses at this time as almost evil. However, if these children had been living outside the workhouse system, their treatment and hard labour would have been be far worse, working in appalling factory conditions from the age of eight or nine with no possibility of an education. In the workhouse, even with its huge social issues, both girls and boys were educated and received three meals each day.

Lunatics

At the heart of the poor law, the question of classification was fundamental. Before 1850, workhouse officials received little guidance on the provision for inmates certified as 'unsound mind'. The 1834 Act permitted the maintenance of insane paupers in workhouses as long as they were considered harmless; dangerous inmates were removed to the county asylum.

The original buildings erected in 1832 were later to become the wards for lunacy, although severe cases were removed to Cheddleton, some distance away. In 1878, the Board of Guardians complained that there was no inducement for them to provide accommodation for lunatics and idiots, with the need for special wards and attendants. They pointed out *in many large workhouses, no accommodation has been provided for this class of pauper, all lunatics being immediately taken into the county asylum.*

By the late 1860s, it became abundantly clear that the crisis of accommodation within asylums had put an end to any hope of eliminating the use of the workhouse as a receptacle for the insane. In 1889 the board commissioner for lunacy reported overcrowding in the lunatic section of The Spittals workhouse, with an over-spill into the main building. An attempt to provide further accommodation for the lunatic classification was made in 1893-4 when the Board of Guardians built two pavilions designed by Charles Lynam, at a cost of £11,340, to accommodate about 140 cases.

Male lunacy wards built 1894

Vagrants or Casuals

Stoke workhouse was situated adjacent to the main highway from London to Carlisle and therefore it became the obvious choice for the travelling poor. Vagrants, or casuals as they were more commonly called, were dealt with in a different way from the inmate. First, a ticket of admission was obtained from the porters office, in order to gain entrance at 6.00p.m. Clothes were removed and disinfected, a 'luxurious bath' followed. The bathrooms were described as *warmed by steam pipes, commodious, well lit and scrupulously clean.* The casual was then provided with a night-shirt, three quilts and a straw pillow, and then taken to a sleeping cell, lighted by gas. There was also an electric bell in each cell, for emergency use only, as the casual was locked in for the night.

In the 1842, 1,915 casuals passed through the workhouse. By 1849, the number had increased to 2,342. Casuals, whose reputations were associated with crime and disease were hated, and it became necessary to place them as for away as

Overnight cells for vagrants

possible from other inmates. It was ordered by the Board of Guardians on the 17th January 1844 *that the masters of the workhouse do set every able adult person that is relieved in the workhouse in return for food and lodging afforded to perform the following tasks of work.*

Breaking 3½ feet of stone or working at the water pump or mill; women to pick 3¾lbs of oakum provided that such persons shall be detained against their will for the performance of these tasks for any time exceeding four hours from the hour of breakfast.

In 1842 there are reports that have survived in the National Archives of burials of inmates at Stoke Church, when in fact their coffins have been empty except for sawdust. This came to light when the sexton of the church was alerted to the fact that certain coffins were much lighter than others. Upon his insistence the coffin were opened and there was found no body but a coffin rather full of sawdust and wood chippings. Reports were sent the Board of Guardians but even after extensive enquiries were made, there was no answer as to who was responsible and where had the body or bodies had been removed to. It may be assumed that they were used for medical experiments.

On the same subject the following is of interest. After the building of the new parish church in Stoke, there are reports of 'grave snatchers' working at night following quickly after a burial. For a period, guard was kept and then certain burial techniques were employed to deter theft.

The annual report for 1866 paints a savage picture of the conditions within Stoke. The burial ground at Stoke Church was becoming full and a reference was made to the fact that paupers should no longer be buried there but have their own burial ground near to the parish workhouse. The hospital was sadly too full, containing an average of 125 cases a day, twenty more than the previous year.

Although pauperism had decreased from the numbers of 1865, there remained in excess of 6,000, one in 18 in the parish and the evils arising from defective sanitary arrangements, crowding of population, and smoke and the large amount of sickness and mortality the majority of the properties were rated between £4 and £5 p.a. which represented one fifth of the community. Deaths in the parish had exceeded those of births. The overcrowded, inconvenient and unhealthy dwellings led to the explosion of public houses and beer houses, numbered at 528, one for less than forty adults.

Out-door relief for the poor had increased from £4,242, in 1863, to £6,134 two years later, probably as a result of the system whereby paupers had to fetch their provisions from the workhouse being changed, to the provisions being obtained directly from traders in the town by vouchers from the relieving officer. Furthermore, the guardians lost the sum of £1,592 4s 3d when the Longton Old Bank failed. The overseers of the poor collected the sum of £24,835 in revenue during the year of 1865, the majority of which was spent on the maintenance of the poor in the workhouse or those receiving out-door relief.

In 1895, the Board of Guardians met to formalise again the dietary needs of the inmates. A table was subsequently compiled showing the allowance of food in different categories, able bodied, the aged, infirm and imbeciles, children from 2-5 years, 5-9 years and 9-16 years.

The charts prepared show that for able-bodied men, the main meal would consist of 4ozs of cooked meat to be served on a Sunday, Wednesday and Fridays. There were no vegetables. Porridge was to be served four days a week, whilst bread, a variable amount between 5 and 7 oz every other day, was to be served. No more than 2oz of cheese given on four days. For breakfasts, gruel, 1½ pints of it, was the order of the day, every day supplemented by 1 or 1½ oz of bread. Supper consisted mostly of bread and cheese and tea, coffee or broth.

For a child, between the ages of 5 and 9, dinner would consist of 4 oz of meat three days a week, vegetables of 12 oz to be served the same day and bread of 2 oz four days only. For breakfast it would be just bread and milk, and supper bread, 5 oz, supplemented with either milk on three days, or tea or coffee on the other days.

By 1895, the guardians had to consider a completely new vagrants' block together with a porter's lodge by the main entrance to the highway. These were completed in 1899 in the same year as electric lighting was introduced. The cost of this amounted to £6,650 and the electricity provided by its own dynamo.

Casual accommodation was not free, except to those who were too old or too ill to work. Meals were supplied to the casual although only the basic bread and water. For the evening meal on the day of reception, 8 oz of dry bread and water was given. For breakfast it was either 6oz of bread and 1 pint of gruel, or 8oz of bread and water. For dinner, 6oz of bread and 1½oz of cheese were allowed. Under the old system, casuals were only permitted to stay over for one night, and first thing in the morning they were required to break three cwt of stone, to be finished by 9.00 a.m.

Under this system, 15,320 casuals acquired accommodation during the year 1899. From March 1900, the system changed to a more stringent method of earning board and keep. After breakfast, the casual was transferred to another cell, to the rear of his sleeping cell, where ten cwt of stone was to be broken, small enough to fit through a grating. If this work was unsuitable, because of age or ill health, the alternative was to pick 3lbs of oakum. A maximum of two nights' accommodation for one day's labour was the arrangement. For women casuals the task was to pick 2lbs of oakum.

Women picking Oakum

A brief report by Mr R J Dansey, a Local Government Inspector dated the 2nd November 1897, makes grim reading regarding sleeping arrangements. *The workhouse is inadequate as regards to accommodation for able bodied men, twelve of whom were sleeping two in a bed at the date of my visit. The practice of sleeping two in a bed must be stopped. I have called attention to it before and it would be well for the Board now to write to the Guardians and inquire what steps they intend to take in the matter.*

In an attempt to gloss over the reality of workhouse life at the turn of the century a writer for a local newspaper states: *It was the opinion of the Board of guardians that the policy was not too harsh or too great for the food and accommodation offered in return. The system, according to the Board of guardians was flexible, according to the casual's ability. Good behaviour will sometimes lighten the work, but the casual that gives unnecessary trouble need not look for sympathy, for none he deserving.* The report continued: *a direct result of the firm policy of work and reward the number of casuals in 1900 reduced sharply to 1,680.*

A further insight into the workhouse two years later dated July 1899 comes from a report made by the Commissioners for Lunacy. Apart from the workhouse providing accommodation for the destitute, it also provided care for the lunatics of that period. The reports makes interesting reading:

Visiting the workhouse this morning, I found 39 men and 58 women classed as persons of unsound mind. There was also a man and a woman who were not on the list who were under observation under 14 days orders. Of the classes, inmates 11 men and 25 women are epileptic, and 10 and 15 respectively are idiots. The idiots are mingled with the other inmates. It would be more satisfactory if they could be separately lodged and in this connection I am glad to hear that the Guardians contemplate arrangements in conjunction with other local authorities for the provision of separate buildings for idiots.

In addition to the classed inmates and the 2 cases under observation I found in the lunacy wards 11 men and 10 women none of whom are considered to be certifiable cases and who are placed in the wards for want of space elsewhere. None of the classed inmates appeared to require asylum treatment. They all had opportunity of speaking with me and I spoke to all of them and had received no complaint of any kind and only one applied for discharge.

All who are physically able work in various ways and go for weekly walks beyond the workhouse grounds. They are all neatly dressed and tidy; their rooms and bedding were clean, comfortable and in good order. The airing courts have been improved; the centre parts being laid down in turf and kept in good order. The bathing now provided a separate bath for each patient weekly, the workhouse having recently improved its water supply by additional services from the Corporation Works.

The Guardians have decided upon improving the ventilation of the padded rooms and the heating of the visiting rooms in accordance with the suggestions made by Dr. Cooke last year and the work will shortly be taken in hand. Attention is paid to their comfort to the amusement of the inmates, and a fair supply of toys are found for the idiots. The addition of a musical box on each side would, I am sure, add to their few pleasures and of some easy chairs in the day room.

The lunatics and idiots appear to be well cared for and properly treated. According to the records only 1 male since the last visit has been mechanically restrained for 14 hours to prevent staff injury.

Unfortunately the same cannot be said in a report dated the 5th January 1899 regarding the state of sanitation at the workhouse. It refers to several outbreaks of diphtheria and other infectious diseases at the workhouse. In the July and August period of the previous year there were measles, ophthalmia and diphtheria of which seven cases were fatal. This was followed by a second outbreak commenceing in the October where there were 16 cases of diphtheria reported. This was followed by a third outbreak, this time it included the resident medical officer, the Master's son, a woman and 5 boys, two of which died.

This situation was put down to poor sanitation at the workhouse, and subsequently a five page report was submitted by the County Medical Officer, Geo. Reid in March 1899, recommending wholesale changes and improvement to the systems.

It was not until a school report of February 1897 commented on the standard of teaching children at the workhouse that consideration for the first time was given for the use of external schools. The workhouse school consisted of 153 children, of which only 104 sat any form of test. The test concluded that only 34 had passed standard 1 for reading, 36 for writing, and 36 for arithmetic. For religious knowledge, 'very fair' was the comment. In July the same year, it was proposed by the guardians to educate the children within the School Board of Stoke-upon-Trent at Penkhull and Stoke. The school board wrote to the Local Government Board asking if they would pay at a reduced cost for the education of the children attending these schools.

Chapel

No particular form of religion was forced upon the inmates. Roman Catholics were allowed to attend the local church. Dissenters were allowed to hold worship in the workhouse chapel each Sunday morning. The chapel (still remaining) was built in 1886, to the design of Charles Lynam providing seating for 400 and catering for the segregation of the sexes which prevailed within the workhouse system. There were separate entrances for male and female and a small gallery, probably reserved for staff. The chapel was run by the Church of England, who held services there on Sunday afternoons and Wednesday evenings. By 1900, Rev J Edwards was the paid chaplin to the workhouse.

In 1900, the local Guardians of the Poor decided to adopt the new method of accommodating pauper children and pursued the policy of 'cottage home' separation. Until 1901, children were accommodated at The Spittals workhouse along with their parents, a situation considered unhealthy

The Chapel built 1866 designed by Charles Lynam

for young children. In December that year new accommodation for children and for babies once weaned, was to become a new style of separate houses (cottages) each with their own foster mother. A separate chapter covers the history of Penkhull Cottage Homes.

By 1902, it was decided to demolish parts of the 1842 workhouse, and in its place erect a new dining hall, capable of seating 500 inmates, kitchen, storerooms, bake house, mess room, offices and a new master's house. The total expenditure was estimated at £27,000. Unfortunately, despite best intentions, these plans did not materialise. There were recorded in this year in excess of one thousand inmates, of whom 426 were over sixty years of age and unable to perform any work. The rest of the inmates, except the sick, had work given to them each day and speaking generally, they got through their duties in a happy and contented manner. Four meals a day were provided.

A writer in 1902 continues in an attempt to present the human side to life in the workhouse: *No intoxicating drinks are allowed, excepting when specially advised by the medical officer. The old men, by the kindly consideration of the Guardians are given 1oz of tobacco each week, and in lieu of these old women get 2oz of tea and 8oz of sugar extra each week. The question of entertainment is not overlooked, for nine concerts are given during the winter months. In addition to this, the Institution is provided with several different musical instruments, including a phonograph and a gramophone.*

The miners' strike promoted serious consequences in the pottery towns of 1912. Hunger and starvation shadowed the marchers, and every street in the city would bear the cost of no work, no money. The Board of Guardians realised the consequences of such, the demand for both out relief and the need for accommodation in the workhouse could be overwhelming.

On the 27th March 1912, a special meeting was held to consider what measures could be put into place for the relief of distress arising out of the industrial trouble. As a result instructions were given to each relieving officer to communicate with the Divisional Secretaries of the Mayor's Distress Fund, with a view to co-operation and prevention of overlapping the work of the relieving the prevailing distress within the union. At this meeting, a letter was circulated from the Local Government Board, Whitehall regarding the action that should be taken with regards to the shortages of coal and its supply due to the dispute in the coal trade and the consequent stoppages of work in various industries.

As a result, an action plan was devised based upon the communication from London.

The superintendent relieving officer reported that since the commencement of the strike, he had been in daily consultation with the relieving officer as to the condition of affairs in their respective districts, and had ascertained what was being done by the Distress Committee in towns to alleviate distress. Application for medical assistance were dealt with by the Relieving Officers, and applications for assistance from able-bodied men by the Distress Fund.

Coal Strike 1912. Minors and families pick for coal on an open slag heap.

In addition to the relief afforded by the Mayor's Fund, the Distress Committee had issued notices that they were prepared to provide work for a number of men, and the committee were of the opinion that it was not at present necessary for the Guardians to take any special action. In the event, however, of a continuance of the strike for much longer period, these agencies would probably be unable to cope with all the applications, and it would then be incumbent upon the Guardians to act. It was decided that out relief should be earned through work and not doled out. If the situation got worse, permission would be granted to modify the Workhouse Test, a Labour test, or either or both of them. In this event the following was recommended.

As a result, a Labour yard would be established at the workhouse, and the following tasks of work to be prescribed: *Every male person shall perform on each of the days on which he is set to work (not ordinarily being less than five days in each week in respect of which relief is given) the following task of work, that is to say: Excavations for the construction of a water storage tank or removing a large mound of soil to a tip and levelling, or sawing and chopping wood.*
Provided that the full amount of work shall not be required from any person to whose age, strength, and capacity, it shall not appear to be suited. Hours of attendance, 8 a.m. to 5 p.m. with an interval of one hour for dinner, men residing more than two miles from the workhouse to be allowed 20 minutes per mile for walking time to the labour yard. Saturday 8a.m. – 12 noon.
Scale of relief to be as follows, with dinner daily in each case and an extra day's allowance on Saturdays to those who have worked for five days during the week, half the amount to be given in money and half in kind.

Class 1. Man and wife, or man, wife and 1 dependent child 1/4d per day
Class 2. Man and wife and 2 children 1/6d per day
Class 3. Man and wife and 3 children 1/8d per day
Class 4. Man and wife and 4 children 1/10d per day
Class 5. Man and wife and 5 children or more 2/- per day

Tickets for provisions and money to be distributed daily. Single men to be excluded.
Men who do not attend the labour yard for at least three days in anyone week, not to be again admitted without a fresh order from the relieving officer.
Applications for admission to the labour yard from old men unlikely to obtain work, and from other men unable to obtain work through physical defects, to be treated by the relieving officer as ordinary applications for relief. No admission order to be given in any case in which the income at the home of the applicant is sufficient for the support of all its occupants without relief of any kind.
Any man who wilfully refuses or neglects to work whilst employed at the Labour Yard will be liable to be proceeded against under the Vagrancy Act. Relieving officers to be authorised to give orders for the Labour Yard, and to report to his committee for confirmation each week.

In 1914, following the Miners' strike of 1912, new regulations were brought in for The Spittals workhouse covering the area of admission, bathing and feeding and the keeping of regular hours.

Regulations relating to the admission and searching of inmates

Every person on admission to the Institution shall be searched by the officer appointed for the purpose providing that a male shall only be searched by a male Officer and a female only by an officer of that sex.
Any articles prohibited by the regulation of the Guardians shall be taken from the inmate, and disposed of in accordance with those regulations.
Any articles of value found upon the inmate shall at once be deposited with the Master for safe custody. Every inmate admitted shall be informed that any money or value security in his possession will, if the Guardians so direct, be taken for his maintenance in the institution.
A careful record of the clothes and articles taken from the inmate shall be made and entered in the 'Inmates Property Register', and the entry in respect of each inmate shall, when completed, be read over to him.
The following articles are prohibited from being brought into the institution and if found in the possession of an inmate will be immediately confiscated: cards or dice, letters, cards, articles or written or printed matter of an obscene or improper character. Matches or other combustible articles. Spirituous or fermented liquors, or any drug or poisonous matter.

Regulations regarding bathing of inmates. *Every inmate shall be bathed on admission to the institution unless the medical officer gives direction to the contrary. Except in cases which the medical officer considers that it is undesirable, every inmate shall be bathed at least as frequently as once a week.*

No inmate shall be bathed except under the direct supervision of an officer of the same sex, excepting that children of either sex, under the care of female officers, may be bathed under the supervision of such officers.

A bath for each inmate shall be prepared as follows: The cold water shall be turned on first, and the water shall be thoroughly mixed. The temperature shall then be taken and no inmate shall be bathed in water of less than 88 Fahrenheit and no more than 98. No additional water, hot or cold, must be added while the inmate is in the bath. In case of a thermometer being inefficient from injury etc., all bathing operations shall be suspended until another is obtained.

The inmate is to be well cleansed with soap. The head of the inmate shall not be held under water. A clean towel must be provided for each inmate and the bath towels must always be washed before being used again. Fresh water must be used for each inmate.

The keys of the hot water taps where provided, shall on no account be let out of the possession of the officers. They shall not be used by the inmates and shall not be allowed to remain on the taps.

Regulations regarding hours and places of meals and work,

and the hours of rising and going to bed. *Meals shall be taken in the dining hall by all the inmates except the sick, the children and infants, persons of unsound mind, persons too infirm, inmates of the Receiving Wards or Vagrant Wards, and save and excepting any other class of inmates in respect of whom the guardians by resolution otherwise direct.*

Hours of Rising Etc.

Rise	Breakfast	Work	Dinner	Work	Supper	Bedtime
April to September						
5:45	6:30-7	7-12	12-1	1-6	6-6:30	8
October to March						
6:45	7:30-8	8-12	12-1	1-6	6-6:30	8

The male inmates shall be employed in such places and at such work as the master or the labour master may direct, and the female inmates in accordance with the directions of the matron or labour mistress.

Only the necessary work shall be performed by inmates on Sunday, Good Friday and Christmas Day. An inmate who is pregnant or recently confined or suckling an infant, shall only be employed at such work and for such hours as the medical officer may approve.

An inmate who shall refuse or neglect to work after being required to do so, shall be deemed disorderly and may be punished accordingly.

By 1920 the days of the workhouse system were numbered. The use of the site by this time was combined between the case of several hundred sick patients and even more still retained under the system of care in the workhouse. The Board of Guardians still had a duty to care for the destitute, and the punitive attitude originally urged on the guardians towards the 'idle' poor was increasingly regarded as inappropriate when applied to orphans, the ill and the elderly. The official title of workhouses by this time had almost disappeared as some time they had been called 'Poor Law Institutions'. The Spittals finally become known as The London Road Hospital or the Union Hospital in London Road before it was taken over by the City Council in 1929. From this date it was known as The City General Hospital, now the University Hospital of North Staffordshire.

Dates of Original and Additional Buildings

1832 Main block
1842 School house
1842 Parish hospital
1842 Vagrants wards and porters lodge
1866 School block
1866 Chapel
1875 Hospital
1884 Hospital
1894 Female imbecile wards
1894 Male imbecile wards
1899 Male vagrants block
1899 Female vagrants block
1890s Farm buildings and farmer's cottage
1900 Cottage Homes for Children
1902 Laundry
1902 Nurses' home
c1907 Fire Station, bakery, administration block, wood chopping room
1910 Corn mill
1913 Children's hospital
1924 Additional homes, Cottage Homes
1929 Taken over as The City General Hospital

Chapter 20
Penkhull Cottage Homes.

The concept of a 'cottage home' type accommodation for children was the brainchild of Jane Senior who produced a report on the treatment of pauper girls in London. Her report submitted at the request of the president of the Local Government Board dated 1873, was a landmark in the history of official policy in favour of small cottage homes.

She was the first woman in Whitehall and in January 1873 was appointed as a poor law inspector, tasked by the president of the Local Government Board, Sir James Stansfeld, *to visit and inspect Workhouses, and District Schools for inquiring into the operation and influence of the present system of education in those establishments upon pauper girls.*

She was asked, as a woman, to report on the effect of poor law education on girls. Senior took advice from Florence Nightingale on how to compile a statistical analysis of the information she gathered. She used a team of women investigators to try to trace the current whereabouts of over 600 girls who had left pauper schools the previous year. Stansfeld accepted her report and in January 1874, her first action as a permanent civil servant was to try to stop the corporal punishment of female pauper children.

Until this report and for many years after, children admitted as paupers to the workhouse and babies born whilst their mothers were interned, were accommodated in separate buildings from adults. They were educated within the institution and all their needs, which were then considered few, catered for by the workhouse system. They were not allowed contact with their parents.

Senior's advocacy of Cottage Homes, alongside other policies such as boarding-out should be seen in the context of the growing strength of the campaign for the *family system,* that of parents and children living together. This was something the Poor Law Act of 1834 failed both to recognise but actively worked against, during the 1860s and 1870s, which in the end would only encourage more families to seek care from the parish. In 1878, another official report was issued promoting the adoption of the home or cottage system of training for pauper children. Between the years 1870 and 1914, nearly two hundred such homes were authorized to be built by local guardians of the poor countrywide.

At the same time, others were raising the issue of the neglect and mistreatment of children. Although England during the 19th century was experiencing considerable growth as the industrial revolution evolved almost unstoppably, it was often at the expense of the poorer classes and - even worse - of the exploitation of children.

Few, if any, were aware of the cruelty inflicted upon children and the dreadful conditions in which they lived and worked. The state in all the Potteries towns was no different from any northern industrial town. Locally, Charles Shaw's autobiography, *When I Was a Child,* compiled as a series for the Staffordshire Sentinel in 1892, illustrates a number of these characteristics. He talks of harsh punishment both by his employer and within the parish workhouse, where discipline was merciless and administered with unfailing regularity. On a national scale, Charles Dickens wrote *Oliver Twist,* which like Shaw's book, describes the appalling conditions of the time, where boys dependent on the parish could be sold into hard labour.

In addition to the progress being made by Jane Senior, Hesba Stretton wrote to *The Times* in January 1884 bringing to the attention of its readers: *Few people have any idea of the extent of active cruelty, and still more of the extent of neglect towards children among our degraded and criminal classes.* In the same year the London Society for the Prevention of Cruelty to Children was founded by Benjamin Waugh. After five years of campaigning by the London SPCC, Parliament passed in 1889 the first ever UK law to protect children from abuse and neglect. In 1889 The London SPCC was renamed the National Society for the Prevention of Cruelty to Children.

Although the conditions of the Poor Law Amendment Act were pressed hard at the workhouse, there was encouragement to make separate and less hard provision for pauper children. One reader of the North Staffs. Mercury wrote: *the homes are a very acceptable alternative to the "barracks" system where the children are reared in one large building and where, however careful, the authority may be to prevent the children from becoming pauperised, whether by the use of uniform clothing or the atmosphere of barracks life, a certain taint frequently managed to creep in.*

It is from this background of public awareness and concern, that in 1899, the local Guardians of the Poor decided to adopt the new method of accommodating pauper children and pursued the policy of cottage home separation. Records from those early days have survived both locally and nationally. The minute books for the Spittals Workhouse remain in the city archives, whilst other records for the poor up to 1900 are stored in the National Archives at Kew. Records after that date were sadly destroyed by the blitz during the Second World War

The first notice of the intended Cottage Homes appears in a letter dated 17th March 1899 from the Local Board to the Board of Guardians in London enclosing an outline of the proposals. The proposals, which were yet to be finalised, cost £7,500 in addition to the building of a Muster Hall at £950. The work was to be carried out by means of a Government loan. There were to be twelve cottages in six semi-detached blocks designed to house twelve children in each. There was also proposed the Muster Hall, measuring 60 feet x 20 feet, two classrooms, and accommodation for the superintendent. The cottages, it was stated, were well designed and of a substantial character each with a day room, living room, sitting room, lavatory on the first floor and outside w.c. There were also two large bedrooms, a mother's room and a spare bedroom. A receiving house with similar accommodation was also to be built. The architect appointed was Mr Charles Lynam of Penkhull.

The first known photograph of Penkhull Cottage Home c1912. A cottage family

Comments from Whitehall, who had the last word on all things, stated that the plans were generally satisfactory but the kitchens and living rooms should be larger, and that a door linking the two sides of a cottage block be provided on the first floor in case of an emergency. Correspondence continued. A letter from the Stoke-upon-Trent Union to London, dated the 23rd May, enclosed a further set of outline plans accommodating the suggestions made previously to include bedrooms of equal size, sinks and baths upstairs and a washhouse for the use of the combined homes. The response from London was favourable, although comments regarding the low cost of the project were made; Mr Lynam assured them that the costs were correct. A loan over a period of 30 years was suggested.

By July 1899, the plans were completed and submitted for final approval by the Local Government Board at Whitehall. Once outline approval had been authorised, a meeting was called of the local guardians on the 8th November 1899 to confirm the arrangements for the building of the Cottage Homes. Also to be built at the same time were farm buildings, adjacent to the workhouse, and a new boiler house for the Spittals, to which the Local Government Board had affixed their seal. The total expenditure on these items would not exceed £12,000. Agreement was confirmed to the borrowing of the funds required. The financial statement produced to the board showed that, since 1875, they had borrowed a total of £33,142, of which £28,402 remained outstanding. This was in addition to this further loan of £12,000 for the new projects.

Additional land purchased in 1907

A letter from the Local Government Board dated the 7th December 1899, confirmed that building work could commence. At this time, there was no Hilton Road, only fields with little to separate the new cottage homes from the Spittals Workhouse, a few hundred metres to the southwest of the proposed site. A suitable site was found on land already in the ownership of the Guardians, just off Newcastle Lane purchased from Miss Elizabeth Coombe in 1880. An additional plot was purchased from the same person in 1900 for the sum of £1,008 11 6d situated to the east of Grindley Hill Farm.

Grindley Hill farm was still owned by Sir Thomas Boughey, and during the building of the new homes, part of the field belonging to the farm had to be fenced off and an agreement made with Sir Thomas to erect a fence for which Sir Thomas made a charge of 1/- for each fence post erected. By 1911, the Board of Guardians had purchased the farm as they discussed the desirability of giving notice for the farmer to quit the farm so that the land could be used as a recreation field adjacent to the new homes.

An additional parcel of copyhold land was purchased by the guardians between the children's home and the Spittals Workhouse in 1907, and the following year was the subject of a freehold grant by the Duchy of Lancaster, in consideration of a one off payment of £116 16 0d.

Even at this early stage of development for the Children's Homes, an eye was focused to the future and the acquisition of additional adjacent land. The following year a substantial amount of land consisting of more than 22 acres was purchased from the trustees of the late Frederick Bishop, formerly of The Mount for the sum of £4,000. This land included the site of the present St. Peter's High School, which was then occupied by Franklands Farm. As a result, the Board of Guardians became its landlord with responsibilities. On the 5th July 1903, the board met to discuss a request from Mr Henry Gifford, the farmer, regarding certain repairs that needed to be made to the buildings. The farm was recorded as being *adjoining the cottage homes and belonging to the Guardians.* The issue was referred to Mr Miller for a report and to the building committee for action.

It was in 1903 that the guardians sold a section of this land to Stoke Borough for an extension of the cemetery at Hartshill at a cost of £250 per acre. Sadly, the transfer of the copyhold land did not conform to the legal requirements of the Duchy of Lancaster. Therefore, in February 1904, steps were taken to obtain the enfranchisement of the lands from the Duchy and have the transaction entered upon the Manor Court Rolls.

The minutes contain just a few references to the building arrangements. That new gates to the avenue would be fitted at a cost of £55 supplied from George Cotton, of Holmes Chapel, and that the walls of the cottages and the Muster Hall would be painted with coloured distemper. Contractors appointed were Samuel Peake of Stoke. The cost of furnishing the new cottages amounted to £2,912.

Arrangements for the transfer of children from the Spittals Workhouse to the new homes were put in hand. The boys were to be transferred on the 6th November 1904, and the girls shortly afterwards.

The system in the new cottage homes was that the children were boarded in large detached houses, each with its own foster mother, which, it was claimed, would enhance the happiness of ordinary family life. There had, it was reported at the opening ceremony, been considerable criticism of the expenditure to the ratepayers. The guardians proceeded with their plan as it was thought that the results would give children a far greater chance in life. Here children would be able to dress as other children did, and attend local Board schools in the village of Penkhull and Stoke. There were now twelve homes, a muster hall and a house for the superintendent, Mr Till, whose wife was the matron. By the time of the opening, each house was full with 140 resident children.

New boots, shoes, and clothes were to be purchased for the children ready for the grand opening. Boots and shoes were obtained from Wallace Bros, of Newcastle at a cost of £97 5 10d and the purchase of boys clothing amounted to £85 5 10d from Staffordshire Tailoring Company, of Hanley. Six women were to be employed one day a week to take care of all the washing at a wage of 2s a day.

The object of the cottage homes was to provide, as near as possible, a family life for each child with a house mother, then much later on in the 60s a father. The father would go out to work as normal, but the duty of the housemother was to care and provide for the children. Each mother ran independently, and as a result, there were no two cottages that were run the same. From the opening of the Homes, it

was decided that older children should have regular daily duties to perform. Furnishings were basic with few soft furnishings until after the Second World War when more modern and comfortable beds were purchased.

The need for foster mothers for the new homes can be identified by advertisements and recruitment. By September, the following staff had been appointed at an annual salary of £20 rising by annual increments of £2 to a maximum of £30, with uniform and rations provided: Lydia Yearsley, aged 28; Eliza Brookes, aged 25; Edith Green, aged 25; Clara Wharton, aged 25; Elizabeth Ellen, aged 29; Alice Collister, aged 33; Emily Davies, aged 33; Agnes Walsh, aged 26; Rose Roman, aged 29; Mary Davies, aged 29; Mary Cordall, aged 39 and Laura Price, aged 28.

Penkhull Cottage Homes were formally opened on Friday, 19th December 1901, by the Right Hon. Henry Chaplin., M.P.

The press report reads: *the children parade under the leadership of Superintendent Till, to meet the gathered company, the boys in blue cloth caps and neat dark suits, which had nothing of the "old workhouse garb" appearance. The girls wore spotless white pinafores, frocks of different colours and tams of light blue and red wool. The children looked remarkably healthy and what is equally important, they looked decidedly happy. The snow on the ground showed them up well and the invigorating atmosphere gave their cheeks a decisively warm glow. A foster mother was to be run each cottage home.*

Boys are recorded at the Penkhull Senior School as having time off for the transfer from the workhouse to the new Cottage Homes.

November 6th 1901

All Newcastle Boys away this afternoon: being transferred from Union to newly erected Cottage Homes.

At the time of the opening, the accommodation at the homes was full, and this was a situation that continued to cause concern to the Board of Guardians.

January 1902	77 boys, 69 girls	Total 144
April 1903	88 boys, 72 girls	Total 160
August 1903	93 boys, 65 girls	Total 158
January 1904	90 boys, 87 girls	Total 177
February 1904	97 boys, 85 girls	Total 182
March 1904	99 boys, 84 girls	Total 183
April 1904	93 boys, 72 girls	Total 165
March 1925		Total 240
December 1939		Total 205
July 1947	119 boys, 75 girls	Total 194

Visiting was only allowed on the first Saturday of the month, between the hours of 3pm. and 5pm.

It was to these children's homes that all babies over the age of one year were sent. Under the rules of the homes, natural mothers were only allowed to visit once a week.

The grouped house system of cottage homes was not without its critics who recommended several alternatives, including *scattered* houses dispersed amongst ordinary residential districts, and boarding the children out in ordinary working-class homes to be grafted into *normal* families. This last suggestion had been carried out for many years under the old workhouse system and the National Archives hold much correspondence on this matter. Even with the new homes providing accommodation for around 150 children, the need continued for additional spaces, as demand exceeded available beds. In 1902, it was reported that bedrooms designed for six children were accommodating up to nine, and the dining tables were inadequate for the number of children to dine together. In October of the following year, the situation became so bad that to relieve the situation, a number of orphaned and deserted children, as a special measure, were sent to *certified* homes.

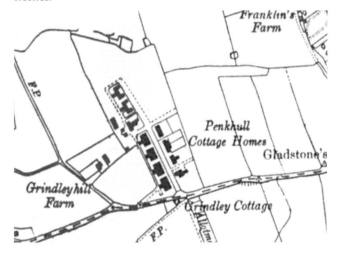

Under this new, and at the time, progressive way of caring for children, many other unions were unable to provide anything comparable. So much so, that Unions in Stafford, Stone and Leek sent children to Penkhull. In 1902, a charge of 3s a week was paid for the care of a child housed at Penkhull but later the same year a charge of 2/6d per week was charged for the maintenance of Jane Billingham from the Leek Union. It may be that she was an older child and therefore a larger fee was charged.

It would appear, for whatever reason, this was a two-way process, and the Stoke Union was sending children to other places. For bad behaviour, George Alcock, in July 1902, was sent to the Certified Industrial School at Standon Bridge. In April 1903 two boys, Walter Jones and William Bagnall, were transferred to Dr Barnardos in London whilst a further

three boys were sent to St. Paul's Home for boys at Coleshill. In May 1911, the guardians received a note that the weekly charges had been increased from 5/- a week to 5/6d per week for boys held in the Stratford-upon-Avon Industrious School. These industrial schools were almost the same as the modern day borstal, designed and administered specifically for children with behavioural problems. Their objects were *Custody and detention with a view to their education, industrial training and moral reclamation of such boy as lawfully committed.* Corporal punishment would be a part of their moral reclamation.

With the passing of years, the system continued. In December 1922, the Children's Aid Society from the Gordon Memorial Home at Nottingham, a home for destitute children, wrote asking for the removal of a boy because of his continued misbehaviour and bad habits. Again, in 1924, four boys were transferred to Father Hudson's Home at Birmingham, and other boys sent to a training camp.

From the outset of the Cottage Homes some children were placed into places of work, fostered, or accommodated with families. In July 1901, an application was made from Mr James Fox, a farmer from Longton, applying for Arthur Lycett, a boy of 15 years, to be a farm apprentice. It was agreed that he should be sent for a month's trial. In February 1904 the numbers increased, Joseph Cartwright, aged 14 years, was also sent for a month's trial to work for Mr William Crewe, a tailor of Hanley, with a view of being apprenticed, and the same month Robert Stattham, aged 4 years, was boarded out with a Mrs Rigby of Holly Place, Fenton, just to name a few.

For girls, the only future before them was *in service,* and in reality; this was the same for the vast majority of girls from working class backgrounds. In August 1903, Ellen Philips was sent to a Servants Training School at the convent of the Holy Child Jesus at St Leonard's on Sea. Many other girls followed over the years. Mother Superior of the Convent in December 1922 wrote about three girls, Mary, Elsie and Kate all in training. It was agreed by the committee: *that in accordance with the request of the Mother Superior that the three girls are returned to Penkhull immediately.* No reasons were given. Why so many girls were sent such a distance and into a very strict Catholic setting can only be guessed at, as other girls were sent to the Girls' Training Home at Shelton.

The sending of children to be placed into care elsewhere was standard practice for the time. Once a child was adopted by the Board of Guardians under the 1899 Act, they came under the jurisdiction and authority of the board until they were 18, and had to do their bidding. Hundreds of children were taken into Penkhull Cottage Homes each year on this basis as orphans, or from parents that were either incapable of looking after their children, mostly because of abject poverty, unemployment, family breakdowns, death, or in many cases the parents just did not care. For example, for one month, in 1911, 63 children were deserted by their parents, just left at the door of the receiving officer, and a further 10 were admitted, as their parents were deemed unfit to care for them. These figures are not unusual or out of keeping with the general patterns of admissions at that time.

Emigration.

For probably hundreds of boys and girls over the life-span of the Cottage Homes, a new life abroad was to be their future. It is only now that representations are being made nationally with regard to this policy for dealing with unwanted children. The first reference found in the National Archives precedes the opening of the Cottage Homes and confirms the practice of emigration of children from a much earlier date than first thought.

The report is dated July 1897, and was obtained by the guardians of the poor through the Colonial Office. It contains reports submitted by the Canadian Immigration Officers regarding the settlement of paupers. For 18 children it details their occupations, education, church-going, work, and states who they are living with.

The first recorded is Peter Bolderstone, aged 12, who was placed with William Gordon at Cushendall P.O. (Province of Ontario). It was a farm. Peter was reported *as working about the house and farm, in good health, attends church and for three months in the year attends school. He was of good character, received board and clothing but no wages.* Peter had a younger brother, Joseph, aged 10. He was placed with Mr J. Boyd of Mountain View P.O. also a farmer. The report was similar to that of Peter, with the exception *that he did not yet attend school and told lies.*

Most of the boys were between the ages of 12-14 years. The eldest was Richard Myatt, aged 17, who was placed with Mr Lucius Reed, of Corleyville P.O. He was a farmer. Richard was *settled into a comfortable home, employed around the farm and house, in good health, attended church and school, of good character, and paid £4 a month during the summer.* Henry Mallard, aged 14, was paid the sum of £25 per annum and placed with a farmer Mr J.S. Sutton of Shannonville P.O. The report confirmed that *he was in a comfortable home, working on the farm, in good health but had a bad habit of chasing sheep and must be closely watched to keep him at work.*

The report contained the names of seven girls, the youngest being 11, the eldest being 15 years. Charlotte Barlow was aged 12, and placed with Mr William Oke of Harloch P.O. It was reported *that she was employed in light housework, in good health, attended church and Sunday school, of good character with the exception of being untruthful.* She would

receive free board and clothing until 15 years, followed by wage of £3 per month until 17, when the sum was increased to £4 per month, until the age of 18. In an attempt to understand the circumstances of these children, the 1881 census has been used. Charlotte was born at No.1 Crown Passage, Fenton. Her mother was widowed by the age of 33 and left with six children to care for. Unable to cope, she faced the stark choice of either to enter the workhouse or starve to death. No doubt, all of these children in this report come from circumstances very similar, if not worse. There was only one from the 18, which had been adopted; Emily Harrison, aged 11, who went to live with Mrs R Miller, Harrisburg P.O.

The first record of emigration for Penkhull Cottage Homes is dated 1911 when Dorothy Philips and Minnie Leek, both aged 14, left for a new life in Canada under a scheme organised by the Catholic Emigration Society. Vast numbers of such organisations were set up from the turn of the century to deal with the emigration of paupers or orphans. The Canada connection came from a visit to that country by Fr Banns and Mr Chilton Thomas from the Liverpool Homes of Rescue and their conclusion was that Canada was the most inviting field of emigration in the world for Catholic children. Other children followed later that year. One case is recorded, - that of PH, - a boy, aged 15, who in December 1911 was sent to Canada. In February 1912, it was reported to the Board of Guardians in Penkhull that a letter had been received from the organisation dated September 1911, that PH had absconded from his home in Cedarville, Ontario and his present whereabouts were not known. One can only guess at the circumstances.

Despite this, and the possible implications of poor treatment of the boy, in the following June, it was agreed to send two further deserted children to Canada; JM, aged 13 and FM, aged 12. The board agreed to cover the cost of transport for the two boys amounting to £33 9 3d. The meeting agreed that they were to be sent immediately. A further case recorded in 1923 of WB, a boy aged 12, whose new address in Canada was submitted to the Board of Guardians. So too was a letter referring to AB, a boy aged 15, on how well he was doing.

The Church Army, a branch of the Anglican Church also ran a scheme whereby boys were sent from Penkhull Cottage Homes from the early 1920s to Wallingford Farm Training Colony or similar institutions, to learn a trade, before being sent to Australia

In the days before child guidance clinics, when the name of Freud had an unsavoury connotation in the minds of respectable people, there was a remarkable man called William Henry Hunt, who was in charge of Wallingford camp for, what used to be called, maladjusted youths. The colony at one point housed up to 250 rejects of the Poor Law system. Hunt learnt that harsh physical discipline was derived from fear and that aggression only produced aggression; that the strong-arm methods of many of the staff in children's homes only led from violence to violence which was seldom more than a transitory deterrent, if that, and not a cure. Hunt, in some ways, appeared to form a bridge between the care and the work of nineteenth-century precursors. His colony might well be considered a forerunner of the rehabilitation centre, were it not for the fact that about three quarters of its inmates were adolescents. Hunt organized the boys in squads of eight or nine, each with an elder 'brother' who shared their life work and was responsible for their well-being. He always insisted that the 'brother' should be the 'stroke oar' of his squad, but that his primary duty was to love his charges.

Further boys were dispatched to the colony, a charge being made to the guardians of 25s a week for their board. The records provide evidence that many boys still went through this system of emigration until the after the First World War. In 1925, H.A. a young boy had to undergo a medical examination before being sent to Queensland. The passage for him was £22, plus a £2 landing fee. He also required a new set of clothes costing a further £8 of which the Church Army agreed to contribute £3. The sad part was that the boy was to first return to Penkhull to visit his blind mother at the Spittals Workhouse to say his goodbye. It is doubtful if he ever saw her again. The guardians continued to *process* children through the Church Army Farm Colony for many years, as it did with the Catholic Emigration society. The Church Army continued to receive children from Penkhull for emigration to the dominions until at least March 1944, by which time the charges had been increased to 29/9d per week. Records show that boys were still being sent to the training farm up to 1948.

However, this treatment of the young did not end here, there was even a worse alternative for many boys, that of going to sea. The first account is dated 6th November 1912 when the Master of the training ship *Clio*, reported that two boys, Martin and Lee, who had been chargeable to the Union, had been discharged and placed in berths on the liners Canada and Merion. The governors' approved this action.

The *Clio* training ship was moored off Bangor, North Wales, and was lent by the Admiralty, from 1822, to provide accommodation for 260 boys of all religious backgrounds. Boys typically joined ship at the age of 11 or 12, and stayed until they were around the age of 15 years. Discipline would be harsh and strict, boys often being birched to enforce it. Food was limited in quantity and variety, biscuit, potatoes and meat with occasional green vegetables. By the 1920s the training ship Exmouth was used by the guardians to send

boys for training as future sailors. It was to these ships that many boys from Penkhull Cottage Homes were sent. Others were sent to the Lancaster National Sea Training home at Wallasey from the late 1920s and the National Nautical School at Bristol. Records show that boys were still being sent for sea training in April 1939 at Wallasey, as the guardians were charged £36 8s for each boy per annum until the late 1930s. A number of boys opted to join the army from the age of 14 years.

Training ship Clio

Training ship Exmouth

Serious overcrowding of the Cottage Homes became an ever-increasing problem. Unemployment and poverty experienced in the pottery towns following the end of the First World War created unprecedented pressure on both staff and guardians. In 1922, it was reported that there were 202 children between the ages of 3-16, and 12 children under the age of 3, all resident at the Cottage Homes, which were only designed for around 140. The problem boiled over into 1923, when in March it was ordered that all efforts should be made to alleviate the overcrowding by boarding out, and that every effort be made to obtain suitable homes in which a number of orphans and deserted children could be housed.

It was at the same time in March 1923 that consideration was given to the extension of the Cottage Homes. By September, Messrs Ball and Sons of Stoke had received the contract and work had commenced. By early 1924 the architect reported that painting work was being undertaken, and that new cooking ranges, four feet high by the name of 'Harold', had been agreed upon for fitting in the kitchens; and that Mr George Fleet of Stoke had the contract for fixing the linoleum for £4 1s 6d for each new cottage.

Progression was slow and despite the architect pressing for a hand-over date in November the matter remained unresolved until in January 1925, when at last the Ministry of Health visited the homes for final approval suggesting changes to the bathrooms before children could be accommodated. The new cottages were soon filled from the scattered homes, and Basford Hall, where accommodation had been provided for a number of years to remove some of the pressures at Penkhull.

The Outside Impression

Unfortunately, the local perception of Penkhull Cottage Homes was that it was full of naughty children. The image projected was that those children living at the home were not there because of social deprivation, but were there because they were bad and that they had ended up there because of something they did. This led to low esteem and under achievement by many of the 'inmates', a sad word to use for young children but that is exactly how they were recorded. Many felt that they were guilty of something, and overall they were quite badly treated almost as if the Cottage Homes were a Borstal institution.

The impression that Penkhull Cottage Homes was a place that bad children would be sent to was a general view of most within the Potteries' towns. Children were brought up in fear of the threat of being sent to the Cottage Homes unless they behaved and did as they were told. The vast majority did not understand anything about it, or even where Penkhull was. The only thing they knew was that, no matter how bad things were in their home life, a period in the Homes would be far worse.

The minute books and admission books have survived and are located in Hanley Archives and come under the 100-year rule for access and confidentiality of names, therefore special permission has been obtained to view these minutes. Unfortunately they are not like school log books, which tend to recall the daily events of a school life, these in turn contain much about administration, staffing, buildings and about children being boarded out, and the general running of the home. From 1948, the Children's Committee of the local authority administered the Homes.

The object here is not to name and shame, but to provide a permanent record of the life of the many children who passed through the care system of the time. To obtain the truth, past inmates and staff were sought and interviewed sharing their good and bad experiences and names of the foster mothers. It was felt that no benefit would be gained by sharing names because there is no other evidence available to substantiate or otherwise check what has been freely said. There is no reason whatsoever to doubt any of the evidence given. It is taken as a true account of life in the home.

Inmate's recollections

The compilation of this chapter has been long and difficult. It has taken several months of research locally and at the National Archives in London. Seeking out and interviewing children who were taken into care and house parents has taken its toll and in some cases was quite disturbing.

The vacated St. Christophers Avenue waiting for a decision on its future following its closure.

All came forward as volunteers to share their story and experiences so a permanent record is made before memories fade and the former residents pass away. Most were local and the majority were elderly but none the less willing to contribute. For all but one they were resident from just before the Second World War when there was just a house mother in charge. From the sixties, married couples were encouraged.

The methodology used was simple. As expected, much of what was recorded was identical such as diet, school, daily routine and clothing of which little if anything would have been achieved by quoting each statement of repetitive information. These have been summarised by broad statements under various subject headings, but where experiences differ from each of the interviewees, these have been credited to that person and listed as an example of one experience or memory alongside that of another. Not one had any suggestion of an answer placed before them. All agreed to have their names attributed to answers. Some of those interviewed found it difficult to share in the first instance, but all found that inner confidence to do so, because of the knowledge that it could help the healing process of the time spent at Penkhull Homes. One or two felt the need for the interview to take place in the company of a husband or wife so they would also have an opportunity to learn for the first time of their partners' childhood experience. Others found it exciting to share of the care they received by the foster mother's, but others still carry the emotional scars of their childhood experience to this day.

The archives at Hanley hold the minute books for the Poor Law administration at the Spittals Workhouse. From 1901, a section within the minutes is devoted to matters relating to Penkhull Cottage Homes each month. Some are general comments over administration or staffing, some are of social interest. From the mid 1950s, the minutes contained little of any use to the social historian. As previously stated, all come under the 100 year Confidentiality Act. The same restrictions apply to information obtained from the National Archives.

Regarding the interviews that have taken place, all have agreed that their names can be acknowledged with their comments. Where the names of staff are recalled in connection with punishment, the decision has been made not to include these because of any possible future legal action except one where the contributor insisted.

As stated before much of the material from interviewees is by its nature describing events repetitive such as holidays, Christmas or activities, so these comments have been included together and not attributed to individual people. They are found under the various sub-headings. Identification is used for personal reflections on the circumstances of being in the workhouse and the treatment

received, no matter whether good or bad. These comments cannot be verified or otherwise.

New admissions

Children entering the home came from varying circumstances, all tragic. Most were unwanted; orphans with no relatives prepared to offer care, some came from situations of abstract poverty, physical abuse, some were ill nourished or from single mothers or even fathers where the mother had run off. They entered into care by many means; just taken to the Penkhull Cottage Homes and left there, others being collected by an officer of the poor law direct from school with no 'goodbye' to parents or siblings, or there was simply a knock on the door and the child was removed as they stood. Others left as orphans would be taken for a walk to Penkhull by a relative or neighbour and just deposited there without a word of explanation. It was very easy to release oneself from the responsibility of parenthood and so the system was abused.

First place of call, The Admissions Home

The matron carried out the administration for admission into the home centrally in a room attached the Muster Hall. When a new child was admitted he or she was taken to the sewing room and given a completely new set of clothes consisting of: three pairs of shoes and two blazers, one for school, one for best. They were also provided with a raincoat and two further coats, again one for school, one for best.

Boys: Best pair of grey flannels, second pair for daily use and three other pairs of trousers, a best pullover, school pullover and jersey, winter shirts and jerseys, two pairs of pyjamas for older boys, two nightdresses for smaller boys.

Girls: Tunic and day blouses for younger girls, skirts and Dayella blouses for older girls. Cardigans and blouses, two nightdresses, pinafores were also provided. Many of the clothes were made 'in-house' whereas the majority of the woollens were purchased from the Blind Workshops at Fenton. As and when the children reached the age to leave school they would receive a completely new outfit. Once a month, a 'condemning day' was held when old clothes or those badly worn would be discarded to make way for new. The same also applied to cracked or chipped crockery.

To ensure that children were in good health, each child underwent a medical examination every three months. They were weighed, measured and examined. This was in addition to the medical given upon arrival at the home and prior to leaving.

Each housemother had to make frequent reports on the children under their care. This was submitted to the City Children's Committee. The questions consisted of name, age, etc. followed by more personal questions - reactions on admission if recently admitted, personal habits, and attitude to staff and to other children in the home, recent development and progress, school attended and educational ability and the child's health. These were then followed by other questions such as interests; whether mother, father, other relatives or friends visit and how often; whether the child visit other children or home, and for how long. None of these records have survived.

The daily routine of each home was kept the same to maintain a regular pattern of times and duties. At 7.30 a.m. breakfast was served. After this, the younger children would go out to play while the older children would then commence their daily tasks. Lunch was served at 1.00p.m. tea at 5.00p.m. A cleaner was employed at each house from 9.00a.m.–2.00p.m. as it was impossible for the housemother to look after the children, as well as prepare meals. After tea, the younger children were prepared for bed by the older ones. In some homes, older children were allowed to stay up a little later, but before going to bed after they prepared the tables for the following morning's breakfast.

A typical menu for the day would consist of:

Breakfast – cereal, bacon sandwiches for the younger children; bacon, egg and coffee for the older children. Dinner – Stew, peas, potatoes, cabbage, followed by either egg custard or stewed apple and custard. Tea, beans on toast, or tomato and ham sandwiches, jam and bread, cake and milk.

Differing Circumstances.

To categorise why children were admitted into Penkhull Homes is not possible, some were wanted and loved and it was the circumstance of the time such as unemployment, poverty or family breakdown that forced children to be delivered or taken into the homes. Many were given up at birth by single mothers and placed into care. Others clearly were not loved and were neglected. Each child would have their own story to tell of the reasons why they were placed into care.

Brian, for example was born in a squalid area of the city. His bedroom contained one bed and one cot. His father was unknown as his mother 'entertained many different men'.

So bad was the property, the council re-housed the mother with Brian and a young baby to a modern home with all mod cons. Soon, the conditions were just as bad as the previous home, and Brian was subsequently taken into care in need and protection and placed into Penkhull Homes in the early 1950s.

For Michael, the story is different. His mother had a nervous breakdown after his birth. Subsequently she would never allow Michael to grow up: he was much easier to cope with as a baby in a cot and pram. The situation worsened and Michael was taken into care whilst his mother became more seriously disturbed and ended up in St. Edward's mental hospital at Cheddleton. Because of his early neglect, Michael was not allowed to attend the local school because of a very low IQ. He was sent to a special school at Blythe Bridge.

In many cases, all the children from one family would be admitted. Yvonne, Pat, Jean and Timmy were one such family group. They came from Yorkshire with their parents and their mother's sister. The father then ran off with his sister-in-law. Mother could not cope, so the children were placed into care in Yorkshire, later to be transferred to Plymouth where their mother was thought to be living. As there was no contact with their mother, and their father was found to be living at Hanley, the children were moved to Penkhull.

Brothers David and Michael came from a difficult background. Their mother and father had each re-married. Two other children from the same family were resident in another cottage in the homes. A further younger sister was living in care at The Grove nursery Penkhull. The father was by now in prison and the mother had started to live a life of prostitution. Originally, two of the children were placed into care to remove some of the burden, but still mother could not manage proper care of the children. Finally, in spite of every assistance, further children had to be taken into care.

Then there were children who were taken into care as infants and their full stories, after all these years, have never been revealed. In the early 1940s, Dorothy was aged 2 or 3 years old when she was placed into the nursery until aged five when she went into the home of Miss Billingsley. *I stayed in the home until I was 18 working with children and then returned as a foster mother in later life. To me it was the only home and mother I knew.*

Heather was born illegitimate in 1946. Her father lived in Penkhull, her mother came from Doncaster. *I don't know why, but my father was taking care of me, but obviously not doing a very good job as a neighbour, Kathleen Whitehurst, noticed that I was being neglected and developed whooping cough. Kathleen took me to the children's home. It was standard practice to remain in the nursery until five and then be placed into another home with other girls. On occasions, my father used to come and visit, then for the odd weekend I was allowed to stay with him and his new wife.*

When they had their first child, I never visited again. At the age of around eleven years, my mother came to see me from Doncaster. The following Christmas I went to Doncaster and stayed with her sister, my aunt for two weeks. I was then taken back to Penkhull and have never heard of my mother since.

Many children never knew the outside world even from birth. When a young girl was found to be pregnant, her family would disown her. Who would take them in to bring shame on the family? The only shelter was the workhouse so on many birth certificates The Spittals; No.576 London Road was the address. This was the situation for Mike born in 1946 and at the age of six weeks, he was taken into care by the local authority and placed in the nursery at Penkhull Cottage Homes.

Doris, like Mike, was born in the workhouse. *Who the father was I never knew. I ended up in the home at the age of three and stayed there until sixteen.* William likewise never knew who his father was. He as admitted along with his brother when he was three and remained in care until fourteen, when his grandmother then took him in.

Kenneth was placed into the care of the local authority in 1941. He and his elder sister were placed first into the receiving home for assessment, and then placed into different homes because mixed sexes were not allowed in one home. Kenneth was around six years of age and stayed there until he was 18. His mother was murdered by a soldier lover, and his father killed by a tram in Leeds. They had only one aunt, living in Hope Street. She already had a large family, so into the Penkhull Homes they both went.

Brian went into the cottage homes twice *the first time was in 1956 when I was around four years of age. My father had died two years earlier, but then mother got pregnant with twins, so mother could not cope and the cottage homes was the only answer.*

Mother had scarlet fever and father was nowhere to be found, so Ann, at the age of six, ended up in the homes as her mother could not cope. She stayed there until she was old enough to go to work.

For Barry, life was tough: *we lived in a small two up and two down in London Road Stoke, on the corner of Union Street. There were six of us, my parents and two lodgers taken in to bring in some money. Following my father's death in 1957 from T.B. my mother could not cope and so just left, leaving us there to fend for ourselves. My eldest brother Eric wrote a note and sent my younger brother Alan to somewhere in Princes Road, Hartshill.*

Either later that day or the next day, someone called at the house and four of us were taken into care. It was a revelation to me. When we arrived, we were given clean clothes and went upstairs to the bathroom, a new experience. So too was the switching on of an electric light, almost by magic and for the first time we ate proper meals. The following four years were without doubt the best four years of my young life.

Bill came from Chell. His father was a prisoner of the Japanese, working on the building of a bridge in Burma. Bill was born while he father was away and as a result, upon his return, when Bill was about three months old his father found there was a new addition to the family. He was always referred to as his 'bastard son'. *My father suffered badly during the war and as a result took out much of his frustrations and anger for his wife becoming pregnant by another man, out on me.*

He frequently got into drink, smoked a lot, and consequently had no money to feed his family. The dining table was an old wooden tea chest with an old rag over as a tablecloth; oil cloth on the floor, gas lighting downstairs, nothing upstairs. Food consisted of half-a-loaf of bread and a bit of jam for the week. There were six of us but we survived, just. In around 1954 when I was about nine years of age a large car pulled up outside and we were ordered get inside. The journey from Chell seemed to take forever. We were taken to the reception home; I was about nine and we were all in need of care and protection so taken into care. We were all split up, my younger sister to the nursery and my brothers into different homes than me. This was the first time I had had a proper cooked meal in my life and until then I always thought that socks and pants were for posh people. Now I had my own. There was still food rationing, but at the home, we never went short of anything.

Certainly different from all the others was Gordon Chan who is Chinese. He was sold as a child to a distant relative whose gave him to his son whose marriage was childless. After the necessary paperwork was sorted in Hong Kong Gordon arrived for a new life in the UK at the age of around nine and lived at 62 Liverpool Road Stoke where his 'alleged' uncle Mr. Chan, ran a Chinese laundry. *The treatment I received at their hands does not warrant thinking about it was simply dreadful. Finally, it all came to ahead when they were prosecuted and I was taken into care in need of protection. This brought me into Penkhull Cottage Homes in around 1963 at the age of thirteen, being placed in home No.25.*

Muster Hall.

The Muster Hall, situated half way down the avenue was the central focal point for activities. It was built as part of the original plan for the Cottage Homes. It was a large room, with a small stage at one end. The hall was used most days for activities by the children, board games during the winter and indoor sports. Each age group had its own club. National events were also celebrated there, and at Christmas time and New Year there was a party for all.

Despite the fact that children were described as 'inmates', an unfortunate and sad word to use for children, entertainment was provided at the homes on various occasions. In March 1911, the Grove Prize Choir provided entertainment in the Muster Hall. This was followed in June by the purchase of a gramophone and records at a cost of £4 0s 10d. Later there were regular film shows for the children, and various groups and organisations came to offer their services in entertaining or inviting children from the homes to visit other private homes.

To raise funds for the children's holidays, the building was also used for public whist drives, and social evenings. The cost of the whist tables amounted to £15. The hall witnessed the celebration of coronations and other special national occasions. During the year, many outside groups, singers, drama and musicians used to come to the home and entertain the children in the Muster Hall.

Mr Ernest Tew, of Trent Valley Road, also used to come on a regular basis during the 1940s and 50s to show films on his projector. Most were 'Cowboys and Indians' and 'Laurel and Hardy'. Local children were allowed to the film shows free of charge. The children from the homes were seated first and the outside children admitted and seated afterwards, having to sit to the rear of the hall. Mr Owen, the superintendent, was always standing at the door keeping a careful eye on events.

The first building on the right in the Avenue was the
Superintendants Home

This was later replaced by a central television for all the children to watch, but even then, both subject matter and times were restricted.

It was in the Muster Hall that children had to line up once a month for a short back and sides by local barber Frank Wedgwood who was employed for the day. It was still used

for this in 1961, when the charge made was increased from 1/- to 1/3d for each boy. In 1934 Lodge Road and other roads were built nearby and then each year, the Muster Hall was used as a polling station on election day.

Activities.

It was the policy of the new style of care for children to involve them where possible in activities outside the home. This was arranged by the superintendent, or by invitation to the children. In May 1903, all went to the Victoria Hall, Hanley to attend the afternoon performance of the *Shelton May Festival*. Exactly what this involved is not recorded or how the children got to Hanley. They probably walked, as they did the following July to visit the annual horticultural show at Hanley Park. Here Mrs Collins (*of Pat Collins fairground amusements*) gave all the children free use of the rides. It is again recorded in 1925, that Mr Pat Collins invited the children to attend the Hanley Park Fête *and to be freely entertained*.

From the opening of the homes, it was the custom to parade the children, two abreast, up Newcastle Lane to Penkhull Church every Sunday morning. The older children had to hold the hands of the younger ones. Sunday clothes were worn for the day. All were all given 1d each by mother for the collection. Just as in the homes where children were divided into different cottages by gender, the same applied to church. The boys sat in the pews to the left hand side of the church, while the girls sat in the pews to the right. It was the opinion of a number of children that the general congregation ignored them. All have strong memories of Vicar Aston. After lunch, once more the procession made its way into the village for the Anglican Sunday school held in the old infants' school. The Homes children accounted for majority of children attending with few other local children, as most of them would have attended the methodist chapel.

Mr and Mrs Jim Goodier ran the Sunday school. Most years the children were involved in a church pageant designed and organised by the Goodier's. For one organised in the mid 1950s, a photograph has survived. The Goodier's were so committed that all the children did their very best for them. In the evening, the children walked up to the village once more for Evensong, then back home to do their jobs in preparation for the following morning, then off to bed.

As early as 1903, the children played an active and committed role in the activities of the Anglican Church. Boys, if they had a good singing voice became part of the church choir at Penkhull and as such would accompany the choir on its annual trip to the sea. Permission was first sought from the guardians before being allowed, and this was recorded in the minute book.

Sunday school Pageant organised by Mr and Mrs Jim Goodier

In one year, August 1903, four boys were allowed to visit Colwyn Bay. In the same year, 55 children received prizes for regular attendance and good conduct at the Sunday school. In June 1924, to enable six children to dress appropriately for confirmation, a new sewing machine was purchased for the making of special white dresses for the occasion. Any boy with a good voice, especially a boy soprano, would soon find themselves in the choir under the leadership of Ken Gleaves, while others could find themselves as an altar boy.

Little information exists concerning attendance at non-conformist churches, apart from an occasion in June 1924, when the Primitive Methodist Chapel in Penkhull requested the guardians to contribute towards the cost of transport of Homes children on a Sunday school treat to Clayton. This short entry implies that a number of children from the Homes were attending the chapel. Roman Catholic children were housed separately from the other children, having one cottage to themselves. This was No.1, where first Miss Hawksworth then Miss Durose, were housemothers. In the early years, under the supervision of a Catholic mother, the children were not allowed to talk with non-Catholics until they were outside the Homes gates. Until her death, Miss Durose would have regular visits from girls formerly in her care. These would then take their own children to visit the lady who had become the only mother many of them knew. One of those children, now in her late 70s recalls how well they were all treated. *Mother was a wonderful mother, a good cook and cared for us Catholic children. Yes, she was strict, and we were punished like all children in those days. That was life then - very different from that of today. I still have a cherished Bible that Miss Durose gave to me when I was in the home. I was treated so very well there, good food, nice clothes, a holiday at Southport each year in an old army comp, a wonderful Christmas, all bring such very happy memories for me. In fact, conditions for us children were probably far better than most children living outside the home during those years following the Second World War.*

By February 1924, some Roman Catholic children were not housed in No.1 because of the pressure of numbers. As numbers exceeded availability it was agreed that any orphan or deserted child of that faith be transferred to Father Hudson's Home at Birmingham. It could well be that the situation was influenced by a shortage of Catholic mothers as reference was made in the minute book the following month *to re-advertise the vacancy for a foster mother in the Roman Catholic Home.* The advertisement bought a response of three applicants. Even so, in October 1925, there remained accommodation issues. A father of two children in the home complained that even though his children were of that faith, they were not supported in a catholic home. Once more, a number of children were transferred to Fr. Hudson's Home at Birmingham to alleviate the problem.

The level of involvement and costs for any national event was first approved by the Board of Guardians. For the coronation of King George V, on 22nd June 1911, the board agreed to authorize a change from the strict diet at the home for two days. In addition, the sum of £2 was to be granted for prizes for the children's sports afternoon in celebration, and the additional allowance of 6d per child to be spent on extras. The sum of £15 was given towards the cost of a party for staff and officers and lastly £5 was put towards a staff outing.

National occasions were always marked in one-way or another. V.E. day was celebrated, as elsewhere, by a proper street party even though the Muster Hall could have been used. Tables and chairs were placed down the avenue, each cottage having their own table as a family. Food was somehow found in abundance even though rationing was in operation. After the party, community games were held, and to finish off, as with all other street parties, there was a huge rendering of *God Save The King.*

It seemed only a few years after V.E. Day that celebrations for the Coronation of Queen Elizabeth II were to be arranged. This time they were held in the Muster Hall, any attempt for a street party being abandoned as it rained all day. All the children were given a celebration mug and the boys a Dinky Toy model of the Queen's golden coach. A huge bonfire followed these celebrations on The Croft, and fireworks completed the day.

In addition to their weekly pocket money, a handful of sweets were given out to the children on a Saturday morning and most managed to save a few pence to visit the Victoria Cinema at Hartshill for a Saturday afternoon matinee at a cost of 2d. The elder boys were allowed to go unattended, keeping to the footpaths. If younger ones wanted to go, they would accompany the older children, who would be responsible for their care. The other cinema used by the 'Homers' was the Prince's Picture House in Wharf Street, Stoke. The cinema backed on to the canal, so sometimes during the showing of the film a scuffle was felt around the ankles as rats sought any food that had been discarded. Metal discs were the 'admission tickets' and at the front of the stalls there were benches instead of seats for children.

Outside interests for boys included The Church Lads', Brigade. Again, approval had to be given by the guardians for 20 boys to attend a summer camp in August 1911, at a cost of 15/-per boy. One thrill for the group was to attend as guard of honour for a civic procession in June 1911 for which they received 1/- each. The same year saw the establishment of the Cottage Homes' own Boys' Brigade Company. For the enrolment in the organisation, the Homes had to pay £1 to its organisation. By the 1920s, boys joined the Penkhull group of Boy Scouts. On many occasions, the Scout Group were invited to the Home to provide entertainment for the children. By 1925, in a further attempt to involve children into a *normal family* situation there was established a Cottage Homes' football team, which competed with other local teams. The guardians agreed to pay any reasonable tram fares to encourage more to take part.

The main highlight of that year was when King George visited Stoke-on-Trent to confer the status of city. Arrangements were made for all the children to watch the King in procession to the Kings Hall in Stoke, and on other occasion, they were lined up when Royalty visited the North Staffs Royal Infirmary.

Sometimes the Theatre Royal provided free tickets for the children especially for the Christmas pantomime, and the Regent Cinema in September 1953 provided free seats for the children to enjoy the film *Peter Pan*.

In the 1920s, Grindley Hill Farm was finally demolished and replaced by a huge playing field behind the Muster Hall and offices. It is here that most of the after-school hours and holiday times would be spent. Most of the 'foster fathers' including David Prince would encourage their own cottage children to take part and enjoy the sport. As a result, relationships were forged in a manner that had not happened in the early years of the Homes. Use of the field was restricted to children from the Homes. In many ways Homes' children had better sporting facilities than other children who had to kick a ball or a tin can in streets or back-alleys with makeshift goal posts made by brick ends.

All had a job to do

From the early age of five years, children in each home were expected to play their part in the running of the home. Mother's job was not to clean, scrub, wash and tidy every day. It was considered that the discipline for children, as in most homes, was that each child should have some responsibility for its upkeep.

First, the older children, in both the girls and boys' homes, were expected to feed the younger children and teach them how to use knives and forks. When a little older they would take the first steps of laying the breakfast table, then getting ready for the evening meal which was a little more complicated. Each child had to make their own bed and get on their knees to scrub and polish with Ronuk the wooden bedroom floors, as well as the landing, stairs and the hall. No fitted carpets in those days.

The breakfast consisted mainly of porridge. This was not only made the previous evening by the older children but also served by them in the morning. Before school, all would have to be cleared away and dishes washed. In the early days, the homes had cooking ranges with open fires. Each evening the ashes and sometimes even the burning coals, if they had not burnt away, had to be removed and the fire re-set for morning. It was also the children's responsibility to chop the sticks and break the large lumps of coal into smaller pieces. Hard work for young children.

A messy job was the 'black-leading' of the cooking ranges once a week by the children. All this was in addition to the general cleaning and dusting in the home. The boys were also expected to help the Cottage Homes gardener in the vegetable garden behind the receiving home, and on a good day many could be seen on a front door step peeling potatoes. The girls were often employed sewing or darning socks. The older a child got the more responsibility was placed upon them, especially in caring for the younger children.

Every evening after the meal, school shoes had to be polished and placed in rows in the hall ready for the next day. The pocket money in 1960 was; under 7 years 6d; 7-9 years 2/-; 9-12 years 2/6d; 12-14 years 3/6d.

Around and About.

The homes had its own sewing room situated near to the administration block at the side of the Muster Hall. Here four women were employed to provide the clothes for the children, and uniforms for the staff. A great deal of trouble was taken in providing a suitable dress for young girls, whilst the boys received standard jackets brought in from outside suppliers.

The house parents were responsible for ordering their weekly groceries on a standard form, providing an adequate and varied diet. The food was held in a central store in the admin. block and delivered upon demand to each cottage home several times a week. Storage of fresh supplies was a problem until refrigeration came, so food was purchased locally. The minutes contain a few references, for example in February 1903 that the beef and mutton supplied by Messrs Woolliscroft, butchers of Stoke, had been returned because of inferior quality. In 1911, Good Friday was celebrated with the addition of hot X buns, and in the same year, contracts were placed with The Maypole of Stoke for margarine, whilst Williams of Longton were contracted to supply the butter.

The Children's Home employed three gardeners who maintained vegetable gardens and greenhouses to provide fresh vegetables when in season. On average, each child had four eggs per week and one pint of fresh milk each day. Fish was on the menu each Friday and alternate Tuesdays. The other mid-week feast was sausages in place of fish. The food store was situated to the rear of the Muster hall. From here meat, sausages, and the weekly provisions would be supplied. Bread was in the form of very long loaves that were cut as required. The housemother would keep a weekly record of all meals supplied.

Cake and sweets were also provided, cake on a Thursday or Friday, and sweets mostly on a Saturday. All the former children of the home agreed that they received three good meals a day, probably far better than those of many children outside.

Home No.............
City of Stoke-on-Trent Children's Committee
CHILDREN'S HOMES, PENKHULL

REQUISITION TO THE SUPERINTENDENT
for the supply of Provisions for

...............Children and...............Staff, for the

week commencing ....

....Housemother.

Article	Quantity	
Bacon		
Butter		
Baking Powder ...		
Bisto ...		
Biscuits ...		
Beans, Baked ...		
Barley ...		
Bovril & Marmite ...		
Cornflour ...		
Custard Powder ...		
Cake Mixture ...		
Cereals ...		
Cheese		
Cocoa ...		
Coffee ...		
Eggs ...		
Flour ...		
Fish (tins) ...		
Fruit, Dried ...		
Fruit Drinks...		
Jams & Marmalade		
Jellies ...		
Lard ...		
Macaroni ...		
Margarine ...		
Milk, Tins ...		
Meat, Tins ...		
Meat & Fish Paste ...		
Mustard ...		
Oats ...		
Peas ...		
Pepper ...		
Pickles ...		
Pilchards ...		
Pudding Spices ...		
Rice ...		
Sago ...		
Salt ...		
Salmon ...		
Sardines ...		
Sauces ...		
Semolina ...		
Soups, Tins ...		
Stuffing ...		
Suet ...		
Syrup & Treacle ...		
Sugar ...		
Tea ...		
Tinned Fruit ...		
Vegetables, Tins ...		
Vinegar ...		

Home No.........

City of Stoke-on-Trent Children's Committee
CHILDREN'S HOMES, PENKHULL
—
...............day of.........................195....

REQUISITION TO THE SUPERINTENDENT

Articles	No. Required	Memoranda
Boot Polish ...		
Brooms, Hair ...		
„ Bass ...		
„ Handles ...		
Brushes, Shoe ...		
„ Stove ...		
„ Scrub ...		
„ Hand ...		
„ Nail ...		
„ Hair ...		
„ Lavatory ...		
„ Tooth ...		
Combs, Dressing ...		
„ Tooth ...		
Cloths, Floor ...		
„ Dish ...		
„ Emery ...		
Dusters ...		
Floor Polish ...		
Harpic ...		
Kleenoff ...		
Mirro Powder ...		
Matches ...		
Metal Polish ...		
Mops ...		
Pan Scourers ...		
Soap, Hard ...		
„ Soft ...		
„ Toilet ...		
„ Powder ...		
„ Flakes ...		
Soda ...		
Step Stones ...		
Tooth Paste ...		
Toilet Rolls ...		
Wash Leathers ...		

BREAD ORDER Home..............

Loaves, Large................... Small............... Brown...............

Names of admissions and discharges

....

....

....

....

Other items and repairs

....

....

No. of Children.................... Date....................

Education

From the outset, it was the policy of the Board of Guardians that, wherever possible children should be incorporated in the local community. This included education. The process of local education was put into place before the homes were opened. An application to the National School (Church of England) in Penkhull was refused but an application to the Stoke School Board at Cross Street was accepted.

At the Spittals workhouse, children were institutionalised and taught in buildings within the site, although in later years boys were taught in local Board Schools. The earliest record appears in November 1898 when it was reported that fifteen boys from the workhouse were not in school because of an outbreak of diphtheria at the Spittals. Six weeks later when the boys had returned, the head teacher, wrote: *that because of their physical condition it was difficult to guess their approximate ages.*

Education at the workhouse was lacking in every respect. The children were sent to the new senior school in Princes Road when it opened. The log books paint a sorry story of many of the children attending as the following extracts from the log books show.

August 29th, 1898

Admitted 60 boys from the Stoke Union (Spittals Workhouse, Nr. Newcastle-u-Lyme) Cannot get proper dates of birth The boys are well fed, very well dressed, and apparently well behaved. Mr. Greatbatch in

August 31st 1898

Examined the Workhouse Boys. I was prepared to find them very ignorant but am dumbfounded at their deplorable condition and think it is a public scandal that a body with rates to fall back upon should turn out such boys.

September 28th 1898

Lady and gentleman visited to see one of Workhouse boys — Uncle and Aunt to boy — seem in good position. Some of poor ratepayers complain that the Workhouse Chn should be so well clothed and fed and those who pay the rates in some cases have not enough to eat

June 9th, 1899

the way these boys (of 7 to 11 about) have been educated or rather not been educated. 24 of them could not tell a single letter from a large type primer and when put to write a or m. from a copy made a series of incoherent scribbles!!! Yet some of these have been in the Union 2, 3, 4 years and in a few cases more!! This was when they were admitted; they are progressing fairly we but they are still so backward I am afraid we shall be blamed. We keep losing a few and getting another uncultivated batch "while father is in prison", "till mother come out of hospital" &c &c.

In June 1901, it was reported that the Cottage Homes children were absent for a day because they were invited to the Hanley Floral Fête. It would appear than many parents of other children complained about the unfair favourable treatment that Cottage Homes children received. Again, in January 1904 the *Homers* were off school once more to

September 1898

60 Workhouse Boys.

Reading
60 {
- *18 did not know their letters perfectly*
- *26 boys read badly or moderately i.e. would not pass in St I*
- *16 boys read fairly i.e. about equal to a poor pass in St 1 or 2; in a few cases St 3.*
}

Writing *Several boys on being asked to make a copy of long letters wrote a slate full of the letter "a".*
60 {
- *44 wrote wretchedly*
- *6 — moderately*
- *10 — fairly viz = to a low quality*
}

Arithmetic *Easy Tests : e.g all who had been taught in St I and II had these sums (dictated not am.*

$$\frac{27}{15} \qquad \frac{160}{205} \qquad \frac{57\, hrs}{30\, mins} \qquad \frac{24\, hrs}{14\, mins}$$

Out of 41 boys 36 had none of these right
Notation almost unknown 27 written 2007
60 {
- *50 had little or no knowledge*
- *4 worked a small portion right*
- *6 did fairly*
}

A very little. Scripture, Geography and Mental Arith. know

attend the pantomime in Hanley. The first note of any Cottage Homes girls attending the school is dated March 1909, when eleven were admitted to Class 5G. An inspector's report on the standard of English at the school pointed a finger at the new admission as they *pulled down the standard somewhat.* The children at the cottage homes were to be educated alongside other children at Penkhull and Trent Vale infants, and at Cross Street and Penkhull Senior Schools.

The school log books, especially for Penkhull Senior School, do not convey a good image of *'Homers'* as Cottage Homes children were called. *April 6th 1909 Admitted Louise Blundred from the Cottage Homes aged 12 years, weight 7 stone 12 lbs can scarcely read words of one syllable. Has been neglected and must have been out of school for years.* In May the same year there were 32 boys and 24 girls on the school registers but reported that during the year only 38 children were in school for more than six months and only 28 for twelve. *Not much can be done for 'in and out' children, but those that remain a year or more benefit considerably. The Cottage Homes children are much below the average in attainment but the children come to school clean, neat, well dressed, exceedingly well fed, and generally well cared for.*

The following year, saw the Penkhull senior school over-subscribed. Accommodation was at a premium and the head teacher refused to accept four boys at the beginning of term in September because *the school was full, there being 618 on the book with accommodation only for 590.* The following day a letter was sent by the Matron of the Homes stating that in future all children from the infants should be found a place at the Senior School and not other senior schools. The matter was referred to the Director of Education.

By June 1910, the number of children, attending the school had fallen to 15 boys and 20 girls and although the comments reiterate those of 1909 regarding appearance etc, the attainment of the children was recorded as much below the average. Two years later, in a report dated July 1912, the children were recorded *as being illiterate, about the level with class 2 in the infants' school. It is therefore difficult to know where to place these children but the main point is that they have been in school apparently about a quarter only of their school life. They could not even read words such as 'that' or 'and' and could not add up 6+6. Many neglected children of this kind come from the Hanley district.*

These facts reflect the poverty in the pottery towns and, on occasions, the low value many parents had of their children. Many children were simply unwanted and burdensome, therefore the Cottage Homes provided, sadly, a convenient opportunity for parents to unburden themselves of the responsibility of children.

There are numerous references to children at the Cottage Homes being ill. Sometimes quarantine was imposed which led to all children being kept from school. In 1927 for example, all the Homes children were kept away from school because of a serious outbreak of scarlet fever at the Children's Home.

Despite all these reports and concerns, the Board of Guardians recognised children who stood out and achieved good results. One such boy, James Jones in May 1911 was allowed to attend evening classes at Stoke Art School, his fees being paid for by the board. Another child, JB, aged 14, an office boy at the Homes was allowed to attend the City School of Commerce on a part-time basis for instruction in shorthand and typing the following year. In August 1923, the guardians also agreed to pay for books required by RC to attend evening classes. Many girls attended The Elms Centre at Shelton to be trained in domestic service, the main occupation for young girls.

Personal evidence of treatment in schools often reflects the same perception as to why children were in the cottage homes. One boy, Mike Shaw, who attended Penkhull Senior School records that the *'Homers'* were treated very badly. *We were singled out constantly for punishment, both for the cane and the slipper for no apparent reason. We were never encouraged but the opposite.* Another boy, Kenneth Wakefield attended Cross Street School where the cane was administered freely to the boys from the Cottage Homes. On the other hand, Brian Tomkins recalls that although *'Homers'* became their brand name *there was little prejudice against us* and Ann Amison who went to St Peter's Girls in Stoke says: *even though we were treated differently at times, probably because we had free school meals, but most of the times we were treated no differently than any other child.* On one occasion, Heather

Perry who also attended St Peters was treated badly, and Mr Marshall, the assistant superintendent at the Home, went to see the school about the treatment of the children there. Bill Bratt shares the same view *that as 'Homers' we were not treated much different from other children. Remember that all children would be punished by the cane or slipper, it really did not matter which home you came from but from what I remember, it did none of us any harm.*

Other boys, William Mason and bothers Karl and Paul Bateman, thought school was not that bad. *The difficulty was that because of how we were dressed with a striped tie, grey flannels and jacket all knew that we were 'Homers' and therefore identified as being different. Some of the teachers took advantage by picking on us but overall we were treated within reason.*

However, some children, not *'Homers'*, are adamant about the appalling treatment some of the boys received especially at Penkhull Senior School. *They were treated so badly by some of the teachers* recalls John Evans. *They were flogged and picked on for no apparent reason simply because they had no parents to come to the school and complain. The boys were not bad lads they always were clean and smart and so well turned out. They simply did not deserve to be leathered as though they were second-class.*

For Gordon Chan, he was singled out at Penkhull Senior School by the head teacher, Mr Thirlwall, as an inspiration to others, because of the Chinese work ethic, coupled with exercise, as dictated by Chairman Mow. Gordon at school assembly was expected to address the school on a regular basis regarding the distance he walked to school each day and the dedication to study in China.

As would be expected, the Homes had a number of children with serious learning difficulties. Despite all efforts at the home to provide a caring environment for these children, their futures were far too obvious, for at the age of fifteen, Stallington Hall, the mental hospital at Blythe Bridge was to become their home.

Christmas.
From the early days of the workhouse, Christmas was celebrated with the prospect of additional fare and perhaps entertainment. The new cottage homes were to be no exception. In January 1902, all the children visited the pantomime at the Theatre Royal at Hanley and Dr Hind, the medical officer for the Homes, gave picture books to the children, together with toys donated by Messrs Holdgate and Small, and Messrs Vyse and Hill of Stoke.

Money was short and the guardians were careful, but in 1920 they agreed an additional expense on food for each home to the value of 2/6d, and the purchase of one toy per child not exceeding 1/-, and the standard apple and orange.

All were placed in the children's stockings for Christmas morning. By the 1950s there were improvements, as each child could be purchased one toy at a cost not exceeding 2/-. Additional food could however be purchased to the sum of 2/6d per child. Staff were given an extra 5/- in cash for the purchase of Christmas Fare.

After the Second World War, Christmas became the highlight of the year. Presents were distributed to each child by means of a pillowcase full on Christmas morning. Civic visitors would make an early visit around the cottages following a special house dinner. Later in the day, a large party would be held in the Muster Hall. Thistley Hough Grammar School for girls, across the road from St. Christopher's Avenue, also provided an evening of entertainment along with refreshments. The boys looked forward to this from September onwards as every boy would have a girl allocated to look after them for the whole evening. There were invitations to so many parties in their honour from Creda, the Michelin works, the police, the list was endless. The local Rotary Club would also organise the annual outing to the pantomime at the Theatre Royal in Hanley, the week after Christmas. The minute books for 1948 read that many Christmas gifts, toys, money and books had been sent to the cottage homes, and that the children had been entertained.

As with many social enterprises of the day, civic dignitaries and clergy would pay a visit to the home on Christmas morning. The Lord Mayor of Stoke would give each child a silver sixpence. By 1960, the allowance for a Christmas gift for each child rose to 10/- and an additional 7/6d for the housemother.

Gordon Chan remembers with joy the number of gifts waiting for him in the dining room on Christmas morning, mostly all donated from charities, companies, groups and individuals. *I had never seen so many presents before,* he said.

Mrs Dorothy Hill, even at the age of 80, remembers Christmas very clearly. *We had lovely Christmases. Each foster mother did her own thing. She would make a Christmas cake all secret; only the eldest girl in the house would help her. No Christmas decorations would go up until Christmas Eve. We would all be sent off to bed early, after a bath, having to have our tea in bed, which was so exciting. Mother and the girl would then decorate the dining room with decorations and a Christmas tree. We were so lucky to have a bath because most children outside would not have that luxury. Mother used to get us to write a letter to Santa with three items we would like but Mother said we might be lucky and get just one. Most would ask for writing or drawing set or perhaps a toyshop, little things like that or a game, but it was not an expensive one like today. I never knew about the finance, I believed it was Santa but then I found out years after it was Mr Victor Tipton, the husband of Mrs Tipton, who* ran the working boy's home in Stoke. He would come to each home with his sack dressed as Santa. He would knock at the door; we would all be sitting in the dining room waiting. He would bring the sack in. All the presents were wrapped with our name on, just so thrilled. Our foster mother would also prepare a stocking, which was hung on the fireguard at night, and then in the morning it was found at the bottom of our beds with an apple, orange, a few chocolates; a new penny, nuts and a sugar mouse. There was a little book or something. We thought the world of these. Mother used to prepare the dinner in the house, beautiful all together with crackers on the table and a tree. The yearly message from the King was listened to from the radio in mother's sitting room, then we had to sit and play with the toys we had. Later on we had a large party in the house, cake, jelly, then after tea we had party games. Cllr. Doris Robinson, chairman of the Children's Committee would come around to each home during the day and give us all a new shilling to spend.

Barry Broadhurst and Bill Bratt also have such fond memories of Christmas, just the excitement of it all and the expectation of a present from Santa. Both could not believe the amount of food provided by mother on that day as they all sat around the table for dinner.

Clothing

Without any doubt, one thing that the cottage homes will be remembered for was the strict attention it paid to the appearance of the children, both in cleanliness and clothing apparel. From the early days, there was a sewing room situated to the rear of the Muster hall employing four women. Here girls' dresses and other items of clothing were made from a choice of materials and styles. The staff would undertake a fitting before completing the job to ensure a good fit.

Those clothes no longer wanted - worn out or perhaps outgrown were returned to the sewing room for re-use, and if worn out, cut up for dusters or floor cloths. Others were checked over, washed and stored as *hand-me-downs* for other children. Girls' school clothing consisted of a grey gymslip and a white blouse and striped ties. For a boy, grey flannel short trousers, white shirt, striped tie and pullover.

For shoes, Mr Shaw was in charge of the stores, which were opened for children on a Saturday morning. Most children used to try their luck in complaining about the old pair so to have a new pair, any excuse. All had house slippers, little shoes, school shoes, and best shoes, and a pair of Wellingtons for wet weather.

In 1911, the main contractors were Moseley Bros. of Newcastle, Huntbatch of Hanley and George Fleet of Stoke. The repair to clothes was an important function of the sewing room, but on occasions, various items would be sent to shops for repair. This was the case in 1911 when thirty infants' knitted jackets were sent away for new sleeves to be fitted at a cost of 1/- each. At the same time Messrs Moseley Bros. of Newcastle were offered the contract to supply boys' tweed suits at 7/3d each and boys' corduroys breeches at 2/9d. In November of the same year, a full set of requirements for the cottage homes was made and tenders requested. Some of the items make interesting reading: *Lustre lining, white, blue scouring flannel, serge, shirting, boys collars, gatatea, machine cotton, hat and garter elastic, grey twill sheeting, turley twill, madras muslin, white and black tape, calico, hessian, braces, circular twill crash towelling, braces and linen buttons.*

In March 1923, 48 girls' hats were obtained from the Co-Op in Wigan and boy's knickers at 6/3 per pair, were to be purchased.

Laundry was collected every week in large wicker baskets, all children's clothing had a name label inside and some of the boys during the school holiday would have fun helping with the process of collection and delivery to each cottage.

Top - Parties held in the Muster Hall
Below - Staff of the Children's Home

Medical Matters.

Dr Hind of Trent Valley Road was appointed the first medical officer for the new Cottage Homes at an annual salary of £30. Before any operation could be carried out on any child, permission had to be sought first from the Board of Guardians. Such permission was granted in July 1903 for Dr Hind to operate on three children with defective eyes at the workhouse hospital. These were the days before the NHS and therefore any treatment at the North Staffs Royal Infirmary had to be paid for, so again approval had to be obtained. Later the same year there was a major epidemic of scarlet fever at the homes and children had to be moved to the Bucknall Isolation Hospital for treatment. This was followed the same year by several cases of chicken pox.

Earlier in the year of 1903, there was also an epidemic of Typhoid fever for which most of the children were immediately vaccinated. However, one boy, Herbert Roberto was not vaccinated as his father who was in Longton Cottage Hospital refused his consent. Additional washerwomen had to be employed in an attempt to cope with all the soiled bed sheets.

One unusual entry is dated January 1911. Mr J A Jones, dentist to the home, recommended that children should be supplied with tooth powder for cleaning of their teeth. This may imply that prior to this date, it was not expected that teeth should be cleaned, or that one brushed without powder.

On occasions, blind children were admitted into the homes. It was general practice that these should be transferred to The Mount, residential school for the blind and deaf at Penkhull. If a child became ill while living there, they would be returned to the cottage homes for treatment. In 1904, William Roden was returned suffering from whooping cough.

In May 1923, issues had been raised by the Ministry of Health following an inspection of the Homes regarding the arrangements for allotting separate towels, toothbrushes, hair brushes and combs to the children. In 1948, there were many case of ringworm in the Homes, so much so that the medical officer requested that the committee set aside one cottage to isolate those children affected. The reply from the committee was *that the request not be tolerated*. However, in June the same year, the committee agreed that home 19 could be opened for the treatment of children with measles, as they could not be accommodated at Bucknall Isolation Hospital.

Bath night was once a week in those days, either Saturday or Sunday. The fire in the kitchen would be stoked up to heat the water and each child would take its turn. Life Buoy soap was used. The younger children were always inspected afterwards to make sure that had washed themselves correctly.

Bedtime was a matter left to the housemothers. There was no set time or policy. Some varied the time for bed with ages. It could be anything from 7.00 to 8.30pm or even 9.00pm then again it depended if the children were on holiday or at school. If the housemother was strict, and many were, the same time of 7.00pm would apply to all children. Talking, once into bed, was almost a criminal offence to some mothers, who would liberally apply the leather strap to anyone who disobeyed her orders.

The War Years.

The first reference to the Second World War was when an application was made for the use of a vacant cottage for the housing of Czech refugee children who had managed to escape by train. Two cottages were allocated for different families, No.19 and No.20, with the Dash family living in one. They looked after themselves, the parents going to work and the children attending the local schools where they made many friends. They did not involve themselves a great deal with the Home activities. However on one occasion the Dash family gave a concert in the Muster Hall with members of the family giving an insight about the German brutality. Mr Dash supplied all the music and acted the part of a SS official and son Hugo acted as a member of the Hitler Youth. Dr Dash later became the Stoke Schools' dentist, and his son followed in his father's footsteps in that chosen profession

Mr. Hugo Hertz with his charges after escaping from Poland, sailing from Gotenberg, Sweden to Tilbury and arriving in Penkhull in 1939. Rudi Hertz is far left on the picture

Air raid shelters were erected at the top of the field behind the Muster Hall to provide safety, and the Penkhull detachment of the ARP were asked to provide wardens for the homes, two or three nights a week. With the restrictions placed on school spaces after war, it was declared the Muster Hall was to be used as a schoolroom to alleviate the problems at the Penkhull school. In the field below the Homes there was an underground air raid shelter constructed for the Homes.

Czech refugees housed at The Cottage Homes

The children were all issued with gas masks, which every night were hung in a row in a hall along with a cape and shoes, all ready for a quick evacuation from the homes if needed.

Holidays.

The first documentary evidence that children from the new Cottage Homes had an annual holiday comes as early as June 1911, when the superintendent of the home submitted a claim for his expenses in accompanying the boys to a summer camp at Skegness. He was paid £2 15s. To undertake such a distance at such an early period would have been long and difficult. To place this into perspective with other children in the area, even to think of a holiday would have been out of this world, let alone to actually go on one.

Little evidence exists to indicate if this holiday was a one-off holiday or an annual event. A further holiday was much nearer home. In March 1923, it was decided to fund-raise for a children's summer outing by holding a whist drive and dance in the Muster Hall. What form the outing was to take is not recorded but it was probably to Rhyl, as later in the year, a recommendation was made to purchase of plot of land near to Rhyl for the purpose of establishing a summer holiday camp for the children.

Plans for this site did not materialise, probably from the lack of funding as the country was starting to feel the depression in trade and employment. In 1924, arrangements for a holiday were in hand by March, as the need for straw mattresses was expressed although at this point no destination had been decided. In May, it was agreed to go to an unnamed seaside camp at a cost not exceeding 15/- per child. This idea was eventually replaced by a Cheshire campsite at Winsford Broads, not far from the Potteries, probably because of financial restraints. The committee also reviewed the arrangements for the services of Mr W S as resident assistant at the camp for its duration, at a wage of £1 per week, plus board and keep. Where possible,

provisions would be taken with them and were obtained from Penkhull Village Stores; any fresh produce needed to be purchased locally in Winsford. Permission by the guardians was given to vary the diet of the children as necessary. The holiday extended from the 5th – 25th August, and at the September meeting of the guardians a most favourable report was submitted of the camp's success.

Before boarding houses could be afforded, old army camps and schools were used. Southport and Llandudno were popular choices in the 1940s and 50s. Dorothy Hill remembers going to Llandudno and Southport: *At Llandudno we stayed at a school near to the Little Orme, sleeping in the classrooms on palletises with just a blanket over us. We would all line up in the avenue. The boys would go the first week, and the girls the second. Used to have 2d a week pocket money and we tried to save from that for the holiday. We were lucky we went for a week to be extended to 10 days later. Now after all these years I realise how fortunate we were. At Southport, the camp was not far from the beach, an army camp or something. It was very basic but good fun.*

Heather Perry also remembers those holidays at Southport. *I recall the wooden hut was like an army hut. The boys would sleep in the tents and the girls in bunk beds inside the huts. It was good fun as we shared with children from other Homes, but we had to cross a field to get hot water. I remember the first evening meal when there were six cream cakes on the plate, something we had never seen before. One mother said you will all have a cream cake before the end of the holiday and made sure that a different six children had one each evening. It was so difficult to wait for my turn.*

Another year we went to Lowestoft. That was a camp also, but it was better, as we did not have to fetch the water but we still had bunk beds. Then we started to go to Blackpool in boarding houses but that was not as much fun, as at the camps where we were free to run around in the fields and the beach. The mother's seemed to join in more then and took turns making custard and porridge in buckets etc.

We used to go after the war to Llandudno hiring a bus where we had to take straw mattresses to sleep upon but the cooking was done for us recalls Doris Palmer. *Another year we went to Southport. It was an old disused army camp at Weld Road, near to the entrance of Birkdale on the north shore, where we played a lot. First, the boys would spend a holiday and then the girls would follow. One year the highlight for us children was when comedian Sam Costa, who was appearing at the theatre in Southport came and visited us.*

The minute book confirms that Southport was the chosen holiday resort for many years with children being taken there from the end of July until the end of August.

Happy holidays spent at Southport, Blackpool and Llandudno in the 1950s

William Mason also remembers with pleasure the holidays spent in the schoolrooms at Llandudno and the campsite at Southport. *They were like billets. On odd occasions, we were allowed to visit the pleasure beach with 6d. Used to go on the 'roll a penny' in the hope of winning a fortune, but like most, lost nearly all my 6d.*

Out of all those interviewed, the memories of holidays always brought a smile and a thought of past happy times where simple pleasures were the best. Blackpool was a first boarding house destination; No.54 Osborne Road to be exact was one comment. It was the same place every year to the same boarding house landlady for two weeks recalls Brian Tomkins. *We saved the best we could from our weekly pocket money, as we were not given any extra for the holiday. There were no shows or ice creams, just happy times playing on the beach but I remember that we did go to the Tower Circus one year.* Ann Amison has a different recall of Blackpool *I hated it, but when we went to Rhyl that was much better. I don't know how it was paid for but one year we travelled to Liverpool to catch the boat to the Isle of Man, we did that twice.* Bill Bratt also recalls a number of holidays at Blackpool, with most of the time being spent on the beach or going on long walks. *I used to think to myself, I would have never had such a good time, or even a holiday, if I had still been at home.*

Barry Broadhurst also remembers Rhyl with fondness as his favourite destination. *All of the children from our home went together like a huge family and would take over nearly all the boarding house for our annual trip. I remember pestering our housemother for casual wear for the holidays and finally we had jeans and open ended sandals to go away with. That was special as for just a short time we were like normal kids.*

One young lad, who certainly had adventure in his veins, remembers his holidays with great gusto. Mike Shaw certainly liked to do something different. *We always had two weeks holidays in August, either Southport, Llandudno, Blackpool or Gt. Yarmouth, where apart from Gt. Yarmouth we stayed in a boarding house. At Gt. Yarmouth, things were different; we stayed in an old army camp, which was something different and adventurous. Our food was prepared though, and we only had to make up our beds in the morning. At Blackpool, as a young boy of eight or nine, somehow I found myself helping on one of the stalls which sold shoes each day. We were allowed to 'do our own thing' or go around with the others. I recall that I received my very first 10/- note as wages which I promptly spent on an aeroplane trip around the town which cost me the whole of the 10/-. That was something so I only told the odd friend for if my housemother found out, I would have been grounded for a month.*

A Birthday celebration party in one of the homes

298

Pictures around and about Penkhull Cottage Homes

Another boy, William Mason remembers more fondly the Llandudno holiday in a school in the middle of the town. *This was exciting, we all slept on mattresses placed on the floor, and the best part was that we had no household jobs to do for the ten days we were there. All the meals were provided and some days if we went out walking we could have a packed lunch. Just for one night we were allowed to visit the pleasure ground, the flashing lights and the music added to the excitement but sadly we could only spend a few pence on the roll a penny on a square game and lost even that. But good memories. Another year we stayed just outside Southport in Billets, an old camp or something. Here again it was fun being in bunk beds. This time the mothers had to do all the cooking.*

House parents Margaret and David Prince always organised two weeks holiday wherever the children wanted to go. *We took our 'family' to Skegness and Great Yarmouth as well as other places. Having eight children was not an easy thing, finding a boarding house to take us was the first problem. We booked on a B & B and Evening meal basis. To visualise the children even after all these years at Stoke Station as we took those first steps to the train brings tears to my eyes, they were so excited. Money was short and each child received 5/- pocket money. We could not afford to shop or go to the fairground therefore it was always a daily visit to the free Punch and Judy show on the prom or long walks, none of which cost money. On occasions, we would try to persuade proprietors of children's activities to allow us in free because the children were from a cottage home. The weekly pocket money varied from 1/- to 2/- a week depending upon age.*

Below - V.E. Day football game

Punishment.

The writing of this section of the chapter has remained until the end. It has been the most difficult and disturbing. Unfortunately, there are no records of punishment administered available. The monthly meeting of the Board of Guardians referred to the 'punishment book' but no details were given. It is doubtful if much was entered in there anyhow. The book has not survived, and before anyone draws the wrong conclusion over this, to lose a book when a building is closed down is quite common. There are no medical records either and it is doubtful that those were ever compiled in the first place.

In some attempt to put physical punishment into context for the period, it should be remembered that, a period is often viewed and judged on the knowledge of today, not on the understanding of the period in question. This can be very misleading, and muddy the waters of the time in any attempt to comprehend, or to contemplate, the issues and therefore many wrong judgements can be made with the appropriate consequences.

These comments are not made to quantify and qualify any treatment of children at Penkhull Cottage Homes. Some children in care were, according to the evidence from later interviews, well treated. The children can compare legitimately with the treatment often administered to children outside, which in many cases was far worse. However, there were many instances where it would appear this was not the case, and although it is difficult to estimate what was normal and what was acceptable, it is apparent that some foster mother's went far beyond any reasonable approach to the matter. Corporal punishment remains for many a matter of debate, especially for its use in schools where six strokes of the cane or the slipper was frequently administered.

To make one point clear, in the records, both locally and nationally there has never been the suggestion of sexual abuse, not even a whisper or suggestion. Furthermore, all interviewees have been asked that very question and each have responded that there has never even been a rumour to that affect.

For most children their experience at Penkhull was good, giving order and some form of stability to their lives where previously there was none or little at the best. Upon reflection many former children now consider themselves even luckier than many children outside with regard to clothes, food, comforts, holidays and general care. Sadly some children, for whatever reason, were damaged upon arrival; others became unfortunate victims of a system of institutional care.

Dorothy Hill, was, as others aware that certain mothers made their wards' life a 'living hell', but no one dared to speak out for fear of even worse things happening to them. To most, it was considered normal. Dorothy recalls *that some of the boys were beaten and yet the Superintendent did nothing about it. Some children were made to stand in a corner, have their legs or bottom smacked with the back of a wooden hairbrush.*

On the other hand, Heather Perry recalls with pleasure when she got her own back on her housemother. *One day when it was snowing, one housemother who had a bad reputation appeared stuck in the snow. She did not half get a pelting with snowballs, but wow did I suffer the next day.*

I still have memories, after all these years, of being sent to bed on Christmas day for just a silly thing. Missed my meals and the jelly, which was a special treat. It was after the evening meal when I was allowed up to open my Christmas present. I just lay there crying all day long.

For Kenneth Wakefield, he thought the treatment, although hard and strict was acceptable. *As boys, we expected nothing less than what we deserved in most cases. If we were naughty, we were made to stand on a chair in the cold hallway for hours, there were restrictions on our playtime and our weekly sweet allowance, and lastly we were sent to bed early.*

Derek Tipton, whose mother ran the working boys, home in Spark Terrace, has strong memories of the homes. *There were certainly a number of housemothers that I could name who were, frankly, sadistic. It was terrible some days to learn just how cruel some of the mothers had been. We all knew it went on behind closed doors.*

Yvonne Wilson can substantiate these comments from Derek. She was a housemother for just a short while in 1961. *I can to this day recall many mothers that were almost like prison officers, like sergeant majors in charge of a regiment, not just a few young children. The whole scheme of things was most distressing and yet although other mothers knew it was going on behind closed doors, no one would lift a finger to bring it to a halt.*

So distressed over the going on, and seeing these poor children suffer so badly in particular by one mother, Miss Beach, I went to the head office in Stoke, the old Registrar's Office to protest to the head of children's services. Within a couple of days, the person concerned was removed.

Checking the minute books for the year 1961 there is no mention of this matter recorded. Heather recalls also Miss Beach, almost with fear. *I think she was the worst of a bad bunch, even on holidays at Southport the poor boys in her care were treated badly. They were not allowed to wear casual clothes* and play around in the fields or the beach like the other children. Even when we visited the town, they had to be dressed up to the hilt and marched in a row. She was terrible.

Roland Goldman told me many years ago of his time in Penkhull Homes. Rowland in later life became a waiter at the B.P.M.F. Club in Stoke. He recalls that he considered that he was one of the lucky children to have been placed into the homes. *I never knew my parents but I never regretted being brought up in the children's home. The discipline and respect I was taught certainly stood me in good stead for my career even to the polishing of my shoes each day. It was strict and a thick ear would not go amiss on occasions, but through that, it showed me to be polite and respect others. I recall with sadness though when I was about 10 years of age how the superintendent, Mr Sheldon, called me into his office one day and introduced me to my sister, Pearl. We'd been living in the same home, but in different blocks all that time and they never told us. It was most strange to meet my twin sister for the first time; even now, I don't know how to describe my feelings. We certainly looked alike. At 15, Mr Sheldon found me a job at Trentham Golf Club where I found myself moving in very exalted circles. I helped in the bar and served at table in the restaurant. I felt comfortable because my upbringing at Penkhull taught me how to behave.*

Even now after all these years Doris Palmer feels that the treatment she received was good. *In fact, when the time came I was sorry to leave. I had a number of housemothers, some were very strict but for me I felt I was treated so very well. Yes, I would admit that I was punished at times but I probably deserved it. Even when I left, I used to go and visit mother on a regular basis. Even for my 21st birthday, she put on a special party for me.*

For William Mason it was a different matter, for his life at the home was a bitter experience. *The lasting memory I have is that there was never any expression of love, compassion, real care or concern given by my mother. She was cold through and through. Even when ill in bed there was never any kindness shown, just pure hatred for us boys in her care. The sad thing was that all the boys in my home thought that the whole world treated children like this. On occasions we had the mopping up bucket placed over our heads and was told to stand in the hall. All of us, no matter what age, had to get ready to bed after doing the house jobs at 6.30p.m and then into bed by 7.00p.m. Woe-betide-us if we spoke after that, and you did not, because of the threatened belting with her leather strap.*

Punishment came in all forms, from the back of a wooden hairbrush on the back of the hand or even worse across your knuckles recalls Brian Tomkins. I am sure there were broken bones because of that but we did not regard the belting with the leather strap as anything but normal. There were little or no feelings or emotions shown by my mother, we were just expected to get on with it even when we felt so ill.

I still have visions of boys, whose faces were absolutely battered, blood running from the nose because of a housefather punching a kid in the face. Of course, none of this is recorded. One of the punishments, which hurt me the most, was when I had grown out of my short trousers and had my first pair of long ones. I did something wrong and my mother took my new trousers away. It was six months before I got a new pair from the store. That was a punishment. Another punishment was standing in a cold hall all night.

The memories of Gordon Chan almost mirror those of William Mason. *By the time I went into the Homes, there was a mother and a father. In our home, the 'father' went to work during the day, but even in the evenings or weekends he never got involved in the life of us children. Not once do I recall him playing football with us on the playing field like other fathers. One thing I do remember about mother is that she was always on about money and finances. That is probably why only one tin of baked-beans had to feed seven or eight growing boys. I just wonder where the rest of the provisions went, as they were readily available from the stores?*

Where punishment was concerned, she could render a good right-hand slap across the head that would keep you quiet for hours. But life was like that even outside of the Homes so I could not complain.

My reflections now are that my house parents were only 'in it for the money'. They were firm and strict. Mother ruled like a rod of iron. We were all lined up before school in the hall for the daily inspection of cleanliness. We all had our daily chores to carry out no matter how we felt.

The one thing I remember above all is that there was never any love or affection given to us young children. Birthdays were never even mentioned. Mother was spiteful and vindictive whereas the relief mothers were so different. You could tell that they cared. One was a Christian, full of life, excitement and loads of love to share.

I remained at the Cottage Homes until I was seventeen. The Christian relief housemother invited me and a friend to visit her and her mother for tea and cake at Ball Green. We cycled all the way. It was here for the first time in my life that I was treated as 'normal' and received my first ever 'hug'. It was a wonderful experience to feel wanted and realised this was God at work and later I became a committed Christian.

For Bill Bratt, punishment was certainly there, but like so many others, he considered it less than he would have received at home. *To me, I probably deserved to be strapped by mother, and yes, it was painful, but I know that this was the same administered to all children at that time. Even now after all these years, I remain strong in my belief that I owe my life today to Penkhull Cottage Homes. They probably saved me from many years of unbearable torture by my father. There is no doubt* that he would probably have murdered me. Following my experience at the Home, I just don't believe some of the stories that go around about the severe punishments, I just don't. On a few occasions, the social worker said it would be OK for me to return home as things had improved. Each time I returned to Penkhull grateful for the security I had found there.

Brothers Karl and Paul Bateman had a bad time of things and, even today, they bear the emotional scars. *We would be placed into the hall with a galvanised bucket over our heads, not only that a wooden spoon would be knocked on the bucket every time mother passed or encouraged other children to do the same. Then another punishment was horrible, we had sponges, rubbed first in soap, stuffed into our mouths.*

However, one of the most painful was when we were told to lick out our tongues and mother then would knock us under chin so we would bite our tongue. Our mother always had the belt ready for administration keeping it in the front pocket of her uniform. It was frightening.

Probably the worst treatment for anyone recorded here was laid out to Mike Shaw. *I remember my mother sending me from the homes to Mr Brunt's shop in Penkhull for ½ lb of chocolate digestive biscuits. They were sold loose in those days. Never having tasted these before, I tried one, which led to another and another. Upon being asked about the shortfall, I told mother that was all Mr Brunt had given to me. As a result, I was told to return to the shop. How could I, so I told another lie stating Mr Brunt said that the weight was correct.*

As a result, the biscuits, (what were left of them) were crunched up in a dish with olive oil. This mixture was then forced in my mouth despite my protests. This punishment was not sufficient to deal with the matter so was followed by a thrashing. On one occasion I was given a meal I did not like and was told to eat it or else. I did, but then vomited. Therefore, mother held my nose and I was force fed with both food and vomit.

Like many other children, we were to bed early and if caught talking you were in big trouble. On one occasion, I was ordered onto the cold landing and ordered to stand there with my hands on my head until told to return to bed. I stayed there in that position until around 3 a.m. when mother got up to go to the toilet, she had forgotten about me. I was so stiff I could not move my arms. Then if I wet the bed, my nose was rubbed into it and I would have to wash the sheets myself. All this was in addition to having to stand on a chair in the hall for hours upon end.

I remember on one occasion I was forced lie on the back door coconut mat with no clothes on as punishment; I was about 8 or 9 at the time. But no, I ran outside and there I stood freezing with no clothes on until around 11p.m. My mother was so cruel; she would even keep back my weekly alloware of sweets and my pocket money if I was naughty. On another occasion, there was a girl in one of the Homes and she was staying out late one night to meet a boy. *Another girl promised to leave open the bathroom window for her return. This was done. When the girl got inside the home, the superintendent, deputy matron and mother were all waiting. That poor girl was beaten by all three. She was moved from the home and we never saw her again.*

One of my jobs was to peel the potatoes for the deputy matron. I am sure she was aware of the treatment that I was receiving so somehow, rather than challenge the situations, she had me moved to another children's home in Somerset.

Children in the playing field at the bottom of St. Christopher's Avenue

Working Boys' Home.

It was recognised by the guardians that there was a need for alterations in the system once children gained employment. They would remain under care in some form or another but it was felt necessary to encourage self-dependency. The way forward was an arrangement called a Working Boys' Home.

Sir Stanley Matthews on one of his visits to Penkhull Cottage Homes

Boys, once gaining employment, would leave the Cottage Homes and move into accommodation with other working boys as boarders, under a housemother who would be there to provide a secure and stable environment for young people, whilst they adjusted to working life.

The superintendent of the Cottage Homes first mooted the idea as early as March 1911, and approval was sought from the Local Government Board. By September, a large, end-terraced property, ideal for the purpose was located at No.1 Park Terrace, Stoke (now Spark Terrace). Agreement was reached with the landlord and various alterations were put into hand before it could be occupied. These included a fire escape to the rear and the division of the scullery, to accommodate four wash hand basins for the use of the boys at a cost of no more than £15.

Progress was slow, and in January 1912, the owner of the house, Mr G Barlow wrote to the guardians demanding rent for the house even though it remained un-occupied. The guardians replied stating that no rent would be paid until the house became occupied and that no deviation would be made from the original contract. The new accommodation was to provide a home for around seven to nine boys at any one time, although attendance registers show that the number was frequently increased to around twelve.

For many years, Mrs Goodall, a widow, ran the Home. The property was large and two rooms were allocated to the boys, a back bedroom that contained five single beds, and a front corner room containing six. On the ground floor was a communal kitchen, a dining and living room. The house parents had their own private accommodation.

Just before the Second World War, Mrs Francis Tipton took over the running of the Home for Working Boys'. Mrs Tipton had been employed already for a few years at Penkhull, first in the reception home for Catholic children, then for a short period as a foster mother at No.3. Mrs Tipton remained in the position at Spark Terrace until she retired on health grounds in the late 1950s. Mrs Green then undertook the running of the home.

Derek Tipton who lived with his parents at Spark Terrace remembers the home well. *It was a very happy atmosphere, the boys had loads of good food, and a cleaner would come into the home each week and clean the boy's rooms and the communal area. All the boys' were out by 8 o'clock to return at some time after 5.00p.m. Jobs were much easier to get in those days and many of the boys were apprentices to skilled jobs. Out of their pocket money they were encouraged to save in 'the Post Office' but some was spent on going to the pictures at the 'Princes' picture house in Wharf Street, Stoke.*

The matinee performance on a Saturday cost only 2d. At Christmas, we all celebrated around the table sharing gifts. One year, before television one boy managed to bring an old projector and show some old black and white silent films. Such a wonderful occasion.

Every Friday evening was payday and each boy would go and see Mrs Tipton in her own sitting room and hand over their wage packet. Out of this, depending upon the age of the boy and the amount of their wages were deducted board and lodgings, a clothing charge and savings. Only their weekly pocket money was given back. All was written down in a ledger.

Mrs Tipton was strict, but fair standing no nonsense from the boys. Punishment would involve having to go to bed early or the stopping of pocket money and probably the occasional slap for a boy who deserved this. Visits to the Billiard Hall, over Burton's Tailors in Stoke, were barred. The guardians considered the venue as an unsuitable place for young men. Mr Sheldon, the Homes superintendent was brought in to lay down the law over this, but even so, a number of the boys continued to visit the hall.

During the war, many of the older boys went off to serve. For them, the working boys' home, or the Cottage Homes before was the only 'home' they had experienced. *Often when on leave the boys would return, asking if they could stay with us again* recalls Derek. *No one was ever refused even if it meant sleeping two in a bed or on the sitting room floor. Once having left the working boys home, many would still return to see mother and at Christmas time, a number of the boys would come and spend the day at Spark Terrace because they had nowhere else to go. During the summer, we still managed to have the occasional holiday. For a number of years the boys', together with my family managed to borrow tents and go off to Dovedale for a camping holiday.*

Although life in the working boys' home was different from the Cottage Homes, until they became 18 years old, those adopted as babies or young children were legally under the care of the Board of Guardians, later the local authority. It was recognised that once employment was gained there was a need to alter the provision made for them in such a way to encourage self-dependency. At the age of 18, boys were encouraged to find lodgings for themselves. Boys once working frequently discovered that their parents whom had had no contact with them all their lives suddenly made contact again. This was considered to be down to the fact that that the boys were now earning money.

In conclusion, despite the fact that there is now considerable support for struggling parents and education over the last fifty years we should have created a society with a better understanding of how to treat and care for children. Health and living conditions have been transformed beyond recognition, from even when I was a child. Much legislation has been undertaken to ensure that children are not exploited and abused, but cared for. However, taking all this into consideration, makes it even worse that some sections of society fail in their treatment of its children where they continue to be abused, tormented and beaten and have no stability or order in their lives.

So many children are simply not loved or wanted and society is the far worse for it.

St. Christopher's Avenue 2010

Chapter 21
The War Years.

It is now nearly forty years since, along with my good friends Ron Foster and Ken Nutt; I decided to make a concerted effort to record memories of those people in Penkhull who wished to share their experience of life during those years of 1939-45. A number had seen service in the Home Guard, 'Dads Army' as it is affectionately now called. For those involved in the defence of our land, along with members of the ARP and other units it seemed all too possible that a day might come - and soon - when Penkhull had to be defended at all costs.

The material used to compile this chapter is not mine but belong to others most of whom are sadly gone: Major Campbell, Bill Gott, Miss Ashwell, Frank Walker, Bill Cliff, Ernest Tew, Hilda Littler, Miss Maskery, Frank Marsden, George Hulme, Doug Jervis, Alice Pattinson, Bert Pattinson, Winnie Roberts, Roslyn Peake and Betty Burrows the last three being the only people still remaining. Each contribution is invaluable and priceless. It is right that they should be shared.

I have also used many church magazines for the period, together with the PCC minutes of that time. In addition, I have a collection of hand-written notes of Rev. VG Aston, which will be used where appropriate.

Prelude to War

The events leading up to the start of World War II have been well documented over the years, but to place this chapter into context perhaps it is right to allow the story to unfold from the point where Penkhull experiences its first taste of war with promises rather than action from our Government as Hitler and the Nazi Party had grown from a small group of disillusioned soldiers and extremists in 1933 to the largest party in the Reichstag.

Gaining prominence through mass rallies and political agitating, Hitler had come to be viewed by many as the Saviour of Germany, a man to lead the people out of the shame of Versailles. He sought to rebuild Germany with new autobahns, greater industrialisation and labour projects all having a great relevance in military terms.

Conquest was at the heart of both Hitler's foreign and domestic policies since the beginning of his political career. He believed that war showed a nation at its finest and that through war a perfect state could be created for the new Germany. It became apparent that regardless of the policy of appeasement and actions of all other outside parties the intentions of Hitler were set firmly from the day he came to power and in that respect war was inevitable.

In 1935 conscription was introduced in Germany. This broke the Treaty of Versailles, but Britain and France did nothing. Britain and France continued to sit in the wings when Hitler invaded the Rhineland on 7th March 1936. After encouraging Austrian Nazis to demand union with Germany in 1938, he then invaded Austria. This again broke the treaty of Versailles but once more Britain and France took no action. In the summer of that year Nazi sympathisers began to enter Czechoslovakia and the Sudetenland to fight with their traditional enemies, the Communists, Social Democrats and Socialists, and to focus attention on the supposed plight of the ethnic Germans. Hitler demanded the Sudetenland from President Eduart Benes. Benes turned to Britain for help. Prime Minister Chamberlain failed to comprehend the circumstances in which he lived. He sought to appease Hitler and flew to Munich on September 29th to discuss the Czech crisis.

Chamberlain along with France essentially sacrificed Czechoslovakia on the altar of appeasement and returned to the UK with a signed treaty for 'peace in our time'. Six months later on 15th March 1939 Hitler's troops marched into Prague.

Following Mr Chamberlain's smiling announcement of peace, a group of deaf children who had recently been evacuated from Greenwich to The Mount School for the duration of the anticipated war were within a week on their way back home,

Neville Chaberlain returns with a promise 'Peace in our time'

as the threat of war was now 'over' and everyday life as we knew it could resume.

It was following the Germanisation of Sudetenland and the threat to the ethnic minorities in Czechoslovakia that a massive campaign was launched by Sir Nicholas Winton and others to evacuate from Europe thousands of children whose parents desperately wanted to protect their children from Nazi persecution. In September 1938 when Chamberlain signed the Munich Agreement, the area of Teplice was formally ceded. In January of 1939 Charles and Hannah Strasser emigrated from Teplice to the UK. Charles worked in the pottery industry in Czechoslovakia and so he made his way to Stoke-on-Trent to seek work. Others fled Teplice to Prague where they explored opportunities to further escape from the country. Somehow they came into contact with Sir. Nicholas Winton or his team who arranged for trains to take children out from Prague to the UK, but each child had to be accepted, with money being put up first by families in the UK. The Strassers knew the family of Dash well and so gladly agreed finance the journey.

These children and others from Czechoslovakia came to be housed in what was Penkhull Cottage Homes (now St. Christopher's Avenue). They arrived by courtesy of the Czech Children's Refugee Committee in 1939. Amongst these children were Hugo Dash later to become a well-known local dental surgeon and his sister Lisa who attended Thistley Hough Girls School. Later Charles Strasser became the head of the national company, Photopia.

Czech refugees housed at The Cottage Homes

Mr Hugo Hertz with his charges after escaping from Poland, sailing from Gotenberg, Sweden to Tilbury and arriving in Penkhull in 1939
Rudi Hertz is far left in the picture

At first local people were apprehensive and objected to having refugees on their doorstep, recalls Ken Nutt who later became a friend of Hugo: *because they dressed differently and spoke differently they were treated differently, but after awhile they were accepted and started to join in local activities.*

In a tape recording done some forty odd years ago, I recorded Miss Phyllis Ashwell who used to live at Beech Grove. She was then into her late 80s and remembers them well. *I recall the Czech children, Hugo, Hendrick, Frizz and Lisa well from the Cottage Homes. They used to come for tea at Beech Grove bringing their musical instruments with them. They were all so musical and after tea, often outside on the lawns we would sit and have a jolly good time listening to them play.* As part of preparations for war, Hartshill Boy Scouts were employed in the filling of hundreds of sand bags at the NSRI The Czech boys by this time had joined the group.

Preparations for war commenced long before September 1939. It was clear that the news from Europe was not good

and in March 1938 war seemed inevitable, as Germany demanded the return of the Sudetenland and the Government decided that local councils should commence preparations. On 1st January 1938, the A.R.P. Act (Air Raid Precautions) came into force, compelling all local authorities to set up ARP schemes.

Hartshill Boy Scouts filling sand-bags for use at the hospital

In Penkhull a number of old cottages in Rothwell Street, one of which was the home of Winnie Alldis were demolished to make way for large water storage tanks. These were to be used in case of incendiary bombs starting fires if dropped on the village. Other preparations such as deep trenches being dug in Richmond Street Park and air raid shelters for the first time were being thought of. In April 1939, conscription was introduced; increasing the British Armed forces by more that 1.5 million. All British men aged 20 or 21, were required to take six months' military training. This was further increased to all men between the ages of 18 and 40 being called up for service.

Just two weeks before war was declared, *The Evening Sentinel* reported that there was an urgent need for more than 1000 volunteers in Stoke-on-Trent and 400 in Newcastle to bring the service to the required efficiency. Mr L Bunn, Chief Constable wrote with some urgency that only half of the volunteers to date had been trained and a serious deficiency was experienced in maintaining medical services. In the case of war there would be a deficiency of 554 ambulance drivers and attendants. The list continued showing serious staff shortages for rescue and demolition, decontamination and special constables.

All possible active men were to be mobilised. I recall Doug Jervis telling me that he was pressed *into night fire watching* at Thistley Hough High School, but had to return back to the farm early to get his cows out to pasture. He later admitted that on many occasions during calving that he would not turn up for duty but managed to persuade Mr

Swetnam the local organiser to sign his attendance book the next morning. On the other hand Mr Frank Peake of Kirkland Lane, and many others in Penkhull, became early volunteers to join giving up two or three nights a week and then having to go to work the next morning. Mr Peake with other members of the ARP. used to meet in Penkhull Infants School. His daughter Roslyn recalls clearly her father in uniform, but could *never understand what use a bucket full of sand would be in case of fire that her father had to carry around!*

Probably one of the most notable memories of war years was the Anderson Shelters attributed to the Home Secretary John Anderson. The idea of producing a cheap domestic shelter, for protection from bombing had been of concern for some time. They consisted of corrugated iron forming a shell six feet high by just under four feet wide and six feet long. They were fitted free for all earning less than £250 per year and those above that income contributed £7.

Anderson Shelters

Those in Penkhull with gardens and even some with only brick backyards got to work installing their own shelters. Even today many still remain hidden by the undergrowth of sixty years. *The biggest problem was that after heavy rain they often became flooded* recalled Roslyn, as I talked to her about

them. Even so, most made the best of the situation making bunk-bends and keeping blankets, oil lamps and a supply of water and food - just in case! And not forgetting a radio to keep in touch with the outside world.

The Local Authority had the responsibility for providing public air raid shelters. *The Evening Sentinel* published lists of places that would provide underground shelters for workers and shoppers. None in Penkhull were listed but it did include those near to Penkhull and the town of Stoke.

The entrance to the Air Raid Shelter beneath Stoke Meat Market in South Wolfe Street, Stoke

In Hartshill Road there was Midlands Hotel where accommodation was provided for 200. The School of Art in London Road 50, The Red Lion and the Noah's Ark in Hartshill both providing 50. At Oakhill Hall there could be 150 housed in the large cellars beneath the building.

For the vast majority of people of Penkhull living in terraced houses, the pantry with three steps down beneath the stairs provided the only protection from air raids unless they had purchased the Morrison Shelter. These were in the form of a heavy steel table with steel mesh sides. With a large tablecloth placed over, it went un-noticed although I have not heard of anyone in Penkhull having one.

It was not until after war had been declared that the go-a-head was given to the provision of air raid shelters for schools. The Emergencies Measures Committee of Stoke-on-Trent met on the 9th September to decide on the action necessary. They were to meet the following day with the ARP Committee to finalise arrangements.

As with all events that happen, even those for the worst, such as war, there are always those who can make a few pounds as a result. The manufacture of air raid shelters was a typical example. Soon there were numerous companies around Stoke only too willing to supply them. The nearest to Penkhull was in Copeland Street, Stoke.

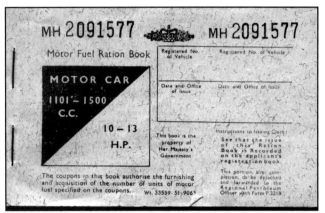

Fuel Ration Book

The Government announced on August 1st petrol rationing in the event of war. By this time coupons had already been distributed. Mr Lloyd, the Minister of Mines, stated that in view of the vital importance of petrol and other petroleum products, a comprehensive scheme would be implemented for the maintenance of supplies. Special arrangements would be announced for the supply to ambulances, fire brigades and the ARP.

Petrol rationing was responsible for most privately owned motor vehicles being placed into storage for the duration of the war. Petrol was always in short supply and hard to find. Initially the ration was three gallons of petrol per week, so all but the shortest of trips were out of the question. The only petrol filling station in Penkhull

Harold Rowland

was that of Harold Rowland in St Thomas Place, and in reality car ownership was almost non-existent, probably amounting to no more than fifty and no petrol could be supplied without coupons. Mr Rowland kept his business going during the war despite loss of trade, and like other properties suffered the effects of war with two incendiary bombs being dropped onto the roof, with nothing more than a bucket of sand and a stirrup pump to put out the fire. The storage area at the back of his garage was used to store a number of cars *laid off* for the war years.

Talking to Mrs Betty Burrows (nee Rowland) she remembers her father obtaining his petrol supplies from 'Pool Petrol' based at Etruria. Penkhull Filling Station was the major supplier to doctors at the hospital who received additional allowances because of their work. Mr Rowland maintained his service contracts with many doctors including Dr and Mrs Ramage, well-known supporters of Penkhull Church,

who then lived in Queens Road. Betty tells me that for a few favours, the odd gallon of petrol could go unnoticed and mean probably the addition of a few extra rashers of bacon, or extra butter, to the table at weekends from many of their customers.

Although public sector vehicles received special petrol allowances, many ingenious alternative fuel devices such as gas storage bladders and generators were employed. The single-decker corporation buses were surmounted with enormous gasbags in some towns. People, who could afford one and were lucky enough to find them, equipped their automobiles with similar devices. The commercial sector, milkmen, coal deliveries etc. were encouraged to use horse drawn vehicles wherever possible.

War Declared

Throughout all this the PMT kept the 'Penkhull Circular' going, that public service from the Majestic cinema in Stoke, through Oakhill, Penkhull and Hartshill, to return to Stoke and commence the whole process again.

War commenced with Germany on the 3rd September 1939, but August was a holiday period for many thousands of 'Potters'. In those days Stoke Railway Station was bursting at the seams conveying tens of thousands from Stoke-on-Trent to digs in either Blackpool or North Wales. This was in addition to numerous day trips undertaken during the first two weeks of August. *The Evening Sentinel* reported: *Joyous Holiday Trek for Wakes Week - Crowds pour from North*

Staffordshire, 36,000 leave the district', probably most thinking that this might be the last holiday they would experience for some years.

With over £250,000 of holiday money clutched firmly in workers hands, Stoke and Penkhull were deserted. The Territorial Army had gone off to their training camps. There was a Carnival of Queens in Hanley Park, floral splendour at Shrewsbury, and the famous Goldin, the illusionist was confusing audiences at the Theatre Royal in Hanley.

And yet to all these families it would be a very different Stoke and Penkhull that they returned to. They left with lights blazing, but they returned to a trial blackout as North Staffordshire was included in a 28 county trial, claimed to be the worlds greatest and the nearest thing to reality of war Britain had ever known in peacetime.

The Evening Sentinel promptly reported the event on the 11th August: *Railway and road traffic necessitated by the return of thousands of holiday makers from excursions impaired the effectiveness in Stoke last night of the blackout for a period from 1.30 a.m. - 4.00 a.m. An ARP official summed up the event by stating that all drivers co-operated fully with the request to turn off their headlights. Headlights were only allowed at important junctions and roundabouts.*

By the end of August, the painting of kerbstones had taken place; street lights were blacked out and hundreds of gallons of black and white paint had been sold for the purpose of painting out roof lights and the blackening of windows in shops and houses.

On the domestic front, Winnie Wyse and Betty Burrows remember having to place brown sticky paper cross ways across all the windows of the house to reduce the risk of shattering glass. In addition to this there was a huge demand for black material to make curtains for the downstairs at least. And where from? Harrison's of Church Street, Stoke or the market. No light was to be let out during the war in case of enemy attack. It was an offence even to show a crack of light through the curtains. Some homes just made linings

for existing curtains and each evening the ARP patrol would walk every street just to make sure orders were followed. Cars had a special cover fitted over the headlights with just a little slit making the light shine only to the road. Once more Mr Rowland was kept busy making these in his garage. If you did have to go out, a torch was a must because everything was so black.

The church did not escape either, or the school at the top of Trent Valley Road. Both had to be blacked out after war was declared. The windows of The Greyhound were also covered over as seen in an old photograph. If any events were organised, they would coincide with a *full moon* so people had the benefit of natural light whilst walking in the village.

One thing followed another, there was no let-up, and the issue of gas masks became necessary to all. It was the responsibility of the ARP to issue these. For those in Penkhull they were distributed at the school, which was by this time the official H.Q. for the ARP. All residents had to go and collect theirs, a normal size respirator for adults whilst babies under the age of two had to endure (if the necessity arose) a

Picture as it appeared in *The Evening Sentinel*

GAS!

THE ECONOMIC LEAGUE
1941
War Series No.20

Have you got a Gas Mask?

Is it in good condition?

Do you carry it regularly?

IF NOT — WHY NOT?

whole unit complete with air pump at the side for mother to keep a supply of air within the unit. All gas masks were supplied with thick cardboard-like boxes with string for carrying over the shoulder or around the neck of children.

It became standard practice to carry in the box Horlicks tablets, just in case anyone was caught in a raid without food for any length of time. The problem was that children used to eat them as fast as they were distributed. However, in the early days people ignored the importance of carrying their masks with them, so much so, that the Chief Constable gave out a warning that appeared in *The Evening Sentinel* stating that: *all must wear their masks said Mr Bunn* and at the same time it was announced that the City had formed a 'Food Committee'.

I recall Frank Marsden who lived at 100 Newcastle Lane, talking to me one evening of an incident of a *light showing* in what was Commercial Row just off Penkhull New Road. It was late at night and a small patrol was sent to investigate after Fenton wardens had rang through to Penkhull to inform them that a light was showing. The usual warning of *turn out that light* was shouted from the pavement. Upon hearing this, a rather stout lady came to the window and responded with the words (or something similar) *if you don't clear off, you will get this lot over you.* Not to be outdone, the ARP wardens replied only to be showered with the contents of a chamber pot that had been quickly retrieved from under the nearest bed. Frank remembers it well as all concerned had to be sent home because of the unbelievable stink.

So how did Penkhull receive the news that war had been declared with Germany? Many stayed at home that morning from church to listen to Chamberlain declare that he had received no assurances from Berlin and subsequently we were at war with Germany. Those who did attend church received no sermon from Rev Aston that morning, instead as the deadline approached, a portable radio was 'hooked up' in church by Mr Frank Bell. *At the 8.00 a.m. service prayers were offered for peace. The mood was sombre, hopes faint and eyes turned to our first boy in uniform* wrote V G Aston.

The news at 10.00 a.m. offered no improvement. The time limit of the ultimatum to Germany was to expire in one hour. The Prime Minister would speak directly to the nation on radio at 11.15a.m. The 11.00a.m. service consisted of a few prayers, the radio broadcast and two hymns. The children's Sunday school was cancelled. At 3.00p.m. village boys asked if they could prepare the schoolroom for games as all public amusements were cancelled. V.G. wrote: *at 6.00 p.m. we hear the voice of our beloved King. "With God's help we will prevail".* Sunday Evensong reflected the mood of the village. The hymns, appropriately chosen were *Oft in Danger; Holy Father, in Thy mercy, and O God our Help.* It was a real test and many

shed tears at that service wondering just what lay ahead. The real first blackout found a strange acceptance of what was to be, but resolution and courage were the real marks of the first day at war for those of Penkhull.

So what was showing in the local cinemas in Stoke the night before war was declared? The Hippodrome in Kingsway was showing Tyrone Power, the heartthrob of the thirties in *Jesse James* for the first half of the week, and George Formby and Googie Withers in *Trouble Brewing* for the second half. There were, however strict conditions to the reopening. All premises must be in readiness, with a fire squad, together with full fire-fighting equipment including sand, long-handled shovels and means of dealing with incendiary bombs. A person must also be on duty throughout the whole period for the purpose of listening for air raid warnings. And yet, despite all this people flocked once more from Penkhull to the 'flicks' at Stoke, not only to see the films on show but also to see the Movie News, as there were no televisions in those days.

Tyrone Power

Goodie Withers and George Formby

Football matches were also allowed to play from Saturday 16th September, but only friendly games, no league matches because they would attract too many people. Stoke played Coventry at a packed Victoria ground and *The Evening Sentinel* reported that Stoke had nineteen players available to play.

Baker, Stoke City's outside left; heading the ball gave City the lead in their friendly match with Coventry. Baker's header followed a free-kick by no less than Stanley Matthews. Stoke 3 Coventry 1. (Baker, Peppitt and Sale scoring.) And the cost of a Saturday afternoon's entertainment? Boothen and Butler Street stands 2/-, Butler Street corners 1/6d, Boothen and Butler Street paddock 1/6d, Ground 1/-, Boys 6d and soldiers in uniform were to be admitted to the ground for just 6d.

Stoke v Coventry. Stoke won 3 -1

The following week, the residents of Penkhull saw the delivery of National Registration forms through their doors.

'National Registration Day', as it was known, would be held the following Friday, September 29th. By midnight every person living in each household would have to be listed on the registration form giving their occupation and other particulars. On Saturday and Sunday, following registration day, enumerators would collect the completed forms, and

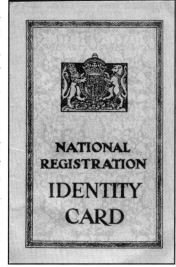

there and then, issue Identity Cards to every member of the civil population.

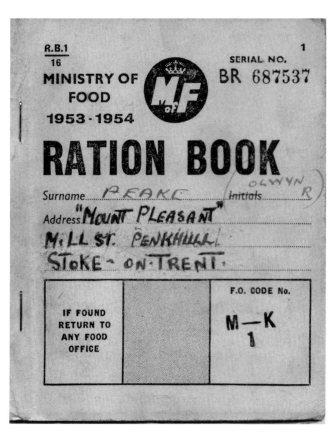

The National Registration compiled, served as the basis for food rationing. In Stoke-on-Trent there were no fewer than a 250 enumerators, responsible for a district each comprising of about 300 houses. The North Staffs Infirmary had an enumerator to itself.

National Registration was not confined to British Subjects. All persons had to complete and those whose nationality was seen as in conflict would be interned for the period of the war. One such person from Penkhull was Mr Delducia, the Italian ice cream man from the cottage that stood down the passage at the side of Penkhull D.I.Y. shop in Newcastle Lane. Even though he had been brought up in the UK and was considered by his friends as not a threat to national security, but because of his nationality he was still interned.

Just a few weeks after the declaration of war, Penkhull Parochial Church Council met to discuss the urgent need for blackouts in the church, which would conform, to the new regulations. V.G. Aston stated that the best way would be to board up the three stained glass windows from the outside but it would be far too expensive, and if all the windows were painted it would mean the church would always be in darkness. It was finally proposed by Mr Dobson that the matter should be left in the hands of the vicar and wardens to sort out.

Civil Defence and School

It was in March 1933, that local authorities had been chosen as the agencies to be responsible for the local organisation of the Civil Defence Services. Under that umbrella, a sub committee was formed called the Air Raid Precautions sub committee. This small committee had actually operated in secret from 1924. When in March 1935, Germany announced that she had re-established her air force; the ARP department went to work and began to issue instructions to local authorities. In January 1937, the first ARP broadcast was made and an appeal was made for volunteers. In the first years of their existence, the ARP personnel had only a helmet, a silver ARP badge and an armband.

As soon as war was announced, all schools were closed initially; Penkhull Infants School at the top of Trentham Road was no different from all others. What was different, was, that it was designated to become the headquarters of the ARP. The PCC minute book confirms that the sum of 8/- (40p) per week would be paid by the ARP for the use of the rooms. At the same meeting after war had been declared, it appears that more concern was expressed as to whether it was more important to pay the fire insurance premium on the scenery used for the annual Revue!

Another good friend of mine, George Hulme, was aged seven in 1939, but remembers clearly the events of the day. *The school appeared closed for some time after the six weeks school*

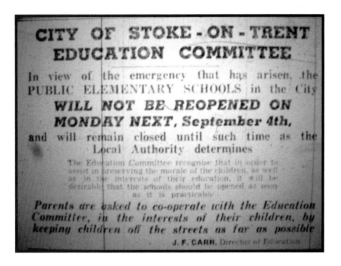

summer holiday because the air raid shelters had not yet been built. Eventually there was a shift system of attendance. Some classes went to school in a morning and some in the afternoon and then they alternated. You can imagine the confusion, children often turning up on the wrong shift. Some children were transferred to the Cottage Homes for lessons.

After several weeks, a few classes were transferred to the Close School, where dividing the assembly hall had created an additional classroom. Here there were two large cellars, plus a new concrete tunnel and air raid shelters in the grounds. George remembers at least three air raid warnings when pupils were evacuated to the shelters, which usually meant a sing-along with the teachers and a welcome break from lessons. Surprisingly George recalled the exercise books being of grey paper and not white as re-cycled paper was used. And it goes without saying that he was delighted for a welcome 'snooze' on folded arms on the desk at school along with all the other children if their previous night's sleep was disturbed by air-raid sirens.

Still looking fit, in 2010; Gilbert Richards of Barnfield recalls that he was one of the early volunteers as a young lad to join what was known as the ARP Messengers. *It never*

really got organised but the idea was that if ever the telephone lines were down, the messengers would be the first call to carry out the service of transferring information. At first we were based in the Penkhull School, the room to the left just as you go in. The building was fitted out with thick black curtains and the windows were all taped up. Later the messengers moved to the control room in the basement of what used to be the Electricity Offices in Kingsway. This was the HQ for the Civil Defence.

We worked on a rota basis, a few nights a week, most of the time just playing cards. Many would fall asleep whilst on duty. I recall Earnest Tew who worked so hard as an ARP warden and also Ken Nutt of Queens Road. The senior warden in Penkhull was Stan Mansfield. There was also Mr Harthern, the preacher from Franklin Road. He also served as an ARP warden and was in charge at Stoke H.Q. At Kingsway the one attraction was the canteen, a good meal for a matter of pence. There was no skimping on rations there, which was probably the attraction for many young lads to join.

Winnie Wyse, whose father was the caretaker of the school, recalls: *all the extra work involved in keeping the school clean and tidy. By night the ARP, and later the Home Guard used the school at night and by day children. There was no end to the hours my dad spent at the school during the war, it was tough for him* remembers Winnie. Miss Roslyn Peake of Kirkland Lane remembers that her father, Frank gave up two or three nights a week as an ARP warden. *He was self-employed therefore could make up his sleep the following day if he was not busy. He, like the other wardens would walk the streets making sure that curtains were closed and no light showing.*

He always carried with him a bucket of sand in case of incendiary bombs dropping on Penkhull. Like all the other young children in the village we had to go to the school to collect our gas masks and at the same time receive our quota of Ovaltine tablets in case of emergencies.

Full time ARP wardens were paid the sum of £3 a week for men and £2 for women. Later in 1939 all part time wardens received payment and those in the rescue teams received more.

'War Work' for Women

It was only a few months following the outbreak of war, or early in 1940 that women were 'called up' to serve in those jobs deemed necessary for the war. One such person in Penkhull, amongst many others, was Mrs Cecily Beech (nee Platt) of 58 Oxford Street. Who talks of the initial shock at being suddenly called-up. *One day the letter just came through the post,* she explained, *I had no choice; I had to go to Swynnerton. I was just seventeen, and came home from work on the first day after being picked up by bus in Princes Road*

ARP Messengers on Parade in Kingsway 1941. Gilbert Richards central front

at 5.30 a.m. and said to my mother, *I'm not going again.
However the next morning I was there waiting for the bus at
5.30a.m. along with other girls from the village. We all had our
part to play for the war effort so I could not refuse.*

*We worked three shifts and earned 10/6d a week for working
with yellow powder on the tracer bullet production line. You were
searched on the way into work every day to make sure you weren't
taking matches or cigarettes into the factory. I remember one time
I had a match in my pocket. I had to take it back to the main
hut and leave it there. I could have been suspended for it though.
It was quite strict there. You couldn't have any time off without
a Doctor's note. We used to wear green overalls. I wanted to take
mine home to wash and left it on under my coat, but I got caught
and searched. I do not recall having holidays either.*

But all told, they were happy
times. The mention of Workers
Playtime on the wireless with
Wilfred Pickles and his *'Give
em the money Mabel'* phrase
brings back so many valued
memories. But munitions were
not the only occupation
women were called to do.
Many had to work in factories,
especially those producing
guns and machines for the

Wilfred Pickles and Mabel

war. Others were called to jobs working for the local
electricity company the, Civil Defence or for education as
unqualified teachers. Many ended up working on farms out
of the district or on the buses.

Nearer comes the War
Penkhull Survivor of HMS Courageous
IN FIRST LIST OF SAVED

read the heading on the front-
page headlines of *The Evening
Sentinel* only a matter of days
after war was declared. On
Tuesday 19th September, it
reported the sinking of aircraft
carrier 'Courageous' by enemy
submarine where only 681
survived the attack out of a total
crew of 1,260. Amongst the first
to be listed as saved was
Leading Signalman John
Siddorn of 150 Oxford Street,
Penkhull where he lived with

John Siddorn

his parents. Like many others, he had served in the Navy for
a twelve-year term until the previous May, but after three
months of civilian life he was recalled to service to serve on
the 'HMS Courageous'.

St. Thomas' Church, like so many parish churches, became
the focus for people to express their thoughts and to receive
whatever comfort they could in times of national trouble or
conflict. The Vicar, Rev V G Aston commenced writing a
war diary in the church magazine, which gave an insight to
events, and expressions of concerns as seen though his eyes.

To bring home the thoughts of the loss of our young men, he
wrote on Tuesday 5th September, *that the troops from
Hartshill barracks passed through Penkhull at 5.00 a.m.
marching to their training camp. We learn of the R.A.F. raid at
Kiel.* He mentions also, *that for that week choir practice was
forbidden, owing to the new lighting blackout order.* Although he
continues to discuss the efforts of redecorating the church, he
recalls rather sombrely that at Sunday evensong the cross
was carried by a soldier, and prayers were offered for two
village lads who were to sail to France the following day,
ending the sentence vividly *Thus nearer comes the war.*

VG comments on events near and far as the first months of
the war continued. Concerned with the news reports of the
treatment of the Poles by Germany and the horrific, almost
unbelievable atrocities against humanity being carried out
in that country he proclaims . . . *God help them in their
struggle.* But he returns to local issues by stating that the
busiest part of the village was the school with the ARP, and
on a personal note, reflects with some humour, how he
collided with the church wall (to the detriment of the former)
during the first week's blackouts. He concludes his notes for
that week with the news that Russia was now *invading
Poland and finally crushing those brave people. Their end is
certain now!*

Other activities in Penkhull responded to the call. The
Penkhull and Hartshill depot for the Red Cross Hospital
War Supplies was established at The Mount blind and deaf
school. The depot was open two days a week for
contributions for the purchase of materials. The chairman
was Mrs N S Follwell of the school, and the secretary Mrs W
Johnson of Tilson Avenue.

In the month of November, V.G. again gives us an insight
into village life with his Parochial War Diary. This was to be
the last, as restrictions on publications, war efforts and
recordings for security reasons and propaganda applied to
church magazines equally as to the newspapers and the
wireless.

*The day schools (Church Hall) are being further prepared for a
long tenancy by the ARP. The children are to attend other schools
in shifts. The first of many Church Parades during the war and
after took place on Sunday 24th. Many of our boys are present
under the command of Major Piggott and they joined heartily in
the service* wrote V.G.

Once more V.G. recalls the struggle in Poland with the fall of Warsaw. *Was there ever the like? The place was bombed out of existence* he concluded, and finally passes comment on the war with the fact that the Germans were sinking neutral ships.

On the local front, butter was to rise to 1/7d per lb. and V.G. was visiting many troops in the parish with the comment *they are a fine lot* and asking for any gifts to be passed on to him. On Sunday 1st October it was announced that many of Penkhull's young lads were to be *called up,* as the age was now to include those of 22 years.

The Home Guard

Most of us have, at some time or another, enjoyed the BBC television series 'Dad's Army', with its somewhat lighthearted look at the Second World War's Home Guard. However, despite this portrayal, in its time, the Home Guard represented a formidable force of willing volunteers ready to give up their lives in protection of their country.

I recall that in around 1967, I took my portable tape recorder, and with a deep breath, knocked on the door of Major George Campbell, M.C. of Queens Road and asked if I could interview him for his memories of the Penkhull Home Guard. Welcoming me in, he talked at length of his involvement and how it all started.

The Home Guard all came about following the invasion of northern France by 2,000 German tanks under Lieutenant-General Heinz Guderian. Anthony Eden, the secretary of State for War, called for a Local Defence Volunteer Force (LDV). He asked for men aged 17 to 65 to serve in this new force. Before the broadcast was made, men were volunteering, and within twenty-four hours, a quarter of a million men had come forward. In August 1940, Winston Churchill renamed L.D.V. the 'Home Guard'.

Winston Churchill

Major Campbell, in an instant recalled all the facts: *Eden's call to those who were in the First World War bought a quick response. Following the broadcast I went down with the first group of volunteers from Penkhull to the Drill Hall in Booth Street, Stoke, where Lt-Col A R Moffat was in charge. I was furious and almost shouted at Moffat "I've got all these people outside, done a day's work and no one here to receive them." In the first place the H.G. was certainly not very organised.*

The idea was to have one battalion for the whole city, and the HQ was to be at Victoria Square Barracks in Shelton.

Penkhull formed a part of Stoke Company, which also included Stoke, Hartshill and Hanford, and under the commanding officer Mr C J Noke where Major Campbell was placed in charge of the Penkhull Platoon. The correct title was 'C' Company and its officers included the following: Major Campbell, Lieuts. W E Gott; C Bellamy; J Taylor, J A Jolly, P C Edwards and R W Cranham. Within the first year Major Campbell was promoted and Mr W Gott took command.

Major Campbell knew Rev V G Aston quite well and asked if the newly formed Home Guard could use the Church steeple every night as a lookout.

The P.C.C. minute book dated Thursday 13th June 1940 confirms - The vicar stated that: *the local defence corps have asked for the steeple to be used as an observation post to assist them in their duties in protecting homes against possible landings by enemy parachutists.* He then gave an account of what this entailed, and the matter was thrown open for discussion. The feeling was that every help should be given to the government in their prosecution of the war, and Mr Meiklejohn proposed that *This council is of the opinion that the Defence Corps shall have the use of the tower as an Observation Post* and that *this resolution be submitted to the Archdeacon for approval.* This was seconded by Mrs Ramage and carried. Note was made also that the church insurers should be notified of this action.

Two other interesting items worthy of mention, for at that meeting the only lady there was Mrs Ramage, all others sent their apologies because they were attending the weekly whist drive (at war and all they could think of was a whist drive!) and as the vicar was using his car to visit soldiers it was agreed that he should be reimbursed for the petrol.

In the first instance Penkhull's Dad's Army only had an armband proudly displaying the initials LDV - weapons were to come much later. *While on patrol in those early days we had to improvise,* recalls Earnest Tew, *with such things as pikes, truncheons, pick axes, broom handles and anything else that easily came to hand.*

Fred Marsden of Newcastle Lane recalled his memories, referring to the use of the church steeple as a lookout. *There was a wooden platform built around the inside walls so we could see from the window slit at the very top of the steeple. I recall many names, Fred Maskery, Spencer Furber, a young Ken Nutt, Mr Sidney Payne, Dick Pattinson and Mr Shufflebotham. It was certainly cold up there and we had measuring instruments provided and Bill Gott managed to get hold of some large maps of the area. There would always be two of us up there and one on guard below at the church doors. We would go up the narrow stairs from the porch to the first level. Then via a rope ladder* that took us up through the trap door to join the pigeons on the top floor. We were relieved from duty every two hours.

My old friend Frank Walker remembered that rope ladder only too well. *Some of those on guard used to nip into The Greyhound for a quick pint (or two) when it was available. The problem was climbing the rope ladder again which was not an easy task for anyone, even when sober. The other problem was that alongside the rope ladder dropped the bell rope. All church bells were silenced during the war unless there was an emergency. After a few pints it was not unknown that those unsteady on their feet would grab out to the bell rope to steady themselves and as a consequence the church bell would clang, bringing with it householders from the neighbouring streets and the ARP stationed in the school opposite.*

In the first week of the church tower becoming part of the war effort, there was trouble with V G. The problem was that an over zealous Defence Volunteer refused to allow him in to his own church. Major Campbell recalls. *I gave orders to the sentry on duty that no one was to enter the church apart from the DV. The young guy wrongly included the Vicar much to the annoyance of V.G. He came knocking at my door in a terrible state, demanding all sorts of things. I quickly went to the church to sort out the guard, only to be told, that it was my orders not to allow anyone in church. Totally dumfounded, all I could say was that that didn't include the Vicar you fool.* Or should it have been 'stupid boy'.

In 1953 a booklet compiled by F S Jones, gave a short history of the North Staffs Home Guard entitled 'Remember Those Days'. This account lists those members of 'C' Company who were Penkhull Home Guard. Capt George Campbell

MC, was a family member of Campbell Tile Co. in London Road and lived in Queens Road. Others were Lieuts Bill Gott, C Ballamy, J Taylor; 2/Lets. W R Hook, G P Windsor, W T Hardiman. After a while Capt. Campbell was later promoted to 2nd in Command of the Battalion. Afterwards Capt. Bill Gott took charge of the 'C' Company until it was ordered to 'stand down'. Mr Gott lived in Trent Valley Road and was a leading figure in Penkhull church choir at its height along with Colin Simpson.

The amusing thing was that during the first phase of Dad's Army, the only identification was a khaki armband. On the 3rd of July, two suits of khaki denim overalls were issued to each of the five companies' patrols. Unfortunately there was only one set per two volunteers, so they had to share with the patrol on the earlier rota, having to disrobe in the church hall H.Q.

The big event that Frank Walker remembered so well was when they learned that five rifles and ten rounds of .303 ammunition became available but only in for an emergency. *Owing to the impossibility of proper training during those early days and the dire emergency which threatened, it was usual for patrols to be composed of at least one ex-Service man of the First World War, with one new recruit. Major Campbell sent out a personal directive to all members of the Home Guard informing them that five rifles were on their way. The big day came and the new rifles arrived at Stoke Station. The five were allocated to Penkhull and turning to the Major Campbell I asked what use would only five be if Penkhull was suddenly under attack. I would not like to repeat what he said. Then someone asked the question, never previously thought of 'where are we going to keep them?'*

Penkhull Home Guard following Church Parade

The regulations were that they must be under close guard at all times which meant simply that we had to have an armoury, and fast. The school was no use as children used this during the day. It was not suitable in the church or chapel. After much deliberation we decided that the Greyhound would be the best place available. The landlord of The Greyhound inn was Dick Pattinson, who, despite representations from his wife Alice agreed that a small bedroom over the bar would be an ideal place to keep the rifles.

There were thirty-five men standing outside to receive just five rifles. They were quickly taken upstairs to a room that Dick had allowed us to store them in. First we had to draw up a rota on who was available to clean them. Dick who was a sergeant in the First World War knew all about rifles. You should have seen all these thirty-five men cramped into one bedroom, cleaning those instruments asking where does this bit and where does this other bit go. It was remarkable that they were ever put back together again.

Anyway, at last the job was done and all back together. Then the real fun commenced with firing practice at Sideway where, near to the Michelin factory, there was a small firing range. So off we all went carrying our new 'toys' almost like the crown jewels. It was typical of Dads Army with the older men trying to teach the young how to load, point and fire. Eventually, we got a further fifty rounds of ammunition, to become for the first time proper soldiers. Later, there were more rifles, ammunition and hand grenades. Alice used to say 'if ever a bomb dropped on the pub, all of Penkhull would blow up'.

Frank then continued: *Alice was a good cook and often she would make a large cake or rabbit pie and bring it across to the school late in the evening. Two sisters who kept the Allotments Chip Shop used to come along sometimes and bring up a big parcel of chips on dark nights.*

Bill Gott, as deputy to Major Campbell, was placed in charge of military instruction; some men were well over 60 and others about twenty. You can imagine some interesting parades with such a diversity of age and ability. Keeping in step was almost impossible.

Once more Frank Mason talks about the uniforms: *a part of the full uniform was shoes. Both Dennis Edwards from Thistley Hough and Ron Street from Penkhull Terrace wore size 14. We had no end of trouble going from shop to shop with only limited wartime stocks available . . .*

As in the TV series, those involved in the Home Guard made their own fun, sometimes with very serious consequences. Frank Marsden talks into my recorder all that time ago (what a blessing I have kept all these tapes): *On one occasion Dennis was larking around in the back room of the school where the ceiling is very high and climbed upon to the beam, probably twenty odd feet high up with the intention of dropping on Ron's*

back as he entered the room. 'Serve him right', Dennis said to the others, as he was always late for parade. However on this occasion he was later than usual and when the door opened and a person in uniform walked in, thinking it was Ron, Dennis dropped from the beam onto the flipping shoulders of the Col of Western Command. Words cannot express the atmosphere at the time, but now we can all see the amusing side of things.

After duty one evening, Bill Gott and myself went to join Dick in the Greyhound Inn for a pint. Beer was on the pumps that week as the previous week they had been dry with war shortages. It was just after ten o'clock when a stranger who was in there buying drinks for many local people and asking all sorts of questions. We had all been warned by Churchill not to talk with strangers and so returned quickly to the H.Q. across the road and telephoned down to Booth Street in Stoke. Before I could walk back across to the pub the military police were there, arrested the man and took him off for interrogation. That's what life was like during the war. You could trust no one.

A meeting of the Home Guard held at Thistley Hough School

Ernest Tew, also good at recounting stories recalls: *From the observation post in the church tower we saw a light shining in Clayton. I organised a small patrol to investigate and to find a man signalling to German bombers. He had got both bicycle and map marked for some reason with a red cross in the locality of the Michelin. Quickly we returned to Penkhull H.Q. with the man and his equipment and sent for Major Campbell who organised a small patrol to escort him, bicycle and map to Booth Street. The following day he was sent to London and never heard of again.*

Frank Walker, never short of a word or two, continues to talk: *one incident that I recall was when Penkhull Home Guard was informed that a mock invasion was to take place during a Saturday night or Sunday morning. On the Saturday night the card games in both the church tower and the school were forgotten, and a sharp watch was kept for the 'enemy'. The enemy attacked about nine o'clock on the Sunday morning, and a fierce battle raged in Penkhull as never before in all its history. Eventually, the umpires decided that the observation post was taken and that Dick Pattinson (Landlord of the Greyhound) would be taken prisoner of war. Dick's wife Alice, heard the news and stormed to The Greyhound entrance, turning to the umpires in her usual* form of address *'If Dick's a prisoner'* she said at full voice, *'how the bloody-hell are we to open at twelve o'clock?'*

It was known locally that the Greyhound had a quantity of good ale in its cellar, so after a rather hurried conference between the 'enemy' and the umpires, and the serious consequences if Dick remained detained, both for Home Guard and regulars it was decided to parole Dick providing that he took no further part in the battle.

At twelve o'clock on the dot an end came to the battle, victors and vanquished dead and wounded almost spontaneously gathered together as long lost friends to be refreshed by a smiling Dick. But on a serious side Frank concluded: *Many of the stories of the Home Guard are humorous but I, and so many more are quite sure that, had the occasion arose, the men of Penkhull would have defended their homes with their lives.*

Dick Pattinson was often referred to as the Yeoman of Penkhull and when he died, Frank wrote the following, which was used by VG in his address at the funeral.

The yeoman arms that held both sword and plough,
In peace and war, in peace are folded now.
I pray you shed no sad or lonely tears.
For he, defending truth these many years,
Defended not with sadness, but with deeds
No soft approach used he to meet the needs
Of those he thought in need, nor did he bend
Before adversity. Thus at the end,
The yeoman did not die, but left this sod
To take up his appointed place with God.

School

George Hulme remembers as a young lad the amusing side of the war years while he attended the Senior School.

Mr Banks was the head master and other teachers were Mr Faram and Mr Foreman. By this time it was 1943 and the air raids had ceased to be a problem although we had surface shelters of brick and concrete in the playground. The curriculum had to be adapted because of the shortage of male teachers and as such, cookery lessons were firmly on the agenda.

Because of food rationing we had to take our own utensils and ingredients, but worst of all as young lads we too had to wear an apron. I recall one amusing incident during a lesson when the teacher searched for a gas leak with a lighted taper. Mr Faram hid under the workbench just in case there was an explosion.

We were all encouraged to be a part of the war effort and so 'dig for victory' became a reality. The senior school had a plot of land in the grounds of the Mount School for the Deaf and Blind. The produce from this ground was sold off in the autumn to staff and pupils. Some of the older boys were allowed to go potato picking at harvest time. They were picked up by the bus at the school gates and taken to local farms.

Other events in the early years of the war are recorded in the school log book: 25th June 1940 *Last night the district had its first air-raid warning of the war but there were no planes overhead.* It was not until Monday 1st July that we read about the bombing at Penkhull - *many children absent today owing to the air raid in this immediate district. Many thousands of people spent their Sunday viewing the damage.* The school, like many other buildings suffered damage during the war albeit very limited. On January 16th 1941 we can read - *an incendiary bomb was dropped on the school last night doing a certain amount of damage to the roof.*

Probably the most memorable thing for the children during the war years was to carry gas masks with them everywhere, even though many were defective. On the 21st April the Log Book records - *The usual beginning of term inspection of gas masks revealed that one hundred children have defective masks, mostly broken eye pieces and punctured face sections. Asked for replacement glasses - told could have only 24 at a time. Will take five weeks to arrive.*

Losses

Sadly, whilst perhaps we see the home side of events during the war, it was war overseas that our country was fighting, and as such had terrible consequences to the lives of many families in Penkhull. VG wrote something of the pain that war created, and the few facts that may be gleaned from the pages of the church magazine reflect the grief suffered by many during those sad years.

For the many families in Penkhull who lost a loved one, the day they received a letter from the War Office meant sad news with either a loved one being taken prisoner, lost in action or worse killed.

Somehow it is the impersonality, the stark nakedness of the news conveyed by a few, formal cold words with names inserted where appropriate, that would remain in the hearts of loved ones for ever. And yet this is exactly the reality of war, which was encountered on a daily basis.

One such letter was received by Mrs Thorley of Portland Street (now Oriel Street) informing her of the loss of her son Fred which shows the clinical approach at the time to such matters. This small piece of paper came to represent the whole life of Fred. It was read, re-read and read again. It was wept over many times and passed around family and friends, all offering their support and sympathy. The fact remained that Fred would not be returning.

The anxiety of waiting and of not knowing was distressing and VG would spend much of his time visiting those who were experiencing this. One family among hundreds was the Gifford Family. Their son Norman was first recorded missing in May 1941. In the June edition the news was better, as a report had been received that he had been saved from his ship and was a prisoner of war. His mother Alice kept a

Issued by the Ministry of Information in co-operation with the War Office
and the Ministry of Home Security

Beating the INVADER

A MESSAGE FROM THE PRIME MINISTER

IF invasion comes, everyone—young or old, men and women—will be eager to play their part worthily. By far the greater part of the country will not be immediately involved. Even along our coasts, the greater part will remain unaffected. But where the enemy lands, or tries to land, there will be most violent fighting. Not only will there be the battles when the enemy tries to come ashore, but afterwards there will fall upon his lodgments very heavy British counter-attacks, and all the time the lodgments will be under the heaviest attack by British bombers. The fewer civilians or non-combatants in these areas, the better—apart from essential workers who must remain. So if you are advised by the authorities to leave the place where you live, it is your duty to go elsewhere when you are told to leave. When the attack begins, it will be too late to go ; and, unless you receive definite instructions to move, your duty then will be to stay where you are. You will have to get into the safest place you can find, and stay there until the battle is over. For all of you then the order and the duty will be : "STAND FIRM ".

This also applies to people inland if any considerable number of parachutists or air-borne troops are landed in their neighbourhood. Above all, they must not cumber the roads. Like their fellow-countrymen on the coasts, they must "STAND FIRM ". The Home Guard, supported by strong mobile columns wherever the enemy's numbers require it, will immediately come to grips with the invaders, and there is little doubt will soon destroy them.

Throughout the rest of the country where there is no fighting going on and no close cannon fire or rifle fire can be heard, everyone will govern his conduct by the second great order and duty, namely, " CARRY ON " It may easily be some weeks before the invader has been totally destroyed, that is to say, killed or captured to the last man who has landed on our shores. Meanwhile, all work must be continued to the utmost, and no time lost.

The following notes have been prepared to tell everyone in rather more detail what to do, and they should be carefully studied. Each man and woman should think out a clear plan of personal action in accordance with the general scheme.

Winston S. Churchill

STAND FIRM

I. What do I do if fighting breaks out in my neighbourhood?

Keep indoors or in your shelter until the battle is over. If you can have a trench ready in your garden or field, so much the better. You may want to use it for protection if your house is damaged. But if you are at work, or if you have special orders, carry on as long as possible and only take cover when danger approaches. If you are on your way to work, finish your journey if you can.

If you see an enemy tank, or a few enemy soldiers do not assume that the enemy are in control of the area. What you have seen may be a party sent on in advance, or stragglers from the main body who can easily be rounded up.

CARRY ON

2. What do I do in areas which are some way from the fighting?

Stay in your district and carry on. Go to work whether in shop, field, factory or office. Do your shopping, send your children to school until you are told not to. Do not try to go and live somewhere else. Do not use the roads for any unnecessary journey; they must be left free for troop movements even a long way from the district where actual fighting is taking place.

3. Will certain roads and railways be reserved for the use of the Military, even in areas far from the scene of action?

Yes, certain roads will have to be reserved for important troop movements; but such reservations should be only temporary. As far as possible, bus companies and railways will try to maintain essential public services, though it may be necessary to cut these down. Bicyclists and pedestrians may use the roads for journeys to work, unless instructed not to do so.

ADVICE AND ORDERS

4. Whom shall I ask for advice?

The police and A.R.P. wardens.

5. From whom shall I take orders?

In most cases from the police and A.R.P. wardens. But there may be times when you will have to take orders from the military and the Home Guard in uniform.

6. Is there any means by which I can tell that an order is a true order and not faked?

You will generally know your policeman and your A.R.P. wardens by sight, and can trust them. With a bit of common sense you can tell if a soldier is really British or only pretending to be so. If in doubt ask a policeman, or ask a soldier whom you know personally.

INSTRUCTIONS

7. What does it mean when the church bells are rung?

It is a warning to the local garrison that troops have been seen landing from the air in the neighbourhood of the church in question. Church bells will *not* be rung all over the country as a general warning that invasion has taken place. The ringing of church bells in one place will not be taken up in neighbouring churches.

8. Will instructions be given over the wireless?

Yes; so far as possible. But remember that the enemy can overhear any wireless message, so that the wireless cannot be used for instructions which might give him valuable information.

9. In what other ways will instructions be given?

Through the Press; by loudspeaker vans; and perhaps by leaflets and posters. But remember that genuine Government leaflets will be given to you only by the policeman, your A.R.P. warden or your postman; while genuine posters and instructions will be put up only on Ministry of Information notice boards and official sites, such as police stations, post offices, A.R.P. posts, town halls and schools.

FOOD

10. Should I try to lay in extra food?

No. If you have already laid in a stock of food, keep it for a real emergency; but do not add to it. The Government has made arrangements for food supplies.

NEWS

11. Will normal news-services continue?

Yes. Careful plans have been made to enable newspapers and wireless broadcasts to carry on, and in case of need there are emergency measures which will bring you the news. But if there should be some temporary breakdown in news supply, it is very important that you should not listen to rumours nor pass them on, but should wait till real news comes through again. Do not use the telephones or send telegrams if you can possibly avoid it.

MOTOR-CARS

12. Should I put my car, lorry or motor-bicycle out of action

Yes, when you are told to do so by the police, A.R.P. wardens or military; or when it is obvious that there is an immediate risk of its being seized by the enemy—then disable and hide your bicycle and destroy your maps.

13. How should it be put out of action?

Remove distributor head and leads and either empty the tank or remove the carburettor. If you don't know how to do this, find out now from your nearest garage. In the case of diesel engines remove the injection pump and connection. The parts removed must be hidden well away from the vehicle.

THE ENEMY

14. Should I defend myself against the enemy?

The enemy is not likely to turn aside to attack separate houses. If small parties are going about threatening persons and property in an area not under enemy control and come your way, you have the right of every man and woman to do what you can to protect yourself, your family and your home.

---

diary of the camps where he was detained as a prisoner, one was for some time Stalag XB-Marlag in Germany where he served as a cook. Norman returned home in April 1945.

In July 1941, Richard Pattinson, Kenneth Till and Eric Rushton were recorded as missing since the evacuation of Greece.

In February 1944 we read that *our hearts were filled with gladness when we heard that cards had been received from Michael Campbell and Tony Littler.* In 1943 VG wrote: *After many months of weary waiting we have heard of their safety. Both of these young lads were missing after the Japanese invasion.*

Norman Gifford 3rd row 2nd from right as a cook in Stalag XB P.O.W Camp

In later years Tony became a close friend of mine, and I know that that he never fully recovered from his time as a Japanese prisoner of war. The horrors of that time retained a hold on him until the day he died.

VG recorded the homecoming of Cll. Piggott after his term of five years as a prisoner of war. And in the June 1943 issue, VG wrote: *Last month we had, with regret, to chronicle the fact that Reg, the son of our good friend Mr Shufflebothan was reported missing. He has now had an official letter regretting to inform him that his son did not return from an operational sortie.*

And yet on occasions the news was good. On one such occasion VG wrote about Victor Reynolds from East Street. *It was good to see Victor after his experience in Africa. He has seen in a few months what people do not see in a lifetime, and we are glad that, save for some effects of his wounds, he is fit and well again.*

There are many accounts of boys who did not return to the village and who gave their lives for *King and Country* and these names are proudly recorded on the war memorial plaque by the organ in Penkhull Church. This war memorial to those who died took the form of rebuilding the church organ and to lay out the churchyard as a 'garden of rest'.

German raiders hit North Staffordshire for the first time in June 1940 - and by a strange trick of fate the first casualty was a four-year-old London evacuee.

A few nights later, on midsummers night, a sole German bomber, probably heading for Shelton Iron and Steel using the line of Penkhull Church spire and the Infirmary chimney as landmarks, dropped four bombs in the vicinity with the death of one person.

Penkhull Home Guard was manning as usual the church tower and heard the plane coming distinguished by its sound. Frank Marsden was the sergeant on duty that night and records that fearful moment of the realisation that they were about to be hit. *I could hear the plane and instinctively knew that it was a German Messerschmitt, we had been trained to listen out for. It came from the south, just over Thistley Hough and then suddenly the whistling sound of the bomb dropping brought fear to all of us high up the tower. Instinctively, we crouched down holding on to our tin helmets fearing the worst and then we heard the explosion nearby. My first thoughts were 'thank God', but then the reality of what had happened quickly turned our thoughts to both casualties and damage. With speed, never before witnessed, myself and the three others on duty that night dropped down the rope ladder. I sent one off to Queens Road to inform Major Campbell. The other guy and myself ran quickly to the site somewhere in Newcastle Lane.*

To our horror it had dropped on the front of the home of Mr Harry Beeston, Manager of Boots Cash Chemist in Stoke, and Church Warden. He had retired early leaving his wife down stairs. The blast had demolished the front of the house, the contents of which were strewn all across the road. Where was Mr Beeston I thought but it was only a matter of seconds before we heard the cries from the rafters where the fifty pound bomb had blown him to.

When I interviewed Mr George Campbell some forty-three years ago, his memories were as strong as though it had happened only the previous night. *I heard one plane and knew that it was not one of ours and then no sooner felt the shake of the ground, as I lay awake in bed, in fact many of the bits from the home of Mr Beeston came into my garden. My wife jumped so quickly out of bed that she put two legs in to one leg of her slacks and fell over shouting 'get up, get up'. The next minute there was a banging at the door, 'Major, Major, bombs dropped' cried the voice of one of those on duty that night. My reply was 'I've heard it and thought of going back to bed' when my wife shouted at me 'my God, you don't want to talk to these men like that, go and see for yourself'. So upon that sharp rebuff I quickly dressed to go to see for myself that terrible sight just around the corner'.*

In my archives I have the original notes written of the event by VG. His son Dennis gave me these years ago.
I was awakened by my son Dennis and the reverberating shock of the bomb too near to be comfortable, and having dressed hurried to the school warden's post to receive first reports. I was informed that the new nurses home had been hit and the end completely demolished. Thank God that no nurses were yet in residence.

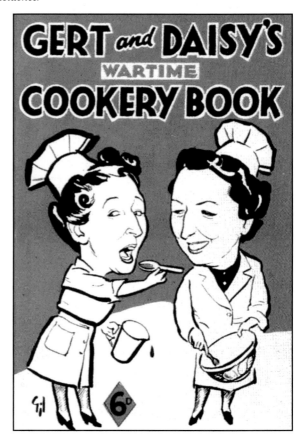

I visited the hospital to find that part of the eye operating theatre had also been caught in the raid but found that all the patients has been removed with promptitude and skill to the lower floors. Indeed they were all singing, 'It's a long way to Tipperary' in the typical British way when faced with adversity. I was next told that Quarry Avenue had had it and at once I saw the wreckage of the house, one of which I knew to be Mrs Bagnall's. Hurrying through the debris I fully expected a gruesome sight, but to my surprise I did not see the wounded and dying, but the brave and smiling face of my friend as she sat amongst the wreckage wrapped in blankets, and would you believe it, reading that night's 'Evening Sentinel'.

Bomb damage at Quarry Road

Mr Harry Beeston was admitted to the City General Hospital badly injured with a smashed pelvis and internal injuries. He died of his wounds on the evening of the 7th August. VG wrote of Mr Beeston later *only those who have seen him daily will know the fight that he has put up and the perseverance that he has shown. I visited him in the ward and often took books for him to read. He was a spiritual man and loved his church. He was a great man of the people with a responsible position. He was later removed to Oswestry for treatment but was not to recover from his injuries. After his death he was bought back to Penkhull Church and placed 'in the shadow of the Cross', we had our Requiem service at which many friends came and made their Communion. We lose from the church militants one of the greatest of Great Hearts.*

The wooden oak panelling beneath the organ chamber, probably hardly noticed today, was donated in memory of Mr Harry Beeston, the only person in Penkhull to have died as a result of enemy action upon our village.

Another old Penkhull character Bill Cliff also recorded for me all those years ago: *there were thousands the following morning in Newcastle Lane to view the damage caused by the bomb. It was a frightening sight seeing all the interior of the house exposed and bits of brick and mortar together with personal possessions strewn all over the gardens and road. Mr Beeston was a wonderful gentleman and well respected by the parish. We all miss him.*

Partly demolished new Nurses Home

However, as luck would have it, the new Nurses Home off Queens Road was not yet occupied. It was officially opened only two days before by Lord Horder otherwise the casualties would have been extensive. Also the eye operating theatre took a direct hit but all the patients had moved to the air-raid shelters in time. The blast caused other damage to windows in the near vicinity. At the Mount Blind and Deaf school where there were over 130 resident children, there were over fifty windows shattered along with those of many houses in nearby Greatbatch Avenue and Princes Road. Although this air raid was a comparatively small one, a considerable amount of damage was done to other properties.

The war brought grief and heartache to many families in Penkhull and the first recorded tragedy is found in November 1940 when VG wrote: *A sad blow has befallen our parish in the death of a soldier boy George Forrester. He was clearing debris away in London and was killed by an unexploded bomb and this splendid young man was taken from us in the saddest of circumstances. They bought his body back home and to church just as Evensong was commencing and we sang a hymn as they entered.*

Many others were reported missing Sapper A E Hill from Honeywall also Harry Harvey, whom everyone in the village knew so well. He was serving in the R.A.S.C. in the Middle East in August 1942. In May 1943, we read that the son of Mr Shufflebotham is missing. It appeared that he was on night duty and taking part in a raid over Germany. He was reported missing the next morning when his plane did not return. In the next month's issue of the magazine VG wrote that a telegram had been received, stating that it is *with deepest regret that the Ministry has to write to say that no further news has yet been received.* - Such hard times for all, and now, sixty years after, it is only right to remember, not only those who lost their lives from Penkhull, but those left at home who even now have never got over their loss.

But there were happier times, Roy Owen was offered congratulations in obtaining his commission to the R.N.V.R. at the same time as the news came in April 1943 that the black-out curtains could be removed from the church windows to allow in *'Gods good sunlight'* and concluding with the note: *May Hitler soon squirm at the sound of the bells of victory.*

In November 1941, the church magazine reported that the choir had not had an outing since the war began. Arrangements were then put in hand for a supper, as far as rationing would permit, at The Greyhound. Messrs Gleaves, Gott and Owen provided entertainment. Visitors included Mr Ramage of Queens Road. The young boys were taken to the Theatre Royal as there was not sufficient food under rationing to feed them as well.

For all families the war years meant that food was in short supply. Lord Woolton, the Minister of Food came up with recipe suggestions using ingredients everyone would have, e.g. Woolton pie. Instructions were distributed along with advice on: Recycling - bones for soap, glue and fertiliser; bottles.

Many people in Penkhull started to keep rabbits and hens in their backyards. Rabbits and roosters were kept for meat, hens for eggs and dead birds for their feathers and fat. Groups of people came together to keep a pig; many built small pigsties on their allotment or a shelter for chickens or turkeys. Winnie Wyse recalls:

We were lucky because we had our own poultry, both hens and turkeys that were kept in allotments where the Donald Bates home stands at the top of Garden Street. Often we would swap a chicken for a piece of pork with a neighbour who kept pigs. Pig waste was collected from most homes in the neighbourhood that contains scraps of food, peelings, etc. in pig bins kept in the back yard.

"He grabbed my ration-book, Officer, and tried to pinch my Personal Points!"

This was a valuable sauce of food for the animals, with many people benefiting when the animal was slaughtered in the cold months. Every part of the pig could be used, even the trotters. They also produced manure that could be used on the garden.

Roslyn Peak and Betty Rowland also talk of food bought with ration tokens changing hands as well as tokens being exchanged to cater for families differing in needs or tastes. At the beginning of the war, there was less choice of biscuits, with one type whereas there had been ten before the war started. Secondly, food changed shape to reduce transport costs, e.g. meat was de-boned or dehydrated, and eggs were dried and powdered. Some food was replaced with not very nice substitutes, e.g. dried milk and powdered eggs. The national loaf arrived, made with low quality flour and with calcium and vitamin B1 added. The war years also saw the arrival of products from the USA like Spam, which was very popular due to its versatility.

For many in Penkhull their gardens were dug up - as well as tennis courts and bowling greens. Those situated in Barnfield were a typical example, and for thousands, an allotment made the difference between basic rations and more food on the table, as well as helping the war effort. It was quite surprising how ingenious people suddenly became in making sure the family had a decent meal. All sorts of leaves were chopped up for salad including dandelion leaves, nasturtium leaves and turnip tops, all neatly arranged in a bowl in patterns with grated carrot to form a contrast.

Anything that could be preserved such as; eggs in isinglass, beans in salt, cabbage, onions and shallots pickled they were all placed in airtight jars with rubber seals then stored on the cold stone at the bottom of the pantry. No Tesco then, or refrigerators! Fruit from the garden and hedgerows was preserved, and jam made.

Morale during the war was often difficult to maintain especially in towns such as London and Coventry. I recall a number of people telling me of the night they stood along Penkhull Terrace to witness the terrible bombings at Coventry as the glow from that onslaught could be seen from that view point.

The BBC prepared most efficiently for the - wrong war. It had been assumed that for the first seven weeks the public would want nothing but news bulletins with record and theatre organ fill-ins. Instead there was a clamour for entertainment. Forces Programmes provided an alternative to popular music and variety programmes. Remember 'Sandy's Half Hour' on the home service? But the programme no one dared to miss on a Saturday

evening was Band Wagon with Arthur Askey and his phase 'Hello, playmates'. For the young there was 'Dick Barton, special agent', and smash hits like 'There'll Always Be An England' all those memories come flooding back.

The cinemas in Stoke were thriving; the Majestic, Danilo, Hippodrome and the Princes all showed films that had been especially produced to help morale. Charles Laughton in *Goodbye, Mr Chips*, with Robert Donat, *Where's that fire*, with Will Hay and those fantastic comedy films of *Old Mother Riley* starring Arthur Lucan – all such wonderful memories. One alarming symptom of low morale was the growing number of people who listened to Lord Haw-Haw, the chief German broadcaster in English. His real name was William Joyce

Arthur Lucan (Old Mother Riley) and his wife Kitty

and he was a Fascist. In Penkhull, however, few if any listened and morale remained high in the small community who retained a focus on events but were determined to support each other through the difficult times. VG worked hard to visit and support all those who called upon his services.

The use of the school by the L.D.V. brought a positive side to the church finances by the sum of one shilling a week rent charge, although it was acknowledged by the church this sum was 'purely as a token sum'. The church invested in War Savings with the sum of £100. In December 1940, the temporary blackouts to the school were in need of replacement and Mr Meiklejohn reported that this was to be paid for by the L.D.V. In January 1941, the Government had contacted the church regarding rent due for the use of the school by the Home Guard, but it was decided that the charges should be left to the government to state what could be charged. Even though the war had been in progress for fifteen months it was at this same meeting that it was decided to purchase stirrup pumps, buckets, sand and one spade for the church, just in case of 'Fire Blitz'.

By March 1940, V.G. commented that the Day School account showed a marked improvement as a result of the ARP rent and further strengthened by subscriptions from the Home Guard.

The use of the school by the ARP and Home Guard bought with it significant additional work for the caretaker Mr Alldis in clearing up each morning before school commenced. He wrote to the PCC in September 1943 asking for consideration of a pay rise. It was quite surprising then, after all the financial benefits the church had received during the war, that they refused his request, stating that *he was paid sufficiently for the work he did* but agreed to pay him just 5/- a week extra as a war bonus. This decision was even more surprising in that Mr Alldis, had almost single handed put out a church roof fire after an incendiary bomb had set fire to it twelve months earlier.

Peace
On March 7th, 1945, the Western Allies crossed the Rhine after having smashed through the strongly fortified Siegfried Line and over-run Western Germany. On the 30th April 1945, realising all was lost; Adolf Hitler committed suicide in his bunker along with Eva Braun, his long-time lover and, briefly his wife. On 4th May, British Field Marshall Montgomery accepted the military surrender of all German forces in Holland, Northwest Germany, and Denmark. The war with Germany was over.

For five years and eight months the people of Penkhull had looked forward to the day when the war against Germany would end - and when it finally did come, no one knew when the celebrations should begin. For a time it appeared that the war-weary people had to pinch themselves to believe that peace had arrived at last.

Plans for **Victory in Europe Day** for Stoke-on-Trent were discussed on the 2nd May and a committee was appointed. There were to be concerts in all the town halls, bands in parks, street parties and an appeal went out to all shopkeepers and business people to put as much decoration on their buildings as possible. The corporation was to give all employees two days off with pay. As a result of this, the pottery manufacturers followed suit but the workers would be on flat pay of £1 10s 0d a day men and £1 0 0d for women.

All restrictions on cinemas were lifted. At the Majestic in Stoke, Greer Garson and Walter Pidgeon were to be seen in *Mrs Markinson* while at the Hippodrome Charles Boyer and Irene Dunn were starring in *Together Again.* In the town centres, there were to be short thanksgiving services and the singing of the National Anthem, and at St Peter's Church in Stoke, there was to be a special service of thanksgiving conducted by Rev Percy Hartill.

Unfortunately confusion arose throughout the land because all were waiting for the official announcement not knowing whether to go to work as usual that day, or whether it would be declared a national holiday. Thousands sat glued by their wireless sets for some sort of announcement. (Most of these were run in those days by an accumulator, recharged each week at Whitakers of London Road, Stoke) Others waited for the Sentinel Victory Edition. Flags of all sorts, colours and shapes appeared almost like magic and the centre of Hanley and of Newcastle suddenly became gridlocked with people just wanting to celebrate.

The official announcement of the end of hostilities in Europe was made at 3.00p.m in a short broadcast by Mr Churchill. The King and Queen appeared on the balcony of Buckingham Palace with the Princesses at 3.11p.m. His Majesty the King was to broadcast to the Empire at 9.00p.m. There was bell ringing throughout the land and Penkhull was no exception, although I have not been able to find out who was the first to pull the bell on such an important occasion. There were bonfires, fireworks and torch light processions. The largest fire was at Trentham Park, where, ironically, the German prisoners of war who were interned there had collected the logs for the bonfire.

The official VE-Day was on May 8th 1945, and was the signal to break out from a time of restrictions and rationing and to celebrate. Tables and chairs appeared from all directions for the numerous street parties. Suddenly all those goods stored on top shelves and in pantries and cupboards were ransacked of their meagre contents to provide the necessary for the celebration parties and the hardships, struggles and difficulties of past years were exchanged for a brief moment of happiness.

Penkhull celebrated like the rest of the country with many street parties but unfortunately this was not recorded on movie film. House to house collections were held both for food and money contributions, and in some case parochial boundaries were almost fought over! Frank Marsden recalled to me that he lived in Newcastle Lane and gave a generous donation of £5 towards the party in Whalley Avenue, but because he lived around the corner was not allowed to attend despite his generous donation.

There were other parties in Tilson Avenue; Croft Crescent and the Methodist chapel all captured on film where they all let their hair down for the day. VG commented that once war was over, the sacrifices, hardships and dangers endured would be soon forgotten, but in those happy days of May 1945 gratitude was deeply felt for all those who had helped to bring about the end of war, the celebrations were as much for them as for us.

Penkhull Methodist Chapel V.E. Day Party

Tilson Avenue V.E. Day Street Party

The Home Guard, now almost certainly doomed, was stood down. The night duties at the church tower had ceased at the end of August the previous year. It had not operated in fact since November 1944. There had been an announcement on September 11th as Mr Frank Marsden recalls that *Stand Down* was imminent and there would be no more compulsory parades. In a conversation with me he spoke softly as he said *'we have been a happy company and the*

Croft Crescent V.E. Day Street Party

announcement makes us feel we have lost something we greatly valued. With a sense of frustration we realise that this is the end of the Home Guard'. On December 3rd, the Company marched for the last time with the Battalion to the parade ground, where Lord Harrowby addressed them. As a fitting conclusion, a dinner and dance was held by the Company, to which all ranks and their wives were invited.

VG wrote in the church magazine after VE-Day: *At last in God's good mercy part of the war is over. It is fitting therefore that we should assemble and meet together to give thanks for our deliverance. Only history will show the magnitude of that and the indomitable will of Mr Churchill when he called us to toil with sweat and blood and tears in 'England's finest hour'. We may not be sure that we are God's chosen race - there is far too much evil still amongst us for that - but we are certain that God has delivered us for some great purpose. We cannot celebrate fully as yet many still remain captive as the war continues with Japan.*

VE-Sunday was celebrated by a special rendering of the Te Deum by the choir, no doubt to a packed congregation mixed with both joy and a time of reflection. VG wrote: *May I, in your name, express our sincere deep thanks to the choirmaster, the organist and the members of the choir for what was a most memorable Act of Praise and a fitting conclusion to the War.*

This was followed later by a choir party arranged by Mr Albert Lawton of Penkhull New Road at which Colonel Piggott and Mr Slater attended, probably through the good offices of Bill Gott, both a member of the choir and Captain of the Home Guard. This was held in the upper room of The Greyhound like many other church choir activities, and thanks were expressed to Mr Pattinson and to Mrs Pattinson and Mrs Dolby for their hard work in preparing the evening.

To this event came former prisoners of war as well as soldiers. One, Richard Pattinson, the son of Burt and Alice had only just returned the previous day as VG spoke *Long have we waited, but our joy was very full when late at night he arrived home. Also - Bradbury is back, 'they did it for us'.*

The following month (September) saw more return, and brought news of others who were feared dead. VG wrote: *Fred Ellis returned from the Far East after four years. Ronald Dobson is home on leave after being away for three years. He passed right up from El Alemain to Italy. George Dolby suffered a broken leg serving in the Middle East. Roy Owens who is on leave and has seen more in his period in the Navy than most of us all our lives. Several others are likely to be back after much hardship, and we look forward to the time when those prisoners in the hands of the Japanese will be home again.*

By the following month there was further good news for the parish, as both Michael Campbell and Tony Littler were known to be safe. From each had come the message that they soon hoped to be returned home to Penkhull. *For long years they have been in the hands of the Japanese, and we were all very anxious when we read of the terrible atrocities,* concluded

VG. It was to be a further two months before they returned home as the December Magazine records: *We are extremely grateful to God for the safe return from great dangers of more of our men. Tony Littler and Michael Campbell, who have suffered more than we can tell in the Far East are now safely amongst us once more. So is Selwyn Crosby and others.*

Tony Littler went on to become a church warden of St Thomas's but like so many who returned he never got over the treatment he received at the hands of the Japanese. God Bless him. As soon as the war was over, VG suggested that a fitting memorial should be made to those from Penkhull who had lost their lives during the conflict. VG wrote in the September issue of the magazine: *In our parish there are a score or more who have laid down their lives for us, and if we forget them, we should deserve all the bitter feelings that the bereaved might offer. But we have no intentions of forgetting. Already I have spoken of the War Memorial for our Village and Church. We hope to accomplish two things: to rebuild our organ first, a matter which must have prior attention by the fact that it is in a thoroughly bad condition; secondly to lay out the Churchyard as a Garden of Remembrance. These we feel would be fitting memorials to our lads, and soon we shall appeal for funds.*

The organ was restored and the console brought down from above the choir stalls to its present position at a cost of over £2,000. It was consecrated in September 1948. However it took much longer with the churchyard and the legal process in transferring it to the safe keeping of the city council. The cost, a further £2,000, but the job was not completed until 1956. What a pity that this a memorial is not recorded, as such, anywhere in the church grounds.

Finally to conclude this chapter it is right to list all the names of those from Penkhull who died as a result of enemy action during the Second World War.

To the Glory of God and in Memory of Harry Beeston, George Brodie, Roger S Burne, Reginald Carr, George Forrester, Peter Gatensbury, Arthur Hopkins, Eric Johnson, Donald W Kemp, George R Leason, Albert E Leigh, Lawrence Lovatt, Douglas Newman, Richard Owen, Thomas Plant, William Rushton, Stephen Sayers, Ernest Sherlock, Reginald Shufflebothem, Philip J Simpson, Harry Tunstall, Albert Wilson. Harry Beeston, died as a result of enemy action in Penkhull.

For some reason two names of Penkhull lads who died in Service to King and Country do not appear on the Memorial. They are Norman Corbishly from Trent Valley Road and Eddie Crosby from East Street. I was assured in 2005 that these names would be added to the memorial in church. It is sad to record that at the time of writing nothing has been done but at least these names are now recorded within these pages.

Chapter 22
Urbanisation of Penkhull.

By the latter part of the 18th century, Penkhull had become established as a residential area for both wealthy and the working-class as the industrial towns of the Potteries became swallowed up in a swathe of pollution, cramped housing and unsanitary conditions. The expanding and increasing mobile population of the area brought with it social implications experienced by most industrial towns of the north. Nineteenth century in Penkhull opened with a period of rapid change. Little urbanisation had taken place for over three hundred years except encroachments upon the Lord's waste. Now with the expanding industrialisation of the Potteries there were workers, and the demand for work encouraged immigration and the subsequent need for housing.

By the turn of the century, Josiah Spode had already acquired Penkhull Farm and established himself as a gentleman, with farming, property and manufacturing interests. His vision was to see Penkhull as a retreat from the town of Stoke below.

In rural, un-commercialised Penkhull, Spode had an opportunity to follow in the footsteps of his predecessor, John Harrison, who had acquired substantial land and property in the district, first by rental then, as the opportunity came, purchase. By 1789, Harrison had built a handsome gentleman's residence in the centre of the village. With the growth of Spode's factory in Stoke, there came the need for cheap working-class housing. Already Stoke was congested by a maze of potworks and small, poorly built back-to-back houses and court-type dwellings clustered together. Conditions were poor with communal privies, ash pits, and limited piped water in the form of stand pumps. The atmosphere was polluted as bottle ovens belched out thick black smoke almost encapsulating the towns shutting out sunlight and fresh air. Spode viewed Penkhull as a place set apart from the industrial town, where he himself could live grandly but also build housing for his workers in a congenial atmosphere.

Before unravelling the subject of urbanisation, first it is necessary to place into context the properties and living standards within the period. They were not good, and in most cases, the poorer working classes suffered in silence as they coped with the daily grind of life with almost no sanitation or clean water, facing hunger and death. This to many, was their status in life, not to argue or fight against, but to accept!

Robert Rawlinson, a Government inspector gives an important snapshot of the prevailing conditions that were found in all of the pottery towns in his report of 1848.

Whatever was recorded for Stoke could be mirrored many times over in each of the other Potteries' towns without exception. The first section is written by Mr R Garner, surgeon.

I would state in the first place, generally, that many parts of the town of Stoke-upon-Trent, of Stoke Lane, (Hartshill area), of the Soap-works (Oakhill), with Boothen etc. are, and have been for many years, in a very defective state in respect to sanitary regulations; and I believe that the consequent loss of life, and amount of ill-health, is such as to be deeply deplored. The places where these circumstances are to be observed are, Stoke Lane, where fever is now, and has always been during the 15 years which I have known it, prevalent and fatal; the Soap-works, the houses limited in number, but of late at least, very bad in the respect mentioned; and in Stoke, Welsh Street, Wharf Street, the three Cliff Squares (the bottom of Honeywall), Thomas Street, Pleasant Row and several streets leading out of Liverpool Road. The fatal complaints here are fevers, infantile and adult pulmonary affections, diarrhoea, erysipelas and sloughing in case of wounds and sores. Diarrhoea and dysentery have been extremely prevalent for two or three years, more so that I ever witnessed or hear of, frequently fatal, particularly to children and the infirm. The cause of these complaints are the usual ones, of course poverty and destitution being excluded in this inquiry are the usual ones, dirty interiors, open privies, heaps of rubbish, piggeries, houses not open and the back and drains stopped up. In Stoke proper are dwellings with only one privy to six or eight houses and until lately, one to ten all without back doors; heaps of manure and cinders in courts, privy-pools above the common level oozing through the walls, or, in wet weather, overflowing the yards. But as for Stoke proper there are two circumstances in comparison with which all the nuisances above enumerated sink into insignificance; I mean the existence, almost in the centre of the place, of a piece of waste land several acres in extent, consisting of a muddy marsh, occasionally inundated, but never dry. Secondly, the inundation, after floods, of most of the cellars in the lower part of Stoke by filthy water from the Foulhay Brook, with no means in many cases of afterwards carrying it off. Some cellars are never dry, others have been filled up with clay from the inmates finding out they were affected with rheumatism, purpurea in the legs, and pulmonary affections; whilst the marshy land evidently produces dysentery, pneumonia and fevers by its emanations.

When in this chapter, the numbers of infantile deaths are quoted they should be placed in context with the living conditions of the day; harsh, cruel, filthy and unhealthy. The village of Penkhull with the majority of its housing being built specifically for factory workers from Stoke there would little difference, if any from Mr Garner's general description in his report except from those who suffered from flooding.

Trent Valley Road formerly Trentham Road

This ancient road led from the south into the village of Penkhull then continued down Honeywall to the north of the city. From its southern junction with London Road at Oakhill there were no buildings apart from Stoke Lodge, which dated from the early 18th century. It was demolished in the 1920's to make way for the Sutton Housing estate. The current New Lodge is situated near to the location of the old Stoke Lodge. It is not shown on a map of 1848 and was probably built just after the sale of the land in 1853. A copyhold transfer dated 1859 lists New Lodge. In 1866 the copyhold records list it as follows: *all that dwelling house called The New Lodge, together with the stable, coachhouse, garden and pleasure grounds situate near a place called Stoke Lodge formerly in the occupation of John Goodwin and then Richard Pratt and afterwards F E Pratt.*

Stoke Lodge

From this point until where Brisley Hill is reached were only fields until the early 19th century when Penkhull Square was built by Josiah Spode. Nothing else was found until the old church school and Victoria Buildings, formerly the old Stoke Parish Poor House.

Stoke Lodge

In February 1907, the top section of land to the left of Trent Valley Road between Penkhull Square to Victoria Buildings was owned by Miss Angelina Reeves of 20 Penkhull Terrace. This was in addition to a large piece of land to the rear of Penkhull Square. The whole area consisted of 4,271 square yards and in the middle of the section bordering Trent Valley

Bottom of Trent Valley Road 1910

Road between the Square and Victoria Buildings were piggeries run by Mr Bills, a plumber from Hartshill. Later the area was used for allotments. In 1911, Miss Reeves paid to the Duchy of Lancaster the sum of £43 1s to transfer the land from copyhold tenure to that of freehold. The section of land running parallel behind the previous plot covering the area of the old Donald Bates House and a part of what is now Jeremy Close, was transferred from copyhold tenure to that of freehold at the same time in the name of Sir Thomas Edward Milborne Swinnerton Pilkington. He had purchased this site in April 1903. He was already in ownership of the adjacent plot occupied by Penkhull Farm.

Penkhull Square

One of the early developments designed specifically to house the working classes was Penkhull Square. It was a group of twenty cottages built on a courtyard plan and approached by a single arched entrance into a cobbled courtyard in the middle of which stood a stand-up water pump. The structure was of brick and tile construction reminiscent of many courtyard housing developments in the area.

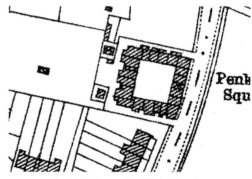
Penkhull Square, Trent Valley Road

Only the dwellings bordering Trent Valley Road had their frontages facing the outside, those on the other three sides of the court faced inwards. At the front were casement windows, at the back tiny sashes. The cottages consisted of a living room and a small scullery with two corresponding bedrooms above approached by a stairway from the main room below.

The second bedroom was too small even to contain a full-sized double bed. The small projecting sculleries to the rear of the cottages were not added until 1907. The privies, a short distance behind the Square were approached through a

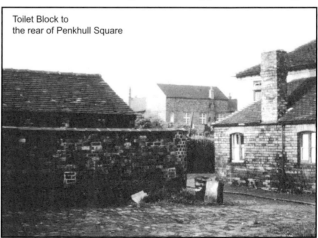
Toilet Block to the rear of Penkhull Square

328

Views from the road and inside of Penkhull Square.
Built by Josiah Spode for his pottery workers.

narrow opening at the back of the square, or from the front around the side. There were two sets of communal privies in block form, one-marked boys and other girls, which drained out into an ash pits situated further down into the field.

The land upon which Penkhull Square stood was purchased by Spode II in 1802 only a few months after his purchase of substantial property from the estate of John Harrison. The manor court entry reads: *October 25th 1802, John Jones, (Trustee for Lovatt as in preceding Recovery), to Josiah Spode of Stoke upon Trent Esq. All that copyhold dwelling house and barn, and all land called the Great Hough and Far Hough in Penkhull, which said pieces of land were formerly in three parts and then called the Three Hough's, were formerly in the holding of Richard Heath, afterwards of John Slaney, but late of John Townsend and were late the estate of Thomas Lovett previously of William Lovett, and formerly of Joseph Lovatt otherwise Lovatt the younger; fine 1s/5d.*

As Spode was engaged in the building of The Mount from 1803 to 1804, it is unlikely that there was any progress on the building of Penkhull Square during that time. In reality, it may not have been until after The Mount had been completed in 1805/6 that work commenced on the building of Penkhull Square. This assumption is supported by the parish lune book for 1807-8, which records that five out of the 20 dwellings remained unoccupied. The early occupants were Messrs Eaton, Taylor, Hatton, Dinney, Bird, Smith, Mason, Martin, Williams, Robinson, Yates, Parker and Spooner. The amount paid to the parish was assessed at 1s 3d for each dwelling.

In a schedule of all the property owned by Spode compiled after his death in 1827, Penkhull Square is described as follows: *And also all those twenty messuages standing at a place called The Square near the south end of the Village of Penkhull now or lately in the holdings of Ann Shaw, John Pugh, Samuel Harding, Ann Shaw the widow of William Shaw, John Steele, Samuel Davis, Thomas Underwood, Robert Hollinshead, Richard Pye, Joseph Bird, Thomas Ridgeway, Samuel Simpson, Thomas Critchley, William Robinson, Thomas Forrester, Richard Ball, Myatt Brookes, William Spooner and John Ridgeway or their under tenants with outbuildings yards, gardens etc.*

The 1841 census return makes interesting reading. All properties were occupied. The occupations included potters, labourers, wheelwright, bricklayer, cordwainer and a shoemaker. The total number of people living in the square numbered 110, an average of 5.5 per dwelling. The numbers varied from a family of three to that of ten. As there were only two bedrooms, one too small to contain a double bed, the living conditions would have been cramped.

Results found in the 1861 census are similar to those of 1841: pottery workers, a widow, Mary Tunstall a domestic servant, aged 51 with 8 children, five of whom went to work. An exception was George Herritt, aged 47, an army pensioner. He came from Cheadle, married an Irish wife and one of his children, Margaret, aged 15 was born in East India.

The 1871 census continues the theme of pottery workers, although one occupation is that of a pig dealer, George Horne, aged 55, who came from Leek. He was in possession of both No. 19 and 20 Penkhull Square but the census records that he was taking in a lodger, William Roberts as well as his wife and daughter. The largest occupancy was that of Mr John Wright, aged 38, a potter's presser, who with his wife and nine children from 1 year to 16 years of age, all managed to live in such a tiny house. They were still in occupation in 1881, although the three eldest children had left home, but in the intervening ten years a further two children had been born.

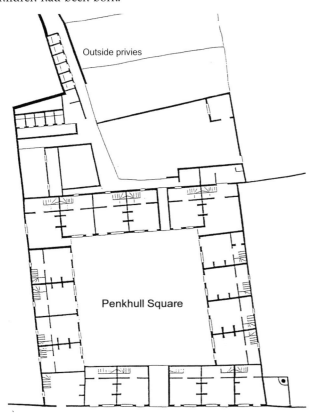

Penkhull Square

Outside privies

Evidence extracted from the census returns show that there was a high turnover of occupiers because the properties were built to a very low standard. Coal for example was kept at the side of the open fire, up a corner, there being nowhere else to store it. Bath night, once a week on a Friday was with a tin bath on the hearth, cleanest first.

The 1911 census provides a further snapshot of the Square, its occupants and social status. The occupations had changed from the early days when most were potters, but now a wide variety of unskilled workers. No tenant remained the same as recorded in the previous census. The average age of the head of families was low at 36 years, the majority were small families compared with previous census returns.

At No 1, James Moss, aged 54, was the eldest head, a potter's labourer. At No.2 William Ball was 46 years. His wife Elizabeth was aged 41. Six children were recorded as living at home from the ages of 6 months to 15 years although a total of twelve were born during their 20 years of marriage. The highest occupancy by a single family was found at No.4. Here, Thomas Wright, aged 44, a telegraph wireman and his wife, Susan, aged 36, had produced seven children who were all still living at home.

For the first time, the 1911 census records how many children were born to a family and how many had died. The totals reflect the times, poor diet, poor housing and bad sanitation and health services that few could afford. Out of a total of children born to the families listed as living in Penkhull Square, there were 56 children born, of whom, 34 died either at birth or in infancy, representing a 61% mortality rate. In comparison, Brisley Hill across the road with a mortality rate of 26%.

A report by the sanitary inspector in 1865 illustrates the seriousness of the problem: *There were twenty-one houses in the square with seven privies, six of them connected and placed in gardens behind the houses. The contents discharge into open receptacles in the adjoining fields. The large ash pit is full and there are no back doors to the houses. About one hundred people live there.* The inspector also noted that the square was conspicuous by the number of deaths recorded from typhus and other fatal forms of fever. In 1865, there were 26 burials in Penkhull churchyard followed by 48 in 1866. All were from Penkhull Square.

Trentham Road, late 1940s

Church Procession and Boys Brigade Band c1910

At the time of mass demolition of Penkhull in the mid 1960s, there were considerable protests against the demolition of the Square. Yes, they were in their existing form unfit for habitation, but the uniqueness and the historical value made them a target to be retained. Ian Nairn, a Daily Telegraph correspondent wrote in 1963. *That Penkhull Square itself must be saved, as reconditioned, it would be tailor-made for old people and childless couples and for anyone who wants to live in a place with some identity to it.*

Yet again, despite protests against the proposals on the grounds that it could indeed be converted into substantial old people's secured housing, with a central square with seats and flowerbeds, the thoughts were ignored by the city council. The powers that be at the town hall ignored every approach and proposal, only to confirm one thing - compulsory demolition.

Almost across the road from Penkhull Square and just below stood Brisley Hill.

Brisley and Bears Hill

Walking southwards down Trent Valley Road today, Brisley Hill is to the left, just past what used to be Penkhull Square on the right. This row of old cottages represented almost the boundary of the old village. The name is the last reminder of the name for the hill itself. Today, the road remains un-adopted and is bounded on the right by the rear of houses now facing Colverly Place, the original row faced into Brisley Hill.

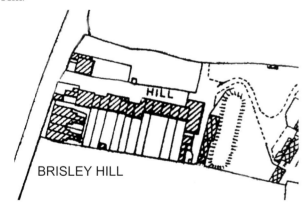

The first two groups of houses are identified in Hargreaves' map of 1832 and again on the Tithe map of 1849. There was firstly a group of four terraced houses followed by a group of five. The group of four were owned by John Hill and in various occupations listed as *William Sutton and others*, whilst Allen Foster the younger owned the group of five. Foster had inherited the property, and in 1853 mortgaged them for the sum of £300 from Richard Godwin, by which time the five had become six. They were recorded as in the occupations of Allen Foster, John Millington, Jesse Buckstones, Joseph Jarvis and Isaac Roberts. Isaac Roberts can be identified in the 1851 and 1861 census. So too can Joseph Forrester and his family.

Brisley Hill, off Trentham Road

The occupations of the heads of families in 1911 are of the lower working class. No.1 John Beardmore, aged 37, colliery banksman; No.2 Albert Cooper, aged 31, earthenware figure caster; No.3 Peter Prendergast, aged 38, bricklayer and his family consisting of five sons from 10 months to 11 years; No. 4 Albert Briggs, aged 49, warehouseman; No.5 George Stretton, aged 46, saddler; No.6 Elizabeth Alerton, aged 54, a widow who took in two boarders, Annie, aged 29, single a charwoman form Leek, and John Goldstraw, aged 19, a basket maker from Stoke; No.7 Benjamin Cheadle, aged 72, and still working as a lodge keeper for a pottery manufactory. His wife Caroline, aged 65, was at home with their four daughters and one son between the ages of 22 and 34. A further three children had died in infancy; No.8 Elizabeth Deakin, aged 42, a widow, pottery enameller with her daughter, aged 12; No.9 William Lowe, aged 40, a carter, his wife and four children all at school; No.10 William

Chapman, aged 27, a paver, his wife and three children aged between 2 months and 4 years of age; No.11 Thomas Wilshaw, aged 26, waggoner, his wife and three children; No. 13 George Stretton, aged 80, a retired coach maker and his wife Martha, aged 77.

A separate group of terraced properties standing on an elevated terrace over-looking Trent Valley Road bear the date 1850. It would be reasonable to assume that the mortgage of £300 was to pay off the debt for building the row of terraced properties as they also belonged to Allen Foster.

In Brisley Hill, there were thirteen houses in number but in three sections. They were initially a row of four and a row of five properties with a space in between but shortly after 1851, this space was built up to complete a row of thirteen. The land was formerly called Bears Hill belonging to Daniel Cotton, a potter from Cliffe Bank. Cotton surrendered a section of Bears Hill at a court held in November 1807 to William Hill who already owned land and premises in the centre of the village. The court entry refers to restrictions on building that no property should be built within six feet of the boundary of the plot. It also states that a new road was to be built but no more than twelve feet wide.

Brisley Hill had various owners throughout the years. In October 1925, Arthur Collis acquired them. In 1933, they had passed to Mrs Daisy Fletcher (nee Collis). An estate map of that date shows that Daisy Fletcher owned all the land bordering Trent Valley Road to its junction with Hunters Way and including the area which is now Colverly Place. The last photographs taken of Brisley Hill are not complimentary and point the need for demolition. They were demolished under a scheme for the whole village in May 1967.

The old cottage still standing on the corner of Brisley Hill facing on to Trent Valley Road was also shown on Hargreaves' map of 1832. A copyhold court held on the 28th September 1854 shows that prior to that date it was in the ownership of William Bell, as the mortgage holder of the sum of £160 loaned to Mr John Evans. The loan was taken out in 1835. In his will he left premises described as: *and all that dwelling house erected on part of a piece or land situate in Penkhull called 'Little Meadow' late Lewis's together with a plot of land at the back now in the occupation of Charles Foster.*

A previous court entry links the two documents. The first is dated the 12th November 1807 and may provide the actual date that this little cottage was erected. Once again, the owner of the land Bears Hill, was Daniel Cotton of Cliffe Bank, a brick manufacturer. He surrendered to the court: *all that plot of land, as the same is marked out of a close of land in Penkhull called little Bears Hill into the hands of John Evans, builder.* In

1861, it was in the occupation of James Brammer and his family. James was employed as a gardener.

The origins of the name of Bears Hill is not the easiest to explain. It sits neatly with the title of a nearby field called Hunter's Croft, (hence the name of the current road Hunter's Way). Sadly, romanticism in this case is probably not the answer. Most names come from the name of a person, and Hunter's Croft is no exception. The surname has its origins locally back in the 15th century with John Hunt senior being recorded in 1414 as holding land. In 1416, William Hunt had inherited the property. A John Hunt is recorded again in 1459, Robert in 1543.

Probably by accident in a document dated 1571, John Hunt is referred to as John Hunter, and this could have been the start of the name given to lands in the occupation for centuries by the Hunt family. Land belonging to a family called Hunt would certainly be called Hunter's land. In 1615, there was a house called Hunters House, no doubt occupied by a family by the name of Hunt. The name of Hunters Croft appears regularly in the manor court rolls from 1605.

The area known by the name of Bears Hill is extensive, extending from Trent Valley Road crossing over to below Hunter's Way, and from almost the centre of the village to the south down Trent Valley Road to the junction of the current Hunter's Way. The land is elevated and the eastern side resembles a ridge overlooking the valley of the Trent, while below, almost by a sheer drop, lies The Villas, a mid 19th century housing development designed by Charles Lynam.

The further name of Bearswall first appears in the manor records of 1580, then 1598 and in 1606 when it went by the name of Bearswall Croft a name which continued to almost modern times. In 1618 it was referred to as Bearswall Waste in the ownership of John Tittensor. An authority on the origins of place names Dr Ian Buckley, gives his point of view: *Sometimes it means 'barley' (OE = 'bere')... but it can also mean 'hill' or 'fort' or again a personal name.* Unfortunately, there is no certain answer. The explanation of a hill fort certainly fits the physical appearance of the area, a subject covered in chapter one. A hill fort would have had a defensive wall. Could therefore the name Bearswall be a left-over from the past?

Victoria Buildings, the old parish workhouse

The old parish poorhouse or workhouse situated opposite the village green was purchased after it was replaced by The Spittals workhouse in 1834. It was then converted into five three-storey properties by Mr George Thomas Taylor. The first public census of 1841 is not very helpful as although Victoria Place is named, unfortunately the area of Victoria

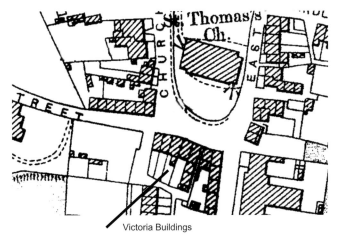

Victoria Buildings

Place included the whole area between the old workhouse, known as Victoria Buildings, and Victoria Place now St Thomas Place to its junction with Greatbatch Avenue. Mr Taylor purchased the old poor house, along with what is now The Greyhound Inn. A mortgage amounting to £820 from John Wickes Tomlinson and Frederick Wright Tomlinson enabled the purchase.

In April 1841, Mr Taylor put up for auction the old workhouse, by then converted into eight properties. The auction took place at the Wheatsheaf Inn, Stoke on Monday 19th April at seven o'clock in the evening. The sale consisted of: *those eight cottages situate in Penkhull in the occupations of Thomas Owen, Richard Bagnall, James Perry, Herbert Hill, Ann Bird George Henny, Charles Peake and Stephen Serjeant with yards, gardens thereto belonging. They are advantageously situated near to the site of the intended new church at Penkhull.*

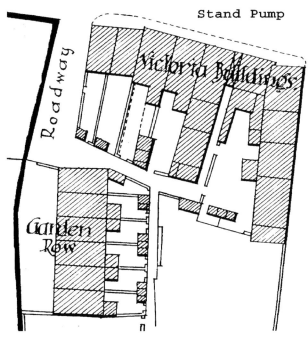

Not only was the old workhouse up for auction, but also The Greyhound Inn. The manor court entry of 13th September 1841 makes interesting reading as it confirms that Mr Taylor converted the old workhouse building into the cottages. *And also all those eight several messuages with the shops and other buildings belonging situated in Penkhull which have*

been constructed and formed out of an edifice or building known as the workhouse or house for the reception of the poor for the parish of Stoke upon Trent or have been built upon the land adjoining and belonging to such workhouse. To the use of William Baker the younger, late of Fenton, but now of Highfields in the City of Chester.

At the time of the 1861 census, the group of houses went by the name of *Old Workhouse* being occupied by George Wright, William Eardley, Ralph Taylor, Hannah Turner and John Clowes.

Looking at old photographs of the row of cottages, No.1 shows a small shop window, although there is no evidence that it was ever occupied for that purpose. However in 1871, No.3 was used as a grocers shop in the occupation of Ralph and Ellen Taylor and in 1887, George Emery. By 1891, the old workhouse was called Victoria Buildings and No.3 was occupied by Herbert Parkes, aged 49. He worked as a potter's miller while his wife Elizabeth, aged 47, ran the grocer's shop. They had four daughters and four sons between the ages of four and 17 years. The rest of the occupants of Victoria Buildings worked in the pottery industry. Ten years later Herbert Parkes was working as a labourer in a brickyard but a trade directory of 1900 lists him as running the grocery business.

Victoria Buildings, the Old Parish Poor House

By 1911, Herbert had died and the grocer's shop was being run by his widow Elizabeth, then aged 64. She lived with two daughters and their husbands and one grandchild Samuel, aged 13, employed as an errand boy. From 1891-1911 the number of children born to the five households in Victoria Buildings totalled 44. Elizabeth Parkes had given birth to fourteen children, of whom ten had survived. At No.2 Thomas and Martha Bradley had eleven children of whom three had died and lastly at No.5, Alfred and Ann Banks who had been married for twenty-seven years had nine children out of whom only one remained alive in 1911. Out of the total of 44 born, 19 had died representing 43% infantile deaths.

Victoria Buildings

Following on from Elizabeth Parkes the shop was run by Mrs Sidley, followed in the early 1940s by Mrs Hilda Smith. By 1947, she employed as an assistant Norman Hill, to whom she sold the business later that year. At the same time, Mrs Smith purchased the old fish and chip shop at the top of Penkhull New Road from Mrs Hemmings. Both Mrs Smith and Norman Hill were renting the front shop while the rear was occupied by David and Marion Dix. Names that appear as residents in 1930 are No.1 Furber; No.2 Fradley; No.4 Webster and No.5 Banks. At this time, Miss Lowe of The Views owned the whole of Victoria Buildings. By the 1950s most of the occupants had changed. At No.1 it was Ernest Wright; No.4 John Webster and No.5 Arthur Nash.

Norman Hill in his old shop in Victoria Buildings

Norman Hill quickly became a popular figure in the village, expanding his business to take in greens as well as groceries. He started by borrowing the initial £200 from local resident Mr Tony Littler, of Trent Valley Road. Norman recalls: *it was only the front shop and a stock room, the back room is where Mr Dix lived. The property was old and very dilapidated. For years,*

Miss Lowe collected the rent and then she sold it to someone from France. At that point I was evicted but my good friend Jack Burton allowed me to use one of his new shops he had built to replace his old cobblers shop in Manor Court Street. From there I moved location to run my business in a pre-fabricated building on land next to the DIY shop in Newcastle Lane for two years until the council served notice on me to quit. Sadly, I then had to finish altogether.

A compulsory purchase order was confirmed on Victoria Buildings on the 29th September 1961 but it was not until January 1967 that they were finally demolished by the city council.

Garden Street, formerly Farm Lane

When Penkhull Square was completed, Spode proceeded to develop further workers' dwellings in the village of Penkhull. In May 1810, he acquired two sites with existing properties owned by Thomas Chapman, a resident of Penkhull, who lived in an old property called Doody's in what was then known as Victoria Place. The first site contained five old cottages described as being *the inheritance of Joseph Bourne and afterwards his sister Margery Chapman.* These five cottages stood in what was Farm Lane and were either demolished or converted into six cottages by Josiah Spode.

The new or converted cottages were built in a similar layout to those described for Penkhull Square. At the rear was a communal yard with shared privies, ash pit and one shared water pump. Even with the lack of facilities compared with other houses built by Spode, the occupants were charged the same rent as those houses in Ten Row at 8s 9d, subsequently creating a high turnover of tenants. The second acquisition by Spode was at the same copyhold court, where a further five cottages, described as *comprising of a barn the same having been many years ago converted into dwelling houses in the respective occupations of. . .* Spode demolished or converted this row of cottages and in its place constructed a row of ten workers' dwellings, appropriately known as Ten Row at the top of Penkhull New Road.

The census of 1841 for Garden Street lists six families the heads being No.1 William Smith, aged 30, potter, with six children; No.3 John Smith, aged 40, potter, with six children; No.5, Thomas Hulme, aged 30, with five children; No.7 William Sutton, aged 25, potter with three children; No 1 Victoria Place, Ellen Ball, potter, with four children; No.2 Victoria Place, Thomas Swetnam, aged 30, potter with five children.

Census returns every ten years show a different set of tenants by 1891. Firstly, the house numbers had changed but by this time they were under a private landlord, and no longer tied to the pottery industry as the occupation of the tenants varied. Samuel Beardsley, aged 29, general labourer, born Rochester; Martha Plant, widow, aged 56, potters presser, born Stoke; John Ridgeway, aged 35, potters presser, born Penkhull; George Horne, widower, aged 76, pig and cattle salesman, born Penkhull; James McPherson, aged 33, drayman, born Scotland. James McPherson occupied both No.12 and 13 Garden Street.

Views of Garden Street, formerly Farm Lane

James was married to Elizabeth, aged 37, who came from Warwick. They had two daughters Emma and Rose. There was also a visitor staying in the home as well as a border, Richard Cabry, aged 23, from Leicester. His occupation was also a drayman. It can be assumed that he worked alongside James at the brewery and therefore found accommodation with James and his family.

By 1901 there was no change as to details, apart from ages. James died in 1905, aged 48, leaving Elizabeth, a widow. It is probably through a change of circumstances that she

commenced business and converted her front room into a beer off-licence in addition to selling groceries and sweets.

Trade listings of 1907 and 1912, confirm Mrs Elizabeth McPherson as grocer and beer retailer. The business continued through the First World War after which, with a change in the law, it was not possible to sell beer alongside groceries and sweets. By this time Elizabeth had acquired two properties around the corner Nos. 3 and 4 Church Street (now Manor Court Street) and decided to build a lean-to adjacent to No.4 from which she could continue to sell few groceries and sweets.

When the sweet and grocery business ceased the small shop was next listed as in the occupation of William Smith, boot and shoemaker. This is once more confirmed in the trade listings of 1912 and the rate assessment book of 1914. The records state that No.3 was rented out to Elizabeth Hemmings and No.4 to Henry Ball.

Out- door off-licence and small grocers shop.
Proprietor Mrs Elizabeth McPherson

Garden Row

Garden Row is situated just off Garden Street and appropriately so called because it overlooked allotments, which lay between the small row of terraced houses and Penkhull Farm. The land was acquired by Josiah Spode and added to the site of the old parish poor house. With the building of the new workhouse at The Spittals, the site became vacant and subsequently sold in 1835 by the new owner of the Spode estate, William Taylor Copeland, to George Thomas Taylor. *Together with the six dwelling houses and the outbuildings thereof recently erected by the said George Thomas Taylor upon the said piece of land and now in the occupations of James Perry, William Sharp, Aaron Simpson, Henry Brown, John Beech and John Daniel or their several under tenants. To which before described plot of land comprising the site of the said dwelling houses the said George Thomas Taylor was admitted tenant at a court held on the 5th November 1835.*

Garden Row, off Garden Street

In 1861, the houses were occupied by Messrs, Joseph Till, Mary Jackson, Walter Heath, John Sutton, John Swetnam and Aaron Keeling. Occupations varied: two worked in the pottery industry, one a point's man on the railways, a crate maker, bricklayer and agricultural labourer. The largest family lived at No.3, Walter Heath, aged 45, along with his wife Sarah, four daughters and one son, Thomas, aged 13. By 1881, apart from Joseph Till, all were new tenants, five of whom worked in the pottery industry, and the other, Fred Williams, aged 25, worked as a blacksmith.

A similar picture to the previous returns were found in 1911 when three worked in the pottery industry, one on the railways, a builder's labourer and George Lyth a milk dealer who just a few years after 1911 transferred his business to No.3, Victoria Place. The largest family lived at No.5 Elijah Tunstall, a bricklayer, aged 45, who was born in Penkhull. He was married to Elizabeth, employed as a washer-woman, aged 45. They had nine children of whom six remained at home, three daughters and three sons. One child died in infancy. Next door, Samuel and Isabella had three children but only one was still living.

Manor Court Street and Malt House Buildings

Both Manor Court Street and Malthouse buildings were once a part of a large section of land in the centre of Penkhull bounded by Manor Court Street, formerly Church Street, Garden Street, formerly Farm Lane and Newcastle Lane. Originally it was all part of the estate of Greenhead House, now The Greyhound Inn, a full account of which can be found under the chapter 'The Greyhound Inn'.

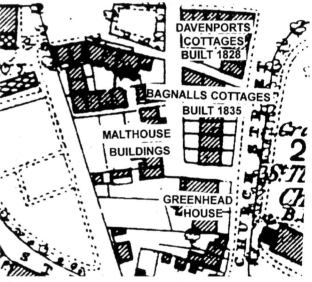

The last person to occupy this large house and and its surrounding land was John Townsend, who, for financial reasons, decided to sell off the land in plots. By 1806, he had already mortgaged the property with a loan from Robert Smith of Grindley House for £350 but the terms were rearranged transferring the mortgage to William Adams of Cobridge, earthenware manufacturer. Townsend further secured an additional mortgage in June 1813 when he borrowed £150 from John Brown of Knutton.

Even with these two loans, John Townsend was unable to meet his financial commitments therefore the only answer was to sell part of his estate to pay off his debts. The first sale of land came in 1812, a decision that had the effect of changing the medieval agrarian village centre forever. To Michael Baxter, he sold the maltkiln and accommodation situated to the rear of the farmhouse together with land amounting to 1036 square yards for £360. The maltkiln had been part of the assets of the large farmhouse and was referred to on many occasions from the late 17th century belonging to Greenhead House.

At the same time, John Townsend sold two further parcels of land the first to John Burgess. This consisted of 1,144 square yards for £328. The second parcel of land was to Thomas Bird, a builder, consisting of 550 square yards for £103.

By 1826, Baxter had built four cottages together and one separate house on the land, no doubt to house the workers of the maltkiln. They were situated at right angles to Manor Court Street, just to the rear of the houses in Newcastle Lane. These may have been financed by a mortgage for the sum of £500 loaned from Elizabeth Kirkham of Horden Cottage, Stoke (Kirkham's Pottery, now Portmeirion). They were brick with long gardens to the front. There was no rear. They had two rooms on the ground floor, a room for daily family use with the stairs off, and a small kitchen. The stairs led directly into the larger of the two bedrooms. Candles later to be replaced by gas originally lit the cottages.

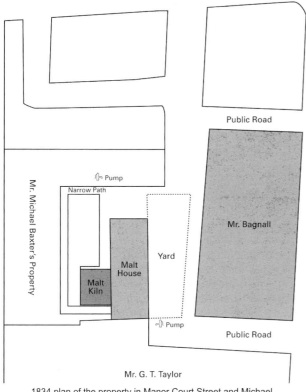

1834 plan of the property in Manor Court Street and Michael Baxters Malt-house

The access road still remains and is referred to in the sale document as in co-ownership with John Townsend and Michel Baxter and their respective heirs and assigns. In 1861, two of the cottages Nos. 2 and 3 were occupied by the Baravale family, parents in one, and the son with his family in the other. The largest family was at No.4; John Leigh, aged 36, a potter's saggar maker who originated from Biddulph. His wife, Martha, aged 36; working in the potteries came from Pershall, together with their five sons, one daughter and the sister of Martha. Ten years later in 1871, the cottages were occupied by a different set of tenants except where John

Leigh and his family had moved from No.4. At No.2 was Thomas Broomfield, aged 30, he was a potter's oven man, and his wife Louisa. They had two young children. At No.3 was the widowed mother of Thomas Broomfield, Susannah, aged 62, along with her son and daughters and two grandchildren. At No.4 lived James Broomfield, aged 36, also the sons of Susannah together with his wife and four daughters and lastly at No.5 lived the other son, Henry Broomfield, aged 39, his wife Harriett and their three daughters.

By 1901 these six cottages were occupied as follows No.1, Martha Meakin, a widow, aged 32, her two illegitimate children Fred and Amy Burrows and three other children. At No.2 was Edward Corn, aged 22, a potter's warehouse man and his wife Ada. No.3, Samuel Burrows, aged 28, a bricklayer's labourer. From this surname, he may be suspected of being the father of the two illegitimate children living at No.1. At No.4 William Riley, aged 42, also a bricklayer's labourer. He came from Shrewsbury. His wife was Ann who was born in Stoke. Lastly at No.5 was Martha Bird, a widow, aged 55, but working as a potter's lathe turner. She was born in Penkhull and lived with her two sons, aged 22 and 29, and a boarder Alfred Prince, aged 25. By 1912, the occupants were No.1 Henry Foster, a sanitary presser; No.2 Amos Bethell, labourer; No.3 Frederick Mason, waggoner; No.4. James Turnock, a stonemason; and No.5 Margaret Bird, a widow. In 1914, the occupants were the same and the cottages were owned by Michael Baxter junior. The rent varied; No.1 the largest at £8 p.a; No. 2 and 3 £6 p.a; and No's 5 and 6 £5 6d p.a.

The old cottages were still occupied in 1955 by: No.1 William Talbot; No.2 Amos Bithell; No.3 Daniel Evans; No.4 John Brandall and No.5 William Underwood.

Manor Court Street

The second parcel of land sold by John Townsend in 1812 was to Thomas Bird, a builder, and consisted of 550 square yards. The sum of £103 was the purchase price. This land was situated facing Manor Court Street, abutting to the left side of Greenhead House. At the time of his death in 1824, Thomas Bird had built two cottages and left them to his wife Susannah.

In June 1837, the cottages and shop (one had been altered) were sold to Joseph Reeves the younger. In February 1849, Reeves mortgaged the cottages and shop for the sum of £80, from a society known as the Horticultural Lodge of the United Free Gardeners. By the turn of the century, the two properties had been purchased by Elizabeth McPhearson who owned an outdoor beerhouse in Garden Street, which also sold sweets and a few groceries. After the First World War regulations changed with regard to the sale of foodstuffs not being compatible with the sale of beer. As a result Elizabeth McPherson decided to sell sweets from the small premises in Church Street. Elizabeth built on to the side of No.4 Church Street a small lean-to. In 1907, this small addition was occupied by William Smith, a boot and shoemaker. He still occupied the shop until 1912. In 1922, another boot and shoe repairer had set up in business by Harry Chell at his home No. 27 Newcastle Street. Harry had served in the Great War and lost both his legs as a result. His small advertisement in the parish magazine makes interesting reading as he refers to *'Lest we Forget'* I served King and Country, the legless boot repairer.

By the following year, Harry Chell had taken up the premises at 4a Church Street and he again advertised as the *'Legless Shoe Repairer'*. It is from Mr Chell that Jack Burton took over the business as village shoe repairer in December 1930, and purchased the property from Mrs McPherson at a cost of £200.

The old cobblers shop demolished mid 1960s

In 1901, Nos 1 and 2 Church Street were owned by the executors of William Mountford who also owned the property at the other end of Church Street. No.1 was occupied by Calbe Farmer, aged 33, a potter's placer and his wife and one child, aged 2 and No.2 was occupied by John Mayor, aged 37, a general labourer and his wife Edith. They took in two lodgers. The occupants at No.3 were Henry Bradbury, aged 53, a self-employed coal carrier and his wife Annie. They had seven sons living at home. There was the same number of children living at No.4 where Harry

Johnson, aged 47, was the head of the family and a tile layer with his wife Susannah, aged 45.

Old cottages and Shops in Manor Court Street

Next to this was an old property, originally a farm house and used as the Manor Courthouse. In 1865, it was occupied by Richard Ball a local man, aged 41, a pottery packer with his wife Mary, aged 42, also born in Penkhull. They had two children. By 1891, the old building was occupied by Thomas Mayer, aged 60, a potter's printer born in Penkhull and his wife Sarah, aged 58, a potter's paintress. They had two children; a son, aged 19, and a daughter, aged 17, both still at home. In the 1930s the last occupant was Mr Bert Pattinson, who was the brother of Dick, the landlord of the inn next door.

The Greyhound Inn was occupied by Joseph Webster, aged 31, who worked during the day as a potter's painter as well as opening up the pub in the evening. His wife was Ann, aged 32. They had three children and employed a servant, Elizabeth Edwards, aged 21.

Proceeding northward from the Greyhound Inn, there was an orchard and gardens belonging to the property until John Townsend sold the plot to Michael Baxter for the sum of £280 paid directly to John Brown of Knutton in full and final settlement of the mortgage that Townsend had earlier taken out from him. The plot extended north from the orchard and included outbuildings and garden, together with three terraced houses already built on the land facing the roadway. At the time of the sale, John Townsend had left Penkhull and was living at Croxton. The old farmhouse and these three dwellings were the subject of a public auction held at the nearby Marquis of Granby on the 26th November 1828 following the death of John Townsend in the previous August at the age of 74. He is buried in Kingsley where the sole executor of his will lived.

The advertisement describes the sale as follows: *Those three newly erected brick and tile dwelling houses pleasantly situated in the centre of Penkhull, with garden containing 150 square yards adjoining, well adapted for building purposes, occupying a frontage of thirty-eight feet. Also, an old respectable Farm House, contiguous to the above, now occupied in three dwellings, commanding an extent of fifty eight feet in front, with a back yard, in which is a stable for two horses, pigsty, coal house and other conveniences and an excellent garden of about eight roods adjoining at the back of the same, all in a ring fence, the whole late the property of John Townsend, deceased.* At the auction, the old farmhouse was purchased by George Thomas Taylor.

This information points to the fact that John Townsend had started to develop Manor Court Street just before he died. Perhaps this was the reason that he sold other plots of land to raise the finance. Hargreaves' map 1832 confirms that development had taken place, both facing the road, and behind, where the malthouse buildings and cottages were situated.

In 1835, this road facing parcel of land and three cottages were sold to William Bagnall of Boothen Cottage. This finally extinguished the remaining agricultural land situated in the centre of the village overlooking the green as he built a further three terraced houses to complete a row of six. In a mortgage document dated 5th November 1835 the additional dwellings are described as: *and also those three other messuages lately erected and built by the said William Bagnall together with the concurrent use in conjunction with the occupiers of the malthouse and cottages and the property formerly of John Townsend and the well of water and pump at the back of the said premises.*

Bagnalls Row, Manor Court Street. Berrisfords Butchers to the right

Apart from two occasions when they were mortgaged, the row of cottages remained in the hands of William Bagnall and then his family. In 1914, they were all owned by Sarah Bagnall but by 1958, the remaining trustee of the estate of William Bagnall was Emma Bagnall Fleet. The last house in the row, No.12, after 1901 opened as a small grocer's shop run by Mr Harry McLean. In 1914, it was run by William Clarke but by the mid 1950s by Edna Myatt.

Manor Court Street c1950

The final development of Manor Court Street was the last section, following Bagnall's Row, to the north of the small pathway. Despite the plot being enclosed and used as a garden by John Townsend he found that the land was still listed as manorial waste belonging to the Duchy of Lancaster when he came to sell it. Therefore before any sale could take place Townsend first had to pay to the Duchy the sum of seven guineas to purchase the copyhold status. It was then described as: *At a special court held on 14th April 1827 to this court comes John Townsend of Penkhull and in consideration of seven guineas of lawful English money paid by him to the Lord of the Manor, doth grant to the said John Townsend . . . . a plot of land now enclosed and used as a garden, bounded on the north by the road leading to Knapper's Gate, on the east by the road leading from Penkhull to the lodge turnpike gate and on the west by a private road leading to Michael Baxter's maltkiln and houses being part of waste land in the village of Penkhull.*

Manor Court Street looking towards Victoria Buildings c1950

After the situation regarding ownership had been resolved, Townsend completed the sale on the 6th March 1828 to Joseph Mountford, yeoman of Penkhull for the price of £60 17s 6d: *All that parcel of land, now enclosed containing 487 sq yards, bounded on the north by a road leading from Penkhull to Knapper's Gate, on the south by a road leading to the premises of John Townsend and on the west by a private road leading to the property of Michael Baxter.*

In the following July, Joseph Mountford mortgaged the land for the sum of £100 from Rupert Masely of Dilhorn. At a manor court held on the 5th February 1841, it was reported that Joseph Mountford had failed to repay the loan, and in fact, increased his debt by borrowing a further £250 from Timothy Dimmock and Robert Kidd. Because of these debts, Mountford transferred the parcel of land, described then as: *together with six houses erected thereon by the said Joseph Mountford.* As a result of the debts, the houses and land were transferred to Messrs Dimmock and Kidd. Following this transfer the properties were then used to secure a mortgage for themselves in July 1860 for the sum of £463: *together with eight cottages, two of which having been recently built.* The loan was taken out from William Bridgewood. By September 1866 the land and property was sold to John Royal, *two cottages of which have been lately converted into one and used as a beer house occupied by William Benbow, and the remaining six in the occupations of Henry Gifford, Thomas Lambert, Samuel Bird, Eliza Dixon, Ann Mould and another.* Four years later, John Royal sold them to William Bradbury for the sum of £525.

A final document is dated 30th June 1898 when David Shenton, formerly of the Royal Oak decided to sell the properties to Angelina Reeves of Penkhull Terrace. Angelina Reeves then passed on these premises to her sister Julia Lowe. By this time, David Shenton had moved to Campbell Road, Stoke. The document makes interesting reading as it refers to the Royal Oak in some detail. In consideration of £550, Shenton surrendered all those six messuages, 6, 8, 10 Newcastle Street, and numbers 13, 14 and 15 Church Street:

The Royal Oak Beer House on the right

together with two other dwelling houses converted into one and used as a beer house, known by the sign of The Royal Oak in the occupation of David Shenton. And also the use of the private road leading to what were formerly Michael Baxter's maltkiln and house together with the right of way at all times over and along the back passage and also the use of the ash pit.

Local grocers run by Mr. Brunt

Angelina Reeves also owned a number of properties in East Street and Penkhull Terrace. Her last years were spent living at The Views with her sister, Julia and brother-in-law and two nieces. As a reflection of her wealth, a large granite stone marks her burial plot in Hartshill Cemetery. She died on the 10th April 1932, aged 77.

It was not until the turn of the century that a number of retail shops started to appear in this group of houses from No.13 onwards. The first record comes with the census return of 1891 when Louisa Comley of No.14 was listed as a small shopkeeper, a widow, aged 42. She lived there with her four sons, one daughter, a visitor and a boarder. Her name appears later in 1901 when she moved to another shop in the village on the corner of Seven Row. The other premises were occupied as domestic houses.

By 1901, changes had taken place. At No.13 a butchers had been established, run by Arthur Salt, aged 28, from Longton; and No.14, a grocer's shop was established by Mary Gibson, a widow, aged 31. By 1907, the butcher's had changed hands to Mr James Berrisford, a family name that held the business until the mid 1980s. Next door at No.14 had opened as a sub-postmaster as well as a confectioner.

Newcastle Lane, formerly Newcastle Street

The origins of this old lane go back as far as the beginning of Penkhull itself. It would be the 'way' that early settlers would walk to the valley and forests below on their daily kill for food, or to fish in the Lyme Brook. It would also be the 'way' that early peddlers would use going from hamlet to hamlet, selling their wares of pots and pans, bottles of elixir that would cure all, followed on by the knife-grinder offering his services to whoever would pay a farthing or halfpenny for him to sharpen their household knives or farm implements.

Until the late 1930s, almost the whole of Newcastle Lane from Franklin Road to Hilton Road was steeped on both sides by high banks on the top of which were footpaths, not laid but on soil or stone. The road was an earth surface like a country lane. The present lower section joining into London Road is the last section which today remains, as it has always had been narrow, with high banks on either side.

Newcastle Lane c1910

In early documents, no name is given to the lane being described only as 'the road from Penkhull leading to Newcastle'. Early references to the lower section refer to its being called Grindley Lane after the fields, house and farm in that area. The first real name appears in the census of 1841 when it is referred to as Castle Street. This name was later changed to Newcastle Street followed by that of Newcastle Lane in 1950.

Although Yates' map of 1775 gives no details of properties in the lane, Hargreaves' of 1832 shows a small number on the north side near to the top from its junction with Franklin Road. A Duchy map drawn up specifically to identify cottages, which had encroached upon the Lord's waste without permission, lists five properties, situated where currently stand a group of modern town houses at the top of Newcastle Lane. The first three leading down from the top of the lane were owned by James Burne. The following two properties were owned by William Fox and John Hancock. There were a further two properties listed, the first just below facing the junction of Franklins Road belonged to George Cowper, and the other standing almost on the site of the present Pear Tree Cottage was owned by Mrs Mary Cowper.

The Lower Section of Newcastle Lane at the entrance to Grindley House

The Half Timbered Cottage

It was not until the group of cottages situated at the top of Newcastle Lane were in the process of demolition in February 1965 that a secret hidden for over four hundred years began to unfold. *The Evening Sentinel* recognising their

Bottom of Newcastle Lane at its junction with London Road

importance reported this together with a photograph. *What is believed to be a 16th century cottage in Newcastle Lane has been discovered among properties being demolished at Penkhull. Mr Richard Holland of the Architectural Dept. at Keele University says he believes the cottage is worthy of preservation as a matter of historic interest.*

'It has a most interesting gable end' says Mr Holland. 'Obviously at one time it was a half timbered cottage, unusual in that area which has been built on afterwards. Probably at one time, it had been a thatched roof. It is the sort of thing which if found in the country would fetch a great deal of money because of its romantic association. Similar structures are to be found in the Nantwich area'.

Mr J W Plant, the Stoke-on-Trent Reconstruction officers and City Architect told the Sentinel that he would go and look at the cottage. The cottage, which is on the top of the hill near to the church has the roof off and is in the course of being demolished. The demolition people are burning some of the ancient wooden beams because of it being badly infested with wood lice. Other timbers are in a good state of preservation. No nails have been employed in the construction all the woodwork being fixed with wooden dowels.

Originally, the cottage was probably a single storey building. It was constructed of sandstone, probably extracted from the surrounding area. The stones are bound together with mud and between the timbers is plaster made from animal fibres, lime and twigs. The original cottage has been covered with brickwork and at sometime a second storey has been added in brickwork.

Mr Plant either failed to recognise the significance of this ancient cottage or it may have been a political decision to take no action to save this cottage for to do so may have had serious consequences to the already controversial clearance order for the village. The city council were not interested in any form of preservation or conservation. Whereas in other parts of the country many councils had grasped the issue with both hands. In Stoke it was low on their agenda.

Early references to this group of cottages are hard to come by, probably because it was built on the Lord's waste and

Early construction of cottage that the council did not wish to know about

therefore not recorded in the normal way through the copyhold courts. However, in January 1828, a court was held transferring them from Anne Simcock to John Burgess, gardener. The document first refers to the fact that the cottages were erected by permission of the Lord upon wasteland formerly in the occupation of John Bond, George Fox and subsequently Robert Simcock. The cottages on either side were occupied by Anne Moore and Edward Broad. The condition of sale to John Burgess was that he paid immediately the sum of £4 5s and then the sum of 1s 6d weekly for the rest of the life of Anne Simcock as a form of rental or pension.

The following letter written by a Commissioner of Oaths upon the instructions of Edward Broad produces evidence of the cottage's history. It is dated 12th July 1841. *I Edward Broad of Penkhull, potter, do solemnly and sincerely declare as follows, that is to say that I am 74 years of age, I am the son of the late Richard Broad of Penkhull, grocer, deceased, (he was buried in Stoke churchyard on the 25th December, 1799) by his will dated 4th January 1799 left me and my heirs forever the house with the shop in which he inhabited and dwelt and which are situated in Penkhull and front the road leading from Penkhull to Newcastle. I was born on the premises and have lived there all my life. My father died soon after making his will in 1799, my mother lived with me on the premises until my marriage, when I turned the premises into two dwellings.*

Avalon, the cottage to the left of the picture in Newcastle Lane

I and my wife lived in one part and my mother in another part. After her death I allowed my daughter Ann, who is my only child and who married Daniel Tatton of Penkhull, potter, to come and live there and she and her husband have lived there ever since. My mother died about twelve years ago at the age of 94. I remember that my father's mother lived with us when I was a little boy and that she died at the age of near 100 years.

I have never paid or have been called upon to pay any acknowledgement or equivalent or other payments (except Land Tax), or have done or have been required to do any service to the Lord of the Manor or any person in respect of the premises but have always enjoyed them as my own freehold. Have never heard it said that the premises are copyhold or had even been taken up in the Copyhold Court. They might have been originally waste but no acknowledgement whatsoever has been paid for them during my life.

I heard my father often say that the premises belonged to his mother and that upon her decease they descended to my father as her heir but I never heard my father say how my grandmother became possessor of them and I make this solemn declaration believing them the same to be true.

Old 16th century cottages in Newcastle Lane

Without explanation somehow these premises, even though recorded as being on the manorial waste in 1777, were never transferred to copyhold tenure from that of waste. There is no reference in the Wasthold Book of the Manor where such a transaction would have been confirmed.

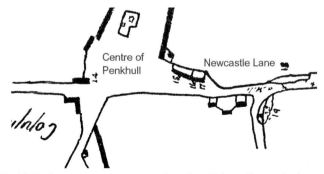

In 1841, the property was transferred to Edward's son-in-law, Daniel Tatton. The census of that year lists Edward Broad, aged 40, potter living in Castle Street. Daniel Tatton is recorded in 1871 as living at a cottage, then No. 14 Newcastle Street. He was aged 70 and widowed and lived with his

unmarried children, George, aged 39, and Hannah, aged 47, *who kept house.* By 1874, the property was recorded as being converted back into one house. In 1911 Thomas Harris, aged 45, a mill labourer was living there with his wife Sarah, aged 54. They took in boarders, David Reeves and his wife, with their six children.

The old Garden Nursery House c1950

Under a clearance compulsory purchase order the house was purchased on the 25th January 1965 by the City of Stoke-on-Trent Council for the sum of £800. The council moved very quickly to demolish the row of cottages as an officer from the Ministry of Housing had already found the property to be sound.

Adjacent to this row of cottages and attached to their walls were a further two late 19th century terraced cottages. Then next down Newcastle Lane came Penkhull Nurseries and Elm Street House with a barn butting out into the road at the junction of Garden Street. Both of these properties have been discussed in other chapters.

Below the barn, just opposite Franklin Road and Pear Tree Cottage stood an old brick cottage. This belonged to Penkhull Nurseries and was recorded as early as the late 18th century. Early occupation is not possible to find but by 1929, it was occupied by Ann Alcock or Joseph and Florence

The old barn used as the retail outlet for Penkhull Nurseries

Toplass followed by Mr Evans. The last person to live there was Ken Plant. It was a small but delightful old cottage and Ken, with the support of his family, repaired and refurbished the cottage. It was demolished in the early 1950's.

Old cottage opposite Pear Tree Cottage

The land below this cottage was owned for many years by Sir Thomas Edwards Milborne Swinnerton Pilkington who rented it out to tenant farmers. Until the building of Penkhull Garden Village most of the land was occupied by Penkhull Farm. However, a section comprising of 29 acres around the area of the present Harpfields Road junction with Newcastle Lane was occupied by Mr John Sant who also kept a number of pigs. Mr Sant was given notice under the Public Health Act both in 1875, and again by the Chief Sanitary Inspector in 1930, in respect of the nuisance caused by insanitary conditions at his smallholding. The foundations and cellar to the old property were uncovered in 2007 whilst workmen were excavating near to the junction of Newcastle Lane and Harpfields Road.

An historical walk down Newcastle Lane; north side, paints a different story of urbanisation. On the corner overlooking the churchyard were two old cottages built to the east of the chapel in 1836 for the chapel caretaker. These were demolished in the 1950s. Below the chapel is the Penkhull DIY Emporium, now No. 12 but originally No.5 Newcastle Street. The plot of land was part of the estate belonging to

Robert Archer of The Grove and was sold in 1838 to John Aidney, a potter. Aidney built a house on that plot of land the following year the first tenant being John Sutton, but by February 1841, the property was unoccupied. The 1841 census lists John Aidney as living in Castle Street, then aged 40, with his wife Sarah and his three children not at No.5 but at a further dwelling further down the lane. Aidney sold No.5 to Daniel Wiggins in the February of that year. Wiggins was living with his son John, aged two, and Dorothy Goodhall, aged 20. Wiggins borrowed the sum of £40 as a mortgage from Samuel Keeling in whose ownership the property remained until 1884, when after his death it was inherited by his son Herbert, described as a *common brewer*.

However, the property had various occupants and by 1871, it was in the hands of Mary Ridgway, a widow, aged 47, who did washing to make ends meet. She had four children, the eldest being William, aged 17, who worked as an oven man while his younger sister, Susannah, aged 15, worked as a potter's paintress. The two youngest were still at school. In December 1884, Keeling sold the property to Henry Turnock, a potter's fireman who, like previous owners, tenanted out the house. The last occupant in 1897 was Eliza Ratcliffe, but at the time of sale the house was unoccupied with vacant possession.

The first reference to the premises being used as a shop comes in 1911 when Emma Simpson, aged 39, was running a small grocery business, no doubt to support her unemployed father, aged 67, and a daughter, and niece. Miss Simpson was still running this grocery business in 1929 when she purchased the building from Miss Carpmail for the sum of £275, and continued to run the little grocer's shop until her death in April 1934.

In 1938, the property was purchased by Miss Martha Sanders, who rented out the shop to Mr Davenport who ran

PENKHULL

Wynns Oatcake Shop. Now Penkhull DIY Store

a fish and chip shop from the front while a Mr Heath lived in the premises behind. In 1957, Miss Sanders sold the premises to Mr Thomas Billings of Franklin Road and it then became *Wynns Oatcake Shop* until Mr Billings died intestate in June 1964. His widow, Evelyn, sold the property in 1965 to Mr Jack Beech, painter and decorator, who already had an established business at the top of Penkhull New Road and it became what it is today, a DIY emporium. Jack Beech died on the 12th December 1981 but his wife, Gwenfyl, continued to run the business for a further seven years until it was sold in 1988 to Mr Geoff Dulson but is now owned by Mr Tes Bansal.

Down the path between the DIY shop and the chapel, there were two old cottages facing the rear of the shop. These were built around 1800 and known as No.1 and 2 off Newcastle Street. The records show that they were owned by John Aidney, who, in 1838, purchased the land in front of the cottages and built No.5 Newcastle Street. After Aidney's ownership, the cottages were occupied by various tenants until 1923 when one was sold to Mr Pietro Delduca for the sum of £90. The other was occupied by Sidney and Ethel Potts. After the death of Pietro Delduca in April 1953, the property was transferred to his widow, Mrs Laura May Delduca. The family was Italian, their son was an expert in laying mosaics but his father Pietro, is remembered for his playing of the piano organ. He used to visit the Ashwell family at Beech Grove on a regular basis to entertain them, but he also used to stand on the corner of the entry to his house in Newcastle Lane playing his hurdy-gurdy collecting in a tin cup a few pence from passers-by. He was supported in this enterprise by a monkey. Another regular spot for business was outside The Grapes Hotel in Stoke. During the war, he was interned. The cottages were sold under a compulsory purchase order and demolished in 1965.

The land around and below the junction of Newcastle Lane which now forms Queens Road was acquired from Thomas and William Ward in May 1789, along with other property and land by John Harrison, with the condition that he would pay a proportion of the costs for the repair of Out Lane, now Franklin Road. This section of land was sold to William Johnson, timber merchant of Stoke, in September 1803.

An indenture discovered at the Duchy of Lancaster Office, dated the 29th September 1881 paints a picture of land and its ownership. The document is a grant from *The Queens Most Excellent Majesty* for a change from the tenure of copyhold to that of freehold. The area on the north side of Newcastle Lane was called Townsend, both Little and Great, but the document refers to Blakeman's Croft, which extended from the west of Doncaster Lane including the home of Michael Baxter, a cottage that was situated just around the corner from Newcastle Lane in Queens Road. The land occupied the area from the present Queens Road to Franklin Road and had been purchased, probably for investment purposes, by Frances Elizabeth Coombe of Burnham, Essex.

From the ownership of Baxter, Blakeman's Croft passed into the hands of Burgess and Kent, gardeners who resided just across the road. Below the DIY shop, there were no other buildings until the mid 1870s with the exception of a group of cottages situated at the corner of Newcastle Lane and Franklin Road. Here before the corner, standing back from the lane, stood a row of four low sandstone buildings, to the north and left side of which were a further three old cottages. The old 16th century cottages were demolished at some time after 1901 but before 1920. In front of this row, there was a further row of six properties probably dating from around 1800 and shown on Hargreaves' map of 1832. All these would have been built at the height of the gardening business run by Burgess and Kent and therefore may have been built for their workers. The present row of 13 terraced houses do not appear on the 1891 census but do on the 1901 census.

Old cottages off Newcastle Lane

Franklin Road formerly Out Lane

Around the corner is Franklin Road, which previously went by the name of Out Lane, despite its not being a direct road out of the village as it terminated at Frankland's farm. Nevertheless, the name is intriguing and could possibly be linked to the hill fort that once occupied the hill of Penkhull. Already the significance of one entrance to the hill fort at Honeywall has been discussed under a previous chapter. Indeed, from this small road to the north the ancient village led to the villages of Wolstanton and Chesterton.

On the right of the road stood Gladstone's Terrace, which later went by the name Gladstone's Row consisting of five

Gladstone's Row, off Newcastle Lane

old terraced houses approached by a narrow pavement and a deep step down from the front doors.

The properties do not appear on Yates' map of 1775 but do on Hargreaves' of 1832. Looking at the style and shape of the buildings, they probably date from around the 1780s. They could have been built by Thomas Harrison, potter, of Beech Grove for his workers as he once had a mill at the bottom of Out Lane.

The 1841 census return shows that only two were occupied, the first by Mary Burgess, a laundress, aged around 45. The second was occupied by John Hackney, aged around 40, together with his wife Mary and seven children ranging from 1 year to 17. By 1881 they were occupied by general workers, potters, labourers and Mary Tennant, a widow, aged 49, who did washing to make ends meet. The largest family was that of Wright, John and Jane. They had five sons and two daughters all in a two-bedroom cottage.

Things did not change. The 1911 census repeats the image with labourers, a washerwoman and pottery workers. As with most of Penkhull, these cottages were part of the 1960s clearance order. A compulsory order was placed upon them by the council and the sum of £50 was paid by the city council in 1970 as compensation to the owner Mr William Hassall of Douglas, Isle of Man.

Pear Tree Cottage

Pear Tree Cottage before restoration

From Out Lane to where Lodge Road now stands was a section of Townsend. It belonged to the Burgess family and passed down to Elizabeth Walmsley Jones a descendant of Burgess. On the corner of Newcastle Lane opposite to Gladstone's Row (but now a group of garages) stands Pear Tree Cottage, little altered from probably a 200 years ago.

Norman Gifford with his mother on weekend leave from the Navy.

The cottage is shown on Hargreaves' map of 1832 but the exact date that it was built is not known, as it was a part of the Burgess and Kent estate. In a document dated 1926, the cottage is named and is described as *formerly in the occupation of Mary Burgess, afterwards of Thomas Kent late of Fanny Holland and now (1926) of John Wright*. The cottage was purchased by Mrs Alice Gifford, the mother of the last owner, Norman in 1930 from Elizabeth Walmsley Jones. Mr John Wright is recorded as the last occupant before Mrs Gifford purchased the cottage. The fields below the cottage were rented out to Mr Arthur Jervis of Penkhull Farm, the father of Doug.

Pear Tree Cottage after modernisation

Following the sale of Pear Tree Cottage came the sale of plots for the building of the properties below for the first few years of the 1930s. The city council purchased the land to the rear of these houses at a cost of £735 for building of council properties in 1933. The building contractor was J W Thorley and Son's of Glebe Street, Stoke. Just below Lodge Road was a gravel pit situated about where Whalley Avenue stands.

Rothwell Street, formerly East Street

At the turn of the century, the centre of the village remained manorial waste and was known as Penkhull Green. On the other side of the green opposite to the Manor Court, a road ran through the village which became known as East Side of Church. This later became East Street and is now Rothwell Street named after a previous vicar of Penkhull. Prior to this, it was incorporated in the general name of Victoria Place, being a continuation of what is now St. Thomas Place.

The gradual process of urban development commenced at sometime before 1776 when a large house, on the south side of the old infants school was sold. It is recorded that Samuel Bridgewater surrendered this house to Samuel Marlow of Hanford, yeoman.

The old post office in Penkhull

Cottages next to the school in East Street

This large house was later converted into two cottages No.1 and No.2 East Street. In 1959, they were purchased by the city council under a compulsory purchase order from the owner Mrs Alice Pointon of Walton on the Hill, Stafford, for the sum of £25. In 1794, William Hill purchased a plot of land formerly Bowyers Meadow from Miss Terricks measuring 195 square yards. The court records present a snapshot of Penkhull at that time as it describes the location of the newly enclosed plot: *from a mark made on the outside*

of the garden wall to a certain cherry tree in the garden belonging to Michael Henney in Penkhull, and near to the said garden hedge. Shortly afterwards, five additional houses were recorded as *recently built* and belonging to William Hill. A large barn situated near to these dwellings and of *an ancient date* did not however, give way to further housing until after 1834.

Further developments in East Street took place during 1866 when Nos. 12 to 16 were built. The old post office and out-door beerhouse No's 24 and 25 East Street could well have dated from the first quarter of the 18th century and built by William Hill. They were again subject to a Compulsory Purchase Order in 1967 by the city council who paid the sum of £285 for the two properties.

By June 1805, William Hill was admitted tenant to a property formerly in the holding of Henry Brassington. In a later court entry, reference is made to the properties adjoining, one of which was a shop. These later became known as No's 28 to 30 East Street. Many elderly residents recall that the middle section of East Street for decades went by the name Bobbie's Row, because the village policeman used to occupy No.14.

Built by Mr. George T. Taylor in 1866

The 1871 census identifies by name East Side of Church. Earlier census returns do not give any address that can easily be found. In fact, the 1871 census calls a section of East Side of Church, Malthouse Row presumably because of having connections to an earlier building in that vicinity. There are 23 houses, which can be identified from this census. In keeping with tradition James Walker, aged 31, the village policeman, who came from Lichfield, occupied No.14. He lived with his wife Tamar, aged

Rothwell Street, view taken from the church tower. View late 1950s

30, a dressmaker and two children, aged 2 and 3 years. Most of the other properties were occupied by workers in the pottery industry but there were also two house painters, a brick maker, and a sawyer. There was at No.24 an out-door beer and grocers shop run by Charlotte Hill, a spinster, aged 32. Her niece, Mary Taylor, aged 8, was also living at the address.

In 1901 the village policeman was John Machin, aged 30, from Church Eaton and his wife, Eliza Ann, aged 28. In the following census of 1911 the house was occupied by George Hopkiss, aged 37, a railway signalman and his family.

Rothwell Street c1950s

By 1891 there were 24 houses listed. At No. 14 lived the village policeman, Thomas Hutchinson, aged 35, with his wife Harriett, aged 34. Thomas came from Yoxall and Harriett from Walsall. Other residents came from far and wide, no doubt in an attempt to find employment: Shropshire, Manchester, Warwick, Bilston, Worcester, Middlewich as well as most of the pottery towns. Previously occupations as were dominated by the pottery industry but for the first time we come across a miner, Joseph Sawyer at No.7, aged 28, who came from Burslem. Other occupations included a blacksmith, cabinetmaker, and charwoman.

Part of Rothwell Street that was at a right angle to the road

At this time, houses in this row started to attract occupations other than those of potters. There was a brewer's drayman, a boiler riveter, a grave digger, a railway guard and boilermaker. However at No.2 George Paulson ran his own hairdressing business. From this last available census it shows that from 24 families a total of 83 children were born, out of which 16 had died representing a 19% death rate.

The new houses that now occupy the site were opened on Thursday 2nd May 1963 with much acclaim especially about a large water feature in front of a section of the properties. Unfortunately, this feature was not valued by residents as it was frequently used as a litterbin for cans, bottles and paper. It became a magnet for youngsters, who shouted and caused a nuisance in that area. Residents, in particular Mrs Brenda Hughes, of No.25 in a press report dated March 1968, demanded that the city council should either fill it in or remove it. Subsequently the pond was filled in and planted with shrubs and trees.

New housing in Rothwell Street, opened 1963

Opening by the Lord Mayor Cllr. E. Holloway
3rd May 1963

Eardley Street

Eardley Street runs southeast at an angle from Rothwell Street. It was represented by the first quarter of the 19th century by a group of six terraced properties to the right of the unmade road. They had add-on kitchens and outside privies. At the entrance to Eardley Street nearest to East Street, stood for many years, a wooden building which became Ernest Holt's shop.

The road was just a short path from the village green but was occupied by at least one property from the mid 17th century. The first reference comes in 1748 when Richard Ball acquired a property, together with orchard and garden, from Samuel Renshaw. By 1775, this old property had been replaced by two newly erected houses in the occupations of Jeremiah Smith and John Smith. In April 1805, the formal admittance of Richard Ball, the son-in-law of Samuel Astbury, deceased as joint tenant with Richard Astbury, the eldest son of Samuel. By this time, the property had expanded to include two shops. One of which can be seen in an old photograph where it joins East Street.

The end of Eardley Street showing a section of the old shop. c1900

The property remained in the hands of the Astbury family until February 1833 when it was purchased by George Bagnall. Bagnall lived in an old cottage in Farm Lane: *To this court comes Richard Astbury of Lower Lane in the Parish of Stoke, shoemaker in his proper person and in consideration of the sum of sixty pounds to him in hand paid by George Bagnall for the absolute purchase surrenders into the hands of the Lord all those two dwelling houses with the gardens to the same belonging situate in Penkhull in the occupation of William Sharp and Thomas Hulme.*

In 1919, the land was purchased from the estate of George Bagnall by Mr. Hanney and described as follows: *All that piece of land described as part of the site of certain premises copyhold to the manor of Newcastle.* Mr Harvey then proceeded to erect a wooden shop where he sold fish, fruit and game, as advertisements in the parish magazine confirm. Four years later in May 1923, Mr Harvey sold the property and business to Mr Earnest Holt of No. 7, Barnfield, a fitter by trade. Mr Holt paid the sum of £150 for the entire package containing: *the said piece of land together with the wooden buildings now erected thereon to the purchase price of £150.*

Many in the village still remember Mr Holt coming around the streets once or twice a week with his horse and cart selling his fruit, poultry and wet fish at the door. Mr Holt later became known as 'Pop Holt' and continued to trade until his death.

His widow, Henrietta, sold the business to a near neighbour, Mr Stanley Wright, of 6 Eardley Street, a commercial traveller. The price was £350, which Mrs Holt agreed to provide a mortgage which with interest, amounted to equal quarterly instalments of £26. The final payment was made on the 2nd March 1960. Mr Wright continued to trade from this site until the new row of shops were built in Manor Court Street. These premises are now occupied by the Co-op Village Store.

The Tithe Schedule of 1849 records four cottages belonging to John Whalley. It would seem that these houses were demolished before a new terrace of seven was built. Little information exists with regards to exact dates but the 1871 census records them in detail.

The interesting thing is that at this time, the street was not called Eardley Street, but Whalleys' Row for obvious reasons, Whalley being the owner. They were occupied as follows:

No.1 John Alerton, aged 50, a pig dealer, his wife Jane, aged 50 and three children.
No.2 Jus. Ainsworth, aged 30, a cabinetmaker and farmer, his wife Lavinio, aged 30, and three children.
No.3 Samuel Lowndes, aged 29, a shoemaker, his wife Kezia, aged 28 and three children.
No.4 Thomas Dudley, aged 38, potter, his wife Frances, aged 26, and 2 two children.
No.5 John Stewart, aged 34, potter's presser his wife Louise, aged 32, and their one child and his mother in law.
No.6 Elizabeth Greatbatch, widow, aged 64, formerly burnisher, her niece and a lodger.
No.7 Joseph Glover, aged 40, potter's slip maker, his wife Ann, aged 34, and five children.

Eardley Street with Holt's wooden shop to the right of the picture

Ten years later, the street name was changed to Eardley Street. Three of the houses had different tenants and No.1 had become No.8 where Mr John Alerton lived, then aged 60. He was still working as a pig dealer but his daughter Mary had married Thomas Forrester, aged 21, a potter, who was listed as head of the family, whilst John effectively became a lodger.

An explanation of the change from No.1 to No.8 can be found in the 1901 census as No.1 Eardley Street was also known as No.11 East Street. It was the shop on the corner, jutting out into the road. The shop was run by William Amison and his wife Sarah. She worked full time, while William worked also as a general labourer.

The properties remained in the ownership of the Whalley family until the row of seven cottages was sold to Mr E J Forrester on the 28th August 1913 for the sum of £420. The occupiers were listed as Jas Reynolds, Mary Deakin, Josiah Bennett, Herbert Smith, William Lawton and Henry Smith. The weekly rent charged was 3s 11d and William Lawton at No.6 was reported to be 1s 9d in arrears.

Details from the 1911 census inform us that from 24 children born to the families living there, seven had died representing 29% mortality. Apart from two adjacent families who were related coming from Worcester, all others came from Penkhull. Two heads of families were employed in engineering but the other three were employed in the pottery industry.

Under the redevelopment plan for Penkhull, the old Whalley Row of cottages was demolished. The bulldozers commenced on the 17th May 1967. Under a thin slab of concrete found in the kitchen of the end house, a well was discovered. Mr Jim Kelly, the city archaeologist was consulted. His report stated: *There was no wall around the well and from the rope grooves, about three on either side of 1¼ inches deep, it appeared that there had never been a wall around it or supporting headgear to raise the water. The well was stone lined and dropped into natural red stone to a depth of about thirty feet, which from the markings on the side had been lowered at three different times.*

A well would only be located there to serve a nearby property or a group of properties. Perhaps it was the four cottages mentioned earlier. On the other hand it could have been Bowyers house, which stood where The Views now stands. An exact date could not be placed on the well, but it could have been originally sunk at some time during the 16th century or even earlier.

St Thomas Place

Until 1957, St Thomas Place went by the name Victoria Place. It is probably difficult to imagine that at one time this area would be as wide as the distance between Rothwell Street and Manor Court Street. In fact, the manorial waste would have continued from this point to the top of Honeywall at the same width. The encroachments onto the edge of the lord's waste over the centuries have created the narrowness in St Thomas Place with properties built on either side.

The far end of St Thomas Place, facing the old senior school, was called Penkhull Croft but was known locally as *the shrubbery* until the present houses were built in the 1930s. It covered the area to the north of Victoria House. A narrow path opposite Greatbatch Avenue leads to a group of workshops currently in the ownership of Peter Taylor. The plot of land was formerly part of The Mount estate and was the subject of a sale by Messrs William Henry and Frederick Sillery Bishop, the sons of the late Frederick Bishop in March of 1902.

It was sold to Mrs Catherine Brunt of 24 Hill Street, Stoke for the sum of £398 14s and consisted of: *all that plot of land called Penkhull Croft and garden situated on the south side of the road leading from Penkhull now called Penkhull Street and contains in measurement 2,658 square yards*. At this time there were no buildings, these were subsequently built by 1908 then described as containing a coach house and piggeries (now converted into workshop, stores and office by Mr Taylor).

In 1908 Mrs Brunt mortgaged the plot to borrow the sum of £600 from Stoke-on-Trent Permanent Building Society but was described differently: *All that plot of land together with coach piggeries and buildings*. Three years later in 1911 Mrs Brunt used the land as the security to borrow a further £60. Then again in 1919 an additional loan was taken out for £120. Most of these loans were used to finance the purchase of other properties in Market Place, Cross Street and Hill Street Stoke. Altogether there were thirteen different loans taken out.

In 1931, as the demand for houses grew, the land became a valuable asset and Catherine Brunt decided to divide the plot into two, the front for development, leaving the rear as it was with its own access from the main road. The front section was sold to Mrs Jessie Holloway in July 1931 who in December of the same year sold it to Mrs Daisy Steele of 3 Doncaster Lane. By March the following year, the city council awarded a *Certificate of Habitation* to Messrs Holloway & Co, of Church Street, Stoke for the houses built on the land.

Victoria House

The large house, which stands detached, Victoria House, takes the name from the highway, Victoria Place. The site in early records was referred to as Doody's messuage.

In his book of the Staffordshire Potteries 1829, Simeon Shaw records that in 1600 *there were at Penkhull three manufactories producing coarse brown pottery; one of which belonged to Thomas Doody.* The manor court records show that Doody held extensive lands in and around the area. The Reeve book records Thomas Doody, junior, as holding the office of Reeve for *his own house in Penkhull.* In a further entry of 1778, the Reeve book states: *that ancient messuage, formerly of Thomas Doody, now Joseph Bourne,* to which entry was added in 1836: *this house is where Chapman lives, purchase by Spode now Mrs Eliza Bree.*

The manor court records of 1810 throw further light to the early occupation of Doody's messuage. *Whereby Richard Lovett surrendered into the hands of Josiah Spode all that messuage known by the name of Doody's Messuage now in the holding of John Chapman and all barns, stables, gardens, orchards, crofts etc.* Thomas Lovatt the nephew of John Doody died in 1740. Thomas Lovatt, was named as a trustee in his last will and testament. Richard Lovatt could well have been his son.

Thomas Doody died on the 26th December 1725, aged 75 years. He is buried in Trentham churchyard. On the 27th April 1726, the appraisers of his estate after death were John Bowyer and Thomas Dale. From this inventory, it appears that Thomas Doody was wealthy as extracts show:

In the little parlour
Two feather beds, two chaff beds, four blankets, one rug, bedsteads and hangings, five blankets and hangings.

In the hall chamber
Six covered stools, a box, two covered chairs, one set of red hangings and a chest. Dozen and a half of napkins and three towels, seven pairs of fine sheets and four pairs of round sheets. Five fine tablecloths and four round ones, a dozen of fine napkins, and seven pillow biers and six silver spoons, and some head linen.

In the parlour
Six large pewter dishes, seven other little dishes and eight pollingers, four pewter candle sticks, two salt flagons one tankard,

a pewter pot, two brass candle sticks, two skimmers, one brass ladle, hanging spit and a pair of tongs.
A cart and wheels. Money upon speciality and note £235.

A court transaction for the same premises is recorded 76 years later on the 3rd April 1812, but this time it is John Chapman that makes the surrender and not Richard Lovatt. *In consideration of the sum of £958 surrendered all that messuage by the name of Doody's Messuage, formerly in the holding of Thomas Whitehurst, afterwards of Samson Bagnall since in the possession of Joseph Bourne and now or late of John Chapman.* There were also included in the sale Hassells Croft, Hall Croft and others. Admitted Josiah Spode.

Following the death of Josiah Spode II in July 1827, a schedule was compiled of all the land and properties he held. Within this lengthy document lies the answer to what happened to this ancient property. *And all that messuage or dwelling house with barns, stables and outbuildings for several years in the holding of Thomas Sutton*

Victoria Place
Hargreaves Map 1832

and since George Hemmings which house was erected by Josiah Spode on the site of the ancient tenement which was pulled down formerly in the holding of Joseph Bourne and John Chapman.

This entry shows that Spode built Victoria House at some time between 1812 and 1827. It is recorded on Hargreaves' map of Penkhull dated 1832. There remains next to the house a sandstone building converted into a study by its last owner Alec Smithers. It probably dates from the 17th or 18th century and could well be the remains of Doodys potworks. Currently (2010) the house is undergoing a total internal reconstruction by the new owners with ceilings, floors, internal

Probably the remains of Thomas Doodys Potworks

walls and plasterwork being removed. This means that evidence of any previous alterations becomes visible.

Victoria House, built by Josiah Spode

There are indeed features that are worthy of note. Currently there is evidence of a lintel over a bricked-up doorway to the left of the present front door. In addition, the buildings to the rear have been added to at least twice, may be three times. Certainly the last bedroom at the back of the house is the last addition, as both the brickwork and roof beams confirm. Below was the old kitchen which can be seen by a bricked-

Bricked up old doorway

Victoria House under reconstruction 2010

up window, and a doorway, situated in an internal wall. This once led directly into the rear yard. Later a utility room/kitchen was built in front taking over part of the yard. These changes are old dated around the middle of the 19th century.

Even now I am not convinced that this old kitchen was part of the original building as a doorway of the stairs to the first floor has been discovered in a room at the front of the building. This room, with the old entrance now bricked up, may have been the original kitchen.

What remains unexplained are the entrance pillars and the huge stone wall to the property. They date from the time when the house was originally built. It could be assumed that when Spode built the house that the first occupier was someone of importance either at his works, such as an artist, or some other professional.

Unfortunately, deeds have not survived but the census returns tell us who was in occupation. In 1841, it was occupied by Elizabeth Hughes, of independent means, and John, her son, aged 20. Eight years later the tithe return states that the property was owned by William Cardland and occupied by Joseph Stringer. In 1851, Joseph is recorded as aged 40, employed as a clerk in a potworks, and from Northampton. He lived with his wife, Maria, aged 38. They had seven children starting with Frederick, at seven months, to Joseph, aged eleven. They employed one servant, Mary Stokes, aged 21, from Uttoxeter. By 1861, the house was occupied by Frederick. Rice, aged 40, a teacher of drawing; his wife, Frances, aged 30; a daughter, aged 27; and one servant.

By 1871 the house was occupied by Joseph Walklate, aged 45, a grocer employing one man and two boys. He had a large family the eldest son, Thomas, aged 16, was working in the family business. There were also four daughters, a further son and a servant, Mary Bloor, aged 19, who came from Stoke. The occupancy changed hands frequently but in a way no different from other rented accommodation. In 1891, William Harrison, aged 55, a potter's presser and his wife Harriett, occupied it. The eldest son was William, aged 32, a butcher, and their eldest daughter, Harriett, aged 26, was a school teacher. They had seven other children. Ten years later, their son William was head of the family and still living at Victoria House. He was un-married and lived with two sisters and a younger brother. All were single. Again, William is recorded as the occupier of Victoria House in 1881 and 1891.

The butcher's shop was situated at No.39 Commercial Road and a trade directory of 1884 lists William as still living in Victoria House. By 1889, the house was in the occupation of Miss Elizabeth Harrison, a governess. The last census available, that of 1911, there was but a single occupant, Elizabeth Buxton; a widow, aged 68, described as a lodger who had her own private income. Probably the family was elsewhere on that night.

Nicholls Row

Doody's messuage did not just consist of the main house, it comprised of all the land and other properties attached to the house. The records include the area from its junction with Penkhull New Road, including the area of Kirkland Lane, Penkhull Terrace and West Bank to Honeywall and then returning to St. Thomas Place. The whole of this was called Hassells Croft. The only exclusions were the old Marquis of Granby and two other adjacent properties and the windmill.

A long barn stood facing Penkhull New Road. This was converted by Spode into ten small terraced houses, going by the name of Ten Row. There was another large property, standing back from the highway and facing St Thomas Place. This now forms four cottages converted from one.

Unfortunately, the records are not very conclusive. It could have been assumed that this building, long and narrow was a barn or a group of stables, but evidence from the manor court rolls point to the fact that it was more likely to have been one dwelling house owned by Thomas Doody.

A further entry then provides the necessary evidence: *a dwelling house has for many years been subdivided into and occupied as four dwelling houses, which servants belonging to the family of Josiah Spode and his late father now deceased.* This conversion must have taken place after 1811 and before 1827 as the successive names of Moss, Atherton, Burbridge, and Maskery are recited as tenants. Further evidence of this is contained in the copyhold record for November 1858 when the owner James Dean finally paid off the mortgage on the cottages: *All those four several dwelling houses situate in Penkhull, lately converted out of a certain dwelling house known as Doody's Messuage.* The next record is dated June 1899 when the court records make note of the fact that Richard Nicholls, a timber merchant from Stoke had died the previous year.

The 1841 census records Richard Nicholls, a sawyer living with his wife Anne in High Street, Penkhull. (It had not yet been named Victoria Place). He had four sons, Thomas, Richard, Benjamin, John and a daughter Mary. By 1851, Richard senior was listed as a grocer from Stoke who with his wife Anne, aged 53, had handed over the timber business to his son Richard. Twenty years later in 1871, Richard junior was the only son left at home living with his widowed father. From the document dated 1899 it would appear that the row of cottages were purchased at some date before then.

The largest cottage of the row of four nearest to Victoria House was No.3, Victoria Place is where the Nicholls family lived. It was much extended at the rear. Richard later left Penkhull after his father's death and moved to No.7 Winton Terrace, Shelton, an exclusive area at that time and married Caroline. By 1881 he had died and Caroline, then aged 41, was recorded as a widow.

Upon the death of Richard senior, Richard junior, a timber merchant inherited his estate and built up a formidable property portfolio. By the time of his death he had acquired property in Newcastle, Shelton, Boothen, Stoke and Penkhull the latter being described as: *all that plot called the Garden Plot bounded on the west by Elizabeth Hughes on the east by a road called Mill Street leading out of the highway from Honeywall, to the north by land owned by Mr Whalley but now the North Staffs Waterworks, to the south premises formerly belonging to Mr Alderman Copeland but now of Ellis Roberts and called Ten Row and four other cottages known by No. 3, 5, 7 and 9 Victoria Place in the respective occupations of Hughes, Brunt, Johnson and Gibson.*

Nicholls Row, Victoria Place

For many years, the row of cottages were known as Nicholls Row.

Richard Nicholls junior left part of his estate to his nephew Robert Nicholls of Hartshill. Robert worked in the family business and lived at Hartshill Hall, now called The Close. Even with his new-found wealth, he ended up a bankrupt. His life became tragic and his wife died an alcoholic. During those years of poverty, he turned his hand to historical research and published a number of small books, one of which was *The History of Penkhull-cum-Boothen* in 1929. It was only a small book quoting a number of historical records for Penkhull extracted from the William Salt Collection. Nevertheless, his contribution was interesting for the period.

At sometime after 1914 the four cottages were sold to Edwin Cocking Bennett, who owned the Hanging Gate Inn, Newcastle, and at the time of his death were occupied by Messrs Hughes, Brunt, Johnson and Gibson. The cottages all remained in the hands of the Bennett family until 1946 when No. 3 was sold to Andrew Cross for the sum of £400.

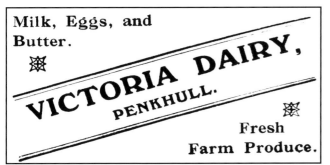

Milk, Eggs, and Butter.

VICTORIA DAIRY, PENKHULL.

Fresh Farm Produce.

From at least 1917 when an advertisement first appeared in the church magazine under the heading of Victoria Dairy, No.3 was occupied by Mr George Lyth who ran a retail dairy business from that address. Deliveries were done by a horse and milk float, kept in the old stables to the rear of the house. This float was replaced in the 1930s by a motorcycle and sidecar from which he delivered his dairy products to the surrounding streets. Many still remember the house as *The Dairy*. Before moving to Victoria Place, George Lyth lived at No.4 Garden Row and is recorded in the 1911 census as a milk dealer. He was 28 years of age and lived with his wife Florence and his son George, aged 7 years. George junior later took over the business from his father.

Six years later the cottage was sold to Mr George Medd of Newcastle for the sum of £1,300 but it was then known by its new address, 35, St Thomas Place. Mr Medd then sold

the cottage to the city council in March 1956. The purchase price was to pay off the remaining mortgage and interest totalling £1,030. The council subsequently rented out the house to Mr and Mrs Sheldon who lived there until the mid 1960s when the council decided that it was unfit for habitation because the gable end had become unstable.

Residents made accusations that this was a move by the council to demolish the end cottage. Had this been done it would have affected the remaining three, which would have followed the same process. Deaconess B Smee mounted a campaign to stop this, writing strongly to the Ministry of Housing and Local Government in August 1968. A reply from the ministry followed on the 30th September explaining that the city council could not just condemn a property without going through a strong procedure. In February 1969, the ministry communicated again with Miss Smee, stating that the council was accepting offers for the property from anyone, and would be willing to give an improvement grant to any prospective purchaser.

One such prospective buyer was Mr N Gilbert of Hunters Way, but he did not go ahead with the purchase, as the list of repairs stipulated by the council would have cost far more that the cottage was worth. However in September 1969, the cottage was sold to Mrs Gribbin of Clayton for the reduced price of £250 making the repairs, alterations and a new gable end viable. The property was fully restored.

Mr. Gilbert and the "old bit" of Penkhull he claims would be too costly to restore.

The old Dairy, now fully restored

Mr. Lyth delivered milk in a motor-cycle side-car

At the other end of the row stands No.11 and No.13 Victoria Place, with a side path extending to Rose Cottage. The earliest of properties on this site are recorded in 1772, when they were described as: *previously in the ownership of Richard Hewitt.* Hewitt had acquired the houses at some time before 1768. Hewitt occupied one and Mr William Hewnett the other. They were demolished in 1828 after being purchased by James Bragg in 1823 from the estate of Thomas Oakes for the sum of £45. The original cottages probably dated from the early 16th century and like so many other properties of ancient date we demolished.

It would appear that the two cottages now standing to the front of Rose Cottage were built by Bragg in 1828 as the court records states: *comes James Bragg of Penkhull and surrenders all those two dwelling houses situate in Penkhull now untenanted with gardens adjoining which houses have lately been erected and built by and at the expense of James Bragg on the site of two old houses which were previously in the occupation of James Bragg and Mary Gretton.*

Rose Cottage

Behind these two houses stands Rose Cottage. It is not included in Hargreaves' map of 1832 but a document dated 1887 recites: *and also that other cottage erected by James Bragg on part of the gardens for the two dwelling houses, No. 11 and 13 Victoria Place, and known by the name Rose Cottage and in the occupation of John Gifford.* It is impossible to identify Rose Cottage until 1861 when Joseph Bacon was the occupier, aged 35, an artist at the school of art. He came from Dublin and lived with his wife, two daughters, his sister-in-law, a cousin and a servant. In 1911, Rose Cottage was occupied by Arthur Sproston, aged 36, a school caretaker, his wife Hannah, aged 40, his mother-in-law and two young children aged 3 and 4.

Doncaster Lane

The first recorded name of this lane was Swynnertons Lane probably taking its name from Thomas Swinnerton who once occupied an 'ancient messuage' near to to the top of Doncaster Lane. The messuage was later occupied by Joseph Booth.

Most of the land in this area later became part of the The Mount Estate. In 1890, the Church Commissioners purchased a plot from Frederick Bishop, then owner of the Mount to add land to the new parsonage. Joseph Turner owned the cottages that remain at the bottom which date from 1773. There were also two cottages standing where the old Parsonage now stands.

Originally, Doncaster Lane continued as a footpath to Hartshill, skirting the boundary wall of The Mount. The pathway came out just past the large house before the BCRA

annex, from where it crossed fields to where the cemetery lodge now stands. From here, it continued roughly in the line of the present Queens Road and then behind the 1930s houses at the end of the road to the left, coming out opposite Hartshill Church. The path from the end of the current Doncaster Lane was closed in 1892 and replaced by a narrow path between the houses into Queens Road.

At the top of Doncaster Lane stands Penkhull Service Station. It was built by Mr Harold Rowland who ran his garage business from 1922 until the late 1970s, a well respected gentleman with a vivid memory of old Penkhull. Mr Rowland built his garage on the site of an old barn, which remained at the fringe of Mount Farm where it occupied the near end of what is now Greatbatch Avenue.

The original stables for The Mount at the end of Greatbatch Avenue

On the opposite corner from the garage there was an old building, standing in the garden of Beech Grove. It was originally called Grove Cottage, but later became known as Doncaster Buildings or Works..

The first reference to Samuel Doncaster is found in 1800, when Mary and Elizabeth Terrick sold a section of Bowyers meadow to him. Doncaster was described as already in occupation of the land situated next to land owned by Michael Henny.

The lower section of Doncaster Lane

The following year in 1801, he acquired: *three of the four shares of a blacksmith's shop, together with the piece of building adjoining now used as a paint house.* In a further transaction dated October 1827, Doncaster sells this plot of land for the sum of £190 to Edward Candland, innkeeper of Penkhull. Candland owned the Marquis of Granby. By this time, two houses had been erected on the plot by Doncaster and were tenanted out to Hannah Hudson and John Baddeley. In an additional document Henny is listed as holding a blacksmiths shop and the malt house, from which information it can be ascertained that the land Samuel Doncaster purchased was situated next to the Marquis of Granby.

In the auction held at The Marquis of Granby in 1802 to sell off the assets of John Harrison, bankrupt, who lived at Beech Grove, Samuel Doncaster purchased the following: *All that piece of land at Penkhull called Little Townsend containing 2 acres and 22 perches and is a parcel of a certain farm late belonging to John Harrison.*

Samuel Doncaster, (1772-1842), was the son of Samuel and Martha, originating from Stone. He had two brothers, Henry, born 1768, and the Rev John Doncaster, born 1769, who resided at Newcastle. Samuel and Henry were both engravers and worked together at the workshop in Swynnerton's Lane. They employed three people, Hancock, Greatbatch and Smith. Greatbatch went on to work for Mr Minton and Smith for Mr Spode (note Greatbatch Avenue). Brothers Henry and Samuel, produced work for Spode, Minton and Davenport. In 1821, they moved to Bleak Hill, Waterloo Road, Burslem for a short period followed by Overhouse. Henry Doncaster assisted another engraver, Mr Turner, in the development of the plates for the Willow Pattern for Mr Minton. In the account books of Minton there are numerous entries of payments to Mr Doncaster for work carried out on their behalf. For many years until the late 1970s, the engraving tools once belonging to the Doncaster brothers remained in regular use by his great, great, grandson.

Shortly after the purchase of land from the estate of John Harrison, the Doncaster brothers placed a section of the land on the open market for sale, advertising the same in the Staffordshire Advertiser on the 2nd March 1805.
The healthy and pleasant village of Penkhull in the Staffordshire Potteries. To be sold by Private Contract. About one acre of rich, loamy land, calculated for either the erection of a genteel family house; or on which Streets may be laid out for small houses, that are much wanted in this truly increasing and now populous neighbourhood.
The estate commands a very extensive and diversified view of the hanging wood of the Most Noble the Marquis of Stafford, at Trentham; from whence it is but about three miles. The borough of Newcastle-under-Lyme too, is within view, and but a small distance from it. The neighbouring markets are well and abundantly supplied with all the delicacies and substantials in season, and there is not within the circle of twenty miles a more respectable neighbourhood. Applications to Samuel Doncaster, at Penkhull. Note that there is no mention of the heavily polluted and cramped housing conditions of the town of Stoke below!

In 1806, Samuel Doncaster occupied what was known as Doncaster Buildings for his engraving business just around the corner to the left, at the top of Swynnerton Lane, a site now occupied by the garden of new properties in Thomas Ward Place.

Cottage still standing at the bottom of Doncaster Lane

Four years later in 1810, Doncaster sold a section of the land to Daniel Murrell for the sum of £64. Again the court minutes make interesting reading as it gives the measurement of the plot, the name of the street, the attached land that was for sale and other cottages already built: *containing in length to the front of the lane called Swynnerton Lane, 16 yards and in depth into the field 32 yards and forever maintaining a quickset hedge in order to fence in the said plot from the remaining piece at present unsold. To erect his intended dwelling house in a lineable manner with the buildings already erected on each side of the said plot of land.* The census return of 1851 lists Daniel Murrell, aged 60, living in Doncaster Lane.

The first record of the name 'Doncaster Lane' did not appear until 1841. Doncaster mortgaged the property obtaining a loan to the value of £260 from Richard Timmis of Crewe. The court minute gives an insight to the property: *And also all that messuage or dwelling house and all outbuildings thereon lately erected and built by, and now in the tenure of Samuel Doncaster.*

In November 1812, Samuel Doncaster takes out a second mortgage for £100 in addition to the previous one of £260 from Richard Timmis.

Finances appear to be strained for on the 16th October 1813, Doncaster, then in debt to Mr Timmis for a total of £360 decided to sell his estate and property in Penkhull to Josiah Spode consisting of: *all that messuage and all buildings thereon erected and now or late in the occupation of Samuel Doncaster, and also all that other dwelling house standing near thereto called Nelson's Crescent.*

For reasons unknown, the transaction was not confirmed until the 1st March 1833 when William Baker, potter of Fenton, was arranging a mortgage to the value of £10,000 to satisfy the executors of Josiah Spode. The court minutes record: *formerly belonging to Henry Doncaster, containing one acre, three roods and 34 perches for some time used for the site of four messuages the remainder thereof for several years been occupied as garden ground by many different tenants and now standing upon the last mentioned close formerly in the occupation of Henry Doncaster but now in the holding of. . .*

Henry Doncaster died in August 1821 and is buried at Burslem. Samuel was recorded as living at No.9 Waterloo Road, Burslem in the 1841 census, an engraver, aged 70. He died the following June and is buried at Wolstanton. He had three children, Maria, John and Henry. Both sons continued in the business of engraving. The records suggest that his residence was in Burslem from at least 1807.

Doncaster Lane, still retains its original setting

Kirkland Lane, formerly Mill Street and Penkhull Terrace

With urbanisation of Penkhull, the demand for building land grew, and therefore a plot of land central to the village became a target for development. The land was situated behind the old row of cottages in St Thomas Place and stretched down the hill to below what is now West Bank.

Immediately behind St Thomas Place, there was a track which lay across the field to the old windmill linking Penkhull New Road and the top of Honeywall. This area of land originally formed part of the estate of Thomas Doody, Doody's messuage. After Doody, its ownership passed to Joseph Bourne, followed by John Chapman. In May 1810, the whole estate was purchased by Josiah Spode. By 1849, the field, Hassells Croft, to the east of what became known as Mill Street, was owned by George Whieldon, who sold it in July that year to William Dean of Stoke, James Dean of Audley, and John Gilbert of Hilderstone as joint owners. The land was described at the time of the sale as: *all that plot of land in Penkhull, part of a certain croft called Hassell's Croft formerly parcel of Penkhull Farm but now set out in Lots for building purposes.*

Apart from providing access to the mill during the late 18th and the 19th century, the roadway had no other purpose. It originally went by the name of Joe's Lane, probably after Joseph Bourne, one of the early owners of the land, who also built the windmill. Later the new owners of the land Messrs Dean, Dean and Gilbert took advantage of the existing roadway, for early housing development and re-named it Mill Street. What the new owners decided to do was to create two roads with properties facing both but backing onto each other. Both Mill Street and the new road, The Terrace, were divided into building plots, the former for working class properties but the latter for dwellings for trades and professional people as the demand for this type of property was increasing from the polluted and over-crowded town of Stoke.

Mill Street was never successfully developed even for working class housing. It was 1853 before three properties were erected by Thomas Moreton, Thomas Robinson and Thomas Morris. The corner plot adjoining Penkhull Street was sold on the 31st March 1853 to Mr John Leigh. The census returns of 1861 show that a further three houses were completed. Like many other properties in Penkhull, all were occupied by the lower social ranks, washerwoman, brick maker, warehouseman and three potter's pressers. The largest household was that of Thomas Morton, aged 53, a

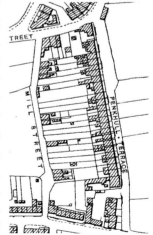

Mill Street & Penkhull Terrace

widower. He lived with three sons, two daughters, one single, the other married, along with her husband John Davenport, aged 23, a potter's turner. Thomas had one grandson by the name of Morton, and three by the surname of his married daughter, Elizabeth Davenport.

By 1881 things had changed, there being thirteen properties in the road. Seven heads of families worked in the pottery industry, three as bricklayers, one a railway clerk, one a commercial clerk, and one a labourer. Most of the families were large. Two had eight in the family, one had seven, two had six, two had five and the remaining properties were young families with only two or three children.

Mill Street now Kirkland Lane

In 1911, there were twelve properties occupied. For the first time there was a shop selling groceries at No.3 run by Henry Lymer, aged 55. There were six families working in the pottery industry. At No.4, Elizabeth Foster, a widow, aged 60,

View along Kirkland Lane late 1950s

with Annie, her unmarried daughter, aged 36, went out to work as washerwomen, but they were lodgers. The head of the household was Jane Woolley, aged 68, a self-employed dressmaker and her daughter, aged 18, was a domestic servant. The largest family was at No.16, William Jefferies, aged 45, and his wife 42. William was a flour miller with four sons and one daughter, but also took in a male boarder, aged 34, who came from Durham.

In 1912, only ten properties are listed, Mr Lymer remains a grocer at the corner shop at the junction of Mill Street with Honeywall. Next door at No.9 Samuel Smith had opened up as an outdoor off-licence. Later the premises became No.32 Kirkland Lane following re-numbering (probably after the development of the west side of the lane). Most of the old properties were demolished under a compulsory order in the early 1960s.

These households were all on the east side of Mill Street, backing onto Penkhull Terrace. The western side remained in the ownership of the Nicholls family who owned No.3 Victoria Place as part of their estate. It was called *the Garden Plot*. In 1912, the land was sold to Mr Edward Cocking Bennett but by 1924, it had passed into the hands of Walter Edwin Bennett for the price of £100. Walter Bennett built a bungalow, No.15 Kirkland Lane in the same year, 1924. It was built of timber, probably because building materials were in short supply for years following the end of the First World War. In 1928, following the death of Walter Bennett, the land and bungalow were passed on to his children. Later the same year, it is recorded as in the occupation of Vernon and Mary George. Next door, No.11 was also of a timber construction.

George Lyth used this plot for many years as a market garden, growing vegetables when he lived at No. 3 Victoria Place. Later when Andy Cross lived at No.3, he purchased the garden plot and built a bungalow in the centre of it around the late 1950s. Subsequently over the last few years the property was sold and a large section to the south of the garden given over for further house building. Regrettably, here now stands a house the size and height of which is totally out of proportion to those surrounding it.

No. 11 Kirkland Lane. Bungalow built from timber

Most of the other properties on the western side of Mill Street date from the either the late 1920s or mid 1930s and are typical of that period. The need for a change of street name came in 1967, as there was in the town of Stoke another street by the name of Mill Street, which caused difficulty with the post office. The council suggested the name of Blakeman Street. However, residents did not view the suggestion lightly and Mr Francis Peake of No.9 pressed the council to change to name to Kirkland Lane, the name by which it has been called since February 1967. It is a poor choice as Kirkland is Scottish for churchland, and this area of Penkhull (nor any other area of Penkhull) was never church land by ancient date.

Corner Grocers shop later to become a Ladies Hairdressers

Penkhull Terrace

Penkhull Terrace, known originally by the name of *The Terrace* situated below Mill Street, is one of those rows of properties that do not conform to the general layout of the area at that time, rather resembling a promenade at some seaside resort such as Llandudno than a housing development in the midst of working class properties. The line of Penkhull Terrace, appropriately named because of its elevated position overlooking the town of Stoke, may well follow the outer perimeter wall of an earlier Iron Age fort which would have continued to the south from this point along Hunters Way.

As previously stated all this land became the possession of Josiah Spode in May 1810, and is recorded with the same details as that of Mill Street from 1849. The first transaction following the purchase of the land took place on the 27th May 1852 after its purchase by Dean, Dean and Gilbert with the sale of Plots 1 and 2 to Mr Charles Simpson, an engraver from Shelton and described: *all that two several plots of copyhold land called Hassell's Croft formerly part of Penkhull Farm but now set out in building plots, No.1 and 2, in consideration of the sum of £41 12s.* These two plots form the land for the large property No1. Penkhull Terrace. The sale of the following four individual plots to Messrs Lawton, Holdcroft, Barcroft and Buxton took place at the same time. The following month, June, saw a further four plots sold one to Mr W Carter, one to Mr B Nicholls, and three to Mr Charles Mason. It was March 1853 before the completion of a further two plots which were sold to Messrs Jackson and Tatton, followed by those to Messrs Greaves and Smith. It was not until August 1855 that a further two plots were sold to a Mr. Ralph Jackson.

Between the years 1852 and 1855, 17 of the 21 were developed. By 1861, the entire undertaking had been completed and the houses occupied. A condition of sale was that: *each building to be erected shall be backwards from Penkhull Terrace by two yards to leave a clear space which shall never be built upon but enclosed by a dwarf wall with stone coping and surmounted with iron palisades and all building shall be uniform in height and width.*

Comparing the names on the original plan of 1858 and the census return of 1861, only six properties were occupied by the same people involved in the copyhold transfer. This suggests that the majority of the houses were built-to-let, a practice that dominated the housing market until relatively modern times. The same census return also shows that nine of the properties were occupied by either skilled or professional middle-class. Five properties employed live-in servants, emphasising the status enjoyed by the residents of Penkhull Terrace. Despite the fact that the properties in Penkhull Terrace were for the middle-class it was not until May 1866 that a sewer was laid costing £51 15 9d.

By 1891 the number of households employing servants had fallen to one at No.19. Unfortunately census returns do not list servants who do not reside in the houses. Therefore, in all probability more than one house employed servants but were not resident. At No.19 lived Elizabeth Taylor, aged 67,

Penkhull Terrace, still a desirable area

a spinster living *on her own means* who came from Liverpool. She employed Hannah Jones, aged 25, from the town of Stoke. There were out of 26 properties, seventeen whose head of family could be classed as professional. There were potter's engravers, a cement manufacturer, inspector of weights and measures, assurance agent, retired grocer, brickworks manager, manufacturer's clerks, watchmaker, coal dealer, designer of tiles, wholesale newsagent and two drapers. There were no working class people living there. The largest family lived at No.7; the Gifford family, William, aged 35, the inspector of weights and measures. His wife Mary was aged 33, and their three sons and three daughters ranged from the ages of 4 to 13 years.

Penkhull Terrace c1930s before the flats were built. Notice the number of bottle-kilns and chimneys below in the town of Stoke

By 1911 those that could be classed as professional or trades persons were reduced to 14 and consisted of a hay and straw merchant, brick foreman, fruit dealer, bookkeeper, clerks, merchant, school teacher, retired letterpress printer, pottery manager, hardware dealer, engineer and two builders from the same family, father and son by the name of John Meiklejohn, a family that has remained involved in the life of the village until this day. The father originated from Stirling and is recorded as clerk of works for the local authority, an important position. The vast majority of residents came from within Penkhull or from other pottery towns, while others came from further afield such as Lincoln, Hereford and Chester.

Surprisingly, considering the better quality of housing over other properties in Penkhull, and a better standard of living, the child mortality rate was high involving 31% of the families. From a total of 45 children born, a total of 26 had died representing 58% mortality. The largest number is found at No.25 where eight children had died out of ten born.

West Bank

This is one of those small rows of elevated terraced houses which are almost hidden away from the rest of Penkhull. The history of this row reflects that of Mill Street and Penkhull Terrace, once all being part of Doody's meadow sold to Spode in 1810. The first reference comes from the Tithe Map of 1849 when a row of six houses were in the ownership of different people including Rev Thomas Minton and James Glover and occupied by Jessie Buxton, Thomas Starkey and others.

The large house overlooking the Falcon pottery below (now Portmeirion) was built by John Johnson but occupied by Mr George Jones. The census of 1851 records him as, aged 27, a pottery agent who was born in Nantwich. He lived with his wife Frances and three children. They employed a servant. He was soon to set up his own business producing ware in the town of Stoke, which was later to become Crescent Pottery in South Wolfe Street. In 1851, he had two of his children Francis and George baptised in Penkhull church. By 1853, Mr Jones was living in the largest house in The Villas, Rosemount.

Documents give a good introduction: *All those copyhold dwellings in a street called West Bank (formerly called Copeland Terrace), which runs out of Penkhull New Road together with gardens and outbuildings being parcel of land called Doody's Meadow.*

William Taylor Copeland purchased the assets from the infant Spode IV's trustees in February 1833 and it is he who would have sold the land to George Whieldon, who in turn sold it to Messrs Dean, Dean and Garrett. The terrace was probably named Copeland Terrace, not because of the ownership, but simply to give the properties some credibility and prestige.

The 1861 census records the properties as West Bank. At No.1 lived one of the most important architects in the Borough of Stoke, if not the city, Charles Lynam, aged 32, with his wife, Lucy, aged 27, and his family consisting of two sons, Charles and Robert, together with two servants, Abigail, aged 22, from Shropshire and Isabella, aged 13, from Hartshill. Lucy was the daughter of Mr Robert Garner, a local respected surgeon. In that year a total of four properties in the row employed servants.

Mr Garner borrowed the sum of £800 in February 1888 to purchase the entire six properties. Two years later Mr Garner died and he left all his estate to his daughter Lucy. In 1897 the mortgagee Mr James Best also died, followed shortly afterwards by Mrs Lucy Lynam in 1906. Two years later Mr Charles Lynam, the son had paid off the mortgage and took ownership of the row of houses.

By 1911 a chartered accountant, George Walters, aged 57, with his wife Christina, aged 48, occupied the same house. They had three single daughters still living at home. By this time none of the six properties employed any servants. The occupations, railway brakes man, blacksmith, carter, colour mixer and two with no occupations reflect a decline in the standing of the road. A directory of 1912 confirms the reduction in status.

Across the road at West Bank Cottage lived Mary Burrow, a widow, aged 60. She had two daughters and two sons, all with good positions, school teacher, and railway clerks. Mary took in three boarders. These were all young girls listed as scholars. A servant, Charlotte, aged 12, from Stoke, was also living in the house. In 1867, it was listed as a Ladies School, which confirms that the three boarders were in fact scholars. Thirty years later the same house was occupied by John Robinson, aged 58, a railway district agent. He was a widower and living there was his sister-in-law, as his housekeeper together with his niece and one servant.

Penkhull New Road

A view of Penkhull New Road taken from the churchyard

A brief outline of Penkhull New Road comes under the chapter headed *Early Road Network*. Today the road combines a mixture of open spaces and properties from different periods but this was not the situation at the turn of the 19th century. The new bottom section of the road reflected a period of growth and expansion from the town of Stoke, but it also represented sub-standard dwellings built for the working classes and a few premises for minor traders.

Josiah Spode who held considerable land in Penkhull, acquired what was formerly Doody's Messuage, which extended from St Thomas Place to Penkhull New Road. This estate included a large barn adjacent to Penkhull New Road.

View looking down Penkhull New Road

After Doody, the ownership passed to Joseph Bourne to John Chapman, before being sold to Josiah Spode on the 25th October 1802. In a survey of land ownership dated c1833 most of the area was still retained by the trustees of Josiah Spode but rented out to George Hemmings. The list was substantial and fields covering either side of Penkhull New Road were: *Hassells Croft, Long field, Doody's meadow, Waste, Moor and Hall Meadow*

Ten Row

In a description dated 1810, a part Hassell's Croft comprised of *a barn formerly having been many years ago converted into dwelling houses and which are now in the respective occupations of Thomas Evans, John Jordan, John Fox, Thomas Baddeley and Margaret Smith.*

The exact date that these five cottages were converted into ten is not known. A trade directory dated 1822/23 lists the following occupants but the house numbers have been added from the 1861 census.

27. Joseph Blackburn, painter
28. Vacant
29. George Hulme, dipper
30. James Davenport, fireman
31. John Sutton, presser
32. Ralph Myatt, turner
33. Thomas Plant, painter

Ten Row, Penkhull New Road

34. Thomas Brunt, fireman
35. James Grocott, warehouseman
36. Joseph Lycett, bricklayer.

An elevated pavement in front of Ten Row

View looking at first Ten Row and then Seven Row

Following the death of Josiah Spode III 1829 a list of all his properties was prepared and transferred at a court held on the 13th May 1831. Under the description of lands and property formerly owned by Chapman is the following:
And also all those ten other messuages or dwelling houses, with the outbuilding gardens and appurtenances to the same respectively belonging, situate and being in the village of Penkhull aforesaid, near to a messuage formerly called Doody's Messuage, which said ten messuages and premises last mentioned are now or lately were in the several holdings of Joseph Blackburn, William Hammersley, George Hulme, James Davenport, John Sutton, Ralph Myatt, Thomas Plant, Thomas Brunt, James Grocott and Joseph Lycett, or their undertenants, and the same ten messuages have been newly erected on the sites of or otherwise converted or altered out of five messuages, formerly in the holdings of Thomas Evans, John Jordan, John Fox, Thomas Baddeley and Margaret Smith.

As Ten Row was built on a steep hill, they were approached by a narrow blue-brick terrace with a number of steps at one end. They were in typical Spode style of brick and tile, each with its own ashpit, privy and small garden to the rear. The rent reflected the quality of the houses, 8s 9d per month compared with 7s for Penkhull Square. These houses had

their own privy at the bottom of the garden, not communal. This in its time was quite a status symbol.

Because of the better quality of house, the turnover of tenants was far less than for other properties such as Penkhull Square. By 1841, the front room of No.35 had been converted into a out-door beer house run by Ann Grocott for which she paid a higher rent than the others. By 1861 only three of the 1822 residents remained: Joseph Blackburn, aged 64, who was still working, but his four unmarried daughters from the ages of 17 - 26 still lived at home. At No.29 still lived William Hulme, aged 42, with his wife, Mary. He had three sons and four daughters between the ages of 4 and 20 years. William was a bricklayer but his children all of working age worked in the pottery industry.

The last census of 1911 reflects a changing occupation. No longer did they all work in the pottery industry as only two are recorded. Others are: one stonemason, two working on the railways, two house painters, one a miner, and at No.67 Absalom Hollins, aged 42, from Silverdale, recorded his occupation *as navvy working on the Garden Village.* He was married to Florence, aged 32, *at house duties* and all children three boys and three girls, were attending school.

Looking at the number of child deaths, there were a total of 35 children born of whom nine had died representing a death rate of 26%, which, compared with that of Penkhull Square at 61%, was good.

Seven Row

Below Ten Row, on the other side of Kirkland Lane was Seven Row, so called because there were seven terraced houses. It was part of Commercial Road, Penkhull New Road formed only the lower section of the road until at least 1890. The terraced cottages were fronted by a blue brick terrace pavement mounted at the lower end by a steep set of steps. They were built in the early years of the 19th century by David Bostock, an iron founder from Stoke, and were similar in size and design to those of Ten Row.

Mr. Albert Lawton's shop and Seven Row

Under the old numbering system of the road, they continue from No.37 Commercial Road to No. 43. At No. 37 lived Maria Brunt, aged 42. Although she was married, there was no mention of her husband. She worked as a potter's slip maker and lived with her three daughters, a son and a son-in-law, all working in the potteries. No. 38 was vacant and the remaining five families all worked within the pottery industry. The seven cottages were served by communal lavatories, the night cart calling weekly to empty the privies on a Tuesday morning at 6.30a.m.

Steps leading to Seven Row

By 1891 the name had been changed from Commercial Road to include the whole length into Penkhull New Road. At the same time No. 51, the first property after Kirkland Lane, had been converted into a small grocer's shop run by Louisa Comley, a widow, aged 53. She lived there with her two sons, a daughter and son-in-law. Before keeping the shop, she lived at the Marquis of Granby where her late husband George, was the landlord recorded in 1881 but he

died in December of that year and is buried in Penkhull churchyard.

The proprietor of the grocer's shop in 1911 was Albert Swetnam. Albert was then aged 23. Together with his wife, and ran this small business. With limited potential, because of its situation in 1912, he purchased an empty property in Manor Court Street, which had formerly been the old Royal Oak beerhouse. This Swetnam converted into a shop and he opened up the premises as a high-class grocer. Surprisingly, by this time, none of the houses in Seven Row were occupied by pottery workers, there being a coal miner, a locomotive fireman, two house painters and a railway engine stoker.

Following on from Mr Swetnam in Seven Row was Mr S E Lawton advertising himself as a high class grocer and provision dealer. After his death, the business continued under the name of James A Lawton.

In 1929 No's 171/181 Penkhull New Road (Seven Row) were sold by Charles and Elizabeth Holdgate to Harold Taylor Robinson. The end property, No.183 was sold to Mr. James Lawton in May 1936, but in March 1968, like the other properties in the row were sold to the City Council under a compulsory purchase order. The rest of the cottages remained with the family until 1937 when John Addison and Eileen Jones became the owners for a short period as 1942 they passed into the hands of their trustees who held the properties until they were sold to the city council in May 1965.

This now vacant plot was purchased from the council in October 1968 by Mr Eric Deakin for the sum of £750 who built a large detached house which was sold the following year to Charles and Millicent Shaw for the sum of £5,000.

Richmond Hill
Below Seven Row, on the opposite side of the road stands Richmond Hill a neat row of genteel terraced properties with small raised gardens approached by steps to an elevated terrace path. On the wall of the first house is a large plaque bearing the words Richmond Hill, J A 1871. Despite this title, records and census returns refer to the group of properties as Richmond Terrace. This title flows on from North Terrace and Penkhull Terrace, names that create an air of fashion and desirability.

The account of the urbanisation of this former farmland comes in September 1866 where at a court the land was surrendered to Mr John Astbury: *All that copyhold land called The Hall Meadow adjoining Penkhull New Road which land William Dean, James Dean and John Gilbert were admitted at a court held on the 31st July 1851 on the surrender of George*

Whieldon, Robert Garner and Josiah Spode. John Astbury was a glass and china dealer, living in Liverpool. In November 1869, he secured a loan of £1,200 to help finance the building of the row of houses.

Richmond Terrace, Penkhull New Road

The names of the early occupants of Richmond Terrace are not available. There is no evidence to suggest that John Astbury ever lived in the row, rather the opposite. The 1871 census does not list the row as it came too early to include Richmond Terrace so unfortunately it is nearly ten years before a snapshot becomes available for us to assess the status of the occupants within the community. The largest of the row was the top house, No.92 Richmond Terrace, but it was originally under No.146 Penkhull New Road.

In 1881, the house was called Richmond House and occupied as a boarding and day school for girls under the principalship of Miss Ann Booth, aged 42. Miss Booth was assisted by Helene Bennett, described as a French governess, aged, 28, who was born in Cheltenham. The subjects taught were wide-ranging; English, maths, French, German, Latin, organ, piano, violin, singing and other subjects. There were eleven scholars who varied in age from Jane Tomlinson, aged six, (who with her sister Beatrice, aged 11, came from Sheffield) to Edith Pitman, aged 19, who came from Birmingham. Other areas included Worcester, Leek, Derby, Norton and Stafford. Miss Booth employed two servants, Ann Cooke, aged 26, from Gloucestershire, and Anna Williams, aged 14, from Gnosall.

RICHMOND HOUSE, PENKHULL,
STOKE-ON-TRENT.

HIGH-CLASS
Boarding & Day School for Girls.

ESTABLISHED 1849.

PRINCIPAL:—MISS BOOTH,

Assisted by Certificated English and Foreign Resident Governesses and Eminent Professors.

The course of Instruction includes English (with Mathematics), French, German, Latin; Organ, Piano, Violin, Musical Theory (with Harmony), Singing; Perspective, Freehand and Model Drawing, China and other Painting; Dancing.

Pupils prepared for the Cambridge, Royal Academy and other Examinations.

The School year is divided into Three Terms of Thirteen weeks each. Punctual attendance on the first day requested.

Proceeding down the terrace from No.92 other occupants in 1881 were Ralph Jackson, a commercial traveller; Alfred Dalley, clerk; Frederick Dudley, railway agent; Samuel Alcock, potter's artist; Matilda Parkes, artist; John Maskery, clerk; Annie Booth, no occupation; Desire Lerdy, flower painter, originating from France; Arthur Simpson, potter's artist from Middlesex; Daniel Dale, clerk, Macclesfield; John Smith, hairdresser, from Manchester; Louis Warner, potter's engraver from Stafford. In addition to the boarding school a further two houses had resident servants.

It is not known when the school closed, but by 1891 George Wright, aged 54, a pottery manager, occupied the house. He lived with his wife Martha, aged 49, and four sons and five daughters from the age of 24 down to Gilbert, aged 4. Also Martha's sister Hannah, aged 58, lived with the family. All the children were single in 1891 and their occupations reflected the status of living in such a well appointed house; a solicitor's clerk, assistant pottery manager and a commercial clerk. The remaining children remained in education.

By 1911, the house was used as a Manse for Rev. William Bickley Haynes, aged 67, resident minister at the Baptist church at the foot of the hill in London Road. He came from London, as did his wife, Isabella, aged 62. They lived with their daughter Clara, aged 34, born in Stafford, probably where her father was resident minister at the time. She had been married eight years but there is no mention of her husband or children in the census so she may have just been visiting. A further daughter was living at home, Violet, aged 22, a single woman, employed as a teacher by the Borough of Stoke. The Rev William Haynes was still in residence the following year.

John Astbury died in Liverpool in April 1878. The properties were then passed down through the family until the late 1920s when they were individually sold off. No. 92 was the largest of the houses and had two front bays. At some time around 1929, Leah Bromley, who was the last in line to inherit the premises, had converted the house into two No.92 and No.92a.

A directory of 1912 lists the occupants of Richmond Terrace as follows: No. 68 Mr Gifford, No.70 William Jones, joiner and builder; No.72, Thomas Simpson, labourer; No.74, vacant; No.76, John Sheppard, sugar boiler; No.78, W Dukes, music teacher; No.80, William Gresty, gardener; No.82 Harry Hammersley, manager; No.84, Mrs Sarah Maskery, widow; No.86, Frank Maskery, clerk; No.88, S. Alcock, Artist; No. 90, Thomas Smith, engraver and No.92, Rev. Haynes, Baptist minister.

Commercial Row and Buildings

This little row of three cottages stood opposite the entrance to Kirkland Lane, just above the present entrance to The Views. In its early years, at the far end of the row was a gated entrance to No1 and No2 The Views. In Commercial Row between houses, No.1 and No.2, a narrow pathway gave access to the rear of those properties No's 104-110 Penkhull New Road, a common yard, with a row of water closets. These properties were later re-numbered to 180-186 Penkhull New Road.

Top section of Commercial Road c1950s

The first record of the cottages in Commercial Row is from 1898 when they formed part of the transfer of The Views from the trustees of Daniel Greatbatch to Edwin Brett. The same applies to those old shops and cottages forming the top of Penkhull New Road. These could date from the late 18th century. Mrs Tompson acquired them from the estate of Edwin Bratt. Two years later Mr Dale sold them to Mr George Foster of Holywell, in Flintshire, for the sum of £485. It has proved an almost impossible task to identify in any detail the old buildings from Commercial Row to the top of

Mr. Frank Wedgwood the gents barber 1930s

Penkhull New Road. Yates' map of 1775 shows some buildings around that area, but Hargreaves' map of 1832 shows that the whole corner from the top of Penkhull New Road to just above The Views had been built up. From old photographs it would be reasonable to assume that they were built around the turn of the 19th century or even earlier, but by whom it is impossible to state. The layout was clumsy with no conformity. In 1911, the three terraced properties were occupied by John Forrester, paver, Caroline Peake, widow, aged 63; and Richard Beech, aged 22, an apprentice earthenware dipper.

The corner of the old Commercial Road where it comes into Penkhull

A further three cottages No.'s 182-186 Penkhull New Road were the subject of a sale in 1932 when Mrs Mary Thomson, then living at No.1 Commercial Row sold them to Mr John Dale of Hanley for the sum of £550. Like the greater part of Penkhull, all these properties were subject to a compulsory purchase order in 1965/6. Two of the houses, No's 182 and 184, were then owned by Mr Percy Burt of Newcastle and were sold to the council under a compulsory order for the sum of £50. At No. 182 was the local newsagent run by Mr W Stuart but later occupied by Mr Jack Beech, painter and decorator, who moved to No.12 Newcastle Lane in the mid 1960s. At No.186 stood the gents hairdressers belonging to Mr Frank Wedgwood.

Houses and The Terrace Inn just before Commercial Row

Honeywall

The origins of Honeywall and its name can be found within the chapter 'Early Road Network'. The hamlet of Honeywall was situated on the bend where the White Lion Inn stands. Hargreaves' map 1832 presents a picture of suburban isolation with just a few isolated cottages distant from the village of Penkhull and the urbanisation of the town of Stoke, while Yates' map of 1775 portrays a hamlet with even fewer properties.

Honeywall

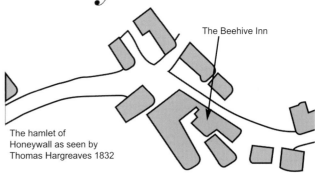

The Beehive Inn

The hamlet of Honeywall as seen by Thomas Hargreaves 1832

Simeon Shaw, 1829, describes Honeywall: *at Honeywall between Stoke and Penkhull, are a number of houses, pleasantly situated on an elevated tract of land possessing a fine view of the eastern side of the district.* At the period of Shaw's writing the views across Stoke would have been exceptional with the old Saxon Church still standing and just a few potworks with workers cottages clustered around.

Starting from the top of Honeywall, the first group of buildings that once stood on the bend to the left went by the name of North Terrace. Why North Terrace? The answer lies with the commercial success of Penkhull Terrace as a group of well-proportioned and salubrious properties aimed at the middle class.

North Terrace, Honeywall

The row built in 1861 was situated to the north of Penkhull Terrace, on the other side of Honeywell and could therefore have been considered as an extension of the former in an attempt to attract the right clients. The land was part of The Mount estate once owned by Josiah Spode and purchased after his death by Frederick Bishop.

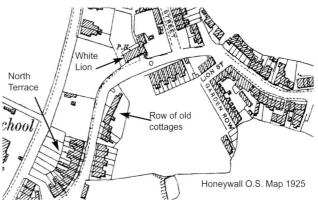

Honeywall O.S. Map 1925

The row containing seven cottages was found on the right of Honeywall, just on the first bend. There were originally seven, being a three and a further four, just on a slightly different line, probably to accommodate the bend in the road. This row of cottages is shown on the 1775 and 1832 maps of Penkhull almost opposite The White Lion and surrounded by fields.

By 1861, the cottages can be identified as those between the Beehive Inn and Penkhull Street as no other houses had been built by that date. They were, with the exception of one, occupied by pottery workers the other by a railway pointsman.

Old Cottages demolished early 1960

All but two cottages remain the others were demolished as part of a clearance order. One of those, No.149 though in a dilapidated state and quite uninhabitable, was not demolished because it gave support to the property next door which was declared fit for habitation. This was the life-saver for No.149.

The exposed gable-end

Unfortunately the first document that lists these old cottages in Honeywall is not dated until 1901 when they were held by Albert Pointon of Oakhill, but who had mortgaged them to Jane Goodall of Eccles. The properties, at least four of them, remained in the Pointon family, Thomas and Alice Pointon who sold the four cottages on the 3rd March 1961 to the city council under a compulsory purchase order for the price of £100. This followed a closure order issued on the properties on the 14th March the previous year.

Three of these were demolished, one remained to support the last cottage, No.151 Honeywall. Finally 18 years later in March 1979, the council decided to sell No.149 to two young men Gerrard Snow and Paul Bould for the sum of £475 on condition that it was renovated for which they received an improvement grant. Following the restoration the property was sold to Mr and Mrs Morrison who then purchased the strip of land on the north side from the council for the sum of £500.

The house now goes under the name of Beekeepers Cottage a title that reflects the name of the road, Honeywall and the nearby inn, The Beehive. This was suggested by myself to the two young men who renovated the property. There is no suggestion that the cottage was ever occupied by a beekeeper despite its title.

Old Cottage in Honeywall c1930

As to the history of the cottage the building was almost able to talk for itself. The tale-tail signs of its past construction became more and more visible as re-construction continued. Firstly the building was originally only one storey high, the apex of the former roof became visible once the old plasterwork had been removed from inside and a bricked-up doorway discovered leading into the next cottage showing at one time they were one property, undivided.

The exposed gable-end showed that the original apex of the first building contained only two rooms suggesting that the original purpose may not have been as a dwelling but as a outhouse or stabling, perhaps for the nearby inn, The White Lion. Furthermore, the rooms to the rear were a later addition, probably in the 19th century creating a two up and two down dwelling.

What now forms Gresty Street was not created until the early 1900s. There were originally just fields below until Lion Street and Garden Street which were situated to the side and behind what is now The Beehive Inn. They, like most of the properties below, were a consequence of the industrialisation of Stoke from the late 18th and early 19th century, providing accommodation for the workers of the town.

Yates' map of 1775 indicates isolated properties on either side of Honeywall below the area of the present Beehive Inn. Subsequently Hargreaves' in 1832, although lacking in any detail, shows considerable developments since 1775. In a trade directory, dated 1818 there are 26 properties listed showing a mixed development of trade and dwellings. The trade premises included a dressmaker, farmer, shopkeeper, baker and flower dealer. The remainder were listed as potters. A further directory dated 1822 records there were 49 names showing in a short period how Honeywall was expanding. As in the previous list of 1818, the grocer remained; there was a blacksmith, tailor, bricklayer, earthenware dealer, plasterer, mason and two joiners. For some reason many of the firemen working in the ovens at the potworks lived in Honeywall. There are ten listed, five turners and six printers. The rest were employed in various semi-skilled jobs within the potworks in Stoke.

The 1861 census lists 71 properties, almost all of which are occupied by pottery workers. The terraced properties were built to a very basic standard, two up and two down with outside privies on the same side. Below The Beehive, there were small courts numbering No.1 to 5, each consisting of two or three properties built without any rhyme or reason, water supplied first by well until it was replaced by a single stand pipe.

One well remained open until the 1880s when it was ordered to be closed as unhealthy. Sanitation was almost non-existent. In 1899, the medical officer for Stoke gave notice on the owner of No. 61-73 to close the properties as being unfit for human habitation. In 1901 there were 79 properties with the address of Honeywall where the overwhelming majority of residents were employed within local potworks.

By 1912, probably at its height of population, the following shops are recorded: No.19 R Edwards, grocer and beer retailer; No.37 Leon Dawson, beer retailer; No.53 A J Beech The Beehive Inn; No.56 H G Barkby, grocer; No.57 Harry Brereton, baker; No.59 Lewis Swinnerton, butcher; No.61 S Picken, greengrocer and Harry Howell at The White Lion.

Most of the properties remained until after the Second World War, to be demolished in the 1950s. I recall myself entering these empty properties awaiting demolition as a young boy, such small dilapidated houses. They were originally built for workers of pottery factories in the area such as Spode, Harrison, Booth, Bird and others.

In the copyhold court records for Honeywall it is not easy to distinguish one plot of land from another, except at the bottom of Honeywall where pottery manufacturers owned them. One entry however is interesting, dated 1803: *and also all those eight other messuages standing on the south east side of the road leading from the village of Penkhull to Cliff Bank with outbuildings, yards and gardens now or lately were wholly or in*

great part rebuilt by Josiah Spode the elder on the sites of five cottages purchased by him from Samuel Turner of which Josiah Spode was admitted on the 19th May 1800.

John Harrison and his Potworks

At the bottom of Honeywall at its junction with Hartshill Road stood a potworks shown on the Duchy of Lancaster map of 1777 as in the occupation of John Harrison. This is the same John Harrison who built and lived at Beech Grove in Penkhull until he became bankrupt in 1802. I am grateful to both Peter Roden and Rodney Hampson whose previous research has assisted in the compilation of this short account of Harrison's potworks.

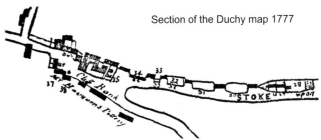

Section of the Duchy map 1777

Harrison's was just one of three potworks that occupied that site. Two of these were adjacent to each other but the position of the third cannot be clarified as adjacent or not. The use of the copyhold court records is invaluable in any attempt to unravel the history.

The first manor record is dated June 1753 when John Alders (sometimes referred to as Aldersea) first raised a mortgage for the sum of £60 from Thomas Pickin on the property described: *all that house of his the said John Alders in Penkhull and all houses, outhouses, pot ovens, workhouses and warehouses etc. which was late the estate of Symon Vinson and were by his will devised to his, the said John Alders.*

To place this entry into context, John Alders had inherited some land from Simon Vinson of Erdington, Warwickshire, whose will was presented in the manor court on the 11th April 1733. It was in June of the same year when Alders was formerly admitted to his inheritance. John died and was buried in Stoke churchyard on 29th July 1779. In April 1782, Elizabeth, the wife of John Alders, and her daughters Anne and Mary, and Joseph Baker, the husband of Mary, sold the potworks. Perhaps Joseph Baker was the second husband of Mary as the will mentions two grandchildren John and Thomas Astbury.

The property was sold to George Carr of Penkhull, maltster on the 5th April 1782 and described as: *all that house or tenement late in the possession of John Alders and afterwards of Eliza Alders and all gardens, folds, potworks, outbuildings etc.* There was no further mention of these works but in the following June, George Carr mortgaged the property back to Elizabeth Alders for £250. The intention was to convert the property into a malthouse: *and all that house or tenement with the malthouse now erecting, late in the possession of Eliz Alders, widow and now of George Carr.* Elizabeth Alders died in 1799 and is buried in Stoke churchyard.

The adjoining potworks belonged to Thomas Alders, the elder brother of John. It was first recorded in the court records on the 30th December 1751 when he raised a mortgage of £60 from Joseph Whitehall and Thomas Knight on the security of property described as: *All that house or tenement in the possession of Thomas Alders and all warehouses, workhouses, ovens and hovels to the same belonging.* It was in August 1775 when the mortgage of the property was released, and Thomas Alders then proceeded to transfer the potworks in October 1777 to his son-in-law Joseph Warburton, potter of Cobridge. It was he who sold this potworks to John Harrison the younger of Cliff Bank, potter on the 21st July 1788. Despite this transaction, they were often referred to as Warburton's Works.

The problem we have here is that there were three successive members of the same family that were called John Harrison. John Harrison, the younger was well known, as his father was already in business at the potworks next door, which is the third potworks to be described on this site. Both the father and grandfather had the name John Harrison, so a generation previous, it is the father who was described as *'the younger'* in transactions of 1751.

On the 16th January that year John Harrison I first acquired property in that area from Michael Henney consisting of: *all that cottage and appurtenances situated in Penkhull in the possession of Michael Henney and barns, stables, gardens, orchards and backsides belonging.* From the court records it seems that this was only part of the land owned by Henney as two further cottages were acquired later the same month on the 30th of January from John Plant of Botteslow (Plant was the mortgage holder for this section of property in the occupation of Michael Henney), followed by a further two cottages on the 20th November from Moses Stockley and Thomas Rowley. Harrison probably converted these two cottages into his first potworks.

The first reference in the manor records to father John Harrison's potworks is found on the 1777 Duchy of Lancaster map of encroachments showing the potworks consisting of four buildings - Mr Harrison's. This potworks was not an encroachment and as there are no references in the copyhold records until after his death in 1798, therefore it may be assumed that he built the potworks himself. (He held two properties Nos 36 on the 1777 map) the one situated on the south side of the turnpike road from Stoke to Newcastle, and a further opposite on the north side where he resided.

Jewitt (1878) refers to the partnership of Harrison with Wedgwood c1752-1754 but describes Harrison as a man possessed of some means, but little taste and not a practical

potter who was taken into partnership by Wedgwood for the advance of capital. Simeon Shaw wrote in 1829: *Mr Wedgwood here entered into partnership with Mr Harrison, a tradesman of Newcastle, (father of the late John Harrison, Banker of Stoke) and at Mr Aldersea's manufactory, he made different kinds of pottery scratched and blue, then in demand; and probably here began to employ his talent for speculation in different articles; for, Mr H., being unwilling to supply further funds, a separation resulted.*

An unpublished biography of Josiah Wedgwood by John Leslie written before 1800, states: *He engaged in partnership with Mr John Harrison who was disposed to transfer his capital from another trade to that of pottery. The manufacture was accordingly begun at Cliffe Bank, in 1752. But its success did not fully answer the sanguine expectations of either party. Mr Wedgwood, finding his plans extremely cramped, determined at the end of two years, to dissolve the contract.*

When Shaw (above) describes Mr Harrison the younger as being a banker, he made an error. This should have read a bankrupt. Also, the name of Aldersea was a name sometimes used for that of Alder but in fact, the two are the same person. The term 'scratched' and 'blue' may be interpreted as white salt-glazed stoneware decorated with 'scratch-blue' or 'Little Wedgwood Blue'. John Harrison I lived from 1717 to 1798.

Base to pottery kiln uncovered on the former Harrison site

John Harrison the younger could well have been originally working at his father's potworks probably until 1781 as only John Harrison II was listed as 'Potter of Stoke' implying that John Harrison I, by then, aged 64, ceased business and that his son had taken over the business. In 1788, he purchased the old Thomas Alder's potworks from Joseph Warburton and his financial credibility was probably supported by the reputation of his father, John Harrison, the elder. On the 1st May 1789, he bought a large 42-acre estate in Penkhull and mortgaged it for £1,000 in August 1793. By the 25th March 1797, and now in severe financial difficulties he re-mortgaged both his estate in Penkhull and the potworks which he owned, for £1,500 to Thomas Haywood of Penkhull, gent,

His father died in 1798 and his will was presented in the manor court on the 9th July 1801. So severe were his debts that within a week, John Harrison was surrendering all the property he had inherited from his father, including the potworks, and a few weeks later his bankruptcy proceedings commenced. The sale of the potworks by Harrison's assignees in bankruptcy was undertaken and following clarification that John Harrison the younger had owned the two potworks, they were sold on the 23rd October 1805. One was purchased by William Kenwright of Stoke-upon-Trent, timber merchant, and the other he purchased was included in: *all that messuage or tenement with potworks belonging at Cliffe Bank in Penkhull formerly the estate of Thomas Alders, and afterwards of Joseph Warburton and late of John Harrison the younger.*

One week after, Kenwright passed some of the property to his partner William Johnson, a timber merchant from the town of Stoke-upon-Trent. The name of Johnson was later given to one of the squares of terraced properties, Johnson's Square. It was a further two years until in December 1807, Harrison's assignees sold the other potworks to Josiah Spode described as: *and also those potworks and other erections whatsoever at Cliffe Bank, contiguous to the said dwelling house and commonly called Harrison's Works.*

The old works were subsequently demolished and replaced by a further square of terraced pottery workers' houses, two up and two down serviced only by a water stand pipe and shared privies and known as Upper and Lower Cliff Bank Squares the two being divided by a path which continues today into what is now Richmond Street.

A report to the general Board of Health prepared by Robert Rawlinson in 1850 gives a snap-shot of living conditions: Cliff Bank - *The ground slopes towards the houses; there is a narrow passage out of this street, betwixt the houses, which is full of refuge; the houses are very much crowded; the privies and middens are confined and dirty; they are opposite the doors of the houses.*

Houses belonging to Alderman Copeland - *The yards are confined; there are no drains, but there are privies, cesspools, and ash-heaps close to the houses; the rent of these cottages is 8s 9d per month; the supply of water is from a pump, and has to be carried some distance.*

Lower Square, also belonging to Alderman Copeland – *There are no drains; there is a large open midden in the centre of the square covered with filth; there is a pump close to it for the supply of the district. The square is unpaved and very dirty, and the channels are immediately in front of the cottages; there is only one privy for twenty houses; in front of these are large heaps of ashes and refuse from the cesspool. I was informed this refuse was emptied out by Mr Copeland's men, and had been left here in the state I witnessed for a fortnight. The tenants near this place complained very much about this.*

The 1901 census makes an interesting comment with regards to 13 uninhabited properties: *Condemned by the Corporation, unfit for habitation. (Johnson's Square).* In 1911, the infantile death rate was 23%. Despite the houses being small (and I remember seeing the footings during an archaeology exploration of the site prior to redevelopment in 2004 and therefore confirm the smallness), one family at No. 13 Upper Cliff Bank consisting of parents by the name of John Bromley, aged 48, a potter's presser and his wife Mary had three daughters, six sons, John's brother, aged 30, his wife and their two children, a total of 15 living under one roof.

By 1906, part of Cliffe Bank Square had been demolished and a daughter mission church from the parish church of St Peter's in Stoke had been built, consecrated to St Andrew. It was sold in 1957 and demolished in about 1962. A new development of three-storey town properties now dominates the area.

Byrd or Bird, Booth and Adams.

On the opposite side of what is now Hartshill Road from the potworks of John Harrison and its junction with Shelton Old Road stood what later became known as The Cliff Bank Works. The surname 'Bird' or 'Byrd' occurs quite often in the entries of Stoke Parish Church registers.

Daniel Bird is not listed as holding any property in the manor encroachments plan of 1777, but his predecessor Hugh Booth is. Occupation was not of copyhold tenure, but an illegal occupation of the manor waste and as such, there are records of Daniel Bird in occupation. In 1751, a thirteen-inch plate of buff clay with the inscription '*William Bird made this mould in the year of Our Lord 1751*' was produced has survived in the 'Greg Collection' of ceramics at Manchester. The plate is decorated with a figure of a man standing wearing a hat, wig and frock coat, bands, breeches, stockings and shoes and the inscription is written on the reverse.

This in itself is no evidence that a William Bird was producing ware at that time only that he made the mould and that could have been under supervision. There is no way of knowing. The parish listing of 1701 lists a family of 'Bird'. Elizabeth Bird, widow, aged 34, and her children; Thomas, aged 12, Mary, aged 10, William, aged 7, Anne, aged 5 and Daniel, aged 3.

Parents William Bird and Elizabeth Meer were married at Stoke Parish Church on the 20th November 1686. Unfortunately, the registers list no occupation. Daniel was baptised on the 13th February 1697. It has not been possible to locate the marriage of a Daniel Bird to a Mary for the early part of the 18th century, which would fit in with the period.

As both the names of Daniel and William Bird appear within a single family in 1701 points to the suggestion that they are the same Daniel and William potters. Certainly their ages are consistant with the late 1750s.

Daniel Bird manufactured agate knife shafts and buttons besides earthenware. He was known as 'the flint potter' because of his having discovered the right proportion of flint and clay needed to prevent the ware from cracking in the oven. Simeon Shaw (1829) wrote: *At the top of Stoke, called Cliff Bank, is a manufactory, now occupied by Mr Thomas Mayer where Mr Daniel Bird first ascertained the exact proportion of flint required by the several kinds of clay to prevent the pottery cracking in the oven; and for which he was first called the 'Flint Potter'. His remains lie under a dilapidated tomb at the steeple end of the old church; and the inscription mentions that he was by accident killed at Twickenham.*

Daniel Bird was killed in an accident in Twickenham in November 1753 and was buried at Stoke on the 10th. His widow Mary then came in possession of his potworks. On the 12th June 1754, Mary Bird bought a plot of land from Benjamin Lewis: *All that copyhold land adjoining to the building and potworks of Mary Bird, widow, adjoining the lane leading from Newcastle to Shelton, and the meadow lying at the bottom of the said piece of land.*

Immediately following this purchase, Daniel Bird II was formerly admitted as son and heir of Daniel Bird I, *to his entire father's copyhold property comprising of twenty acres, about sixty statute acres.* Sadly, Daniel II died young, and in April 1766, his four sisters were admitted co-heirs to his property.

Four years after the death of her husband, Mary Bird married Hugh Booth at Whitmore on the 14th September 1757. He was described as a 'potseller of Stoke'. In marrying Mary Bird, Hugh Booth became the stepfather of Daniel Bird's son, also named Daniel and his four daughters. Hugh Booth was producing china glazed ware and earthenware at the works in the 1780s.

Hugh Booth was buried in Stoke churchyard on the 15th June 1789. A large memorial was placed on a wall within the old church in his memory. When the old church was demolished, the memorial was removed and is now situated high up on the wall to the north of the chancel arch in the present St Peter's church. In the will of Hugh Booth, he made bequests to the four daughters of Daniel Bird, two of whom were recorded as married.

His will also gave his brother, Ephraim, a life-long interest in all his property, and thereafter some was left to Ephraim's sons, (Hugh's nephews). The the potworks, were given to Hugh as the eldest nephew. It was he who was admitted to the copyhold inheritance on the 16th March 1808. Later the name changed to Booth and Sons, as Ephraim was running the business with his two sons Hugh and Joseph between at least 1792 and 1802. Hugh and Joseph ran the works between at least 1805 and 1808. A lease was held by Thomas Ward and Company by 1815 (Ward and Davenport in 1822) and by Thomas Mayer from at least 1826.

The firm of William Adams and Sons took over from Mayer c.1837 and held the works (described as 'small, dilapidated and old') until the 1850s. It then passed to Minton, Hollins and Company, who were still the occupants in 1889. The factory was pulled down in 1914.

Hugh and Joseph were the sons of Ephraim. Joseph, following the bankruptcy of John Harrison, purchased his former home, Beech Grove in 1802. Hugh and Joseph traded until around 1808. Joseph went to live at Whitchurch in 1812.

Cliff Bank Works. Honeywall is shown top right of the picture.
Below Honeywall 2010

Chapter 23
The Destruction of Old Penkhull.

Walking around the village today with its well-kept lawns, the old Greyhound Inn standing almost to attention as it has done for over four hundred years it is hard to believe that a battle was fought here some fifty years ago. From the Inn the property line is followed by a mixture of 60's shops then a small group of 19th century shops. Neither of these have any impact on the surroundings and almost cry out for order, design and uniformity.

The first group of shops following to the right of The Greyhound Inn are typical of the period with no architectural merit to speak of. These are followed by a mixture of non-impressive shops and houses all bearing the scars of renovation and alterations without any form of cohesion. Sadly, none of these add anything to the debate on the merits of town planning.

On the other side of the churchyard is Rothwell Street, far better maintained and attractive than in recent years, but the architecture cannot be classed as modern, striking yes, with its skyline resembling a wartime ammunition factory roof from the late 1930s. These replaced an earlier group of terraced houses, set back from the road with long neat gardens and set at unusual angles to enhance a small village setting, all facing the church. These old houses were sacrificed on the block of social engineering for the sake of a lawn, inside facilities and a damp course.

The 60's properties that replaced them have a small section of lawn to the front and that all important inside lavatory and a proper bath without the need to boil a kettle to fill once a week the tin-bath dip in front of the kitchen fire. This is exactly how the vast majority of post war Penkhull lived.

Perhaps too critical, perhaps unsympathetic, that is for the reader to decide. But what we have today is a result of the folly of politicians with little, or, if I dare say, no expertise or knowledge of what was required to have made the decision to demolish the centre of Penkhull in one foul swoop. It could be likened to a tidal wave of destruction, flattening all in its path without fear or retribution. And yes, there was another side to the reasoning, that it was an early attempt at social engineering by the ruling Labour Party of the day. Strong words and yet true!

I suppose it was inevitable that one day there would have to be demolition in Penkhull as many of the properties were old; they were becoming a liability requiring modern facilities such as bathroom, inside toilets, central heating and a damp course.

In the church magazine of September 1956, the Vicar, Rev V G Aston wrote, rather prophetically that *change must happen* but emphasised that the frontages, the facades of the old cottages should be retained. This was just two months before he retired to Worcester on the ground of ill health in the November.

Demolition of unfit houses has already accounted for changes in the village. There is no doubt that some of these houses were in a very bad state, and nothing could be done to restore them. No doubt, too, there will be others that will follow, but we are deeply concerned lest the whole facade of the village is changed. Penkhull is one of the few remaining villages in the City that bears the marks of that era in which the great potters of the past lived. We know that Minton, Spode, Harrison, Mason, Twyford and Wedgwood used to walk around the village discussing business and probably their latest designs as they would meet in the 'Manor Court House' when dealing with the affairs of land or property.

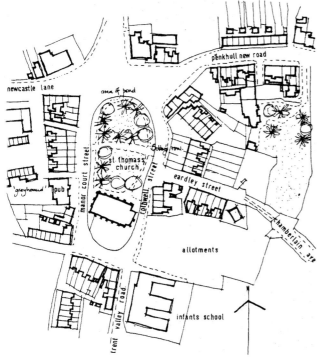

Plan of Penkhull Village 1958

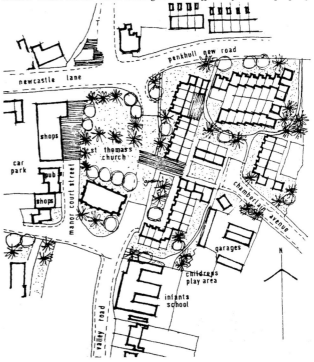

Proposed Plan for Penkhull 1966

Most, if not all of the houses that remained in the 1950s were built between the years 1700 and 1890 and all were focused on the old Court House and the Church, preserving much of the atmosphere of that time. What then of the other property? What we are struggling for is to preserve the outward look of the village. We realise that much will have to be done to bring many houses to the standards required but nevertheless we believe that this could be done without, completely altering the shape of these houses. And it is good to know that the reconstruction officers are willing to look at the question in this way. We sincerely hope that all our efforts will meet with success.

We shall not cease to struggle for these ends, and we hope that we shall have the backing of everyone. It would be terrible to envisage our Church and The Greyhound flanked and fronted by modern buildings quite out of keeping. Every bit of help is needed. All old things are not bad, neither are all modern ones good. Changes must come, but with these changes there must enter care for tradition, and kindness towards human beings. I feel sure that our Councillors will see the wisdom of doing everything they can towards preserving for all time something in the City of the days of those great men who made Stoke what it is. To this end we must dedicate all our resources.

It is my hope that all living around the village and the planners could come together and create a package of changes that would be acceptable to both sides.

But VG was not a well man. In December of the same year a new Vicar was to be installed to take over the reins of St Thomas's church. The appointment was Rev Arthur Perry, he was a city councillor and a member of the Labour Party and was shortly to become the Lord Mayor of Stoke-on-Trent and it is he who took these plans forward to transform the old village into what we have today.

It is quite remarkable that correspondence from both V G and Arthur Perry was to end up in my hands. Mrs Aston gave me all of V Gs notes and after the death of Arthur Perry, Michael his son handed over to me further correspondence.

It was less than one year after taking charge of the parish on the 13th September 1957 that he wrote to Rev. VG Aston explaining and listing in detail all the plans for the new village.

Dear VG

Things are fairly well in the parish and we are kept pretty busy also with Civic Engagements. The old Terrace is now closed and most of us are sad at the ending of something that has contributed to Penkhull, as we knew it.

The new look' for Penkhull is now on the drawing boards after much thought and conference between the experts and myself. When it comes off the drawing board there will be another examination of it and then it will be passed on to the committee stage and then to the Council. If it is not altered much in committee it will be briefly as follows:

Demolition of most of the property around the church; on one side of the top of Chamberlain Avenue; on another side to Barnfield to another down to Lewis' Nursery. This, as you will understand opens up a kind of close around the church and in that close will be built of

'approved design and architecture', bungalows for old folk, flats for single professional folk, village hall, extension of the school playground, playing space and some shopping premises and some houses. In all there are some 120 houses well below standard. Building will commence next month on land between Penkhull New Road and Honeywall and will have 108 houses erected. So if all goes according to plan no family which desires to remain here will leave.

I am content that a good job is projected and while it may mean a few more headaches and perhaps heartache or two, the future glory in some measure will surpass the old. Penkhull offers the best proposition which will come to the planners in this generation and what is to be done will most likely set the pattern for village rebuilding for the whole City and more likely for the whole country.

I hope this had not wearied you and I trust you may be interested. If you want to know what is being dome parochially, I send for your information the letter, which is now going around the village. I hope that you are both well and look forward to seeing you soon. Love ARTHUR.

The contents of this letter leave questions unanswered. Perry opens by stating that the plans are drawn up between himself and the local planners. No mention of any other parties represented or consulted. The words of 'approved design and architecture' are underlined, but who was to approve them? Certainly, not the residents of Penkhull. There was no mention of consultation, except that by the Committee and full council who were the judges and imposers of change. The new properties referred to as being between Penkhull New Road and Honeywall are the flats in Penkhull Terrace and the houses in Boon Avenue and Sillitoe Place, both named after senior city councillors which says it all.

VG was distressed at receiving such a letter, listing in almost alphabetical order the changes that were going to take place in his beloved Penkhull. Just three days later he wrote to Perry pleading with him to fight the planners to retain Penkhull as it was. Even at this point VG did not comprehend that it was actually Arthur Perry himself who was leading the move for change.

The Reverend V G Aston replied to this letter and in his words can be seen the anguish in his heart at the destruction of his OWN VILLAGE, which he loved so very dearly and where he had devoted so faithfully 25 years of his life to its spiritual well being and preservation. There is no doubt, if he had still been vicar at this time, the village would be standing today. Indeed, he received many letters asking him to return to his village and to help to save it from the whim of a few, but failing health prohibited him from doing this.

My Dear Arthur,
Tell me no more, it breaks my heart, is this to be the end of my struggles to save the village.

Please Arthur, please be big enough to save the sacred ground where Spode, Minton and Wedgwood walked and talked. Save the old village with its Greyhound, save it from the 'Subtopia' which desecrates and destroys everything that will not conform to the officialdom of the drawing board, blueprint, sub-standard and all the finalising, canalising, the horrible jargon which conceals the lack of historical sequence or traditional symbols in our national or local history.

Jump in and save it that your name may be blessed for evermore. Must the planners with their slide rules and compasses, and their neatly drawn geometrical figures be allowed to cry 'CARTHAGINEM ESSE DELENDEM' and thus destroy Penkhull for the bathroom which could even now be fitted, whilst still retaining the facade of the one village left in the City?

Must the word 'substandard', be the 'open sesame' to the transformation of Old England into another star on the flag of the U.S.A. Have we no pride in our traditions? Perhaps you and only you, in your double capacity - in your unique capacity – can save at least the facade and therefore the glory of our Domesday Book village, of its Mintonian background.

Is not Penkhull Church almost a private chapel of the Minton's? Does that mean anything to the 'experts'? 'Expert' in what? Ye high heavens, there remains but one more thing to do - to rename the ancient 'Pinchetel' ICHABOD - the glory hath departed.

If you and the planners cannot save my old village, then I shall be content to pass away from the sight of man with it. Please tell me no more. Oh, my Arthur, 'If thou canst'.
Yours affectionately, VG.

In a letter I received from Mrs Lilly Aston in June 1971, she

wrote to me saying that if only her late husband had been

well enough he would have fought to stop the changes planned for the village. Sadly he was not well enough to return to pick up the gauntlet and challenge all that had been planned. He was a sick man.

From 1957, little or nothing had been heard further about the development of Penkhull until a bombshell appeared in the Sentinel in September 1961 that knocked local people sideways. It was the bombshell that all dreaded as the press reported the notice for the demolition of 120 dwellings around the centre of the village. It was a complete community relation's disaster for the City Council. They were all most inept in the way they conducted the correspondence to the residents involved.

Dated the 29th September 1961 the official compulsory notices were distributed to all homes affected. It was formal, to the point of being dictatorial and intimidating. *The Council have now decided to make the above compulsory purchase order which affects the property in which you are interested.*

The list contained all the houses to be demolished. A number in Trent Valley Road, all in Penkhull Square, Victoria Buildings, Garden Row, the old cottages at the top of Garden Street, Rothwell Street, the top of Penkhull New Road, Ten Row and Seven Row, cottages in Manor Court Street, a number in Newcastle Lane, Back Newcastle Lane No.3 the Views and the old cottages at the top of Franklin Road.
The enclosed Notice is intended to explain to you that if you desire to object to the making of this order you should do so in writing to the Minister of Housing and local Government during the course of the next three weeks or so. The Council will, at any inquiry into this matter, submit that the houses included in the order that rising and penetrating dampness exists. It will also be alleged that the staircases are, for the most part, steep and entered directly off the living rooms and that the houses are of the terraced type and of very high densities to the acre.
For these reasons and by reason of the detailed defects that the public Health Inspector will provide, if required, these properties are considered to be unfit.

The letter then continued to list all the properties involved which apart from the remaining few shops in Manor Court Street and the Greyhound Inn included removing all the properties in the centre of the village giving an almost clean canvas from which to start. Such a unique position would have been relished by many local authorities, but for Stoke Labour councillors and planning officers, they were totally out of their depth by the enormity of the scheme they had created with no vision except to create a further council estate amongst a community they considered elitist. Many local residents openly stated that Hitler did not achieve this during the 2nd World War, but Stoke-on-Trent City Council was preparing to do just that.

In the following November, two months after the notices had been served on residents, Perry wrote in the church magazine

CITY OF STOKE-ON-TRENT

HARRY TAYLOR
TOWN CLERK
CLERK OF THE PEACE
TELEPHONE 48241

REF   AJR/BC

TOWN HALL
STOKE-ON-TRENT

29th September, 1961.

Dear Sir or Madam,

STOKE NOS. 29, 30, 31, 32, 33, 34 AND 35
CLEARANCE AREAS COMPULSORY PURCHASE ORDER, 1961.

The Council have now decided to make the above
Compulsory Purchase Order which affects the property in
which you are interested.

The enclosed Notice is intended to explain to you
that if you desire to object to the making of the Order
you should do so in writing to the Minister of Housing
and Local Government during the course of the next three
weeks or so.

I am instructed to inform you of the general grounds
upon which the Council seek to include your property in a
Clearance Areas Compulsory Purchase Order. The areas
affected by the Order consist of properties in Brisley
Hill, Trent Valley Road, Penkhull Square, Garden Row,
Garden Street, Manor Court Street, Victoria Buildings,
Rothwell Street, Eardley Street, Penkhull New Road,
Commercial Row, The Views, Mill Street, Newcastle Lane,
Franklin Road and Laburnum Cottages, and comprise a total
of 135 dwellinghouses, 5 dwellinghouses and shops, and two
dwellinghouses and off-licences which the Council allege
to be unfit for human habitation. The total area involved
is a little under 5 acres.

The Council will, at any Inquiry into this matter,
submit that the houses included in the first part of the
schedule and coloured pink on the map are generally old,
in disrepair and that rising and penetrating dampness
exist. It will also be alleged that the staircases are,
for the most part, steep and entered directly off the
living rooms and that the houses are of the terraced type
and of very high densities to the acre, i.e. 32, 25, 27,
24, 30, 26 and 62. For these reasons and by reason of the
detailed defects which the Public Health Inspector will
provide, if required, these properties are considered to
be unfit.

Letter sent to all residents whose properties were to be demolished

STOKE NO. 29

Dwellinghouse	-	45	Trent Valley Road
Dwellinghouse	-	1	Brisley Hill
Dwellinghouse	-	2	Brisley Hill
Dwellinghouse	-	3	Brisley Hill
Dwellinghouse	-	4	Brisley Hill
Dwellinghouse	-	5	Brisley Hill
Dwellinghouse	-	6	Brisley Hill
Dwellinghouse	-	7	Brisley Hill
Dwellinghouse	-	8	Brisley Hill
Dwellinghouse	-	9	Brisley Hill
Dwellinghouse	-	10	Brisley Hill
Dwellinghouse	-	11	Brisley Hill
Dwellinghouse	-	12	Brisley Hill

STOKE NO. 30

Dwellinghouse	-	52	Trent Valley Road
Dwellinghouse	-	54	Trent Valley Road
Dwellinghouse	-	56	Trent Valley Road
Dwellinghouse	-	14	Penkhull Square
Dwellinghouse	-	13	Penkhull Square
Dwellinghouse	-	12	Penkhull Square
Dwellinghouse	-	11	Penkhull Square
Dwellinghouse	-	10	Penkhull Square
Dwellinghouse	-	9	Penkhull Square
Dwellinghouse	-	8	Penkhull Square
Dwellinghouse	-	7	Penkhull Square
Dwellinghouse	-	6	Penkhull Square
Dwellinghouse	-	5	Penkhull Square
Dwellinghouse	-	4	Penkhull Square
Dwellinghouse	-	3	Penkhull Square
Dwellinghouse	-	2	Penkhull Square
Dwellinghouse	-	1	Penkhull Square
Dwellinghouse	-	46	Trent Valley Road
Dwellinghouse	-	48	Trent Valley Road
Dwellinghouse	-	50	Trent Valley Road

STOKE NO. 31

Dwellinghouse	-	6	Trent Valley Road
Dwellinghouse	-	4	Trent Valley Road
Dwellinghouse	-	2	Trent Valley Road
Dwellinghouse	-	1	Victoria Buildings
Dwellinghouse	-	2	Victoria Buildings
Dwellinghouse and Lock-up Shop	-	3/3a	Victoria Buildings
Dwellinghouse	-	4	Victoria Buildings
Dwellinghouse	-	5	Victoria Buildings
Dwellinghouse	-	6	Victoria Buildings
Dwellinghouse	-	7	Victoria Buildings
Dwellinghouse	-	1	Garden Row
Dwellinghouse	-	2	Garden Row
Dwellinghouse	-	3	Garden Row
Dwellinghouse	-	4	Garden Row
Dwellinghouse	-	5	Garden Row
Dwellinghouse	-	6	Garden Row

One page of the compulsory order. The list is four pages long

in an attempt to put a spin on the whole affair.

There has been much activity in the village on this matter which was announced in the Evening Sentinel some weeks ago, and I hope that most of it has been without bitterness. I am among those who believe our village can be made a much better place to live in, by giving the people better houses, but I also believe most of the work can be done without expecting our people to leave the place where they have grown up in and love.

There are spaces on which houses can be built before any are taken down, and if this is done, then people can be transferred to them and their old houses taken down and others built in their places. We also need in this parish one or two groups of old people's houses for there are many who are living on their own and who may be, at times, in need of some help.

I have seen a sketch of the new layout and think it a good one and if it is as good when it become a fact, I think all those who now have proper misgivings will be well content. Such a large plan cannot be done without some inconvenience, but it is my hope that no one will be compelled to leave Penkhull who wishes to stay here. The planners have a wonderful opportunity and I believe they are anxious to take it and well able to make of this village something which not only will be pleasing to the people who live here, but will set a very high standard for any future developments in like conditions.

Arthur Perry was becoming the target of people's frustrations as it was considered that he was only paying lip service to the problem. The subject was on the tongues of all who lived in the village being the only topic of conversation in pups, shops and the back of church and chapel. The demolition of Penkhull and the central part in the scheme played by Arthur Perry caused him to once again write in the next issue of the parish magazine on the subject and he referred to the bitterness in the hearts of local people.

Magazine December 1961

The Evening Sentinel article has been much discussed, as indeed it deserved to be, not only for what was in it, but also because of what it left out. Old buildings are not necessarily good because they are old, nor are new ones necessarily good because they are new. I do not see much of historical interest, nor of architectural beauty in most of the houses, which it is proposed for demolition. There is nothing beautiful in having pots and pans to catch the water on a rainy day, nor in walking down a dark backyard on a cold winter's night to go to the toilet, and that is made a lot worse if the toilet is not working.

The new houses which have already been built in Penkhull are quite attractive and of a better construction than many of the old ones. Some of those who signed the petition did so because of the fear of the unknown. I understand that they do not want to be pushed out to some new estate and I share their view, that is why I said in last month's magazine that the builders should build on the spare land around here before any of the present houses are pulled down. This is so that our folk may stay where their roots

Party officials deny 'political motive in Penkhull plans' claim

City plan will NOT 'destroy' Penkhull

BUT RESIDENTS OBJECT AT PUBLIC INQUIRY

Claiming that many old houses in Penkhull had no architectural merit and contributed little to the picturesque village scene, Mr. E. J. Evans, Senior Assistant Solicitor to Stoke-on-Trent Corporation, declared at a public inquiry at Stoke to-day that with suitably-designed new houses Penkhull would be preserved and be just as attractive as it was at present.

Pointing out that the Corporation had carried

"Different"

Suggestions that Stoke-on-Trent's Socialist-controlled City Council have political motives in their redevelopment plans for Penkhull were scoffed at to-day by officials of the two political groups concerned.

The suggestions are contained in a letter to the Ministry of Housing and Local Government from Mr. Clive Howson, who signs himself as co-founder of the Potteries Civic Society and former Parliamentary candidate for Stoke-on-Trent South.

He complains of the council's "vandalism" in applying for compulsory purchase order to enable demolition of The Views, birthplace of Sir Oliver Lodge.

New flare-up is anticipated over Penkhull scheme

The Penkhull redevelopment controversy, which has been simmering since the City Council's scheme for remodelling the "village" was hacked by the Ministry of Housing and Local Government, may flare up again.

The latest proposals, put forward by the council, would involve compulso

'NO BID TO MAKE LABOUR AREA'

"RESTRICT THE WRECKERS TO SPECIFIC SITES"

To the Editor of the "Sentinel"

SIR,—May I support the move of the Potteries Civic Society to preserve The Views, Penkhull, birthplace of Sir Oliver Lodge?

PULLING DOWN PENKHULL

SIR,—I have been sub-postmistress of Penkhull Post Office for the last 18 years. I was born in the village more than 50 years ago, and have lived and worked there nearly all my life.

Butt Lane.   RAMBLER
(Name and address supplied)

CROCKS AND CRAZES

Worried Penkhull is asked to be patient

PENKHULL, one of the oldest inhabited parts of the city, is still awaiting the next step in the planning of its future, and the mystery will probably remain unravelled

A community set amid the city's working class

ONE of the oddest things about the meeting Penkhull this week to explain the redevelopment plans for the area was the revelation Penkhull is a genuinely middle class community set down among working class

BIG CUT-BACK IN PLAN FOR 'NEW PENKHULL'

Stoke-on-Trent Corporation's much revised and often criticised plan for the redevelopment of Penkhull is now likely to be presented in considerably reduced form.

A report which the City Council will receive at

"Some reservations" over Penkhull skyscraper

The amended scheme for the redevelopment of Penkhull—approved in principle by the City Housing Committee, but still awaiting approval by other departments—provides for the erection of 240 dwellings and 84 garages.

This is shown in the committee's report to the City Council, who, on Thursday, will be asked to approve a decision calling for the compulsory acquisition of land and properties—which are not

377

Brisley Hill comes down

Top of Trent Valley Road and most of Manor Court Street gone.

Penkhull Square all boarded up

are.

The work which is proposed for Penkhull gives a wonderful chance to those whose task it is to do the designing and building, and I think the officials at the Town Hall realise very fully the importance of making a good job of it, and are fully qualified to

do so.

Finally, as a result of public pressure an Inquiry was held at Stoke Town Hall on the 23rd January 1962 that was duly reported in the Evening Sentinel under the headlines of 'City plan will NOT destroy Penkhull, but residents object at Public Inquiry'.

Mr E J Evans, Senior Assistant Solicitor presented the case on behalf of the city council who stated that with suitably designed houses Penkhull would be preserved and be just as attractive as it was at present. Miss D R Lane, an inspector from the Ministry of Housing and Local Government, conducted the inquiry. The plans for Penkhull included around 100 new dwellings, a row of shops and a car park. A total of fourteen streets in the vicinity would be affected.

To press the case further, Mr Evans gave details that a total of 142 properties had been judged by the council as being unfit for habitation and a further 18 properties were added to the scheme because the land was required for the satisfactory development of the area. Shops for Manor Court Street were to be suitably designed for the locality and the closure of the street was also planned making it free from traffic.

Representing two objectors from Garden Street, their representative, Mr W A L Allardice said that *in view of the amount of money his clients had spent to improve their homes, they took a very hard view of the fact that they had been deemed un-fit by the council.* He continued *Penkhull is one of the oldest inhabited areas in the city. All that would remain in existence after redevelopment would be a church surrounded completely by new buildings apart from the Greyhound Inn. It is a pity that a plan had not been considered leaving some of the old houses and then adapting the development around them*

Mr R F Atkins, a Liverpool solicitor acting on behalf of a number of residents told the Inquiry that *most other cities received this treatment which the City Council intends from the Germans during the war, but Stoke-on-Trent is doing the same to itself.* Mr Atkins agreed that shortcomings were very evident in the village. The cottages in the majority were Victorian with no intrinsic architectural merit, but were very much in keeping with the older plan of Penkhull which gave it its charm He urged that the plans should be submitted to the most searching opinions and thought.

To put the track record of the authority to date into context, Mr Atkins referred to the fact that since the war, the council had produced nothing which has commanded the attention of anybody outside the city apart from the Burslem face-lift.

In his concluding comments Mr Evans said that *the large*

Public Inquiry held at Stoke Town Hall 20th September 1967

rethink and a reduction in size of the scheme, which if went ahead would completely change the face of Penkhull forever. The council would have to re-think the whole scheme.

The cries for a new vision, the voices expressing discontent and the requests for experts to be consulted in the Penkhull reconstruction was heard throughout the city, would no one listen in the corridors of power at the Town Hall? One group called the New Potteries Society listened and one of its committee members, Mr Clive Howson expressed the groups concerns at a monthly meeting of the local Inter-Varsity Club held on the 28th March 1962. *Penkhull must be one of the most dramatic and satisfying sites in the country* he said. *We want to try and get the best young brains in the country to design it as a town village as a design competition. The idea,* he concluded *would create such an interest in the whole region that people would come from miles around to see Penkhull.*

attendance at the Inquiry showed there was considerable public interest. Therefore, we have got to be particularly careful how we move from this point onwards and, if the minister approves the scheme, I am quite sure the council would engage outside advice so that the best could be made of a fine opportunity.

Writing in the following month's church magazine, Arthur Perry took the opportunity to put on record his own feelings on the subject taking the stance that he wanted to demolish the old village. *It is a very good thing that people have been ready to discuss the matter and we can only hope that it has been, and will continue to be, without any bitterness that could lead to misunderstanding of motive. We are all entitled to our opinions and it is one of the freedoms, which must be preserved, that we shall all continue to be able to express them.*

There is little of the 'old world' in this village, the Greyhound Inn is probably the oldest, and that fortunately, is not included in the demolition order. The church is not an old building for it was built in 1842, 120 years ago and as all can see the church needs to be restored, then what can be said about the property around it? Property, which in the main had little spent on it for many years past, except that which is owner-occupied.

The report of the Government Minister Miss D. R. Lane, rejected the full plan making suggestions for a radical

These comments differ greatly from the assertions of Perry when he stated earlier, *that the plans for Penkhull will most likely set the pattern for village rebuilding for the whole City and more likely for the whole country.*

Once more the subject came to a head in April 1963 when Ian Nairn, British Architectural critic and correspondent for the Daily Telegraph, together with topographer Kenneth Browne took up the challenge as more details of a new plan became known following the report of the Minister. They criticized the plans: *For the potteries, Penkhull is something special. The local council realized this, and proposed a complete plan for a new village, intending it to be their showpiece. The spirit was excellent, but the results will be deplorable. Everything is moved apart, the tight enclosures of the old buildings around the church have gone; it will only be a hill village on paper, incorporating hardly any of the old buildings, and none of the old spaces.*

The article continued with a series of sketches, showing the existing and the proposed and how the whole outlook would change drastically by a policy of openness, with bland rows of stereotyped houses and shops as almost duplicate copies of any city council estate. It stated that the old cottages in Manor Court Street should be retained and those to the east of the church to be replaced, one section at a time, not departing from the old shapes without good reason.

The same article can now be found within the library at Harvard University design school, no doubt as a reference on how not to design villages. It concluded. *It is all a far cry from the council's original plan, but it is what Penkhull and hundreds of villages like it must have if they are not to be killed with kindness; smothered by the 'this is a good for you dear' ministrations of an over-possessive aunt. One day a week from an architectural assistant would do it, provided he feels for the place. Surely, Stoke-on-Trent, a city of a quarter of a million people, can afford that?*

A further editorial in a local magazine called 'Unit 7 The Potteries' dated 1963 makes an interesting comment that planners of today should take to heart. *The villagers of Penkhull haven't shown much enthusiasm for the plans to modernise their village on a hill overlooking Stoke. Undoubtedly the central area of Penkhull has a charm unmatched by anywhere else in the potteries. St. Thomas' church, neatly set on a wooded island plumb in the centre might have been contemporary with the village's first mention in the Domesday Book.*

To the villagers themselves, who are prepared to overlook the dismal state of many of the houses and cottages in the central area, the business-like approach of the planners hasn't endeared itself. The town planners seem to them to be indiscriminate wielders of compulsory purchase orders, bent on modernising the village in their own image. Unfortunately, many of the misunderstandings of the planners' intentions have arisen because there is no adequate machinery for bringing together the planners and those being planned. Until this is created one side will continue to respond obstructively out of weakness and the other side will react by imposing their views as the people who know best.

As vicar, Rev Arthur Perry decided to catalogue the progress of the demolition gangs and the re-building programme in the church service books. The bulldozers started on the 8th June 1964 and ceased on the 21st May 1967, three years of dust, noise and tears. It must have been one of the unstable periods in modern history for those people living in the adjacent streets, watching as cardboard cutouts on a windy day.

May 1964	Slum clearance began today at Brisley Hill, demolished Eardley Street and part of Rothwell Street started to clear.
28th June 1964	Top of Penkhull New Road started to clear, the old Terrace Inn gone.
6th July 1964	Manor Court Street started to clear.
10th July 1964	Meeting with shop keepers, Vicar and

	Councillors. Delay in enforcing notices.
16th July 1964	Mr Lawton's old shop is down at the end of Seven Row in Penkhull New Road.
22nd July 1964	Meeting between vicar, shopkeepers and the Reconstruction Committee.
27th July 1964	Shop notices for compulsory purchase not to be confirmed, further thoughts to shopping in Manor Court Street.
23rd May 1965	Foundations for new houses in Brisley Hill began eight houses to be built.
13th June 1965	House building in Newcastle Lane begins.
January 1966	Houses in Brisley Hill let.
20th March 1966	Three houses in Newcastle Lane let.
10th April 1966	Houses in Franklin Road now completed.
19th May 1966	Demolition of Penkhull Square commenced.
9th June 1966	Public Meeting on housing development around the church.
July 1966	Bulldozers demolish Garden Row the site for the Church Army Flats after a wait of eight years.
25th Jan. 1967	Victoria Buildings being demolished, this was the old workhouse for Stoke.
12th Feb. 1967	Building commenced on the old Ten Row at the top of Penkhull New Road.
26th March 1967	Bulldozers levelled off Rothwell Street, Eardley Street in preparation of new housing.
23rd April 1967	Foundations for building in Rothwell Street and Eardley Street being made.
14th May 1967	Discovery of well in old Eardley Street. Beautifully stone lined 43 feet deep, 3 feet of water. Rope marks on the side.
21st May 1967	The well, said to be 400 years old filled in so housing can proceed.

By this time, correspondents to the Evening Sentinel had turned up the heat. A number of letters were submitted claiming that the redevelopment of Penkhull was an elaborate plot to further socialism in the city by the transformation of Penkhull into a council housing estate similar to that of Bentilee and Ubberley.

It was only a matter of weeks after the first demolitions that local traders became anxious as their livelihoods were being threatened. Because of local concern an emergency meeting

Penkhull Square, all now but a memory

Victoria Buildings, the old parish workhouse

Garden Row, off Garden Street

Corner of Garden Street and Manor Court Street

was called between traders, Rev. Perry and officers from the planning department and held on the 26th July 1964 and a compromise to the plans was arrived at which meant that the last block of shops in Manor Court Street would remain. The plan to pedestrianize Rothwell Street and Manor Court Street with the traffic going via Thistley Hough was also abandoned under mounting pressure so leaving the street as we find it today.

Again, the Evening Sentinel dated 2nd July 1965 reported the charges by the Potteries Civic Society, that the council intended purchasing by compulsion the village of Penkhull in order to impose their unpopular plan of development into a council house estate. The charges were made in a protest letter to the Ministry of Housing and Local Government in which they ask for a further public inquiry into the whole affair.

The article continued to press the city council to draw back from its high-handed decision and in particular the withdrawal of the notice on the owners of The Views. In typical fashion, the council's response was predictable saying that the *charges by the society were an exaggeration* and that *compulsory power were being sought to acquire property but certainly not the whole village in order to carry out carefully planned comprehensive redevelopment.* Further to this they added that *The Views, historically and architecturally is classed by the Minister as only grade three.*

This whole rumpus had blown up because the housing committee, after negotiations to acquire property had failed, and therefore decided to seek compulsory powers to do so.

Mr Clive Howson, from the Potteries Civic Society made a number of interesting observations that are note-worthy, and show the determination of the city council to over-ride any thoughts or wishes of the local community. Remember that Arthur Perry was a part of the inner circle of senior councillors with influence and power, sufficient to have changed the political agenda for the transformation of Penkhull but he failed to intervene and remained in full support of the projected vision as he was determined to see the project come to a conclusion.

Again Mr Howson continued. *The revised Penkhull scheme has not been submitted to the people of Penkhull for their views, nor have the Society been invited to see plans or models to give constructive comments. The corporation's intention goes entirely against the decision of the Ministry after a previous inquiry, that compulsory purchase procedure should not be used.* The article continues with further damning claims against the local administration. *It is surely not too late for the council to draw back from this cynical and high-handed decision and to withdraw in particular their notice of seven days to the owners of The Views. Its members were elected, one supposes, to be the*

Cottages in Manor Court Street ready for demolition

The rear of cottages in Manor Court Street

Rothwell Street, most properties are now down

guardians and not the destroyers of the historic dignity of this city and the rights of its citizens.

As chairman of the Reconstruction Committee Mr Arthur Cholerton responded: *At all times, the city council has given the utmost thought and consideration to the question of unnecessarily disturbing property owners. The decision to proceed by compulsory purchase order had been taken only with great reluctance and in the light of a vital need to include The Views within the proposed scheme.*

The following comment probably sums up the total inadequacy of councillors and officials at the time as it became clear that a decision had been made to demolish the vast majority of Penkhull without first a plan and second without consultation.

Mr Cholerton added that *at the moment it was not possible to place something definite before the people of Penkhull but a public meeting would be called at which models and plans would be on view and at which they would be able to express their opinions.* A city reconstruction department spokesman followed with the comment: *it was very unkind to suggest that the council's plan for Penkhull was that of a council estate.*

In a Letter to the Editor dated 29th July 1965, Mr R. Carr of Hunters Way wrote referring to the comments of the Vicar: *Sir, the Vicar of Penkhull counsels patience over the redevelopment of Penkhull. The patience of some of the ratepayers of Penkhull has already been exhausted by the damage the city planners have done to existing owner-occupied property by the senseless rebuilding now being carried out at Brisley Hill.*

Included in the original plan for the redevelopment of the village there were two blocks of eight storey flats. I am not sure they were in the first draft for the village but in a press report dated the 26th October 1965 there is reference to an amended scheme for Penkhull which would include two blocks of flats, and that the meeting of the city council the following Thursday would be asked to approve the decision of compulsory purchase of properties so the buildings could go ahead. Once more the council is observed in this report to be secretive and divisive as the locations of properties to be compulsory purchased were not named. At the same time it was reported that a total of *15 dwellings and 17 garages, not included in the stage one of the original plan had all ready being built.* One critic replied that he *failed to understand at this point who was actually running the council?*

It was only four weeks following this report that the Evening Sentinel reported that a further amended plan had been prepared whereby the proposed blocks of flats had been withdrawn and that the full council would be asked to approve the new plans. Mr Jim Westwood, the Housing Committee chairman was not satisfied and stated that if the flats that were being built elsewhere in the city were a success, the council might feel justified to return once more to Penkhull. But even while all this was going on, there had been no public meeting to discuss the issue. However Mr Cholerton did express his desire to hold one in January so the committee could explain everything to local residents. Despite assurances, the meeting was not held until the 9th June 1966, two years almost to the day after the first properties were demolished. It was held in the old Senior

Public Meeting held on the 9th June 1966 at the old Senior School

School in Princes Road and presided over by the Lord Mayor of Stoke-on-Trent Alderman James Evans. Members of the public occupied every available seat and lined the walls as members of the council and officials explained the plans and answered questions.

The Lord Mayor responded to the anxiety which had been expressed about the plans and what they actually meant to residents but proclaimed that the city council *did not share their view* and continuing to state *that the central area of Penkhull, with its charm unequalled anywhere else in the city with its church and pubs had never been forgotten and if the proposals could be implemented with the co-operation of residents it would have been a worthwhile achievement.*

Councillor Cholerton told the meeting that *the Penkhull proposals were not revolutionary in any way. They provided for properties of medium density and also for the diversion of traffic. Mr Plant, the City Architect stated that the first 27 houses were ready to be built at a cost of £3,000 each, the costliest houses the council had ever built.* Various questions came from the floor and at times the speakers on the platform were interrupted to the point where Mr Cholerton rebuked one member of the public for *lack of dignity.*

Following a further public inquiry changes to the original plans would now include the demolition of 'The Views'. The city council decided that it required the land occupied by The Views for once demolished it would enable the strip of land at the top of Penkhull New Road to be increased in depth, thereby allowing council properties to built.

The Views
In the centre of Penkhull, a new battle of survival had

Rothwell Street comes down

Rothwell Street is next to be demolished

Last deliveries of fresh milk. End of Ten Row

The home of the Village Bobby comes down

Ten Row under demolition

Seven Row in Penkhull New Road

The rear of Ten Row

Seven Row, now down

Old Commercial Buildings. The Terrace Inn to the right

commenced in view of this latest twist by the city council. They appeared arrogant, they appeared dictatorial and starting lines were put into place. Two residents Deaconess B. Smee of No.2 and sisters Miss Lowe and Mrs Townsend of No.1 the Views decided to fight all the way to protect their homes. They rose to the challenge and, like so many groups or residents throughout the land, wanted to protect their little bit of England against the mighty power of the local authority. In September 1967, the council placed an order on The Views to have them demolished, and like the proposed plans for the village it went to public inquiry. It was here that the claim was made by the council that there was a large demand for rented properties within the Penkhull area as well as in other parts of the city.

The Evening Sentinel reported on the 8th September under the headline 'Sir Oliver's Old Home Must Go, say Council'. Despite protests from the Potteries Civic Society and individuals, the city council was pressing ahead to include The Views in their redevelopment plan for the village. The new scheme was a result of an earlier Ministry Appeal in 1962, which caused that plan to be abandoned because of fierce opposition. Even so, an amended plan introduced later that year made no mention for the acquisition of The Views and did not appear into the council's schedule until February 1966.

As a result of increased pressure upon the city council a Ministry of Housing and Local Government Inspector came from London to see the Georgian house for himself. The Inspector Mr A G Kelly following a visit to The Views held nine-hour public inquiry at Stoke Town Hall on the 26th September 1967.

At this inquiry the council officers made their case for demolition. Mr Burt, the Corporation's Housing Manger said *the area was needed to provide vital extra housing* and Mr James Jones, Assistant Deputy Planning Officer confirmed: *in my opinion the house has little to offer Penkhull. It has no great architectural value. We would be prepared to build a memorial to Sir Oliver to take its place* he concluded.

In addition to the two owner-occupiers of The Views, the Potteries Civic Society, the North Staffordshire Field Club, artist Mr Arnold Machin and a total of 585 petitioners made representations.

The Government Inspector took four months to submit his findings to the city council. The announcement was made on the 8th February 1968 in an eight hundred-word document. The conclusion reached was that The Views and the grounds immediately to the rear and front should be preserved on historical grounds and left in private ownership. However the Ministry agreed that the city council should be allowed to acquire some of the outbuildings and garden belonging to No.1 bordering Chamberlain Avenue for the purpose of erecting a number of pensioners' bungalows.

At the opening ceremony of the new houses in Rothwell Street on the 1st May 1968, the Chairman of the Housing Committee, Mr James Westwood could not resist the temptation to have a go at the critics who had censured the scheme because of their looks. *Houses are built to live in and not to look at,* he declared and continued. *I am of the opinion that these houses will provide excellent accommodation.* To make a bad situation worse, he then congratulated the city architects department for the way they had planned the development in conjunction with the church.

As expected a number of Letters to the Editor appeared in the Evening Sentinel. One such letter was from Werringtonian dated the 9th May 1968 *Sir, As an emigrant Lancastrian living thankfully outside the jurisdiction of your City Housing Committee, I read with dismay the statements made at the opening ceremony of the Penkhull housing scheme that houses are supposed to be lived in and not looked at. Councillor Westwood would do well to ponder on the fact that what his committee plan and build today will be the future town that your children inherit from you, and that visual appeal must be considered as well as functional.*

Conclusion

Looking back at what happened nearly fifty years ago and

SIR OLIVER'S OLD HOME MUST GO, SAY COUNCIL

Despite protests from the Potteries Civic Society and individuals, the City Council still intend to include The Views—birthplace of Sir Oliver Lodge in their redevelopment plan for part of Penkhull.

The council intend to state their case at a public inquiry on September 26th, when they will seek powe compulsorily. to purchase The Views and about an acre of adjoining land.

Plans for the site involve the demolition of Sir Oliver Lodge's old home.

The present scheme is the remains of a much earlier one, dating from 1962, which was severely cut by the Ministry and finally abandoned because of fierce local opposition.

Early in 1965, The Views was added to the Ministry list of "buildings of architectural and historical

The birthplace of Sir Oliver Lodge. The

Ministry reprieve Sir Oliver Lodge house Council over-ruled

The Penkhull birthplace of famousscientist Sir Oliver Lodge is to be spared from demolition in a Ministry decision that cripples part of the city's housing plans.

trying to balance the arguments. I suppose with a new incumbent, political influence, position, authority and socialist principles that change was in fact inevitable. Arthur Perry came with his new ideas and with his friends in high places on the city council who in those days had unlimited power without being challenged and because of his own political standing and influence was in a position to see the plans through to fruition.

Reflecting somewhat on the whole dilemma with deeply held concerns held by local residents and the intractable dogma of the city councillors more concerned to force their socialist principles *that one coat fits all* and bring down the aspirations of those living in Penkhull to a for more subservient community, the problem as I see it was that Penkhull became too old, just ten years too early.

Within that ten year period, the whole ideology and political

agenda had changed to that of conservation and preservation and I believe that if the architects and planners had put their heads together in the mid 70s we would have ended up with a village very different from that which we are left with today.

If the same situation arose now we would have certainly ended up with a unique village with houses built in architecture of around 200 years ago. There would be little neat gardens in the front; there wouldn't be the row of clumsy architectural deficient shops in Manor Court Street. Penkhull would have been rebuilt, but would have retained its old world village atmosphere that V.G. Aston knew and loved, as others did of that time.

If nothing else this chapter serves to record forever the disruptive and indiscriminate way the people of Penkhull were treated by those elected to represent them and will stand as a warning to other villages in our lands that for whatever reason may find themselves in a similar situation.

Yes, we still have an atmosphere. People still love living in Penkhull and at the end of the day, life is about people and people should have homes that reflect the needs of the time, but things could have been very different in the end.

Mr. F. A. Cholerton, Chairman of the City Reconstruction Committee indicates features of the village to the Lord Mayor, Alderman James Evans and other city officials before last night's public meeting on the redevelopment of Penkhull.

Council aim to retain village character,

The people who were responsible for the destruction of old Penkhull

Appendix i
Glossary of terms

Admittance: the procedure by which a new owner of a copyhold property became a tenant of the manor.

Advowson: the right of patronage of an ecclesiastical office, which during the subject period meant the right to present a clergyman to a benefice. The word is used for the appointment of a Rector to the parish of Stoke-upon-Trent.

Appurtenances: meaning anything appertaining to or belonging to a property.

Attorney: someone who is authorised to attend court to represent and act of behalf of an absent plaintiff.

Behoof: an ancient word, now obsolete, meaning use, benefit or advantage.

Constable: a local government official appointed for each township, or part thereof by the **Court Leet**. At times the name changed to that of **Headborough** or **Thirdborough.**

Demesne: land within the manor retained by the lord of the manor for his own use. However, villagers would be responsible for its cultivation etc. as a form of rental in the case of an absentee lord as in Penkhull.

Duchy of Lancaster: the part of the Sovereign's Crown estate which owned the manor.

Encroachments: properties which had been built upon land belonging to the Lord of the Manor, and thus encroached onto his property. These encroachments usually appeared on the road-side or upon the manor waste land.

Feather: A small piece of land.

Frankpledge: Frankpledge was the name of the part of the Anglo-Saxon system of local government which became regulated within the manorial Court Leet under the description of View of Frankpledge which dealt with no more than to hear the presentments to the court.

Headborough: see Constable.

Hereditaments: means any inheritable property.

Heriot: the name of the local tax payable to the Lord of the manor upon death of a copyhold tenant.

Land: A 'land' was a unit of the open field. It varied in size from one part of the country to another depending upon the nature of the soil. On light soils it was a full twenty-two yards wide but on heavy soils it may not have exceeded three yards. On flat lands it might run the full 'furrow-long' of 220 yards and more; on land sharply contoured or in awkward spots it may not have extended a quarter of that length. The term may also go under the name of 'strip' or 'strips'

Math: the OED defines a math as a mowing or the amount of a crop mowed, and it was also used as a term to describe an area of land by how long it took to mow which could have regional variations. A land could be valued or described as 'the two day math' or more or less.

Messuage: A dwelling house with some adjacent land. A word still in use today.

Paines or Paynes: the name given to what would now be described as fines imposed by a court.

Procurator of St. Mary: The Procurator was the legal representative of St. Giles old church at Newcastle. The Rector had three assistants, known as Chauntry priests, deputed to the Chauntries of St. Mary, St. Leonard, and St. Katherine, all situated within the great church. It was the procurators duty to collect the rents and other dues, including tithes and then transfer the profits to Rome. He was a man of some standing, well versed in the law, and would enjoy a considerable degree of wealth. In many cases land owners would leave a part of their estate to the church for prayers to be offered for the redemption of their souls after death.#

Reeve: an official of the Court Leet assisting with the administration of the manor.

Seisen: a term meaning possession rather than ownership which probably pre-dates the Norman Conquest and sometimes spelt seizen.

Socage: 'In socage' was a term to describe the tenure of a piece of land in feudal English property law by which the tenant lived on his lord's land and in return rendered to the lord a certain agricultural service or money rent. At the death of a tenant in socage (or

387

socager), the land went to his heir after a payment to the lord of a sum of money which in time became fixed at an amount equal to a year's rent.

Surrender: the procedure by which the owner of a copyhold property passed title to another on a permanent or temporary basis, either which could be subject to various conditions for various purposes.

Waste: The land in the manor which had never been brought into regular cultivation. This was often situated on the edges of the open fields or where the landscape was difficult to cultivate. Often taken up by people moving into the area and erecting cottages without permission from the Lord of Manor, squatters.

Appendix ii

Survey of Penkhull 1414

The aforesaid procurator holds a third of one acre of land of waste formerly held by the said John pays per annum at the same terms 2s 8d

Raph Gent holds one land and a half of demesne formerly held by the aforesaid John pays 3d

The aforesaid procurator holds half a land [1d] and one feather of demesne [½d] and one and a half lands of socage [1½d] formerly held by the aforesaid John pays 3d

Roger Fenton chaplain holds one quarter of one acre of land of waste [1½d] 2½ lands of socage [2d] formerly held by the aforesaid John pays 3‰ d

Thomas Bothes holds one half-land of demesne formerly held by the aforesaid John pays ‰ d

John Bothes holds one half-land of demesne formerly held by the aforesaid John pays 1d

John Nikson holds 2 lands of socage formerly held by the aforesaid John pays 2d

Henry de Lyme holds 3 halflands of socage formerly held by the aforesaid John pays 1‰ d

John Bateson holds one land of socage formerly held by the aforesaid John pays 1d

William Skydby holds one half-land of socage formerly held by the aforesaid John pays ‰ d

William de Lake holds one half-land of socage formerly held by the aforesaid John pays ‰ d

William Pesedale holds one half-land of socage formerly held by the aforesaid John pays ‰ d

Henry Bateson holds one half-land of demesne formerly held by the aforesaid John pays 1d

John Bateson holds one land of socage formerly held by the aforesaid John pays 1d

Thomas Bothes holds one oxen [4d] and 5 lands of demesne [10d] and one quarter of one acre of waste [1½d] 4

lands of waste [2d] 19 lands of socage [19d] and one half-land of socage ½ was formerly held by the aforesaid John pays 3s 1d

John Milwarde holds one acre of land of demesne [11½d] one cottage [1d] 42 lands and a half of socage [3s 6½d] pays 4s 7d

John Bothes holds one land of socage formerly held by John Milwarde pays 1d

Henry de Lyme holds one land of socage formerly held by Robert de Weson pays 1d

John Bateson holds one quarter of one acre of land of waste formerly held by the aforesaid Robert pays 1‰ d

The same John holds one feather of socage formerly held by the aforesaid Robert pays 1d

Roger Gent holds one land of demesne formerly held by the aforesaid Robert pays ... d

John Nicson holds half a messuage [5d] 18 lands except one feather [17¾d], 2½ lands of demesne [5d], one cottage [1d], half a land of socage [½d] and one feather [½d] formerly held by Roger Nicson pays 2s 5‰ d

Alan Bateson holds 4 lands and one feather formerly held by the aforesaid Roger pays 4... d

Roger Gent holds 2 lands of demesne formerly held by the same Roger pays 4d

John Tupp holds one quarter of an acre of land of waste formerly held by the aforesaid Roger pays 2d

Thomas son of Henry Bothes holds a parcel and one feather of waste formerly held by the aforesaid Roger pays 1... d

William Tyttensor holds one parcel of waste formerly held by the same Roger pays 1d

John Machen holds one cottage formerly held by Thomas Machen pays 1d

John Nicson holds one messuage [3d] 11½ lands of socage [11½d] half an acre of demesne except one feather [5½d] formerly held by John Bothes pays 20d

Roger Gent holds the twelfth part of an acre of land and one feather of demesne formerly held by the aforesaid John pays 1‰ d

The same Roger holds half an acre of land of demesne formerly held by John Nicson pays 6d

Roger Fenton chaplain holds one messuage, 16 lands of socage and 4 lands of demesne formerly held by William Wroo pays 20½d

William Pesedale holds 2 lands of socage [2d] and one rood of waste [1½d] formerly held by the aforesaid

Roger Fenton holds 2 lands [2d] and one feather of socage [¼d] and a half acre of waste [3d] formerly held by the said William pays 5¾d

The Procurator of the Blessed Mary holds half a land of socage formerly held by the aforesaid William and pays ½d

William Tyttensor holds one land of demesne [2d] and half a land of socage [½d] formerly held by the said William pays 2½d

John Bateson holds one land of demesne [2d] and half a land of socage [½d] formerly held by the said William pays ½d

William de Meer holds 2 lands of socage formerly held by the aforesaid William pays with 2d for land recently brought under cultivation 4d

William Atte lake holds one feather of socage formerly held by the aforesaid William pays ¼d

Roger Gent holds half a land of demesne formerly held by the said William pays 1d

Roger Peyntor holds 3 feathers of demesne formerly held by the aforesaid William pays 1½d

John son of Henry Bothes holds one feather of demesne formerly held by the aforesaid William pays ½d

The Procurator of the Blessed Mary holds one acre and the fourth part of one acre and one feather of demesne [15¾d] 3 cottages [3¾d] 16 lands of socage land [16d] at 1d; 6 lands of socage land at a halfpenny formerly held by Personilla Mason pays 3s 2½d

John Hochon holds one and a half acres and one feather of land of waste formerly held by the said Personilla pays 10d

Nicholas Potter pays 23d

Memorandum re-Manor lease renewal 1781 Memorandum

The following memorandum is attached to the Duchy of Lancaster's plans dated 1777 which show the location of all the wasthold properties belonging to the Duchy in this Manor. The plans give every property a reference number, and the key to these references is provided by schedules which list each property, its area, annual rent and the name of the occupier.

The Lease of these premises was renewed to the Right honourable Granville Leveson Earl Gower on the 2nd day of March 1781 for 31 years to 1812; and although the buildings erected and lands enclosed from the waste appear by the foregoing survey to be of the improved annual value of £275 10s 8d, yet they were rated on setting the fine at no more than one tenth part of that rent, being equal to 45s per acre per annum for the land itself. The reasons for this reduction were that the buildings have been erected on the waste by and at the expense of the reputed owners thereof, with the sanction as well of the officers and lessees of the Crown, as of the Inhabitants having right of common on the waste, all of whom promoted and encouraged such erections for the increase of population whereby the Manufacture of potters ware and china lately set on foot might be carried on to public advantage, and which is now like to become of general importance.

The inhabitants would not have suffered the waste but has been converted to such uses for the benefit of the Crown; they permitted it for the increase of trade and commerce. The officers of the crown or the lessee could not without great approve or exact the value of the buildings in rent, nor in justice more than the worth of the ground. To have demanded more would not only have been injurious, but the utter ruin of man who had borrowed to enable them to build, depending on their industry to repay it. It would also have greatly obstructed the future increase of the manufactory. At present every body who chooses is permitted to build on the waste on payment of a small acknowledgement to the Lessee.

As to the Lessee himself, it would have been highly dishonourable in him to have demanded the Value of these buildings in rent, after having permitted them to be erected.

It was on a full consideration of these circumstances, and after many conferences with Thomas Gilbert Esq. on behalf of the lessee, that the Duchy Officers thought it just to value the premises upon this Renewal at the value of the land only, and the more especially as the manufactory is but lately established and the buildings new, and many of them not yet finished.

	£	s	d
	8	15	0
	49	5	0
	40	0	0
	275	10	8
Total	**£373**	**10**	**8**

In process of time, it may not be unjust to increase the rate or value, but it would be highly injurious to the country to discourage the manufacturers in the present infant state of their undertaking.

As to the casual profits of the manor, they do not on a fair calculation produce more than the rents of £8 1s and 14s reserved for the same by the Lease.

The quit rents also amount to just the sum reserved for the Castle Manor and Royalties, viz. £49 5s

The collieries on a real survey were estimated at £40 p.a.

The real improved value of the Incroachments rated on this renewal at only £27.1s

Penkhull Church and Churchyard Petition for Consecration.
To the Right Reverend Father in God, James by Divine permission Lord Bishop of Lichfield.

The Reverend Thomas Webb Minton of Darlington in the County of Durham, do humbly present unto your Lordship, that the population of the Parish of Stoke-upon-Trent and within your Lordships Diocese amounts to thirty six thousand persons and that the existing Parish Church and the Chapel within the said Parish of Stoke-upon-Trent do not afford accommodation for one third of the inhabitants of the said parish to attend divine service therein according to the Liturgy of the United Church of England and Ireland, which fact is verified by a certificate under the hands of George Lynam an Architect and in order to provide further accommodation and to permit the public worship of Almighty God according to the Liturgy, I have under the powers and provisions of a certain Act of Parliament passed of His late Majesty King William the Fourth instituted An Act to amend and render more effectual An Act passed in the seventh years of the reign of his late Majesty entitled An Act to amend the Acts for building and promoting the building of additional churches in the populous parishes duly given notice to William Moor Esq. Frederick Wright Tomlinson Esq. William Taylor Copeland Esq. and the Reverend John Wickes Tomlinson, Clerk being the Patron of the Parish Church of Stoke-upon-Trent and to your Lordship as informing of my intention to build and endow a Chapel in the Township of Penkhull with Boothen in the Parish of Stoke-upon-Trent and to provide the sum requisite for the repairs of the same, independent of and in addition to a further sum of five pounds percent of the sum of the Chapel and that such Chapel should contain sittings for five hundred persons of which one third at least should be set apart and appropriated for ever as free sittings pursuant to the requirements of the said Act, I further represent unto your Lordship that the said William Moore, Frederick Wright Tomlinson and William Taylor Copeland hath not entered into the Bond required under the said Act within the time specified and by virtue of a certain Deed of Conveyance being the date the third day of October instant the most Nobel George Granville, Duke of Sutherland did hereby freely and voluntarily and without any valuable consideration grant, convey and release and for ever enfranchise unto John Smith of Springfields, Herbert Minton of Hartshill and John Goodwin of New Lodge all within the Township of Penkhull in the Manor of Newcastle there hairs or assigns all and singular the Parcel or Plots of land partly of Copyhold Tenure and partly waste lying within the village having an oval shape outlined upon the plan or may drawn on the said Deed, and includes altogether about three thousand, two hundred and forty three yards, to hold the same as joint tenants upon Trust to cause the said land together with the building thereon erected to be with all urgent dispatch consecrated as a Church or Chapel with Churchyard or Burial Ground thereto and the same to be for ever thereafter devoted to Ecclesiastical purposes.

I further represent unto your Lordship that aided by public and private Subscription and a Grant of four hundred and ten pounds from the Lichfield Diocesan Church Extension Society, I have built upon part of the said plot of land a new church containing within the walls sixty one feet in length and twenty five feet in width and a gallery at the West end and the same is furnished with a communion table of the Holy Sacraments, Pulpit, Reading Desk, Pews and seats and sitting places a font for baptising children a bell and all things necessary for a Church, and which church together with the land around hath been enclosed by a wall or strong fence and ready for Consecration and the said Thomas Webb Minton further represents unto your Lordship that I have provided a sum of one thousand pounds by way of endowment of the said church, to be placed in trust to the Queens Anne Bounty, for the augmentation and the maintenance of the Poor Clergy. I further have invested the sum of ninety pounds for the purchase of Capital Stock by way of a repair fund for the said church.

A further sum of four pounds, ten shillings is intended to be reserved annually out of the Pew Rents, to be added to the repair fund capital, and I further represent unto your Lordship that one hundred and two sittings in the body or ground floor and the whole of the sittings in the gallery being one hundred and seventy and containing together two hundred and seventy two sittings are to be set apart as free and open seats and sitting places, or to be let as such low rents as your Lordship may direct, and that three pews in the church containing twelve sittings are to set apart for the use of the Minister, his servants and the Churchwardens respectfully and that the remainder of the pews being fifty five in number and containing two hundred and sixteen sittings are to be let apart as a Stipend for the maintenance of the Minister of the said church according to the sale of Pew Rents to be approved by your Lordship and to be deposited in your Lordships Registry.

I therefore do hereby promise and bow before Almighty God that the said newly erected Church and Churchyard or Burial Ground thereto shall not be hereafter put to any purpose or secular uses whatsoever, and I earnestly desire your Lordship to dedicate and consecrate the said Church by the name of St.Thomas the Apostle for the worship of Almighty God. I beseech your Lordship that upon these conditions and promises hereto made, I have subscribed my name and which I request may be registered and remain upon your records in your Registry of your Lordships Diocese will be pleased to proceed in your Holy Function, dated this (blank) day of October in the year of our Lord, one thousand eight hundred and forty two.

Thomas Webb Minton of Darlington
by Herbert Minton

Proposed Parish of Penkhull dated 1843

Whereas it hath been represented unto us John by Divine permission Lord Bishop of Lichfield that under the powers of a certain "Act of Parliament" passed in the session of the first and second years of the reign of his later Majesty King William the Fourth, entitled "An Act" to amend and render more effectual and Act made in the seventh and eighth years of the Reign of His late Majesty King George the Fourth entitled "An Act to amend the Act for Building and promoting of additional churches in populous parishes". A church or Chapel at Penkhull in the Parish of Stoke-upon-Trent, in the County of Stafford and within the Diocese of Lichfield hath been built and endowed with the respective sums for the repairs, thereof duly provided as required by the said Act of Parliament and hath been subsequently consecrated by the name of Saint Thomas the Apostle.

And Whereas we have the Petitioned by the Reverend Thomas Webb Minton of Darlington, in the County of Durham, the Patron and the Reverend Samuel Minton the Perpetual Curate of Penkhull in the County of Stafford to assign a District to the same under the authority of the said Act of Parliament so far as regards to the Visitation of the Sick and other pastoral duties and determined whether Churchings and Baptisms should be solemnised and performed in the said Church. AND WHEREAS the consent of the Reverenced John Wickes Tomlinson, the Rector of Stoke-upon-Trent hath been obtained to the assignment thereof. Now know all men, that We John by Divine permission, Lord Bishop of Lichfield under the authority of the above recited Act of Parliament, do hereby assign the following district to the said Chapel of St.Thomas the Apostle in Penkhull in the County of Staffordshire and within our Diocese "(namely)"

Commencing on the South and beginning from that Close of land called The Meadow and numbered as in the plan by the new District of Hartshill on the west by the Parish of Newcastle on the south west by the Parish of Trentham and by the south west side of the Turnpike Road from Newcastle to Trentham as far as the point in the said road opposite to where the foot road therefrom passes through the Great and Little Holden from that aforesaid point marked P in the plan it is bounded by the said footpath as far as the said road from Penkhull to Penkhull Hollow where the boundary crosses that road and runs thence through the flat, the Thistly or White Hough and the Eight Acre Field to the road from Penkhull to Trentham. There it runs along the west side of the said road which it crosses in a straight line with the east boundary between the Boothen Wood Field and Bearshill from that point it is bounded by Boothen Wood Field by a line crossing between Big and Barkers Meadow parallel to the road from Trentham to Stoke and joining the east or south east fence of Far Hunters Croft thence by Big and Barkers Meadow, Upper Barn Field, Upper Vine Field, The Croft and Bowling Green, Upper Vine Meadow, The Moore and a line crossing between Moor and the Waste a line drawn from south eastward of Dowdies Meadow, through Longfield to the west fence of Hob Croft and by a line from west fence thereof to a road from Honey Wall to Stoke which road the boundary crosses and passes to the west close behind the houses along the said road being bounded further by Big Meadow, Great Long Hough, Square Piece, Upper Slang and Lower Slang, which adjoins the Meadow first named at the beginning of this description and which district is more particularly described in the map or plan hereto annexed and tinted pink. And We do hereby direct and order so far as by Law, We may or can that the Minister or Curate thereof for the time being shall and may officiate in the visitation of the sick and other pastoral duties within the said district and also that Churchings and Baptisms that may be Solemnised and performed therein be duly kept for the same.

In Witness whereof, we have hereto set our Hand and Episcopal Seal this twelfth day of October in the year of our Lord, one thousand eight hundred and forty four.

Letter from Dennis Aston, the son of V.G. talking about his memories of 'Penkhull Belles'

Thank you for your two letters requesting our presence at the get together of the Penkhull Belles. I regret that it will be impossible because of her frailty now 82 years of age. Even writing letters has become burdensome to her and that's why I am corresponding with you. Hello Bunty and all the gathered old friends. Mother, although old in years has a remarkably clear picture in her mind of the names of the Belles and all those associated with the shows behind the scenes, and it gives her much pleasure to be able to reach them all in this way.

Although father and she worked like trojans to perfect the performances she admits that nothing could have been achieved without such people for instance as Tom Meiklejohn who stage managed the whole shows and provided those elaborate 'props' so needful for the professional touch. I remember quite clearly the fountain placed on the stage with jets of water rising from it while the dancers cavorted hither and thither in flimsy costume - the coloured lights meantime high up in the wings, adding to the gaiety and loveliness of that extraordinary scene. However Mr. Meiklejohn managed in the small space allowed putting on such a splendid spectacular passes my comprehension!

But of course mother had worked hard for months with the children and it was the number in the programme entitled 'The Children's Ballet' which always brought warm applause from the audience. Bunty and Irene Phillips were her speciality dancers. I remember Bunty very well a name which comes back to my mind straight away from the distant past. It is so very nice that she is now able to meet all her childhood friends once more. Another young dancer who had great promise was Peggy Skellern, who now I believe has a dancing school of her own at Penkhull. Well, she made her debut at Penkhull. Vera Hassle (Mrs. Evans) helped mother with the training of the children; she had charm and great capacity. Mother says she owed a great debt of gratitude to the ladies who worked for weeks as a Sewing Party, making the costumes for the children. This lady's sowing group was led by Mrs. Phillips the mother of Bunty and Irene with other ladies of the parish. Apparently these frocks had to be pressed and to save a great deal of labour of heating the old irons so Miss. Charlesworth from the corner sweet shop in Princes Road volunteered to sit on them and if any of you remember dear Miss. Charlesworth, you'll know why no irons were necessary.

It goes without saying that the Belles were the star attraction with their sprightly dances, kicking high their graceful legs to those wonderful tunes. Thank heavens we were spared the dreary dirges that go for popular music today. Some of these tunes linger in my mind to-day - Give yourself a pat of the Back; Happy days are here again; Easter Parade; Spread a little Happiness; There's something about a soldier and so on. But those girls were great and what is more important for a troupe of dancers; they were 'smashers'.

Unfortunately for me I was just too young to be really in the act. I was still at school and although I was about 15 or 16 years of age, you weren't considered worth bothering about. (From a young ladies point of view until you were say 19 or over). Sadly I had to admire their beauty at a distance, but I can picture them in my minds eye as it were at this very moment. I don't think I have seen any of them since I left Penkhull 36 years ago except for one of you - Grace Ellis and that was some years back - she hardly had changed and she was still as beautiful as ever.

Mother received great help with the training of the Belles from Phyllis Beresford and Ida and Beryl Lawton. I remember well the Dobson girls Jean & Peggy because their father Percy Dobson was churchwarden for many years at Penkhull. Oh and there were Unis Dobson and I seemed to remember something about her and a motor bike? Then there was Freda wasn't there (Grace's Sister)

And then of course there was the originator of the whole thing my inimitable father 'V.G.' a man of very many talents. Not only did he devise and write those shows, but he also composed much of the incidental music and scored all the orchestral parts with his own hand which was a mammoth task in itself. often all this effort coupled with his work as vicar of the parish laid him low, and on more than one occasion he was in bed with illness. Most of the members of the 'Belles', whether actors, dancers, stage hands, seamstress etc. were practising Christians and I can recollect vividly the great numbers who attended the Sunday services then - it was most inspiring.

The shows didn't all consist of dancing and singing - another name while thinking of singing Hilda Hesbrook, she sang most attractively. As I said it wasn't all dancing and singing and plenty of comedy too. There was Billy Bishop - he was a first rate comic who always earned generous applause for the way he galvanised the show into uproarious laughter. Ah! There are many other faces I can see but the names just won't come.

What happy days. They pass away before you realise it. Some have made a success of their lives others, alas a mess, but successful or otherwise it must be joyous for you to unite in fellowship once more and chat over old times. For me personally, I'd rather just remember you all as I can so easily as you were in your prime, full of vigour, charm and beauty. Perhaps that's how you would have it with mother.

How good of you Winnie and your friends to arrange this reunion. I and mother wish you all a most enjoyable evening. Let's keep those happy memories green in our thoughts. She sends her deepest love and affection to all of you and like the song that one of you sang on one of those unforgettable shows she would say.

There's nothing left for me of days that used to be, they're just a memory among my souvenirs

And that about sums it up. Regards to all my old friends.   May 1975

1701 Parish Listing for
Stoke-upon-Trent

	Age
Thomas Allen, Rector	29
Anne Allen, his wife	27
William Hyde	33
Uriah Leigh	26
Margaret Buckstones Servants	45
Elizabeth Terrick	23
Margery Allen, widow	62
Margery Allen, her daughter	25
Thomas Bourne, Schoolmaster	19
Mary Tittensor, Servant	29
John Ward, Curate	35
Michael Ward, Widower	83
John Poulson, Clerke	28
Margaret Elkin, Servant	19
Margaret Sale Spinsters	55
Elizabeth Sale and twins	55
Phillip Fenton .	5
John Fenton Parish Boys	3
John Swoaringon	37
Hellin Swoaringon, his wife	32
Mary Swoaringon)	6
Elizabeth Swoaringon Children)	4
Newton Swoaringon)	½year
Elizabeth Mills, servant	20
Sara Cavanaugh, Sojourn	28
John Leigh, Blacksmith	36
Ellin Leigh, his wife	32
John Leigh	12
Ellin Leigh)	7
Sarah Leigh Children)	4
William Leigh)	1
John Shawe, Musician	38
Anne Shawe, his wife	34
Anne Shawe)	11
Elizabeth Shawe Children)	9
John Shawe)	7
Ellin Shawe)	2
Edward Shawe	½year
Sara Class, widow	76
Mary Whittaker, pauper	20
John Bird, Baker	34
Dorothy Bird, his wife	35
John Bird, young child	½year
Margery Thornton, pauper	13
Henry Cooper, widower	92
Mary Ratcliffe, widow	55

	Age
Elizabeth Cooper Spur. ejus.	19
Henry Cooper, Mary's nephew	15
Elizabeth Hatton, widow	64
Jane Hatton	31
Elizabeth Hatton children	20
Abigail Hatton, spur. Jane's	5
William Hatton	2weeks
Robert Austin	32
Elizabeth Austin, his wife	35
William Proston, her son	9
Richard Fenton, widower Yeoman	70
Richard Fenton, batchelor	32
Catherine Fenton, servant	30
William Thomas, Cutler	70
Elnor Thomas, his wife	75
Anne Thomas, daughter	19
Ellin Skellott, single woman	54
Frances Gerard, widow & pauper	72
Mary Sutton, widow	50
Paul Sutton, her son	15
Mary Walton, widow	60
Jane Walton, her daughter	29
Joseph Ward	42
Mary Ward, his wife	38
Joseph Ward)	6
Thomas Ward)	4
Ellin Ward Children)	3
John Ward)	1
John Knight, Weaver	32
Alice Waste, servant	25
Anne Bird, widow	64
Thomasin Butterton, widow	62
Samson Hazells	38
Margery Hazells, his wife	32
Mary Hazells)	10
Maria Hazells)	9
Sara Hazells Children)	7
Richard Hazells)	5
Dorothy Hazells)	4
William Hazells)	2
Henry Stevenson	42
Mary Stevenson	11
Sarah Stevenson	3
Thomas Stevenson	5
Pricilla Slany, widow	57
Pricilla Slany)	24

Walter Slany Children	)	17
Elizabeth Bird, widow		34
Thomas Bird		12
Mary Bird		10
William Bird		7
Anne Bird		5
Daniel Bird		3
William Leigh, pauper		29
Ursulah Leigh, his wife		27
William Leigh their child		2
Joseph Hewitt		38
Anne Hewitt, his wife		50
John Hewitt, their son		18
John Fox		51
Catherine Fox, his wife		43
John Fox		19
Thomas Fox	)	6
Catherine Fox Children	)	13
James Fox	)	11
William Fox	)	7
Elizabeth Standley, single woman		60
John Mare, Batchelor		52
Ellin Mare, widow		54
Lydia Pipper, servant		20
Thomas Tittensor		38
Alice Tittensor, his wife		40
Margaret Tittensor		8
Elizabeth Tittensor		5
Mary Tittensor		3
Jane Tittensor, servant		23
Margaret Tittensor, widow		64
Margaret Tittensor, her daughter		28
Elizabeth Woolf, widow		42
Margery Alerton, single woman		19
Thomas Wildblood		44
Mary Wildblood, his wife		40
Mary Wildblood	)	10
Hannah Wildblood Children	)	4
Elizabeth Wildblood	)	1
Samuel Astbury		28
Elizabeth Alsop servants		30
Mary Dawson		19
Thomas Blakeman, widower		58
Ellin Blakeman		25
John Blakeman		20
Thomas Blakeman		17
Aaron Blakeman Children	)	15
Moses Blakeman	)	12
Alice Blakeman	)	10
John Phillips, weaver		61
Ellin Phillips, his wife		61
Anne Phillip s.	)	20
Sarah Phillips, Children	)	18
Anne Hassall, widow		75
Elizabeth Spencer, widow		80
Jane Browning, illegit		16
Robert Nelson		46
Mary Nelson, his wife		42
Catherine Nelson		10
Margaret Nelson Children		6
Mary Nelson	)	4
John Coleclough, collier		42
Anne Coleclough, his wife		35
John Coleclough, his son		9
Susanna Adams, widow		71
Richard Slany		44
Mary Slany, his wife		43
William Slany Children	)	12
John Slany	)	2
Thomas Doody		68
J oane Doody, his wife		68
Elizabeth Doody Servants		19
Jane Doody		15
John Bowyer Yeoman		66
Anne Bowyer, his wife		49
Jolm Bowyer .	)	23
Anne Bowyer Children	)	19
Thomas Walker Servants		29
Mary Proctor		23
Mary Thornton, single woman		17
Richard Buckstones		24
Elizabeth Bqckstones, his wife		28
Thomas Buckstones, child		2
Thomas Fenton, pauper		10
Thomas Astbury		30
CatherinvAstbury, his wife		32
Catherine Astbury	)	6
Samuel Astbury Children	)	5
Elizabeth Astbury	)	5 months
William Shawe		50
Susanna Shawe, his wife		60

Name		Age
Ralph Adams		34
Mary Adams, his wife		35
Bridgett Adams	)	7
Elizabeth Adams Children	)	5
Ralph Adams	)	2
Lydia Tittensor … Robti		51
Hanna Tittensor	)	19
Lydia Tittensor Children	)	16
Mary Tittensor	)	14
Thomas Dale, yeoman		69
Margery Dale, his wife		56
Thomas Dale, gentleman		28
Mary Dale .	)	22
Margery Dale Children	)	18
Edward Quaile		28
Joseph Skelton, servants		20
Mary Ankors		20
Mathew Clewlow		26
Elizabeth Clewlow, his wife		34
James Clewlow, son		2
Mary Edge, her child, illegit.		7
Ralph Bourne Yeoman		70
Anne Boume, his wife		72
Alice Dale, widow		80
Joshua Bourne Sojournes		22
Ellin Bourne		9
William Bourne Servants		17
Anne Cooke		30
Roger Tittensor		54
Anne Tittensor, his wife		34
Thomas Tittensor	)	10
John Tittensor	)	8
Mary Tittensor	)	6
Joseph Tittensor Chlldrcn	)	4
William Tittensor	)	2
Daniel Edwards Yeoman		44
Jane Edwards, his wife		42
Deborah Edwards	)	16
Hanna Edwards	)	15
Jane Edwards	)	13
Catherine Edwards	)	11
John Edwards Children	)	10
Thomas Edwards	)	8
Richard Edwards	)	7
Elijah Edwards	)	5
Elizabeth Edwards	)	4
William Edwards	)	2
James Foster		34
Susanne Foster, his wife		30
James Foster	)	11
Peter Foster	)	9
J osias Foster Children	)	7
Elijah Foster	)	5
William Foster	)	3
Moses Foster	)	1
Elizabeth Dixon, widow		42
Elizabeth Dixon	)	14
Anne Dixon Children	)	9
Mary Ward, widow		61
Elizabeth Ward		23
Anne Ward	)	19
Hannah Ward Children	)	15
Elizabeth Brett, pauper		57
J ohn Terrick		33
ElizabethTerrick, his wife		33
John Tarrick .	)	4
William Terrick Children	)	2
Ellen Terrick, widow		58
Daniel Parton Servants		20
Sarah Haines		21
Thomas Knapper		29
Jane Knapper, his wife		26
Anne Knapper .	)	3
Mary Knapper Children	)	1
Mary Cooper, widow		30
John Cooper, her son		4
Thomas Edge, widower		74
Hugh Edge		32
Sarah Edge, his wife		30
Steven Edge, Spur: Joan Edge		11
John Tittensor		56
Elizabeth Tittensor, his wife		38
Elizabeth Tittensor	)	6
John Tittensor.	)	4
Francis Tittensor Chlldren)		2
Richard Muchell		73
Elizabeth Muchell, his wife		52
Elizabeth Muchell,		9
Mary Muchell		4
John Knapper		65
Anne Knapper, his wife		60
Roger Townsend		59
Mary Townsend, his daughter		36
Thomas Elkin		54
Alice Elkin, his wife		44
Mary Elkin	)	12

Alice Elkin Children) 7
John Elkin) 4

William Proctor, apprentice 18
Margaret Johnson, 84

Richard Smith 60
Margaret Smith, his wife 60
Catherine Smith) 30
Robert Smith.) 27
Edward Smith Children) 27
Richard Smith) 24

Richard Hammersley, farmer 30
Sara Hammersley, his wife 23
Richard Hammersley .) 2
Mary Hammersley Children ½ year

William Ormes 34
Elnor Proudlove, servant 29

William Podmore 58
. . . Podmore, his wife 61
Mary Podmore, daughter 26

Richard Hewitt 37
Mary Hewitt
Annie Hewitt Children) 2
Richard Hewitt)
Elizabeth Degg, servant

Thomas Bloore 29
Elizabeth Bloore, his wife 28
William Bloore) 6
Thomas Bloore Children) 4
John Bloore) 4 months

John Pattison 34
Anne Eardley, servant 22

Ralph Bucknall 60
Elizabeth Bucknall, his wife 43

Ellin Woodnott 55
Elizabeth Woodnott, her daughter 22

Edward Baggiley 31
Margaret Baggiley, his wife 37
Mary Baggiley 8
Margaret Baggiley 3
Thomas Baggiley ½ year

William Barratt 35
Elizabeth Barratt, his wife 36
Elizabeth Barratt, child 5
Elizabeth Barratt, widow 61

John Barratt 25
Mary Barratt, his wife 34
William Barratt, child 5 months

John Foster 32
Sarah Foster, his wife 28
Bridgett Foster, child

Laurence Simpcock Yeoman 34
Dorothy Simpcock, his wife 30
Thomas Simpcock) 10
Samuel Simpcock) 8
Laurence Simpcock Children) 3
Dorothy Simpcock) ½ year
Benjamin Wesson) 22
Thomas Sale Servants) 20
Mary Lilley) 17

Thomas Ratcliffe 42
Joane Ratcliffe, his wife 39
Elizabeth Ratcliffe) 14
Samuel Ratcliffe) 12
Alice Ratcliffe Children) 7
Thomas Ratcliffe) 3
William Ratcliffe) ½ year

James Ratcliffe 70
Dorothy Ratcliffe, his wife 62
Elizabeth Ratcliffe Children) 25
Rebecca Ratcliffe) 18

Sampson Skelton, pauper 81

Richard Coleclough 56
Jane Coleclough, his wife 29
Mary Coleclough, daughter 3

Mary Massey, widow 45
Elizabeth Massey) 14
Anne Massey Children) 11
Catherine Massey) 5

John Hollinshead 29
Alice Hollinshead, his wife 24
Thomas Hollinshead) 4
John Hollinshead Children) 2
Anne Allen, virgo, sojourn 20

Thomas Poole 49
Martha Poole, his wife 57

William Reinolds 46
Elizabeth Reinolds, his wife 40
Catherine Reinolds) 8
Margaret Reinolds Children) 5
Amey Reinolds) 3
Mary Reinolds single woman 32

Jolm Reinolds, spun her son		12
Elizabeth Johnson, widow		51
John Johnson	)	21
Sarah Johnson	)	19
Elizabeth Johnson Children	)	13
Marjory Johnson	)	8
Thomas Jolmson	)	5
John Johnson, pauper		80
Dorothy Johnson, his wife		76
William Fowler		48
Elizabeth Fowler, his wife		52
William Cartlitch		36
Margaret Cartlitch, his wife		34
Parnel Cartlitch, daughter		
Elizabeth Hemmings, widow		45
Margaret Wright, single woman		50
Thomas Barker		45
Catherine Barker, his wife		36
William Barker	)	16
Thomas Barker	)	12
Richard Barker Children	)	10
John Barker	)	5
Daniel Barker	)	3
Catherine Barker	)	5 months
John Barnshawe		45
Ester Barnshawe, his wife		38
Ester Barnshawe		15
John Barnshawe	)	13
Elizabeth Barnshawe Children	)	10
Hannah Barnshawe	)	7
William Barnshawe	)	4
Charles Bamshawe	)	5 months
John Berrisforde		36
Mary Berrisforde, his wife		34
Mary Berrisforde	)	10
Anne Berrisforde	)	8
John Berrisforde Children	)	6
Robert Berrisforde	)	3
Samuel Berrisforde	)	½year
Edmund Clitheroe		32
Sarah Clitheroe, his wife		30
John Clitheroe, child		3
Thomas Bell		32
Jane Bell, his wife		31
Anne Bell	)	6
Elizabeth Bell Children	)	4
Thomas Bell	)	1

Edmund Clitheroe	69
John Clitheroe, his son	29

ANCIENT MESSUAGES IN PENKHULL : as described in various records for the doing service for the Office of Reeve of the Manor

Ref.	Year	Source	Details
-	1579	Fenton Bk	[blank]
-	1582	Fenton Bk	[blank]
10	1585	Fenton Bk	Robert Tittensor for his messuage in Penckhull.
11	1588	Fenton Bk	John Bradshawe's house in Penkhull.
3 ??	1591	Fenton Bk	Roger Machin Senr for Wood's house in Penkhull.
13 ?	1594	Fenton Bk	Randall Boothes for one of his 2 services in Penkhull.
15	1597	Fenton Bk	John Hitchen for his house up in the towne in Penkhull
16	1600	Fenton Bk	William Turner for Hitchen's house in the lane in Penkhull
-	1603	Fenton Bk	[blank]
1	1606	Fenton Bk	Thomas Tittensor up in the towne for his messuage in Penckhull. [corrected from 1605]
2	1609	Fenton Bk	Roger Machin for one of his messuages in Penckhull, vizt Bate Lake house
16 ??	1612	Fenton Bk	William Turner for his owne messuage in Penckhull
6	1614	Fenton Bk	John Boothes hired by John Brett Esq. to serve for Bowyer's house in Penckhull
7	1618	Fenton Bk	Thomas Fenton for John Doodie's messuage in Penckhull
4 ??	1621	Fenton Bk	Roger Dale for Willm Turner.

Prior to 1624, the subsequent rotation within Penkhull of messuages' service as Reeve is not obvious

Ref.	Year	Source	Details
8	1624	Fenton Bk	Mr. Jo^n Terrick for Badeley's messuage in Penckhull served by Cranage Wilcockson.
9	1627	Fenton Bk	Roger Dale for Jo^n Dale's messuage in Penckhull
10	1630	Fenton Bk	Willm Hill for Thomas Tittensor's messuage downe in the Towne.
11	1633	Fenton Bk	Henry Shawe hired for Henry Stevenson to serve for Bradshawe's house & land in Penckhull.
12	1636	Fenton Bk	Nicholas Woodcocke for Nickson's house and land in Penkhull.
13	1639	Fenton Bk	Willm Hill hired by [written above- Mr Jo^n Terrick] Roger Machin of Bate Lake & others to serve for one of the houses & lands called Boothe's land in Penckhull.
14	1642	Fenton Bk	Roger Machin of the Greenhead for one of Boothe's his service in Penkhull vizt for an ancient meese place called Duncott Leigh. This now belongs to Mr John Fenton of Shelton.
15	1648	Fenton Bk	John Simkin for one of the Hichen's [written above - Hichen of the greene] his land in Penckhull now Richard Huett's house. Now sold again to Thomas Astbury.
16	1651	Fenton Bk	Roger Dale for the other Hichen's land in Penckhull vizt Hichen's in the lane since Turner's in the lane & now Thomas Dale's.
17	1654	Fenton Bk	Robert Machin for Wood's house in Penckhull (alias Machin in the lane) served by Thomas Doody being one of his 4 services in Penckhull.

Dates for service as Reeve by Penkhull messauges in 1657 and subsequently is given DL30/516

Ref.	Year	Source	Details
1	1657	Fenton Bk	Thomas Tittensor for his messuage in Penckhull up in the Towne, served by Thomas Machin of
2	1660	Fenton Bk	Robert Machin for Bate Lake house being one of his 4 services, served by Thomas Doody.
3	1663	Fenton Bk	Robert Machin for his messuage wch formerly was his grandfather's wch is now pulled downe heretofore called the Little Beare Yard.
4	1666	Fenton Bk	Thomas Dale for old Turner's alias Ingram's house in Penkhull being one of his three services in Penkhull aforesaid.
5	1669	Fenton Bk	Thomas Dale for an antient messuage standing heretofore in Hunters Croft being his third service. This is now sold unto Robert Machin.
6	1672	Fenton Bk	John Bowyer Junr for his father's house in Penkhull.
7	1675	Fenton Bk	Thomas Doody Junr for his owne house in Penkhull.
8	1678	Fenton Bk	John Terrick of Penckhull for his messuage antientlie one Baddilye's, served by Richard Cartwright of Fowlea at the wages of 2$^£$ 15^s.
9	1681	Fenton Bk	John Dale for the Draw Well house served by Richard Cartwright of Fowlea at the wages of three pounds besides the aforesaid 24^s
10	1684	Fenton Bk	Roger & Jno Tittensor his sonne for their messuage in Penckhull served by Richard Cartwright aforesaid, at the wages last aforesaid; this was Tittensor downe in the towne of Penckhull
11	1687	Fenton Bk	Robert Machin for Bradshaw's messuage & lands in Penckhull : the messuage house long since stood in Robert Machin's Bradshaw's yard but not within the memorie of man. Thomas Stevenson usually serveth or hireth the offices served for the said messuage & lands because he hath most of the lands now knowne to belong to the said messuage & he hired Thomas Dale to serve the Reeve's office for the said messuage & lands this present year, at the wages of three pounds besides 24^s allowed from the Kings Auditt.
12	1691	Fenton Bk	Woodcock's messuage in Penkhull, served by George Hanson aforesaid, for the wages of three pounds six shillings and eight pence, besides the 24^s due from the Auditt.
13	1694	Fenton Bk	Mrs Elizabeth Machin for a messuage in Penkhull, formerly Boothe's, and served for before 1639; now executed by George Hanson
14	1698	Fenton Bk	John Bowyer for the place in Penckhull where the messuage called Duncott Leigh formerly stood; served for before Ano. 1642

ANCIENT MESSUAGES IN PENKHULL : as described in various records for the doing service for the Office of Reeve of the Manor

Ref.	Year	Source	Property descriptions for Reeve Service
			Details
15	1701	Fenton Bk	Thomas Astbury for ye house on ye Green in Penkhull; formerly Hitchen's and serv'd for before 1648; now executed by Thomas Astbury, assistente Tho. Doody Senr
16	1704	Fenton Bk	Thomas Dale for his house in Penkhull, once Hitchen's in the lane then Turner's and serv'd for before 1651
17	1707	Fenton Bk	Mr Roger Machin for an house now demolished (formerly inhabited by one Thornton), lately standing in Penckhull and serv'd for before Ano. 1654; now serv'd by John Terrick
1	1710	Fenton Bk	Mr Thomas Doody for the house in Penkhull lately purchased by him of Thomas Tittensor and serv'd for formerly Ano. 1657; the office now executed by Richard Fenton.
2	1713	Fenton Bk	Mr Roger Machin for the Bate lake house in Penckhull; serv'd for before 1660; executed by himselfe
3	1716	Fenton Bk	Mr Thomas Machin for the Beare Yord in Penckhull, serv'd by George Machin his father, and serv'd for before 1663
4	1719	Fenton Bk	Thomas Dale for one of his services in Penckhull, viz. an house formerly Ingram's, and serv'd for before viz. 1666
5	1722	Fenton Bk	Rebecca Machin, widd' of Roger Machin, for the Hunter Croft Head in Penckhull, formerly serv'd for 1669; executed by Cleaton Lea
6	1725	Fenton Bk	John Terrick for the messuage in Penkhull lately by him purchased of John Bowyer serv'd for before 1672.
7	1728	Fenton Bk	John Doody for his messuage in Penkhull serv'd for before 1675; serv'd now by Mr Jenkinson.
8	1731	Fenton Bk	Mr John Terrick for his ancient mess' in Penkhull (formerly Baddiley's) serv'd for before 1678.
9	1734	Fenton Bk	Mr Wm Bourn of Chell for the Draw Well House in Penkhull, (serv'd by Tho. Marsh) serv'd for before
10	1737	Fenton Bk	Mr Tho. Pickin for his house in Penkhull, serv'd for ante 1684.
11	1740	Fenton Bk	Mr Benjamin Hewit (who now is intitled to Steveson's estate in Penkhull vid. ante 1687), for Bradshaw's yord in Penkhull. Serv'd by Richd Hewitt.
12	1743	Fenton Bk	Mr Tho. Lovat for a messuage in Penkhull form'ly called Woodcock's, serv'd for before 1692 and now executed by Mr Tho. Pickin. [entry on a different page :] Tho. Blakeman for a messuage in Penckhull now belonging to Mr Lovatt of Fulford & Jno Terrick, & served by them alternetly; it was formerly Halton's, Nicson's & Woodcok's
13	1746	Fenton Bk	[space] for a mess' in Penkhull now or lately Machin's and formerly Boothe's, served for before 1694 and executed now by [space]. [entry on a different page :] Robert Machin for Boothe's messuage in Penchull, now Whalle's
14	1749	Fenton Bk	Mr Terrick for Duncott Lee in Penkhull. [entry on a different page is the same]
15	1752	Fenton Bk	Thomas Astbury for a messuage in Penkhull late Hitchen's, serv'd by Henry Mounteford. [entry on a different page :] Tho. Astbury for a message in Penckhull, served by Henry Moontford; it was late
16	1755	DL30/516 start	An Antient Messuage called Turner's in the Lane, now Mr Joseph Lovatt's.
17	1758	DL30/516 start	An Antient Messuage called Hutchin's in the Lane, now Mr Whaley's
1	1761	DL30/516 start	An Antient Messuage, formerly Thos Titensor's, now belonging to Mr Lovatt of Fulford.
2	1764	DL30/516 start	An Antient Messuage called the Bate Lake, antiently Roger Machin's, now Mr Whaley's,
3	1767	DL30/516 start	An Antient Messuage called the Beare Yard of late Mr Machin's, now Mr Whaley's
4	1771	DL30/516 start	An Antient Messuage, formerly Turnor's or Ingram's, now Mr Joseph Burns.
6	1774	DL30/516 start	An Antient Messuage, formerly Bower's, now Mr Terrik's
5	1777	DL30/516 start	An Antient Messuage called Hunters Crofthead, formerly Machin's, now Mr Whaley's.
7	1778	DL30/516 start	An Antient Messuage, formerly Thos Doody, now Mr Joseph Burns
8	1783	DL30/516 start	An Antient Messuage, formerly Baddely's, now Mr Terrick's
9	1786	DL30/516 start	An Antient Messuage called Drawwell, formerly Dale's now Mr Alsager's
10	1789	DL30/516 start	An Antient Messuage, formerly Roger Titensor's, now Mr Joseph Burns
11	1792	DL30/516 start	An Antient Messuage called Bradshaw's Yard, formerly Machin's, now to be served by Mr Benjamin
12	1793	DL30/516 start	An Antient Messuage, formerly Woodcock's & Blakeman's, now to be served by Mr Lovatt of Fulford & Mr Terrick ['alternately' deleted].
13	1799	DL30/516 start	An Antient Messuage, formerly Roger Machin's called Booth's, now Mr Whaley's.
14	1802	DL30/516 start	An Antient Messuage called Duncot Lee, formerly Bowyers, now Mr Terrick's
15	1807	DL30/516 start	An Antient Messuage called Hutchin's in the town, now Catherine Astbury's
16	1812	DL30/516 start	An Antient Messuage called Turner's in the Lane, now Mr Joseph Lovatt's.
17	1815	DL30/516 start	An Antient Messuage called Hutchin's in the Lane, now Mr Whaley's

Index